**Neuropsychological Rehabilitation**

# Neuropsychological Rehabilitation

**Manfred J. Meier** PhD
Professor and Director, Neuropsychology Laboratory,
Departments of Neurosurgery and Psychiatry,
University of Minnesota Medical School

**Arthur L. Benton** PhD DSc
Emeritus Professor of Psychology and Neurology,
University of Iowa

**Leonard Diller** PhD
Professor of Clinical Rehabilitation Medicine,
New York Medical Center, and Chief of Behavioral Science,
Rusk Institute of Rehabilitation Medicine

THE GUILFORD PRESS
NEW YORK LONDON

Published in the United States in 1987 by The Guilford Press
A Division of Guilford Publications, Inc.
72 Spring Street
New York, NY 10012

This edition of *Neuropsychological Rehabilitation* is published by arrangement with Churchill Livingstone, Edinburgh.



Printed in the United States of America
***Last digit is print number*** *9 8 7 6 5 4 3 2*

**Library of Congress Cataloging-in-Publication Data**

Neuropsychological rehabilitation.

Includes bibliographies and index.
1. Brain—Diseases—Patients—Rehabilitation.
2. Neuropsychology. I. Meier, Manfred J. II. Benton, Arthur Lester, 1909- III. Diller, Leonard.
[DNLM: 1. Nervous System Diseases—rehabilitation.
2. Neuropsychology. WL 103 N4934]
RC386.2.N489 1987 616.8′046 87-154
ISBN 0-89862-702-8

# Preface

---

The rapidly expanding clinical neuropsychological literature and the marked rise in survivors of acute and severe neurological disorders, such as closed-head injury and stroke, have prompted a more deliberate and (hopefully) productive relationship between the traditional rehabilitation disciplines and clinical neuropsychology. The challenge for rehabilitation professionals in the treatment and management of these patients is enormous and has stimulated more interest among neuropsychologists who are relatively new to the rehabilitation team. Clinical neuropsychology's growth over the past few decades has established a conceptual and empirical base for developing new interdisciplinary relationships and neuropsychological applications in rehabilitation. As a consequence, neuropsychologists are increasingly entering the rehabilitation arena, with the hope of solving major rehabilitation problems or at least of having a significant impact on team efforts to address these problems. This has resulted in substantial expansion of the role of neuropsychologists in the assessment and treatment of disabled individuals with the neurological disorders and has heightened the awareness of professionals in both areas of the growing relationship of clinical neuropsychology to rehabilitation.

The impetus for developing a volume devoted to neuropsychological aspects of rehabilitation came from individuals in this expanding activity network. It began in response to an expressed need for more information about activities in various clinical settings and countries. It evolved into a more comprehensive examination of the current status of this evolving relationship. Thus, the volume was designed to yield an account of the conceptual and methodological foundations of neuropsychological applications in rehabilitation, representative hypotheses and findings of both basic and clinical researchers, and descriptions of developments in various countries where an identifiable program or set of programs expressed a readiness to provide descriptions. It was hoped that the volume would help clarify the current state of knowledge and application in this area and encourage researchers and clinicians to focus their energies toward pursuing a major new direction for both neuropsychology and rehabilitation. Whether this volume succeeds in fostering new activities to validate the role of neuropsychology in rehabilitation remains to be seen. Hopefully this effort is not premature or too convoluted to reflect both the current status and future directions implied in the potential shown to date.

In any case, this effort reflects a sincere desire to assist the many dedicated individuals working toward this goal. As an international venture, extended planning and development was necessary, particularly with the already heavily scheduled commitments of the contributors. The process would have been even more elongated except for the outstanding assistance of Edna Maneval who reviewed each contribution for style and grammar and of Barbara Lea Skon whose immense secretarial skills, and willingness to manage the many details, prevented more disorganization than such an expansive effort could otherwise readily entail. Lastly, thanks are due to the many contributors, particularly those who submitted early and then waited patiently for the process to reach fruition.

Minnesota M.J.M.
Iowa A.L.B.
New York L.D.
1987

# Contributors

**Anna Basso** PhD
Associate Professor, Centre of Neuropsychology, Institute of Neuropsychology, Milan

**Arthur L. Benton** PhD DSc
Emeritus Professor of Psychology and Neurology, University of Iowa

**Yehuda Ben-Yishay** PhD
Associate Professor of Clinical Rehabilitation Medicine, New York School of Medicine

**Nelson Butters** PhD
Chief, Psychology Service, San Diego Veterans Administration Medical Center; Professor of Psychiatry, University of California School of Medicine, San Diego

**Laird S. Cermak** PhD
Boston Veterans Administration Medical Center; Neurology Department, Boston University School of Medicine

**Anne-Lise Christensen** PhD
Clinical Psychologist and Director, The Center for Rehabilitation of Brain Damage, Copenhagen

**Ulla Tarp Danielsen** Cand Psych
Chief Psychologist, Department of Neurology, University of Copenhagen

**Leonard Diller** PhD
Professor of Clinical Rehabilitation Medicine, New York Medical Center; Chief of Behavioral Science, Rusk Institute of Rehabilitation Medicine, New York Medical Center

**Howard Gardner** PhD
Research Psychologist, Boston Veterans Administration Medical Center; Professor of Neurology, Boston University School of Medicine; Co-Director, Harvard Project Zero

**Rosamund Gianutsos** PhD
Director, Cognitive Rehabilitation Services, Sunnyside, New York; Adjunct Associate Professor of Neurology, New York Medical Center

**Felicia C. Goldstein** PhD
Instructor, Department of Neurology, The University of Texas Medical Branch, Galveston, Texas

**Gerald Goldstein** PhD
Director, Neuropsychology Research Program, Highland Drive Veterans Administration Medical Center, Pittsburgh; Associate Professor of Psychiatry and Psychology, University of Pittsburgh

**Harold Goodglass** PhD
Professor of Neurology (Neuropsychology), Boston University School of Medicine; Director of Psychology Research, Boston Veterans Administration Medical Center

**Wayne A. Gordon** PhD
Assistant Professor of Clinical Rehabilitation Medicine, New York University Medical Center, Rusk Institute of Rehabilitation Medicine

**Ritva Laaksonen** MA
Chief Psychologist, Department of Neurology and Part-Time Lecturer, Department of Psychology, Helsinki University

**Anton Leischner** MD
Professor and Emeritus Director of The Rhine State Clinic for Speech Disorders, Bonn

**Harvey S. Levin** PhD
Professor, Division of Neurosurgery, The University of Texas Medical Branch, Galveston, Texas

**Muriel D. Lezak** PhD
Associate Professor, Neurology and Psychiatry, Oregon Health Sciences University, Portland, Oregon

**Pauline Matheson** MA
Head Injury Recovery Center, Milford, Pennsylvania; Department of Psychology, Adelphi University, Garden City, New York

**Manfred J. Meier** PhD
Professor and Director, Neuropsychology Laboratory, Departments of Neurosurgery and Psychiatry, University of Minnesota Medical School, Minneapolis, Minnesota

**Margaret G. O'Connor** MA
Department of Psychology, Boston University, Boston Veterans Administration Medical Center

**Eugene B. Piasetsky** PhD
Co-Director, Head Trauma Program, and Supervising Psychologist, Institute of Rehabilitation Medicine, New York Medical Center

**Michael I. Posner** PhD
Professor of Neuropsychology, Departments of Neurology, Neurosurgery and Psychology, Washington University, St Louis, Missouri

**George P. Prigatano** PhD
Chairman, Section of Neuropsychology, and Clinical Director, Neurological Rehabilitation, Barrow Institute, Phoenix, Arizona

**Robert D. Rafal** MD
Division of Neurology, Brown University, Roger Williams General Hospital, Providence, Rhode Island

**Graham Ratcliff** DPhil
Neuropsychology Consultant, Harmarville Rehabilitation Center, Pittsburgh; Clinical Assistant Professor of Psychiatry, Neurology and Psychology, University of Pittsburgh

**Jack Rattok** PhD
Director, Psychserve; Senior Consultant in Cognitive Rehabilitation, International Center for the Disabled, New York

**Ivar Reinvang** PhD
Psychologist and Professor of Applied Psychology, Sunnaas Hospital, Norway

**David P. Salmon** PhD
Psychology Service, San Diego Veterans Administration Medical Center; Neuroscience Department, University of California, San Diego

**Sumiko Sasanuma** PhD
Director, Department of Rehabilitation Research, Tokyo Metropolitan Institute of Gerontology

**Xavier Seron** PhD
Professor of Neuropsychology, University of Louvain; Co-Director of The Centre of Neuropsychological Rehabilitation Clinics, St Luc, Brussels

**Silvia Strauman** MS
Research Fellow, Neuropsychology Laboratory, University of Minnesota Medical School, Minneapolis, Minnesota

**W. Gary Thompson** PhD
Neuropsychology Laboratory, University of Minnesota Hospital, Minneapolis, Minnesota

**Lance E. Trexler** PhD
Director, The Center for Neuropsychological Rehabilitation, Indianapolis, Indiana

**Barbara Wilson** BA MPhil PhD
Principal Clinical Neuropsychologist, Charing Cross Hospital, London

**Maria Ester Zanobio**
Speech Therapist, Neuropsychological Centre, Milan University

# Contents

# **Part one:** Assessment and Methodological Issues

 *Leonard Diller*

# Neuropsychological rehabilitation

The relationship between neuropsychology and rehabilitation has been uneasy. Is there a field of neuropsychological rehabilitation with a body of knowledge and professional identification? The purpose of this volume is to indicate a sufficient understanding and interest to provide a substantive base for integrating both.

In the past there has been little interaction between workers in the neurosciences and rehabilitation disciplines. Workers in neurosciences tended to view rehabilitation as associated with charity, and 'soft' human services, important, but of secondary interest to diagnosis, disease, and prognosis of central nervous system disorders. Quality-of-life issues, the essence of rehabilitation activities, may be neither unique nor substantive to neuropsychology and, therefore, have been relegated to the background. Workers in the field of rehabilitation have viewed neuropsychology as a diagnostic enterprise that generates data which, once a diagnosis has been established, are basically peripheral to the tasks of living with a disability. Most contemporary neuropsyschological methods have been developed in neurology or neurosurgery settings to identify pathology. Their applications to rehabilitation have been afterthoughts or derivatives. Indeed, only in the past 15–20 years have 'interdisciplinary' conferences, organized around a given disease or syndrome (e.g., stroke, brain-damaged children, Alzheimer's disease), attempted to bridge this gap. Typically, the neurosciences were presented early in the conference, while those related to rehabilitation were presented at the end of the conference. Little attempt was made to integrate them.

Rapprochement is being shaped by a number of changes in the field of health care including:

1. The growth of the number of professionals who deal with brain-damaged people after acute care is terminated. These individuals are concerned with issues of management, e.g., the National Head Injury Foundation Directory lists more than 220 programs that are focused on the management and rehabilitation of those with closed-head injury.
2. Patterns of reimbursement for services to people with disabilities by which funding agencies pay for therapies; as well as:

3. Public awareness and concern, e.g., the 'epidemics' of head trauma and Alzheimer's disease capture the imagination of the public, just as the concern with polio did three decades ago. Consequently, there is a demand for treatment as well as prevention.
4. Advances in technology: computers have been introduced as tools in the study of cognition. They serve as prosthetic aids in remediation of cognitive deficits as well (Gianutsos & Grynbaum, 1983; Lynch, 1982).
5. The development of sophisticated imaging techniques, e.g., CT scans, evoked potentials, NMRs (nuclear magnetic resonance), etc. may alter the needs for information traditionally supplied by neuropsychologists via behavioral testing.

While these clinical diagnostic procedures may prove useful in sorting patients into pathological entities, issues of management are too fine-grained and complex to be addressed by the mere identification of pathology. The differences between neuropsychology and rehabilitation have to be recognized (see Table 1.1).

The primary language of neuropsychology is one of impairment. Impairments are deficits which are dysfunctions in underlying mental or physical structures. Deficits are identified by responses to standardized tests. The primary language of rehabilitation is one of disability. Disabilities are limitations in actual functioning in daily activities (Halpern & Fuhrer, 1984). In the case of a cognitive problem, a complaint is analyzed by weighing it against responses to a battery of tasks tapping different dimensions of cognition. There are no data which indicate that a cognitive impairment must be related to a cognitive disability, e.g., a loss of 40 points on a memory scale does not indicate the severity/extent of the patient's functional memory loss, i.e., how the memory loss impacts day-to-day functions. Can an impairment measure be used to indicate that an individual is not competent to practice a profession or sign checks? The neuropsychologist has a problem in translating the language of impairment into a language of disability without a complex chain of assumptions. While the neuropsychologist can categorize the complaint, the data are too non-specific to illuminate management issues at more refined levels.

The primary activities of clinical neuropsychologists are conducting

**Table 1.1** The different bases of neuropsychology and rehabilitation

| | Neuropsychology | Rehabilitation |
|---|---|---|
| Language | Impairment | Disability |
| Knowledge network | Neurosciences/biology | Education/social sciences |
| Methods | Experimental/psychometric | Ecological/work sample |
| Locus | Laboratory/clinic | Natural environment |
| Forms of activity | Diagnostic | Intervention |
| State for management | Acute | Chronic |

diagnostic studies or experiments to help elucidate and clarify the nature of impairments. The primary activities of rehabilitation workers are in remediation of impairments and teaching people to manage their disabilities. Diagnostic activities in neuropsychology are generally based on tasks designed to be sensitive to individual differences. The items used in intelligence tests (Wechsler, Stanford Binet) are derived from 19th-century experimental psychology laboratories. Other tasks are borrowed from vocational psychology – e.g. Purdue Peg Board, Minnesota Clerical Test, and educational psychology – e.g. achievement tests. Patterns of failure on these tests are used to detect the presence and/or locus of brain damage. The primary tasks which rehabilitation workers use are samples of behavior involving motoric components of activities of daily living such as dressing and walking or work activities derived from job situations used to assess employment potential. The neuropsychologist draws from the laboratory, those in rehabilitation draw from observations in natural habitats. While experimental psychology is the knowledge base for neuropsychology, ecological psychology (Willems, 1976; Willems & Halsted, 1978) provides the knowledge base for rehabilitation psychology. Neuropsychology has empirical and conceptual ties to the neurosciences while rehabilitation psychology has ties to the social sciences.

The challenge of neuropsychological rehabilitation is to develop concepts and tools to bridge these different centers of interest and to demonstrate their validity and utility. To put it another way, the clinical assessment in neuropsychology is the application, extension, and refinement of the neurological examination. It provides a more precise description of people with brain damage to establish etiology and prognosis leading to a management plan. Clinical assessment in rehabilitation is designed to survey problems in daily function in order to develop ways to help handicapped people to become more independent in the real world and increase their options. Granted an overlap, the examination in neuropsychology may seek to identify pathology. The examination in rehabilitation may seek to identify assets. While the history of neuropsychology is based on a history of accumulated knowledge, the history of rehabilitation is marked as much by changes in legislation as it is by scientific advances. The value systems behind these histories may overlap, but they are quite different.

## THE TASKS OF NEUROPSYCHOLOGY IN RELATION TO REHABILITATION

The neuropsychologist interested in rehabilitation is in a position to pull together diverse information from the biological and social sciences. On a theoretical level, a psychology of rehabilitation without a biological underpinning leaves open many questions about individual differences which affect clinical management. A neuro-psychology which does not deal with rehabilitation ignores important domains of behavior which limit its usefulness. How does functional reorganization following brain damage modify learning and teaching? Do different loci of brain damage suggest different styles of teaching for individuals with different disabilities who have to learn a common task? For example, right and left brain-damaged hemiplegics may have equal difficulty in learning to transfer from bed to wheelchair; however, the correlates of success may differ. For the right brain-damaged person success may be related to one set of abilities (visuospatial), for the left brain-damaged person it may be related to another (language). Shouldn't the teaching of patients with different loci of brain damage differ (Diller et al, 1972)?

The neuropsychologist might also be involved in reconceptualizing the idea of activities of daily living (ADLs). This major measurement device in rehabilitation is used to set criteria for admission and discharge, and to assess progress. ADLs for neurologic patients have generally been based on motor-dependent features of behavior such as dressing, feeding, walking, and toileting. These scales, which were designed for the more general class of motorically handicapped people, may not meet the needs of people without motoric handicaps or people with primary cognitive impairments. Thus, there needs to be a way of examining neuropsychological impairments as they impact their daily living activities that is not based on motor behavior. While neuropsychological analysis has provided useful insights into academic disorders in terms of identifying subsyndromes of deficit, it also might be useful in understanding the cognitive/emotional task demands of living, and might even lead to suggestions for environmental management. Thus, concern for the physically handicapped has led to a reconsideration of geographical barriers for non-handicapped people. Indeed, every major city has curb cuts on sidewalks to permit access to wheelchairs. It is conceivable that systems designed to aid cognitively impaired people might be useful for a broader range of populations. For example, studies of the perception of the vertical plane show that hemiplegics who respond poorly to the perception of the vertical improve their performance when the task is repeated in a well-lit room as opposed to a dark room (Birch et al, 1961). Perception of the vertical plane has been shown to be correlated to falling behavior in the elderly (Tobis et al, 1981). It might, therefore, follow that hospital corridors or long passageways where hemiplegics or elderly people walk require more intense illumination in order to prevent falls. The study of disabled people in their natural habitats raises further questions for neuropsychology. We cite three examples. First, there is a low correlation between gains as measured by tests of aphasia and by ratings of functional language by a speech therapist (Sarno & Levitta, 1971). Furthermore, there are few data relating language measures to how much an aphasic talks at home. (For that matter there is little data with regard to how much non-aphasic spouse pairs talk at home.) From a functional standpoint one can raise the question what is the practical aims of speech therapy? To increase vocabulary, or grammar, or to get people to talk more. Second, consider a study of cerebral palsied pre-school children which revealed that teachers interacted less and provided less feedback to these children than they did to children with other disabilities, e.g, spina bifida, amputees, etc., who were of equivalent mental age (Gordon et al, 1972). This raises the issue of whether neurologically impaired children received altered interpersonal feedback. Perhaps such feedback may contribute to 'immaturity' noted in developmentally disabled neurologically impaired children. Relating different dimensions of classroom behavior to neurological impairment may provide useful information on the ecologic consequences of deficit of information processing.

Hemiplegics while undergoing rehabilitation sustain more accidents than do other populations of physically disabled people. In a population of left hemiplegics, those who had two or more accidents were found to have difficulties in scanning their environments, as manifested by many errors of omission on a visual cancellation test. Left hemiplegics with one or no accidents made few errors on a visual cancellation test. Right hemiplegics who had two or more accidents tended to make few errors on a visual cancellation test, but were very slow in performing the task. Right hemiplegics with one or no accidents performed the task close to normal time limits (Diller & Weinberg, 1970). Thus, two different patterns of aberrant performance on the same task were observed in patients with the same functional problem which could interfere with rehabilitation. These studies serve as illustrations of how neuropsychological perspectives can be applied to situations in life outside of standard testing situations.

The neuropsychologist is beginning to address issues of behavior aside from traditional measures of cognitive skills, which are relevant to concerns of rehabilitation. Recent work on the neuropsychology of emotion (Heilman & Satz, 1983; Ross, 1981) suggests that some affective disturbances in people with brain damage may have a neurological basis. For example, it has been traditionally thought that people with right hemisphere damage tend to show indifference or denial reactions. However, recent studies suggest that on self ratings of affect, right brain-damaged patients are more depressed than other population groups in rehabilitation including people with cancer and spinal cord injury. The data also suggests that these very same brain-damaged patients have difficulty in understanding and expressing emotion (Ruckdeschel-Hibbard & Gordon, 1985). The person who states that he/she is sad in a bland, indifferent way might be misleading a clinician, because the manner of self-presentation might mask the severity of the mood disorder. One consequence of this observation is the requirement on the part of clinical workers to separate style and content when assessing affective behavior. This is surely pertinent to management. Similar observations with regard to disturbances in arousal in populations with closed head injury (Van Zomeren et al, 1984), Parkinson disease (Mayeux, 1983), and stroke (Heilman & Satz, 1984; Ruckdeschel-Hibbard & Gordon, 1985) suggest that there may be a neuropsychology of arousal disturbance in brain-damaged people. From a rehabilitation standpoint, knowing that affective and motivational problems may have a neurologic base poses an immediate diagnostic and therapeutic challenge. Conventional methods of management are immediately brought into question.

Major areas of impact of neuropsychological impairments remain to be explored. For example, in the world of work it is clear that standardized vocational tests or even current approaches to vocational exploration which have been developed for populations of handicapped people, e.g., job samples, may not be helpful in the vocational assessment/placement of individuals with closed head injury (Oddy, 1984). For closed head-injured populations, (a) little work has been done in teasing apart automatic overlearned skills versus volitionally related skills in performing a job; (b) once an individual is placed in a job, there may be difficulty in holding on to it because of neurobehavioral problems; (c) fears of employers in retaining a brain-injured person at work may play an important role. In addition, repeated studies have pointed to problems of a family in living with a closed head-injured person (Brooks, 1984). The psychosocial consequences of brain damage are fields of clinical investigation where neuropsychologists and rehabilitation workers may have common interests. Traditional neuropsychological assessments are based on samplings of disturbances in responding to sensory, motor, language, and computational tasks but not to interpersonal tasks. Typically, these tasks are short and the responses are too brief to provide an adequate sample of behavior. One can only infer how the individual will respond to situations which cover several days or weeks. While neuropsychological testing has advanced by trying to become more narrow and precise in the individual skill areas which are sampled, in rehabilitation it must retain a broader perspective on activities performed outside of the laboratory and the clinic.

On the other side of the coin, the neuropsychologist can direct the attention of the rehabilitation worker to the emerging findings on the biology of individual differences and their consequences for damage to the central nervous system. For example, factors such as gender, laterality, age, and education may affect the organization of the brain and patterns of cognitive functioning (Bryden et al, 1983; Geschwind & Galaburda, 1985; Inglis et al, 1983). Because of lack of normative data bases, current approaches to comparing population groups in rehabilitation settings lack a firm footing. Indeed, Bakker (1984) has noted that while neuropsychologists have viewed the brain largely as an independent variable affecting behavior, recent studies indicate that the brain might be modifiable by environmental influences.

## INTERVENTIONS

Neuropsychologists can participate in treatment in rehabilitation by addressing some of the therapeutic issues in the sensory motor and language problems in daily living areas which are traditionally part of occupational and physical therapy. For example, applications of biofeedback to improve the functioning of a plegic extremity (Gianutsos et al, 1978) or to improve the balance of people with gait problems is only one area that is currently being explored (Gianutsos, 1984). Neuropsychologists similarly might contribute to areas of skill retraining in the areas of dressing and feeding. Much of the exercise and skill training in rehabilitation lacks an adequate empirical basis for its efficacy. Nor are there data to show how often, how long, and with what intensity should therapies be administered. The neuropsychologist operating in a rehabilitation setting might also translate the task demands of ADL into a suitable neuropsychological framework to retrain individuals, e.g., people with different levels of cognitive impairment may respond better to different types of instruction. Gordon et al (1972) have shown that teachers use verbal versus demonstration styles with brain-damaged children depending on level of mental age. If a rehabilitation setting can be pictured as a type of school where people are taught to master disabilities, the neuropsychologist might contribute by leaving the 'testing' room and participating in the class activities as a database for observation.

An expansion of these concerns of neuropsychology agrees with a shift taking place in contemporary educational psychology. Farnham-Diggory & Nelson (1984) have noted that early educational psychologists were interested in curriculum, content, and instruction in school. These interests were muted by the rise of the testing movement after the First World War. Only in the past 5 years has there been a return to these interests. This is easily demonstrated by a survey of titles of papers in the *Journal of Educational Psychology* over the years. Similarly, it may be argued that neuropsychology has been fixated on testing, but now should be concerned with the content of the retraining programs used for people with brain damage.

An additional interest of a neuropsychologist in rehabilitation is in direct intervention for cognitive deficits. While some neuropsychologists are skeptical with regard to the theoretical and scientific bases for remediation, others are moving ahead trying to create a clinical discipline where none now exists. Before accepting or dismissing these developments in an unequivocal way, considering the complex series of decisions to be made in conducting an intervention. Each decision touches an important question which can be addressed scientifically. (1) What cognitive deficit is being treated? (2) How is the deficit operationalized in measurable terms? (3) What are the stimuli which elicit the deficit and how can they be manipulated to make them easier or harder? (4) What are the responses which serve as indicators of the deficit? (5) What is the content of the treatments, how are they administered, how often, what standards are set for continuing, altering or stopping the program? (a) how are issues of non-compliance managed? and (b) to what behavior or family of behavior do the gains generalize (Diller & Gordon, 1981)? These procedural issues are clearly not trivial, from a practical standpoint as well as theoretical one. An intervention program must be carefully planned as a good experiment where the attainment of a goal should not be sabotaged by faulty procedures. While current accounts of remediation have been criticized as lacking a theoretical base, it might be more accurate to state that remediation must take into account several theoretical bases including a biology of individual differences, a neuropsychology of cognitive impairments, an ecologic psychology of functional behavior, and a psychology of learning and teaching. On a common-sense level further questions are also raised.

## What does one treat?

This can be considered in several ways. For example, are assets or impairments treated? Weinberg et al (1977), in discussing a treatment for hemi-neglect in right brain-damaged people argue that one must treat the visual scanning problems which are the deficit area of function. Even if one uses a verbal auditory modality, it is in the service of habit in a deficit area of skill. On the surface this would appear to be contrary to conventional mental health and rehabilitation principles which emphasize accentuating assets by bypassing defects. However, it may be argued that the conventional principles apply when the individual can identify the problem, but cannot overcome it. However, when an individual is not aware of the problem and the lack of awareness is a major obstacle to treatment, then the person must be made aware of the problem before treatment can be initiated. Addressing the deficit area also fits into the notion that failure on a complex task may be correlated with a more simple underlying deficit. For example, failure on the Raven's matrices, a test of visuoperceptual functions, in a right brain-damaged person is related to a deficit in scanning (Piasetsky, 1981). Treating the scanning will help performance on the matrices. Finally, one might argue that ignoring the deficit simply fosters denial.

On the other side of the coin, one might note that individuals who perform poorly, in a given area of skill, find that acquisition of cues is more difficult than individuals who perform well (Ben-Yishay et al, 1970). It may therefore prove unprofitable to attempt to teach in areas of weakness. This would be supported by the study of Stanton et al (1983), who attempted to teach wheelchair competence to a right brain-damaged person by the use of verbal cues, i.e., asset abilities rather than impaired abilities. This rationale would fit those who argue that rehabilitation consists of utilizing the intact hemisphere to solve problems usually undertaken by the impaired hemisphere. This rationale would also fit the argument behind melodic intonation therapy for aphasia (Albert et al, 1973), i.e., the use of the more intact musical skills rather than the language skills which are impaired in aphasics. Indeed, one might push this argument to its outermost boundary and argue that speech therapy might be harmful because it treats areas of weakness rather than areas of strength in aphasics.

If one addressed the defective structure underlying the complaint how does one think of the problem from both the standpoint of pathology and remediation. A sophisticated statement of treatment issues would note that remediation approaches may involve different models of pathology and treatment (Seron, 1982). These include deficiency models, interference models and absence models.

Deficiency models are based on the idea that atypical behavior is due to an absence of proper experience as a result of neurologic impairment of lack of use. The aims of this model are to treat the deficiency by providing enriching experiences, and by providing the effective tasks and environments to bring about learning. This model is in accord with the recent studies which suggest that experiences enrich brain function (Bakker, 1984; Bach-y-Rita, 1980). Treatment may differ in terms of structure, i.e., from the highly structured where one might 'force' or encourage the hemiplegic to utilize the paralyzed limb rather than become dependent on the intact limb, to the unstructured where one would expose the individual to a general set of experiences without explicit response demands. It might be possible that degree of structure which is most helpful to the patient might be related to neurologic diagnosis. Clinically, one might expect that individuals who are poor in certain abilities are fearful of exploring tasks in the skill domains in which they fail. The therapeutic task is to encourage continued experiences in the domain of skills which is difficult.

The interference model argues that lack of competence is not a function of lack of experience. Competence does not arise from sheer exposure, repetition, or enrichment. This view is in accord with the neurologic notions of disturbance, e.g., in excitation/inhibition or the cognitive psychologist's concerns with disturbances in selectivity of attention as manifested in difficulties with figure ground problems, or those neuropsychologists who argue that damage to one hemisphere disinhibits the actions of the other. For this framework remediation must be sensitive to the antagonism between different modes of performing a task which might not be apparent in intact people, but become apparent in brain-damaged people or in young children. For example, the compelling Gestalt features of a word learned under the 'look-and-say' method may interfere with learning and using a code for the percept. Interference models involve the notion of hierarchy of learning. In general these models are in accord with the idea that removal of the interference by techniques of suppression, isolation, and bypassing of distractors aid good performance. There are, for example, a large number of studies showing the conditions under which the maximum performance of impaired children can be elicited (Bortner and Birch, 1969). Interference models place less emphasis on competence. Competence is viewed as only one dimension of performance. Other dimensions such as style of performance manifested by impulsivity, rigidity, and distractibility are equally important.

Absence models are invoked to describe states due to an intrinsic lack. The blind, the deaf, and the retarded represent deficit states. In these conditions one assumes the defect itself cannot be ameliorated, nor will exposure to the environment help the basic defect. Remedies lie in developing substitutes (a blind person relying on auditory cues) and prosthetic devices (using a cane). Wearing a watch or a ring to identify which hand is used may be of help in teaching a child to discriminate left from right when one does not wish to go through the steps of training the discrimination.

**What treatment procedures are to be used in neuropsychological rehabilitation?**

The models used to describe the problems suggest certain techniques. While these techniques may appear to be exclusive with regard to the model, in clinical practice they can be blended. The model provides a tentative guide.

The deficiency model suggests that exposure to the task will be useful. While exposure with repetition in some instances may be sufficient, in indiviudals with severe impairments it is necessary to break the task into graded levels of difficulty to facilitate a successful response. Ben-Yishay et al (1971) have shown that it is possible to perform analyses of task difficulty in tasks as widely divergent as block designs, peg boards, and verbal reasoning. While the contents of these domains differ, the underlying principles of analysis are similar. The remediators use a method of saturated cuing by which individuals who fail are provided with graded degrees of task-specific support to assist in passing. The nature of the support will, of course, depend on the task. The degree of support required is directly related to the individual's innate level of competence. With increasing competence there is a decrease in support. At the level of maximum support, tasks are highly 'structured' in the sense that there is a limitation of degrees of freedom in searching for response options. To put it another way, Fredriksen (1984) argues that a problem is well structured when the elements for its solution lie within the problem. It is poorly structured (as are many problems in life) when the individual must go outside of these elements. Saturated cuing provides a systematic approach to retraining. It is based on a combination of phenomenological and statistical analyses of task difficulty. It makes little presumption about how skill hierarchies are developed or interfered with by brain damage. It has been shown to be useful in enhancing psychometric performance. In theory it can be applied to the analysis and teaching of functional skills in brain-damaged people as well.

The interference model has found its largest number of examples in experiments which demonstrate conditions under which brain-damaged people can improve their performance when task conditions are altered. Perhaps the most well known of these studies which have generated a body of literature include (a) involving the utilization of mnemonic devices (Aeschelman & Snoy, 1982; Bellaza, 1983; Rose et al, 1983), via visual imagery techniques and verbal rehearsal to improve memory, and (b) presenting information to the more intact modality (auditory/visual) to improve responses in unilaterally brain-damaged people. In effect, systematic methods for presentation of stimuli or for transforming stimuli are used to bypass reliance on modes of perception and memory which can inhibit performance in brain-damaged populations. Other examples of techniques to improve performance by altering conditions of task presentation can be found in Table 1.2. This approach assumes the brain-damaged person is capable of the correct response, but is inhibited from performing it by a break-down in information processing. The intervention is designed to bypass the breakdown. This model draws most

**Table 1.2** Techniques used to overcome 'interference' in brain-damaged people

| Author(s) | Method | Principle |
|---|---|---|
| Birch, Belmont, Reilly, and Belmont, 1961 | Hemiplegics improve on rod/ frame by (a) removing frame, (b) turning on lights | Varying intrasensory input can improve performance |
| Birch, Belmont, and Karp 1967 | Hemiplegics overcome extinction by changing timing of stimulus | Information dampened by impaired hemisphere can be transmitted by presenting it first |
| Bortner and Birch, 1960 | Hemiplegics/CPs select correct blocks although they fail a block design task | Failure not in perception, but in translating into action |
| Birch and Bortner, 1967 | Brain-damaged children abstract when competing stimuli are reduced | Response capability submerged by competing options |
| Shapiro, 1951, 1952, 1953 | Brain-damaged adults improve block designs when viewing target through a pinhole of light | Peripheral perception degrades performance in brain damage |
| Weinberg et al 1977, 1979 | Force neglect patient to pay attention to the left side of space | Anchor start of gaze to the left to overcome 'pull' to the right |

CPs = patients with cerebral palsy

fully on a notion of information processing dependent on a nervous system which is continuously mediating and regulating information. Since neuropsychological experiments reveal methods of altering behavior under different conditions, it lies close to an important core of neuropsychological thinking.

The absence model assumes that simple exposure and practice are not sufficient. The correct response must be elicited by an external source of information such as a computer which serves as an external prosthetic device.

Furthermore, there are also instructional issues which await more detailed study by both the neuropsychologist and the rehabilitation worker. These issues are part of the bread-and-butter concerns of the individual remediator. The tasks of the remediator, the goals for the student, and some clinical issues which require continual monitoring are indicated in Table 1.3. There are few studies which have attempted to supply data to yield insight into these issues for populations of people with brain damage. The field of instructional psychology (Frederiksen 1984), which is developing rapidly following the growth of cognitive psychology, provides a useful resource for students of remediation.

Finally, as the neurobehavioral dynamics of problems of emotions and motivation are more completely explicated (Tyerman & Humphrey, 1984), one can expect to see intervention programs for phenomena such as empathy, self-regard, self-control, depression, denial, and failure to initiate for people with brain damage (Long et al, 1984; Novack et al, 1984; Wood, 1984). For many

**Table 1.3**

| Remediator's preparations | Goals for student | Clinical issues which require ongoing intervention |
|---|---|---|
| 1. *Induction* | | |
| (a) Explain the task | To understand what is wanted | Establish felt need; denial |
| (b) Relate task to complaint or clinical problem | | |
| (c) Clarify (demonstrate) task demands | | |
| 2. *Organizing the activity to elicit success* | | |
| (a) Selecting content | To engage interest and master | Wanders off task |
| (b) Calibrating task demands | | |
| (c) Criteria for success/failure | | |
| (d) Criteria for plateau | | |
| (e) Cuing procedures for failure | | |
| (f) Feedback | | |
| (g) Encouragement | | |
| 3. *Generalization* | | |
| (a) Practice success | To use skills automatically without effort; to internalize | Cannot self-monitor efforts and principles |
| (b) Awareness of errors | | |
| (c) Self-monitoring | | |

years it was noted that conventional neuropsychological tests were insensitive to behavioral problems of individuals with frontal lobe damage, although personality problems were readily observable. Recent work suggests that rehabilitation programs can address the problems of people following closed head injury, including those with frontal lobe damage, with some success (Prigitano et al, 1984). As therapeutic gains are noted clinically, there is a pressing need to develop assessment measures to keep pace with clinical observation.

## SUMMARY AND CONCLUSION

The rehabilitation of individuals with neuropsychological impairments poses a major scientific and professional challenge. For the neuropsychologist it presents an opportunity to observe how individuals with residual effects of brain damage lead their lives, and to develop methodologies for helping them. In order to maximize the opportunity the neuropsychologist will have to understand some of the issues in providing rehabilitation services and trying to ameliorate deficits. For the rehabilitation worker, neuropsychology provides a rational base for understanding some of the phenomena which are observed and treated. Both must look at the following questions: How does one know what to research in this field? How does one know what to diagnose? How does one know what to treat? A moment's reflection suggests that the answers to each question will depend on the answers to the other questions.

## REFERENCES


Aeschelman S R, Snoy M D 1982 Enhancing the recall of prose in a brain client with mnemonic instruction. Human learning 1: 165–170

Albert M D, Sparks R W, Helm N A 1973 Melodic intonation therapy for aphasia. Archives Neurology 29: 130–131

Bach-y-Rita P (ed) 1980 Recovery of function: theoretical considerations for brain injury rehabilitation. University Park Press, Baltimore

Bakker K 1984 The brain as a dependent variable. Journal of Clinical Neuropsychology 6: 1–16

Bellaza F S 1985 The spatial arrangement mnemonic. Journal of Experimental Psychology 75: 830–837

Ben-Yishay Y, Diller L, Gerstman L J, Gordon W A 1970 Relationships between initial competence and ability to profit from cues in brain damaged individuals. Journal of Abnormal Psychology 75: 248–259

Ben-Yishay Y, Diller L, Mandleberg I, Gerstman L J 1974 Difference in matching persistence behavior during block design performance between older and brain damaged persons: a process analysis. Cortex 10: 121–132

Ben-Yishay Y, Diller L, Mandleberg I, Gordon W A, Gerstman L J 1971 Similarities and differences in block design performance between older normal and brain damaged persons. A task analysis. Journal of Abnormal Psychology 78: 17–25

Birch H G, Bortner M 1967 Stimulus competition and concept utilization in brain damaged children. Developmental Medicine and Child Neurology 9: 402–410

Birch H G, Belmont I, Reilly T, Belmont L 1961 Visual verticality in hemiplegia. Archives of Neurology 5: 444–453

Birch H G, Belmont I, Karp E 1967 Delayed information processing and extinction following cerebral damage. Brain 90: 113–130

Bortner M, Birch H G 1960 Perception and perceptual motor disassociation in cerebral palsied children. Journal of Nervous and Mental Diseases 130: 49–53

Bortner M, Birch H G 1969 Cognitive capacity and cognitive competence. Paper presented at American Association of Mental Deficiency, San Francisco, 12 May 1969.

Brooks N (ed) 1974 Closed head injury: psychological, social and family consequences. Oxford University Press, Oxford

Bryden M D, Hecaen H, DeAgostini M 1983 Patterns of cerebral organization. Brain and Language 20: 249–263

Diller L, Gordon W A 1981 Interventions for cognitive deficits in brain injured adults. Journal of Consulting and Clinical Psychology 49: 822–834

Diller L, Weinberg J 1970 Accidents in hemiplegia. Archives of Physical Medicine and Rehabilitation 51: 358–363

Diller L, Buxbaum J, Chiotelis S 1972 Relearning motor skills in hemiplegia. Error analyses. Genetic Psychology Monographs 85: 249–286

Farnham-Diggory S, Nelson B N 1984 Cognitive analyses of basic school tasks. Applied Development a Psychology 1: 21–73

Flavell J H 1979 Metacognition and cognitive monitoring: a new area of cognitive development inquiry. American Psychologist 24: 906–911

Fordyce D J, Roueche J R, Prigitano G D 1983 Enhanced emotional reactions in chronic head trauma patients. Journal of Neurology, Neurosurgery and Psychiatry 46: 620–624

Frederiksen N 1984 Implications of cognitive theory for instruction in problem solving. Review of Educational Research 54: 363–407

Geschwind N, Galaburda A M 1985 Cerebral lateralization – biological mechanisms, associations, and pathology: I. Hypothesis and a program for research. Archives of Neurology 42: 428–450; 521–552; 634–654

Gianutsos J 1984 On teaching balance in gait training - progress report. NIHR - Research Training Center, New York University - Head Trauma and Stroke, (unpublished)
Gianutsos J, Grynbaum B B 1983 Helping brain-injured people to contend with hidden cognitive deficits. International Journal of Rehabilitation Medicine, 5: 37–40
Gianutsos J, Eberstein A, Kraselowsky G, Goodgold J 1978 EMG feedback in the rehabilitation of upper arm extremity function. Single case studies of chronic hemiplegics. INS Bulletin (proceedings) December, 12 (abstract)
Gordon R, White D, Diller L 1972 Performance of neurologically impaired preschool children with educational materials. Exceptional Children 39: 428–437
Halpern A S, Fuhrer M J (ed) 1984 Functional assessment in rehabilitation. Brookes, Baltimore
Heilman K M, Satz P 1984 Neuropsychology of human emotion. Guilford Press, New York
Heilman K M, Schwartz H, Watson R T 1978 Hypoarousal in patients with the neglect syndrome and emotional indifference. Neurology 28: 224–232
Inglis J, Ruckman J S, Lawson A W, McLean W, Monga T N 1983 Sex differences in the cognitive effects of unilateral brain damage: comparison of stroke patients and normal control subjects. Cortex 19: 551–555
Long C J, Gouvier W D, Cole J C 1984 A model of recovery for the total rehabilitation of individuals with head trauma. Journal of Rehabilitation 16: 39–45
Lynch W J 1982 The use of electronic games in cognitive games in cognitive rehabilitation. In: Trexler, C (ed) Cognitive rehabilitation: conceptualization and intervention. Plenum, New York
Mayeux R 1983 Emotional changes associated with basal ganglia disorder. In: Heilman K M, Satz P (eds) Neuropsychology of human emotion. Guilford Press, New York
Novack T A, Daniel M S, Long C J 1984 Factors related to emotional adjustment following head injury. International Journal of Clinical Neuropsychology 6: 139–141
Oddy M 1984 Head injury and social adjustment. In: Brooks N (ed) Closed head injury, psychological, social, and family consequences Oxford University Press, Oxford
Piasetsky E 1981 A study of pathological asymmetries in visual spatial attention in unilaterally brain damaged stroke patients. City University of New York; unpublished doctoral dissertation
Pratt J A, Higbee K L 1983 Use of an imagery mnemonic by the elderly in natural settings. Human Learning 2: 227–235
Prigitano G, Fordyce I J, Zeiner H K, Roueche J R, Pegging M, Wood B C 1984 Neuropsychological rehabilitation after closed head injury. Journal of Neurology, Neurosurgery and Psychiatry 47: 505–513
Rose M D, Cundick B P, Higbeck K 1983 Verbal rehearsal and visual imagery: mnemonic aids for learning disabled children. Journal of Learning Disabilities 16: 352–354
Rosenthal M, Griffith E R, Bond M R, Miller J D 1983 Rehabilitation of the head injured adult. Davis, Philadelphia
Ross E D 1981 The aprosodias: functional anatomic organization of the affective components of language in the right hemisphere. Archives of Neurology 38: 561–589
Ruckdeschel-Hibbard M, Gordon W A 1985 Affect comprehension deficits in right brain damaged stroke patients: a refinement of the literature. INS (bulletin) 23: 10 (San Diego)
Sarno M T, Levitta E 1971 Natural course of recovery in severe aphasia. Archives of Physical Medicine and Rehabilitation 52: 171–178
Seron X 1982 The reeducation of aphasics: the problem of the reeducation strategies. International Journal of Psychology 17: 299–317
Shapiro M B 1951 Experimental studies of a perceptual anomaly. I: Initial experiment. Journal of Mental Science 97: 90–110
Shapiro M B 1952 Experimental studies of a perceptual anomaly. II: Confirmatory and explanatory theory. Journal of Mental Science 98: 605–617
Shapiro M B 1953 Experimental studies of a perceptual anomaly. III: The testing of an explanatory theory. Journal of Mental Science 99: 394–409
Stanton K M, Pepping M, Brockaway J A, Bliss L, Framal P, Waggner S 1983 Wheelchair transfer training for right cerebral dysfunctions; an interdisciplinary approach. Archives of Physical Medicine and Rehabilitation 64: 276–281
Tobis J, Novak L, Hoehler F 1981 Visual perception of verticality and horizontality among elderly fallers. Archives of Physical Medicine and Rehabilitation 62: 619–625

Tyerman A, Humprey M 1984 Changes in self concept following severe head injury. International Journal of Rehabilitation Research 7: 110–123

Van Zomeren A N, Brouwer W H, Deelman B G 1984 Attentional deficits: the riddles of selectivity, speed, and alertness. In: Brooks M (ed) Closed head injury: psychological, social and family consequences. Oxford University Press, Oxford

Weinberg J, Diller L, Gordon W A, Gerstman L J et al 1977 Visual scanning. Training on reading related tasks in acquired right brain damage. Archives of Physical Medicine and Rehabilitation 58: 480–486

Weinberg J, Diller L, Gordon W A et al 1979 Training sensory awareness and spatial organization in people with right brain damage. Archives of Physical Medicine and Rehabilitation 60: 491–497

Willems E P 1976 Behavioral ecology, health status and health care: applications to the rehabilitation setting. In: Altman I & Wohlwill J F (eds) Human behavior and environment. Plenum, New York

Willems E P, Halstead L S 1978 An eco behavioral approach to health status and health care. In: Barker R G (ed) Habitats, environments, and human behavior. Jossey-Bass, San Francisco

Wood R L 1984 Behavior disorders following severe brain injury: their presentation and psychological management. In: Brooks N (ed) Closed head injury, psychological, social and family consequences. Oxford University Press, Oxford

# 2

Gerald Goldstein

# Neuropsychological assessment for rehabilitation: fixed batteries, automated systems, and non-psychometric methods

## INTRODUCTORY REMARKS

This chapter will examine the value of using so-called fixed neuropsychological batteries in rehabilitation planning, how the use of computers can expedite the planning process, and how non-psychometric methods, largely direct systematic behavioral observation, can supplement formal neuropsychological testing in the formulation of rehabilitation plans. Thus, the focus of the chapter will be on how empirical, objective, and data-oriented methodologies can contribute to the task of restoring function to brain-damaged patients. There are actually two kinds of fixed batteries in neuropsychology: specialized and comprehensive. The specialized batteries assess some aspect of behavior in detail, such as language or motor skills. Probably the most well-known specialized batteries are the aphasia examinations, such as the Boston Diagnostic Aphasia Examination (Goodglass & Kaplan, 1972) and the Western Aphasia Battery (Kertesz, 1979). This chapter will not concern itself with the fixed specialized batteries since the areas they assess are well covered elsewhere. Rather it will concentrate on the two comprehensive fixed batteries that are currently most widely used in the United States: the Halstead-Reitan (HRB) (Reitan & Davison 1974) and the Luria-Nebraska (LNNB) (Golden et al, 1980) neuropsychological test batteries. An attempt will be made to demonstrate how these standard, quantitatively oriented procedures can be used in productive rehabilitation planning, and how their utilization may have some advantages over the so-called flexible or qualitative approaches to neuropsychological assessment. Following that discussion, I will attempt to demonstrate how judicious use of computers can aid the assessment process, particularly with regard to the capacities the computer may have for rapid scoring and preliminary interpretation. I will not be discussing the use of computers in rehabilitation itself, but only in assessment. Finally, I will attempt to develop the position that rehabilitation planning may be significantly enhanced through direct behavioral observation in natural environments, as long as such observation is planned and implemented in a systematic fashion.

## THE STANDARD COMPREHENSIVE BATTERIES

For those readers unfamiliar with the HRB and LNNB procedures, I will provide brief descriptions here. More detailed descriptions and reviews are available for both the HRB (Reitan & Davison, 1974; Reitan, 1966; Boll, 1981; Russell et al, 1970) and the LNNB (Golden, 1981). Reviews of both procedures may be found in Jones & Butters (1983) and Goldstein (1984). Both procedures have standard administration and scoring methods and both, in greater or lesser detail, provide evaluations of the various cognitive, perceptual, and motor abilities that typically constitute a neuropsychological assessment. These areas include general intelligence; abstraction and related conceptual abilities; attention; language; memory; visual-spatial abilities; and a variety of perceptual, motor, and perceptual-motor skills.

The HRB has as its core Halstead's (1947) measures of 'biological intelligence' that were developed in his Chicago laboratory during the 1930s and 1940s. The most well known and widely used of these tests include the following:

1. *The Halstead Category Test*: A measure of abstraction and related conceptual abilities in which the subject must identify a number of concepts through a series of trials in which geometric forms and some verbal stimuli are presented on a screen. The subject presses one of four keys indicating the correct response. A correct response is followed by a chime, while an incorrect response is associated with a rasping buzzer. The subject's task is that of identifying the proper concept through the feedback regarding the pattern of correct and incorrect responses.
2. *The Tactual Performance Test*: A modified version of the Seguin–Goddard formboard, in which blocks must be placed in the proper recesses on the board while the subject is blindfolded. The procedure is repeated with the dominant hand, non-dominant hand, and both hands. Performance is timed. The subject is also asked to draw the board from memory with the drawing reflecting not only the shapes of the blocks but their proper location on the board.
3. *The Speech Perception Test*: The subject listens to a tape recording containing a series of 60 nonsense words. On a four-choice answer sheet provided, the word heard must be underlined. The incorrect three words in the multiple-choice set are always similar to the word spoken on the tape, in that all the words have 'ee' digraphs at their centers (e.g. geend).
4. *The Seashore Rhythm Test*: Thirty paired sets of rhythmic patterns are presented on a tape. The subject must mark on an answer sheet whether the two members of each pair are the same as (S) or different from each other (D).
5. *Finger Tapping*: A test of motor speed in which the subject must tap as rapidly as possible with the extended finger on a key attached to a mechanical counter. Sets of 10 second trials are administered for both the right and left hands.

The following tests were subsequently added to the battery by Reitan and various collaborators.

6. *Reitan Aphasia Screening Test*: A brief survey of major language and language-related functions including naming, spelling, repetition, articulation, writing, comprehension, right–left orientation, narrative speech, and reading.
7. *Trail Making A and B*: In Trail Making A, the subject must connect as rapidly as possible a series of circled numbers printed in random locations on a sheet of paper. The numbers must be connected in numerical order. In Trail Making B numbers and letters must be connected in their appropriate order, alternating between them (e.g. 1 to A to 2 to B, etc.). The test is timed and errors are recorded.
8. *Perceptual Disorders*: A number of tests of elementary perceptual skills including measures of the ability to discriminate among one's fingers; to identify numbers written on the fingertips; and to perceive simple tactile, visual, and auditory stimuli under single and double simultaneous stimulation conditions.

In addition to the above procedures it is customary to administer the appropriate Wechsler Intelligence Scale (Wechsler-Bellevue, WAIS, WAIS-R, WISC, or WISC-R) as part of the HRB. Many users also include an achievement test, usually the Wide Range Achievement Test (Jastak & Jastak, 1965). Over the years, individual laboratories have added numerous other tests to the HRB core, including such procedures as the Weschler Memory Scale, the Klove Grooved Pegboard, perimetric examination of the visual fields, and dichotic listening procedures.

Various scoring systems are available for the HRB, but all of them incorporate some form of impairment index, a global score representing overall level of performance. Individual test scores may be converted into T scores or ratings so that the results can be profiled, and inter-test comparisons can be conveniently made. Interpretation of the test data is generally done clinically, although several automated interpretation procedures have been devised (Finkelstein, 1977; Russell et al, 1970) for the HRB. Several efforts are currently in progress related to computerization of administration, scoring and preliminary interpretation of the HRB or HRB-like batteries.

The LNNB is a standardized procedure based on the administration of a set of items described in Christensen (1975). These items consist of brief tests said to have been used by Luria and colleagues in their examinations of brain-damaged patients. The current version of the battery consists of 269 of these items, which are divided into 11 major ability scales: motor skills, rhythm, tactile, visual, receptive speech, expressive speech, writing, reading, arithmetic, memory, and intellectual processes. There is also a pathognomonic scale, based on particularly sensitive items, and sensory-motor right and left hemisphere scales. Each item may be scored as 0 (normal) or 2 (abnormal). Some items may be scored 1, reflecting a borderline level of performance. The raw score for each scale, the sum of the item scores, is converted to a T score with a mean of 50 and a standard deviation of 10. Several alternative methods of scoring the items are available, including empirically derived localization scales and a set of factor scales based on a series of factor analyses of the battery. Scores may be adjusted for the anticipated influence of age and educational factors on neuropsychological test performance. A so-called "baseline" score is computed by means of an equation provided in the test manual which shifts the individual's average T score, which is 50 in the general population, up or down depending upon age and educational level. Scores that are one standard deviation higher than this computed baseline score are viewed as abnormal. The equivalent of the impairment index is the number of abnormal scores above the so-called 'critical level'; i.e. the value that is one standard deviation above baseline. The procedure has been published by Western Psychological Services. The interested reader is referred to the manual (Golden et al, 1980), and to various review chapters describing the battery (Golden, 1981; Goldstein, 1984).

## THE USE OF STANDARD COMPREHENSIVE NEUROPSYCHOLOGICAL BATTERIES IN REHABILITATION PLANNING

### General considerations

By their very nature, standard comprehensive batteries are always administered in the same way to all patients. That is, the same tests are given to all patients utilizing the same administrative procedures. Content of the battery, the nature of the test instructions, and the manner in which the battery is scored is the same, regardless of the referral question or the status of the patient. Of course, the nature of the interpretation may vary in response to the referral question and related matters, but the testing procedure is constant. When the procedure is administered by technicians they are trained to adhere to standard procedures, and to attempt to get every patient through every test. While this method has been criticized as being overly rigid, inefficient, excessively lengthy, and deficient with regard to its capability of generating specific rehabilitation plans for individual patients, I will try to demonstrate here that these criticisms are not entirely warranted and, furthermore, that there are distinct advantages in using quantitative, standard procedures in rehabilitation planning.

The use of standard batteries in planning represents a departure from the traditional medical model. Thus its assessment methodology is not necessarily aimed at identifying pathology through detection of symptoms or syndromes, and recommending or prescribing treatment on the basis of that identification. The approach is not based on the logic that one only has to find out what is wrong with the patient in order to prescribe treatment. Rather it is an approach that considers both what is wrong and what is right with the patient. Thus it considers both assets and deficits, particularly since the examiner is 'forced' to administer all the tests in the battery. It is highly likely that the average patient will do well on some tests and poorly on others, and it is this combination of assets and deficits that often provides the information needed to formulate an effective rehabilitation plan. Advocates of specialized testing or qualitative, syndrome-oriented approaches often suggest that they also look at the patient's assets, but they typically do not do so in a manner that provides usable information to those engaged in rehabilitation. For example, take the following passage describing an assessment based on Luria's qualitative methodology.

> The manifestation of a distinct disturbance in all tasks that include spatial elements forms the background for a focal diagnosis, according to the theory of the functional systems. The reliability of the diagnosis is obtained by the double dissociation principle of H. Teuber; all other functions are intact. (Christensen, 1979, p. 246).

While an analysis of this type may provide a very exact characterization of the patient's deficit, it may not provide very adequate information for a rehabilitation specialist attempting to work with this patient with regard to employment, educational, or functional considerations relevant to everyday living. The phrase 'all other functions are intact', while being a significant statement within a medical framework, is essentially meaningless from the standpoint of psychological assessment.

The major advantage of standard procedures is that they provide quantitative measures of performance levels in areas that may be problematic for the patient, but also in areas in which the patient does not have deficits. Often the rehabilitation plan must involve capitalization on just those areas; on those abilities at which the patient does well. It is therefore not sufficient to indicate that these abilities are 'normal' or 'intact.' One has to know how normal and how intact. That is, one needs to know how well the patient is doing relative to the normal population in order, for example, to determine how well he or she can compete for educational or employment opportunities. Clinicians in medical settings may be familiar with the situation in which the resident making a case presentation is told by the impatient consultant to 'just give the positive findings'; i.e. 'just report what is abnormal.' Such an approach, while quite reasonable in a medical framework, is quite inappropriate within the framework of behavioral or psychological assessment. If one grants that neuropsychological assessment is a form of psychological assessment, and not a form of medical examination, then it seems clear that the principles and methods of psychological testing/assessment that have developed over many years, and have a long tradition, should be employed. The use of standard procedures of proven validity and acceptable reliability would appear to be as appropriate for neuropsychological assessment as for other forms of psychological assessment. Psychology has a rich testing literature (Anastasi, 1982; Cronbach, 1971; Goldstein & Hersen, 1984) that clearly makes a case for objectivity, quantification, and standardization based on appropriate normative studies.

The case could be made that while one should employ well-standardized tests, those tests may be selected on an individual basis in order to respond to the referral question, or the particular characteristics of the patient. In other words, if one adopts the use of only quantitative procedures, one need not administer these procedures in the form of one of the standard batteries. The difficulty we would have with this approach is that, in the typical clinical situation, it is often not a simple matter to administer both those tests that the patient is likely to do poorly on, plus those tests on which he or she will probably perform within the normal range. The temptation is clearly to administer those procedures that are most likely to clarify the patient's presenting problem. That is a perfectly reasonable procedure when doing diagnostic assessments, but assessment for rehabilitation planning is another matter. There, I would take the position that it is crucial to obtain quantitative measures of ability levels, even though those levels may be well within the normal range. The utilization of a standard battery as a routine clinical procedure would appear to make it easier to obtain the desired profile of assets and deficits. In this regard, clinical neuropsychology may have a good deal to learn from the fields of educational and vocational planning and rehabilitation, in which the use of standard batteries is commonplace.

## Philosophies of rehabilitation

The above comments may be viewed as suggesting a certain stance toward the rehabilitation of brain-damaged patients that requires some explication. It is our view that the philosophy of rehabilitation expressed by such authorities as Luria (1973) and the NYU group (Diller & Gordon, 1981) are individual theoretical orientations that do not necessarily reflect some set of commonly agreed upon goals. For example, the philosophy of rehabilitation associated with Luria's functional system theory suggests that the task of neuropsychological assessment is that of identifying the defective link in the functional system involved so that it can be replaced with an intact link, thus restoring, at least to some extent, the system as a whole. Thus, for example, acoustic analysis may be replaced by tactile analysis in the mediation of some behavior. In other words, the concept of 'rehabilitation' is rather tightly associated with specific restoration of function. On the other extreme, it is also possible to view rehabilitation much more globally, perhaps in terms of restoring the impaired patient to some form of productive living or by providing an improved quality of life. The latter approach may not involve specific restoration at all, but rather may involve the identification of some area in which the patient may be productive, despite his or her neuropsychological deficits. Thus, the aphasic patient may be rehabilitated by painting houses, while the amnesic patient may be taught to work in a situation in which recent memory is not crucial for optimal performance.

With regard to neuropsychological assessment, our position would be that if one takes the latter approach it is not sufficient to simply select an unimpaired area as the rehabilitation focus. More must be known about the status of the unimpaired area. One must know how good the aphasic patient is at house painting, and not simply that aphasia would not appear to greatly impair one's ability to paint houses as long as working channels of communication are established. Standard neuropsychological assessment, in combination with other methods, could be of great value in determining vocational capacities in situations of this type. In any event, the goals of rehabilitation might best be formulated in terms of rehabilitating a person rather than a system, and effective treatment may not simply be a matter of restoring some specific mechanism, even when such restoration is possible. With regard to the latter point, the currently available data only reflect an extremely modest level of success with regard to restoration of specific functions unaided by natural recovery processes (Hamsher, 1984). Although the degree of efficacy of treatment is a controversial issue (Helm-Estabrooks & Holland, 1984), few authorities would deny that it is extremely difficult to separate out the effects of active, specific treatment from what is accomplished by nature. However, the chronic, persistent presence of certain symptoms does not preclude the possibility of rehabilitation in terms of exploiting preserved abilities. Difficulties in rehabilitation often emerge when no program is instituted for the patient when his or her specific symptoms are viewed as untreatable. While that view may be correct, efforts made in directions other than attempting to treat an untreatable condition could have been productive. In other words, rehabilitation in a sense broader than attempts at specific restoration of function could have been accomplished. My view is that the comprehensive neuropsychological assessment batteries, because of the broad range of abilities they tap, could be quite useful in exploring alternative approaches to the patient.

## REHABILITATION AND THE HALSTEAD–REITAN BATTERY

We can identify two approaches to rehabilitation planning based on assessment with the HRB. One of them was developed by Ralph Reitan and is known as the REHABIT system. The other approach is reported in Goldstein & Ruthven (1983). REHABIT is an acronym for Reitan Evaluation of Hemispheric Abilities and Brain Improvement Training. The system is as yet unpublished, but information describing it has been provided in Reitan's workshops. The REHABIT system involves three phases: (1) HRB evaluation, (2) use of the tests themselves as training devices and (3) specific training utilizing a broad variety of training materials, such as the Frostig developmental program or various pegboards and card sets containing conceptual, verbal, or visual-spatial material. The program is organized into five tracks: (a) language and verbal skills; (b) language and verbal skills with an element of abstraction and logical analysis; (c) reasoning, organization, and abstraction; (d) abstraction with an emphasis on visual-spatial and manipulatory skills; and (e) fundamental visual-spatial and manipulatory skills. In his descriptive material for REHABIT, Reitan points out that a comprehensive assessment is necessary in rehabilitation planning because while some neuropsychological deficits are quite specific, more often than not they are general, involving several abilities. The REHABIT system has not yet been evaluated in a research context, but appears to be a promising and comprehensive approach to the rehabilitation of brain-damaged patients.

Goldstein & Ruthven (1983) used the HRB to recommend the class of vocationally oriented rehabilitation to be used by a series of brain-damaged patients in a sheltered workshop setting. Great emphasis was placed on the distinction between left hemisphere or language-related programs, such as mail sorting, and right hemisphere or visual-spatial programs, such as assembly manufacturing tasks. Clients who did not have a specific language or visual-spatial deficit (mainly individuals with diffuse lesions) were placed through exploration in a number of alternative tasks. These authors report that the program was successful, in that there was significant post-testing improvement relative to what was found for a control group. More significantly, however, while none of the clients was engaged in work or educational activities prior to the program, many of them found jobs or went back to school after its completion. The post-testing data indicated that the improvement tended to be found on the more non-specific procedures, such as the Category test, rather than on the measures of relatively discrete abilities. Perhaps the Goldstein and Ruthven study stands as an illustration that successful rehabilitation can be achieved without restoration of specific neuropsychological deficits. Many of their clients had such deficits, but rather than treating them formally, the clients were put to productive work either because their assignments may have sharpened their skill levels in relatively intact areas, or because the work itself served as a means of retraining in defective areas. However, without a comprehensive neuropsychological assessment, appropriate placements among alternatives available in the sheltered workshop setting may not have been possible. Sometimes the work program was supplemented by formal treatment such as speech therapy or training in attention or visual–spatial skills. The neuropsychological assessments were also useful in identifying treatment needs of that type.

The use of the HRB in rehabilitation planning is a new and relatively unexplored area, but several rationales for its use have been put forth, and there are some promising data. The need is clear, however, for further program evaluation and demonstration of efficacy. Because of their use of comprehensive assessment systems, both the REHABIT and Goldstein and Ruthven approaches do justice to the complexity of neurological dysfunction, and the fact that most brain-damaged patients do not have single, isolated deficits. Indeed, much of the early literature in clinical neuropsychology and behavioral neurology, particularly the case literature, mistakenly reported such deficits in patients because of failure to obtain comprehensive data. Thus, deficits that may have been present in such patients, and contributory to the symptoms reported, were not detected because they were not investigated. Perhaps the clearest example of this difficulty is to be found in the case of the so-called 'Gerstmann Syndrome' (Benton, 1961).

## REHABILITATION AND THE LURIA-NEBRASKA BATTERY

To the best of my knowledge there have been no formal efficacy or program evaluation studies of rehabilitation planning with the LNNB, probably because the LNNB is a relatively new procedure, its manual only appearing in 1980 (Golden et al, 1980). Of course, Luria wrote a book on restoration of function many years ago (Luria, 1963; original publication date 1948), but the contents of that book have absolutely nothing to do with the use of quantitatively oriented comprehensive neuropsychological assessment batteries in rehabilitation planning. Indeed, they did not exist when Luria wrote his book. In any event, Luria's approach to rehabilitation has been presented elsewhere (Christensen, 1984; Luria, 1963) and whether developers and advocates of the LNNB would take the same approach to rehabilitation planning as did Luria and his co-workers is debatable. The case example of rehabilitation assessment based on Luria's procedure (Christensen, 1984) does not mention the use of standardized tests in the neuropsychological evaluation. More likely the approach to rehabilitation planning taken by LNNB users would resemble the HRB approach associated with REHABIT, or perhaps the Goldstein and Ruthven method.

There has been some suggestion that the LNNB may be better for rehabilitation planning than the HRB because of the relatively discrete nature of the 269 items that make up that procedure. These separate pieces of information may have the potential of indicating in detail just what the patient can and cannot do. That may or may not be the case, although there have been no demonstrations of that purported advantage. There is one area, however, in which the LNNB would have superiority – memory. The absence of formal memory testing as part of the standard HRB has been noted by many observers (Goldstein, 1984; Russell, 1981), while the LNNB does have a Memory Scale. While we would not support the view that this scale provides comprehensive information about a patient's memory in order to formulate a rehabilitation plan, at least it provides the opportunity to identify a memory deficit that can be assessed further with more refined procedures. Somewhat disconcerting is the fact that while memory training is perhaps the most widely used and intensively studied form of cognitive rehabilitation (other than speech therapy), one of the most widely used comprehensive assessment procedures provides no systematic evaluation of it. However, many clinicians, recognizing this lack, have added formal memory tests to the HRB. Many clinicians use the Wechsler Memory Scale or similar procedure as a supplement to the HRB. The modifications proposed by Russell (1975) and Kaplan (1980) are also frequently used to provide assessments of aspects of memory that are of great neuropsychological interest, notably the status of delayed recall ability. Recently, Golden (1984) wrote a chapter on the LNNB and rehabilitation, but it does not describe an efficacy program. Golden does provide a case example, however, of how the LNNB may be used in rehabilitation planning. The patient was a young woman who had sustained a severe head injury. While she demonstrated generalized impairment on the LNNB, her major difficulty appeared to be in the area of visual perception. She was placed into both speech and occupational therapy. In speech therapy efforts were made to have her describe pictures, while in occupational therapy she was trained to match objects to pictures and to sort objects by use. Later, as she recovered, her writing was emphasized by having her write letters and verbalize them while her eyes were closed, since she retained the ability to use kinesthetic cues in writing. Gradually, she could write more and more with her eyes open. Arithmetic and memory training were also attempted, with mixed results. Unfortunately, this program was instituted while the patient was recovering from her trauma and so it is impossible to evaluate its efficacy. While it was quite appropriate clinically to initiate treatment at that time, the evaluation of treatment efficacy may be accomplished more unequivocally utilizing case examples with more stable conditions.

Based simply on consideration of the content differences between the HRB and the LNNB, each procedure has advantages and disadvantages. If rehabilitation is being contemplated in the memory or language areas, then the LNNB might be the procedure of choice, since it contains some formal memory testing and provides a more extensive language evaluation than does the HRB. On the other hand, the HRB would appear to be better for conceptual problems and visual-spatial disorders, since it contains more extensive and challenging tests in those areas. In any event it is impossible to evaluate the efficacy of the LNNB in rehabilitation planning or evaluation, since the appropriate studies have not been completed. Furthermore, there has been no system or methodology worked out of the REHABIT type, or of the kind of programs developed by Diller and his collaborators, such as the Block Design or visual scanning training programs (Diller & Gordon, 1981). One could also attempt to apply some of the programs described in Luria's book *Restoration of Function After Brain Injury* (Luria, 1963), but to the best of my knowledge that has not been attempted.

## AUTOMATED SYSTEMS

Considering the small amount of work done in rehabilitation planning utilizing the comprehensive batteries, it would be premature, to say the least, to speak of computerizing or automating those procedures. One might imagine the results of an automated assessment going into a computer, which returns a comprehensive rehabilitation plan, but currently such a procedure is science-fiction and not science. However, since the publication of Russell et al (1970) many clinicians have used computers to score and provide preliminary interpretations of neuropsychological tests. There have been several attempts at automating administration of neuropsychological tests, but thus far they have been less than successful. Since it is difficult to distinguish between the use of computers in rehabilitation planning specifically and in assessment in general, I will examine both areas of them together. I will take the position that while computerized testing has numerous problems with regard to administration and interpretation of neuropsychological tests, it has many advantages.

### Computers, in many crucial respects, are faster than human beings

The implication of this point is simply that test material can be processed much more rapidly with computer support than without it. Tests can be scored more rapidly, word-processing systems can prepare reports more quickly, and data can be transmitted more efficiently. In certain clinical situations, things not done rapidly are sometimes not worth being done at all, and to the extent that computer support can expedite processing of information it may substantially improve services to patients. This idea is well supported in the recent trend toward computerization of many modern hospitals and clinics.

### Computers are less biased and often more accurate than humans

Despite our best efforts we are subject to error when tests are scored by hand. The situation could be aggravated as we go more into use of complex multivariate tests with complicated scoring systems. Since the early work of Rosenthal (1966) we also know that recording of data may sometimes reflect the biases of the examiner. The absolute accuracy of computers in regard to calculation, and their lack of bias as long as the data are entered correctly, provides real advantages.

### Computers have the capacity to store, tabulate, analyze, and retrieve large masses of data rapidly and efficiently

This point requires little elaboration. In evaluating rehabilitation programs the capacity to record and instantly retrieve previous assessment or treatment data is clearly advantageous. In doing general neuropsychological rehabilitation research the use of computers has essentially become a necessity. The capacity to monitor treatment data periodically with a computer is a very valuable asset.

### In addition to data, computers can store large amounts of clinically relevant knowledge

Professionals in various specialities of clinical practice have made extensive use of computerized databases to quickly obtain information that they may not have immediately available. Numerous interactive 'advice-giving' systems have been developed in medicine that provide the physician with information crucial for diagnosis and prescribing treatment. While no such systems are currently available in clinical neuropsychology the computers provide the opportunity to develop such systems in the future.

## Computers can be more precise than humans

When one enters the realm of the more detailed aspects of neuropsychological assessment, sometimes it becomes necessary to make rather refined measurements. Reaction times, detection of thresholds, and related psychophysical measurements can often be accomplished with extreme accuracy utilizing the timers and counters that are parts of many computer systems. Additionally, more refined measures may be obtained from our standard clinical tests through automation. For example, it is now possible to obtain measures of fluctuation on finger tapping tasks in addition to simple number of taps. Recently, Butcher & Keller (1984) have reported on a computerized device that records response latencies and key pressure to MMPI items (Stout, 1981). These more refined measures may ultimately greatly enhance the sensitivity of psychological assessment. While some clinicians may insist that they are sensitized to these subtleties, and regularly observe them in their face-to-face evaluation of patients, we suspect that these individuals would lose to computers in any contest concerning accuracy levels.

## Computers have a future

While criticisms have been raised concerning the premature and perhaps exploitative use of computers in administration and interpretation of neuropsychological tests, it would seem foolhardy to insist that technologies not currently available may not become available in the future. Our computer scientists and engineers may eventually develop a technology that will provide a very satisfactory means of administering many neuropsychological tests, despite the fact that such a goal has not yet been achieved. Whether computerized administration is used exclusively or as an adjunct to the experienced clinician will depend on preference and technological advances. Advances will surely be made in computerized test interpretation, relative to the rather primitive systems available at present. Again, acceptance or rejection of computerized test interpretation is a matter of personal preference, but it would appear unwise to reject potential future developments on the basis of what is currently available.

*Caveats*: Having outlined these advantages of computer applications in neuropsychology, disadvantages or dangers must be acknowledged. There is one major disadvantage that is, in fact, a genuine danger, that various computer 'packages' for administration and interpretation may be provided to individuals who are not fully competent to utilize them in clinical situations. Such individuals may also not have the necessary expertise to evaluate these 'packages' in terms of their capacity to fulfill the claims made for them. Recently, various organizations have formed oversight committees to monitor these developments in computer technology and to provide guidelines for ethical professional practice. This development is probably a desirable one and may contribute substantially to the scientifically and professionally sound development of computer technologies. We are aware that there are also those clinicians who suffer from computer phobia, or who adhere to the belief that their established clinical techniques and skills can never be replaced by computers. This latter group may cite some method of observation or assessment along with the claim that a computer could never accomplish it. While being sympathetic with those who feel uncomfortable being around computers, I would take issue with the claim that computers can never perform certain tasks, simply on the basis that these matters are impossible to determine. We cannot predict the future with any degree of certainty.

*Summary*: I view automated systems in neuropsychology primarily as something for the future. What we have now are primitive beginnings of questionable general applicability. There are some very useful scoring systems available, but attempts at computerized interpretation have been limited to the making of rather basic decisions, while attempts at development of computer-administered batteries are clearly in their infancy. I have tried to outline some of the advantages that could accrue for neuropsychology through increased application of computer technology, and have pointed out a major danger of going in that direction. However, that danger can be overcome through mature professional behavior and practice.

## NON-PSYCHOMETRIC METHODS

Typically and traditionally, neuropsychologists have learned about their patients through tests; either through analysis of test scores or observing the patient while he or she is taking a test. Thus far in this chapter I have written in favor of objective, quantitative tests administered in some organized fashion; i.e., as part of a comprehensive battery. However, the utilization of objective, standard, and quantitative methods need not be limited to psychometric testing. There is an extensive literature, generally characterized as involving behavioral assessment, that utilizes objective and quantitative methods in the direct observation of behavior (Hersen & Bellack, 1981). The application of behavioral assessment in clinical neuropsychology is a relatively new departure, but I feel that it holds great promise for the fields of neuropsychological assessment, and for rehabilitation planning in particular. The techniques of behavioral assessment involve direct and indirect methods (Nelson & Hayes, 1981). The direct methods include observation of the individual in a natural setting, or in an analogue situation and self-monitoring; while the indirect methods involve interviewing, ratings by others, and self-reports. For present purposes I will restrict my discussion to the direct method of observation in natural settings. Thus, I will be concerned with what is learned about the patient through systematic, unobtrusive observation of behavior on the ward or in other treatment/rehabilitation settings in which we typically find patients. It should be pointed out at the beginning that I am not talking about casual, anecdotally reported observations. Rather, I am addressing myself to the establishment of a number of structured, quantitative techniques developed over the years in connection with the development of behavior therapy programs. While most behavioral assessments are conducted before, during and after some treatment intervention, discussion here will be largely limited to the pre-intervention phase of the process.

The behavioral assessment procedure is initiated through identification of some target behavior to be observed. The observation methodology is then determined. It can be in the form of a time sample in which the patient is observed for a fixed time period during which the incidence of the targeted behavior or behaviors are recorded over established units of time during the sample period. For example, recordings can be made for every minute of a 10-minute time sample. Observations of this type are generally brief, and are made at several times during the day. The time sample is actually a form of interval method, in which the behavior is simply rated as present or absent. The dependent measure in this case is frequency of occurrence. However, it is also possible to measure duration or intensity of the target behavior when assessing a behavior. Perhaps the most crucial aspect of a behavioral assessment involves the determination of the conditions under which the behavior occurs. Generally these are environmental contingencies that serve as reinforcers for the target behavior. Behavior therapy is often a process of altering those contingencies through the establishment of some form of treatment program. Thus, in very brief summary, behavioral assessment of the direct observation type involves systematic observation and recording of some parameter of a target behavior, and of the circumstances under which the behavior occurs. The view that certain aspects of the behavior of brain-damaged patients are determined by the neuropsychological deficit, while other behaviors are under environmental control, requires some elaboration from the point of view of rehabilitation philosophy.

## Further remarks on philosophies of rehabilitation

I will propose and briefly elaborate on two ideas. The first may be viewed as a variation of Lewin's formulation that behavior is a function of the individual interacting with an environment ($B = f\ [P,\ E]$). In the case of the brain-damaged patient we would say that brain damage can alter behavior, but not all of a brain-damaged individual's behavior is determined by the brain damage. Much of it may be controlled by environmental contingencies, as would be the case for everybody. Within neuropsychology, there has been an emphasis (perhaps an over-emphasis) on organismic determinants of behavior, with little attention paid to the influence of the environment. Thus, neuropsychologically oriented rehabilitation programs have focused on restoration of functions rather than on person–environment interactions. The application of methods derived from behavioristic approaches to personality and psychopathology, notably behavioral assessment and behavior therapy, may provide more of a balance in our treatment modalities.

The second idea is that a distinction can be made between two kinds of rehabilitative treatment which I will describe as generic and specific. In generic treatment a general skill is trained in anticipation of generalization to a variety of specific behaviors that utilize that skill. In specific treatment the specific behaviors themselves become the target of the treatment program. Thus, for example, visual-spatial skills may be taught so that the patient may be more effective at tasks that require that skill such as dressing, eating, reading maps, making assemblies, and performing related tasks. Specific training would select one of those individual tasks and deal only with it. For example, the program may be directed toward teaching the patient eating skills. In general, generic training has been largely associated with clinical neuropsychology and particularly with those neuropsychologists involved in cognitive rehabilitation or retraining. Specific training is much more highly associated with behavior therapy, and particularly with those aspects of it that address themselves to mentally retarded and psychiatric patients (Hersen & Bellack, 1978). It would probably be fair to say that most neuropsychologists focus on organismic variables and generically oriented rehabilitation, while most behavior therapists involve themselves largely with environmental variables, and their treatments tend to be rather specific. Some time ago (Goldstein, 1979) I made an appeal for collaboration between neuropsychologists and behavior therapists with a focus on treatment of brain-damaged patients, and I would like to restate that appeal here.

Behavioral assessment methods are most appropriate for the planning of specific training in that they are oriented toward observation of discrete target behaviors and the environmental contingencies that maintain them. My view is that a strong case can be made for the extensive application of specific training to brain-damaged patients. First of all, the empirical evidence for generalization to activities of daily living from generic cognitive retraining is relatively meagre. Much of the positive work in this area has been done by the New York University (NYU) group (Diller & Gordon, 1981) who were able to demonstrate that their block design and visual scanning training generalized to improvement in occupational therapy (OT) activities and in the organizational aspects of eating. However, studies of that type are few and far between, with efficacy of treatment generally evaluated within the framework of the treatment itself. Second, there have been extensive and impressive demonstrations of the efficacy of specific, behavior therapy-oriented treatment programs with psychiatric (Hersen & Bellack, 1978) and mentally retarded (Matson & Mulick, 1983) populations. In that schizophrenic and mentally retarded patients share many of the cognitive disorders found in brain-damaged patients, one might express some optimism concerning the efficacy of behavior therapy in its unexplored application to brain-damaged patients. Finally, there are practical considerations. If a patient has difficulty eating, why not simply teach him or her to eat, rather than teach a visual-spatial constructional task with the hope that the results of that training will generalize to certain aspects of eating? The mental retardation literature reports substantial success with this form of practical training in such areas as dressing, certain aspects of language skill, toileting, and social skills. Why wouldn't these methods work with brain-damaged adults? Brain-damaged patients frequently exhibit problematic behaviors that, while specific, reflect some interaction between their neurological impairment and events taking place in the environment. The assaultive patient may have become assaultive following a severe head injury, but his or her assaultiveness may be modulated in relation to the amount of provocation taking place in the environment. The incontinent patient may achieve better control when an episode of incontinence is not followed by an increase in attention paid to him or her by the nursing staff.

We understand that the hope for cognitive training was that it would be an efficient means of teaching general skills that could be applied in a number of contexts, and for that reason may be more efficient than teaching each separate skill separately. However, the data available suggest that while training of this type is often effective in terms of meeting the educational goals of the program itself, there is little evidence that these procedures actually assist patients with their everyday activities. On the other hand, the existence of severely disruptive or disabling behaviors of a specific nature may, in some cases, be remediated with the educational technologies provided by the behavior therapists. Elsewhere (Goldstein & Ruthven, 1983; Goldstein et al, in press) we have provided demonstrations of the efficacy of such methods in individual cases.

## The interface between standard comprehensive neuropsychological assessment and behavioral assessment

Thus far I have considered two rather diverse assessment methods: the standard neuropsychology batteries and behavioral assessment. However, my view is that they can be used together productively in rehabilitation programs. Here I would like to outline how this might be implemented. In my experience, and probably in the experience of many clinical neuropsychologists, the majority of brain-damaged patients do not have single specific deficits. When such deficits occur they most often are in the context of some degree of generalized intellectual impairment and a series of rather specific behavioral problems. Within institutional settings for chronic patients it is usually the behavioral problems that perpetuate institutionalization, and not the deficits themselves. For example, the amnesic patient may remain institutionalized not because he or she has a poor memory, but because of wandering behavior resulting in getting lost and not recalling how to get back home. Non-wanderers with memory problems of equal density may not become institutionalized. Within this context, there may be a major difference from the standpoint of rehabilitation between the patient in a rehabilitation hospital who is in treatment during the period immediately following an acute episode, generally associated with trauma, stroke or conditions treated surgically, and the patient with chronic illness, inside or outside of an institutional setting. These differences involve diagnostic matters, behavioral manifestations, prognosis, motivational considerations, and neuropsychological findings. The role of natural recovery processes is also quite significant here, in that rehabilitation of a patient with an evolving condition, particularly when the direction is toward recovery, is quite different from rehabilitation of an individual with a stable or progressively deteriorating disorder.

In view of this diversity, it is difficult to suggest that one form of rehabilitation planning is best for all patients, in all settings and under all circumstances. There are, first of all, practical constraints. Patients in certain settings may not have the time needed to take the Halstead–Reitan battery. Behavioral assessment is a person-intensive method, and staff may not be available to make the necessary observations. There are general patient-related variables. Some patients may be too ill, feeble or impaired to take a full comprehensive assessment procedure. There are ethical considerations. Active rehabilitation efforts may not be appropriate for patients suffering from progressive illnesses, since, despite the patient's and therapist's best efforts, the advancing disease process may perpetually cancel out the treatment effects obtained. For example, one might have qualms about providing memory training to patients with Huntington's disease or multiple sclerosis. There are certainly appropriate treatment strategies for individuals with progressive illnesses, but they may not be of the cognitive retraining–restoration of function type. Indeed, this area of treatment deserves great attention, but its consideration here would take us far afield from our present topic. However, despite the diversity, we generally all work with patients who have patterns of cognitive, perceptual, and motor strengths and deficits, as revealed by testing, as well as characteristic behaviors, attitudes, and motivational states, that can be assessed through observation in natural settings. Thus, the patient with a frontal lobe wound might demonstrate conceptual impairment on neuropsychological tests, but might also be inappropriately sexually impulsive, something that would not generally be made manifest through performance on the Category test.

The above somewhat facetious illustration contains the essence of our recommended approach. Under relatively ideal conditions, that is when time is available, the patient is testable and cooperative, staffing is adequate, etc. it is highly desirable to administer a comprehensive neuropsychological test battery and conduct an appropriate behavioral assessment as integral parts of the rehabilitation planning program. The utilization of comprehensive assessment is important since these procedures tend to do justice to the combination of deficits usually found among brain-damaged patients, and, as indicated earlier, allow for the systematic and quantitative evaluation of strengths and weaknesses. We would agree that the available comprehensive assessment batteries may not provide sufficiently detailed information about specific areas of cognitive function, and additional specialized testing may be necessary in many cases. The comprehensive assessments also provide information about general level of performance, and such information is of crucial importance in determining the level at which to approach the patient. The behavioral assessment provides information concerning the visible manifestations of the patient's underlying cognitive deficit as well as the role of environmental contingencies in maintaining problematic behaviors. Once these data are in, an informed decision can be made about the treatment approach, and a rationally based treatment plan can be formulated. What happens at this point can be conceptualized as a decision tree. One would first determine whether a generic, specific, or multimodal approach should be taken. There are several considerations here. The patient's overt behavior may be so disorganized or disruptive that there is little choice but to intervene pharmacologically, behaviorally, or both to deal with that behavior. There is often a pre-rehabilitation phase of treatment during which the patient's affective or behavioral difficulties must be addressed before systematic rehabilitative efforts can even be contemplated. Deciding upon a specific approach implies identification of a target behavior, followed by formulation of a treatment design and collection of appropriate baseline data. The neuropsychological tests may be helpful here, particularly with regard to level of performance considerations. For example, a design involving delayed reinforcement and the use of tokens may not be appropriate for the patient with such severe conceptual impairment that the association between the appropriate behavior and issuance of the token as a secondary reinforcer cannot be appreciated. In our experience we have found that there can be genuinely productive relationships formed between neuropsychologists and behavior therapists in this regard. The behavior therapists tend to be particularly skilled at designing treatment programs, but sometimes need to be reminded by the neuropsychologist that their program may not work, for example because they are dependent on recall of the reinforcement history and the patient has dense amnesia. In some cases I have found that these exchanges ultimately led to the formulation of programs that did work.

Branching to a generic approach may be based on a number of considerations. Perhaps the most important one is that the major deficit is so severe that little can be done to improve the patient's general condition until it is dealt with in some way. The densely amnesic and aphasic patients are good examples of this situation. If the patient cannot remember anything, or cannot communicate, little can be accomplished. It is therefore necessary to attempt to restore at least some aspects of memory or language in order to significantly assist the patient to resume as many normal life activities as possible. Alternatively the relatively rare patient with an isolated deficit and without significant behavioral problems may be an ideal candidate for generic cognitive retraining. The model here would be the child with a specific learning disability who may benefit greatly from formal remedial education without intrusion into any other aspects of his or her life. In planning programs of this type the neuropsychological assessment is helpful in its traditional role as a diagnostic instrument. It can help to identify the specific nature of the disability, delineate the profile of intact and impaired abilities, estimate general level of performance, and provide material for making inferences concerning the nature of the relevant brain–behavior relationships. Thus, for example, if the client is viewed as preferring to process information with the right cerebral hemisphere, then that information can be productively used in determining the form of remediation to be used. I would grant that for this kind of treatment planning the standard assessment batteries may not provide all the information needed to formulate the program. However, I would argue they are necessary but not sufficient, in that they can provide significant information that may not be available through specialized, targeted assessment of only the area in which there is an obvious deficit. In this regard, I would agree with the general philosophy implicit in formulation of approaches of the REHABIT type. However, I strongly suspect that users of that program will find the core Halstead–Reitan battery may not be fully adequate, in at least some cases, to answer pertinent assessment questions, and that supplemental tests will have to be employed, particularly in the language and memory areas.

In a general way, I can conceive of rehabilitation as change, but changes can take place both in the patient and in the patient's environment. The former alternative corresponds, more or less, to Diller & Gordon's (1981) psychometrist and biologist models of rehabilitation, while the latter generally corresponds with their engineer model. When questioned about the wisdom of attempting to rehabilitate patients with medically incurable or perhaps progressive illnesses, one response I have made is that while one may not be able to change the patient or the condition that the patient suffers from, one can change the world in which the patient lives. In more behavioral terms, one can work toward the alteration of environments and environmental contingencies in a manner that increases performance levels and improves quality of life. Such approaches can even be taken with patients who have progressive disorders, as in the case of the substantial effort now being made to improve management of patients with Alzheimer's disease. As we know, the field of clinical neuropsychology contains both optimists and pessimists with regard to the efficacy of rehabilitation for brain-damaged patients. The available data are, as yet, inconclusive, and suggest that modest but demonstrable changes may come about through systematic cognitive retraining. The extent to which the efficacy of these retraining efforts can be improved through formulating the training program on the basis of the results of neuropsychological testing also requires further evaluation. I am fully aware that many clinical neuropsychologists firmly believe their test findings are of major significance for rehabilitation planning, but there has been little consideration of the impact on outcome of how the findings are communicated to educators and rehabilitation specialists. The traditional written report phrased in technical neuropsychological terminology may not be the optimal method. In general, I have had better luck through working directly with nursing personnel and specialty therapists in implementing the formulations and recommendations derived from the neuropsychological assessment.

In order to make these views more explicit, I can provide the following general rehabilitation overview with some brief examples. The first consideration is that I use the term rehabilitation in a comprehensive sense, and do not limit its definition to the area of restoration of function. A rehabilitation program is more than restoration of specific functions. Conversely, effective rehabilitation can sometimes be accomplished without restoration of function. For example, blind individuals are often successfully rehabilitated without restoration of vision. Within this context, brain-damaged patients frequently have both cognitive and perceptual deficits involving impairment of some formal process or of some content (e.g. language) that can be elicited with neuropsychological tests. However, they are rarely totally disabled, and may have some well-preserved abilities, which can also be measured with tests. In this regard I use the term 'measured' advisedly, and have little use for the statement that these functions are 'normal' or 'intact.' Aside from these deficits, brain-damaged patients also have what may be described, admittedly inadequately, as behavioral problems, that cannot be measured with tests, but that can be evaluated with behavioral assessment techniques. While these behaviors may have been associated in some way with the brain damage, they may also be associated with factors in the patient's social history or with ongoing environmental contingencies. My general view regarding rehabilitation planning is therefore that it is generally desirable to do comprehensive neuropsychological testing in order to obtain quantitative measures of ability in both preserved and impaired areas, and to do a behavioral assessment in order to evaluate problematic behaviors that could significantly interfere with the patient's adjustment to more independent living. In this regard it is particularly helpful to make a determination of the extent to which these behaviors are solely the consequence of brain disease, and which may at least be modulated by environmental events. Following the completion of the data collection phase of the assessment, a decision can be made with regard to the most promising route to pursue. In general, the decision initially is reduced to whether it is best to pursue some form of behavior therapy, cognitive retraining or a combination of the two. Once that decision is made, the specific treatment strategies can be devised.

As an example, I may mention the case of a young man with Huntington's disease. The neuropsychological tests provided clear evidence of the intellectual impairments commonly associated with this disorder (Boll et al, 1974). On the ward the patient would frequently have temper tantrums, and would go on hunger strikes if he did not get his way. In one particular incident he went on a hunger strike when a nurse he was particularly fond of was unavailable to take care of him. Since he had used this behavior before, and since he typically achieved his goals since nutrition is particularly important with Huntington's disease patients, we appeared to have a reinforcement history that was the basis for the incident with the nurse. The treatment team determined that, while this patient had significant cognitive deficits, it would be wrong to attempt cognitive retraining because of the progressive nature of his illness. However, the staff recognized that some form of behavior therapy was necessary to deal with the hunger strike problem. A very simple intervention was utilized in which the patient was informed that he would not be permitted to starve, but that the nurse would not be made available to him despite his behavior. The hunger strikes soon disappeared, and it became possible to work with this patient along more productive lines. In this case the neuropsychological tests were important because they suggested a level at which to approach this patient, but the treatment itself, simple as it was, was along behavior therapeutic lines.

In a second case a somewhat different approach was taken. The patient was a 25-year-old man who, after sustaining a head injury in an automobile accident, developed an anomic aphasia that was present 4 months after the accident, when we tested him. The Halstead–Reitan results reflected the effects of the language deficit as well as some degree of generalized intellectual impairment. However, the most pertinent findings for the discussion here are the following. He obtained a WAIS verbal IQ of 46 and a performance IQ of 89. While his scores were below average for most of the performance tests, he obtained a Block Design score of 11, which is above average for the population. Furthermore, his drawings were of good quality and he correctly recalled 7 of the 10 Tactual Performance Test blocks; a performance level that falls within the normal range. Therefore, despite the language deficits and the generalized intellectual impairment, the patient apparently had good visual-spatial abilities. While the patient received speech therapy for his aphasia, another aspect of rehabilitation planning was assisting him with his education so that he might become re-employed. Here, the performance test data became quite useful because the patient's artistic talents were noted, and the vocational rehabilitation specialists wanted to know whether he had the general capacity to pursue training in art work. We felt that he did, because of the good performances noted. He was placed into a commercial art school and I understand that he did well.

I bring this case up not because of its successful outcome, but for two other reasons. First, if a specialized, 'targeted' assessment had been done with this patient it probably would have reached a sophisticated understanding of the aphasia, but may have missed the good visual-spatial ability, except, perhaps that there may have been some indication that it was 'intact.' Second, as noted, it is not sufficient to declare a function as 'intact' for purposes of rehabilitation planning. The quantitative measure of performance on Block Design indicated not only that the underlying visual-spatial ability was intact, but that the patient could perform at a level sufficiently high to allow him to compete with the normal population for limited educational and vocational opportunities. Therefore, in this case, a comprehensive battery was useful because it clearly provided a quantitative measure of an asset that was productively used in rehabilitation planning. This approach to rehabilitation also reflects a very different model from the functional system, syndrome analysis oriented approach. That latter approach may have been quite appropriate for planning for treatment of the patient's aphasia, but may have been less effective for the more comprehensive rehabilitation program that was implemented in this case.

## SUMMARY

In summary, there may be certain advantages in using the standard, comprehensive neuropsychological assessment methods in rehabilitation planning, as long as the opportunity is provided for other indicated forms of assessment. The assessment process can be expedited, made more accurate and, to some extent, more informed through utilization of computers, but we have not yet reached the stage at which the automated interpretative systems can replace clinical judgement. However, the computerized interpretation programs can make preliminary statements of proven validity, and the rapid generation of such statements may be quite useful during the early stages of assessment. In addition to specialized neuropsychological assessment, I have indicated that various types of behavioral assessment may be highly relevant to rehabilitation planning and evaluation. Within my framework, rehabilitation is conceptualized not only as restoration of function through the application of various educational methods, but is a broader process that involves treatment of specific behavioral problems and alterations of environmental situations as a means of coping with those problems. As pointed out, many patients may be aided in improving their adaptive functioning and capacity for independent living through the application of methods derived from behavior therapy, particularly when behavior therapists and clinical neuropsychologists collaborate on the assessment, design, and implementation phases of rehabilitative programs.

## REFERENCES

Anastasi A 1982 Psychological testing. Macmillan, New York

Benton A L 1961 The fiction of the Gerstmann syndrome. Journal of Neurology, Neurosurgery and Psychiatry 24: 176–181

Boll T J 1981 The Halstead-Reitan neuropsychology battery. In: Filskov S B, Boll T J (eds) Handbook of clinical neuropsychology. Wiley-Interscience, New York

Boll T J, Heaton R, Reitan R M 1974 Neuropsychological and emotional correlates of Huntington's chorea. Journal of Nervous and Mental Disease 158: 61–69

Butcher J N, Keller L S 1984 Objective personality assessment. In: Goldstein G, Hersen M (eds) Handbook of psychological assessment. Pergamon Press, New York

Christensen A-L 1975 Luria's neuropsychological investigation. Spectrum, New York

Christensen A-L 1979 A practical application of the Luria methodology. Journal of Clinical Neuropsychology 1: 241–247

Christensen A-L 1984 The Luria method of examination of the brain-impaired patient. In: Logue P E, Schear J M (eds) Clinical neuropsychology: a multidisciplinary approach. C. C. Thomas, Springfield, IL

Cronbach L J 1971 Essentials of psychological testing. Harper, New York

Diller L, Gordon W A 1981 Rehabilitation and clinical neuropsychology. In: Filskov S B, Boll T J (eds) Handbook of clinical neuropsychology. John Wiley, New York

Finkelstein J N 1977 BRAIN: a computer program for interpretation of the Halstead-Reitan Neuropsychological Test Battery. Dissertation Abstracts International 37: 5349B. (Doctoral dissertation, Columbia University, 1976. University Microfilms No. 77–8, 8864)

Golden C J 1981 A standardized version of Luria's neuropsychological tests: a quantitative and qualitative approach to neuropsychological evaluation. In: Filskov S B, Boll T J (eds) Handbook of clinical neuropsychology. Wiley-Interscience, New York

Golden C 1984 Rehabilitation and the Luria–Nebraska Neuropsychological Battery:

introduction to theory and practice. In: Edelstein B A, Couture E T (eds), Behavioral assessment and rehabilitation of the traumatically brain damaged. Plenum, New York

Golden C J, Hammeke T A, Purisch A D 1980 The Luria–Nebraska Battery manual. Western Psychological Services, Los Angeles, CA

Goldstein G 1979 Methodological and theoretical issues in neuropsychological assessment. Journal of Behavioral Assessment 1: 23–41

Goldstein G 1984 Comprehensive neuropsychological assessment batteries. In: Goldstein G, Hersen M (eds) Handbook of psychological assessment. Pergamon, New York

Goldstein G, Hersen M 1984 Handbook of psychological assessment. Pergamon, New York

Goldstein G, Ruthven L 1983 Rehabilitation of the brain damaged adult. Plenum, New York

Goldstein G, Ryan C, Turner S M, Kanagy M, Barry K, Kelly L 1987 Three methods of memory training for severely amnesic patients. Behavior modification (in press)

Goodglass H, Kaplan E 1972 The assessment of aphasia and related disorders. Lee & Febiger, Philadelphia, PA

Halstead W C 1947 Brain and intelligence: a quantitative study of the frontal lobes. University of Chicago Press, Chicago

Hamsher K deS 1984 Specialized neuropsychological assessment methods. In: Goldstein G, Hersen M (eds) Handbook of psychological assessment. Pergamon Press, New York

Helm-Estabrooks N, Holland A L 1984 Spontaneous recovery and efficacy of therapy in aphasia. In: Goldstein G (ed) Advances in clinical neuropsychology. Plenum, New York

Hersen M, Bellack A S 1978 Behavior therapy in a psychiatric setting. Williams & Wilkins, Baltimore

Hersen M, Bellack A S 1981 Behavioral assessment: a practical handbook, 2nd edn. Pergamon, New York

Jastak J F, Jastak S P 1965 The Wide Range Achievement Test: manual of instructions. Guidance Associates, Wilmington, DEL

Jones B P, Butters N 1983 Neuropsychological assessment. In: Hersen M, Bellack A S, Kazkin A E (eds) The clinical psychology handbook. Pergamon, New York

Kaplan E 1980 Boston neuropsychological adaptation of the Wechsler Memory Scale. Presented at the 88th Annual Convention of the American Psychological Association, Montreal, Canada, September 1980

Kertesz A 1979 Aphasia and associated disorders: taxonomy, localization and recovery. Grune & Stratton, New York

Luria A R 1963 Restoration of function after brain injury. Macmillan, New York (original in Russian published in 1948)

Luria A R 1973 The working brain. Basic Books, New York

Matson J L, Mulick J A 1983 Handbook of mental retardation. Pergamon, New York

Nelson R O, Hayes S C 1981 Nature of behavioral assessment. In: Hersen M, Bellack A S (eds) Behavioral assessment: a practical handbook. Pergamon, New York

Reitan R M 1966 A research program on the psychological effects of brain lesions in human beings. In: Ellis N R (ed) International review of research in mental retardation. Academic Press, New York

Reitan R M, Davison L A 1974 Clinical neuropsychology: current status and applications. Winston, Washington, DC

Rosenthal R 1966 Experimenter effects in behavioral research. Appleton-Century-Crofts, New York

Russell E W 1975 A multiple scoring method for the assessment of complex memory functions. Journal of Consulting and Clinical Psychology 43: 800–809

Russell E W 1981 The pathology and clinical examination of memory. In: Filskov S B, Boll T J (eds) Handbook of clinical neuropsychology. Wiley-Interscience, New York

Russell E W, Neuringer C, Goldstein G 1970 Assessment of brain damage: a neuropsychological key approach. Wiley, New York

Stout R L 1981 New approaches to the design of computerized interviewing and testing systems. Behavior Research Methods and Instrumentation 13: 436–442

# 3

*Muriel D. Lezak*

# Assessment for rehabilitation planning

## THE NEED FOR ASSESSMENT IN PLANNING

In planning for behavioral rehabilitation, two questions must be kept in mind: (1) What are realistic treatment goals? and (2) What is the patient's capacity to benefit from available treatments? Although the answers to these two questions will, in some measure, depend upon the same observations, they will also be based on such different observations that they should be considered individually.

### Identifying realistic treatment goals

The nature and extent of brain damage plays a predominant role in determining the kinds of deficits and behavioral alterations the patient will experience (Lezak, 1983; Lishman, 1978; Smith, 1981). Moderate to severe brain damage – particularly when prefrontal, right hemisphere, or limbic system structures are involved or the lesions are multiple or diffuse – tends to compromise the patient's capacity to function independently in our complex society. Thus, in planning a rehabilitation program for the moderately to severely impaired patient it is necessary to evaluate what the patient's ultimate needs will be. For example, it is wasteful and probably unkind to enter a patient into a vocational training program when brain damage has rendered him or her incapable of meeting the day-to-day requirements of getting to work on time, behaving appropriately, monitoring the work product, or even finding a job independently.

The identification of realistic treatment goals requires the evaluation of two aspects of the patient's behavioral repertoire: (1) the capacity for taking an abstract attitude; and (2) the integrity of the executive functions. *Abstract attitude* refers to the capacity to take a perspective different from one's own: e.g., to appreciate the point of view of others; to be aware that there is an ongoing world outside of one's immediate perceptual field; to be free from the constraints of concrete thinking and literal interpretations of experience (Goldstein, 1948; Stuss & Benson, 1984; Walsh, 1978). The ability to take an abstract attitude is not the same as the ability to reason abstractly. Many bright brain-damaged patients can get high scores on tests that ask for interpretations of proverbs or generalizations from particulars, and yet have lost the ability to empathize with others, or to take into account the facets of a situation that are not immediately present. *Executive functions* are those capacities inherent in directed, effective activity (Lezak, 1982, 1983; Luria, 1966). They include the capacity to *formulate goals* (i.e., to *have an intention*), to *plan and organize goal-directed behavior,* to *carry out goal-directed behavior fully and effectively,* and to *monitor and self-correct one's behavior as needed.* When capacities for taking an abstract attitude or for executive functioning are compromised, the patient is disabled for social independence. Obversely, many patients can function autonomously with even such handicaps as deafness, blindness, paralysis, even aphasia, so long as they can still take the abstract attitude, can still initiate, plan, carry out, and monitor their activities.

Unfortunately, unlike some cognitive deficits that improve with rehabilitation training, an impaired capacity to take the abstract attitude and defective executive functioning often prove to be permanent handicaps, stubbornly resistant to even the most sophisticated and intensively applied treatments.[1] It should not be difficult to see why this is so from a purely pedagogical viewpoint: retraining of these functions or capacities requires the patient to have in mind what no longer comes to mind or what he or she no longer appreciates as missing. For example, if nothing comes to the apathetic patient's mind, that patient will continue doing nothing until activated externally or by autonomic impulses. Training such a patient to look for environmental cues for initiating activity will come to naught so long as, when left alone, it never occurs to the patient to look for the cues that could prompt activity. By the same token, when the patient no longer takes an abstract attitude, training for empathy or to consider the actions of others when making decisions may work for specific situations or in specific settings, but the patients will be unlikely to appreciate that the abstract attitude is lacking when confronted with a new situation, and thus will typically deal with it as concretely and obtusely as if training had never taken place.

Deficits in these areas thus present a much different kind of rehabilitation challenge than do deficits that are appreciated by a patient whose sense of self and not-self is well-defined, who is aware of events outside of immediate experience, and whose executive functions are intact. In the latter case, treatment planning can focus on retraining impaired functions or assisting the patient to develop and use compensatory techniques. However, when the abstract attitude is impaired and one or more of the executive functions is compromised, the patient may need to be prepared for something less than full

[1]Few substantial data have been published on long-term and generalized effects of cognitive retraining programs, much less on the social or vocational adjustment of moderately to severely brain-damaged patients after undergoing retraining. Most of the literature on cognitive retraining programs tends to be speculative rather than informational. Most studies that are reported consist of a single case typically involving some specific deficit (see Gummow et al, 1983 for a discussion of this problem). Moreover, when reading such reports closely, there is usually some evidence that despite improvements in those behaviors under treatment the subject has remained socially dependent, and/or some specific evidence is contained in the report indicating that impaired executive functions continue to be the central obstacle (e.g. Craine, 1982; Haffey, 1983).

independence. No matter how high are a patient's scores on formal tests of cognitive functioning, if that patient is socially regressed or unable to maintain a complex behavioral sequence without prompting, he or she is also unlikely to get or keep a job. It makes little sense to put such patients through an arduous and time-consuming series of training exercises that would develop employment skills. Rather, when socially dependent patient's limitations have been identified, rehabilitation efforts can be directed toward working with the persons responsible for the patient in selecting an appropriate living situation for the patient and in learning how to organize that living situation so as to make the most of the patient's residual capacities. Work with the patient can then be focused on improving skills of everyday living, including social skills, and on the retraining of those cognitive, perceptual, or motor disorders that interfere with the patient's social interactions, efficiency, and enjoyment of life, wherever practical.

## Assessing the capacity to benefit from treatment

Generally speaking, the major neuropsychological limitations to a patient's ability to profit from rehabilitation training are (a) impaired executive functions; (b) loss of the abstract attitude; (c) attentional disorders; and (d) memory and learning deficits. The importance of the contribution of any one of these problems to poor rehabilitation results will naturally vary from patient to patient. The seemingly infinite variations in deficit patterns between patients, even when the underlying neuropathological condition appears to be quite similar, requires that each patient-candidate for rehabilitation be given a thoroughgoing neuropsychological evaluation if treatment planning is to be appropriate for the patient's needs, strengths, and limitations.

*Defective executive functions* interfere with training in much the same way that they make the patient unemployable. For example, it simply may not occur to the patient who cannot form an intention that treatment is needed; nor, if in a treatment program, that schedules need to be followed, practice undertaken, or effort put forth on one's own behalf. Impaired ability to plan and organize activities will show up in erratic attendance; confusion of relevant and irrelevant events or expectations; and difficulty in appreciating that dull, repetitive, or what seems to the patient to be silly or degrading training exercises are means to an end. Problems in self-control or self-regulation may thwart both the therapist's and the patient's efforts to develop good work habits and maintain a useful level of activity. Of all the disorders of executive functions, probably those involving self-monitoring and self-correcting are most retrainable. Here too, of course, the effectiveness of the training will depend considerably on whether it occurs to the patient to check for errors, whether error-checking is generalized to situations outside the classroom, and whether the patient is sufficiently motivated to correct errors with enough consistency to warrant the time and effort invested in training.

Essential for full executive functioning is the capacity for *taking the abstract attitude*. Impairment of this capacity shows up in rehabilitation settings in many ways. Perhaps most frustrating to staff is defective generalizing from one situation to another, even when the new situation is similar in most respects to the original one. When this problem is pronounced, what is learned can only be applied within the same context as it was learned, instructions are taken so literally as to require a different set of instructions for every contingency, and the patient does not profit from experience.

For example, one victim of a motor vehicle accident, a college graduate in his 30s, was wearing an open-necked shirt that revealed a filthy undershirt underneath when he announced that he was on his way to apply for a volunteer position that he very much wanted. He was told not to apply for the post that day, but to wait until he came to the hospital with clean clothes. Moments after he had agreed to follow this reasonable-sounding advice, he was observed continuing in his original direction. When questioned he explained that he fully planned to wear fresh underclothes when he *applied* for the job the next day, but now he was not applying for the job, he was just going to *leave* his application with his potential new supervisor!

*Attentional deficits* plague most victims of moderate to severe brain damage as well as many whose injuries are relatively mild (Gronwall & Wrightson, 1981; Rimel et al, 1981). That they can seriously interfere with rehabilitation efforts is patently obvious. In fact, when attentional problems are severe, the patient may be unable to benefit from rehabilitation even when motivation, reasoning and judgement, and memory functions are relatively intact. Fortunately, some attentional deficits are remediable (Ben-Yishay et al, 1979; Diller & Weinberg, 1977; Gummow et al, 1983); and the effects of others may be ameliorated by such measures as reducing the amount of background stimulation (Lezak, 1978); or slowing delivery of material to be processed by the patient. Thus, a careful analysis of the rehabilitation candidate's attentional deficits is often of primary importance both in evaluating the patient's rehabilitation potential and in determining the order in which training procedures can be most effectively undertaken. When attentional problems are pronounced, they need to be dealt with before any other cognitive retraining efforts can be successful.

*Memory and learning disorders,* too, are among the most common residuals of brain damage. The level of the patient's abilities for new learning and effective recall sets a practical limit on the kind of information and activities the patient can learn anew, the amount and complexity level of new material that the patient can be expected to assimilate, the rate at which new learning will take place, and the efficiency of retrieval. Rehabilitation planning, therefore, must be based on the patient's learning capacity. Attempts to train the patient in areas in which learning ability is significantly impaired, or to bombard the patient with more material than can be effectively processed, will necessarily be doomed to failure.

After repeated failures because their patients have difficulty learning, many rehabilitation workers have thought that memory retraining might solve these problems. However, in proposing to improve memory through training techniques, these well-intentioned persons have overlooked the fact that what they are asking for contains an inherent paradox: if learning ability is impaired, then learning to learn will also be impaired. Moreover, learning does not improve with exercise; it is not a muscle but an anatomically sited, electrochemically based neurophysiological process. It is little wonder, then, that most schemes for improving memory by means of 'cognitive rehabilitation' techniques have not resulted in practical enhancement of memory disorders (Lewinsohn et al, 1977; Miller, 1980; Schachter et al 1985).

Descriptions of some procedures for assessing memory functions of rehabilitation patients are presented in Chapters 12 and 13. These procedures can be used for diagnostic and treatment evaluation as well as for examining treatment potential and for treatment planning.

## Brain damage and time

Since rehabilitation is usually initiated early for patients whose condition was of relatively sudden onset, such as stroke or head trauma victims, time is an important consideration in evaluating assessment data (Lezak, 1983). By far the greatest amount of spontaneous improvement takes place within the first 3–6 months following a stroke or head injury (Bond, 1979; Kertesz & McCabe, 1977). Noticeable spontaneous improvement typically continues throughout the first year and often well into the second, but at a diminishing pace. Within 2–3 years after the event, most patients will have reached a plateau. Thereafter, test performances will change little if any from year to year, providing a relatively substantial basis for rehabilitation planning. Significant gains that take place after the first 1½–2½ years can probably be attributed to training, practice, or some other form of new learning.

Obviously the situation is not as simple during the first months and year or so following brain damage of sudden onset, for the patient's neuropsychological status will be in flux. Moreover, since different neuropsychological functions improve at different rates, observations made on one function or class of functions cannot be extrapolated to other functions. Thus, long-range rehabilitation planning cannot be made on the basis of examination data obtained early in the patient's course. In fact, when rehabilitation is undertaken within the first month or two, the functional areas being dealt with in rehabilitation should be re-examined at relatively frequent intervals (e.g., 1–6 weeks at first), lest spontaneous improvement catches up to or even surpasses original estimates of residual potential. Repeated examinations at less frequent intervals (e.g., 3–4 months within the first year; 6-month intervals in the second year) should be made if the patient is in rehabilitation. While improvements documented in these repeated examinations may be – at least in part – due to rehabilitation, it is difficult to attribute improvement in neuropsychological functioning to rehabilitation in the early stages of the condition when rapid spontaneous improvement is taking place.

## ASSESSMENT TECHNIQUES FOR REHABILITATION PLANNING

### Tests as observational tools

Psychological tests are simply a means of enhancing (refining, standardizing) our observations. They can be thought of as extensions of our organs of perception – the 'seven-league boots' of clinical behavioral observation. If we use them properly, as extensions of our observational end-organs, like seven-league boots they enable us to accomplish much more with greater speed. When tests are misused as *substitutes for* rather than *extensions of* clinical observation, they can obscure our view of the patient much as seven-league boots would get in the way if worn over the head.

Underlying this presentation of some tests and assessment techniques that are applicable to rehabilitation questions is the assumption that tests should serve the examiner, not the other way around. The tests are there for examiners to apply as appropriate for the patient and the needs of the examination; the examiner is not limited by the instructions or norms of the tests. Of course, test administration should be standardized whenever possible. However, when the patient's situation or the circumstances do not allow for a standardized application of a test that might still provide needed information about the patient, the examiner should feel free to use the test anyhow. Obviously, a score obtained in this manner can give at best only a rough estimate of the patient's performance relative to the normative population, if that. Yet the test performance may shed light on strengths or weaknesses that would not otherwise be readily apparent.

For example, in giving a motorically slowed patient a paper-and-pencil tracking task scored for response speed, such as the Trail Making Test, an experienced examiner would know beforehand that the patient's score will necessarily fall into the *defective* range. If the examiner's goal were simply to get a score, giving the test would be a waste of time. However, if the examiner has questions about the patient's mental tracking or visual scanning abilities, or about the patient's capacity to follow a complex set of instructions, then the test might well be given without being timed at all. In this example the test was used not as a measuring instrument but as a device for eliciting some aspects of mental functioning that do not generally show up in interviews or in day-to-day observations. More often, the same examination technique can serve as both a test and an observational aid, so that the examiner gets, in effect, twice as much information for the time and effort (see Lezak, 1983, pp. 135–137 and passim).

### The examination of executive functions

Defective *goal formulation,* like most other neuropsychological deficits associated with brain damage, can range in its expression from severe and obvious to mild and very subtle. A severe impairment of the ability to formulate goals is self-evident as the patient tends to remain virtually immobilized unless prompted externally or aroused to activity by internal signals of visceral needs. In the most extreme cases, even hunger and thirst may not be identified as needs requiring a response.

At the other extreme are patients whose capacity to generate ideas of engaging in goal-directed activity is adequate for viscerally stimulated, familiar, and well-practiced activities. These patients with only a mildly compromised ability to formulate goals can function seemingly normally in most if not all routine matters, but quite literally have no new ideas; experience no promptings to undertake unfamiliar, non-habital ventures. Generally the idea of engaging in an activity will occur to them from habit, from viscerally based drives, and in responses to cues provided by their immediate surrounds. Absent these conditions, they tend to sit in front of the television set or visit a (usually the same) local coffee shop or tavern for hours at a time. If they talk about what sounds like goal-setting, their statements are vague wishes, not actionable goals (e.g., 'I want to get married'; 'I want a job') which turn out, on questioning, to contain no concrete ideas for directing activity. Since so much of what they do seems usual, sensible, and typical to their family and friends, the fact that they do not undertake to find a job, make new friends, or develop activity programs for themselves is frequently misinterpreted as lack of ambition, laziness, or symptomatic of depression or some other serious psychiatric disorder. These misinterpretations of an organically based behavioral deficit can have far-reaching and tragic repercussions when they appear as conclusions in a psychiatrist's or psychologist's disability report to an insurance company or Social Security; or when family members reject the patient as an irresponsible parasite who is too arrogant (or stubborn or selfish or whatever other 'psychological' interpretation they use to account for what they perceive to be a deliberate ploy) to assume normal adult responsibilities.

Assessment of the capacity for goal formulation involves the evaluation of the patient's capacity for motivation and the patient's awareness of self and surrounds; for the generation of motives depends both upon the ability to conceptualize needs and desires before acting upon them and the ability to identify goal-relevant aspects of the world around oneself. The capacity for motivation is best assessed through observations – the examiner's and observations made by others. In the clinical setting the patient can be questioned about likes and dislikes, what kinds of things upset the patient and what gives pleasure. Two questions that I have found useful for this purpose are, 'What do you do for fun?' and 'What makes you angry?' By and large, patients who have diminished motivational capacity on an organic basis are emotionally flat, lacking in strong feelings generally. Many will be unable to answer these questions, or give only a superficial answer based on what they have been told or remember from premorbid experience. For example, a seriously impaired young woman who was – for all intents and purposes – affectively empty, reported in a monotone voice that she liked to play games. On questioning, she recited the names of several card and board games that her family was using to encourage interactional activity. However, questioning also elicited that it never occurred to her to play these games, but rather she had to be engaged by others who told her that this activity was 'fun.'

Reports from family members, caretakers, the therapists who work with the patient, and anyone else who sees the patient in a naturalistic setting can provide invaluable information about the patient's capacity for motivation. Often, naive observers are not aware of the importance of what they have to report; particularly if they mistake the patient's apathy for a personality or character disorder. Thus the examiner may not find it very fruitful simply to inquire whether the patient's drive or goal-formulation ability has changed since the event, for many people do not have well-conceptualized notions of drive or intention. Rather, the wise examiner will ask the family or caretaker to describe the patient's day – what he or she does step-by-step, from morning until night. A critical question for everyday observers and for therapists is, 'What does the patient do when left alone?' Descriptions of long hours of television watching, aimless activity such as pacing or walking around, or just gazing out the window when not activated by others suggest impaired motivation in a patient who is not obviously depressed. Although profound depression can mimic the apathy of persons suffering motivational impairments resulting from brain damage, the profoundly depressed patient will give other evidence of depression, such as self-deprecation, psychodynamically meaningful obsessions, tearfulness, expressions of sadness, insomnia or poor appetite, etc. The apathetic person whose capacity for motivation is more or less compromised will simply appear as more or less affectively flat; the more apathetic they are, the less emotionally toned will be their gestures and expressions and the less emotionally meaningful will be their behavior.

The other aspect of intentional behavior involves appreciation of what may be relevant or important both within and outside one's immediate perceptual focus. This requires self-awareness at many different levels, such as awareness of internal states, awareness of self as a person, and the capacity to view oneself in relationship to the social and objective environment; i.e., the capacity to take the abstract attitude.

Awareness of self and surrounds is typically assessed by the mental status examination (e.g., see Strub & Black, 1977). In addition to providing information about the patient's orientation, the mental status examination may shed light on the patient's ability to identify relevant environmental cues and to integrate them. For example, the patient who looks for a clock when asked the time, or glances out the window if questioned about the weather, demonstrates – at least at this simple level – an appreciation that useful information can be found in the external world.

Observation probably offers the most valuable information about the patient's capacity for self-awareness and appreciation of the environment. Lack of self-consciousness in a once socially effective adult is strong evidence that the patient's self-awareness is significantly impaired. Thus, the sensitive clinician will look for signs of disinterest in appearance or lack of concern about childish or crude behavior, and will take notice of caretaker or family complaints about the patient's grooming and social graces.

Awareness of the value of environmental cues and the ability to use them can also be examined with tests. Among these are 'Problems of Fact' in the Stanford-Binet Intelligence Scale (Terman & Merrill, 1973) in which the subject must reason about such questions as 'What is happening?' when first a doctor, then a lawyer, and then a priest were seen going into a house. Having the patient make up a story about a picture allows the examiner to see whether and how well the patient utilizes the information provided by the picture. The 'Cookie Theft' picture of the *Boston Diagnostic Aphasia Examination* (Goodglass & Kaplan, 1972) is excellent for this purpose because it is a simple line drawing which portrays familiar characters in a familiar setting; another useful picture is 'The Smashed Window' in *The Mental Examiner's Handbook* (Wells & Ruesch, 1969). In order to make up an integrated story the subject must identify the relevant features of the picture and organize them appropriately. Piecemeal descriptions suggest that the patient may be having difficulty integrating what is seen. When the focus is on only one or two items, or the patient deals with both important and unimportant elements in much the same manner, the capacity to identify and use environmental information appropriately comes into question.

It is important that examiners be aware that intentional deficits are more likely to be overlooked or obscured in the typical clinical examination than when the patient is observed in a naturalistic setting. The examiner's questions and directions prompt the patient to respond and guide the patient through the examination proceedings, obviating any need on the part of the patient to form an intention and any opportunity for the examiner to discover what happens – actually, what doesn't happen – when the patient is left to his or her own devices. Family and caretaker's reports, on the other hand, are invaluable for providing descriptions of how the patient behaves when the structure for activity is not immediately available.

*Planning* depends on the integrity of several capacities.Essential for planning is the capacity to objectify experience: to detach one's attention from the pull of immediate experience so that thought can be focused away from the here and now; to perceive oneself as a distinctive entity; to project personhood onto other, i.e., again, to be able to take the 'abstract attitude.' Planning also requires the subject to generate and evaluate alternatives, to think in terms of sequential steps, and to develop a conceptual framework for working out the plan. Also essential for planning are sustained attention and the capacity to inhibit impulsivity.

Planning defects are clearly apparent in impulsive patients, in those who talk about their many goals but cannot keep track of any one of them long enough to come up with a plan, or in those whose plans are unrealistic or frankly silly. More subtle planning defects – in working out sequences or integrating all the facets of a plan – may require formal assessment to be made obvious.

The patient's personal situation frequently provides opportunities for testing the patient's capacity to plan. Hospitalized patients can be asked what they plan to do when they leave the hospital, where they plan to go, and how they plan to get there. Stroke and head trauma patients who want to return to work or indicate a desire to travel can be asked about their plans. The examiner must be careful when questioning the patient about planning activities with which the patient is already familiar, for then the response may simply represent recall of previously learned behavior.

Among tests that have proven useful for evaluating the capacity to plan, the Porteus Mazes was devised especially for this purpose; i.e., to examine the processes involved in 'choosing, trying, and rejecting or adopting alternative courses of conduct or thought' (Porteus, 1959). Tests that require the subject to organize the elements of the task give the examiner an excellent opportunity to see ongoing planning (or lack of planning). Drawing tasks are ideal for this purpose because the patient must structure or otherwise organize the response. In the Complex Figure Test (Osterrieth, 1944; Rey, 1941; Taylor, 1979), for instance, a fragmented or haphazard approach to copying the intricate design suggests poor planning. The layout of the nine Bender Gestalt figures (L. Bender, 1938; Hutt, 1977) also shows how the subject plans the response; e.g., whether all the designs were given sufficient space, whether designs impinged on one another or on the paper's edge, whether they were arranged in order of presentation or randomly.

J. Wasserstein (personal communication) and her colleagues have devised a pictorial form of the popular parlor game, 'Twenty Questions.' This technique makes evident the subject's strategy (or lack of strategy) in figuring out which object of many different kinds in a pictorial array is the target. A simplified oral version of Twenty Questions, such as 'I'm thinking of something in a restaurant,' can be played out in a Twenty Question format. A similar test, Identification of Common Objects, uses a 26.5 × 20.3 card containing 42 pictures (in a 7 × 6 format) of such familiar items as a bee, a bunch of carrots, the sun, and a pair of gloves (Laine & Butters, 1982). The examiner requests the subject to ask 'yes – no' questions in order to 'find the object I am thinking of with as few questions as possible.' Responses are evaluated for the efficiency of the questions in delimiting the field of possible target objects.

*Carrying out activities.* The ability to carry out meaningful behavior and to persevere in, shift, or stop ongoing activities is necessary to translate intentions and plans into constructive responses. In characterizing normal activity as the product of organized *behavioral programs,* Luria (1966) gave us a conceptual framework for understanding the nature of the disruptions of purposive behavior associated with certain kinds of brain damage. Programming disorders prevent a person from carrying out plans, no matter how motivated the planner or how reasonable the plans. Thus even alert, well-energized and goal-directed patients who are unable to program their responses effectively can be thwarted in their efforts to carry out their intentions. Programming disorders may appear in simple motor perseverations or inability to carry out sequential movements, or in discontinuities of discrete motor activities which interrupt sequentially organized acts such as writing, drawing, or speaking. Although large-scale purposive activities may be compromised by programming disorders when programming of discrete activities has remained intact, the reverse is not commonly seen (Goldberg and Tucker, 1979).

When the programming disorder is pronounced, it may interfere with almost everything the patient tries to do. Subtle programming disorders are most likely to show up when the task is relatively open-ended and unstructured. For example, verbal fluency tests, free writing, and free drawing are sensitive to defects in the capacity to generate, maintain, and stop sequentially organized intentional responses. The capacity to shift motor responses will show up on tasks requiring the patient to copy and maintain patterns of alternating hand movements, letter sequences such as *mnmnmn,* or chained geometric figures such as a series consisting of little squares, circles, and triangles (Luria, 1966). At the conceptual level, the capacity to shift can be examined by the Wisconsin Card Sorting Test (Berg, 1948; Lezak, 1983; Milner, 1963) or Halstead's Category Test (Halstead, 1947; Russell et al, 1970).[2]

However, in the usual structured examination, subtle defects in the capacity to carry out purposive behavior tend not to show up since, in these traditional examinations, the patient is typically told what to do, and when and how to do it (Lezak, 1982). As a result, problems in initiating, maintaining, or stopping behavior may never come to the examiner's attention because the examiner assumes all the executive functions for the patient, leaving the patient only the task of being a good patient, i.e., doing unquestioningly what he or she is told. Or, as in the case example below, the examiner documents the executive deficit but makes nothing of it.

Hebb (1942) described one such patient, a 15-year-old boy who became blind and left-hemiparetic as a result of three large abscesses in the right temporoparietal region. On the basis of post-operative encephalograms, it was estimated that 40–50% of the right hemisphere had been destroyed and that intracranial pressure had damaged at least 20% of the left hemisphere. Hebb reported that 'The patient's psychological status appeared to be exceptionally good. The one defect, by informal observation, was his inactivity, and apparent willingness to do nothing for rather long periods. But in conversation he seemed normally alert and responsive, and quite co-operative.' Hebb then went on to report a number of verbal skill scores at *average* and better levels (e.g., vocabulary, verbal subtests of the Stanford-Binet).

The problem of identifying subtle deficits in carrying out activities in the typical structured clinical examination led to the development of an examination technique that puts the responsibility for structuring the test activity onto the subject. In the Tinker Toy test the subject is asked to 'make

[2]A very satisfactory form of the Category Test has been developed by S. D. Kimura (1981). Each item is presented on a 10 × 15 cm card resulting in a pack that can be easily carried, used at bedside, and – not the least of its virtues – is relatively inexpensive.

whatever you want' with 50 pieces of brightly colored wood and plastic knobs, dowels, and connecting pieces of varying sizes. They can be combined into many different constructions in a relatively brief time. On completion the subject is asked to name the construction. In a pilot study comparing the constructions of 35 unselected brain-damage patients with 10 normal control subjects, the patients used far fewer pieces in their constructions, made less complex constructions (e.g., fewer moving parts, fewer symmetrical constructions), and gave their constructions less appropriate names (if any) (Lezak, 1982, 1983). Moreover, a comparison between fully dependent and semi-dependent patients showed that the semi-dependent patients out-performed the fully dependent ones on such measure. Clinical observations suggested that patients who had difficulty initiating or carrying out purposive activities were most likely to use relatively few pieces, although their constructions tended to be recognizable and appropriately named. Those with deficits in goal formulation or planning used relatively more pieces but their constructions were less likely to match the names given them, or they were unnamed. Patients with extensive impairment involving all aspects of executive functioning used few pieces and either made unnamed and unplanned constructions or simply made piles of the Tinker Toy pieces.

*Effective performance.* The performer's ability to monitor, self-correct, and regulate such qualitative aspects of activity as tempo and intensity makes a crucial contribution to the effectiveness of behavior. Brain-damaged patients are particularly prone to performing erratically since self-monitoring and self-correcting capacities are frequently compromised. Some patients cannot correct mistakes because they don't look for them or overlook them; others may perceive their errors and even talk about them, but still leave them be. Self-monitoring defects may show up at any level of performance, from quite basic grooming tasks in which buttons are left unbuttoned or torn off, to careless speech delivery, to computational errors on complex mathematical problems despite unequivocal evidence that the patient understands the mathematics and knows how to solve the problem.

The identification of problems in self-correction and regulation rests on the sensitivity of the examiner's observations of the patient as he or she responds in the examination. Test scores do not contain this information, nor do they provide evidence of idiosyncratic responses, such as cramped writing, that will not lower a score but can interfere with the patient's effectiveness in practical matters. Problems in self-correction and regulation are most likely to show up on tasks in which the patient has to create a response, or tasks which allow the examiner to see how the patient arrives at the solution. Examples of the former are free drawing tests such as bicycle, house, or person drawings; and free writing tests, in which the subject is asked to describe a picture, complete sentence stems, or compose sentences using one or more specified words. Arithmetic calculation problems to be solved on paper represent the latter kind of task. When giving problems for this purpose they should be well within the patient's capability but sufficiently complex to involve several stages of computations (e.g., adding four or five 3-place numbers, multiplying or dividing 3-, 4-, and 5-place numbers).

## The assessment of attentional functions

For neuropsychological assessment purposes, attentional functions can be conceptualized as attention *per se,* concentration, and tracking. *Simple attention* involves awareness and requires relatively little effort. *Concentration* is an effortful activity in which attention is focused and irrelevant stimuli are excluded from conscious awareness. *Tracking* requires the maintenance of attentive focusing on objective stimuli or mental contents that change with time.

Three aspects of attentional functions are relevant in neuropsychological examinations conducted to assess the patient's rehabilitation potential and needs.

1. They are organized on a hierarchical basis such that deficits in the simpler attentional functions (e.g., in span, vigilance, freedom from distractibility) will tend to disrupt more complex attentional activities; but the reverse is unlikely.
2. Mental processing speed relates directly to attentional efficiency (Gronwall & Sampson, 1974; Gronwall & Wrightson, 1981).
3. Significantly better performances on attentional and tracking tasks when the test stimuli are concretely (usually visually) present than when all operations must be performed mentally may not reflect attentional disorders so much as structure dependency.

### *Attention*

The amount of material that can be held in awareness at any given time provides the usual measure of attention. Typically, immediate recall of a string of digits or letters is used for this purpose (Spitz, 1972). Since most adults, at least until the age of 70, can retain six digits in mind long enough to recite them, in young to middle-aged adults recall of only five digits must be considered borderline to normal limits, and four or fewer digits is frankly defective.

### *Concentration*

Two aspects of concentration can be examined: the ability to sustain attention (*vigilance*), and the ability to withstand distraction. Tests of vigilance typically require the subject to attend to a shifting set of stimuli, such as a string of letters, while searching for a defined target, such as a specific letter. The subject may indicate awareness of the target stimulus by raising a hand or tapping when it is read (e.g., Strub & Black's Vigilance task, 1977); or, on paper-and-pencil cancellation tasks, the subject typically marks out the target symbol. The success of the performance may be measured by the time it takes to complete a search of the whole stimulus set (e.g., Letter Cancellation task: Diller et al, 1974); by the number of stimuli attended to in a given length of time (e.g., a cancellation task, that differs from most others in that the target shifts from line to line, Perceptual Speed: Moran & Mefferd, 1959; Lezak, 1983); and/or the number of errors (e.g., the Vigilance task; the cancellation tasks). Characteristic response tendencies may be documented through such scoring refinements as the computation of the relative number of false positive and false negative errors, and on paper-and-pencil tests – when visuospatial inattention is suspected – the relative number of errors to the left and right of the midline (Diller & Weinberg, 1977).

The ability to withstand distraction may show up on cancellation tasks that require the subject to respond only when the target item is preceded by a specified item (e.g., Strub & Black, 1977), although performance on this kind of task may be affected by impulsivity as well. The test most usually used to assess resistance to distraction is the Stroop Test (Dodrill, 1978; Stroop, 1935). Using rows of differently colored printed color names, the subject is first required to read the printed color names as rapidly as possible. A second trial requires the subject to call off the color in which each word is printed, again being urged to respond quickly. Invariably, it takes longer to call off the colors than to read the color names since the printed word is a stronger distractor to color naming than the color is to print reading. Distractible patients tend to take a great deal longer naming the colors than reading the color names than do organically intact subjects.

*Tracking: mental*

Tests of mental tracking require the subject to keep one or more bits of information in mind while performing one or more mental operations. The simplest mental tracking tasks involve reversed sequences. Recalling a string of digits in reverse is probably the most widely used of all mental tracking tasks. It is compounded by the necessity of remembering the digit string (Vernon, 1979), so that subjects with defective short-term memory may do relatively poorly on it even though they can perform other mental tracking tasks successfully. Since the recall of digits forward tests one aspect of attention and the recall of digits backward tests complex attentional functions and has a short-term memory component as well, the wise examiner will never combine performance scores on these two tasks, since that would only obscure the data and makes no neuropsychological sense. Nor will a wise examiner follow a psychometric scheme in which span length has been compounded with a performance reliability score for normalizing a data distribution that does not take the classical bell-shape in nature (e.g., Wechsler, 1981). Here too the compounded score makes no neuropsychological sense, nor can it be meaningfully interpreted. Should the examiner want to know how reliable is the subject's ability to recall digit strings of a given length either forward or backward, the examiner can test for consistency of success at a given length.

Other tests of mental tracking include reversed spelling (M. B. Bender, 1979); reversed familiar sequences, such as the alphabet, days of the week, month of the year; and serial subtraction tests (Lezak, 1983; Luria, 1966). Performances on these tasks can be scored for length of pauses as well as errors. Double addition and subtraction problems also test mental tracking ability. These problems require the subject to add or subtract two sets of items simultaneously; e.g., 'How many apples and oranges will you have if you add three apples and six oranges to five apples and four oranges?'

### *Tracking: complex*

Both visual and mental tracking capacities are engaged in complex tracking tasks. All tests of complex tracking involve a speed component and require the subject to make relatively fine visual discriminations. This makes them not only very sensitive to mental impairments due to brain damage, but to response slowing and a host of visuoperceptual disorders that occur for reasons other than brain damage. As a result, performance on these tests must be carefully evaluated before low scores can be attributed to attentional deficits. However, when age-graded norms are used and the subject has demonstrated adequate response speed and visual acuity on other tests, poor performances on these tests become useful indicators of attentional problems. It is particularly important to give these tests to patients who perform adequately on simpler attentional tests to investigate their capacity to attend to two or more things at once, a capacity that is necessary for one to function adequately in normal social or work conditions.

The best-known of these tests is the Trail Making Test which comes from the Army Individual Test Battery (1944). The administration and scoring of this test have undergone revisions over the years. The procedures now in general use were instituted by Reitan (undated); the recommended adult norms take age into account (Davies, 1968). This is a two-part test in which the first part simply tests visual tracking; the second part includes a mental tracking component. Normal control subjects typically take a little more than twice as long to complete the second part as the first. Abnormal slowing on both parts reflects generally slowed processing and implicates a pervasive attentional disorder. Abnormal slowing of the second part relative to a performance on the first part that is within normal limits suggests that attentional problems are not general but will tend to occur when the patient attempts to do more than one thing at a time or is subject to other stimulation. The Symbol-Digit Modalities Test (Smith, 1973) and the Digit-Symbol subtest of the Wechsler Intelligence Scales (Weschler, 1981) are coding tests that require the subject to work back and forth from a key printed at the top of the answer sheet to rows of items to be coded. These tests have less of a mental tracking component than the Trail Making Test, but involve response speed, visual scanning and tracking and, to some degree, short-term memory. The Symbol-Digit Modalities Test, in calling for a number response, permits two administrations, one written and one oral.

This test enables the examiner to compare performances in these two modalities as well as give the test to persons who are unable to write or to speak. It also has a more demanding visual scanning component than the Digit Symbol subtest as the key to the latter test is organized numerically, from 1 to 9; the key to the Symbol-Digit Modalities Test must be learned as the order of presentation has no *a priori* basis.

The evaluation of performances of complex tracking tasks, too, must take into account qualitative characteristics to be most useful in guiding a rehabilitation program. Thus, the examiner should note whether the subject is aware of errors and corrects them, whether errors occur in some regular manner suggestive of a particular visuoperceptual or motor response problem, and how the subject who has difficulty performing these tasks reacts to evident failure.

## SUMMARY

In the last analysis, regardless of how much potential the patient has for improvement of any impaired cognitive function, the patient's capacity to benefit from rehabilitation training and to apply what is learned depends on the integrity of the executive functions. Skills are of little use if it does not occur to the patient to apply them, or to regulate their application appropriately, or to correct errors as they come up. Cognitive retraining of particular disabilities, e.g., certain aphasic and attentional disorders, and retraining of impaired skills, can promote independence in patients whose executive functions are relatively intact. For patients who are unable to define goals, plan, initiate, or regulate their behavior adequately, it can make living more comfortable and satisfying. However, it will not restore the capacity for independent living to patients whose brain damage has significantly impaired their executive functions. For these patients, cognitive retraining must be viewed as a beginning step toward helping them and their families adjust to the long-term care provisions that they will need, rather than a final step in making a return to normal adult independence.

### REFERENCES

Army Individual Test Battery 1944 Manual of directions and scoring. War Department, Adjutant General's Office, Washington, DC

Bender L 1938 A visual motor gestalt test and its clinical use. American Orthopsychiatric Association Research Monographs No. 3

Bender M B 1979 Defects in reversal of serial order of symbols. Neuropsychologia 17: 125–138

Ben-Yishay Y, Rattock J, Diller L 1979 A clinical strategy for the systematic amelioration of attentional disturbances in severe head trauma patients. In: Working approaches to remediation of cognitive deficits in brain damaged, A supplement to 7th Annual Workshop for Rehabilitation Professionals, Institute of Rehabilitation Medicine, New York University Medical Center, New York

Berg E A 1948 A simple objective test for measuring flexibility in thinking. Journal of General Psychology 39: 15–22

Bond M R 1979 The stages of recovery from severe head injury with special reference to late outcome. International Rehabilitation Medicine 1: 155–159

Craine J F 1982 The retraining of frontal lobe dysfunction. In: Trexler L E (ed.), Cognitive rehabilitation: conceptualization and intervention. Plenum, New York

Davies A 1968 The influence of age on Trail Making test performance. Journal of Clinical Psychology 24: 96–98.

Diller L, Weinberg J 1977 Hemi-inattention in rehabilitation: the evolution of a rational remediation program. In Weinstein E A, Friedland R P (eds) Advances in neurology. Raven Press, New York

Diller L, Ben-Yishay Y, Gerstman L J, Goodkin R, Gordon W, Weinberg J 1974 Studies in cognition and rehabilitation in hemiplegia (Rehabilitation Monograph No. 50), Institute of Rehabilitation Medicine, New York University Medical Center, New York

Dodrill C B 1978 A neuropsychological battery for epilepsy. Epilepsia 19: 236–241

Goldberg E, Tucker D 1979 Motor perservation and long-term memory for visual forms. Journal of Clinical Neuropsychology 1: 273–288

Goldstein K H 1948 Language and language disturbances. Grune & Stratton, New York

Goodglass H, Kaplan E 1972 Assessment of aphasia and related disorders. Lea & Febiger, Philadelphia

Gronwall D M A, Sampson H 1974 The psychological effects of concussion. Auckland University Press/Oxford University Press, Auckland, NZ

Gronwall D M A, Wrightson P 1981 Memory and information processing capacity after closed head injury. Journal of Neurology, Neurosurgery and Psychiatry 44: 889–895

Gummow L J, Miller P, Dustman R E 1983 Attention and brain injury. A case for cognitive rehabilitation of attentional deficits. Clinical Psychological Review 3: 255–274

Haffey W J 1983 A demonstration of Luria's qualitative neuropsychological method of cognitive remediation. Paper presented at the International Neuropsychological Society meeting, Mexico City, Feb. 4

Halstead W C 1947 Brain and intelligence. University of Chicago Press, Chicago

Hebb D O 1942 The effects of early and late brain injury upon test scores, and the nature of normal adult intelligence. Proceedings of the American Philosophical Society 85: 275–292.

Hutt M L 1977 The Hutt adaptation of the Bender-Gestalt test, 3rd edn. Grune & Stratton, New York

Kertesz A, McCabe P 1977 Recovery patterns and prognosis in aphasia. Brain 100: 1–18

Lewinsohn P M, Danaher B G, Kikel S 1977 Visual imagery as a mnemonic aid for brain-injured persons. Journal of Consulting and Clinical Psychology 45: 717–723

Lezak M D 1978 Subtle sequelae of brain damage: perplexity, distractibility, and fatigue. American Journal of Physical Medicine 57: 9–15

Lezak M D 1982 The problem of assessing executive functions. International Journal of Psychology 17: 281–297

Lezak M D 1983 Neuropsychological assessment, 2nd edn. Oxford University Press, New York

Lishman W A 1978 Organic psychiatry. Blackwell Scientific Publications, Oxford

Luria A R 1966 Higher cortical functions in man (B Haigh, trans) Basic Books, New York

Miller E 1980 Psychological intervention in the management and rehabilitation of neuropsychological impairments. Behavior Research and Therapy 18: 527–535

Milner B 1963 Effects of different brain lesions on card sorting. Archives of Neurology 9: 90–100

Moran L J, Mefferd R B Jr 1959 Repetitive psychometric measures. Psychological Reports 5: 269–275

Osterrieth P A 1944 Le test de copie d'une figure complexe. Archives de Psychologie 30: 206–356

Porteus S D 1959 The maze test and clinical psychology. Pacific Books, Palo Alto, California

Reitan R M undated Instructions and procedures for administering the Neuropsychological Test Battery used at the Neuropsychology Laboratory, Indiana University Medical Center, Bloomington, Indiana

Rey A 1941 L'examen psychologique dans le cas d'encephalopathie traumatique. Archives de Psychologie 28, No. 112: 286–340

Rimel R W, Giordani B, Barth J T, Boll T J, Jane J A 1981 Disability caused by minor head injury. Neurosurgery 9: 221–228

Russell E W, Neuringer C, Goldstein G 1970 Assessment of brain damage: A neuropsychological key approach. Wiley-Interscience, New York

Schachter D L, Rich S A, Stampp M S 1985 Remediation of memory disorders:

Experimental evaluation of the spaced-retrieval technique. Journal of Clinical Neuropsychology 7: 79–96

Smith A 1973 Symbol Digit Modalities Test. Manual. Western Psychological Services, Los Angeles

Smith A 1981 Principles underlying human brain functions in neuropsychological sequelae of different neuropathological processes. In: Filskov S B, Boll T J (eds) Handbook of clinical neuropsychology. Wiley-Interscience, New York

Spitz H H 1972 Note on immediate memory for digits: invariance over the years. Psychological Bulletin 78: 183–185

Stroop J R 1935 Studies of interference in serial verbal reactions. Journal of Experimental Psychology 18: 643–662

Strub R L, Black F W 1977 The mental status examination in neurology. F A Davis, Philadelphia

Stuss D T, Benson D F 1984 Neuropsychological studies of the frontal lobes. Psychological Bulletin 95: 3–28

Taylor L B 1979 Psychological assessment of neurosurgical patients. In: Rasmussen T, Marino R (eds) Functional neurosurgery. Raven Press, New York

Terman L M, Merrill M A 1973 Stanford-Binet Intelligence Scale: Manual for the third revision, Form L-M. Houston Mifflin, Boston

Vernon P E 1979 Intelligence: heredity and environment. W H Freeman, San Francisco

Walsh K W 1978 Neuropsychology. Churchill Livingstone/Longman, New York

Wechsler D 1981 WAIS-R manual. Psychological Corporation, New York

Wells F L, Ruesch J 1969 Mental examiner's handbook (rev. edn) Psychological Corporation, New York

*Howard Gardner*

# The assessment of intelligences: a neuropsychological perspective

## STANDARD APPROACHES TO NEUROPSYCHOLOGICAL ASSESSMENT

Over the past decades many impressive efforts have been undertaken to devise batteries of tests for the assessment of organically injured patients. Some neuropsychological laboratories rely heavily on one or two key measures, such as the Wechsler Adult Intelligence Scale or the Raven's progressive matrices, while others favor a more extensive range of instruments, for the purpose of surveying the gamut of cognitive functions. For the most part the selection of tests is based on experience; rather than being inspired by a particular theoretical point of view, clinicians embrace that combination of tests which has proved useful for diagnosis and for treatment. Indeed, the rapid growth of neuropsychological assessment signals both the need for, and the success of, such a pragmatic approach to assessment.

Despite the diversity of approaches which has emerged, certain broad characterizations apply to most clinical testing. For one thing, most neuropsychological tests are relatively artificial; they are a product of the psychological laboratory rather than a reflection of the demands and desires of daily life (Neisser, 1976). These test instruments place a premium on providing short answers, often under strictly timed conditions, and require that the patient move rapidly and without guidance from one context or set to another. While the relative level of performance across item types yields a cognitive behavioral profile, the emphasis on rapid responses in context-free conditions tends to highlight areas of weakness rather than islands of strength.

Perhaps most strikingly, despite their manifold diversity, most test batteries tend to focus heavily on two kinds of tasks: those requiring (1) linguistic skill, and (2) skill in logical problem-solving. Any individual who has relatively spared linguistic and logical capacities will succeed on these tasks: any individual with significant compromise in one or both of these areas will perform poorly. In this sense, neuropsychological assessment today (understandably) reflects the view of cognition and intelligence which dominates Western psychological settings.

Having suggested certain limitations in most current approaches, I put forth here a different view of human cognition, one which has grown out of my studies of intellectual development and breakdown over the past 15 years (Gardner, 1975, 1982, 1983). The approach seeks to survey the full range of human cognitive capacities as they have been realized over the millennia in a wide range of cultural settings. The emphasis falls on behaviors and skills which have proven of value in meaningful settings. The result is a novel approach to cognition, one which has gathered a certain degree of scientific support and has already engendered some controversy. In this essay I first sketch the main lines of the theory and then consider some possible implications for the assessment and rehabilitation of brain-damaged patients.

## A NEW VIEW OF HUMAN INTELLIGENCES

To understand this approach to human cognition, it is desirable to suspend common notions about intelligence. These perceived notions include the following. Intelligence is a unitary construct; intelligence can be equated, roughly, with the ability to succeed in a modern secular school; intelligence, however defined, can be reliably assessed using a short answer instrument, one which can be administered and reliably scored within a brief time; intelligence is, or reflects, a generic property of the nervous system – for example, the ability to synthesize a great deal of information or to respond quickly to a more or less complex stimulus.

Without necessarily passing judgement on any of these assertions, it is salutary to bracket them for awhile. Consider, instead, a survey of the contemporary world and the wide range of adult competences (or end-states) which have been valued by diverse cultures over the millennia. These end-states include the hunter, farmer, parent, statesman, chief, religious leader, sailor, musician, dancer, athlete, seer, scientist, inventor, and many others as well. In my view, a theory of human cognition should be able to account for the skills, or combinations of skills, on which individuals can draw in order to achieve this full spectrum of end-states; indeed, to the extent that a theory of cognition fails to account adequately for this range, that theory is deficient.

In my own case, I began with a belief in the unitary notion of intelligence and in the existence of general intellectual operations *á la* Piaget (1970). However, I found these beliefs to be systematically undermined by my research with normal and gifted children, on the one hand, and with brain-injured patients on the other.

### Definition

Based on my growing realization that there are various kinds of intellectual skills of which human beings are capable, I formulated the notion of *an* intelligence. An intelligence is an ability, or a set of abilities, which permit an individual *to solve a problem*, or *to fashion a product*, which is valued within one or more cultural settings. Note that this definition diverges widely from usual formulations. The definition makes no assumptions about singularity, nor about utility in school, nor about susceptibility to assessment in a short period of time. Rather, the definition rests on the assumption that mental abilities can be marshalled to carry out tasks or to create works of unquestioned cultural value.

## Criteria

Armed with this rough-and-ready formulation of 'an intelligence', I next devised a set of criteria that any intelligence must meet. These criteria entailed an inventory of disparate sources of information, which are relevant to the existence (or non-existence) of certain kinds of discrete mental capacities. Among the sources which my colleagues and I surveyed were information about development in normal and in gifted children; information about the breakdown of mental abilities in once-normal individuals under conditions of organic pathology; data about exceptional individuals, including prodigies, *idiot savants*, autistic individuals, children with learning disabilities, and the like; evidence on the evolution of cognition over the millennia and on the kinds of cognitive capacities found in infra-human (and infra-primate) species; results of psychometric testing, and, in particular, the correlations which obtain among tests; and, finally, results of tests of psychological training, particularly those efforts in which the transfer of a skill to another kind of task was assessed.

My survey proceeded as follows. To the extent that an ability, or a set of abilities, recurred in a review of the evidence from these disparate sources, that candidate skill gained credibility as an intelligence. Conversely, to the extent that a candidate skill failed to appear, or was counterindicated by another source, or always correlated with a more fundamental ability, it lost persuasiveness as a candidate intelligence. Thus, certain once-promising candidates, such as temporal sequencing, or auditory processing, were eventually eliminated from the list because they did not consistently emerge in the surveys. Other initially speculative capacities, like interpersonal skills, become progressively more persuasive.

Ultimately, I performed a 'subjective factor analysis' on these sources of evidence, synthesizing the information in the most adequate way that I could. Such a subjective survey was necessary because acceptable means of testing several of the various candidate intelligences do not yet exist: and so there were no objective scores to feed into a standard factor analysis. Naturally, such an idiosyncratic reading must be deemed as tentative. In my book *Frames of Mind* (1983), I lay out the evidence on each intelligence as best I can. Readers have the option of evaluating the same evidence that I have, and if it appears appropriate, of arriving at a different set of conclusions.

I come now to the list of seven intelligences, my so-called 'multiple intelligences' (MI). I am under no illusion that seven must be the ultimate number, nor that my present list contains only or all acceptable candidates. Clearly, most, if not all of the intelligences harbor several separate skills, and an analysis in terms of much finer-grained categories can readily be conducted. It is important to indicate that no intelligence is cognate with an adult cultural end-state: just as any intelligence can be put to many uses, so any adult end-state will consist of a blend of intelligences working in concert. Finally, while evidence from brain damage contributes to the identification of intelligences, there is no claim that each intelligence (or, indeed, *any* intelligence) must be localized in a particular brain region. While I happen to believe that evidence is impressive for the localization of particular intelligences, separate intelligences can be posited simply in light of functional evidence for their existence (Fodor, 1975, 1983).

In defining each intelligence, and in citing roles in which that intelligence is featured, then, I am not insisting that any particular listing is decisive. Rather, I want to support the *notion* of a plurality of intelligence, each separate from one another, and suggested by the kind of analysis which I have carried out in my research; the case for the exact number and the precise identity of each intelligence can be made at a later date.

**The intelligences**

The first entry, linguistic intelligence, is exemplified in the poet, orator, or lawyer. The second intelligence, logical–mathematical, is exemplified in the scientist or mathematician. I contend that most intelligence tests, whatever their claims, assess these two intelligences, while ignoring or minimizing other ones. To the extent that a case can be made for 'g', or a general factor of intelligence, it entails the ability to handle linguistic and logical forms of information as assessed by standard short-answer formats. While Piaget claimed to be investigating all human intelligences, he actually devoted his work largely to the investigation of logical–mathematical intelligence.

It is important to indicate here that linguistic (and logical mathematical) intelligence are divisions at one level of generality. Within linguistic intelligence one can certainly tease out further subcomponents, including syntactic, semantic, or pragmatic aspects; and certain kinds of more specific skills, such as facility at written expression, at oral expression, in verbal memory and the like. Conceivably one might excel at one aspect of language, while not at the others. In practice, however, extensive involvement in activities featuring linguistic intelligence should bolster linguistic skills across the board (though not, by argument, skills in other intelligences). A similar inventory of subskills, and a similar argument about their tendencies to develop together, can be made with reference to logical mathematical intelligence.

Moving down the list, there is a spatial intelligence, entailing the capacity to represent and to manipulate spatial configurations. Geographers, surveyors, sculptors, painters, and engineers all possess considerable spatial intelligence. Note here that the existence of a strong intelligence by no means predicts which particular occupation an individual will pursue, nor even whether she will be an artist or scientist; but the identification of a strong intelligence allows one to designate the *kinds* of occupations for which she will have gifts. A fourth form, musical intelligence, is exemplified by the composer, performer, or other individual with a keen musical ear and music analytic abilities. A fifth, termed bodily-kinesthetic intelligence, highlights the ability to use one's whole body, or certain parts, like the hands or mouth, to fashion products or solve problems. Dancers and athletes, but also surgeons and craftsmen, are distinguished by considerable bodily-kinesthetic intelligence.

While many psychologists find the first five to be credible candidates (even if they question the term 'intelligence'), they typically balk at the final two on the list. I claim that there exist two forms of *personal intelligences.* Interpersonal intelligence, exhibited by a leader, salesman, or therapist, involves the abilities to understand other individuals, to develop viable models of how they function and how they are motivated, and to act on the basis of that knowledge. In contrast, intrapersonal intelligence, perhaps exemplified by a psychologically oriented novelist, or an individual whose degree of self-insight has been notably enhanced by psychotherapy, involves the ability to know one's own feelings and goals, to create a viable model of one's self, and to act on the basis of this model. I consider individuals such as Dale Carnegie and Lyndon Johnson to have had excellent interpersonal intelligence; individuals such as Mahatma Gandhi, Sigmund Freud, or Feodor Dostoevsky, to have possessed considerable intrapersonal intelligence.

In my view, all normal members of our species have the potential to develop each of these intelligences to some degree. Individuals differ in the extent to which they are 'at risk' or 'at promise' in each sphere. Both genetic factors and early opportunities will determine the extent to which a particular intelligence is fully realized. It is important to stress once again, since this point is often missed, that there is no simple one-to-one mapping between an intelligence and an adult end-state. Individuals with a keen intelligence (say, spatial) can develop in any number of ways and fulfill any number of cultural end-states. By the same token, any particular end-state (say, a lawyer or a scientist) inevitably involves a blend of intelligences. In fact, only freaks ever exhibit a single intelligence completely in isolation from others; any well-functioning human being will inevitably draw upon an amalgam of some (though usually not all) intelligences.

Intelligences are not based upon a single sensory system. With the possible exception of music, which may be yoked to the auditory senses, intelligences feature more abstract forms of information processing which can be applied to data from more than one sensory modality. Thus, spatial intelligence is exhibited even by blind individuals, while linguistic intelligence can proceed through the visual–gestural as well as the oral–auditory modalities.

Finally, each intelligence contains one or more 'core' operations which are relatively autonomous from other 'core' operations in other intelligences. Syntactic and phonological analyses are core operations in the linguistic sphere; sensitivity to number and to causality are 'core operations' in the logical–mathematical sphere. By and large, strength in a particular intelligence does not predict strength (or weakness) in another intelligence. By the same token, given the independence of core operations, it proves difficult to strengthen a given intelligence by exploiting the core operations of another intelligence.

## The novelty of the theory

Without question, this theory has venerable antecedents in the past. Francis Joseph Gall (Boring, 1950), with his belief in different brain regions subserving different cognitive functions, and L. L. Thurstone (1938), with his factor analytic claims about vectors of the mind, certainly have anticipated aspects of this approach, and I in no sense spurn this pedigree. At the same time, however, it is important to indicate that this theory diverges in significant respects from such predecessors.

First of all, the theory is grounded in knowledge about the nervous system, especially that gained from studies of insults to the brain. While Gall made audacious claims about the neuropsychological representation of different 'faculties', he in fact lacked evidence on which to base such accounts. Even as this theory is more firmly rooted in neuroscience than its predecessors, it is also far more dependent on cross-cultural studies. The list of 'end-states' to be accounted for was derived from a cross-cultural study which surveyed many kinds of mental abilities (for example, those exhibited by hunters or by seers): some of these vocational and avocational end-states have rarely been taken into account in our Western schooled setting and certainly have fallen outside the normal orbit of intelligence testing. It is possible, at least in principle, to analyze any end-state in terms of its constituent intelligences; and, as already noted, failure to be able to account for an end-state in terms of its component intelligences would count as a deficit of the theory.

Most psychological theories are based on the assumption of *horizontality* – the assumption that abilities like perception, memory, learning, and the like apply equivalently and in the same manner across the range of contents (Fodor, 1983). On a horizontal account, memory occurs in the same way, independent of the kind of content that has been introduced. In contrast, the theory of multiple intelligences embraces a *vertical* organization of mental processing: on this account memory operates in a characteristic (and perhaps in a characteristically different) way with various kinds of content (e.g., language, music, spatial layout). Therefore, knowledge of an individual's competence in remembering language holds little if any predictive value about that individual's capacity to remember musical or spatial information. At the very least, on a vertical account, it becomes an empirical issue to what extent processes like memory or perception operate in equivalent ways independent of the particular contents to which they are being applied.

Even as the theory questions the viability of a single intelligence, or a single horizontal factor like 'memory' or 'learning', it challenges a belief in general creativity. Creativity is seen as the ability to create a product or solve a problem in a novel way; one which the culture eventually comes to recognize as important and significant. It may well be that an individual can be highly creative with one kind of informational content – say music or language – without exhibiting the slightest ability or inclination to be creative with other materials. One of the most creative individuals of all time, Leonardo da Vinci, appears to have excelled chiefly in logical–mathematical and spatial spheres;

there is little evidence that his abilities in other spheres were particularly notable.

A final feature of the theory is its developmental orientation. To be sure, the theory rejects the Piagetian view that development consists of a series of broad stages which are manifested, independent of the particular content involved. If stages exist, they are likely to be particular to a given content area. That is, within each intelligence there should be distinct developmental stages through which each individual must pass; individuals will differ in the speed with which they pass through these stages and the stage which they ultimately achieve, but the same developmental sequence should be observed in every case. At each developmental stage there will be appropriate means for manifesting an intelligence: thus in infancy an intelligence is manifest through direct perception of patterns - for example, the ability to discriminate among tonal sequences or to count small sets of numbers; in early childhood an intelligence is manifest through an initial mastery of symbol systems - for example, the ability to tell a story or to render a representational drawing.

Relatedly, assessment of intelligences must be carried out in the way that makes sense at each age, or developmental stage; it is unlikely that any particular measure will be applicable across diverse developmental levels. Each intelligence presumably has its own optimal developmental trajectory and this lifeline can be ascertained by extensive study. There are likely to be stages at which development is particularly plastic or especially vulnerable; a search for sensitive periods and for crystallizing experiences which encourage development during such periods should have strong educational implications.

### Summary

To summarize, then, I have introduced a new conception of an intelligence, one which highlights the capacity to create a product or to solve a problem of consequence within a culture. Drawing on a deliberately diverse range of criteria, I have then nominated seven separate intellectual capacities, which all normal individuals have the opportunity of developing to a greater or lesser extent. While this theory bears a certain resemblance to earlier multifactorial approaches, it stands out in various respects: its dependence upon biological and cultural evidence; its rootedness in developmental analysis; its espousal of 'vertical' processes; and its expressed skepticism about the potential for assessing intelligence(s) using conventional paper and pencil measures.

## THE RELEVANCE OF THE THEORY FOR THE NEUROPSYCHOLOGICAL LABORATORY

According to multiple intelligences theory, every normal individual, from early in life, possesses a profile of intelligences; this profile delineates the individual's current developmental level in each intelligence. It should be possible, in principle, to assess this profile and to use it as a guide - whether to lead a preschooler to captivating activities, or to assist a brain-injured adult (or his family) in making vocational, avocational, or other life decisions.

Unfortunately, means for assessing each of the intelligences have not yet been developed. The only possible exceptions are in the linguistic and logical areas where standardized intelligence tests, including measures like the Raven's matrices or the Peabody Picture Vocabulary Test, can provide a rough-and-ready measure of skills. Of course, within particular spheres there are also tests which allow finer-grained analyses of difficulties - for example, the various tests of aphasia or of apraxia. Even here, however, it would be desirable to assess these capacities in ways which are closer to the competence required in daily life. Language competence might be assessed through monitoring the ability to carry out a conversation; logical mathematical intelligence might be assessed by observing how an individual shops for her daily needs. As far as I have been able to ascertain, there are few measures which do a credible job of assessing the remaining intelligences, though there are certainly measures of spatial abilities or personal understanding which might prove relevant.

The very recitation of inadequacies in current testing suggests an interim solution. The therapist or clinician with an interest in MI theory can combine standardized tests, which indicate something about core operations, with informal observations of patients as they cope in milieus which tap intelligences in more naturalistic fashion. Through this combination of standardized and naturalistic measures it should be possible to arrive at a fairly accurate profile of the individual's current abilities and - perhaps - to offer suggestions about which rehabilitation maneuvers might prove effective (see also Holland, 1985).

## One possible regime

Any effort to assess intelligence in brain-damaged patients must, of course, be adapted to the particular kinds of brain damage that has been sustained as well as to any other obvious deficits. With this caveat in mind I would like to suggest the kinds of observations and informal assessments which might provide a tentative profile of intelligence in a range (though by no means the whole range) of organic patients. These suggested assessments will focus primarily on the patient's productive capacities: this is because standardized tests are generally geared to deal with perception and comprehension. It is assumed that this program of testing will be done in conjunction with standardized instruments, including tests which purport to detect damage to particular brain loci, such as frontal lobe or parietal lobe tests. As new means are developed for assessing an intelligence, it might be possible to reduce dependence on short-answer instruments which are often of dubious ecological validity.

*Logical–mathematical.* The ability of a patient to handle money in a store setting, to keep her own books, or to make decisions about her savings or investments are promising ways of assessing an individual's capacities in this sphere.

*Linguistic.* The ability of a patient to converse with familiar and with unfamiliar people, to read and paraphrase a newspaper or magazine, to relate and to understand stories and jokes, to compose or understand a letter, are all means of assessing the degree to which an individual's language capacities remain functional. Our own work indicates the importance of assessing these competences in individuals who have sustained right hemisphere disease (Gardner et al, 1983).

*Spatial.* Probably the best measure of spatial ability is the capacity to learn one's way around an unfamiliar terrain. The hospital, an unfamiliar region in a city, or even a specially constructed site can be employed. Map reading should also be assessed. In cases of severe pathology, the ability of the patient to negotiate his way around familiar spaces should be probed.

*Musical.* In the musical realm the individual's capacity to produce a known piece, either by singing, or by the use of an instrument with which the patient has prior familiarity, proves the most straightforward means for an initial assessment. The ability to criticize performances, or to compare renditions of the same work, provides alternative means of assessment: these prove of particular utility with those individuals whose productive capacities have for one or another reason been compromised.

*Bodily kinesthetic.* The ability of the patient to carry out familiar tasks, like tying a shoe, using a tool, or driving a car, is one way of assessing bodily kinesthetic intelligence. The ability to learn a new task, which uses the whole body (like a dance) or parts of the body (like a toy or tool) provides a more challenging assessment. Apraxia need not disqualify a patient from such tests; a patient may succeed with a task encountered in context, even while he fails with a task which must be executed to command or in the absence of the customary object.

*Interpersonal.* Interpersonal intelligences can be readily assessed by observing how the patient interacts with familiar individuals, such as family members or friends; the ability to understand motivations, pick up intentions, or influence social interactions should be monitored. The ability of the patient to interact satisfactorily with unfamiliar individuals, including examiners, provides a correlative estimate in an unfamiliar context. It is also possible to gain leverage by examining the patient's ability to interpret interpersonal interactions and motivations in a book, movie, play or television drama.

*Intrapersonal.* While intrapersonal instruments which assess an individual's knowledge of self will prove most elusive, every effort ought to be made to assess the patient's own sense of what happened to him, what are his prospects, how well he can plan for himself in the short and in the intermediate run. The fact that a patient can achieve an IQ score in the superior range, yet demonstrate neither self-insight nor the ability to formulate and execute plans, is strong evidence that this crucial component is not tapped by standard tests. Testimony from the family about the individual's self-understanding, self-concept, will to act, and accomplishment of intended acts can be extremely valuable inputs to any assessment of intrapersonal skill.

As should be evident, the ways for assessing these intelligences are straightforward (though not necessarily convenient to carry out); most of the assessments tap facets to which sensitive family members and examiners have always attended. For these very reasons, I wish to stress that such monitoring is all too frequently forgotten, or left out of reports, even though it may contain the most critical information for the rehabilitation specialist or the family. In fact, so long as testing is restricted to short-answer assessments of linguistic and logical skills, patients with severe damage of certain sorts (e.g., right hemisphere disease, or frontal lobe syndromes) may appear deceptively normal in the wake of standardized tests. In the future it may well be possible to evolve means of assessment which are as uniform and objective as those currently used in standardized testing; in the interim period the kind of informal inventory recommended here can be implemented.

It is worth mentioning at this juncture that MI theory is best suited for monitoring local or particular mental capacities. Certain more general abilities – wisdom, judgement, synthesizing capacities, 'common sense' come to mind – are not easily handled within the terminology and assessment apparatus of MI theory. The fact that these most general abilities are not addressed is a genuine weakness of the theory, though whether this lacuna entirely invalidates the theory is doubtful. In any case, these capacities should certainly be monitored when possible.

## Implications for rehabilitation

The theory of multiple intelligence has only recently been proposed and its implications for brain-damaged patients have yet to be worked out in any detail. In my view the theory may prove more useful for assessment than for rehabilitation; and yet, in a volume focused on the latter topic, it may be worthwhile to assay a few remarks.

First of all, adoption of an assessment procedure based on MI theory is likely to highlight the uneven cognitive profiles of most individuals. Rather than revealing an individual who is uniformly strong, or uniformly compromised (perhaps because of difficulties in taking standardized tests), such a pluralistic approach is likely to isolate areas of relative strength and areas of relative weakness. The therapist thus has the option either of trying to shore up weakness or of building up strength. While any comprehensive therapy program will necessarily address both tasks, it is important to indicate the difficulty of shoring up an intelligence if core capacities have been impaired. Other intelligences cannot be readily substituted for an impaired intelligence. MI theory harbors the hint that the therapist ought to play from strength.

The bias in MI therapy falls toward environments of assessment and rehabilitation which are as rich and 'natural' as possible. While it may sometimes be easier to heighten performance through the use of artificial stimulus materials in a constructed environment, such 'contrived' performances very rarely survive in a more naturalistic setting. The recommendation here is to begin efforts of assessment and rehabilitation by working with the most context-rich environment – shopping at the actual store, rather than playing store; an actual conversation with a family member, rather than a ritualized conversation with a trained experimenter; and the like. At the very least, the patient has the opportunity to draw on past skills rather than having to develop wholly new ones; and to the extent that such practice actually improves performance, it will always be possible to move to more artificial settings, should that procedure (for some reason) be indicated.

While it is not easy to replace one intelligence with another, nearly all complex adult tasks and end-states can be accomplished through combinations of a number of intelligences. One may become a successful lawyer by highlighting linguistic, logical–mathematical, and interpersonal intelligences, or (optimally) some combination of all three. This fact holds out some hope for patients: even if the capacity to attain an end-state in one way has been violated, there is still hope for approaching the same end-state *via* another, hitherto underexploited but still spared intelligence.

As with assessment, my suggestions for rehabilitation do not depart from common sense and should already be familiar to a reflective practitioner. I hope, nonetheless, that the positing of a theoretical framework may serve as a useful background against which to carry out assessment and to offer suggestions for therapy in the hospital or aids in a home setting. Indeed, sharing the approach of multiple intelligences with families – even (in appropriate cases) with the patient himself – may serve as a useful way of keeping track of deficits, and of fostering viable performance through some combination of preserved intellectual strengths.

The theory of multiple intelligences grew out of a dual dissatisfaction: dissatisfaction with unitary conceptions of the mind, whether they be Piagetian or Spearmanesque in origin; dissatisfaction with 'short-answer', timed modes of testing (see also Kaplan, 1983). I have sought to fashion a more pluralistic notion of human cognition, and to suggest that cognition can be appropriately assessed through tasks whose relation to daily living need not remain an article of faith.

It has taken decades of research and development involving many millions of dollars to bring standardized intelligence testing to the high art that it has now become; it would take a comparable developmental effort before one could determine whether an alternative approach such as the one I have sketched would be viable. It is, of course, impossible to know whether the opportunity for such development will present itself, or whether, if presented, the current approach will prove even as successful as its barely adequate predecessors. I have tried to suggest that, even now, one can begin to think of patients in terms of possessing multiple competences and to monitor their spontaneous and elicited performances in settings which illuminate their intelligences. In my own work I have found that such a reorientation can be helpful; I hope that other clinicians will find it suggestive as well.

## ACKNOWLEDGMENT

Preparation of this paper was supported in part by grants from the National Institute of Neurological and Communication Diseases and Stroke (NS 11408 and 06209), the Veterans Administration, the Spencer Foundation, and the Bernard van Leer Foundation. I thank Hiram Brownell and Harold Goodglass for advice on an earlier draft of this paper.

## REFERENCES

Boring E G 1950 A history of experimental psychology. Appleton-Century, New York

Fodor J A 1975 The language of thought. Crowell, New York

Fodor J A 1983 The modularity of mind. MIT Press, Cambridge, MA

Gardner H 1975 The shattered mind. Knopf, New York

Gardner H 1982 Developmental psychology. Little Brown, Boston

Gardner H 1983 Frames of mind: the theory of multiple intelligences. Basic Books, New York

Gardner H, Brownell H H, Wapner W, Michelow D 1983 Missing the point: the role of the right hemisphere in the processing of complex linguistic materials. In: Perceman E (ed) Cognitive processing in the right hemisphere. Academic Press, New York

Holland A 1985 The evolution of aphasic syndromes. Paper presented at the Academy of Aphasia, Pittsburgh

Kaplan E F 1983 Process and achievement revisited. In: Wapner S, Kaplan B (eds) Toward a holistic developmental psychology. L. Erlbaum, Hillsdale, NJ

Neisser U 1976 Cognition and reality. Freeman, San Francisco

Piaget J 1970 Piaget's theory. In: Mussen P (ed) Carmichael's manual of child psychology. Wiley, New York

Thurstone L L 1938 Primary mental abilities. Psychological Monograph, no. 1

Manfred J. Meier, Silvia Strauman, and W. Gary Thompson

# 5 Individual differences in neuropsychological recovery: an overview

The spontaneous recovery of higher cortical functions following brain injury or disease is a topic of continuing interest to neuropsychologists and the various rehabilitation professionals. In practice individual differences in spontaneous recovery inevitably become confounded with treatment effects and complicate evaluation of different treatment outcomes. The effectiveness of various rehabilitation procedures may be evaluated primarily on the basis of the degree to which acceleration of spontaneous recovery changes and, hopefully, recovery of function exceeding baseline changes can be achieved. Empirical evaluation of any treatment, retraining, or remediation procedure therefore requires some formal assessment and control for spontaneous recovery factors. An understanding of the determinants of recovery, in turn, may help define the boundaries within which a given treatment may be said to be effective, and lead to more precise prediction of specific individual outcomes, whether with or without formal remedial intervention.

This chapter endeavors to relate neuropsychology as the study of brain–behavior relationships to a general model of individual outcome differences following cerebral involvement. This is necessarily a capsular treatment of a subject area and, therefore, will be limited to an overview of the high points from the clinical neuropsychologist's perspective as a member of the rehabilitation team. Inclusion of a review of brain–behavior relationships was prompted by the centrality of this issue to differential diagnosis. An equivalent emphasis on individual outcome differences was prompted by the observed wide range of individual differences in rehabilitation potential and outcome following head injury or cerebral infarction.

A major role for the neuropsychologist in rehabilitation is the quantitative and qualitative assessment of variables for the prediction of outcome and the delineation of impaired and spared functions early in the recovery process. A review of the vast basic and clinical literature on recovery of function will not be attempted since numerous excellent reviews are available, (Stein et al, 1974; Newcombe & Ratcliff, 1979; Newcombe, 1982; Stein et al, 1983; Brooks et al, 1984).

This discussion is intended to explore the factors that have been shown to contribute to recovery as seen from clinical studies, and to examine possible interactions among these variables to produce the wide range of individual differences observed on dependent 'outcome' variables assessed by means of neuropsychological tests. Representative clinical studies will be described to illustrate particular points. Brief neuroanatomical or neuropathological summaries will be introduced in an attempt to articulate the complexly determined nature of such relationships and to identify how these factors may affect neuropsychological outcomes.

## INDIVIDUAL DIFFERENCES IN RECOVERY

The basis for a general individual differences model may be derived from lifespan developmental psychology as applied to normal aging, for example, (Schaie, 1979). Individual differences are determined by many different classes of variables of a genetic, environmental, social, and biological nature. The large numbers of possible interactions among such variables may result in a wide variety of individual outcomes. Specific neuropathological factors related to the disease or injury constitute the biological determinants of outcome within this configuration of interacting effects.

Of greatest interest are the location of the lesion; the extent or severity of neurological involvement; specific etiological conditions; age at onset; time since symptom onset; the momentum or short-term rate of change in manifestations of the disease process; variations in cerebral organization or dominance that may favor or disfavor the bilateral representation of higher cortical functions in focal lesions; any premorbid environmental or lifestyle factors such as education, nutrition, vocational level, physical health, and psychological health; any detrimental internal and external factors such as alcohol and drug abuse, prior exposure to toxins, and functional psychopathology.

### General concepts

Before summarizing the major behavioral correlates of lesions in differing regions of the cerebral cortex, it might be worthwhile to outline briefly the historical precepts, observations and concepts that have led to current theories of higher cortical function (see Luria, 1980, for detailed discussion).

#### *Strict localization doctrine*

This doctrine prevailed among 19th-century European neurologists. It provided a heuristic view of the anatomical basis for the behavioral syndromes which was useful in diagnosis at the time but generated a relatively static view of central nervous system (CNS) function by overstressing the modal effects of discrete lesions and by ignoring dynamic interactions between regions as a basis for observed neurobehavioral change. Strict localization doctrine underestimated the possibility for recovery of function.

### *Mass action/equipotentiality of function*

The mass action hypothesis simply states that the greater the mass of brain substance affected by a lesion, the greater the disruption of function. It assumes that an organized set of dynamically related structures is responsible for the highest functions of the association cortex. The data generated in support of the doctrine emphasized the importance of the extent of brain involvement (particularly the prefrontal regions) in individuals with impaired abstract reasoning abilities and categorical behavior (Lashley, 1929; Goldstein & Scheerer, 1941). The test procedure utilized in the early studies consisted of a variety of sorting tasks, of which the Wisconsin Card Sorting Test (Milner, 1964) constitutes the most cogent modern example. Emphasis on mass action and equipotentiality tended to underestimate regional differences in the organization of higher functions and provided an overinclusive and overgeneralized view of what appears to be the most elaborated or highest class of cortical functions.

### *Regional localization*

Elements of both theories of higher cortical functioning were integrated on the basis of relevant neurophysiological findings and neuroanatomical studies. An example of this was the observation that pyramidal tract fibers originate beyond the motor cortex. Luria (1980) reviewed the literature showing that 43% of the cortex involves overlapping or interconnected zones. The now classic studies of Magoun (1950) provided the first demonstrations of connections from the cortex to secondary nuclei of the thalamus and to the nonspecific reticular activating system of the brain stem. It followed directly that structures that were anatomically more removed from the sensory motor regions (association cortex) might be significantly overlapping or interconnected to provide an anatomical basis for the recovery of function. Following some early efforts by Hebb (1949) the supporting literature was extensively documented by Luria (1980). Modern regional localization doctrine incorporates a number of concepts of reference to neuropsychological rehabilitation. Functional pluripotentiality relates to the notion that no structure in the CNS is solely responsible for a single function. A given structure may participate in a number of functions or functional systems and, thereby, introduce redundancy and rerepresentation of function. Furthermore, functions are organized dynamically through complex interdependencies and composition of participating structures. Gross differentiation of function on a zonal or regional basis may reflect such complex interdependencies. These may permit the uniting of a mosaic of networks in a common task while, at the same time, yielding differentiated effects that can be described behaviorally as a function of the zone or region involved. Such an integration of discrete localization and equipotentiality of function doctrine is expressed most cogently by the concept of plasticity to account for the variability short- and long-term effects of lesions. Another important concept for regional localization theory is 'autoregulation', which acknowledges that a given function is under both afferent and efferent control, this being a precondition for the systematic unification of components in producing: either behavior that serves as a substitute for the impaired function, or some genuinely new behavior pattern that effectively achieves the same function through alternative neural behavioral means. The ascending or hierarchical structure of the brain and the relationship of structure to behavior has been summarized elsewhere (van der Vlugt, 1979) and is discussed briefly in the section on etiology below.

## Neuropsychological deficits related to association cortex lesions

Most of the neuropsychological research on localization of function has been done on patients with acute, circumscribed lesions due to cerebrovascular infarction and those with focal, static, atrophic lesions (usually of early origin) which have produced focal seizure disorders from an identifiable region of the cerebral cortex. This has permitted the systematic analysis of behavioral effects of these lesions and, in some studies, the longitudinal course of the impaired functions. Three major regions of the association cortex have been implicated in these studies: frontal/prefrontal, inferolateral/mesial temporal, and posterior temporoparietal. It is beyond the scope of this chapter to provide elaborate detailed descriptions of the tests utilized in such studies. Useful references are readily available for such a review (Milner, 1964, 1971; Teuber, 1975; Luria, 1980; Lezak, 1983; Meier & Thompson, 1983).

For present purposes, a brief summary will be provided of (a) the primary anatomical structures involved in these regions, (b) the clinical manifestations of lesions, and (c) the neuropsychological test functions that may be subserved by each region.

### *Frontal/prefrontal*

These regions comprise one-half of the cortical mass and consist of both highly and least differentiated areas of the cortex relative to measurement of higher cortical functioning. These areas have extensive connections to the limbic system via the dorsomedial thalamus, the deeper portions of the centrencephalic or brainstem activating system through the ventromedial thalamus, and the temporal region via the cingula tegyrus and the arcuate fasciculus. By contrast, the motor and premotor areas have a more direct relationship to the peripheral neuromusculature and are relatively more differentiated to subserve contralateral voluntary motor function. Interhemispheric connections are found here through the genu of the corpus callosum and there are rich white matter connections to the posterior association areas. The prefrontal region is the last to myelinate and undergoes a rapid proliferation of maturational changes after birth. The association layers of this region also atrophy rapidly under detrimental conditions of nutrition or oxygenation (Akert, 1964).

Experimental lesions in subhuman primates produce selected effects (Luria, 1980). Individual specialized functions are relatively well preserved if the frontal motor cortex is spared but behavior as a whole is grossly pathological. There is marked impairment of purposeful movements characterized by indiscriminate seizing and chewing of objects, failure to recognize familiar care-givers, easy distractibility, and motor automatisms (e.g., walking in circles). This literature implicates this region for serial operations requiring a preliminary synthesis of the stimulus situation. In humans, extensive involvement leads to loss of abstract attitude and a disintegration of goal-oriented behavior (Goldstein & Scheerer, 1981; Luria, 1980).

Extensive frontal involvement is likely to lead to reduced ability to evaluate the results of actions, integrate new experiences with old, direct one's actions to advantage, evaluate environmental circumstances, make purposeful choices in accord with evaluation, and apply a resulting plan to the setting and pursuit of goals (Luria, 1980). Circumscribed focal lesions may not characteristically produce such a full-blown 'frontal lobe syndrome' but many produce elements of this syndrome.

A summary of focal behavioral effects in the quantitative neuropsychological literature is as follows:

1. There may be a deficit in abstract reasoning and categorical functioning, especially where there is involvement of the lateral convexity. The tests most likely to demonstrate such a deficit include sorting procedures such as the Wisconsin Card Sorting Test (Milner, 1964).
2. Beyond the severe nonfluent aphasic changes introduced by a lesion in Broca's area, there may be less dramatic declines of expressive symbolic functions such as selective changes in verbal associative fluency as measured by the Oral Word Association Test (Borkowski et al, 1967). Comparable changes in associative fluency can be demonstrated with right prefrontal involvement utilizing a figural production task such as generating forms that cannot be encoded verbally (Jones-Gotman & Milner, 1977).
3. Some aspects of attentional dysfunction may appear and may be related to reduced exploratory visual functioning (Teuber, 1964).
4. Impaired regulatory control of more complex psychomotor functions necessary for adequate goal-directed behavior may lead to gross declines in planning and foresight abilities as reflected in reduced maze-solving ability (Porteus, 1959). These may be compounded by disturbances in perceptual organization due to right hemisphere involvement (Critchley, 1953; Benton, 1979a).
5. There may be evidence of an abnormally brief response to personal failure experiences in addition to judgmental lapses, impulsivity, and euphoria associated with orbital–basal lesions (Teuber, 1964).
6. Combined declines in planning, initiative, and elaborate volitional processes may be disabling even in the presence of relatively intact

information processing and general intellectual functioning (Hebb & Penfield, 1940; Milner, 1964).

The relative sparing of information processing and general intellectual functioning may give the misleading impression that the patient is more competent to engage in purposeful choice situations and exercise adequate judgment than is likely to be possible. The challenge in rehabilitation planning relates to the design of neuropsychological interventions that improve goal-directed behavior or planning and executive functions (see Ch. 3). Little is known about the spontaneous recovery of such functions though rehabilitation personnel are often acutely aware of the barriers introduced to the treatment process by such deficits. It seems reasonable to assume that these changes are among the last to recover spontaneously if they are going to recover at all. They are clearly most representative of severe and bilateral frontal lobe disease but may also appear with unilateral lesions (Milner, 1971).

### *Infero/mesial temporal region*

The temporal lobe contains the primary auditory cortex which is bilaterally innervated and not directly related to the inferotemporal and basal/mesial portions of the temporal lobes. This region has been demonstrated to constitute an important zone for mediating complex visually guided functions through connections to the striate cortex of the occipital lobe. The basal or mesial temporal region is a part of the limbic system which also includes the olfactory bulb and stalk, the anterior olfactory nucleus, the hippocampus and associated gray matter, the prepyriform cortex and portions of the hippocampal gyrus, the isthmus of the fornicate gyrus, the amygdala, and the cingulate region. This system also interrelates with the Papez 'circuit' to form a cingulate–hippocampus–fornix–mammillary bodies–anterior thalamus–cingulate relationship. Other regions have been considered to be part of this circuit including the orbital frontal, insular and anterotemporal cortex, and the dorsal–medial nucleus of the thalamus. The latter has been particularly implicated in severe recent memory disorders such as Wernicke-Korsakoff's syndrome.

As with frontal lobe lesions, the animal literature shows that individual specialized functions are relatively preserved. Bilateral removal of the temporal lobes produces a change in behavior as a whole that is characteristically different from that seen in prefrontal lesions (Klüver & Bucy, 1937). Behavior changes include an inability to distinguish between edible and inedible objects associated with a compulsive mouthing of objects. There is reduced fear and aggressiveness. Hyperactivity and hypersexuality are prominent features. Both cognitive and emotional disturbances or alterations of function are implied. There is an extensive animal literature, beginning with the classic studies of Bard and Mountcastle (1948) that have shown that the amygdala and cingulate gyrus play an important role in the placidity produced when all of the neocortex is removed, while sparing the limbic system. Removal of the amygdala produced placidity/rage variations while additional removal of the hippocampus may produce rage and changes in territorial behavior.

The emotional/motivational components of these deeper lesions may well become manifest in humans following a head injury in which the orbital–basal frontal and mesial temporal regions are especially vulnerable. Clinical studies of man reflect these changes since tumors of the septal region have been shown to produce rage-like attacks and increased irritability (Valenstein & Heilman, 1979). Early studies also showed that stimulation of the septal region may produce pleasant and sexually arousing experiences in man (Heath, 1964). Bilateral temporal removals in humans have been reported to produce placidity, consistent with the animal research reports. Anterior temporal lobectomy has been reported to increase sexuality in some patients (Blumer & Walker, 1975) while stereotactic amygdaloidectomy may inconsistently produce rage (Mark et al, 1972). By far the most remarkable consequences of bilateral medial temporal lobe removals are the profound and permanent recent memory impairments produced by such lesions (Milner, 1967). A higher incidence of psychiatric referrals has been noted for individuals with partial-complex seizure disorders of temporal lobe origin (Flor-Henry, 1969). However, it is difficult to isolate or separate the emotional/motivational effects of limbic system origin from the detrimental psychosocial effects of having a partial-complex seizure disorder in these individuals (Stevens, 1966; Meier, 1969).

Nevertheless, the higher incidence of psychiatric disorders in seizure patients may have some basis in CNS dysfunction in some cases since electrical stimulation studies of the temporal lobes in humans have elicited relaxation (amygdala, medial forebrain bundle), dysphoria (hippocampus), disorientation (repeated low-frequency stimulation which is correlated with hippocampal slow wave activity), and post-stimulation withdrawal, signs of depression, tension, and somatic complaints (Valenstein & Heilman, 1979). Also, presence of independent bitemporal spike foci on the EEG of patients with temporal lobe disorders has been shown to be associated with multiple elevations on the MMPI scales inferred to reflect both ideational and emotional disturbances (Meier & French, 1965a).

In general, removal of the temporal lobe in man has been associated with material-specific learning and memory changes that parallel what has been observed in animals. The results of these studies may be highlighted as follows:

1. Lateralized effects on learning and memory are more prominent than those observed after prefrontal lesions. Although these recover relatively well, subtle and persisting deficits in verbal learning and memory have been shown after left temporal lobectomy and nonverbal memory after right temporal lobectomy (Milner & Teuber, 1968; Milner, 1971).
2. These conspicuous material-specific deficits in learning and recent memory functioning are directly related to the extent of hippocampal removal (Milner, 1964).

3. Deficits in verbal and visuospatial processing are not excessive after unilateral ablation and tend to be of little consequence except in larger ablations that may intrude on the posterior information processing zones of the posterior and superior portion of the temporal lobes (Milner, 1964).
4. Evidence for personality disturbances is equivocal for the partial-complex seizure population since many individuals with this disorder do not evidence gross psychopathology. However, selected instances of affective and ideational disturbances may occur as a function of lesion-related factors (Seidman, 1980; Thomas et al, 1980).
5. Although information processing and perceptual deficits are minimal, if at all present, there is some evidence of impaired visual discriminability and facial recognition as well as figural and facial memory with temporal lobe involvement (Meier & French, 1965b; Milner, 1971).

*Posterior temporoparietal region*

In addition to the postcentral gyrus and the superior margin of the parietal lobe, this region includes the superior temporal gyrus and the angular and supramarginal gyri. The anatomical differentiation of this region is variable and there are differential rates of myelination following birth, the latest occurring in the region of the angular and supramarginal gyri and, to a lesser extent, Wernicke's area. Collectively, these structures bear no direct relationship to the periphery and relate primarily to the surrounding sensory regions in what Critchley (1953) has called 'an association area of association areas'. It is somewhat arbitrary where the temporal and parietal lobes meet but it is generally accepted that the posterior association cortex that lies beyond the primary sensory receiving areas is responsible for intermodal syntheses of information being processed, verbal or nonverbal, depending upon the hemisphere under consideration. This region is characteristically somewhat larger in the left cerebral hemisphere in most right-handed individuals (Geschwind & Levitsky, 1968), a finding that may be indicative of a more extensive representation of language processing in the leading hemisphere. However, the corresponding region of the right cerebral hemisphere also has major nonverbal information processing functions of an integrative nature. Lesions of this region produce a characteristic 'parietal lobe syndrome' which is characterized by major visuospatial and visuoconstructual disturbances, constructional apraxia, spatial neglect, dressing apraxia, prosopagnosia (facial recognition), susceptibility to sensory extinction (even with intact sensory motor function), and impaired spatial orientation (Critchley, 1953; Hécaen, 1962; Hécaen & Angelerques, 1962; Benton, 1979a).

Unlike prefrontal and anterior/mesial temporal lobe lesions, posterior association cortex lesions produce readily demonstrable behavioral changes that can be assessed informally or by means of brief neuropsychological tests. Lateralized lesions produce a characteristic Wernicke's aphasia which may be more severe as a function of the extent of posterior temporoparietal involvement. Similarly, the manifestations of right posterior temporoparietal involvement are readily discernible in evaluations of graphomotor and perceptual functioning. Since both verbal and visuospatial deficits can appear in extensive diffuse cerebral disease, however, more extensive evaluations may be needed to differentiate between focal and diffuse changes. Highlights from the related literature are as follows:

1. Unlike anterior temporal and prefrontal lesions, posterior lesions are more likely to produce sizable discrepancies between verbal and visuospatial abilities on conventional intellectual tests and neuropsychological test batteries (Reitan, 1964; Meier, 1970).
2. Verbal–visuospatial discrepancies may be present independently of somatosensory or motor deficits since posterior lesions may spare such functions although they will frequently produce visual field defects (Benton, 1979a).
3. Lesions that invade the somatosensory cortex produce rather discrete changes that are more focally represented in the left hemisphere than the right (Semmes et al, 1960; Semmes, 1968), although contradictory findings have been reported (Carmon, 1971).
4. Nevertheless, posterior lesions produce the most consistent and predictable changes in neurological and neuopsychological measurements of any region within the cerebral hemispheres. For example numerous information processing deficits have been demonstrated for facial recognition (Warrington & James, 1967; Benton & Van Allen, 1972), closure of incomplete figures, letters and shapes (Kinsbourne & Warrington, 1963), rod and line-slope matching tasks (DeRenzi et al, 1971; Taylor & Warrington, 1973) and stylus maze performances (Milner, 1964; Ratcliff & Newcombe, 1973).
5. The presence of visual field defects is associated with more severe deficits of visuospatial and visuoconstructional functioning, presumably on the basis of larger and deeper lesions (DeRenzi et al, 1977).
6. Personality changes appear to constitute a reaction to the more conspicuous deficits associated with posterior association lesions (Friedman, 1950). Though 'denial' of neurological involvement or deficit is an exception, it tends to be seen only in acutely involved individuals after cerebrovascular infarction whose body image distortions may be too severe to perceive the nature of the neuropsychological deficit (Critchley, 1953).

This introductory account of the common behavioral deficits resulting from lesions in the major areas of association cortex is designed to anchor the reader to the range of behavioral changes of neuropsychological significance. The outline is not exhaustive by any means, and is provided as a frame of reference for rehabilitation personnel who seek some anchorage in a clinical context of the behavioral literature as it relates to brain structure. Recovery of function is constrained by location and the extent of the lesion as well as associated neuropathological and pathophysiological factors that arise as a function of the level of CNS involvement encountered in a given disease process. Attention will now be directed at two representative neurological disease processes – namely, closed head injury and cerebrovascular infarction, since they introduce underlying anatomical considerations that differ even when there is similarity in region of the cerebral cortex that may be involved. The size of the lesion, of course, is one factor that relates to the severity of the neuropsychological deficits but circumscribed and critically located lesions may produce profound deficits as well.

## Etiology as a factor in outcome

The development of technologically advanced neurological diagnostic procedures has made it possible to characterize lesions in specific anatomical terms for different etiologies. The correlation between the resulting lesion-localization classifications and neuropsychological test outcomes is not always very high (Kaszniak et al, 1979). Computerized axial tomography (CAT or CT scans), the most widely used direct anatomical localizing technique, does not yield complete neuroanatomical information in all cases. This is more true under some etiological circumstances than others. Neuropathological heterogeneity may exist under different etiological conditions. Different patient subgroups may well dictate different emphases within the configuration of neuropsychological tests used in assessment and in longitudinal monitoring of recovery changes. Two such populations are especially relevant for neuropsychological rehabilitation, both involving an abrupt neuropathological event from which varying degrees of recovery may then occur; closed head injury and cerebrovascular accidents. Patients with other neuropathological changes less frequently become involved in intensive rehabilitation programs, including those with brain tumors and degenerative disorders, since these may produce both progressive and multifocal or diffuse underlying neuropathological changes.

### *Closed head injury*

Closed head injury provides perhaps the most cogent example of an etiological condition that produces a wide range of individual differences in neuropathology. Superficially considered, a head injury might be expected to produce relatively unitary changes of a nonspecific nature. However, there are many difficulties involved in classifying lesions due to closed head injury, as shown by the neuropathological findings reported for nonsurviving cases (Courville & Ames, 1952; Strich, 1961). In the special case of sudden death due to closed head injury, there are frequently no signs of contusions, lacerations, or hemorrhage when the brain is inspected grossly. However, there may be an interesting and peculiar distribution of changes in the white matter, leaving the gray matter relatively unaffected. Although normal in general appearance, such brains characteristically have undergone widespread shearing and tearing of the white matter in the cerebral hemispheres and in the long tracts, both ascending and descending, that relate deeper structures responsible for cerebral activation (reticular activating system) to structures at the level of the cerebral hemispheres. It has also been shown that such changes are likely to be present in surviving cases although perhaps not to the same degree as that seen in nonsurvivors. These changes may not be immediately evident on CT scans, nor can scans readily identify shearing in the long tracts. Retrograde degeneration may subsequently be associated with ventricular enlargement and include lateralized asymmetries in ventricular size. Very complete reviews of the literature, both experimental and clinical, are now available (Ommaya & Gennarelli, 1974; Hardman, 1979). Ommaya and Gennarelli (1974) have shown that shearing and tearing of the white matter may occur even at subconcussive levels in experimental injuries, and that the effects may extend beyond the cerebral hemispheres to involve deeper thalamic and subthalamic structures. Severe impact results in longer durations of coma and post-traumatic amnesia in humans (Russell & Smith, 1961; Smith, 1981). Although not precisely predictive of degree of cognitive and memory impairment or of eventual outcome, measures of duration of coma, retrograde and anterograde amnesia, and post-traumatic amnesia have been extensively studied and reviewed in a growing clinical literature (Benton, 1979b; Levin et al, 1982). Some of these studies will be discussed selectively in the section on recent longitudinal neuropsychological research. In the meantime, it is emphasized that the evaluation of the severity of a closed head injury is still based on these clinical indicators and the corresponding inferred nature and depth of neurological involvement.

Due to the large size and compressible nature of the brain, the changes in the velocity within the head produced by lateral dislocations of the brain and the rotational forces that shear and tear the white matter may vary quite widely. In milder injuries the damage may be limited to extremely subtle shearing effects restricted to the cerebral hemispheres. With more severe rotational injuries involved in acceleration concussions, there are centripetal as well as centrifugal effects that produce increasingly deeper shearing of the white matter as a function of the specific rotational forces resulting at the moment of impact. As the shearing effects become more severe, secondary effects of a more localized nature may occur in the form of contusions, lacerations, and hemorrhages. In turn, these changes may produce impairments of functions known to be affected by focal injuries as seen, for example, in penetrating head injuries or in cerebrovascular accident. These focal changes may be asymmetrical as may be the shearing effects themselves, again depending upon the specific dynamics of force at the time of the injury. In more severe injuries there is also a greater likelihood of damage to the corpus callosum including complete disruption of the fibers connecting the cerebral hemispheres. Among the most common focal effects are those described as 'coup' and 'contre-coup' contusions. These contusions are more likely to involve the orbital–basal portions of the frontal lobes and the temporal poles because of their vulnerability to contact with the cranial fossae, the bony ridges and recesses of the skull. Some rather fundamental principles govern the relative likelihood of coup as contrasted with contre-coup effects. Sudden deceleration of the head, as in the special circumstance involved with the head striking an immovable object, may produce contre-coup effects or prominent injury to the contralateral structures in the hemisphere opposite the side of impact. On the other hand, if the head is stationary at impact, contusions are more likely in regions underlying the point of impact and can then produce greater effects in the proximal rather than the distal hemisphere. In the presence of a skull fracture there is a greater likelihood that the posterior and inferior surfaces of the cerebral hemispheres and the cerebellum will sustain focal effects (Hardman, 1979).

The hemorrhaging that may occur, along with other vascular changes, complicates the task of estimating the extent, depth, and overall severity of the injury. Multifocal complications of closed head injury contribute to the overall severity but may not be directly identifiable, though they may be expressed indirectly through such severity indicators as duration of coma, retrograde and anterograde amnesia, and the resulting pattern on batteries of neuropsychological tests (Levin et al, 1979; Russell, 1971; Russell & Smith, 1961). In order to characterize the lesion on the basis of the inferred brain–behavior relationships involved in a particular case, it is necessary to take specialized radiologic data such as CT scans or increasingly utilized nuclear magnetic resonance (NMR) and positron emission tomography (PET) scans and the configuration of neuropsychological deficits into account. Table 5.1 shows the expected neuropsychological deficits that are likely to be present as a function of the severity of the injury based on neuroanatomical data. Table 5.2 summarizes the focal outcomes that may be present in the more severe instances of surviving closed head injuries where focal effects may be prominent. Thus, severity cannot be understood in closed head injury without considering both the breadth and depth of underlying neuropathological change. Severity has been shown to be an important limiting condition for estimating the likelihood of focal dysfunction in closed head injury (Fahey et al, 1967). An additional important limiting factor is age, which appears to interact with severity in a synergistic manner to affect the recovery course (Carlsson et al, 1968).

**Table 5.1** Probable relations between neuroanatomical and neuropsychological variables in closed head injury

| Neuroanatomical | Neuropsychological |
|---|---|
| Longitudinal tracts (brainstem RAS) | Attention, vigilance, concentration |
| Brainstem/limbic system or deep fronto-temporal connections | Learning, memory, personality disturbances |
| Fiber systems within hemispheres | Subtle subjective complaints |
| Interhemispheric commissures | Possible disconnection phenomena |
| Secondary focal involvement | Superimposed focal correlates |

**Table 5.2** Probable relations between focal neuroanatomical effects and neuropsychological variables in more severe closed head injury

| Neuroanatomical | Neuropsychological |
|---|---|
| Direct and indirect focal involvement | Wide range of possible deficits |
| Superficial and/or deep penetration | Admixture of cortical/subcortical deficits |
| Prefrontal | Abstract reasoning, fluency, personality |
| Frontothalamic | Planning, motivation |
| Anterior temporal | Perception, learning and memory |
| Mesial temporal/diencephalic | Learning, memory, personality |
| Temporoparietal | Complex perception/comprehension |
| Deeper parietal | Cognitive and perceptual integration |
| Occipital | Primary and secondary visual processes |

### *Cerebrovascular infarction*

Thrombotic cerebrovascular episodes are widely known to produce the most circumscribed and sharply localized lesions. Unless there is a history of multiple strokes, the infarction typically has occurred in one cerebral hemisphere. Strokes occur with greatest frequency in the distribution of the middle cerebral artery. For this reason, the lesions are located largely in the lateral convexity of the cerebral hemisphere. Much of the literature in behavioral neurology is based on an analysis of the syndromes that result from such specific and circumscribed lesions (Geschwind, 1965). Cerebrovascular infarctions occur less frequently in the distribution of the anterior or posterior arteries which supply blood to the medial portions of the cerebral hemispheres. Such lesions may lead to predictable consequences behaviorally and pose different rehabilitation challenges. CT scans have been shown to be sensitive to defining the area of involvement following a period of 14–21 days, with utilization of special contrast enhancement procedures (New et al, 1975; Paxton & Ambrose, 1974). Effective prediction of recovery of functions can be made based on CT scan data with reference to the extent and location of cerebral involvement (Rao et al, 1984).

There is a wide variation in the behavioral status of the cerebrovascular patient during the acute and subacute stages before well-defined CT scan findings may appear. Sensorimotor functions show the earliest recovery changes and plateau earliest in the recovery process (Twitchell, 1951). The clinical literature indicates that the highest symbolic and processing functions of the affected hemisphere may show recovery changes as late as 3 years post-episode (Geschwind, 1974). The variability of both behavioral and CT scan findings early in recovery reflects the importance of the time since symptom onset as a covariate. The severe sensorimotor deficits, seen in anterior lesions, may confound the assessment of higher cognitive functions related to stimulus processing, organization, attention, and abstraction. However, immediate outcome and recovery changes may be predictable, at least in part, from neuropsychological test patterns (Meier et al, 1982). These patterns will be discussed in a section on longitudinal studies. Focal cerebrovascular accidents are not limited to the cerebral cortex. For example, subcortical lesions may produce similar but more transient disturbances in the function known to be affected by lesions in the cerebral cortex. Since the cerebrovascular accident patient is typically older than the individual suffering a closed head injury, the importance of age as a covariate in contributing to immediate outcome and potential for recovery must be considered. This introduces the importance of age and time-related factors for estimating the likelihood of a more or less favorable recovery course.

## Age and time-related variables

The significance of age as a key factor in the recovery of survivors of closed head injury became evident in the earliest studies of the natural course of closed head injury. A classic example of age as a primary determinant of the recovery course is seen in the report from Carlsson et al (1968). They followed 496 cases for 10 years. Of these, 34.5% died without regaining consciousness, 1% remained comatose in an apallic and akinetic state, while 64.5% regained consciousness and evidenced some degree of recovery. Recovery was defined clinically as a return to approximate autonomous functioning in the community. Of the 64.5%, 11.5% demonstrated a persisting dementia while the remaining 53% showed varying degrees of recovery, many to an autonomous level of functioning. Autonomous functioning was observed in virtually all individuals below 20 years of age, irrespective of duration of coma. However, subsequent studies have indicated that even at this age, a duration of coma beyond 3 weeks is associated with relatively permanent residual neuropsychological deficits (Levin et al, 1982). Recovery to an autonomous level was noted in virtually all individuals between 21 and 50 years of age but only if the duration of coma was less than 24 hours. There was a sharp reduction to approximately 50% with a duration of coma between 24 hours and 7 days in this age group. Beyond age 50, coma durations beyond a 4–6 day limit were associated with significant compromise of functioning on a permanent basis. There were clinical indications that recovery reached an asymptote later and was more complete in younger individuals. A marked increase in mortality beyond age 40 was noted among older victims when brain damage alone rather than secondary medical complications accounted for the death. The lowest mortality rate was noted in the 1–10-year old age group and clinical recovery was considered quite remarkable as well in many adolescents. These statements from natural history studies, of course, must be qualified to take into consideration the severity of the injury which at extreme levels will produce persisting residuals in virtually all individuals, regardless of age. The introduction of more effective life-saving intensive care programs has increased the survival rate even in very severe injuries so that the incidence of residually impaired function and failure to return to fully autonomous levels of functioning in the community has probably increased. In any case, increased severity, especially in older individuals, appears to be associated with prolonged duration of coma, and increased density and extent of retrograde amnesia (the period during which recall for events preceding the accident is affected). Persisting memory deficits and other indications of anterograde amnesia, attentional dysfunction and confabulatory behavior, and secondary focal deficits across a wide range of cognitive, psychomotor, and personality changes are more likely in older individuals with severe head injuries (Levin et al, 1982).

Some studies, however, provide contradictory findings and suggest that the predictive utility of clinical severity indicators may be limited (Levin et al, 1982). This presents a challenge for neuropsychology and rehabilitation to explore the prognostic significance of behavioral indicators which hold promise as shown in some of the studies summarized in Tables 5.3 and 5.4 Age as a determinant of outcome also appears to interact with etiology. Clinical experience suggests that younger stroke patients (below age 60) have a more favorable recovery course and a much higher likelihood of returning to at least a semi-autonomous level of functioning. Since head injuries occur with greater frequency in younger individuals, the age level for predicting a poor outcome may be much lower. Thus, where there is overlap in age between subgroups of stroke and head injury patients, the outlook would appear to be much worse for a head-injured individual, for example, in the 50–60 age group, other determinants being equal in influence. Similarly, a stroke in the 50–60 age group, other factors assumed equal in influence, might have a much better prognosis. This conclusion is supported by selected data in the quantitative recovery studies below.

A central methodological issue in the study of age differences in recovery relates to the difficulty in establishing functional age gradients in normal aging. As in disease states affecting the nervous system, 'normal' aging occurs differently in different individuals. Facilitative factors may protect against age-related declines in visuospatial, visuoconstructional, and memory functioning with age (Benton, 1981). Individuals with higher initial ability levels tend to survive longer and to achieve higher performance levels as they age (Schaie, 1970; Botwinick, 1977). Similarly, people of higher educational levels may survive longer to achieve the same result.

Neuropsychological tests are characteristically normed on a cross-sectional basis which introduces a higher likelihood of overestimating the degree of deficit that would occur normally with age. Such norms confound age and cohort-related effects and yield an estimate of earlier and steeper decline of function in people in their 60s and 70s (Schaie & Schaie, 1977). In normal aging studies, such declines are seen especially on speeded psychomotor and nonverbal functions which are known to be affected by cerebral involvement in both head injury and stroke. The life-span developmental psychology literature identifies the problems of measurement involved in establishing norms for tests in clinical use, including many standardized neuropsychological tests. Ideally, age norms should be established for new tests being developed.

Valid age norms require that age (ontogenetic), cohort-related (generational), and historical (time of measurement) factors be separated or

Table 5.3 Recent longitudinal studies of neuropsychological recovery in head injury

| Author (year), Location | *N* and description, head injury subjects | Age at injury (years) | Post-injury test intervals | Cognitive measures used |
|---|---|---|---|---|
| Brooks & Aughton (1979), Scotland | *N* = 24<br>'severe' | 15–55 | 1 and 3 months<br>6 months<br>12 months | Ravens Progressive Matrices<br>Mill Hill Vocabulary Scale<br>Logical Memory Subtests (WMS)[1]<br>Inglis, P-A Learning Test<br>Rey Figure<br>Block Design (WAIS)[2] |
| Lezak (1979), Oregon | *N* = 24<br>CHI[3] | 19–41<br>(*x* = 26) | 4–6 weeks (75%)<br>within 1 year<br>during 2nd year<br>during 3rd year | Digits F & B (WAIS)[2]<br>RAVLT[4]<br>Word Fluency<br>Token Test |
| Dikmen, Reitan & Temkin (1983), Washington | *N* = 27<br>mild to severe | 15–44<br>(*x* =24) | when testable (median 16 days)<br>12 months<br>18 months | H-R[5]<br>(FT, Grip Strength, TPT, Rhythm, Speech, Trial-Making, A, B Category Test) |
| McLean, Temkin, Dikmen & Wyler (1983), Washington | *N* = 20<br>mild to moderate/ severe | 15–60<br>(*x* = 23) | 3 days<br>1 month | Selective Reminding Test<br>GOAT[6]<br>Stroop Color Test<br>'self-perception' measures |
| Meier (1983), Minnesota | *N* = 16<br>moderate severe CHI | 17–61<br>(*x* = 34) | 1 month<br>6 months<br>1 year | Porteus Maze Test<br>Grooved Pegboard<br>Blindfolded Formboard (TPT)<br>WAIS<br>Meier Visual Discrimination<br>Prose Passages (short- and long-term)<br>Oral & Figural Fluency<br>Rey Figure & RAVLT |

**Table 5.3**—Contd.

| Author (year), Location | $N$ and description, head injury subjects | Age at injury (years) | Post-injury test intervals | Cognitive measures used |
|---|---|---|---|---|
| Drudge, Williams & Kessler (1984), Vermont | $N = 15$<br>severe<br>CHI[3] | 18–35<br>($x = 25$) | when testable<br>(× 2.6 months)<br>1 year | H-R[6]<br>WAIS[2] |
| O'Shaughnessy, Fowler & Reid (1984), Washington | $NB = 39$<br>minimal<br>to mild<br>CHI[3] | 16–58<br>($x = 28$) | within 1 week<br>6 months | WAIS[2]<br>Erickson Memory Scales<br>PASAT[7]<br>Trail Making Test (A, B) |
| Tabaddor, Mattis & Zuzula (1984), New York | $N = 68$<br>severe to<br>moderate | 15–55<br>($x = 30$) | when DRS[8]<br>reach 100 or at<br>3 months<br>6 months<br>1 year | WAIS<br>Multilingual Aphasia Exam<br>Purdue Pegboard<br>Mattis-Kovner Verbal Retention<br>Benton Visual Retention |

[1] WMS = Wechsler Memory Scale
[2] WAIS = Wechsler Adult Intelligence Scale
[3] CHI = Closed Head Injury
[4] RAVLT = Rey Auditory Verbal Learning Test
[5] H-R = Halstead Reitan Neuropsychological Test Battery
[6] GOAT = Galveston Orientation & Amnesia Test
[7] PASAT = Paced Auditory Serial Addition Test
[8] DRS = Dementia Rating Scale

**Table 5.4** Recent longitudinal studies of neuropsychologiucal recovery in stroke

| Author (year), location | *N* of subjects and stroke criteria | Age at CVA (years) | Post-CVA test intervals | Cognitive measures used |
|---|---|---|---|---|
| Kinsella & Ford (1980), Australia | $N = 31$<br>R and L hemisphere | 33–74<br>($x = 62$) | 4 weeks<br>8 weeks<br>12 weeks | Specific tests not indicated ('measures of USN[1]; constructional apraxia; motor, planning and reasoning skills; memory and learning') |
| Meier, Ettinger & Arthur (1982), Minnesota | $N = 28$<br>hemiplegia<br>$N = 31$<br>+ hemiplegia<br>R and L | 41–86<br>($x = 64$)<br>37–77<br>($x = 59$) | within 1 week<br>2 months<br>6 months | WAIS[2]<br>Porteus Maze Test<br>Token Test & AST[3]<br>Grooved Pegboard<br>Blindfolded Formboard<br>Finger Tapping and Ballistic Tapping |
| Hier, Mondlock & Caplan (1983), Chicago | $N = 41$<br>R hemisphere | $x = 59$ | within 1 week<br>subsequently at 2–4 weeks intervals<br>× to 13.5 weeks | USN[1]<br>'face naming'<br>Block Design (WAIS)<br>Rey Figure |
| Kotila, Waltimo, Niemi, Laaksonen, & Lempinen (1984), Finland | $N = 154$<br>hemorrhagic and infarct<br>R and L | 17–90<br>($x = 61$) | 'acute stage'<br>3 months<br>12 months | WAIS[2]<br>WMS[4]<br>Benton Visual Retention Test<br>'visuo-perceptual tasks'<br>'speech and language subtests' |
| Meerwaldt (1983), Netherlands | *N* - 16<br>infarct (posterior)<br>R hemisphere | 42–70<br>($x = 58$) | 2 weeks<br>6 weeks<br>3 months<br>6 months<br>1 year | Rod Orientation Test<br>Line Orientation Test |

[1] USN = Unilateral Spatial Neglect
[2] WAIS = Wechsler Adult Intelligence Scale
[3] AST = Aphasia Screening Test
[4] WMS = Wechsler Memory Scale

unconfounded in order to provide an accurate expected performance for a given age. Age-related determinants of change and recovery will be necessary to identify, describe, and quantify neuropsychological deficits and to design appropriate intervention strategies to reverse, slow, or facilitate the development of compensatory strategies for coping with neuropsychological deficits.

*Early developmental effects*

There is a growing literature on age and recovery from brain damage in younger age groups. An excellent review has recently become available (Levin et al, 1984). This literature proceeds from earlier misconceptions about the ultimate level of recovery in children who suffered an acquired aphasia due to a left hemisphere injury. Acquired dysphasia in children follows a different recovery course as compared to aphasia in adults. This recovery course has been noted to be rapid with relatively more persistent disturbances in writing and impaired comprehension of written material. The most complete recoveries have been observed in children who sustained left hemisphere lesions during infancy. Recovery does not appear to reflect a linear relationship between age at injury and later language status (van Dongen & Loolen, 1977; Woods & Teuber, 1978) despite the better subsequent development of linguistic functions in children with early lesions. Some cognitive deficits can be demonstrated irrespective of the age at injury (Alajouanine & Lhermitte, 1965; Hécaen, 1976; Woods & Teuber, 1978). Even with the more favorable developmental consequences of early lesions noted in the literature, residual impairments can be demonstrated as task complexity is increased and the information processing demands of the task become greater (Dennis & Whitaker, 1976). Memory deficits seem particularly prominent despite the relatively higher levels of linguistic competence achieved, for example, after a left hemispherectomy, if the lesion occurred during the first year of life. There have been some dramatic examples of recovery of language function after left hemispherectomy in adults, at least to the level of speech expressed in short propositional sentences (Smith, 1977). Previously acquired functions of the impaired hemisphere remain relatively unaffected. Many of the lesions that prompted a decision to perform a hemispherectomy occur early in infancy so that the developing intact portions of the brain may participate in functions that would normally be subserved by the intact hemisphere. The key factor in determining outcome in early lesions appears to be the degree of maturation of the involved tissue since those functions which develop more slowly and reach an asymptote later are least affected by early injury, while highly specialized early functions such as psychomotor abilities seem to be relatively independent of the age at which the lesion occurs. It remains difficult to derive firm generalizations and general principles of the effect of age on recovery since outcome studies have not been consistent and may lead to an underestimation of the quality of cognitive recovery, particularly under more demanding environmental conditions (Levin et al, 1984).

The maxim that early involvement does not necessarily lead to major long-term effects on maturation and development is highly questionable given the recent evidence of readily demonstrated deficits after severe head injury in children for functions such as object-naming latency (Chadwick et al, 1981), confrontation naming, spelling, sentence completion, usage of verbs, and complex verbal comprehension and syntax (Woods & Carey, 1979). After the first year of life, the effects of age on recovery from aphasia appear to be less important than the etiology and severity of the brain damage and the type of aphasia (van Dongen & Loolen, 1977) since more complete recoveries were more common after head injury than with cerebrovascular disease in children. Also, despite the generally more favorable outlook for very early lesions in children, persisting memory deficits may be quite severe and there appears to be a higher likelihood of behavioral disturbances such as hyperactivity, short attention span, impulsiveness, and aggressive behavior (Hjern & Nylander, 1964; Brink et al, 1970). This may parallel the observation reported in adults of persisting memory and attentional deficits even when there has been a relatively strong recovery of information processing and practical reasoning abilities. This may indicate that although the functions of the lateral convexities of the cerebral hemispheres may undergo a relatively favorable recovery course, functions mediated by the deeper portions of the brain, including the orbitofrontal and limbic systems and the brainstem, may account for the ultimate compromise of quality of competence and adjustment observed in many individuals following more severe closed head injuries. Obviously, the interaction between age and developmental factors is extremely complex as revealed in the rapidly expanding experimental animal literature in which time-related factors can be more completely controlled for determining the developmental effects of early lesions (Goldman, 1974; Finger, 1978; Stein et al, 1983). Examination of this literature is beyond the scope of this chapter but is essential reading for any professional working with brain damaged children.

### *Time since symptom onset*

Cerebral vascular accidents and closed head injuries are characterized by an abrupt onset of the insult followed by a prolonged course of recovery. Individual differences in the rate of general clinical recovery are reflected as well in differential rates of recovery for particular neuropsychological functions. A general but somewhat oversimplified rule is that the higher the level of function, the more prolonged the recovery course, the later recovery will reach an asymptote, and the later recovery changes will appear. Spontaneous return of focal neurological and neuropsychological function following onset of a hemiplegia due to stroke, for example, occurs largely within the first 2 months following symptom onset but is characterized by highly variable individual recovery rates. The typical recovery pattern includes variable initial return of motion on the affected side between 6 and 33 days, earlier and more complete recovery of proximal neuromuscular function and lagging recovery in the upper distal extremities, manifest especially in the fine manipulative movements of the hand. The general recovery course for psychomotor functions closely parallels the emergence of neurological changes which, in instances of more complete restitution of function, include the facilitation of voluntary movement by means of proprioceptive and tactile stimulation and elicitation of the proximal traction response (Twitchell, 1951). A challenge for neuropsychology and rehabilitation is the development of early predictors of individual neuropsychological outcomes across functions. Derivation of specific actuarial predictors, using behavioral measurements obtained early in the subacute phase before the critical recovery changes have occurred, would be of both theoretical and practical significance. An example of such a search for predictors of early psychomotor recovery in acute stroke patients suggests that assessment of residual adaptive capacities by means of neuropsychological tests may provide an empirical basis for predicting subsequent degree of motor recovery (Meier et al, 1982).

Early motor recovery, frequently quite dramatic, underscores the need to control for such time-related variables when estimating moderating effects of other covariates to facilitate or predict recovery in individual patients. Neuropsychological test predictors might reveal the relative availability of a neural reserve for the restitution and reorganization of cerebral function and identify patients with high recovery potential. Whatever intrinsic CNS mechanisms may be operating in determining the course of recovery in a given individual, a sufficiently wide sampling of higher cortical functions should favor identification of some that are significantly and perhaps even highly correlated with outcome. The quantitative measurements derived from neuropsychological tests might then yield estimates of the longitudinal course of change in a given function as well as predictions related to the outcome of such functions. Meier (1981) reported moderately to highly accurate predictions of recovery of contralateral motor functions over 2 and 6 months, respectively, on the basis of Porteus Maze and ipsilateral ballistic arm tapping performances in acute stroke patients. Furthermore, these predictors were correlated with recovery of information processing abilities, as measured by standardized intellectual tests such as the WAIS, and auditory verbal comprehension as measured by the Token Test with baseline measurements obtained within one week of symptom onset (Meier et al, 1982).

## Sex

Gender differences in lateral specialization of function in the cerebral hemispheres have been studied extensively in the recent neuropsychological literature (McGlone, 1980; Inglis & Lawson, 1981). Sex differences are reflected in relatively greater superiority of verbal processing abilities in women. Visuospatial integration and abstract nonverbal processes have been favored in males. However, there is considerable overlap in the distributions of these functions in large sample research. Nevertheless, such differences have been demonstrated even in children, and may be related to lateral asymmetries in hemispheric structures (Witelson & Pallie, 1973; Wada, 1976). The influence of gender on recovery is not well understood if the factor plays a role at all. Furthermore, gender may interact with a variety of environmental factors, incremental and decremental, to influence the recovery course. Such interactions may be expressed as differences in aptitude, motivation and strategy (McGlone, 1980). Longitudinal studies of recovery have not revealed striking sex differences, though these warrant continued investigation. The methodological difficulties associated with the definition of higher cortical functions become even more germane in determining sex-related differences (Caplan et al, 1985).

## Demographic variables

Neuropsychological outcomes, irrespective of direct effects of lesions, are related to demographic variables such as education, socioeconomic level, vocational choice, and ethnicity. Methodological consideration for these and other determinants in clinical research and application are discussed elsewhere (Parsons & Prigatano, 1978; Meier & Thompson, 1983). These factors rarely function independently and may interact with the entire range of other determining conditions in assessing and monitoring recovery. Highly overlearned and practised functions may be represented more redundantly and, accordingly, may be subject to less initial impairment and more rapid recovery. Earlier longitudinal studies were not highly revealing of a major effect of demographic variables since there was no relationship found between educational level or occupational status and recovery, for example (Smith, 1981). These variables, however, may help explain unexpected outcomes, both in terms of the initial effects of the lesion and recovery. They may interact especially with age since higher educational and socioeconomic levels have been associated with better maintenance of higher cortical functions in older individuals (Benton, 1981). Thus, these variables may indirectly represent incremental or detrimental environmental effects on neuropsychological functioning. They might usefully be incorporated into clinical formulations by means of the conceptual distinction between crystallized and fluid abilities (Cattell, 1963; Meier & Thompson, 1983). While such variables probably operate with limited influence, their consideration is obviously necessary for understanding atypical or unexpected characteristics of the neuropsychological data, and are particularly relevant for rehabilitation planning and decision making.

## Cerebral dominance

The many covariates, in addition to lesion location and size, that influence outcomes, may contribute to individual differences in the organization of function. Perhaps the most important source of individual differences in the organization of function is cerebral dominance. This is characteristically assessed by self-report, which remains perhaps the best single indicator of lateral dominance (Geschwind, 1974). It is well accepted that most right-handers are left-cerebral dominant for language and right-cerebral dominant for visuospatial and visuoconstructional functioning. Despite the highly lateralized nature of cerebral dominance in right-handers, there are exceptions among right-handers who occasionally are right-hemisphere organized for speech. It is widely acknowledged that left-handers tend to be ambilateral, suggesting that higher cortical functions may be bilaterally represented though perhaps not symmetrically in this group. This may well account for the many reports of more rapid and extensive recovery of language functioning in left-handed aphasics despite the greater incidence of language deficits with lesions in either hemisphere in this group (Sarno & Levita, 1971). Conflicting findings are not unexpected since the effect of any single determining factor among these covariates could easily be overridden by the presence of an alternative factor at a higher level of determination or expression. Nevertheless, due regard for this factor may help explain individual differences in recovery and assist in the design of interventions to enhance any more favorable recovery potential that may be present on this basis.

## Possible CNS mechanisms of recovery

The past two decades have seen an impressive conceptual and experimental analysis of recovery changes in animals. The appearance of the volume on plasticity and recovery of function in the CNS, edited by Stein, Rosen and Butters (1974) marked the integration of the recovery literature to that date. The animal far outweighs the human literature in volume and sophistication, and warrants careful examination by clinical neuropsychologists and rehabilitation personnel. This exciting literature is readily accessible (Luria, 1963; Rosner, 1970; Teuber, 1975; Finger, 1978; Goldman, 1978; Finger & Stein, 1982; Stein et al, 1983). Central to these deliberations has been the concept of 'plasticity' which has acquired various meanings and interpretations. As Stein et al (1983) point out, this concept remains elusive to systematic analysis and investigation due to the difficulties encountered in defining the concept operationally at each level of analysis: anatomical, physiological, and behavioral. Limited to the description of response to injury, the concept seems to be well accepted (Geschwind, 1974). However, the concept may be overly reified when used to explain recovery phenomena and then becomes meaningless. Nevertheless, search for the meaning of the concept has led to much productive work and to the identification of numerous possible mechanisms that intrinsically relate to the recovery process.

### *Diaschisis*

One such mechanism, diaschisis, has received considerable attention in the literature and provides a point of departure for a summary of such recovery mechanisms. Others include the masking effects of cerebral edema during the acute phase of recovery, the resumption of flow following interruptions of cerebral blood flow in local injury or disease, regeneration of neural elements, denervation supersensitivity, substitution of a structural nature, and substitution at the response or performance level. One or more of these mechanisms may be operating in a constantly changing temporal pattern and in interaction with one or more of the above covariates, either singly or in combination. Therefore it seems extremely unlikely that any single factor, extrinsic or intrinsic, will account for all recovery changes seen in a particular patient. Assessment and intervention challenges for both the neuropsychologist and the rehabilitation team can then be seen as enormous. It is these challenges that appear to have heightened interest in seeking a more effective relationship between these disciplines.

Introduced by von Monakow (1914/1969), this mechanism relates to effects of a lesion or disease process on remote as well as on immediate structures. This is most conspicuous in the immediate effects of a cerebrovascular accident, for example, in which there may be considerable swelling of brain (edema) as well as alterations in blood flow through patent vessels. Such acute effects may mask or distort functions in essentially intact regions of the brain. Dissipation of such effects may account for a substantial proportion of early recovery and for some of the dramatic recovery changes seen in selected patients with severe or profound initial neurological and neuropsychological deficit. Indirect evidence for such a mechanism can be derived from observations on serially lesioned animals, for example, who evidence much milder impairments of briefer duration than do animals with comparable lesions introduced in one stage (Adametz, 1959). Even with more prolonged interoperative or postoperative intervals, recovery effects may be quite remarkable even after left hemispherectomy in man, for example, where recovery of language function seems almost paradoxical (Smith, 1977). The validity of this concept remains questionable though most theoreticians in neuropsychology acknowledge that the underlying pathophysiological components are likely to be identified in the future (Teuber, 1975). To distinguish this from other mechanisms, it is important to stress that this concept refers to the progressive re-establishment of neural systems that are incidentally disrupted by the lesion. Thus, if valid, the concept may encompass redundancy of function in the CNS, but would not account for any reorganization of neural systems into new configurations based on other mechanisms, such as modified neural growth and regeneration.

### *Regeneration of neural elements*

There is increasing evidence of at least a potential for selective regeneration of neural elements in recovery (Finger & Stein, 1982). Regeneration is defined as any change in the morphological organization of the nervous system that may occur in response to injury (Moore, 1974). Any growth of neuronal processes would then lead to the formation of new and presumably functional synpatic contact between surviving neurons. Whether such contact would facilitate, inhibit, or disrupt function remains an empirical question. Regenerative sprouting from transected axons and collateral sprouting from intact axons have been identified for some time (Stein et al, 1983). Axons of the central adrenergic neurons have been shown to be most capable of regenerative sprouting and growth following transection. However, it remains of doubtful functional significance in humans and does not appear to account for recovery. Lateral sprouting has been demonstrated to occur from intact neurons and results in some reorganization of the synaptic structure in a denervated area. The collateral sprouting seen in transected axons appears to maintain a relatively constant contact field so that any newly formed terminals, if they are to become functional, do so at the expense of other synaptic connections. Of perhaps even greater significance are recent developments in the basic neuroscience literature that demonstrate the potential for further neural growth in response to presence of transplanted brain tissue (see Ch. 12 for further implications). To the extent that such neural growth can lead to the establishment of new functional systems and can be facilitated by other favorable determining factors, some true reorganization of function may be possible.

### *Denervation supersensitivity*

Some basis for redundancy of function in the CNS might be found in the phenomenon of denervation supersensitivity. Cannon and Rosenblueth (1949) refer to the increased sensitivity to neurotransmitter agonists and antagonists in denervated neurons. This appears to be due to an increase in the number of receptor sites and has been demonstrated in skeletal muscles, peripheral neurons of the autonomic ganglia, and spinal neurons. Recovery of function may be attributable in part to increased sensitivity to the remaining influence of areas of the brain that are partially denervated by the lesion. This might lead to the participation of a partially denervated region subserved by the affected region. The role of this mechanism in the CNS recovery remains questionable, and might be in turn facilitated or inhibited by collateral sprouting from both intact and denervated axons. If potentially capable of enhancing recovery, the phenomenon would add to the potential for reorganization of function.

### *Structural substitution or vicariation*

As applied to CNS structure, this mechanism has been invoked to account for locomotor recovery following unilateral lesion of the motor cortex (Kennard, 1938). This mechanism involves the postulation that an intact structure can assume the functions of an affected structure. Redundancy of discrete or primary sensory and motor functions is seen more frequently in animals than in humans, where recovery of such functions may sometimes be nil. Small lesions that affect the internal capsule may produce relatively permanent and profound hemiplegia though exceptions have been noted (Geschwind, 1974). There are known individual differences in the relative concentration of the pyramidal tract on either side so that some individuals may have substantial ipsilateral control of motor and somatosensory functions. Even an extensive lesion in one hemisphere would then not produce permanent contralateral effects in such individuals (Yakovlev, 1971). Redundancy of function may be more feasible when the function is independent of integrity of primary cortical or peripheral structures. Thus, greater overlap of zones that subserve language, visuospatial, and abstract reasoning functions may account for the fact that some degree of recovery of such functions is seen in virtually all patients following cerebrovascular accidents or closed head injuries. This may be due in part to less discrete involvement of the brain in closed head injury where both focal and nonfocal as well as multilevel effects may be present. Information processing functions may recover to near-normal levels while residual impairments of memory and attention may persist. Structural substitution remains a somewhat nebulous concept and, like 'plasticity' is subject to reification. That is to say, it may have no conceptual meaning beyond the descriptive behavior features of recovery. Redundant representation may exist within a structural system so that it may not be necessary to postulate substitution of systems to account for that portion of recovery that reflects redundancy (Rosner, 1970).

### *Behavioral substitution*

Both the animal and human clinical literature are replete with examples of response or behavioral substitution in which there is a marked increase in efficiency in achieving an end despite the persistence of a psychological deficit. This gives the misleading impression of intrinsic recovery of a function when it is not the function, but rather the strategy used for applying intact functions toward achieving a goal, that is at issue. Thus, a problem that cannot be solved directly since the behavior response may no longer be available can be solved by introducing new strategies or ways for reaching the goal (Stein et al, 1983). Valentino and Stein (1983) examined the relationship between age and staging of lesions of the frontal cortex to produce differences in the ability to select and pursue effective strategies in goal-directed behavior. Young rats with single-stage lesions were more variable than controls but ultimately found and utilized an effective strategy. Young rats with two-staged lesions were virtually indistinguishable from normals in the way in which they adapted and utilized an effective strategy. A contrasting older group of rats, even with two-staged lesions, remain confused and unable to identify the effective strategy for solving the maze. For that matter, age was overwhelmingly the strongest determinant since nonoperated controls were also impaired in this respect.

Most therapists become keenly aware of the need to foster response substitution as a means of improving overall function. Neuropsychological test procedures have not been investigated extensively from this perspective. It is generally accepted that failure to identify a deficit by means of a neuropsychological test of known validity indicates that the individual is unimpaired for that function. On the other hand, rehabilitation personnel who have daily contact with that patient may report that there is a deficiency in the effective execution of that function in particular ecological circumstances. An extremely important area for future investigation is the assessment of preferred strategies and their effectiveness in arriving at particular solutions. As Finger (1978) has pointed out, strategy failures may be simply due to a shift in response preference so that adaptive failures may not be due to a loss of function but rather to the application of a faulty strategy. Alterations of testing and intervention procedures may lead to more enlightened performance of the rehabilitation team in assisting an individual to shift strategies and utilize intact behaviors in problem solving.

In addition to expanding our knowledge of the effects of strategy selection in rehabilitation and recovery, eliciting responses by means of alternate but relevant cues should also favor functional recovery in the ecological context. The neuropsychological literature is lacking in validation studies that emphasize ecological criteria (but see McSweeney et al, 1985). This seems especially important for work with older individuals who may exhibit reduced ability to utilize new strategies or respond to novel stimuli, even in the absence of demonstrable neurological disease.

## QUANTITATIVE LONGITUDINAL MONITORING OF NEUROPSYCHOLOGICAL RECOVERY

Theories of recovery of function in the context of neuropsychological rehabilitation have been elaborated in selected chapters of this volume (e.g. Ch. 11). In addition there is an extensive conceptual base and numerous points of entry into this growing literature (Bond & Brooks, 1976; Long et al, 1984; Bach-y-Rita, 1981; Newcombe, 1982; Rothi & Horner, 1983). Human studies of the longitudinal recovery of function are either cross-sectional or longitudinal in design. Cross-sectional studies examine a given neuropsychological function at a single point in time following a given time interval since symptom onset. Longitudinal studies examine a function or set of functions over time and from a baseline set of measurements obtained at a particular point in time following symptom onset and again at intervals extending over months and years. Cross-sectional studies do not yield a direct analysis of the inferred recovery process and relate more to an understanding of the effects of a given etiology when behavioral outcomes are contrasted with those of an appropriate control group. Longitudinal studies permit inferences about the recovery process but confound time (or developmental) effects with practice due to repeated measurements. Both types of studies yield useful information for predicting the natural course of recovery and for designing intervention strategies that may be adjusted for recovery changes as they evolve in the treatment process. Benton (1979b) provides a summary of cross-sectional studies of the cognitive consequences of closed head injury. Similarly, Levin et al (1982) review both the cross-sectional and longitudinal studies of memory, intellectual, language, perceptual, psychomotor, and psychosocial consequences of head injury. Excellent reviews exist both for basic and applied research on attentional deficits (Gummow et al, 1983) and for the entire range of neuropsychological functions after closed head injury (Newcombe, 1982). The corresponding literature on cerebral vascular disease is not as extensive, possibly due to the less central place of behavioral research has in funded programs. Nevertheless, some primary sources are available (Benton, 1968). Selected chapters in this volume address aspects of this recovery literature as appropriate to their central themes.

The purpose of the concluding section of this chapter is to summarize quantitative longitudinal neuropsychological studies of head injury and stroke since 1980. These studies bear directly on the role of the neuropsychologist in predicting and monitoring recovery changes in the rehabilitation setting. Summaries of these studies, following the format utilized by Levin et al (1982) are found in Table 5.3. Summaries for longitudinal neuropsychological changes following cerebral vascular accident are found in Table 5.4.

## Longitudinal studies of cognitive recovery after head injury in adults

Most quantitative studies of recovery of function are based on group data that mark individual differences, particularly if the patient pool is heterogeneous with respect to the covariates underlying these differences as is typically the case in head-injured populations, for example (Bond & Brooks, 1976). Newcombe et al (1979) examined recovery curves for specific linguistic functions in individual patients and found that there was considerable variability despite overall similarities in the recovery curves. Hiorns and Newcombe (1979) derived a recovery curve that could be described in simple mathematical terms but found that the formula oversimplified the entire recovery process, making the curves potentially misleading when applied to describing specific outcomes for a particular patient. Studies of the natural history of cognitive recovery overwhelmingly show that the mean recovery function reaches an asymptote after an accelerated rate of recovery in the early stages after the injury. The rate of gain slows at 6 months to 1 year. Again, however, there are wide individual differences in the length of time following injury during which recovery changes may occur.

These rather consistent and replicable group curves, however, need to be qualified by the very late recovery changes seen in some individuals, especially for the highest cognitive functions such as language (Geschwind, 1974). Brooks et al (1984) identified some general methodological principles for interpreting sequential studies of neuropsychological recovery. They provide guidelines for the derivation of follow-up schedules, the selection and definition of the functions being measured, the selection of patient and control groups, the control of practice effects and the optimal length of a follow-up study. Their comments apply equally to the design of sequential studies of any etiological group. Methodological issues in single case and intervention research are addressed in Chapter 6 of this volume.

Two of the studies listed in Table 5.3 (Brooks & Aughton, 1979; Lezak, 1979) are included since they did not appear in earlier reviews. Brooks and Aughton (1979) note that their sample of severe head injuries did not comprise a random sample of the general head injury population and required neurosurgical review and, in some instances, intervention. They also question the use of multiple '*t*' tests because of the characteristically large number of functions by tests utilized in this type of research, and emphasized the use of alternative forms of tests (if available). Counterbalancing of test order was introduced to control test-specific changes over time since constant order confounds test differences in difficulty with time. Their battery consisted of widely applied procedures for assessing intellectual, immediate and delayed memory, auditory verbal comprehension, and verbal fluency functions. Persistent deficits in verbal and nonverbal learning were observed in a severe head injury as contrasted with a matched control group, at least on group measures. A relatively wide range of individual differences in the extent and pattern of recovery over 1 year characterized outcome course. Similar results were reported by Lezak (1979) in a follow-up study with the Rey Auditory Verbal Learning Test (RAVLT), a measure of episodic verbal learning and memory. Her data suggest that immediate memory span, as measured by a digits forward procedure, evidenced more consistent and sustained improvement over a 3-year interval than digits backward or auditory verbal learning and memory as measured by the RAVLT. Implied was an interaction between recovery, task difficulty, and severity of the injury in predicting outcome. Age differences were not prominent but the sample only covered a small age range. There were some consistent trends implicating the hemisphere of primary dysfunction that could not be completely explained with the limited neuropathological or pathophysiological data available.

More recent studies involved the Halstead–Reitan Neuropsychological Test Battery (Dikmen et al, 1983) and the Buschke Selective Reminding Test (Buschke & Fuld, 1974) among other instruments (Buschke & Fuld, 1974). This study involved a wide age range and large sample. Recovery changes reported were quite pervasive, occurring on both complex and simple neuropsychological functions and extending beyond 1 year. A major methodological contribution of this study relates to a statistical adjustment for the severity of initial impairment by means of a distinction between constant and deficit-proportional recovery changes. The standard analysis of variance procedure assumes a simple additive relationship between baseline and follow-up scores which fails to adjust for severity of injury or preinjury cognitive status. Recovery is then examined within and between subgroups of differing initial deficit levels. These analyses yield a different recovery function in so far as significant recovery changes appear well beyond the first 6 months, the asymptote shown in earlier studies. Such observations are consistent with the occasional case encountered clinically where extremely late recovery effects are sometimes observed (Mandelberg & Brooks, 1975). Contrasting the results utilizing traditional analysis of variance and a procedure adjusted for initial degree of deficit yielded a more favorable long-term projection across almost the entire range of functions assessed by this battery. The ultimate levels of recovery stretched over a more extended recovery interval, however, may fall far short of normal levels and give the misleading impression that these later changes make a large difference in the most severely impaired patients. Severity probably is the major limiting condition for predicting the ultimate level of recovery.

Thus McLean et al (1983), utilizing a milder head injury group but over a relatively brief (1 month) period showed that the effects of 'minor' head injury remain questionable, though even minor injuries may demonstrate a persisting inability to process information rapidly (Wrightson & Gronwall, 1980) and impairment of learning and memory, attention, and psychomotor functioning (Gronwall & Wrightson, 1974; Rimel et al, 1981). Patients with either a loss of consciousness of 10 minutes or more, or presence of post-traumatic amnesia for at least 1 hour post-injury show a virtually complete recovery (as contrasted with a corresponding control) after 1 month in the McLean et al (1983) follow-up study utilizing a multiple-trial, free-recall memory/learning procedure (Buschke & Fuld, 1974), the Stroop Color Test (a measure of distractibility), and the Galveston Orientation and Amnesia Test (GOAT), a measure of orientation. Although statistically insignificant, even after statistical adjustment for initial deficit level, differences between the head injury and the control groups consistently favored the controls, so that subtle residual impairments might have been present, at least in some cases, to account for this trend. The study highlights the need to pay careful attention to the identity of a control group. In this study, friends of the head-injured subjects, rather than hospital workers or university students, were used. The Selective Reminding Procedure was counterbalanced to minimize practice effects. Density of PTA was a correlate of early impairment for even mild head injuries at the 2-day baseline testing. Whether duration of PTA will be predictive of persisting impairments on more sensitive functions such as paced information processing remains to be seen. There are indications that the duration of PTA is likely to be correlated with permanent measurable residuals on measures of attention and recent memory functioning (Levin et al, 1982).

The most pessimistic group recovery data were reported by Tabaddor et al (1984) for a relatively severe head injury group as measured by the Glasgow Coma Scale (Teasdale & Jennett, 1974). Persisting deficits of general intellectual functioning, language processing, confrontation naming, fine motor coordination, recent verbal and nonverbal memory (both recall and recognition) were characterized. Confrontation naming, perception, language, and memory functioning were particularly impaired. These observations were derived from normative comparisons but did not include a corresponding control group. Subsequent research (Mattis, 1984) indicates that a local control group for the study setting yields a less negative outcome than when a pooled control group from different geographic and demographic settings was utilized. Deficits, when present in such comparisons, are characteristically more severe for memory and confrontation naming (Levin et al, 1979). Except for recognition memory, which usually recovers earliest and more completely, impairments may be material-specific, suggesting selectively more dysfunction of the structures that subserve memory in one hemisphere or the other. Lateralized cerebral dysfunction may also be present on measures of information processing and reasoning abilities, so that individual differences at baseline and over time may reflect subtle lateralized effects as well as deeper periventricular effects (memory) and shearing of the long tracts that relate brainstem to cortical structures (attention). Many neurological variables have been identified as predictors of outcome, including the duration of coma, depth of coma, and duration of post-traumatic amnesia (Jennett & Teasdale, 1981; Levin et al, 1982). Age has not been a consistent predictor of outcome, though the bulk of the evidence points toward an age by severity interaction that is reflected in earlier recovery, higher survival probabilities, and a more extended recovery period in younger patients (Teasdale & Jennett, 1976). Although lateralized cerebral dysfunction may be evident in individual cases, the group data tend to obscure such differences and have led to the conclusion that neuropsychological deficits, even when lateralized cerebral involvement is evident on specialized neurodiagnostic procedures, tend to be relatively generalized. Diffuse effects presumed to involve primarily the white matter and petechial hemorrhaging may be sufficient to mask focal effects in individual test patterns (Brooks et al, 1980; Levin et al, 1982).

The Drudge et al (1984) study involved procedures that do not target memory impairments as completely as selective reminding and related procedures used in other studies. They reported residual impairments after 1 year in a severe closed head injury group as compared to a control group assessed only once. The head injury sample was unique insofar as it included patients with a high severity rating Grady Coma Scale (Cooper et al, 1979) which had been shown to be indicative of severe trauma and impaired intellectual recovery (Williams et al, 1981) even in the absence of focal neurological findings. It is well known that the more severe the injury, the greater the likelihood of focal as well as generalized neurological effects (Levin et al, 1979). Despite lack of a longitudinal control group, the Drudge et al (1984) study adds to the literature on longitudinal recovery since repeated testings in chronic brain-damaged patients and test–retest practice effects are not remarkable on their battery (Matarrazo et al, 1974). This study confirmed earlier reports (Levin et al, 1982) of reduced mean performance IQ, as compared to verbal IQ after head injury, consistent with other indications in the literature of greater impairment of ('fluid') abilities required for processing new information. The HRNB, despite the absence of specific measurements of delayed verbal or nonverbal memory, has shown substantial sensitivity to differences between head-injured and control samples in cross-sectional studies, and appears to be sensitive to persisting impairments across the entire range of neuropsychological functions measured by the battery. In the Drudge et al (1984) study, patients were selected that had been repeatedly evaluated with this battery, a factor that may have selectively biased this sample in the direction of the most severely injured who would be expected to show more lasting deficits. Failure to counterbalance alternate forms of this procedure (which are not available) resulted in failure to control for practice effects. Nevertheless, the failure of a retested sample to reach the initial control group level after 1 year is noteworthy, and adds to the expectation that at least in severe injuries consistent deficits on the battery after 1 year are remarkable. Implied is the presence of extensive generalized cerebral dysfunction in severe head injury, whether or not the deficit pattern includes localized effects.

These recent longitudinal studies emphasize the importance of severity but throw little additional light on the role of age as a factor in determining outcome. Tabaddor et al (1984) found no main effect for age. In a current series of moderately to severely closed head injured patients in this laboratory, as defined by a Galveston Scale Grade III injury (Levin et al, 1982), an age by severity interaction appears to be present (Meier, 1983). Subgroups averaging approximately 45 and 25 years of age differed on the number of subgroup means that underwent either an increase, remained stable, or declined after a 6-month interval on tests designed to measure a wide range of neuropsychological functions. The younger group remained unchanged or improved while the older group declined on 11 of 23 measures. Obviously, further research will be required to establish precise boundaries within which age and severity are likely to interact in determining outcomes from specific baseline measurements on neuropsychological tests.

## Quantitative longitudinal studies of neuropsychological recovery after stroke

Much of the earlier neuropsychological research in this area was done in rehabilitation settings where the baseline testing for subsequent follow-up was done 6 or more months following symptom onset. Many of the spontaneous recovery changes, particularly in sensory and motor functions, have already occurred by that time. Some limited predictability of rehabilitation outcome, nevertheless, has been demonstrated (Anderson et al, 1970; Ben-Yishay et al, 1970) late in the recovery period. The establishment of cerebrovascular research centers in the 1960s permitted investigation of the predictability of behavioral outcomes from baselines established early in the recovery period (Meier & Resch, 1967; Benton, 1968; Meier, 1970). Kertesz (1979) reviewed much of the behavior neurological and neuropsychological literature for recovery from aphasia involving studies with substantial numbers of patients with cerebrovascular infarctions. More recent research focused upon the primary behavioral syndromes is cited where appropriate in other chapters in this volume. This section will focus on a small collection of quantitative follow-up studies involving neuropsychological test batteries since 1980. Table 5.4 summarizes the sampling and procedural characteristics of these studies.

Kinsella and Ford (1980) explored unilateral spatial neglect as a predictor of functional recovery. The procedures were not specified but were alleged to include quantitative measures of functions shown in Table 5.4 plus the Norwick Park Activities of Daily Living (ADL) Index (Sheikh et al, 1979). The finding that unilateral spatial neglect was predictive of poorer ADL outcomes may have resulted from a confounding of lesion size with this clinical sign, since it tends to appear more frequently with larger lesions, particularly in the posterior parietal region. ADL and motor recovery change exceeded those observed for the various cognitive abilities assessed in this undescribed battery. Follow-up interval, however, was limited to 12 weeks, which is not sufficient to determine the extent of cognitive recovery (Meier et al, 1982). The hypothesis that unilateral spatial neglect, independent of primary hemisphere involved, will be predictive of a less adequate outcome remains to be confirmed.

In a follow-up investigation of a nonhemorrhagic, thrombotic stroke sample, Meier et al (1982) confirmed the predictive utility of a Porteus Maze Test age of 8 for predicting psychomotor and cognitive recovery over 6 months. Earlier neurological studies suggested that sensory and motor changes tend to reach an asymptote at about 6 weeks (Twitchell, 1951; van Buskirk, 1954). Repeated measures of fine manipulative dexterity, index finger tapping speed, ballistic arm tapping rates, and tactually guided form placements tended to confirm these earlier impressions since substantial recovery changes, particularly in those patients who had evidenced a Porteus Test age of 8 or more within 1 week of the episode, occurred by the 2-month follow-up assessment on such functions. Isolated patients within the subsamples continued to show some improvement by the 6-month follow-up interval so that recovery varied sufficiently to reduce the overall predictability of change somewhat. Of additional interest is the fact that this cutting score, which had shown some validity in predicting rated neurological outcome, was able to predict beyond chance the recovery of verbal comprehension, language processing, and visuoconstructional functioning in the same patients. These recovery manifestations appeared substantially later toward the end of the 6-month period. This study demonstrates that neuropsychological test measurements can be used as dependent variables to yield a quantitative description of these changes and to predict the subsequent discrete changes.

In a study that was limited to right hemisphere strokes (Hier et al, 1983) the relatively early recovery from unilateral spatial neglect familiar to clinicians was confirmed. However, a paradoxically greater recovery rate from constructional apraxia, unilateral neglect, and motor impersistence was noted in the hemorrhagic subgroup. This subgroup, however, was also shown to have smaller lesions and consisted of younger patients, thus implicating the age and severity factors as confounds. It seems likely that hemorrhagic strokes in surviving patients are likely to be relatively more circumscribed and less debilitating over the long term unless there is some recurrence as seen in multi-infarct dementia, for example. The study underscores the need to control the many covariates that may influence the recovery course. It also confirms the importance of establishing an early baseline for monitoring recovery.

Repeated follow-up assessments were carried out (five over 1 year) in the Meerwaldt study (1983) which was limited, however, to patients with right posterior lesions. The study demonstrated that quickly administered tests of rod (DeRenzi et al, 1971) and line orientation (Benton et al, 1978) can yield a description of the recovery course that correlates with rated neurological changes. Their findings of a relationship between lesion size and recovery speed is consistent with other data. The superiority of the rod orientation test was a better predictor of recovery and apparently provided a more realistic estimate of lesion size. The study confirmed the characteristic course of recovery in the first 6 months after stroke.

The detrimental implications of age, extent of neurological involvement, and degree of impairment of cognitive and memory abilities in predicting outcome was again demonstrated in the extensive study of Kotila et al (1984). The study yielded the characteristic negatively accelerated recovery curve which reached an asymptote at approximately 6 months to 1 year. Like many other studies in this area, the sample included a combination of hemorrhagic and thrombotic strokes. Since these covary with other confounding variables, the neurological and neuropsychological outcomes should be profiled separately. This study provides useful new information insofar as outcome was measured independently by means of ADL and return-to-work criteria. The hemorrhagic subgroup again showed a better recovery though when age-matched with infarction patients the outcome differences were not significant. Despite the use of well-known tests, specific quantitative information was not included in the report, a deficiency that recurs in selected studies in this area. Nevertheless, the results are relatively consistent across the studies, to suggest that quantitative assessment approaches may yield valid predictors of the longitudinal course of recovery in individual patients, particularly when the many coveriates that contribute to the determination of individual differences in outcome can be measured and incorporated into the predictive equations. The challenge to clinical neuropsychologists working in rehabilitation settings implied in this conclusion warrants further longitudinal research utilizing the many new methods and concepts emerging in the clinical neuropsychological literature.

## REFERENCES

Adametz J H 1959 Role of recovery of functioning in cats with rostal reticular lesions. Journal of Neurosurgery 16: 85–98

Akert K 1964 Comparative anatomy of the frontal cortex and thalamocortical connections. In: Warren J M, Akert K (eds) The frontal granular cortex and behavior, McGraw-Hill, New York

Alajouanine T, Lhermitte F 1965 Acquired aphasia in children. Brain 88: 653–662

Anderson T P, Boureston M, Greenberg F R 1970 Rehabilitation predictors in completed stroke: Final Report. Kenny Rehabilitation Institute, SRS Grant No RD-1757-M-68-C3

Bach-y-Rita P 1981 Central nervous system lesions; sprouting and unmasking in rehabilitation. Archives of Physical Medicine and Rehabilitation 62: 413–417

Bard P, Mountcastle V B 1948 Some forebrain mechanisms involved in expression of rage with special reference to suppression of angry behavior. Research Publication Assn Nerv Ment Dis 27: 362–404

Benton A L (ed) 1968 Behavioral change in cerebrovascular disease. Harper & Row, New York

Benton A L 1979a Visuoperceptive, visuospatial and visuoconstructional disorders. In: Heilman K M, Valenstein E (eds) Clinical neuropsychology, Oxford University Press, New York

Benton A L 1979b Behavioral consequences of closed head injury. In: Odom G L (ed) Central Nervous System Trauma Research Status Report, NINCDS, National Institutes of Health, Washington D C

Benton A L 1981 Aspects of the neuropsychology of aging. Invited Address, Division 40, American Psychological Association, Los Angeles

Benton A L, Van Allen M W 1972 Prosapagnosia and facial discrimination. Journal of Neurological Science 15: 167–172

Benton A L, Varney N R, Hamsher KdeS 1978 Visuospatial judgement. Archives of Neurology 35: 364–367

Ben-Yishay Y, Gerstman L, Diller L, Haas A 1970 Prediction of rehabilitation outcomes from psychometric parameters in left hemiplegics. Journal of Consulting and Clinical Psychology 34: 436–441

Blumer D, Walker A E 1975 The neural basis of sexual behavior. In: Benson D F, Blumer D (eds) Psychiatric aspects of neurological disease. Grune & Stratton, New York

Bond M R, Brooks D N 1976 Understanding the process of recovery as a basis for the investigation of rehabilitation for the brain injured. Scandinavian Journal of Rehabilitation Medicine 8: 127–133

Borkowski J G, Benton A L, Spreen O 1967 Word fluency and brain damage. Neuropsychologia 5: 135–140

Botwinick J 1977 Intellectual abilities. In: Birren J E, Schaie K W (eds) Handbook of the psychology of aging, Van Nostrand Reinhold, New York

Brink J D, Garrett A L, Hale W R, Woo-Sam J, Nickel V L 1970 Recovery of motor and intellectual function in children sustaining severe head injuries. Developmental Medicine and Child Neurology 12: 565–571

Brooks D N, Aughton M E 1979 Psychological consequences of blunt head injury. International Rehabilitation Medicine 1: 160–165

Brooks D N, Aughton M E, Bond M R, Jones P, Rizvi S 1980 Cognitive sequelae in relationship to early indices of severity of brain damage after severe blunt head injury. Journal of Neurology, Neurosurgery, and Psychiatry 43: 529–534

Brooks D N, Deelman B G, van Zomeren A H, van Dongen H, van Harskamp F, Aughton M E 1984 Problems in measuring cognitive recovery after acute brain injury. Journal of Clinical Neuropsychology 6: 71–85

Buschke H, Fuld P A 1974 Evaluating storage, retention, and retrieval in disordered memory and learning. Neurology 24: 1019–1025

Cannon W F, Rosenblueth A 1949 The supersensitivity of denervated structures: a law of denervation. Macmillan, New York

Caplan P J, MacPherson G M, Tobin P 1985 Do sex-related differences in spatial abilities exist? A multilevel critique with new data. American Psychologist 40: 786–799

Carlsson C A, van Essen C, Lofgren J 1968 Factors affecting the clinical course of patients with severe head injury. Journal of Neurosurgery 29: 242–251

Carmon A 1971 Disturbances in tactile sensitivity in patients with cerebral lesions. Cortex 7: 83–97

Cattell R B 1963 Theory of fluid and crystallized intelligence: an initial experiment. Journal of Educational Psychology 105: 105–111

Chadwick O, Rutter M, Shaffer D, Shrout P E 1981 A prospective study of children with head injuries: IV: specific cognitive deficits. Journal of Clinical Neuropsychology 3: 101–126

Cooper P R et al 1979 Dexamethasone and severe head injury: a prospective double-blind

study. Journal of Neurosurgery 51: 307–316
Courville C B 1944 The structural basis for the common traumatic cerebral syndromes. Bulletin of Los Angeles Neurological Society 9: 17
Courville C B, Aymes E W 1952 Late residuals of the brain consequent to dural hemorrhage. Bulletin of the Los Angeles Neurological Society 17: 163–167
Critchley M 1953 The parietal lobes. Edward Arnold, London
DeRenzi E, Faglioni P, Scott G 1971 Judgment of spatial orientation in patients with focal brain damage. Journal of Neurology, Neurosurgery, and Psychiatry 34: 489–495
DeRenzi E, Faglioni P, Villa P 1977 Topographical amnesia. Journal of Neurology, Neurosurgery, and Psychiatry 40: 498–505
Dennis M, Whitaker H A 1976 Hemisphere equipotentiality and language acquisition. In: Segalowitz S, Gruber F (eds) Language development and neurological theory. Academic Press, New York
Dikmen S, Reitan R M, Temkin R 1983 Neuropsychological recovery in head injury. Archives of Neurology 40: 333–338
Drudge O W, Williams J M, Kessler M 1984 Recovery from severe closed head injuries with the Halstead-Reitan Neuropsychological Battery. Journal of Clinical Psychology 40: 259–265
Fahey T J, Irving M H, Miller P 1967 Severe head injuries: a six year follow-up. Lancet 2: 475–479
Finger S (ed) 1978 Recovery from brain damage: research and theory. Plenum, New York
Finger S, Stein D G 1982 Brain damage and recovery. Academic Press, New York
Flor-Henry P 1969 Schizophrenic-like reactions and affective psychoses associated with temporal lobe epilepsy: etiologic factors. American Journal of Psychiatry 216: 400–403
Friedman S H 1950 Psychometric effects of frontal and parietal lobe damage. Unpublished doctoral dissertation. University of Minnesota
Geschwind N 1965 Disconnexion syndromes in animals and man. Brain 88: 237–294, 584–644
Geschwind N 1974 Late changes in the nervous system: an overview. In: Stern D, Rosen J, Butters N (eds) Plasticity and recovery of function in the central nervous system. Warren H Green, St. Louis
Geschwind N, Levitsky W 1968 Human brain: left–right asymmetries in temporal speech region. Science 161: 186–187
Goldman P S 1974 An alternative to developmental plasticity: heterology of CNS structures in infants and adults: In Stern D G, Rosen J J, Butters N (eds) Plasticity and recovery of function in the central nervous system. Academic Press, New York
Goldstein K, Scheerer M 1941 Abstract and concrete behavior. Psychological Monographs 53: Whole No. 39
Gronwall D, Wrightson P 1974 Delayed recovery of intellectual function after minor head injury. Lancet 2: 605–609
Gummow L, Miller P, Dustman R E 1983 Attention and brain injury: a case for cognitive rehabilitation of attentional deficits. Clinical Psychology Review 3: 255–274
Hardman J M 1979 The pathology of traumatic brain injuries. In: Thompson R A, Green J R (eds) Advances in neurology, Vol. 22. Raven, New York
Heath R G 1964 Pleasure response of human subjects to direct stimulation of the brain: physiologic and psychodynamic considerations. In: Heath R G (ed) The role of pleasure in behavior. Harper & Row, New York
Hebb D O 1949 The organization of behavior. Wiley, New York
Hebb D O, Penfield W 1940 Human behavior after extensive bilateral removals from the frontal lobes. Archives of Neurology and Psychiatry 44: 421–438
Hécaen H 1962 Clinical symptomatology in right and left hemispheric lesions. In: Mountcastle V B (ed) Interhemispheric relations and cerebral dominance. John Hopkins Press, Baltimore
Hécaen H 1976 Acquired aphasia in children and the ontogenesis of hemispheric functional specialization. Brain and Language 3: 114–134
Hécaen H, Angelerques R 1962 Agnosia for faces (prosopagnosia). Archives of Neurology 7: 92–100
Hier D B, Mondlock J, Caplan C R 1983 Recovery of behavioral abnormalities after right hemisphere stroke. Neurology 33: 345–350
Hiorns O, Newcombe F 1979 Recovery curves: uses and limitations. International Rehabilitation Medicine 1: 173–176

Hjern B, Nylander L 1964 Late prognosis of severe head injuries in childhood. Acta Paediatrica Scandinavica 152: 113–116
Inglis J, Lawson J S 1981 Sex differences in the effects of unilateral brain damage on intelligence. Science 212: 693–695
Jennett B, Teasdale G 1981 Management of head injuries. Davis, Philadelphia
Jones-Gotman M, Milner B 1977 Design fluency: the invention of nonsense drawings after focal cortical lesions. Neuropsychologia 15: 653–673
Kaszniak A W, Garron D C, Fox J H, Bergen D, Huckman M 1979 Cerebral atrophy, EEG slowing, age, education and cognitive functioning in suspected dementia. Neurology 8: 1273–1279
Kennard M 1938 Reorganization of motor function in the cerebral cortex of monkeys deprived of motor and premotor areas in infancy. Journal of Neurophysiology 1: 477–496
Kertesz A 1979 Recovery of associated disorders. In: Aphasia and associated disorders: taxonomy, localization and recovery. Grune & Stratton, New York, 283–316
Kinsbourne M, Warrington E K 1963 Localizing significance of limited simultaneous form perception. Brain 86: 699–702
Kinsella G, Ford B 1980 Acute recovery patterns in stroke patients. Neuropsychological factors. Medical Journal of Australia 2: 663–666
Klüver H, Bucy P C 1937 'Psychic blindness' and other symptoms following bilateral temporal lobectomy in rhesus monkeys. American Journal of Physiology 119: 352–353
Kotila M, Waltimo O, Niemi M-L, Laaksonen R, Lempinen M 1984 The profile of recovery from stroke and factors influencing outcome. Stroke 15: 1039–1044
Lashley K 1929 Brain mechanisms and intelligence. University of Chicago Press, Chicago
Levin H S, Benton A L, Grossman R G 1982 Neurobehavioral consequences of closed head injury. Oxford University Press, New York
Levin H S, Ewing-Cobles L, Benton A L 1984 Age and recovery from brain damage: a review of clinical studies: In: Scheff S W (ed) Aging and recovery of function in the central nervous system. Plenum, New York
Levin H, Grossman R, Rose L, Teasdale G 1979 Long-term neuropsychological outcome of closed head injury. Journal of Neurosurgery 50: 412–422
Lezak M D 1979 Recovery of memory and learning functions following traumatic brain injury. Cortex 15: 63–72
Lezak M D 1983 Neuropsychological Assessment. 2nd edn. Oxford University Press, New York
Long C J, Gouvier W D, Cole J C 1984 A model of recovery for the total rehabilitation of individuals with head trauma. Journal of Rehabilitation 50: 39–45, 70
Luria A R 1963 Restoration of function after brain injury. Pergamon, Oxford
Luria A R 1980 Higher cortical functions in man. 2nd edn. Basic Books, New York
Magoun H W 1950 Caudal and cephalic influences of the brain stem reticular formation. Physiological Reviews 40: 105–112
Mandelberg I A, Brooks D N 1975 Cognitive recovery after severe head injury. Journal of Neurology, Neurosurgery and Psychiatry 38: 1121–1126
Mark V H, Sweet W H, Ervin F R 1972 The effect of amygdalectomy on violent behavior in patients with temporal lobe epilepsy. In: Hitchcock E, Laitinen L, Vernet K (eds) Psychosurgery. C C Thomas, Springfield
Marvin O S M, Schwartz M F, Saffran E M 1979 Origins and distribution of language. In: Gazzaniga M S (ed) Handbook of behavioral neurobiology, Vol. 2. Plenum, New York
Matarazzo J D, Wiens A N, Matarazzo R G, Goldstein S G 1974 Psychometric and clinical test-retest reliability of the Halstead impairment index in a sample of healthy, young, normal men. Journal of Nervous and Mental Disease 158: 37–49
Mattis S 1984 Neuropsychological consequences of head injury. Presented at annual meeting of the International Neuropsychological Society, Houston
McGlone J 1980 Sex differences in human brain asymmetry: a critical review. Behavioral and Brain Sciences 3: 215–263
McLean Jr A, Temkin N R, Dikmen S, Wyler A R 1983 The behavioral sequelae of head injury. Journal of Clinical Neuropsychology 5: 361–376
McSweeney A J, Grant I, Heaton R K, Prigatano G P, Adams K M 1985 Relationship of neuropsychological status to everyday functioning in healthy and chronically ill persons. Journal of Clinical and Experimental Neuropsychology 7: 281–291
Meerwaldt J D 1983 Spatial disorientation in right-hemisphere infarction: a study of the

speed of recovery. Journal of Neurology, Neurosurgery, and Psychiatry 46: 426–429
Meier M J 1969 The regional localization hypothesis and personality change associated with focal cerebral lesions and ablations. In: Butcher J N (ed) MMPI research developments and clinical applications. McGraw-Hill, New York
Meier M J 1970 Objective behavioral assessment in diagnosis and prediction. In: Benton A L (ed) Behavior changes in cerebrovascular disease. Harper & Row, New York
Meier M J 1974 Some challenges for clinical neuropsychology. In: Reitan R M, Davison L A (eds) Clinical neuropsychology: current status and applications. Winston & Sons, Washington, DC
Meier M J 1981 Prediction of neuropsychological outcomes after cerebrovascular infarction. Presented at First International Congress of Neuropsychology, Bogota
Meier M J 1983 Recovery of neuropsychological functioning as a function of age in closed head injury. Presented at annual meeting of the Midwestern Psychological Association, Minneapolis, May
Meier M J, French L A 1965a Changes in MMPI scale scores and an index of psychopathology following unilateral temporal lobectomy in epilepsy. Epilepsia 6: 263–273
Meier M J, French L A 1965b Lateralized deficits in complex visual discrimination and bilateral transfer of reminiscense following unilateral temporal lobectomy. Neuropsychologia 3: 261–273
Meier M J, Resch J A 1967 Behavioral prediction of short-term neurologic change following acute onset of cerebrovascular symptoms. Mayo Clinic Proceedings 42: 641–647
Meier M J, Thompson W G 1983 Methodological issues in clinical studies of right cerebral hemisphere dysfunction. In: Hellige J B (ed) Cerebral hemisphere asymmetry: method, theory, and application. Praeger, New York
Meier M J, Ettinger M C, Arthur L 1982 Recovery of neuropsychological functioning after cerebrovascular infarction. In: Malatesha R, Hartlage L (eds) Neuropsychology and cognition, Vol. 2, NATO Advanced Study Series. Martinus Nijhoff, The Hague
Milner B 1964 Some effects of frontal lobectomy in man. In: Warren J M, Akert K (eds) The frontal granular cortex and behavior. McGraw-Hill, New York
Milner B 1967 Brain mechanisms suggested by studies of temporal lobes. In: Darley F L (ed) Brain mechanisms underlying speech and language. Grune & Stratton, New York
Milner B 1971 Interhemispheric differences in localization of psychological processes in man. British Medical Bulletin 27: 272–277
Milner B, Teuber H-L 1968 Alteration of perception and memory in man: reflections on methods. In: Weiskrantz L (ed) Analysis of behavior change. Harper & Row, New York
Moore R Y 1974 Central regeneration and recovery of function: the problem of collateral reinnervation. In: Stein D G, Rosen J J, Butters N (eds) Plasticity and recovery of function in the central nervous system. Academic Press, New York
New P F, Scott W R, Schnur J A, Davis K R, Taveras J M, Hochberg F H 1975 Computed tomography with the EMI scanner in the diagnosis of primary and metastatic intracranial neoplasma. Radiology 114: 75–87
Newcombe F 1982 The psychological consequences of closed head injury: assessment and rehabilitation. Injury 14: 111–136
Newcombe F, Ratcliff G 1979 Long-term psychological consequences of cerebral lesions. In: Gazzaniga M (ed). Handbook of behavioral neurobiology, Vol. 2. Plenum, New York
Newcombe F, Hiorns R W, Marshall J C, Adams C B T 1975 Acquired dyslexia: patterns of deficit and recovery. In: Porter R, Fitzsimmons D W (eds) Outcome of severe brain damage to the central nervous system. Amsterdam, Elsevier-Excerpta Medica
Ommaya A, Gennarelli T 1974 Cerebral concussion and traumatic unconsciousness. Brain 97: 633–654
O'Shaughnessy E J, Fowler R S, Reid V 1984 Sequelae of mild closed head injury. Journal of Family Practice 18: 391–394
Parsons O A, Prigatano G P 1978 Methodological considerations in clinical and neuropsychological research. Journal of Consulting and Clinical Psychology 46: 608–619
Paxton R, Ambrose J 1974 Proceedings: a review of the results of EMI scanning in the first 650 patients. British Journal of Radiology 47: 515
Porteus S 1959 The maze test and clinical psychology. Pacific Books, Palo Alto
Rao N, Jellinek H M, Harvey R F, Flynn M M 1984 Computerized tomography head scans as predictors of rehabilitation outcome. Archives of Physical Medicine and Rehabilitation 65: 18–20

Ratcliff G, Newcombe F 1973 Spatial orientation in man: effects of left, right and bilateral posterior cerebral lesions. Journal of Neurology, Neurosurgery, and Psychiatry 36: 448–454
Reitan R M 1964 Psychological deficits resulting from cerebral lesions in man. In: Warren J M, Akert K (eds) The frontal granular cortex and behavior. McGraw-Hill, New York
Rimel R W, Giordani B, Barth J T 1981 Disability caused by minor head injury. Neurosurgery 9: 221–228
Rosner B S 1970 Brain functions. Annual Review of Psychology 21: 555–594
Rothi L J, Horner J 1983 Restitution and substitution: two theories of recovery with application to neurobehavioral treatment. Journal of Clinical Neuropsychology 5: 73–81
Russell W R 1971 The traumatic amnesias. Oxford University Press, London
Russell W R, Smith A 1961 Post-traumatic amnesia in closed head injury. Archives of Neurology 5: 4–17
Sarno M T, Levita E 1971 Natural course of recovery in severe aphasia. Archives of Physical Medicine and Rehabilitation 52: 175–186
Schaie K W 1970 A reinterpretation of age-related changes in cognitive structure and functioning. In: Goulet C R, Baltes P B (eds) Life-span developmental psychology: research and theory. Academic Press, New York
Schaie K W, Schaie J P 1977 Clinical assessment and aging. In: Birren J E, Schaie K W (eds) Handbook of the psychology of aging. Von Nostrand Reinhold, New York
Seidman L 1980 Lateralized cerebral dysfunction, personality and cognition in temporal lobe epilepsy. Unpublished doctoral dissertation. University Microfilms International, Ann Arbor
Semmes J 1968 Hemispheric specialization: a clue to mechanism. Neuopsychologia 6: 11–26
Semmes J, Weinsten S, Ghent L, Teuber H-L 1960 Somatosensory changes after penetrating brain wounds in man. Harvard University Press, Cambridge
Sheikh K, Smith S, Meade T, Goldenberg E, Brennan P, Kinsella G 1979 Repeatability and validity of a modified activities of daily living (ADL) index in studies of chronic disability. International Journal of Rehabilitation Medicine 1: 51–58
Smith A 1977 Dominant and nondominant hemispherectomy. In: Kinsbourne M, Smith W L (eds) Hemispheric disconnection and cerebral function. C C Thomas, Springfield
Smith A 1981 Principles underlying human brain functions in neuropsychological sequelae of different neuropsychological processes. In: Filskov S B, Boll T J (eds) Handbook of clinical neuropsychology. Wiley, New York
Stein D G, Finger S, Hart T 1983 Brain damage and recovery: problems and perspectives. Behavioral and Neural Biology 37: 185–222
Stein D G, Rosen J J, Butters N (eds) 1974 Plasticity and recovery of function in the nervous system. Academic Press, New York
Stevens J R 1966 Psychiatric implications of psychomotor epilepsy. Archives of General Psychiatry 14: 461–471
Strich S 1961 Shearing of nerve fibers as a cause of brain damage due to head injury: a pathological study of twenty cases. Lancet 2: 443–448
Tabaddor K, Mattis S, Zuzula T 1984 Cognitive sequelae and recovery course after moderate and severe head injury. Neurosurgery 14: 701–708
Taylor A M, Warrington E K 1973 Visual discrimination in patients with localized lesions. Cortex 9: 82–93
Teasdale G, Jennett B 1974 Assessment of coma and impaired consciousness: a practical scale. Lancet 2: 81–84
Teasdale G, Jennett B 1976 Assessment and prognosis of coma after head injury. Acta Neurochirurgica 34: 45–55
Teuber H-L 1964 The riddle of frontal lobe function in man. In: Warren J M, Akert K (eds) The frontal granular cortex and behavior. McGraw-Hill, New York
Teuber H-L 1975 Recovery of function after brain injury in man. Ciba Foundation Symposium 34, Outcome of severe damage to the nervous system. Elsevier–Excerpta Medica–North Holland, 159–190
Thomas R S, Hauser W, Strauman S, Chern M, Kouri T, Anderson V E 1980 Neuropsychological and genetic interactions in epilepsy. Presented at annual meeting of the International Neuropsychological Society, San Francisco, February
Twitchell T 1951 The restoration of motor function following hemiplegia in man. Brain 74: 443–480

Valenstein E, Heilman K M 1979 Emotional disorders resulting from lesions of the central nervous system. In: Heilman K M, Valenstein E (eds) Clinical neuropsychology. Oxford University Press, New York

Valentino M L, Stein D G 1983 Do rats have hypotheses? A developmental and means–ends approach to brain damage, recovery of function and aging. In: Scheff S (ed) Aging and Recovery of Function. Plenum, New York

van Buskirk C 1954 Return of motor function in hemiplegia. Neurology 4: 919–928

van der Vlugt H 1979 Aspects of normal and abnormal neuropsychological development. In: Gazzaniga M S (ed) Handbook of behavioral neurobiology. Plenum, New York

van Dongen H R, Loolen M C B 1977 Factors related to prognosis of acquired aphasia in children. Cortex 13: 131–136

von Monakow C 1969 Die Lokalisation in Grosshirn und der Abbau der Funktion durch korticale Herde. Bergmann, Wiesbaden, 1914. Translated and excerpted in Pribram K H (ed) Mood states and mind. Penguin, London

Wada J 1976 Cerebral anatomical asymmetry in infant brains. Symposium on sex differences in brain asymmetry. Presented at meeting of the International Neuropsychological Society, Toronto, February

Warrington E K, James M 1967 An experimental investigation of facial recognition in patients with unilateral lesions. Cortex 3: 317–326

Williams J M, Gomes F B, Drudge V W, Kessler M 1981 Predicting cognitive and global outcome from closed head injury using severity measures collected early in treatment. Presented at Fifth Annual Conference on the Rehabilitation of the Brain Injured Adult, Williamsburg, June

Witelson S F, Pallie W 1973 Left hemisphere specialization for language in the newborn: neuroanatomical evidence for asymmetry. Brain 96: 641–647

Woods B T, Carey S 1979 Language deficits after apparent clinical recovery from childhood aphasia. Annals of Neurology 6: 405–409

Woods B T, Teuber H-L 1978 Changing patterns of childhood aphasia. Annals of Neurology 3: 273–280

Wrightson O N, Gronwall M E 1980 Time off work and symptoms after minor head injury. Injury 12: 445–454

Yakovlev P I 1971 Neuroanatomical variants and neurological symptomatology. Invited address to the Department of Neurology, University of Minnesota Medical School

*Wayne A. Gordon*

# Methodological considerations in cognitive remediation

## INTRODUCTION

Neuropsychological rehabilitation is a new field. There are no textbooks on the subject and no graduate training programs or courses focused solely on issues pertinent to cognitive remediation in brain-damaged people. The terms 'remediation' and 'rehabilitation' are often used interchangeably in the literature, although they are not synonymous. Diller & Gordon (1981a) define remediation as a constellation of procedures that are used by a neuropsychologist to provide patients with the skills and strategies needed for the performance of tasks that are difficult and/or impossible for them to complete due to the existence of cognitive deficits. Rehabilitation, on the other hand, involves the organization and delivery of a wide array of interventions that are provided by a health care team (e.g., physiatrists, physical therapists, occupational therapists, psychologists, social workers, nurses, speech pathologists, etc.). Thus, neuropsychological remediation is included under the umbrella of rehabilitation.

Although still in its infancy, neuropsychological rehabilitation has quickly become the focus of increased interest. In the late 1970s, remediation was viewed as a domain which was at the cutting edge of research in neuropsychology (Parsons & Prigatano, 1978). In fact, in 1981 the editors of the *Journal of Consulting and Clinical Psychology* saw fit to include an article on neuropsychological interventions in an issue devoted to neuropsychology (Diller & Gordon, 1981a). Three major reasons for this interest can be cited. First, advances that have been made in diagnosis of neuropsychological disorders have naturally prompted concern with possible remedial treatment. Increasingly, rehabilitation of the cognitive, perceptual and affective deficits of the neurologically impaired offers the clinical researcher a unique opportunity to develop theories and/or build models, which can be used to describe, explain, or elucidate brain–behavior relationships, and at the same time deliver meaningful services to brain-damaged individuals.

Examples of how research in neuropsychology can be used by those interested in remediation include studies by Carson et al (1968) and Ben-Yishay et al (1970, 1974). Carson et al (1968) compared the learning abilities and characteristics of a group of 64 left brain-damaged (LBD) aphasic patients with those in a sample of non-brain-damaged individuals. The findings indicated that: (a) although the aphasics learned at a slower rate than did the 'normals', the shapes of the learning curve of the two groups were similar; (b) the effects of practice were maintained after interpolated periods of practice; and (c) the aphasics could learn rules and transfer what they had learned. Thus, besides offering theoretically relevant findings, this study provided useful information on the learning patterns of aphasics to speech pathologists planning remediation programs.

A similar example of the interweaving of theoretically and practically meaningful research is provided by Ben-Yishay and his colleagues (1970, 1974), who have conducted in-depth studies of the specific breakdowns which occur when right and left hemiplegics are learning to complete items on the WAIS Block Design. This information not only is useful in understanding lateralized brain damage performance (i.e., in what ways performance is initially deficient), but also provides a means for empirically describing those aspects of performance which need to be addressed in intervention programs.

The second reason for increased interest in neuropsychological rehabilitation relates to the advances that have been achieved in health care over the past two decades. The increased longevity in the general population, coupled with decreased birth rates, have generated heightened concern regarding the treatment of the cognitive changes that are associated with the 'normal' aging process. Another way in which improved medical care has influenced neuropsychology is that more people are surviving head trauma, strokes and other forms of brain pathology (e.g., benign tumors, arterial venous malformations). It is therefore not uncommon today to see individuals who have suffered strokes live 10–20% of their lives following the onset of their cerebrovascular accident (CVA). The victims of head trauma, since they are usually younger than those with strokes, are likely to live out a major portion of their lives with their impairments.

A third reason for the increased interest in neuropsychological rehabilitation stems from the emergence of politically active consumer groups which have been organized by head trauma victims and their families. In particular, the National Head Injury Foundation (NHIF) and Mothers Against Drunk Drivers (MADD) have successfully exerted pressure not only on funding agencies (e.g., the National Institute of Communication Diseases and Stroke, National Institute of Handicapped Research) to sponsor programs focused on the development of intervention programs for the brain injured, but also on health care agencies and insurance companies to support specialized rehabilitation programs for the victims of head trauma.

Although Parsons & Prigatano (1978) note that the methological issues facing professionals developing programs to rehabilitate the neuropsychological deficits of brain-damaged individuals are similar to issues which any researcher must confront when conducting conventional neuropsychological research, each field of research has its own set of constraints which are unique to that area. Given the viability and continued growth of neuropsychological rehabilitation, it is important to describe some specific methodological problems commonly encountered, which need to be addressed before undertaking research in this field.

## METHODOLOGICAL PROBLEMS IN NEUROPSYCHOLOGICAL RESEARCH

Several critical methodological issues must be confronted by the rehabilitation neuropsychologist in order to make sure that research in this relatively new area avoids the errors that have been made in the past. Much of the controversy in neuropsychological literature is associated with: (a) inadequate nosology; (b) poor specification of the samples of individuals that are being studied; (c) inappropriate combining of data collected from heterogeneous groups of patients without analysis of whether the findings which emerged were consistent across patients (i.e., the results were independent of the diverse set of neurological entities that were studied); and (d) inadequate specification of multiple deficits in a given sample of brain-damaged patients. Each of these methodological problems will be briefly discussed below.

### Inadequate nosology

One of the more important contributions of neuropsychologists has been the validation of clinical syndromes that are associated with a particular hemisphere of the brain or with a particular structural area of the brain. Occasionally one is confronted with data that challenge one's expectations and understanding of these well-recognized clinical syndromes. A recent study illustrates this point. Egelko (1983b) was intrigued by the observation that verbal cues were useless tools in providing right brain-damaged (RBD) patients the feedback necessary to compensate for their visual–perceptual deficits. It was reasoned that RBD patients might have a coexisting linguistic deficit in addition to their well-documented perceptual disorders. Not only did she find that the sample of RBD patients exhibited a consistent verbal linguistic deficit, i.e., one which was manifested on six of the seven verbal measures that were administered, but also found that this difficulty was independent of the patient's visual scanning deficit. Thus, along with the more commonly diagnosed perceptual problems, a language disorder was noted as well. However, this verbal deficit has been both under-reported in the literature and under-diagnosed in clinical situations. There are two likely reasons for this:

1. In diagnosing a brain-injured person's deficits, the pre-existing mental set of the clinician/researcher will often interfere with observing, understanding, and interpreting the patient's behavior.
2. Researchers often stop analyzing their data when what they are looking for has been observed. Frequently, unexpected findings remain unexplored and uninterpreted.

## Poor specification of samples studied

Unfortunately, too many of the premises of neuropsychologists are based on studies in which the data from patients with diverse types of etiologies of brain damage have been combined to form a 'brain-damaged' group. This methodological problem renders the data derived from such studies uninterpretable. Underlying the combination of data collected from heterogeneous samples is the assumption that there are no differences in the performance of individuals with similar diagnoses. It is often assumed, for example, that the performance of two individuals with a right brain injury will be similar on a given psychometric measure, ignoring possible differences associated with one person's being right brain-injured secondary to a stroke while the other person is right brain-injured secondary to a closed head injury. The validity of the premise of ascribing overwhelming importance to the site of the lesion but little to the etiology of the lesion has not been systematically examined in neuropsychology. Indeed, there are several reasons to question its validity. For example, individuals with head trauma and stroke often differ in the age of onset of their pathology. This age difference has many implications. For instance, when examining the data derived from an older individual who has had a stroke, a determination must be made on what extent the deficient performance is a function of age and how much of the observed deficit function is associated with the brain damage *per se*. Since head trauma victims are younger, deficit performance is more likely to be a function of the brain damage alone. Age also is associated with the speed and amount of skill acquisition. Thus, expectations for the effects of an intervention that are based on experiences with the head-injured often must be altered when one is applying similar programs to individuals who have had strokes.

Another reason to question the validity of combining data derived from diverse neurological disorders is that the speed and extent of recovery of a deficit function might be associated with the etiology of brain damage. Thus, even though two individuals might be similar in terms of diagnosis and length of time since the onset of brain damage, an individual with one etiology might recover faster than an individual with a second etiology. All of the studies described below illustrate this issue.

Gianutsos et al (1983) studied the phenomena of visual imperception in a group of brain-damaged individuals and found that imperception consisted of several independent components. This important finding is undermined by several methodological flaws in the study. First, data were derived from individuals who had mixed etiologies, i.e., head trauma and strokes, and it was not stated whether the findings were consistent across the etiologies of brain damage. Second, in several analyses the data from right and left brain-damaged individuals were combined. Given that the pattern of performance on a visual perceptual test for right and left brain-damaged individuals is bound to differ, the rationale behind this approach was not apparent. Finally, the characteristics of a group of 'controls' were not specified (e.g., were they healthy volunteers or individuals who were hospitalized but without brain damage?).

There are both advocates (Golden et al, 1980, 1981) and critics (Adams, 1980a, b; Spiers, 1981) of the Luria–Nebraska Neuropsychological Battery. Nonetheless, the fact still remains that the test was standardized on groups of brain-damaged individuals with diverse etiologies. Neither laterality of brain damage nor etiology were factors that were considered in the standardization of the test.

Wyke (1971) studied the ability of brain-damaged individuals to learn coordinated movements of the right and left arm. She studied a group of 40 brain-damaged individuals, the majority of whom had either a neoplasm (73%) or a temporal lobectomy (25%). Her results indicated that patients with left-sided lesions had more difficulty learning the task than did patients with right-sided lesions. However, the length of time between operation and testing was highly variable, ranging between 1 month and 9 years (mean = 3.7 years). The potential effect of time since onset was not examined in the data presented. This factor is an important one to consider in a learning situation. Indeed, if time since onset was differentially represented in the left and right brain-damaged individuals, it alone might have accounted for the differences that were reported.

Zihl & Von Cramon (1979) examined the extent to which patients with cerebral blindness could be trained to improve their visual functioning. Twelve patients were studied who had visual field deficits secondary to post-chiasmatic lesions. As in the previous studies, the patients differed in the etiology of brain pathology and the length of time since the onset of brain damage. While the authors make consistent reference to individual differences in performance, they do not mention whether variations in learning were associated with etiology of brain damage, locus of lesion, type of visual field defect or length of time since the onset of brain damage.

The literature in neuropsychology is replete with studies like the ones just discussed that have assumed that patients who are homogeneous with regard to either their neurological diagnosis or syndrome will perform similarly on neurological tests. Unfortunately this issue has not been systematically examined. Indeed it may be found that neuropsychological tests are more sensitive than had been previously anticipated.

## Inadequate data analysis

Discrepant findings in neuropsychological research are often associated with inadequate analysis of data derived from patients who are homogeneous with regard to lesion site, but who are heterogeneous with regard to extent of neurological impairment. For example, while recent research has supported the findings that RBD patients have deficits in affect comprehension, the extent of these affective comprehension deficits in RBD patients is controversial. Heilman et al (1975) have reported that severe auditory affect comprehension deficits were associated with right but not left brain damage. These findings were in contrast with those of Schlanger et al (1976), who found the performance of right and left brain-damaged patients to be equivalent on an auditory affect comprehension task similar to that used by Heilman and colleagues.

These seemingly discrepant findings appear to be associated with the different characteristics of the sample of RBD patients included in the two studies. The right brain-damaged patients who were studied by Heilman et al (1975) and Tucker et al (1977) had severe visual neglect. Only three of 20 right brain-damaged patients examined by Schlanger et al had this type of disorder. Furthermore, the data derived from the three 'neglectors' in the Schlanger et al study were not analyzed separately from those of the remaining 17 patients in order to determine if the data of the former group were consistent with those of the non-neglectors. Thus, the relationship between a perceptual deficit and affect comprehension is unclear. Ruckdeschel-Hibbard (1984) explored this issue by analyzing the affect comprehension performance of RBD patients with and without severe perceptual impairments. The following results emerged:

1. auditory affect comprehension disorders were more likely to be found in right brain-damaged patients with moderate to severe visual neglect; and
2. the performance of right brain-damaged patients without visual neglect was similar to that of left brain-damaged patients on this particular task.

This study illustrates the need to control for severity of concomitant cognitive/perceptual deficits in the interpretation of study findings.

Additional evidence has surfaced for the need to separately analyze data derived from patients who are homogeneous with regard to the extent of their neurological deficit. The literature often associates affect comprehension deficits with RBD (Cicone et al, 1980; De Kosky et al, 1980; Heilman et al, 1975; Tucker et al, 1977) and associates higher levels of depression with LBD in comparison to RBD (Black, 1975; Gasparrini et al, 1978; Robinson & Benson, 1981; Robinson & Price, 1982; Robinson & Szetela, 1981). Contrary to these prevailing beliefs, Ruckdeschel-Hibbard (1984) found that affect comprehension abilities were impaired only in those RBD patients who were more neurologically impaired. She also found that the levels of depression in RBD and LBD patients depended on the way in which depression was assessed (self-report, as assessed by the Beck Depression Inventory, or observer rating, as assessed by the Hamilton Rating Scale for Depression) and the presence of visual field impairment (Table 6.1). Several points can be made based on data presented in Table 6.1.

1. In RBD and LBD patients without visual deficits, there was a congruence between self-report of depression and an examiner's rating of the patient's depression. This was not the case with those RBD patients with visual field defects. This subgroup of RBDs rated themselves as less depressed than did the examiner. Thus, these patients tended to minimize the severity of depression.

**Table 6.1** Depression scores: stroke patients

| | (N = 20) RBD Hemianopsia | | (N = 15) RBD Normal vision | | (N = 19) LBD Normal vision | |
|---|---|---|---|---|---|---|
| | *N* | % | *N* | % | *N* | % |
| Beck Depression Inventory (BDI)[1] | | | | | | |
| Not depressed | 10 | 50 | 8 | 53 | 11 | 58 |
| Mild/moderate | 4 | 20 | 4 | 27 | 7 | 36 |
| Severe | 6 | 30 | 3 | 20 | 1 | 5 |
| Hamilton Rating Scale for Depression (HRSD)[2] | | | | | | |
| Not depressed | 6 | 30 | 10 | 67 | 9 | 47 |
| Mild/moderate | 3 | 15 | 2 | 13 | 7 | 37 |
| Severe | 11 | 55 | 3 | 20 | 3 | 16 |

[1] BDI score less than 9 = not depressed; 10–20 = mild/moderate depression; 21+ = severe depression
[2] HRSD score less than 13 = not depressed; 14–20 = mild/moderate depression; 21+ = severe depression

2. Approximately half of all the patients studied, independent of laterality of lesions, were not depressed.
3. The self-reported levels of moderate depression were similar in all three groups.
4. Self-report of severe depression was more prevalent in RBDs than LBDs.

In addition, for all three patient groups (LBD, RBD with visual field defects, RBD without visual field defects), the severity of depression was unrelated to either affect comprehension or visual perceptual (scanning) abilities.

Similarly, Egelko (1983a) has found that the extent of neurological damage, particularly the presence of a visual field cut, is a critical variable in interpreting neuropsychological performance. Indeed, she found that a sex-differentiated pattern of verbal and cognitive impairments associated with right brain damage (i.e., males suffering more impairment of visual–spatial tasks with females suffering more impairment on verbal tasks) was masked until the data from RBD patients with visual field defects were analyzed separately from those without this impairment.

Both of these studies (Ruckdeschel-Hibbard, 1984; Egelko, 1983b) underscore the importance of visual field defects as a clinical variable that is important in furthering our understanding of the deficits associated with right brain damage. While previous neuropsychological research has not thoroughly examined differences between neurological subgroups (McGlone, 1977; McGlone & Kertesz, 1973), the results of the current studies present strong evidence that the presence of a visual field defect is a critical neurological variable in understanding right brain damage and related cognitive disorders, and should be specifically studied rather than statistically controlled. Separate analysis of the data of those who differ in the extent of their neurological deficits provides a way of examining whether deficits are correlated and if findings are a function of the extent of neurological impairments.

## Nesting multiplicity of deficits

The literature suggesting that specific deficits are associated with damage to a given area or side of the brain is often in conflict because it is difficult to separate deficits that are nested within each other. For example, in severely perceptually impaired RBD patients the extent of the patient's disturbance in processing complex visual information cannot be determined until the person has been taught to compensate for his/her neglect (Weinberg et al, 1977, 1979). Once the primary perceptual deficit, i.e., the neglect of space on the left side, has been remediated, more extensive testing/training can be initiated to determine the nature of the patient's remaining perceptual problems. For example, the extent of a patient's difficulty with reading comprehension cannot be determined until the patient has been taught to at least perform the mechanics of reading, i.e., scanning (Weinberg et al, 1982; Diller & Gordon, 1981a, b). Thus, more complex disturbances can neither be diagnosed nor treated until the primary deficit has been treated.

A different situation exists when diagnosing the multiple deficits that are often associated with RBD. Although several deficits may co-exist in many patients, they may remain unrelated. For example, studies in our laboratory (Gordon & Diller, 1983) indicate that about 70% of those RBDs with visual field deficits and half of those without visual problems are depressed (as measured by both the Beck Depression Inventory and the Multiple Affect Adjective Checklist). Of interest here, however, is the finding that perceptual disturbances are uncorrelated with depression (Table 6.2). This finding was confirmed by Ruckdeschel-Hibbard's (1984) study. The data presented in Table 6.2 also indicate that auditory affect comprehension/expression

**Table 6.2** Intercorrelations of three deficit domains in a sample of 22 RBD patients with visual information processing deficits

| Deficit domain | Arousal | Visual information processing | Auditory affect Comprehension | | Depression | | |
|---|---|---|---|---|---|---|---|
| Variable | C&E Rate | C&E Errors | Comp. | Disc. | BDI[1] | MAACL[2] | HRSD[3] |
| Cancellation rate | – | 0.47* | 0.06 | 0.10 | –21 | –22 | –0.06 |
| Cancellation errors | | – | 0.30 | 0.27 | –0.23 | –0.21 | –0.22 |
| Affect comprehension | | | – | 0.82** | 0.07 | 0.13 | 0.04 |
| Affect discrimination | | | | – | 0.24 | 0.04 | 0.18 |
| BDI[1] | | | | | – | 0.58** | 0.84** |
| MAACL[2] | | | | | | – | 0.59** |
| HRSD[3] | | | | | | | – |

*$p < 0.05$.
**$p < 0.01$.
[1] Beck Depression Inventory.
[2] Multiple Affect Adjective Checklist.
[3] Hamilton Rating Scale for Depression.

competence is not associated with depression, but is correlated with visual information processing disorders (VIP); and hypoarousal is associated with VIP deficit. From the diagnostic viewpoint, the intercorrelations suggest that RBD patients have perceptual problems as well as other cognitive deficits, e.g., hypoarousal, affect comprehension/expression. In addition, these individuals may or may not be depressed.

From the treatment vantage, Table 6.2 suggests several areas for exploration to those interested in the rehabilitation of neuropsychological disturbances. RBD patients display a host of disturbances that extend far beyond the well-recognized clinical syndrome(s) associated with RBD, i.e., perceptual impairments. For example, it has been our experience that the hypoarousal disturbance, first noted by Heilman and his colleagues (Heilman et al, 1978) is a primary barrier not only to perceptual intervention but to medical rehabilitation as well. A clinical manifestation of hypoarousal is drowsiness. In our setting we have observed that RBD patients with severe perceptual problems fall asleep during their rehabilitation classes and the in-patient rehabilitation stay of these drowsy patients is longer than that for non-drowsy RBD patients (95 days vs. 71 days) (Gordon, unpublished). Thus these findings suggest that developing methods to remediate this state of hypoarousal should be a top priority for those entering the field. Indeed, once these procedures are developed they could be useful not only in improving the performance of these patients but in reducing health care costs as well.

## Problems with intervention studies

The simplest interpretation for the failure of an intervention is either that there was a poor match between the deficit and the treatment rendered or that the tasks used to measure the impact of treatment were poorly selected. Additionally, however, the methodological issues previously discussed can be applied to treatment studies and may explain the lack of success experienced by some investigators (Taylor et al, 1971). For example, Weinberg et al (1982) found that, although RBD stroke patients benefited from an intervention program designed to ameliorate deficits in perceptual organization, the treatment effect was less dramatic than had been reported in previous studies by this same group of researchers (Weinberg et al, 1979). The reasons offered for this diminished treatment effect were related to the specific nature of the treatment. A plausible alternative explanation can be posited to account for these findings: eight of the 18 (44%) patients who were in the experimental group had a visual field defect. It was reasoned that, prior to being able to profit from training aimed at improved performance on complex visual perceptual tasks, they would need to be taught to compensate for their visual neglect while performing simple search and stimulus-recognition tasks. Thus, these eight patients were given a brief period of training which was designed to improve their visual scanning abilities. Following this brief intervention to improve visual scanning these patients were re-baselined and given the more complex training in perceptual organization. Thus, the measured performance of the RBDs with visual field deficits was improved, and had become comparable to the RBDs with normal vision on tests of simple visual scanning ability prior to receiving the more complex types of training. However, even though the patients were behaviorally equivalent prior to receiving the more complex training, the RBDs with visual field defects remained more neurologically impaired. While it was correct to train a proficiency in basic skills (scanning) prior to training more difficult ones, the ways these two groups of patients learned, and their capacity to absorb new material, remained different. Thus, the assumption that these two groups of neurologically divergent patients could benefit from the same training program was false. Retraining did nothing to correct the original neurological heterogeneity of these two subgroups of RBDs.

In retrospect, a possibly more appropriate approach to the training of complex visual perceptual tasks would have been to scale down the training stimuli, so that the more impaired patients would initially be trained using easier stimuli than the less impaired. Only at a point where these easier tasks had been mastered would more difficult training materials have been introduced. Separate analyses of the data derived from patients with and without visual field defects may have clarified possible differential treatment effects in this study. In failing to analyze the data in this fashion, it was assumed that equivalent performance on visual scanning tasks implied that the two RBD groups were equally able to learn more complex perceptual material even though those with the visual field deficit were more neurologically impaired.

## METHODOLOGICAL ISSUES IN COGNITIVE REMEDIATION

Given the problems and the complex issues already discussed, what follows are some guidelines which can be applied when planning and implementing future research.

### Deciding what to treat

Typically when patients seek health care from a physician, psychologist, or any other type of health professional, the patient or significant other reports the existence of a constellation of symptoms to the service provider. For example, a person sees a physician to report a persistent fever, cough, ache, pain, etc. A person sees a psychologist when upset, unhappy, etc. In contrast, the neuropsychologist often operates like a detective embarking on an investigation with little evidence to predict the outcome of his/her efforts. In many instances the neuropsychologist is diagnosing a difficulty without the aid of the patient's self-report of the difficulty. Frequently the brain-damaged person is not aware of the existence of the problem. For example, a person with a perceptual deficit does not know that s/he is not seeing the world veridically; a person with an aprosodia may/may not be aware of the fact that s/he is unable to competently understand or express emotion (Ross, 1981, 1982; Ross & Rush, 1981; Ross & Mesulam, 1979). Thus, the complaint presented to the neuropsychologist by the referring agent, e.g., a family member or physician, is rarely formulated more specifically than as a non-specific description of the patient's medical condition, i.e., the patient is brain-damaged.

In most instances in neuropsychology the diagnosis is the end-point of inquiry. The patient's performance on a battery of tests either has helped the researcher in supporting or rejecting the hypothesis under investigation or has aided the clinician in making a differential diagnosis or in describing a pattern of strengths and deficits. Thus, the initial question to be confronted is a variant of 'Is the person brain-damaged?' or 'Does the person have *X* deficit?' However, to those seeking to treat the disorder, diagnosis is only the starting point for further efforts. The question to be addressed becomes, 'Given the diagnosis, what can be done to ameliorate the problem?'

Having defined the problem, several issues are brought into focus. In what types of patients does the deficit occur? In what proportion of these patients is it found? Is the problem associated with a particular site of brain damage? Is it related to the extent of brain damage? Is the nature/extent of deficit altered by the length of time the person has been brain-damaged, i.e., does performance change over time or is it stable? Are there any ancillary deficits that are correlated with the primary deficit? Each of these issues is related to developing an in-depth understanding of the deficit prior to conceptualizing the ways in which it might be treated.

The delineation of a clear diagnostic statement is of primary importance in developing an intervention program. The diagnostic statement defines what gets treated and who gets treated, as well. The diagnosis should be based on three pieces of interrelated information:

1. The defect being treated should be exhibited in the everyday functioning of the person. Thus, for example, a visual field problem may be seen to interfere with reading, writing, and most forms of visual perceptual activity. In a similar vein, a memory problem or difficulty with abstract thinking may be easily observed in daily life activities.
2. The deficit should be able to be diagnosed as part of the standard clinical neurological examination. That is, test results validate the presence of the deficit.
3. The deficit should be observed during neuropsychological testing or be the most parsimonious interpretation of performance on a battery of tests.

## Choosing the appropriate experimental design

Although neuropsychologists often attempt to ameliorate deficits that are the hallmarks of brain damage, the conventional wisdom concerning these deficits is that, since they are manifestations of brain damage, they are intractable to treatment. In order to promote clinical treatment of neuropsychological disorders, intervention studies must first gain credibility to overcome the pervasive nihilism that exists in the field concerning the treatment of neuropsychological deficits. Given this atmosphere, traditional experiments will provide the most convincing evidence to those who doubt the effects of neuropsychological rehabilitation and who maintain a 'show-me' attitude when it is asserted that patients can be helped. In a sense, traditional experiments become the primary weapons of neuropsychologists because many of the arguments used to disparage the efforts of those who remediate can be countered by the scientific evidence provided by well-designed experiments (Campbell & Stanley, 1963; Cook & Campbell, 1979). More specifically:

1. The effects of treatment and non-treatment groups can be compared.
2. The issue of separating the effects of treatment from spontaneous recovery can be examined. This is especially important since it is clear that the natural course of recovery usually results in some degree of improvement.
3. The effects of an intervention are often more readily accepted when they are demonstrated in a large group of patients with a wide range of impairments.

Notwithstanding the need for, and utility of, traditional experimental designs, single case designs have also had wide application in neuropsychological rehabilitation (Diller & Gordon, 1981a, b; Parsons & Prigatano, 1978; Leftoff, 1979; Gianutsos & Gianutsos, 1979; Glasgow et al, 1977). These latter designs are useful for several reasons:

1. Case studies are useful in the clinical demonstration of a given intervention when applied to an individual with an unusual pattern of competencies or to someone who has multiple, severe impairments.
2. Case studies are useful in making points that are of theoretical interest. Case studies by Diller & Weinberg (1977), Denny-Brown et al (1952), Ross (1981), etc., provide excellent models for the ways in which case studies advance theory while at the same time aid in the development of models of retraining.
3. Case studies provide the researcher with a unique opportunity to study relationships among complex arrays of interacting variables.
4. Case studies provide the clinician with an opportunity to view the ways in which treatment generalizes to everyday functioning.
5. For obvious practical reasons, single case designs are useful when traditional experiments are not feasible. For example, the unavailability of a sufficiently large pool of patients to enable individuals to be assigned to treatment and non-treatment groups precludes the implementation of an experiment. Also, experiments are obviously more expensive than single case designs since more patients need to be included. This, in turn, requires more space, staff, equipment, and other resources.
6. Recent advances in the design of single case experiments (Hersen & Barlow, 1976) have greatly advanced the scientific rigor with which they can be applied.

However, for several reasons, single case designs must be applied and interpreted with caution:

1. The experiment may have 'worked' with only one person. Thus, the conclusions that can be drawn and generalizations that can be made are limited.
2. Most single case designs do not enable the examiner to separate the nested effects of recovery, practice and intervention.
3. A performance plateau often is used as the criterion for cessation of treatment. However, whether the intervention has been withdrawn at the appropriate time may be unknown because learning might still be taking place, albeit at a markedly slowed rate.
4. In multiple baseline studies, learning does not stop when an intervention has been removed. Thus, changes in performance need to be carefully examined.

Once the type of experimental design that will be used to study the impact of a neuropsychological intervention has been decided, the next issue that needs to be addressed is determining how the effects of the intervention program will be studied. This touches on two issues: choosing a battery of tests that can be used to measure the impact of the program and generalization of treatment.

## Measurement issues

Selecting a battery of neuropsychological tests that are useful in studying the impact of neuropsychological intervention is a complex task. There are several basic issues that need to be examined. For example:

1. The size of a test battery is limited by the amount of time (both yours and the patient's) that can be devoted to testing the patient.
2. Careful consideration needs to be given to the use of multiple measures of a deficit. A strong case can be made for including multiple measures of the same deficit in brain-damaged patients on the grounds that this will increase the reliability of a given set of findings. A potential problem with this approach is that redundancy might cause the findings to be difficult to interpret. This would be the case if the measures are not found to be correlated or if one measure improves and the other either stays the same or even gets worse.
3. Even when one has chosen to collect data on a control or comparison group of patients, skeptics may still question whether change is due to spontaneous recovery rather than to the impact of intervention. This is especially the case when improvement is observed on most of the tests in a battery. Critics tend to view this type of change as a generalized effect that is more likely to be associated with recovery than it is to be related to the effects of an intervention. One solution to this difficulty is to include in the test battery a group of measures that are unlikely to be affected by the

program. This enables one to specify on an *a priori* basis those tasks on which change is to be expected.

In addition to these points there are several other considerations that need to be taken into account when constructing a battery of tests. For example:

1. Performance on a test must be correlated with the deficit being diagnosed and treated. Thus, the test must be accepted as a valid measure of the impairment.
2. The test must elicit a sufficient range of performance in brain-damaged people. It should be neither too easy for the minimally impaired nor too difficult for the severely impaired. This enables use of the measure to document change in a full spectrum of patients.
3. In order for a test to have diagnostic value, and for it to be an acceptable measure of change, it must be reliable. That is, the performance it elicits must be a stable indicator of a deficit. Such issues as practice effects, the amount of improvement in performance that can be expected as a function of 'spontaneous recovery,' and whether performance is altered by medication, must be considered.
4. The test must have adequate norms so that performance can be compared with that of an appropriate reference group. Defining the characteristics of the reference group is a complex issue involving many different considerations. For example, with whom will the individual's performance be compared: non-brain-damaged people, a homogeneous group of brain-damaged people, the person's baseline, or even an estimate pre-morbid performance? The influences of such factors as age, sex, handedness, and years of education on task performance must be examined in both brain-damaged and non-brain-damaged standardization samples so that the competence can be correctly graded. For example, if performance correlates with both age and sex, it is advisable to have separate norms for males and females group by age. Finally, it is critical to document the characteristics of the brain-damaged reference groups. To say that 'norms' were generated from 'a group of hemiplegics' is inadequate. The experience of those in our laboratory is that performance and the recovery of function in unilateral right, unilateral left, and bilaterally brain-damaged individuals usually differs on most measures.

## Generalization of treatment

An important issue which requires much thought when designing neuropsychological interventions is that of the generalization of the treatment. Generalization may be defined as occurring on three levels:

*Level I*: At the most basic level it is expected that the result of training should persist from one training session to the next, as well as on alternate forms of the training materials.

*Level II*: A more complex type of generalization occurs when improvement is noted on psychometric tests that are (a) similar to and (b) different from the task demands that are being trained.

*Level III*: The highest order of generalization involves the transfer of what has been learned from training to functioning as it occurs in day-to-day living.

Needless to say, when undertaking remediation, generalization at Level I is a necessary but not a sufficient criterion by which to determine the effectiveness of a given intervention.

In most studies in neuropsychological rehabilitation, investigators have been satisfied with the outcomes of their remedial efforts if improvement is noted on Level II tasks, i.e., psychometric tests. There is a problem with this approach to determining the effects of an intervention. More specifically, even if statistically significant pre-test to post-test changes are noted, the question of meaningful change remains unanswered. One needs to anticipate the size of the experimental effect in order to determine appropriate sample sizes and apply power analysis (Cohen, 1977). Due to the myriad of potential sources of individual differences, in neuropsychological interventions it is often difficult to predict on an *a priori* basis the magnitude of the change that is expected. Since this is not possible, many statisticians are willing to accept change of at least one standard error of measurement (Bradley, 1983). Nonetheless, the question remains as to whether the person's actual functioning has been impacted. Thus, while test data are useful for purposes of model or theory building, from the patient's vantage this type of generalization is often inadequate. Indeed, the validity of many standard test measures as indices of day-to-day functioning may be quite poor. For example, Sarno and Levita (1971) found that performance on formal language tests did not correlate with improvements in functional language in a group of aphasics. Patients are often unaware of the changes that have been rendered by interventions, as often it is difficult to translate the test gains into actual day-to-day performance. Consequently, unless rehabilitation has impacted the patient's behavioral repertoire, the exercise will have little, if any, meaning to the patient.

Generalization at Level III should be viewed as the *sine qua non* for judging the effectiveness of an intervention program. Unfortunately, this type of learning has not been given sufficient attention by neuropsychologists. This neglect is probably related to the difficulty of measuring change in everyday performance, both in terms of impact on the person's skills (what the person 'can do') and on activities (what the person 'does do').

### *Skills*

When skill change is the focus of treatment it is assumed that, as an outcome of the intervention, the person will be able to do more things. This type of change is most obvious in a rehabilitation setting where the efforts of an entire rehabilitation team, i.e., physiatrist, occupational therapist, physical therapist, speech pathologist, psychologist, are focused on treating 'activities of daily living' (ADL), e.g., eating, dressing, etc., and their components, e.g., 'cutting with a knife,' 'putting on/removing clothing,' etc.

A rehabilitation therapist looks at skills from a different vantage point than does the neuropsychologist. Those in rehabilitation would examine a function such as grasping in terms of the way it might interfere with holding a utensil that is needed for eating or brushing teeth. The issue in treatment would be to build up strength and flexibility so that the task can be performed unaided, i.e., without the help of another person. The neuropsychologist would focus on gaining a better understanding of the particular motor deficit presented by the patient by looking at such aspects of the motor impairment as speed, accuracy, or reaction time. Although the degree of sensory/motor impairment is correlated with the person's competence at performing an array of ADL tasks, the period of recovery noted in improvement in the functional skills has been observed over longer periods of time than have the recovery periods for the motor/sensory impairment (Twitchell, 1951; Van Buskirk & Webster, 1955; Rusk et al, 1969).

Early studies of Diller et al (1974) provide examples of how skill performance can be used to examine the impact of remediation. Eating was reasoned to be a task involving eye–hand–mouth coordination, in that the patient must not only organize the food on the plate and manipulate utensils so that the food is ready to be eaten, but also must transport the food from the plate to the mouth. Thus, the task demands involved in eating were seen as similar to those needed to complete block designs. Consequently, individuals who received specialized training to improve their ability in completing block designs were expected to show improvement not only on Level II psychometric tasks that are similar in demand to block design but also in Level III tasks: some of the eye–hand skills required when eating. In order to test these hypotheses, a means of recording the maneuvers of patients while they were eating a standardized meal was developed; in order to control for individual differences in meal choice, all patients were provided with the same meal, in which the food was standardly organized on the tray. Following this, the eating behavior of a group of RBD patients who did and did not receive specialized block design training was videotaped and scored by two independent examiners who were unaware which patients had received specialized training. Two samples of eating behavior were videotaped and scored for each patient: one was contiguous with baseline testing and the second corresponded with the time interval of post-testing. Diller et al found that relative to the performance of the control group, the experimental group showed the expected Level II improvement on WAIS Block Design and Object Assembly, Bender-Gestalt, and Motor Impersistence. In addition, the number of organizational maneuvers during eating increased and the number of inappropriate maneuvers and accidents decreased. These findings supported the hypothesis that block design training would improve Level III eating proficiency.

*Activities*

The assumption underlying the use of activities as a means of examining the effectiveness of an intervention is that treatment should have some impact on what the person does. Thus, while skill assessment measures aspects of ability, activity assessment is focused on actual performance. The expectation is that as a consequence of intervention, in conjunction with other mediating variables, the patient will participate in a different array of activities or re-arrange his/her pattern of time usage, e.g., decrease the amount of time sleeping, resting, watching television, or sitting idly, and increase participation in household activities, social interactions, active recreation, work, etc. Time usage is being used with increasing frequency as a measure of effectiveness of intervention with diverse groups of rehabilitation patients, e.g., post-surgical cancer (Gordon et al, 1980), chronic and acute pain (Fordyce, 1978), spinal cord injury (Alexander et al, 1979; Brown, 1982; Norris-Baker et al, 1981) and mental retardation (O'Neill et al, 1981).

With brain-damaged persons few efforts have been implemented to describe the ways in which this group spends its time and how time usage is impacted by impairment. For example, we do not know how much aphasics talk, or how frequently an individual who has suffered a head trauma gets out of the house. Recently, Gordon & Diller (1983) completed a follow-up study of over 30 right brain-damaged stroke victims who had participated in perceptual retraining rehabilitation programs and found:

1. The persons who had experienced a stroke spent approximately 17 hours (or 70% of their time) sleeping, napping, sitting idly and television watching. This is 5 hours more each day spent in such activities than was found in the non-disabled, age-matched comparison group.
2. While both the stroke and non-disabled groups were found to spend 20% of their time in 'quiet recreational activities,' the type of quiet activities differed for each group: the non-disabled group spent more time with hobbies and reading, while the stroke victims were more passive, spending more time watching television.
3. During the average day the stroke group spent less than 2 hours outside of their homes, compared to 6 hours for the non-disabled group.

In another study, Gordon et al (in press) hypothesized that as a consequence of a comprehensive program of visual perceptual retraining, those who received training would read more often and for longer periods of time than those who did not receive the specialized remediation. This hypothesis was not only confirmed, but the differential participation in reading persisted for at least 4 months following the termination of the program and the patient's discharge to their homes. Thus, not only was significant improvement noted on psychometric tests (Level II) but a change in patients' patterns of time usage was associated with the intervention (Level III).

Unfortunately, there have been no studies which have concomitantly examined both skills and activities. Therefore, the relationship between skill and activity change remains an unexplored and potentially fruitful area for empirical investigation.

## CONCLUSION

In concluding this chapter it might be useful to make some specific methodological suggestions to those who are preparing to develop, design, implement, and evaluate cognitive remediation studies:

1. Pre–post changes must be reliably measured, statistically meaningful, and have some impact on the patient's day-to-day functioning.
2. Examination of individual differences is extremely important and is useful in clarifying such issues as who benefits the most and the least from interventions.
3. Subject selection criteria should be carefully established so that homogeneous groups of patients with respect to etiology, time since onset, age, sex, and severity of neurological impairments are studied.
4. Well-specified selection criteria are useful when implementing an experiment because they aid in insuring group equivalence on the dependent variables.
5. The specific relationships between treatment effectiveness and demographic/neurological variables (e.g., time since onset, etiology of brain damage, age, sex, etc.) need to be systematically examined.
6. Accepted clinical syndromes should be challenged and reformulated as new information regarding neuropsychological performance develops. Such reformulation will examine our understanding of the functional organization of the brain.
7. Treatment should be focused on ameliorating deficits that are readily and reliably observed.
8. Treatment should be standardized so that it can be implemented and tested in multiple settings.
9. Multivariate statistical analyses should be adopted to examine the general effects of treatment across many dependent variables and to elucidate relationships among several independent variables and improvement on dependent measures.
10. Clear and well-articulated relationships between what is being treated, the specific intervention program, and the tests that are used to measure program impact need to be defined on an *a priori* basis.
11. The tests that are used to examine the effects of treatment must not only be reliable and valid but must also be ones that elicit a wide range of performance and ones that are well standardized on both brain-damaged and non-brain-damaged samples of people.

## ACKNOWLEDGMENT

The work was supported by Grant No. G008300039 from the National Institute of Handicapped Research, US Department of Education. The author wishes to thank Mary Ruckdeschel-Hibbard, Susan Egelko, Leonard Diller, Margaret Brown, Karen Langer, and Mary Sano for their constructive criticisms of early versions of this manuscript.

## REFERENCES

Adams K 1980a In search of Luria's battery: a false start. Journal of Consulting and Clinical Psychology 48: 511-516

Adams K 1980b An era of innocence for behavioral neurology? Adams replies. Journal of Consulting and Clinical Psychology 48: 522-524

Alexander J L, Willems E P, Halstead L S, Spencer W A 1979 The relationship of functional assessment to evaluation of the quality of outcomes in the rehabilitation process. In: Gremy F, de Dombal F T, Alpernovitch A (eds) Evaluation of the efficacy of medical action. North-Holland, Amsterdam

Ben-Yishay Y, Diller L, Gerstman L, Gordon W A 1970 Relationship between initial competence and ability to profit from cues in brain-damaged individuals. Journal of Abnormal Psychology 75: 248-259

Ben-Yishay Y, Diller L, Mandelberg I, Gordon W A, Gerstman L J 1974 Differences in matching persistence behavior during block design performance between older normal and brain damaged persons: a process analysis. Cortex 10: 121-347

Black F W 1975 Unilateral brain lesions and MMPI performance: a preliminary study. Perceptual and Motor Skills 40: 87-93

Bradley T B 1983 Remediation of cognitive deficits. A critical appraisal of the Feuerstein model. Journal of Mental Deficiency Research 27: 79-92

Brown M 1982 Actual and perceived differences in activity patterns of able-bodied and disabled men. Unpublished doctoral dissertation, New York Univresity, New York

Campbell D T, Stanley J D 1963 Experimental and quasi-experimental design for research. Rand McNally, Chicago

Carson D H, Carson F E, Tikofsky R S 1968 On learning characteristics of the adult aphasic. Cortex 4: 91-112

Cicone M, Wapner W, Gardner H 1980 Sensitivity to emotion expressions and situations in organic patients. Cortex 16: 145-158

Cohen J 1977 Statistical power analysis for the behavioral sciences. Academic Press, New York

Cook J D, Campbell D T 1979 Quasi-experimentation: design and analysis issues for field setting. Rand McNally, New York

De Kosky S, Heilman K, Bowers D, Valenstein E 1980 Recognition and discrimination of emotional faces and pictures. Brain and Language 9: 206-214

Denny-Brown D, Meyers J, Horenstein S 1952 The significance of perceptual rivalry resulting from parietal lesions. Brain 75: 433-471

Diller L, Gordon W A 1981a Interventions for cognitive deficits in brain injured adults. Journal of Consulting and Clinical Psychology 49: 822-834

Diller L, Gordon W A 1981b Rehabilitation and clinical neuropsychology. In: Filskov S, Boll T (eds) Handbook of clinical neuropsychology. Wiley, New York

Diller L, Weinberg J 1977 Hemi-inattention in rehabilitation: The evolution of a rational remediation program. In: Weinstein E, Friedland R (eds) Advances in neurology, 18. Raven, New York

Diller L et al 1974 Studies in cognition and rehabilitation in hemiplegia. IRM Rehabilitation Monograph, New York University, New York

Egelko S 1983a Cognitive sequelae of right cerebrovascular accident: issues of verbal deficit and sex differential patterns in visuospatial and verbal performance. Unpublished doctoral dissertation, Fordham University

Egelko S 1983b Verbal cognitive deficits associated with right cerebrovascular accident. Paper, American Psychological Association, Anaheim, California

Fordyce W 1978 Application of rehabilitation indicators to pain and stroke patients and spouses. Paper, American Psychological Association, Toronto

Gasparrini W, Satz P, Heilman M, Coolidge F 1978 Hemispheric asymmetries of affective processing determined by Minnesota Multiphasic Personality Inventory. Journal of Neurology, Neurosurgery and Psychiatry 41: 470–473

Gianutsos R, Gianutsos J 1979 Rehabilitating the verbal information processing of brain injured patients: a demonstration using single-case methodology. Journal of Clinical Neuropsychology 1: 117–133

Gianutsos R, Glasser D, Elbaum J, Vroman G 1983 Visual imperception in brain-injured adults: multifaceted measures. Archives of Physical Medicine and Rehabilitation 64: 456–461

Glasgow R, Zeiss R, Barrera M Jr, Lewishon P 1977 Case studies on remediating memory deficits in brain damaged individuals. Journal of Clinical Psychology 33: 1049–1054

Golden C J, Hammeke T, Purish A 1980 A manual for the administration and interpretation of the Luria-Nebraska Neuropsychological Battery. Western Psychological Services, Los Angeles

Golden C J, Moses J Jr, Graber B, Berg R 1981 Objective clinical rules for interpreting the Luria-Nebraska Neuropsychological Battery: derivation, effectiveness, and validation. Journal of Consulting and Clinical Psychology 49: 616–618

Gordon W A, Diller L 1983 Stroke: Coping with a cognitive deficit. In: Burish T E, Bradley L A (eds) Coping with chronic disease: research and applications. Academic Press, New York

Gordon W A, Friedenbergs I, Diller L 1980 The efficacy of psychosocial intervention with cancer patients. Journal of Clinical and Consulting Psychology 48: 743–759

Gordon W A, Hibbard M, Diller L, Egelko S, Scotzin M, Lieberman A, Ragnarsson K T 1985 The impact of a comprehensive program of perceptual retraining on right brain damaged stroke patients. Archives of Physical Medicine and Rehabilitation (in press)

Heilman K M, Scholes R, Watson R T 1975 Auditory affect agnosia: disturbed comprehension of affective speech. Journal of Neurology, Neurosurgery and Psychiatry 38: 69–72

Heilman K M, Schwartz H D, Watson R T 1978 Hypoarousal in patients with neglect syndrome and emotional indifference. Neurology 28: 229–232

Hersen M, Barlow D H 1976 Single case experimental designs: strategies for studying behavioral change. Pergamon, New York

Leftoff S 1979 Perceptual retraining in an adult cerebral palsied patient: a case of deficit in cross modal equivalence. Journal of Clinical Neuropsychology 1: 227–241

McGlone J 1977 Sex differences in the cerebral organization of verbal functions in patients with unilateral cerebral lesions. Brain 100: 775–793

McGlone J, Kertesz A 1973 Sex differences in cerebral processing of visuospatial tasks. Cortex 9: 313–320

Norris-Baker C, Stephens M A, Rintala D, Willems, E P 1981 Patient behavior as a predictor of outcomes in spinal cord injury. Archives of Physical Medicine and Rehabilitation 62: 602–608

O'Neill J, Brown M, Gordon W A, Schonhorn R, Grer E 1981 The activity patterns of retarded adults as they move from the institution to the community. Applied Research in Mental Retardatin 2: 367–379

Parsons O A, Prigatano G P 1978 Methodological considerations in clinical neuropsychological research. Journal of Consulting and Clinical Psychology 46: 608–619

Robinson R G, Benson D F 1981 Depression in aphasic patients: frequency, severity, and clinical-pathological correlations. Brain and Language 14: 282–291

Robinson R G, Price T R 1982 Post stroke depressive disorders: a follow up study of 103 patients. Stroke 13: 635–640

Robinson R G, Szetela B S 1981 Mood change following left hemispheric brain injury. Annals of Neurology 9: 447–453

Ross E D 1981 The aprosodias. Archives of Neurology 38: 561–569

Ross E D 1982 The divided self. The Sciences 8–10

Ross E D, Mesulam M 1979 Dominant language functions in the right hemisphere? Archives of Neurology 36: 144–148

Ross E D, Rush J 1981 Diagnosis and neuroanatomical correlates of depression in brain damaged patients. Archives of General Psychiatry 38: 1344–1354

Ruckdeschel-Hibbard M 1984 Affective impairment in right brain damaged individuals. Unpublished doctoral dissertation, New York University, New York

Rusk H A, Block S M, Lowman E W 1969 Rehabilitation of the brain injured patient. In: Walker A E, Caveness W F, Critchley M (eds) The late effects of head injury. C C Thomas, Springfield, Illinois

Sarno M T, Levita E 1971 Natural course of recovery in severe aphasia. Archives of Physical Medicine and Rehabilitation 52: 175–178

Schlanger B B, Schlanger P, Gerstman L 1976 The perception of emotionally toned sentences by right hemisphere-damaged and aphasic subjects. Brain 3: 396–403

Spiers P A 1981 Have they come to praise Luria or to bury him? The Luria–Nebraska Battery controversy. Journal of Consulting and Clinical Psychology 49: 331–341

Taylor M M, Schaefer J N, Blumenthal F S, Grissel J L 1971 Perceptual training in patients with left hemiplegia. Archives of Physical Medicine and Rehabilitation 52: 163–169

Tucker D, Watson R G, Heilman K M 1977 Affective discrimination and evocation in patients with right parietal disease. Neurology 27: 947–950

Twitchell T E 1951 The restoration of motor function following hemiplegia in man. Brain 74: 443–480

Van Buskirk C, Webster D 1955 Prognostic value of sensory defect in rehabilitation of hemiplegics. Neurology 5: 407–411

Weinberg J, Diller L, Gordon W 1977 Visual scanning training effect on reading-related tasks in acquired right brain damage. Archives of Physical Medicine and Rehabilitation 58: 479–486

Weinberg J, Diller L, Gordon W 1979 Training sensory awareness and spatial organization in people with right brain damage. Archives of Physical Medicine and Rehabilitation 60: 491–496

Weinberg J, Piasetsky E, Diller L, Gordon W A 1982 Treating perceptual organization deficits in non-neglecting right brain damage stroke patients. Journal of Clinical Neuropsychology 4: 59–75

Wyke M 1971 The effects of brain lesions on the learning performance of bi-manual coordination task. Cortex 7: 59–72

Zihl J, Von Cramon D 1979 Restitution of visual function in patients with cerebral blindness. Journal of Neurology, Neurosurgery and Psychiatry 42: 312–322

# 7

*Xavier Seron*

# Operant procedures and neuropsychological rehabilitation

Rehabilitation methods based on operant conditioning theory (referred to in this chapter with the generic expression 'behavior modification') were first applied in the field of psychopathology in the 1960s. They have progressively penetrated other areas such as mental retardation, school education, and social deviance. In neuropsychology the direct impact of this therapeutic orientation has been modest. In this chapter I will present the main behavior modification principles and procedures, discuss the limits of this school of thought, and predict the future of this therapeutic orientation.

## GENERAL PRINCIPLES: THE THREE TERMS OF THE OPERANT ANALYSIS

The recent evolution of ideas in behavior modification clearly shows that the conceptual separation is becoming progressively more marked between the practice and the theory of human behavior modification and operant conditioning theory (Fontaine, 1978). Nevertheless, it is still useful to recall some fundamental concepts of the functional analysis of behavior presented years ago by B. F. Skinner. In operant analysis, learned behavior, including learned verbal behavior, is controlled by antecedent events (discriminative stimuli) and consequent events (appetitive and aversive stimuli). By modifying the conditions of occurrence of behavior and its consequences one can affect its frequency and its form. Operant analysis was thus never concerned with units of behavior in isolation, but by the relationships between a unit of behavior (the response), the event that preceded it, and its consequences. A verbal operant is thus a language episode defined by three elements as indicated schematically in Table 7.1.

### The consequent events

Consequent events may influence behavior in two different ways: by increasing the rate or probability of response by positive or negative reinforcement (avoidance or escape) or by decreasing the rate of probability of response by punishment, time-out and extinction.

**Table 7.1** Example of a verbal operant: positive reinforcement

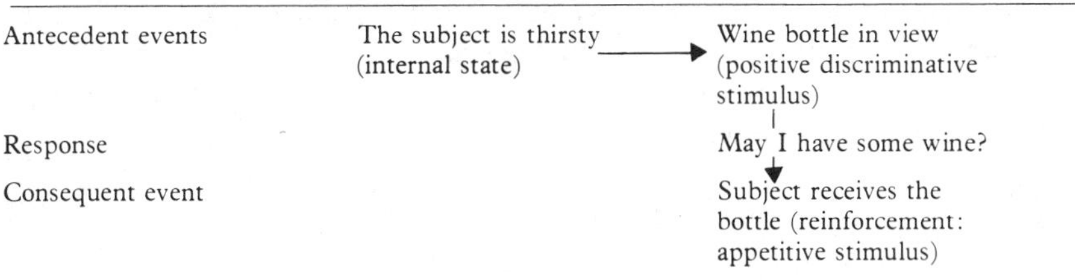

| | | |
|---|---|---|
| Antecedent events | The subject is thirsty (internal state) → | Wine bottle in view (positive discriminative stimulus) |
| Response | | May I have some wine? |
| Consequent event | | Subject receives the bottle (reinforcement: appetitive stimulus) |

Speech therapists frequently present stimuli after the patient has emitted a response, which does not necessarily mean that they 'reinforce' or 'punish.' To be effective (i.e., to modify response frequency occurrence) an event delivered after an act has been performed must obey some rules. One of the more general is that the consequent event must *immediately* follow the response. A delay generally decreases the efficacy of the consequent event, and it is possible that another behavioral unit will appear between the target behavior and the reinforcement and that this intercalary response will therefore be modified instead of the target behavior. Brookshire (1971), for example, has studied the performance of aphasic patients in a probability learning task: he has shown that the aphasics' performance is altered by introducing delays as short as 1 or 2 seconds between responses and reinforcers, although a control group of normal subjects was not affected by such a subtle temporal modification.

In clinical practice, social reinforcers ('Bravo,' 'O.K.,' 'Good,' 'No' and so on) are frequently used, and alimentary or ludic reinforcers ('after an exercise is finished, you may play') are sometimes used with children. The reinforcer may also be the presentation of the correct response, and the correct response may also be presented before the patient's response. This point will be included in the discussion of antecedent events.

One of the most important rules in the presentation of consequent events is that they must be delivered systematically and not at random with no relationship with clearly specified behavioral units. This specificity criterion requires a clear definition of the target behavior.

Positive reinforcement is not encouraging the patient from time to time, during a therapeutic session, but rather is reacting punctually and with precision to a clear preselected behavioral unit. Too often, in non-controlled therapy, a speech therapist will encourage a patient who has just given an inadequate response. Doing so may provoke recurrence of this undesirable response. In the same way, to show disapproval of the fifth erroneous oral repetition will be ineffective, if signs of satisfaction had been manifested for the four preceding repetitions, for then the same response is first positively reinforced and then punished.

Only a few neuropsychological studies have been devoted to the precise influence of different consequent events on learning. For example, Goodkin (1966, 1969) has studied the effect on word and sentence learning by aphasics of consequent events such as verbal reinforcers (approval), token, giving self-reinforcement, auto-punition, or delay of reinforcement. In the same line, Kusher et al (1973) have analyzed the influence of three different punishments in a non-verbal learning task: time-out, response cost, and presentation of an aversive stimilus. The effectiveness of these punishments seems to vary according to the individual subjects.

### The antecedent event

The appearance of a response is not only dependent on its consequence, but these consequences are also expected in some situations. In operant terminology, one speaks of 'stimulus control.' A stimulus (or a pattern of stimuli) the presence of which is associated with a reinforcing consequence is called a positive discriminative stimulus; inversely, a stimulus the presence of which is associated with the absence of reinforcement is called a negative discriminative stimulus.

Let us assume that the objective is to control the logorrheic verbal output of a Wernicke's aphasic. One can, for example, try to induce the patient to segment his utterances. To attain this end, one can decide when one raises one's hand the patient is authorized to speak and is reinforced to do so, but the contrary when one lowers one's hand the patient is urged to be silent. 'When hand is up' is a positive discriminative stimulus, the reinforcement is given; 'When hand is down' is a negative discriminative stimulus, and the reinforcing consequences are suspended.

As noted by La Pointe (1978), therapeutic efforts in neuropsychology have focused on the precise control and manipulation of the antecedent event. Careful selection of prompts and cues may offer the optimal environment for the generation and shaping of the desired responses. The selection and planning of antecedent events will be included in the discussion of therapy administration.

### The target behavior or responses

The main criterion is that the responses to be modified or elicited must be both observable and clearly defined. It is indeed essential to be able to distinguish the target-behavior from other, very similar behavior and to locate its frequency of occurrence and the relevant contexts in which it appears. Depending on the therapy and the program, it is, of course, possible that one is concerned with a class of responses and not with a unique response. In this case it is necessary to be able to place the response unambiguously in the class to which it belongs. This classification must not only be clear, it must also be efficient, i.e., the therapist must be able to react differentially without delay. In one rehabilitation program aimed at training spouses to improve the functional speech of aphasic patients (Diller et al, 1974), different categories of spouse responses were defined. Some examples are:

'*positive feedback,*' words that objectively or subjectively convey that the patient's response was clear or correct (e.g., 'that's right,' 'correct,' 'very good' and so on);

'*negative feedback-objective,*' task-oriented negative feedback (e.g., 'I didn't understand that,' 'You have already said that' and so on);

'*negative feedback-subjective,*' person-oriented negative feedback (e.g., 'Is that all you can say about it?,' 'No good,' 'You should do better than that' and so on).

In such a program the therapist must be trained to immediately identify and categorize the spouse's comments for reinforcement or punishment.

## ELABORATION OF THE THERAPY: PRINCIPLES AND PROCEDURES

### Collection of baseline data

Before designing the therapy, baseline data must first be collected. This consists of establishing and measuring a repertoire of responses as precisely as possible: this level, called the pretherapeutic baseline measurement, becomes the standard against which all progress is measured. The baseline data should not be confused with neuropsychological assessment tests or with functional standardized tests (like the PICA, Porch, 1967; the FCP, Sarno, 1969; or the CDAL, Holland, 1980). The baseline must also include a specific and quantitied examination of responses similar to those included in the training program.

As an example, in their study derived from programmed teaching, Sarno et al (1970) selected patients according to their scores on the FCP. But this functional examination does not constitute the entire baseline measurement, which also includes ten pre-tests specially constructed in function for the particular objectives of re-education (gestural imitation, visual matching, writing, etc.). These pre-tests consist of items selected from the therapeutic programs and cover its range of complexity. After the therapy the baseline measurement test is readministered for the therapy evolution. The elements used in the establishment of a baseline measurement are dependent on objectives of the therapy. In a program dealing with anomia, for example, the pre-therapeutic baseline may be a set of pictures to be named (Seron et al, 1979), and in a program designed to improve communication effectiveness, the pre-therapeutic baseline would be derived from the measurement of different parameters of spontaneous conversation such as verbal fluency, Token Type Ratio, and MLU. A classic requirement for baseline data is stability: to demonstrate the therapeutic effects it is necessary that the pre-therapeutic behavior measurement be stable. Indeed, if there are major performance fluctuations prior to the therapy, what is considered progress may only be a positive oscillation, and what is considered failure may only be a negative oscillation. Take, for example, an aphasic patient who obtains a score of 5 out of 20 on a naming-picture battery. If this score is influenced by fatigue, vigilance level, degree of attention, or an undetermined neurophysiological instability, this patient could well obtain a score of 10 out of 20 on the same battery later on. If this second measurement is not made, one may wrongly consider that a score of 10 out of 20 obtained after the therapy to be a unambiguous indication of this effectiveness (Fig. 7.1).

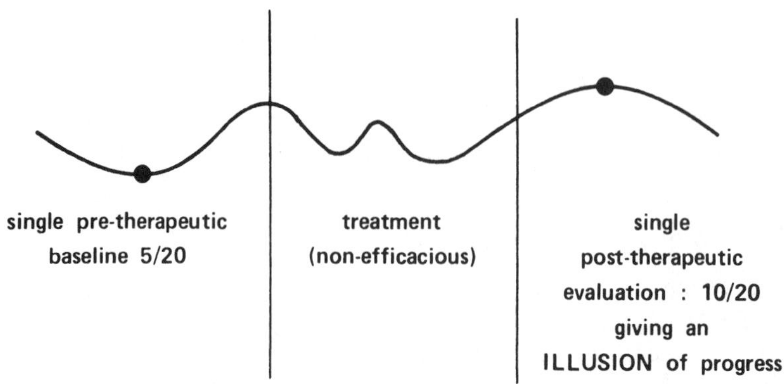


**Fig. 7.1** Level of naming performance.

The establishment of baseline data thus involves controlling the conditions prevailing during behavior measurement (fatigue, motivation, time of the day, etc.) and a repetition of these measurements until the baseline is stable. Of course, a stable baseline is not synonymous with a perfect uniformity in the scores; minor oscillations are acceptable, and the baseline then becomes the mean value of the oscillations. This stability criterion is rarely taken into account in behavioral modification or in other schools of neuropsychological therapy. The baseline may be simple or multiple. It is simple when it concerns exclusively a class of responses to be retaught; it is multiple when it concerns different parts of the behavioral repertoire. The advantages of multiple baseline data are to be found principally in the measurement of transfer learning and the causal analysis of factors at work in the therapy.

*Multiple baseline and transfer learning measurement*

Each time one intends to analyze therapy efficacy in a re-education program, one must ask if this efficacy is restricted to the behavioral units that are part of the program or if one may generalize to other behavior or to other contexts. Various transfer situations have to be examined.

*Transfer of learning to non-trained, identical structural responses* In this case, one determines if the learned performance on a given material can be generalized to cover non-trained material that elicits responses of the same complexity and structure. In two anomia re-education studies, Wiegel-

Crump and Koenigsknecht (1973) and Seron et al (1979) have rehabilitative programs based on a very limited lexicon. For testing the efficacy of the method they developed a double baseline measurement using a list of trained words and a list of non-trained words of equivalent difficulty. At the end of the therapy the two lists (trained and non-trained words) were readministered. The scores acquired on the non-trained words after re-education then indicate if a transfer of learning has occurred (Table 7.2).

*Transfer of learning to different behaviors.* In this case one determines if there is a transfer of learning to behavior other than that trained in the therapy. In most cases there are hypotheses about the existence of common mechanisms underlying the trained behavior and the behavior to which transfer is expected. For example, in a study on the rehabilitation of visual scanning difficulties of hemiplegic patients, Diller et al (1974) analyzed the effect of learning on cancellation tasks that were not used as part of the training and also on tasks considered to be affected by the hemineglect syndrome but that did not require overt scanning behavior (for example, the patient recognizing the midpoint of the back of his body). Absence of transfer suggests functional independence of the two classes of behaviors; existence of transfer suggests the identification of an underlying common mechanism. A multiple baseline may thus be a useful means for testing the specificity of different classes of behavior.

This was, for example, the case in a discussion on the nature of deficits underlying agrammatism in terms of the transfer method used by Kolk (1979), who demonstrated that, after having trained subjects in a story completion paradigm to emit sentences such as *'the lion is able to kill'* where *lion* is the subject of the action no transfer is observed to similar linear word-order sentences such as *'the lion is easy to capture,'* which is syntactically different in that now *'lion'* is the object of the action. Such a result means that the two classes of behavior are functionally independent and that what was learned may not be confused with the surface word-order sequence.

*Transfer to daily-life situations.* The practical utility of therapy may also be questioned. The objective is to determine if training restricted to specified stimuli and responses has an effect on various and not so well-controlled daily-life behavior. Several measurements are possible. For language, there are some functional tests batteries such as the FCP (Sarno, 1969), the PICA (Porch, 1967), and the CADL (Holland, 1980). For other behavior, other scales may be used or constructed by direct or indirect observation in the home or in the care

**Table 7.2** Schematic presentation of transfer of learning to non-trained identical responses

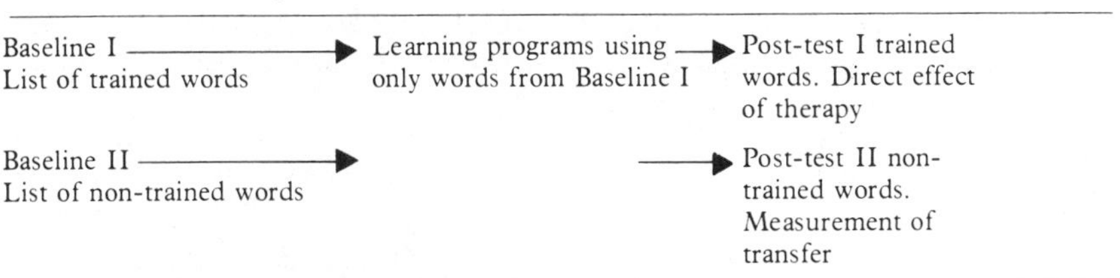

| | | |
|---|---|---|
| Baseline I → List of trained words | Learning programs using only words from Baseline I → | Post-test I trained words. Direct effect of therapy |
| Baseline II → List of non-trained words | → | Post-test II non-trained words. Measurement of transfer |

institution (e.g., the ergo-therapy setting). But, as noted by different authors (e.g., Holland, 1975 and Eisenson, 1981), the question of the relationship between specific therapeutic programs and improvement in daily-life situations is still largely to be documented, and in neuropsychology the measurement of the transfer of learning has most often been restricted to the first two transfer cases cited above.

*Multiple baseline and causal analysis*

Another advantage of the multiple baseline is that it can indicate the extent to which the therapy is the veritable cause of the progress observed without using a reversal procedure. In the classic reversal procedure, therapy is suspended for a period, and if there is an arrest of progress (as shown by an effect plateau when the pre-tests are readministered), one may conclude that the therapy is causing the progress. This effect is most clearly established if, when the therapy recommences, a parallel progress also recommences (this is the ABA paradigm that all therapists should apply when therapy is suspended for holidays). The multiple baseline eliminates the need for total suspension of therapy which can negatively affect the patient's evolution, as only specific treatment programs need be suspended.

Take for example the programming of a course of therapy for a Wernicke's aphasic patient who presents associated deficits such as dyscalculia, left–right confusion, and constructive apraxia. One may elaborate different re-educational programs for verbal activity (reading aloud, phonetic discrimination, syntactic discrimination, verbal memory, and so on) as well as other programs focusing on associated disorders. To each of these different programs corresponds a pre-therapeutic baseline. Instead of managing all the programs at once, one may conduct them in a sequence. During therapy, and at each change of program, the different baselines are readministered to evaluate the specific effects of each program (Table 7.3). If, for example, the performance on the intermediary baselines 1 (e.g., naming) indicates improvement only after the administration of stages 2 and 6 of the therapy, and that during these stages naming behavior has been the specific object of the therapy, then one has been able to demonstrate a specific therapeutic effect without any suspension of the treatment. However, the advantages of such temporal programming must not be exaggerated. Such an approach is logically valid only if there is perfect independence between the different classes of behavior included in the various treatments (cf. supra, the transfer problem) and if what has been learned during a stage has not been sufficient for the patient to establishing a stable strategy he can use to maintain progress without direct treatment. This paradigm is thus not as discriminatory as it might seem at first sight (on the multiple baseline, see also La Pointe, 1977, 1978).

## The therapy

We will limit ourselves here to the discussion of some principles and procedures

**Table 7.3** Succession of treatment with multiple baseline measurement

| Pre-test | Therapy stage 1 | Intermediary measurements | Therapy stage 2 | Intermediary measurements |
|---|---|---|---|---|
| *Different baselines for language* | | | | |
| 1 | Therapy no. 1 | | Therapy no. 1 | |
| 2 | | All pre-tests | discontinued | All pre-tests |
| 3 | No other therapy | readministered | Therapy no. 2 | readministered |
| . | | | No other therapy | |
| . | | | | |
| *n* | | | | |
| *Different baselines for associated disorders* | | | | |
| 1′ | Therapy no. 1′ | | No other therapy | |
| 2′ | No other therapy | All pre-tests | Therapy no. 2′ | All pre-tests |
| 3′ | | readministered | No other therapy | readministered |
| . | | | | |
| . | | | | |
| . | | | | |
| *n*′ | | | | |

specific to the behavioral modification school, without broaching the problem of the therapeutic choices that sustain the logic of the program (selection of the facilitation cues, analysis of the patient's strategies, reconstruction programs versus reorganization programs, and so on).

### *Program progression: the response's criteria*

In behavioral modification, therapy is always concerned with the passing from an initial limited behavioral repertoire to a terminal and more complete behavioral repertoire. In programmed therapy this objective is achieved by passing through stages defined in relation to the hierarchies of the responses to be constructed and with the cues or prompts to be delivered.

The response criterion is the level of response a patient must emit at a step of the program before passing on to the next. These response criteria, of course, vary considerably according to the program and the nature of the task, as indicated in the following examples (Table 7.4).

The use of response criteria has two main advantages: first, it permits continuous appraisal of the progress made by the patient; second, it allows the patient to advance through the program at his own pace. In most cases it is not advantageous to establish too severe criteria, for example, a 100% level of success, as it may retard the re-education, but too lax criteria may result in the failure to build responses that are firm and durable. During the design of the program and its initial applications, one should evaluate and adapt the different criteria of responses. If, for example, a criterion of response at a particular step is too difficult to attain for several patients, the smoothness of the progression at this step in the program may be at fault.

**Table 7.4** Examples of criteria of response

| Response task | Criteria of response |
|---|---|
| Auditory–visual matching of pictures and words | 100% responses on the level of 10, self-correct, or above PICA scoring system (Bollinger & Stout, 1976, criterion step 1) |
| Visual Action Therapy (VAT) program of three levels beginning from tracing to producing pantomimed gestures for absent objects | Nearly 100% success for each step before progressing to the next (Helm-Estabrooks et al., 1982) |
| Melodic intonation therapy | 90% correct responses at each level based on the average of 10 consecutive scores (Sparks & Holland, 1976) |

*Manipulation of antecedents events*

*Prompts and cues.* The use of prompts and cues is, of course, not specific to the behavioral modification approach; most neuropsychological therapies involve facilitation and stimulation procedures. First, it is necessary to select stimuli that facilitate the emission of a response; second, one must manage and organize these stimuli along the program continuum. Selection of antecedent events is one of the most important decisions a therapist must make, but the linkage between fundamental research in neuropsychology and therapeutic practice leaves much to be desired. There are at least two different ways to organize and select the antecedent events: one consists of trying all possible cues in turn and selecting only those having a positive effect; the other is based on the interpretation of the disorders and consists of checking only those cues that are assumed relevant to a theoretical model. The first strategy is currently the most frequently used. Yet, even if it were possible to compile a catalogue of the different cues that have been proposed in the literature for a given disorder, this catalogue would not be exhaustive, and more importantly would not be without contradictions. For example as regards the different variables which seem to influence naming, some authors have observed an influence of the perceptual qualities of the visual referent (Benton et al, 1972; Bisiach, 1966) whereas others have not found such an influence (Hatfield et al, 1977; Corlew & Nation, 1975). The same remark applies to context influence which was reported by Hatfield et al (1977) and Seron et al (1980a) not to have any impact on aphasic naming performance, while the contrary has been observed by Rochford & Williams (1962). Other contradictions exist regarding color influence (Bisiach, 1966; Seron et al, 1980b; Wyke & Holgate, 1973), and it may be that the frequency variable is the only one that always has a positive effect on naming. This lack of consistency may explain why it is difficult to devise homogeneous cuing and prompting methods for such disorders as anomie since this label probably covers several clearly different subjacent disorders. The most economical way to solve this problem is not to try all the imaginable cues one after another (first sound, first letter, first syllable, presentation of a sentence to complete on a non-verbal context, presentation of the word before naming of a semantic associate, presentation of objects, colored pictures, photographs, alternation of words that are easy and difficult to name, and so on). Clearly what we need is more substantive theory on the precise nature of the naming disorders.

The conditions that must be met to clarify this problem will be discussed later.

*Fading.* All therapists agree that the main objective of treatment is to have a patient become as autonomous as possible. Consequently, after having selected efficacious antecedent events, one must provide for the progressive removal of assistance, without of course, a parallel disappearance of the learned behavior. In Luria's terminology this is the passing from external control of the response to internalization or internal control (Luria, 1963). In behavior modification this internal control is instilled by means of a programmed fading of the cues or prompts. The first rule to be respected is that one cannot reduce maximum to less assistance before a given criterion of response has been attained. Several examples of fading are given in the literature; Bollinger & Stout (1976) present progressive fading in a program of verbal designation. Holland (1970) has given examples of fading in her programmed treatment approach. The second rule is, of course, never to pass in a single step from a situation with very effective assistance to a situation without any at all. For example, in a program devoted to articulatory re-education, Dabul & Bollier (1976) propose the presentation of incitations in three steps: the word is first presented segmented in syllables, then in bisyllabic groups, and finally as a whole. Other examples of fading occur in several original forms of therapy, especially in Melodic Intonation Therapy (Sparks & Holland, 1976), in pantomime gesture therapy (Helm-Estabrooks et al, 1982), in therapy for hemineglect (Seron & Tissot, 1973; Diller & Weinberg, 1977) and in therapies inspired by Luria's general approach (Derouesné et al, 1975).

*The response.* In addition to having a clear definition of the responses or the classes of responses to be instilled, it is also important to establish the order in which they are to be elicited. The program here is to establish hierarchies of responses. Such hierarchies are perhaps best developed in the articulatory treatment. All clinicians, for example, realize that it is not wise to start articulatory re-education with fricatives. The literature devoted to the re-education of apraxia of speech contains various articulatory hierarchies that not only take into account different parameters (such as the manner of production, the difference between singletons and clusters, the frequency of occurrence of speech sounds, and sound position in the utterance) but also recommend being sensitive to individual particularities of the patient's difficulties (see for example Rosenbeck, 1978 for English; Lhermitte & Ducarne, 1965 and Lecours & Lhermitte, 1979 for French).

The crucial problem in establishing hierarchies of response is making explicit the underlying logic sustaining its elaboration. This problem is too often neglected in neuropsychological therapy; and one often wonders why this succession of responses is chosen instead of another. Indeed, any definition of hierarchy of responses implies a strict definition of what is simple and what is complex, and a clarification of the criteria used in the definition. Among the best examples of hierarchical programs in neuropsychology are those developed in Melodic Intonation Therapy by Sparks & Holland (1976) and those developed by Diller et al (1974), Bollinger & Stout (1976) and Helm-Estabrooks et al (1982). All these studies present clearly defined and easy-to-follow hierarchies. Finally, it must be added that hierarchies in therapy are not only dependent on the response, but are also defined by the manipulation of the antecedent events.

*The shaping.* The behavior that we hope to reinforce may be not present in its desired final form or may occur so rarely that it would be useless to wait for its appearance in order to apply reinforcement. The solution is to use a shaping process. In this procedure the reinforcement is given after the emission of a response that is in the patient's repertoire and then, in finely graded steps, to responses progressively closer to the desired terminal behavior. In this way one reinforces successive approximations of the final response. Long applied in behavioral modification, and particularly in language therapy with autistic or retarded children (Lovaas et al, 1966), this method is not used extensively in neuropsychology.

Holland (1967) has presented successful applications of the shaping technique. At the beginning of the therapy the patient infrequently emitted a stereotyped verbal response: 'Bah.' First, by differential reinforcement, the therapist provoked an increase in the frequency of this stereotyped verbal emission. Then, when it had become regular, a series of questions was constructed in such a way that the required response resembled the stereotype ('ball,' 'box,' and 'barn'). Then the responses were differentially reinforced until the initial 'bah' response had been transformed to the intended 'ball,' 'box' and 'barn.'

Shaping is not always easy to apply: the successive steps must be sufficiently discrete for the patient to respond to the differential reinforcement (the steps must be not too small or too large), and a great deal is demanded from the clinician since mastering such finely graded progressions may be difficult. In Holland's illustrations the clinician also had to have good auditory discrimination to be able to compare the target with the patient's successive responses. A further limitation of this procedure when applied in isolation is that there must be some relevant responses in the patient's residual repertoire. Generally, therefore, shaping is used in conjunction with prompting and cuing methods.

*Selection and administration of consequent events.* The influence of consequent events (reinforcement, punishment, time out, and so on) has been given relatively little attention in neuropsychology. As pointed out by La Pointe (1978), research has mainly focused on the analysis of the antecedent events and the establishment of response hierarchies. Contrary to some authors (see

Rosenbeck, 1978), however, we think this is a deficiency. Most clinicians underscore the necessity of having recourse to reinforcement, and they generally suggest intermittently presenting social reinforcement during therapy. But this is only a superficial concession and, in the context of apraxia of speech therapy, Rosenbeck reports that the reinforcement is of minor importance in therapy. He suggests following general rules such as avoidance of overt punishment of errors (those responses being best ignored) and adjustment of the level of difficulty in the program in such a way that, after an incorrect response, the patient has a higher possibility of producing a correct one. This non-canonical procedure of reinforcement, called by Rosenbeck the 'good ol' boy' approach, deserves comment.

Although it may be adequate for speech re-education of apraxia of speech, the generalization of such an approach to other pathological contexts seems questionable. In fact it may be important to distinguish the motivational and the cognitive sides of reinforcement. What Rosenbeck clearly assumes is the persistence of an adequate level of motivation. It is in this same line that Brookshire (1978), having shown that too high a percentage of errors seems to reduce the subsequent performance of aphasic patients, suggests designing tasks so that there will be an error rate of no more than 20%. The impact of errors enhances frustration and reduces the patient's motivation to achieve the treatment objectives. The patient is also motivated when confronted with a graph respresenting his actual level of performance. These systems of continuous evaluation (see La Pointe, 1978; Seron et al, 1981) have, of course, a reinforcing value both for the patient and the therapist, when the therapy results evolve positively. But in these cases, the goal is not so much to control the reinforcement of specific behavior but only to maintain motivation.

Nevertheless, in some situations the objective is to shape or maintain specific and well-defined behavior. In these cases differential reinforcement must be delivered precisely and immediately after the desired response has been produced. The reinforcement here is clearly equivalent to 'knowledge of result' as defined by Luria, in that it informs the patient about the quality of his response at a precise step of the program. Such a procedure seems indispensable when the patient is not able to analyze the quality of his response himself; in other words, when the patient is not able to compare his actual production with an internal model of the correct response or with the correct response presented by the therapist. When a patient is not capable of self-evaluation, the presentation of differential reinforcement creates external feedback and thus helps the patient to analyze his errors.

In summary, it is thus necessary to distinguish the motivational and the informative elements of the reinforcement process. In neuropsychological therapy the motivational level is generally insisted on in situations where the patient has some degree of nosognosia; here correct responses are probably self-reinforcing, and progress in therapy is *per se* reinforcing. Yet nosognosia is not always the rule, and the relationship between the level and quality of nosognosia, on the one hand, and the selection and amount of reinforcement, on the other, will have to be clarified (on the role of nosognosia see Wepman, 1958, and on self-correction Farmer, 1977).

## SUMMARY OF THE MAJOR APPLICATION OF BEHAVIOR MODIFICATION IN NEUROPSYCHOLOGY

The influence of behavior modification on neuropsychology includes several aspects. Here I will discuss (1) works devoted to general verbal and non-verbal learning capacities, (2) therapies of language disorders based on programmed learning or on a more functional approach, (3) special therapies: the Premack language and MIT, (4) therapies for other neuropsychological disorders, and (5) extension of some behavioral modification principles to other types of therapy.

### Works on verbal and non-verbal learning

The initial penetration of the psychology of learning into the treatment of aphasia was not directly concerned with therapy, but with more general problems: the evaluation of aphasics' learning capacities and the analysis of their sensitivity to manipulation of reinforcement. Frequently, the tasks devised were non-verbal and visual (Filby & Edwards, 1963; Tikofsky & Reynolds, 1962, 1963; Rosenberg & Edwards, 1964, 1965; Rosenberg, 1965; Brookshire, 1968, 1969, 1971). In these studies the variables such as the nature of the stimuli, the type of reinforcement, the delay between response and reinforcement and the reinforcement contingencies (reversal, or in probability learning, change in reinforcement ratio), were systematically manipulated in order to study their effect on the course of learning. The major significance of these studies is that they demonstrate that learning is possible by most aphasics, even severe cases, and that the aphasic's responses are not arbitrary, but, on the contrary, show a clear sensitivity to modifications or reinforcement contingencies. As Brookshire (1968) rightly pointed out 'the differences observed were not a simple division of subjects into learners and non-learners, but were differences arising from strategies with which subjects attempted to solve the problem presented to them.' But, if important conclusions can be drawn from these studies concerning the management of remedial procedures from a learning point of view, they remain disappointing in that they offer no explanation of the origin of interindividual variability regularly seen in aphasics' learning performance. One can presume that this variability is partially a function of pathological variables such as the type and severity of aphasia and the presence of associated disorders or of psychobiological variables such as sex, age and previous sociocultural level. But, and this may be more important, what is lacking in these pioneering studies is a specific analysis of the coding processes implied in the various learning tasks. For example, in some of the so-called non-verbal learning tasks, there could well be verbal coding of the stimulus. Finally, the question of what conclusions can be drawn from performance in non-verbal learning tasks to performance in language rehabilitation has yet to be dealt with directly.

These shortcomings no doubt explain why so little attention has been paid to these studies in the literature on remedial therapy. Nevertheless, their results should not be disregarded since, as Brookshire (1978) has clearly shown, an accurate analysis of the behavior exhibited in these learning tasks may well be relevant to the design of procedural details in verbal restoration programs.

## Language therapies

### *The programmed teaching approaches*

One can make a distinction here between the first multi-dimensional projects like those of Sarno et al (1970), and Holland (1970) with Holland & Harris (1968) and the more restricted applications of programmed teaching instructions. Sarno and Holland took into account the general principles of programmed teaching: progression by small steps and immediate correction of errors. Sarno's work concerned the verbal behavior of a group of global aphasics (oral and written code, expression, and reception); Holland examined verbal behavior in single case studies. Sarno's therapy for global aphasics was not successful. Holland's results were better, but no systematic comparison with other therapeutic approaches has been made and her cases were generally far less severe than Sarno's. In Holland's therapy the programs were regularly adapted to the progress made by the patient and to his remaining disorders, and the exercise content was selected according to the patient's fields of interest. When programs are so individualized – when they are tailor-made, so to speak – one would expect that it would be difficult to apply them to other patients.

Another problem raised by these studies is precisely what patients learn in these programmed situations. As has been noted elsewhere (Seron et al, 1978), the significance of machine–patient or book–patient interaction for functional verbal behavior is far from clear. These programmed situations are generally not representative of natural conversation, and the reinforcement is generally given in function of the structural adequacy of the responses and not their communicative value. In daily-life situations formal reinforcements (i.e., centered on the quality of the responses) are not the most frequent. Furthermore, the rigid application of a program seems to violate a well-known but less well-documented clinical phenomenon: the irregularity curve of progress in neuropsychological recovery and rehabilitation (Martin, 1977). I will return to these criticisms at the end of this chapter.

In addition to these multi-dimensional approaches, several learning programs have been elaborated with more limited objectives. For writing therapy, programs using automated registration of responses and direct correction of errors have been devised by Pizzamiglio & Roberts (1967) and by Seron et al (1980), who use microcomputer technology. Smith (1974) applied an operant conditioning procedure with two aphasic patients and taught them to use prepositions for expressing spatial relationships. Keenan (1966) developed a program for eliciting spoken and written naming behavior by using visual and auditory stimuli on cards specially constructed for the Language Master System. Holland & Levy (1971) used a programmed instruction procedure to train aphasic patients to use active sentences; these authors observed no clear generalization either to negative and passive sentences or to lexically modified active sentences. Naeser (1974) also used a programmed instruction method to train aphasic patients to produce three basic declarative sentences types (Type I, the verb to be; Type II, a transitive verb; Type III, an intransitive verb). They observed discrete improvement of the basic trained sentences and some generalization to non-trained sentences of the same type. Recently, Helm-Estabrook et al (1981) devised a program for agrammatic patients by using a story completion technique (from the Gleason and Goodglass Story Comprehension test), but there seems to be little transfer of learning to non-drilled sentences. Programmed therapies have been developed to cover virtually all aspects of aphasic disorders, for example, comprehension (Culton & Ferguson, 1979; Flowers & Danforth, 1979), syntax (Holland & Levy, 1971; Naeser, 1974; Wiegel-Crump, 1976; Helm-Estabrooks et al, 1981) and naming (Taylor & Marks, 1959; Keenan, 1966). This list is, of course, far from exhaustive. These more restricted content programs cannot be criticized for not being representative of daily-life situations since they focus on very defined behavior which cannot be easily identified in more natural situations. Such programs may be used profitably as a part of a larger therapeutic program.

### *Functional operant approaches*

In these approaches the artificial character of the more or less automated programmed learning therapies is avoided. The behavioral modification principles are implemented in more natural conversational situations. From a theoretical point of view the functional therapies are more directly linked with Skinner's analysis of the verbal operant in that speech acts (the so-called 'verbal operant') are considered as a function of dependent and independent variables in an environment that includes a speaker and an audience. In such a functional approach the goal is to identify the variables in conversational settings that positively influence the verbal behavior (or the communicative behavior in general) of a patient and to structure favorable eliciting and reinforcing situations. Goodkin (1966, 1969) has applied conditioning principles during oral sessions in which patients respond to structural questions, the objectives being to increase the frequency of understandable words and phrases and to decrease the amount of unintelligible utterances and perservations. Two single case studies with fairly good results were published.

Bloom (1962) and Holland (1970) have also applied operant procedures to group therapy. According to Bloom, the aim of group therapy is to recreate and to structure everyday situations which elicit routine, frequently used forms of speech (for example: greeting behavior, yes/no questions, use of the words 'up' and 'down' in an elevator, and so on). The reinforcements, usually present in natural conversation, were used. In the same line, Diller et al (1974) developed an operant therapy approach with special attention given to the patient's spouse. Their purpose was to teach the spouse to train the patient to improve his or her functional speech. In this unique program the spouse–patient conversational exchanges at home and in more controlled laboratory situations were first subjected to functional analyses. The objectives were then defined and the spouse was given a short introduction to behavioral modification concepts and principles. During the therapy the spouse was trained through earphones to improve his or her communicational feedback in conversation. Curiously enough, the functional therapies which are the most clearly operant in the Skinnerian tradition have not been developed further within the behavioral modification school, and, the most popular communication therapies are being developed in other theoretical contexts (Davis, 1983), often referred to as the pragmatic approaches [see the role-playing technique of Schlanger & Schlanger (1970) and especially the promising PACE method of Davis & Wilcox (1981)].

## Particular therapies: Premack's artificial language and MIT

The work of Glass et al (1973) on training aphasic patients to learn an artificial visual language and the Melodic Intonation Therapy elaborated by Sparks and his colleagues (Albert et al, 1973: Sparks et al, 1974; Sparks & Holland, 1976) merit special attention here because these authors have introduced very original approaches into the repertoire of training methods in aphasiology therapy. The methods are also finely elaborated and have had an impact on numerous subsequent therapeutic designs.

Glass et al (1973) applied the training method developed with chimpanzees by Premack to seven global aphasics who had had a cerebral vascular accident. The uniqueness of the Premack's technique is that, instead of trying to reinstall language on an auditory–phonatory basis, it uses the visual mode and teaches an artificial language based on arbitrary forms cut out of colored cardboard. In their study the experimental program was preceded by a detailed examination of some of the cognitive and linguistic abilities of the patients. The test required making syntactic classifications such as word/non-word distinctions, singular/plural distinctions, sentence constructions and some semantic classifications. While all the patients were severely impaired in the areas of sentence construction, identification of grammatical structures and syntactic classification, they did have some preserved knowledge of word/non-word distinctions and semantic classifications (e.g., animate or inanimate, fruits, vegetables). The actual procedure began with a pre-test to assess the patient's ability to match objects. The errorless procedure began with the distinction between 'same' and 'different' words and the interrogation sign then progressed to gradual expansion of the vocabulary (nouns, verbs, and personal names) and simple sentence constructions (S–V and S–V–O). Although the patients achieved different levels of proficiency, all made some progress in using the code. This is noteworthy since programmed instructions using verbal material have proven inefficient with similar patients (Sarno et al, 1970). Moreover, this program has obvious advantages: the material is chosen according to the patient's interests and the procedure is errorless, but if, nevertheless, a patient does err, the therapist returns to a previous stage. Finally, from a functional point of view the training sessions are structured to resemble natural conversational exchanges in that they are cast in the question/answer, alternating dialogue form.

This approach does have some limits and has been criticized. Some wonder whether acquisition of such an artificial language is useful in that anyone else who wishes to communicate with the patient must also learn this abstract code. To some extent, Gardner et al (1976) answered this question by developing a more usable visual communication system with representational (ideographic) forms in addition to arbitrary geometric forms. This more pictorial code has been used at home by a patient with his family.

But the main point here is that the pioneer work of Glass et al (1973) has demonstrated that global aphasics retain a conceptual system and thus that their cognitive impairment did not necessarily parallel their language impairment. The fact that some of the cognitive processes involved in natural language may be at least partially intact is now at the origin of various other attempts to teach non-verbal language, either as a substitute for language or as a means to re-establish access to language in global aphasics (Visual Action Therapy: Helm-Estabrooks et al, 1982; Bliss: Ross, 1979; Amerind: Skelly et al, 1974; for a review of the literature on alternative and augmentative system communication in aphasia see Disimoni, 1981).

Melodic Intonation Therapy is one of the most spectacular therapies that has been successfully applied with non-fluent aphasics in recent years. At the origin of the therapy is a frequently observed clinical phenomenon: non-fluent aphasics are regularly able to sing or to recite some well-known prayers better than to speak. But methods using group singing have had only discrete effects on propositional speech and thus have gradually been discarded. The originality of the study by Albert et al (1973) is its use of another form of singing, the accentuation of the natural North American sentence intonation contour. The melodic intonation is thus not a song but rather a modification of the three basic elements of spoken prosody: the melodic line, the tempo and rhythm, and the point of stress (Sparks, 1981). The therapy presumes that the intact hemisphere plays a dominant role in melodic production and in the discrimination of intonational contour (Blumstein & Cooper, 1974) and that a functional language can be developed in association with rhythm and melody accompaniment. Sparks et al (1974) described the results obtained with nine patients selected according to precise criteria, mainly good auditory comprehension, marked paucity of verbal output and normal emotional stability.

In MIT the material consists of phrases and sentences selected according to their functional value (frequency of occurrence in daily-life situations) and in reference to the patient's personal occupations. The program is carefully organized along a clearly specified hierarchy of four levels, each level containing several steps. Progression in the program is controlled by precise response criteria and when the patient errs different backups are provided. The first level is non-linguistic, the patient being taught to hum melodies and to hand-tap various rhythm–tempo–stress patterns. At level two linguistic material is incorported in the melodic patterns in four steps of increasing complexity by which the patient learns to repeat and to answer questions. At the third level the complexity of the tasks is increased progressively by the introduction of a delay between the clinician's and the patient's productions in repetition exercises and by gradual fading of the clinician's role. The fourth level is intended to provide return to normal speech prosody by means of the Sprechtgesang techniques and by introducing longer delays.

The MIT is certainly one of the most carefully elaborated methods of re-education in neuropsychology. Its application is spreading in European countries where some adaptations have been proposed (for a French version see Van Eeckhout et al, 1982 and Chapter 20 in this book). There are still some problems with MIT, however, notably with regard to the respective influence of the various components of the method: accentuation of the prosodic line, lengthening of the tempo, exaggeration of rhythm, and stress or arm-movements participation. Finally it is not yet established why MIT works. In addition to explanations in terms of a right hemispheric participation, it could be that the chief reason for its efficacy is that, in focusing the patient on melody, attention is shifted away from the control of the patient's articulatory apparatus. A number of attempts have been made to transfer the learning to natural situations. In France (Van Eeckhout et al, 1982) the family of the patient was present during the session so that the spouse could continue the exercises at home, and in the USA Goldfarb and Bader (1979) present an adaptation of MIT specifically designed for training the spouse to teach the patient at home to emit in context 52 simple questions relevant to daily life situations. All in all, MIT seems to be a very promising therapeutic method. Sparks (1981) has clearly delineated the characteristics of the aphasics considered as good candidates, but extension of these criteria along with specific modifications of the standard method is possible, as Van Eeckhout et al (1982) and Sparks himself (1981) have suggested.

## Therapy of other neuropsychological disorders

Behavior modification has also been applied to praxic, attentional, mnemonic, emotional, and other neuropsychological disorders. But publications in these fields are less numerous than for linguistic disorders and, with the notable exception of the work done by Diller's team in New York, they generally lack a good theoretical foundation. I would note, however, that this neglect in the field of non-verbal disorders is not specific to behavioral modification approaches, but is a general deficiency of the neuropsychological therapy. Certainly Luria's school in the Soviet Union is a notable exception.

The work being done at the Institute of Rehabilitation Medicine at New York is so varied that it cannot be exhaustively presented here, but perhaps the most important therapeutical projects are those concerning the rehabilitation of attentional disorders and the hemineglect syndrome in right and left hemiplegic traumatic patients (Diller et al, 1974). In both cases a classical behavioral modification approach is followed: functional analysis of the disorders, compilation of baseline measurements, elaboration of the re-education procedure, programming of the therapy, immediate and delayed post-test measurement, and evaluation of transfer of learning to similar and non-similar tasks. For attentional behavior, Ben-Yishay et al (1980) present a complete therapeutic program composed of five learning tasks of presumed increasing complexity which they call the Orientation Remedial Module. The five tasks are a conditioned reaction-time task in which the subjects are trained to react accurately to a visual stimulus, a reaction-time that involves the anticipations of the trajectory of a moving target, a rhythm-synchronization task that requires synchronization of external patterned stimuli and the subjects' motor responses, a task requiring continuous linear visual scanning and visual discrimination, and finally a time-estimation task. These tasks are intended to train different attentional processes: optimal wakefulness, anticipation, focusing attention, persistence of concentration, and synchronization to external stimuli. Single-case studies are presented, and the whole program seems efficacious. After having succeeded in such a program, patients are able to follow other more specific therapeutic programs.

The other main project of Diller and his co-workers focuses on the hemineglect syndrome (Diller et al, 1974; Diller & Weinberg, 1977). As observed by these authors, presence of hemineglect syndrome has a negative impact upon motor re-education, and left or right hemiplegic patients who made errors or were slow in visual cancellation tasks were in danger of having accidents in a rehabilitation setting or in daily-life situations (Weinberg & Diller, 1968; Diller & Weinberg, 1970). With the hypothesis that the major causes of attentional deficits in hemiplegic patients are related to difficulties in visual scanning, Diller et al conducted a series of studies to analyze the characteristics of the visual scanning in function of hemiplegic groups, the kinds of stimuli, and the ongoing tasks. Then, on the basis of the results gathered from these preliminary investigations, they developed a rehabilitation program to improve scanning behavior in hemiplegics. The training tasks contain: (1) scanning or cancellation tasks with an anchor assistance in different conditions (slowing down performance, overt verbalization of all stimuli while performing, silent and covert verbalization), (2) looking at the target which moves at different speeds on a scanning apparatus, and (3) searching for a light stimulus located on a panel in front of the patient. Fifteen left hemiplegic patients with cancelling disorders of varying gravity underwent this program, and their results were compared to those of a control group of comparable left hemiplegics. The results show an improvement of the left hemiplegic group relative to the controls, the effect being more marked for the most impaired patients. Positive effects of training were also observed in an occupational therapy setting and with scanning tasks not directly trained such as mid-point personal body identification.

Other therapeutical programs also deserve mention. Derouesné et al (1975) present a rehabilitation program devised for frontal lesion patients. The orientation of the therapy is based on Luria's analysis of frontal lobe disorders. The tasks were the Raven's PM 38, Kohs' block design, and a visuospatial logic problem. The program consisted of sequencing goal-oriented actions beginning with very constraining and detailed verbal instructions that progressively faded during therapy. Post-tests on the trained material indicated a clear improvement of performance for the two single cases examined, but there was little transfer to other situations. The block design task has also been used by Ben-Yishay et al (1978) with left and right traumatic hemiplegic patients. The program contains a finely graded cuing procedure of nine steps ranging from verbal instructions only to visuographic–motoric assistance. The cuing procedure is saturated in that it begins from the most articulated and structured conditions and proceeds to the standard unaided condition. Groups of right and left hemiplegic patients were able to learn to make the block design. Clear transfer of learning was observed for similar alternative block design forms and some carry-over was also observed in other tasks such as the WAIS object assembly subtest, occupational therapy, and eating behavior (for left hemiplegics only). Seron et al (1981) and Bruyer (1981) use more or less direct behavioral modification principles on verbal and visual memory disorders in a clinical setting and with a functional perspective (but see also Jaffe & Katz, 1976 and Lewinsohn et al, 1977).

## Extension of some behavior principles and procedures to other types of therapy

The influence of behavior modification in neuropsychology must not be restricted to the studies presenting all the distinctiveness criteria that justify the label of pure 'operant-programmed therapy' and whose main distinctive traits are probably precise and functional measurement of baseline behavior, selective use of reinforcement, definition of objectives in behavioral terms and careful programming of training. The influence of the behavioral modification school must be appreciated in a more diffuse and tolerant way. With this non-restrictive or academic approach it seems evident that the influence of behavior modification in neuropsychology is becoming considerably more important. Currently, most research in neuropsychology uses some behavioral modification principles or procedures. In fact, influence of the pioneer work of Brookshire, Sarno, Holland, Goodkin, and Diller has been such that many behavioral modification principles have lost their specificity and are now simply considered basic scientific conditions for constructing and demonstrating the efficacy of any kind of therapeutic enterprise. This evolution is due to the fact that, although the behavioral modification principles and procedures constitute a coherent ensemble, they may be dissociated so that one may borrow some of them without paying much heed to the others. It is, indeed, perfectly possible to disregard the utility of establishing precisely the type, amount, or schedule of reinforcement in therapy and still use measurement baseline procedures or conduct therapy without *a priori* programming of exercises and still introduce during the treatment a reversal ABA paradigm in order to evaluate the efficacy of the therapy. This difficulty of establishing clear boundaries is manifest in my review of literature, and some authors may well be astonished to find them here and surely some would think I have gone too far in placing them in the behavioral modification school. But as is almost standard in the history of the psychological sciences, schools evolve and limits are permeable. One of the most significant things that behavior modification has done is certainly sharing with the other schools some of its central virtues; particularly, its rigorus control of therapy efficacy and its analysis of the factors responsible for the changes that occur in therapy. With this in mind I will now attempt to chart the future of behavior modification in neuropsychology.

## CRITICAL COMMENTS: THE FUTURE OF BEHAVIOR MODIFICATION IN NEUROPSYCHOLOGY

Many of the theoretical problems discussed here are far from being specific to the behavioral modification school in that they can be applied to all the other rehabilitative approaches.

### Behavior re-establishment or behavior reorganization

In most of the critical reviews devoted to the logic of re-education strategies, an opposition is frequently advanced between those for whom the disturbances are conceived as a 'loss of function' and those for whom it reflects rather a difficulty of access to knowledge still stored in the central nervous system (Martin, 1977; Sarno, 1981; Seron, 1982; Albert et al, 1981). Furthermore, as rightly observed by Sarno (1981), a link has generally existed between, on the one hand, the pedagogical approach and the 'loss theory' and, on the other hand, the 'stimulation–facilitation' approaches and the 'impaired-access theory.' Although such a division is probably too large and we are clearly not obliged to choose between the two approaches as though one were true and the other false (Seron & Laterre, 1982), it must be emphasized that on the theoretical level there is no necessary linkage between behavior modification and one of these two approaches to the exclusion of the other. Yet, at first sight, behavior modification seems closer to the re-establishment strategy in that the therapy begins with an analysis of the overt behavior repertoire and moves through small steps to a terminal, more complete behavior repertoire. Historically, for the most part, behavior modification interventions have been reconstructive in nature. But, as pointed out by La Pointe (1978) and more recently by Duffy (1981), the so-called stimulation–facilitation therapies can easily support a marriage with behavior modification, as has been clearly demonstrated by empirical evidence from the 'Base-10 Programmed Stimulation' of La Pointe (1977) and in the 'Response-Contingent Small-Step Treatment' of Bollinger & Stout (1976). This could be extended without major difficulty to Luria's school (Derouesné et al, 1975), to the cognitive strategies, and to the socio-therapeutic approach. In fact, the behavioral modification school as far as re-education strategies are concerned is, in a way, neutral. Yet in my opinion, whatever the strategy adopted, something has to be learned in re-education, and the difference between schools concerns the means used in this goal and what precisely is being taught to the patients. In the case of the loss theory, what has to be learned may be defined as a set of behavior similar to that existing prior to the lesion; in the impaired access theory, the insistence is on relearning some privileged S–R relationships; in reorganizing strategies (closer to Luria's school and information processing theory) the goal of learning may be defined as teaching the patient to use some specific mental processes in order to effect reorganization of the sub-processes sustaining an appropriate but different overt behavior. But it remains evident in each case that the patient learns something; and the behavioral modification methodology may be equally useful to construct a specified behavior sample in a reconstructive spirit, to elaborate fine-graded steps of cuing or prompting in a facilitation approach, to implement non-habitual or new mental processes in a reorganizational approach through external helps, and to guarantee that they become progressively internalized. My first conclusion is thus that behavior modification, whatever its historical roots, is not logically bound to any particular school of therapy in neuropsychology.

## The programming dilemma

The well-graded and clearly defined character of the different steps of the programmed teaching involved in behavior modification is frequently stressed. The advantages of such programming are numerous; in programmed re-education one knows exactly what to do, in what order, and at what rhythm, and, in the learning interpretation of re-education, one controls the difficulty level of the response in a continuous and finely graded manner. But some therapists are opposed to such a point of view, which they declare too rigid and invalid. Generally it is argued that aphasic recovery never seems to follow a regular curve of progress as expected in a learning reconstruction perspective and that such a rigid organization cannot take into account the fluctuations of patient performance. Even in the behavioral modification school, Holland (1970) remarks

> programmed instructions is neither an excuse for relinquishing clinical responsibility nor a panacea for the many problems inherent in adequate clinical treatment of aphasia: but it does have a place, perhaps even a considerable place, in the clinician's repertoire of skills.

These oppositions or nuances deserve attention, and two things at least must be said. First, as concerns fluctuations of performance, if it is true that clinicians are generally not confronted in re-education with regular and smooth learning curves and that the patient's performance is frequently variable with sudden periods of progress followed by slow-downs, one still cannot conclude that no learning processes are involved in re-education. There are other, equally legitimate explanations of fluctuations in performances: they may be caused by modification of neurophysiological variables, by the development of covert learning processes, or by sudden changes in the patient's motivation. It may even be that what has been learned by the patient was not precisely what the therapist put in his program progression. Furthermore, for a large part, fluctuations of performance are taken into account in programs by the criteria of response, which can play a regulatory role, and thus the variability of patient performance is not necessarily violated in behavioral modification methodology. But as noted above, each time the progress made by a patient does not follow the progressions proposed by the therapist, the question of the psychological relevance of the plan must be raised. As has been discussed elsewhere in more detail (Seron & Laterre, 1982; Seron, 1982), three different hierarchies are regularly advanced but none of them seems sufficiently demonstrated from a theoretical point of view. They are the developmental hierarchy (see for example Crystal et al, 1976 or Lecours & Lhermitte, 1979, for the treatment of agrammatism), the structural hierarchies based on the supposed complexity of overt behavior (see for example, Corbin, 1951; Dabul & Bollier, 1976, in the treatment of expressive speech, or Naeser, 1974 for aggrammatism), and the neuropsychological hierarchies based on the observation of spontaneous recovery (see Lecours & Lhermitte, 1979; Sarno & Levita, 1971, 1981). But all of these hierarchies have their shortcomings. Neuropsychological disorders are generally not of a regressive nature and thus developmental hierarchies must be questioned, and structural hierarchies may be without any significance in that they confuse the complexity of the topography of overt behavior with the complexity of the mental subprocesses sustaining it. Finally, with some exceptions (Peuser & Temp, 1981; Sarno & Levita, 1981) spontaneous recovery has, as yet, only been described at a phenomenological level without sufficient analysis of the mental processes responsible for the reappearance of some normal overt behavior. Therefore, one of the most important problems facing behavioral modification approaches is the explicit justification of the logic of the progression implemented in a program. Of course, the establishment of hierarchies on the basis of a precise understanding of the nature of the disorders is dependent on the general progress of fundamental research in neuropsychology.

## Bottom-up or top-down strategies

Another divergence in neuropsychological therapy has emerged between re-educative strategies focused on modality-specific, well-delineated disorders (the so-called 'direct approach' of Wepman, 1972) and the emphasis on more general cognitive and communicative processes. This debate is the most vehement in the aphasia field, but it is also carried on in the other neuropsychological disorders. In aphasia therapy the discussion is frequently cast in terms of all-or-nothing, as though it were obligatory to choose between the psycholinguistic-modality approach or the pragmatic-contextual one. The elements of the debate are numerous, but they may be summarized as follows: opponents to the specific approach to the disorders underline the frequent absence of carryover effects, the unrealistic character of the therapies, and the regular motivational difficulties encountered with such artificial activities. Nevertheless, the supporters of the pragmatic approaches have been unable to present a substantial body of significant results, and the only positive data available have been published recently (Holland, 1978; Diller et al, 1974 and Davis & Wilcox, 1981). The opponents of the pragmatic approaches argue that it is far more complicated to analyze precisely what changes occur in complex natural settings and to define the variables responsible for the observed changes. In fact, the relative effectivenesses of the two approaches are difficult to compare because therapists generally evaluate the progress they obtain by means of scoring systems designed to fit their objectives. In the pragmatic approaches, functional tests of communicative abilities are generally used, like the FCP, the PICA, the CADL or other scales of social adjustment, self-evaluation, and so on; in the modality-specific approaches, progress is evaluated by using tests measuring the specific trained verbal behavior. The validations are thus in some ways circular, making comparison difficult. Therefore, considering only the question of the relative efficacy of the two approaches, it seems premature to conclude that we lack sufficiently numerous and clear empirical validations. Although this debate is to a large extent external to the behavioral modification methodology, it is of crucial importance for neuropsychological therapy in general and deserves comment here. As pointed out by Muma & McNeill (1981), both rehabilitation strategies have their origin in theoretical models of language behavior and in the level on which one tries to comprehend the aphasic disorder. The psycholinguistic-modality approach is bounded by linguistically oriented models of language distinguishing lexical, syntactic, and phonological components and their corresponding cognitive processes, whereas pragmatic-oriented therapies are closer to models that consider verbal activity in a larger psychological framework and include the cognitive processes sustaining the communicatory functions of language.

These theoretical relationships may be dangerous in that the question of the level to be chosen for interpreting the aphasic disorder should not necessarily be equated with that of the most efficient strategy for treating those disorders. This relative dissociation I propose explains why, although I think there is currently more evidence in favor of the thesis that the aphasia is principally a disorder situated on the level of the grammatical and the lexical components of the verbal activity, the logical consequence from this is not the neglect of pragmatic approaches in re-education. Indeed as Feyereisen (in press) recently pointed out, there is no clear evidence that aphasic disorders may be more adequately explained in a pragmatic framework. On the contrary, Feyereisen goes on to note, most of the studies at our disposal indicate better preservation of the pragmatic components than of what Bates et al (1983) have modestly labeled more 'conversationally neutral' levels, i.e., the grammatical and lexical components. This is shown in several studies on the receptive level. Wilcox et al (1978) have indicated better comprehension of indirect requests presented in natural communication settings than utterances presented in standard test situations. In the same vein, Stachowiak et al (1977), and Waller & Darley (1978) have shown that aphasics understand utterances better when they are given in linguistic contexts than would be predicted by their scores on the Token test. The same applies on the productive level. Ulatowska et al (1981 and 1983) discovered only quantitative differences between normals and aphasics on the level of discourse structure production, and Bates et al (1983) observed no clear evidence of a pragmatic deficiency in Wernicke's and Broca's aphasics in a study focused on the pragmatic distinction between given and new information. For non-verbal communication, while the data at our disposal are still too limited to be certain (Feyereisen & Seron, 1982a,b), I would share the general position of Davis & Wilcox (1981) that if the ability of aphasic patients to comprehend and produce emotional and pantomimic messages is generally inferior to that of control subjects, it is still better than their linguistic capacities.

Although such evidence is far from being conclusive, it may be suggested that a kind of dissociation exists in aphasia that may be defined in terms of a pragmatic/linguistic distinction: the higher pragmatic components being better preserved than the linguistic ones (dynamic aphasia and jargon-aphasia in the acute state could well constitute exceptions to this point of view, but the studies on the pragmatic/linguistic dimension are too frequently restricted to selected cases of Broca's aphasia and testable Wernicke's aphasia). If such an interpretation is correct, what is the justification for designing therapies situated on a non-relevant level? In other words, what is the sense of training the communicational abilities that are not primarily disturbed on this level? The main answer for doing so is that most aphasic patients have to discover that their language disorders may not be equated with their communicational abilities, and that they can improve their abilties to communicate more than they think they can. The pragmatic communication orientation can also assist the patients to reorganize the means they use to convey messages by modeling, and to develop more adequate strategies, notably by having recourse to different, more efficient communicational channels. Moreover, if we presume the existence of dissociation in aphasic conditions between the pragmatic and the linguistic components of language, such a dissociation is surely only relative and one still has to explore the interactions existing between the different levels. Then, too, the possibility that training communication efficiency has a secondary influence on the linguistic adequacy of the verbal channel must not be disregarded. Such a position has the important advantage of rejecting the pseudo-conflict between the two approaches sometimes put forward in rehabilitation literature. In our opinion aphasia therapy must be conducted in a complementary fashion on the grammatical and lexical levels where the specific disorders can be identified in trying to reorganize their corresponding cognitive processes, as well as on the pragmatic level, to induce the patient to reorganize his communicational exchanges with his social partners and to assume that what has been acquired on the lower specific levels will be used for communication ends.

Nevertheless, this debate does not directly affect behavior modification as such, since behavioral modification methodology may be used just as well in the linguistic-oriented as in the pragmatic approach therapies, the only difference being the processes and behavior to be controlled. In the former, attention is given to the control of well-defined specific verbal behavior; in the latter the objective focuses on communicational effectiveness.

## CONCLUSION

In this chapter I have considered behavior modification as an ensemble of principles and procedures aimed at controlling and favoring change in the patient's behavior repertoire. Interpretation of the disorders, as well as selection of the re-education strategy, are dependent upon neuropsychological theories relative to the organization of the mental subprocesses sustaining the behavior and to their dissociation in pathological conditions. From this methodological point of view (which of course is not shared by everybody who applies behavioral modification methods) the future of behavior modification is not bounded to any specific theory of re-education either along the re-establishment/reorganization spectrum or in terms of the bottom-up/top-down opposition. This position has the advantage of emphasizing the general utility of behavioral modification methodology as a method for systematic and scientific control of the therapeutic efficacy, whatever the theoretical postulate. As Goldfarb (1981) put it, behavior modification is a tool; please use it!

### REFERENCES


Albert M L, Sparks R, Helm N A 1973 Melodic intonation for aphasia. Archives of Neurology 29: 130

Albert M L, Goodglass H, Helm N A, Rubens A B, Alexander M P 1981 Clinical aspects of dysphasia. Springer-Verlag, New York

Bates E, Haby S, Zurif E 1983 The effects of focal brain damage on pragmatic expression. Canadian Journal of Psychology 37: 59

Benton A L, Smith K C, Lang M 1972 Stimulus characteristics and object naming in aphasic patients. Journal of Communicative Disorders 5: 19

Ben-Yishay Y, Diller L, Gordon W, Gerstman L 1978 A modular approach to training in cognitive perceptual integration (constructional skills) in brain injured people. In: Working approaches on cognitive deficits in brain damaged. Supplement to 6th Annual Working Workshop for Rehabilitation Professionals, New York, ch. 4, p. 107–132

Ben-Yishay Y, Rattok J, Ross B, Lakin P, Cohen J, Diller L 1980 A remedial 'module' for the systematic amelioration of basic attentional disturbances in head trauma patients. In: Working approaches to remediation of cognitive deficits in brain damaged. Supplement to 8th Annual Workshop for Rehabilitation Professionals, New York, ch. 3, p. 71

Bisiach E 1966 Perceptual factors in the pathogenesis of anomia. Cortex 2: 90

Bloom L M 1962 A rationale for group-treatment of aphasic patients. Journal of Speech and Hearing Disorders 27: 11

Blumstein S E, Cooper W 1974 Hemispheric processing of intonational contours. Cortex 10: 146

Bollinger R L, Stout C E 1976 Response-contingent small-step treatment: performances based communication intervention. Journal of Speech and Hearing Disorders 41: 40

Brookshire R 1968 Visual discrimination and response reversal learning by aphasic subjects. Journal of Speech and Hearing Research 11: 677

Brookshire R 1969 Probabilty learning by aphasic subjects. Journal of Speech and Hearing Research 12: 857

Brookshire R 1971 Effects of delay of reinforcement on probability learning by aphasic subjects. Journal of Speech and Hearing Research 14: 92

Brookshire R H 1978 An introduction to aphasia. BRK, Minneapolis

Bruyer R 1981 Approche opérante des atteintes traumatiques de la mémoire, effet de la connaissance des résultats sur la performance. Journal de Thérapie Comportementale III: 33

Corbin M L 1951 Group speech therapy for motor aphasia and dysarthria. Journal of Speech and Hearing Disorders 16: 21

Corlew M M, Nation J E 1975 Characteristics on visual stimuli and naming performance in aphasic adults. Cortex 11: 186

Crystal D, Fletcher P, Garman M 1976 The grammatical analysis of language disability. Elsevier, New York.

Culton G L, Ferguson P A 1979 Comprehension training with aphasic subjects: the development and application of five automated language programs. Journal of Communication Disorders 12: 69

Dabul B, Bollier B 1976 Therapeutic approaches to apraxia. Journal of Speech and Hearing Disorders 41: 268

Davis G A 1983 A survey of adult aphasia. Prentice Hall Inc., Englewood Cliffs, New York

Davis G A, Wilcox M J 1981 Incorporating parameters of natural conversation in aphasia treatment. In: Chapey R (ed) Language intervention strategies in adult aphasia. Williams & Wilkins, Baltimore, p. 169–193

Derouesné J, Seron X, Lhermitte F 1975 Rééducation de patients atteints de lésions frontales. Revue Neurologique 131: 677

Diller L, Weinberg J M, 1970 Evidence for accident-prone behavior in hemiplegic patients. Archives of Physical Medicine and Rehabilitation 51: 358

Diller L, Weinberg J M, 1977 Hemi-inattention in rehabilitation: the evolution of a rationale remediation program. In: Weinstein E A, Friedland R P (eds) Advances in Neurology. Raven, New York

Diller L, Ben-Yishay Y, Gerstman L J, Goodkin R, Gordon W, Weinberg J 1974 Studies in cognition and rehabilitation in hemiplegia. Rehabilitation Monograph 50, New York University Medical Center, New York

Disimoni F G 1981 Therapies which utilize alternative, or augmentative communication systems. In: Chapey R (ed) Language intervention strategies in adult aphasia. Williams & Wilkins, Baltimore, ch. 16, p. 329

Duffy J R 1981 Schuell's stimulation approach to rehabilitation. In: Chapey R (ed) Language intervention-strategies in adult aphasia. Williams & Wilkins, Baltimore, ch. 5, p. 105

Eisenson J 1981 Issues, prognosis and problems in the rehabilitation of language disorders in adults. In: Chapey R (ed) Language intervention strategies in adult aphasia, Williams & Wilkins, Baltimore, ch. 4, p. 85

Farmer A 1977 Self-correctional strategies in the conversational speech of aphasic and non aphasic brain damaged adults. Cortex 13: 327

Feyereisen P in press Les troubles de l'expression et les niveaux de production verbale. In: Messerli P, Lavorel P, Nespoulous J L (eds) Pathologie de l'expression orale. Monographies françaises de Psychologie CNRS, Paris

Feyereisen P, Seron X 1982a Non verbal communication and aphasia. Part I: comprehension. Brain and Language 16: 191

Feyereisen P, Seron X 1982b Non verbal communication and aphasia. Part II: reception. Brain and Language 16: 213
Filby Y, Edwards A 1963 An application of automated teaching methods to test and teach form discrimination in aphasics. Journal of Programmed Instruction 2: 25
Flowers C R, Danforth L C 1979 A step-wise auditory comprehension improvement administered to aphasic patients by family members. In: Brookshire R H (ed) Clinical Aphasiology Conference Proceedings. BRK, Minneapolis
Fontaine O 1978 Introduction aux therapies comportementales. Mardaga, Brussels
Gardner H, Zurif E B, Berry T, Bakker E 1976 Visual communication in aphasia. Neuropsychologia 14: 275
Glass A V, Gazzaniga M S, Premack P 1973 Artificial language training in global aphasics. Neuropsychologia 11: 95
Goldfarb R 1981 Operant conditioning and programmed instruction in aphasia rehabilitation. In: Chapey R (ed) Language intervention strategies in adult aphasia. Williams & Wilkins, Baltimore, ch. 12, p. 249
Goldfarb R, Bader E 1979 Espousing melodic intonation therapy in aphasia rehabilitation: a case study. International Journal of Rehabilitation Research 2: 333
Goodkin R 1966 Case studies in behavioral research in rehabilitation. Perceptual and Motor Skills 23: 171
Goodkin R 1969 Changes in word production, sentence production and relevance in an aphasic through verbal conditioning. Behavior Research Therapy 7: 93
Hatfield F M, Howard D, Barber J, Jones C, Morton J 1977 Object naming in aphasics. The lack of effect of context or realism. Neuropsychologia 15: 717
Helm-Estabrooks N, Fitzpatrick P M, Barresi B 1981 Response of an agrammatic patient to a syntax stimulation program for aphasia. Journal of Speech and Hearing Disorders 46: 422
Helm-Estabrooks N, Fitzpatrick P M, Barresi B 1982 Visual action therapy for global aphasia. Journal of Speech and Hearing Disorders 47: 385
Holland A L 1967 Some applications of behavioral principles to clinical speech problems. Journal of Speech and Hearing Disorders 32: 11
Holland A L 1970 Case studies in aphasia rehabilitation using programmed instruction. Journal of Speech and Hearing, Disorders 35: 377
Holland A L 1975 The effectiveness of treatment in aphasia. In: Brookshire R (ed) Clinical aphasiology. Proceedings of the conference. BRK, Minneapolis.
Holland A L 1978 Functional communication in the treatment of aphasia. In: Bradford L J (ed) Communicative disorders: an audio journal of continuing education. Grune & Stratton, New York, vol. 3
Holland A L 1980 Communicative abilities in daily living. University Park Press, Baltimore
Holland A L, Harris A 1968 Aphasia rehabilitation using programmed instruction: an intensive case history. In: Sloane H, MacAulay H (eds) Operant procedures in remedial speech and language training. Houghton Mifflin, Boston, ch. 10, p. 197
Holland A, Levy C 1971 Syntactic generalization in aphasics as a function of relearning an active sentence. Acta Symbolica 2: 34
Jaffe P G, Katz A N 1976 Attenuating anterograde amnesia in Korsakoff's psychosis. Journal of Abnormal Psychology 84: 559
Keenan J 1966 A method for eliciting naming behavior from aphasic patients. Journal of Speech and Hearing Disorders 31: 261
Kolk H 1979 Where do agrammatic sentences come from? Paper presented at the International Neuropsychological Society, June, New York
Kushner H, Hubbard D J, Know A W 1973 Effects of punishment on learning by aphasic subjects. Perceptual and Motor Skills 36: 283
La Pointe L L 1977 Base-10 programmed stimulation: task specification, scoring and plotting performance in aphasia therapy. Journal of Speech and Hearing Disorders 42: 90
La Pointe L L 1978 Aphasia therapy: some principles and strategies for treatment. In: John D F (ed) Clinical management of neurogenic communicative disorders. Little Brown, Boston, ch. 3, p. 129
Lecours A R, Lhermitte F 1979 L'Aphasie. Flammarion, Paris
Lewinsohn P M, Danaher B G, Kikel S 1977 Imagery as a mnemonic aid for brain injured persons. Journal of Consulting and Clinical Psychology 5: 717
Lhermitte D, Ducarne B 1965 La rééducation des aphasiques. La Revue du Praticien 15: 234

Lovass D I, Berberich J P, Perloff B F, Schaeffer B 1966 Acquistion of imitative speech in schizophrenic children. Science 151: 705
Luria A R 1963 Restoration of function after brain injury. Pergamon, Oxford
Martin A D 1977 Processing strategies in aphasia rehabilitation. Paper presented at American Speech and Hearing Association Meeting, Chicago
Muma J R, McNeil M R 1981 Intervention in aphasia: psycho-socio-linguistic perspectives. In: Chapey R (ed) Language intervention strategies in adult aphasia. Williams & Wilkins, Baltimore, ch. 9, p. 195
Naeser M A 1974 A structured approach teaching aphasic basic sentence types. British Journal of Disorders of Communication 10: 70
Peuser G, Temp K 1981 The evolution of jargonaphaisa. In: Brown J W (ed) Jargonaphasia. Academic Press, New York, ch. 11, p. 259
Pizzamiglio L, Roberts M 1967 Writing in aphasia: learning study. Cortex 3: 250
Porch B E 1967 Administration, scoring, interpretation of the Porch index of communicative ability. Consulting Psychologists Press, Palo Alto
Rochford G, Williams M 1962 Studies in the development and breakdown of the use of names: experimental production of naming disorders in normal people. Journal of Neurology, Neurosurgery and Psychiatry 28: 407
Rosenbeck J C 1978 Treating apraxia of speech. In: Johns D F (ed) Clinical management of neurogenic communicative disorders. Little, Brown, Boston, ch. 4, p. 191
Rosenberg B 1965 The performance of aphasics on automated visuo-perceptual discrimination, training and transfer tasks. Journal of Speech and Hearing Research 8: 165
Rosenberg B, Edwards A 1964 The performance of aphasics on three automated perceptual discrimination programs. Journal of Speech and Hearing Research 7: 295
Rosenberg B, Edwards A 1965 An automated multiple response alternative training program for use with aphasics. Journal of Speech and Hearing Research 8: 415
Ross A J 1979 A study of the application of blissymbolics as a means of communication for a young brain damaged adult. Journal of Disorders of Communication 14: 103
Sarno M 1969 The functional communicative profile, manual of directions. Rehabilitation Monograph 42, Institute of Rehabilitation Medicine, New York
Sarno M T 1981 Recovery and rehabilitation in aphasia. In: Sarno M T (ed) Acquired aphasia. Academic Press, New York, ch. 17, p 485
Sarno M T, Levita E 1971 Natural course of recovery in severe aphasia. Archives of Physical Medicine and Rehabilitation 52: 175
Sarno M T, Levita E 1981 Some observations on the nature of recovery in global aphasia after stroke. Brain and Language 13: 1
Sarno M, Silverman M, Sands E 1970 Speech therapy and language recovery in severe aphasia. Journal of Speech and Hearing Research, 13: 607
Schlanger P H, Schlanger B B 1970 Adapting role playing activities with aphasic patients. Journal of Speech and Hearing Disorders 35: 229
Seron X 1982 The re-education of aphasics: the problem of the re-education strategies. International Journal of Psychology 17: 299
Seron X, Laterre C (eds) 1982 Rééduquer le cerveau, Logopédie, Psychologie, Neurologie. Mardaga, Brussels
Seron X, Tissot R 1973 Essai de rééducation d'une agnosie spatiale unilatérale gauche. Acta Psychiatrica Belgica 73: 448
Seron X, Van der Linden M, Van der Kaa M A 1978 The operant school in aphasia rehabilitation. In: Lebrun Y, Hoops R (eds) The management of aphasia. Swets & Zeitlinger B V, Amsterdam, ch. 7, p. 76
Seron X, Deloche G, Bastard V, Chassin G, Herman N, 1979 Word-findings difficulties and learning transfer in aphasic patients. Cortex 15: 149
Seron X, Monsel Y, Van der Kaa M A, Remits A, Van der Linden M 1980a La dénomination d'images chez des patients aphasiques: mesure de l'influence de trois contextes non-verbaux différents. Psychologica Belgica 20: 205
Seron X, Bruyer R, Martha T, Le Jeune A 1980b Influence du contexte sur le manque du mot aphasique: rôle de la couleur. Grammatica VII: 179
Seron X, Deloche G, Moulard G, Roussell M 1980c Computer-based therapy for the treatment of aphasic subjects with writing disorders. Journal of Speech and Hearing Disorders 45: 45
Seron X, Bruyer R, Rectem D, Lepoivre H 1981 Essais de revalidation des troubles

post-traumatiques de la memoire. Unpublished manuscript, Brussels
Skelly M, Schinsky L, Smith R W, Fust R S 1974 American Indian sign (Amerind) as a facilitation of verbalization of the oral verbal apraxia. Journal of Speech and Hearing Disorders 39: 445
Smith M 1974 Operant conditioning of syntax in aphasia. Neuropsychologia 12: 403
Sparks R 1981 Melodic intonation therapy. In: Chapey R (ed) Language intervention strategies in adult aphasia. Williams & Wilkins, Baltimore, ch. 13, p. 265
Sparks R W, Holland L 1976 Method: melodic intonation therapy for aphasia. Journal of Speech and Hearing Disorders 41: 187
Sparks R, Helm N, Albert M 1974 Aphasia rehabilitation resulting from melodic intonation therapy. Cortex 10: 303
Stachowiak F J, Huber W, Poeck K, Kerschensteiner M 1977 Text comprehension in aphasia. Brain and Language 4: 179
Taylor M L, Marks M M 1959 Aphasia rehabilitation manual and therapy kit. McGraw-Hill, New York
Tikofsky R S, Reynolds G L 1962 Preliminary study: non-verbal learning and aphasia. Journal of Speech and Hearing Research 6: 329
Tikofsky R S, Reynolds G L 1963 Further studies of non-verbal learning and aphasia. Journal of Speech and Hearing Research 6: 329
Ulatowska H K, North A J, Macaluno-Haynes S 1981 Production of narrative and procedural discourse in aphasia. Brain and Language 13: 345
Ulatowska H K, Doyel A W, Stern R F, Haynes S M 1983 Production of procedural discourse aphasia. Brain and Language 18: 315
Van Eeckhout P, Pillon B, Signoret J L, Deloche G, Seron X 1982 Rééducation des réductions sévères de l'expression orale: la 'therapie mélodique et rythmée'. In: Seron X, Laterre C (eds) Rééduquer le cerveau, logopedie, psychologie, neurologie. Mardaga, Brussels, ch. 7, p. 109
Waller M R, Darley F L 1978 Effect of prestimulation in sentence comprehension by aphasic subjects. Journal of Speech and Hearing Research 21: 732
Weinberg J, Diller L 1968 On reading newspapers by hemiplegic denial of visual disability. Proceedings of the 76th Convention of the American Psychologists Association 3: 665
Wepman J M 1958 The relationship between self-correction and recovery from aphasia. Journal of Speech and Hearing Disorders 23: 302
Wepman J 1972 Aphasia therapy: a new look. Journal of Speech and Hearing Disorders 37: 203
Wiegel-Crump C 1976 Agrammatism and aphasia. In: Lebrun Y, Hoops R (eds) Recovery in aphasics. Swets & Zeitlinger, Amsterdam, p. 243
Wiegel- Crump C, Koenigsknecht R A 1973 Tapping the lexical score of the adult aphasic: analysis of the improvement made in word retrieval skills. Cortex 9: 410
Wilcox M J, Davis G A, Leonard L B 1978 Aphasic's comprehension of contextually conveyed meaning. Brain and Language 6: 362
Wyke M, Holgate D 1973 Colour-naming defects in dysphasic patients: a qualitative analysis. Neuropsychologia 11: 451

# **Part two:** Representative Research and Application

# 8

*Yehuda Ben-Yishay, Eugene B. Piasetsky, and Jack Rattok*

# A systematic method for ameliorating disorders in basic attention

## INTRODUCTION

This chapter was planned and organized as a companion to the chapter on attention written by Posner and Rafal which appears as Chapter 9 in this volume. In their theoretical chapter, Posner and Rafal have delineated attention into three component processes: (1) alertness, (2) selection, and (3) vigilance or conscious attention. The clinical manifestations of disturbed attention in patients with traumatic head injury in remedial rehabilitation, conform well to Posner and Rafal's layered partitioning of the attentional processes. This presentation will focus on our systematic efforts to develop a method for remediating such deficits.

Specifically, this chapter reviews the development, implementation, and evaluation of a clinical strategy for dealing in a systematic fashion with the assessment and amelioration of attention-concentration deficits in persons who have suffered severe head trauma. The strategy and its present state of implementation have evolved over a period of 10 years within a clinical research and rehabilitation setting. It is part of a comprehensive remedial-rehabilitation program designed for head trauma patients who, despite conventional rehabilitation efforts, remained unable to resume functional social and occupational lives (Ben-Yishay, 1976; Ben-Yishay & Diller, 1983).

The term attention-concentration deficits as used here represents a class of specific clinical neuropsychologic sequelae of head injury, associated with disturbances in the basic arousal domain of the consciousness continuum (Strub & Black, 1977), which impede patients' ability to productively interact with their environment. As clinically identified (Ben-Yishay et al, 1979a) these sequelae include:

1. insufficient alertness, such as when the individual is not adequately awake and, hence, not fully aware of normal internal and external stimuli;
2. fluctuations in attention (in the presence of adequate wakefulness), such that the individual remains unable to selectively attend to specific stimuli because he/she is unable to screen out extraneous or irrelevant ones;
3. disturbances in concentration or manifestations of psychomotor impersistence, two alternate descriptors, which refer to difficulties in sustaining

focused attention over periods of time required to engage in even simple cognitive-perceptual or psychomotor behaviors (Joynt et al, 1962); and
4. response deficiencies such as delayed, poorly modulated, or perseverative responding.

To the extent these disturbances mask and/or prohibit access to the patient's residual intellectual abilities and critical faculties, they constitute a major obstacle to the effective differential diagnosis and treatment of the patient's functional disturbances. A patient's residual abilities and/or potential to learn remain, thus, largely obscured in the presence of basic attentional deficits. For this reason it was of paramount importance to diagnose and ameliorate these disturbances to the point where more effective utilization of intact abilities and, thereby, a basis for the rehabilitation of the patient may be possible.

The Orientation Remedial Module (ORM) consists of five procedures (aided by a series of tailor-designed electronic gadgets) which involve the reception of visual and/or auditory stimuli and the elicitation of a series of simple visuomotor responses with very few demands for higher-level processing of information. This series of tasks was designed on the basis of a phenomenological analysis to form an overlapping hierarchy in complexity of reception/response demands (see Table 8.1). According to this analysis, increasing difficulty is associated with (1) greater need to rely on internal as opposed to external cues; (2) longer intervals of sustained mental effort; and (3) increasing intentional demands. We viewed these tasks as operationalized indices of ordered functional steps along the consciousness continuum. Namely, that when the first task is administered, one taps into the upper limits of a patient's wakefulness, then into his/her full alertness, then attention, concentration (or vigilance, persistence), and finally into the lower limits of his/her higher cortical functions. Each exercise was constructed to address a critical dimension of the generic domain of attention/arousal, while providing for a clinically suitable training milieu. Construction of these exercises was further influenced by the consideration that:

1. they provide for the systematic assessment of respective components of the arousal functions;
2. they permit application of a test–train–test sequence;
3. they provide the patient with simple, direct feedback as to his/her performance (which may be charted to illustrate emerging success); and
4. they have a naturally engaging quality, so as to evoke in the patient the interest and desire to perform.

In the original version, which is the subject of this presentation, electronic instruments were employed to provide the desired stimulus conditions and to accept the patients' responses. These instruments (and associated procedures) were constructed to inhere with sufficient versatility so as to allow for selective and graded cuing. The goal in providing this module, i.e., the five tasks combined, is two-fold:

**Table 8.1** Hypothesis concerning the degree of overlap of component attentional functions of the ORM battery: a phenomenological analysis

| Component functions | Task hierarchy 1 ARC | 2 ZAC | 3 VDC | 4 TE | 5 RSC |
|---|---|---|---|---|---|
| Optimal wakefulness | * | * | * | * | * |
| Anticipation of the onset of the stimulus cycle: | | | | | |
| (a) when cycle is intermittent | * | * | * | * | * |
| (b) when cycle is continuous | | * | * | * | * |
| Focusing attention on: locus/light/sound/'time' | * | * | * | * | * |
| Concentrating or persisting: | | | | | |
| (a) when scan/span is intermittent | * | * | * | * | * |
| (b) when scan/span is continuous | | | * | * | * |
| Self-induction (internal 'countdown'-readiness) | * | * | * | * | * |
| Modulated response: press/lift finger/identify | * | * | * | * | * |
| Decision (whether to respond, now or delay) | | * | * | * | * |
| Discrimination: number/color/beat | | | * | | * |
| Maintaining a rhythm (internal pacing ... ) | | | | * | * |
| Synchronizing (internal with external pacing) | | | | | * |
| Degree of differentiation of simultaneously ongoing introspective–cognitive processes: | | | | | |
| (a) moderately complex | | | | * | * |
| (b) very complex | | | | | * |

* Denotes a degree of overlap in the specified component function.

1. that the five exercises, delivered in sequence, will produce a cumulative enhancement in the patient's levels of alertness, attention and concentration; and
2. that, upon completion of the module, the patient will be sufficiently competent in his/her ability to interact with the environment so as to permit further remedial training in more substantive areas of intellectual functioning.

## METHOD

The following briefly describes the specific treatment objectives and training procedures associated with each of the five ORM tasks. But first, a point of clarification is in place with reference to the electronic instrumentation. From 1983 the application of the ORM by electronic instrumentation has been discontinued since, as the latest phase in the evolution of this training module, the ORM has been computerized (Piasetsky et al, 1983). This provided for:

1. the faithful reproduction, through high-resolution graphic simulations, of the operation of the five original ORM instruments;

2. the incorporation of a graded system of cues, reflecting the spirit and substance of our training methodology;
3. establishing minimum standard guidelines for administering the training; and
4. an extension in the range of ORM training to enhance its applicability to more mildly impaired patients.

While our experiences with this upgraded version have been decidedly positive (and appear to be in line with the findings reported herein), in the present context we will confine our discussion to work completed using the original (i.e. the electronic-assisted) system. The following is a brief summary of the five ORM tasks in their hierarchic order:

## Training the patient to attend and react to environmental 'signals'

The first exercise seeks to stimulate the patient's general level of arousal and enhance attention and responsiveness. A visual reaction time apparatus – the 'Attention Reaction Conditioner' ARC – was specially modifed as a training tool. The modifications made possible simple and direct feedback to patients (as to their performance), which could be automatically or manually engaged. The reaction time paradigm was selected as a milieu for training in that it embodies, at a most basic level, the principal elements which define an active engagement of the environment, i.e., seeking and interpreting the signal(s) – for which to select and apply appropriate action(s). The demands placed on the patient are simplified in two ways: (1) both the signal and appropriate action are simple, well-defined and invariant; and (2) the signal is external to the patient.

## Training the patient to time his/her responses in relation to changing environmental cues

The second exercise seeks to train the patient to effectively screen out distractions and use available environmental cues to determine the most appropriate time to respond. The instrument employed in training – the 'Zeroing Accuracy Conditioner,' ZAC – is an oversized clock-like device with a single sweep hand. The sweep hand is activated by depressing a button. As long as pressure on the button is maintained, the hand will remain in motion. The patient is instructed to make the hand stop (by releasing the button) at a predetermined position on the clock face. During the course of performing the training task the patient is faced with a set of stimulus cues (hash markings on the clock face) he/she must select the appropriate one, remain focused on it, and release the button at the right time, in order to get the hand to stop at the predetermined position.

## Training the patient to be actively vigilant

The third exercise seeks to train the patient to actively scan his/her environment and seek out the presence of signals and identify them. The instrument employed in training – the 'Visual Discrimination Conditioner,' VDC – consists of a 30-inch long horizontal display panel containing two movable cubes. The cube on the left contains a digital display and the cube on the right contains five colored lights. Either or both sources may be activated to display a number, a color, or both. In performing this training exercise the patient must continuously visually scan his environment, fixate on both stimulus sources, and correctly discriminate a variety of specific color/number stimuli. Stimulus duration and the distance between sources can be systematically adjusted to facilitate training.

### Training in time estimation

The fourth exercise seeks to improve the patient's concentration while fostering attention to internal, as opposed to external, sources of cues. The essential task is to estimate the passage of time – TE – in units of one-tenth of a second. The instrumentation employed is a special 10-second stopwatch which is mounted on a small stand containing an activating lever. This enables the patient to start or stop the watch whether it is facing him/her or turned away. The logic of this exercise is to train the patient to internalize the pace of the stopwatch through the use of timed body movements, vocalized, then silent, counting systems, and/or by means of visual imagery.

### Training the patient to synchronize responding with complex rhythms

The fifth training exercise initially focuses on the patient's modulation and basic sequencing of responses (i.e. depressing a telegraph key in the proper rhythm). The final phase of training – on the 'Rhythm Synchrony Conditioner,' RSC – seeks to foster an integration of what has been trained in previous ORM exercises. The stimuli for this exercise are series of morse code-like tones systematically distributed over time. To achieve success on this exercise the patient must learn to: attend to the rhythm formed by the sequence of tones; internalize it; and anticipate each beat so that his/her responses, i.e., depressing the telegraph key, will be of the same duration and in phase with the stimulus tones.

The foregoing descriptions were provided to acquaint the reader with the basic structure of the five ORM training exercises. A more detailed presentation of methods and procedures may be obtained by referring to Ben-Yishay et al (1979a).

Following an initial 2-year period of pilot tests, during which these procedures were clinically evaluated and revised (Ben-Yishay et al, 1978), the ORM sequence was subjected to formal evaluation within the context of a 6-year, holistic, out-patient clinical research study in rehabilitation of chronic severely head injured young adults (Ben-Yishay et al, 1979b; Ezrachi et al, 1983; Ben-Yishay et al, 1985).

## PROCEDURE

As the first cognitive remedial module administered in the setting of an intensive day program, the effects of the ORM training and the interrelatedness of its components could be isolated relatively well. However, as is often the case in clinical research, the larger objectives of the study, plus the special structure of the program, imposed limitations on our ability to adhere to rigorous methods of research design in evaluating the ORM. For example, although, as was already mentioned, the attention training sequence was the first one to be administered, patients were concurrently exposed to the routine of a daily program schedule and participated in supervised and highly structured peer group discussions. Additionally, it was not feasible for us to systematically vary the training order of the five component ORM tasks or otherwise engage in study of the independent effects of each. Yet our study design provided for a particularly good research sample. That is, patients were uniformly chronic (at least 1 year and typically 2–4 years post-injury) and were well 'seasoned' rehabilitation participants. All had previously engaged in various traditional programs of inpatient and outpatient therapies. Moreover, in a separate substudy ($n$=30), we were able to establish that patients' performance on our comprehensive baseline evaluation battery remained stable over a period of approximately 3 months prior to entering into treatments.

The following summarizes the findings obtained on the first 40 patients who participated in our research-rehabilitation programs using the ORM. All received training on the original (as opposed to the computerized) version of the ORM sequence. Data used in the analysis were routinely obtained from the following sources:

1. Upon entering the program, each patient underwent evaluation on an extensive battery of tests including various neuropsychological/cognitive measures, measures of selected intrapersonal and interpersonal functions, and indices of functional adequacy in everyday life. These measures combined yielded 77 psychometric variables.
2. After completing the baseline assessment, and once treatments were commenced, each patient was first trained on the five ORM procedures (ARC, ZAC, VDC, TE, and RSC, in that order). Each was then retested on the ORM sequence under baseline conditions.
3. A subgroup consisting of the first 11 patients was serially evaluated on all five ORM tasks upon completion of training on each. Additionally, these patients were retested 3 months after cessation of training on the ORM, and five of these patients who remained geographically accessible were also retested 6 months after cessation of the treatments.
4. Immediately following the completion of ORM training (and before initiating other modular cognitive remedial treatments) each patient received an interim retesting on four selected measures from the evaluation battery (Visual Reaction Time, WAIS Digit Span, WAIS Picture Completion, and IRM Picture Description).

Analyses were undertaken to address questions pertaining to (a) the overall efficacy of the ORM series as a training module; (b) interrelatedness and stability of training effects over time; and, (c) its psychometric and behavioral correlates.

## RESULTS

### Training efficacy

As reflected in Table 8.2, training on the ORM instruments resulted in significant improvement in performance on all of the tasks in the sequence (Rattok et al, 1982). As a group, patients progressed from initially impaired performance to within the average normal range. Moreover, levels achieved on the ARC and TE tasks following training were marginally better than those observed among non-neurologically impaired adults we tested.

**Table 8.2** Means and standard deviations before and after training on the ORM module and results of correlated *t* tests for differences between means; $n = 40$

| ORM instrument | | Expected score | Pre-training | Post-training | $t$* |
|---|---|---|---|---|---|
| ARC | Mean | 7–8 | 6.32 | 7.82 | |
| | SD | Lights | 0.94 | 0.33 | 11.66 |
| ZAC+ | Mean | 0–2 | 4.49 | 1.88 | |
| | SD | Deviations | 1.73 | 0.81 | 8.89 |
| VDC | Mean | 46–48 | 43.9 | 47.62 | |
| | SD | Correct | 5.43 | 0.77 | 4.54 |
| TE+ | Mean | 0.3–0.6 | 1.06 | 0.31 | |
| | SD | Sec. dev. | 0.91 | 0.13 | 5.25 |
| RSC | Mean | 7.3–9 | 5.68 | 7.25 | |
| | SD | Scaled points | 1.50 | 0.90 | 9.15 |

*All significant at $P < 0.001$.
+Decreasing scores (deviations from zero) reflect improvement.

In considering these results, it is important to note that methods or potential tricks employed by patients to improve their performances on the ORM tasks would necessarily coincide with enhanced attention/arousal and with more effective modulation of one's responses. For, after all, aside from the training on the ORM, there is no other knowledge base of circumvention technique for the patient to fall back on. So, in view of the consistency in improvement with training and the final levels achieved, it may be concluded that the ORM task hierarchy is efficacious as a training system to ameliorate deficits in basic attention, as operationalized by the component tasks of the ORM battery.

Having established that patients can achieve normal levels of performance on the ORM tasks after systematic training, an obvious question arises concerning the generalizability of this effect. Appropriate indices of enhanced alertness, improved orientation to stimuli, crisper responses, greater freedom from distractions (heightened selectivity), and more effectively sustained mental effort, might best be derived from observations on the patient's behavior during specially targeted activities. Where this was systematically undertaken (see case study M.S. in this chapter) positive changes were indeed documented.

As an alternative, for this behavior sampling, we opted to examine patient performances on those psychometric tests contained in our evaluation battery which have been cited as measures of attentional capabilities in the brain-injured. We selected, accordingly, Visual Reaction Time, WAIS Digit Span, WAIS Picture Completion, and our own Picture Description Test (involving the seeking and reporting of major details in a pastoral scene). As reflected in Table 8.3, patients evidenced statistically reliable improvement on all four criterial measures upon completion of ORM training. It is particularly noteworthy that the magnitude of change on the Visual Reaction Time and the Picture Description tests was substantial, suggesting that the carryover of training on the ORM is greater when the criterial tasks are not compounded also by other cognitive functions.

In summary, training on the ORM procedures resulted in consistent and substantial improvement on all tasks in the training sequence. Patients progressed from initially impaired levels to within average normal limits, or above. Statistically reliable improvement was also obtained on four criterial measures selected from our psychometric evaluation battery. These findings support a conclusion that the ORM task hierarchy is an effective training system to ameliorate deficits in basic attention/arousal.

**Table 8.3** Correlated *t* test analysis of performance on critical measures before and after ORM training; $n = 40$

| Variable | | Pre-ORM training | Post-ORM training | Correlated *t* |
|---|---|---|---|---|
| VRT | Mean | 222.55 | 166.95 | |
| | SD | 45.63 | 28.26 | 7.38** |
| WAIS DS | Mean | 9.8 | 10.4 | |
| | SD | 2.6 | 2.1 | 2.17* |
| WAIS PC | Mean | 10.2 | 11.1 | |
| | SD | 2.3 | 2.7 | 3.28** |
| IRM DPic | Mean | 12.8 | 16.0 | |
| | SD | 3.0 | 2.8 | 8.83** |

* $P < 0.05$.
** $P < 0.01$.
VRT = Visual reaction time; DS = The auditory 'Digits' subtest of the WAIS test; PC = picture completion; IRM = Institute of Rehabilitation Medicine; DPic = picture description test.

## Interrelatedness and stability of training effects

A subgroup of 11 patients was serially evaluated on all five ORM tasks upon completion of training on each. Table 8.4 presents mean performance scores of these patients at baseline and following completion of each task-specific training.

Examination of Table 8.4 reveals that, for each specific task in the ORM

**Table 8.4** Mean performance scores at baseline and after specific training; $n = 11$

| Task | Baseline | Post-ARC | Post-ZAC | Post-VDC | Post-TE | Post-RSC |
|---|---|---|---|---|---|---|
| ARC | 5.95 | *7.82* | 7.76 | 7.70 | 7.60 | 7.71 |
| ZAC* | 4.74 | 4.70 | *1.82* | 1.73 | 2.23 | 1.65 |
| VDC | 40.60 | 40.50 | 40.00 | *46.82* | 46.14 | 47.36 |
| TE* | 1.28 | 0.72 | 0.80 | 0.96 | *0.37* | 0.36 |
| RSC | 5.12 | 3.60 | 3.40 | 3.65 | 4.64 | *6.59* |

*For the ZAC and TE tasks, the values represent deviations from zero. Thus the lower the values, the better the score. The numbers in italic represent the mean values obtained (for each of the given tasks) immediately at the end of the task-specific training.

sequence, performance scores remained at approximately baseline levels until immediately following specific training. Mean scores obtained after task-specific training, in all five instances, reflected significant improvement (Wilcoxon $t=0$, $p<0.005$ one-tailed) and remained relatively stable thereafter. In addition, training on one task did not appear to impact performance on others.

Table 8.5 presents mean performance levels of patients on the five ORM tasks measured immediately after completion of training, 3 and 6 months later. Follow-up at 6 months was limited to five patients who remained geographically accessible. It was found that training effects persist, essentially undiminished, up to 6 months following cessation of ORM training.

**Table 8.5** Mean scores on ORM tasks at baseline, on completion of training, and at 3 and 6 months after training

| Task | Baseline ($n = 11$) | Completion of training ($n = 11$) | Three months post-training ($n = 11$) | Six months post-training ($n = 5$) |
|---|---|---|---|---|
| ARC | 5.95 | 7.71 | 7.80 | 7.70 |
| ZAC* | 4.74 | 1.65 | 1.66 | 2.36 |
| VDC | 40.60 | 47.36 | 47.09 | 46.50 |
| TE* | 1.28 | 0.36 | 0.38 | 0.34 |
| RSC | 5.21 | 6.59 | 7.18 | 5.65 |

*ZAC and TE performance measured in deviations from zero. Decreasing scores are improvement.

## Psychometric and behavioral correlates of attentional deficits

The reader may recall that our patients received a comprehensive battery of measures at baseline evaluation which yielded a total of 77 psychometric variables. These variables were composed of neuropsychological/cognitive measures, measures of intrapersonal and interpersonal functioning, and indices of functional life activities. In order to assess the extent to which basic attentional difficulties may impinge upon any or all of these domains, data reduction techniques were employed with each set of measurements in order to extract principal marker variables (i.e., the most representative variables for each domain). Table 8.6 displays rank order correlation coefficients for the five ORM baseline measures with each of the marker variables (Rattok et al, 1982).

Inspection of the pattern of correlations displayed in Table 8.6 reveals that ORM measures are differentially related to performance/functional domains, although the magnitude of relationship, with few exceptions, tends to be low (under 10% shared variability). Significant correlations of the marker variables with RSC were ubiquitous, which tends to support our hypothesis that this task has the highest degree of attentional complexity and also involves modulated responding. Time estimation correlated above-chance levels with various higher level but no lower-level cognitive tasks. This finding is also consistent with our initial hypothesis that TE inheres with complex attentional demands which are predominantly internal. On the other hand, even though the ARC and ZAC involve a rapid initiation of a motor response (a quick depressing and releasing of a button respectively), neither correlated with measures of motor persistence, fine-motor coordination or speeded dexterity. The most plausible explanation for this is that, unlike the RSC, which requires both continuous and modulated responses, the unitary motoric responses required by the ARC and ZAC are not systematically related to fine motor skills *per se*.

**Table 8.6** Significant ($P < 0.05$) Spearman rank order correlations ($R_s$) between the five ORM measures and 19 'marker' variables representing a comprehensive battery of psychometric measures; $n = 40$

| Domain | 'Marker' variables | ORM measures | | | | |
|---|---|---|---|---|---|---|
| | | ARC | ZAC* | VDC | TE* | RSC |
| Basic psychomotor and attention | Visual reaction time* | 62 | 38 | -- | -- | 54 |
| | Finger tapping (30 seconds) | -- | -- | 34 | -- | 51 |
| Finger dexterity | Purdue assembly | -- | -- | 40 | -- | 45 |
| 'Tool use' | Tweezer | -- | -- | -- | -- | -- |
| | Nuts and bolts | -- | -- | -35 | -- | -- |
| Integrative functions | WAIS, block design | 30 | 28 | -- | 35 | 57 |
| | WAIS, picture completion | -- | -- | 36 | -- | 46 |
| | Canc., double | -- | 31 | -- | -- | -- |
| Memory | WAIS, DS backward | -- | -- | -- | 30 | 34 |
| General verbal aptitude | WAIS, VIQ | -- | 40 | -- | 31 | 32 |
| | MAT, vocabulary | -- | 29 | -- | 32 | 35 |
| Behavioral competence index (BCI) | Energy level/initiative | 27 | -- | -- | 26 | 44 |
| | Orientation in family environment | 35 | -- | -- | 30 | 36 |
| | 'Fail-safe' emotional checks | -- | -- | -- | -- | -- |
| | Cooperation | -- | -- | -- | -- | -- |
| Higher-level reasoning | Telegram, selection | -- | -- | -- | 35 | 38 |
| | IRM object sorting category | -38 | -- | -- | -- | -- |
| Interpersonal functions | Self-esteem | -- | -- | -- | -- | 31 |
| | Social cooperation | -- | -- | -- | 29 | -- |

*For consistency, direction (sign) of obtained correlations have been adjusted to reflect improvement associated with decreasing scores (visual reaction time, ZAC, TE). Hence, positive correlations uniformly reflect a tendency to improve or worsen in correspondence.

VIQ = Verbal IQ; Canc. = Cancellation test: a paper/pencil test of cancellation of predetermined digits/numbers from an array of random stimuli; DS = The auditory 'Digits' subtest of the WAIS test; MAT = Metropolitan Aptitude Test

In balance, these results tend to support our original hypothesis concerning the ORM demand hierarchy and, further, suggest that basic attentional deficits impact on cognitive, psychological, and functional life domains in chronic head trauma patients. As such, they serve to underscore the value of assessing intactness of basic attention as operationalized by the ORM methodology (which primarily involves simple psychomotor tasks) in traumatic brain-injured patients. Indications are that including such a battery of measures would:

1. permit a more refined differential diagnosis relating to the presence and impact on various psychometric performances of attentional disturbances;
2. provide for a means of assessing the role of attentional disturbances in skill deficits, problems in everyday life functioning, and difficulties in interpersonal interactions; and
3. augment the process of formulating intervention strategies.

## A case presentation

In this context a case study is presented to illustrate a special application of our attention-enhancing remedial methodology in a clinical setting which differed in some respects from the setting in which our grouped data were obtained.

Different aspects of this case study were already described in greater detail elsewhere (Ben-Yishay et al, 1979a, 1980). We summarize it again to illustrate the systematic use of our ORM methodology as part of, and as an adjunct to, the multidisciplinary interventions which must take place during the early phases of in-patient rehabilitation.

At the time of his injury, M.S. was a 27-year-old, white, middle-class male. Possessing degrees in chemical engineering and in business administration, M.S. quickly attained a high position with a large chemical corporation.

Twenty-one months prior to his admission to the Rusk Institute of Rehabilitation Medicine, M.S. sustained severe traumatic brain injuries in a high-speed, multi-car collision. He was admitted to the intensive care unit of a hospital in deep coma; was unresponsive to stimulation, and was placed on a respirator for the following 21 days. Thereafter, M.S. remained in various states of unconsciousness for the next 4 months. There followed many medical complications, including a double pneumonia.

Upon regaining full consciousness, M.S. was described as intermittently withdrawn and belligerent for about 2 months. Then, as he became more manageable, an active inpatient program of rehabilitation was recommended.

Twenty-one months after the onset of his injuries, M.S. was admitted to our inpatient service to continue his rehabilitation. The admission diagnosis included: severe craniocerebral injury; a severe organic brain syndrome; spastic quadriparesis; bilateral equinovarus deformities; and traumatic optic atrophy of the right eye. While attending the inpatient rehabilitation program M.S.

underwent a series of surgical and multiple casting interventions, which enabled him to gradually regain ambulation skills and the functional use of his right arm. By this time he was described as pleasant, friendly, and cooperative, although he was almost totally disoriented in all spheres and exhibited extreme degrees of physical and mental passivity (manifestations of a severe form of adynamia). M.S.'s adynamic syndrome was coupled with a massive anterograde amnesia; a near-complete lack of awareness of the consequences of his brain injuries (except for admitting lapses of memory); very severe attentional disorders (distractibility, motor impersistence, and inability to maintain focused attention); plus an unrealistic and nearly euphoric sense of optimism about what the future had in store for him. M.S. was in effect untestable at the time because of the severity of attentional problems which prevented a reliable assessment of his true residual intellectual abilities. At any rate, based on results of formal testing (WAIS) his prorated Verbal and Performance IQ scores were estimated to be 83 and 64 respectively.

Although M.S. was exposed to a full and vigorous, but conventional, program of inpatient rehabilitation (physical and occupational therapies, psychotherapy, etc.), it was quite obvious that he was making little or no progress from the standpoint of regaining his competence in the intellectual spheres, and in his daily life functions. The decision was therefore made to supplement M.S.'s regularly scheduled activities with a special program of cognitive remedial intervention. The program was tailor-designed to answer the following questions: (1) Could M.S. be optimally aroused? (2) Could he be helped in becoming more spontaneous and self-initiating (i.e., ameliorate manifestations of adynamia)? (3) Could his severe attention and concentration deficits be sufficiently ameliorated, enabling him to become a pupil again, capable of engaging in systematic learning activities? (4) Would the exposure of M.S. to systematic remedial training exercises result in measurable improvements in his orientation, awareness, and competence in a selected number of functional behaviors on the ward?

Two hours were set aside each day for the special remedial experiment. As a first step, a representative sample of M.S.'s problem behaviors on the ward were identified and carefully assessed (i.e., operationalized and quantified) over a 2-week period of naturalistic ward behavior observations. These behaviors were judged on a clinical basis to have a direct, face valid, relationship to M.S.'s severe overlay problems. They were set aside as the functional criterion measures for assessing the effectiveness of subsequent remedial training. During the same 2 weeks of initial baseline assessment, M.S. was also administered the five ORM tests, plus the WAIS battery and a Visual Reaction Time measure.

Following this initial baseline evaluation and preparation period, M.S. underwent daily (for 2 consecutive hours each day) systematic training on the original electronic version of the ORM battery of tasks. Each day, part of the 2 hours was utilized for the purpose of induction into the tasks; then the actual training was carried out; followed by a brief dialogue which was designed to interpret for him the meaning of the exercises, and to place them in their proper rehabilitation perspective.

After 62 hours of training on the ORM hierarchy (which spanned a period of approximately 3 months), this phase of M.S.'s program was concluded. He was then (1) retested on the standard procedures of the ORM tasks; (2) readministered the other psychometric criterion measures (Visual Reaction Time and WAIS battery); and (3) observed again for the functional ward behaviors, i.e., those set aside as criterion measures before the commencement of the ORM training program.

Table 8.7 summarizes the results of M.S.'s performance on the five ORM tasks, before and after the training. As may be seen, M.S.'s post-training proficiency on all of the tasks had improved; with scores on four of the five tasks reaching the normally expected levels of performance on these measures. It may therefore be concluded that the systematic training on the ORM hierarchy of tasks proved effective as a means of enhancing his attention and concentration, as measured by these tasks.

**Table 8.7** Comparison of M.S.'s scores on the ORM measures before and after the ORM training

| Measure | Expected normal range of scores | Mean score at baseline testing | Mean score after ORM training |
|---|---|---|---|
| ARC | 7–8<br>Lights | 6.0 | 8.0 |
| ZAC | 0–2<br>Deviations | 4.0 | 0.3* |
| VDC | 46–48<br>Points | 21.0 | 48.0 |
| TE | 0.33–0.60<br>Sec. dev. | 1.1 | 0.3* |
| RSC | 7.3–9<br>Scaled point | 7.0 | 8.0 |

*The smaller the value, the better the performance.

Results of M.S.'s pre- and post-training performances on the psychometric criterion measures are summarized in Table 8.8. As shown by the results, M.S.'s performances on the Visual Reaction Time, the Auditory Digits series, and the WAIS Verbal IQ criterion measures, improved dramatically after the ORM training. These improvements, moreover, were not merely statistically significant, but also very important from a clinical standpoint. M.S.'s post-training performance scores on the above three tests were clearly within the above-average range, as opposed to the borderline-to-defective values which were obtained before training. With respect to the WAIS Performance IQ score, the nine-point gain was, of course, within the limits of the normal test–retest variability. Yet, as was evidenced in a qualitative analysis of his work on the WAIS subtests, after training, M.S. was more active and targeted in his overall approach to test demands.

**Table 8.8** M.S.'s scores on selected psychometric measures pre- and post-ORM training

| Measure | At baseline | After ORM training |
|---|---|---|
| IRM, VRT; in milliseconds | 470 | 187* |
| Auditory digits | | |
| (WAIS, Scaled score) | 7 | 12* |
| WAIS, Verbal IQ | 83 | 115* |
| WAIS, Performance IQ | 64 | 73 |

*Denotes a significant improvement in performance scores.
IRM = Institute of Rehabilitation Medicine; VRT = visual reaction time.

We may thus conclude that the ORM training procedure had a demonstrable carryover effect; indicating, thereby, that M.S.'s ability to attend and to concentrate has been generalized to some extent to tasks other than the specific ones on which he was trained.

But perhaps the most dramatic – and from a clinical point of view the most meaningful – improvements were noted in the area of M.S.'s functional behaviors on the hospital ward. The findings were described in detail elsewhere. In this context suffice to restate that following the training period on the ORM battery, M.S. (1) became significantly better oriented to this environment; (2) became more alert, more observant, more active, and better able to respond appropriately to the demands of his physical environment; (3) became better able to reflect upon and more realistically assess his situation; and (4) became significantly better able to reason logically.

Without a doubt, M.S. had become a pupil again; in the sense that he was now capable of actively engaging in a variety of learning experiences; and able to progressively assimilate the cumulative remedial inputs and digest their meaning (as articulated by his therapists). This opened up new possibilities which were exploited in the months that followed M.S.'s initial period of rehabilitation. He was subsequently discharged from the inpatient rehabilitation service and was admitted on an outpatient basis to the Head Trauma program. The results of his treatments in the holistic day program were summarized – under the designation of T1 – elsewhere (Ben-Yishay et al, 1979c).

## DISCUSSION

Our objective in developing the Orientation Remedial Module was to establish a systematic strategy for assessing and ameliorating attentional deficits in persons who have suffered severe head trauma. Our observations, obtained within a rehabilitation context, suggested that these deficits were manifestations of an underlying disturbance in basic arousal functions. As such they were reasoned to manifestly influence, but be independent of, a patient's ability to process information (i.e., content), as such. Insofar as the patient's residual abilities and/or potential to learn would, thus, remain obscured in the presence of attentional deficits, we sought to determine whether these deficits (1) could be effectively isolated through diagnostic procedures; and (2) could be sufficiently ameliorated, so as to provide a basis for engaging in a rehabilitation effort. Our approach was to devise a series of tasks which, on a phenomenological basis, operationalized increasing levels of attentional demand; and which could readily be adapted for use in systematic remedial training. The bulk of this chapter was devoted to reporting results obtained in applying this methodology with 40 head-injured patients.

We found that patients, as a group, evidenced significant impairment on the relatively simple reception/response paradigms which comprise the ORM. We also found that levels of performance on the five component tasks correlated differentially with selected measures of cognitive, interpersonal, and functional-life abilities. Moreover, the pattern of relationships obtained tended to support our original hypothesis concerning the ORM hierarchy. Taken together, these findings support a conclusion that deficits in basic attention constitute a distinct diagnostic entity in traumatic brain-injured adults, which can effectively be isolated on primarily simple psychomotor tasks. Inclusion of these or a comparable battery of measures would therefore:

1. permit a more refined differential diagnosis relating to the presence and impact on test performances of attentional disturbances;
2. provide a means for assessing the role of attentional disturbances in skill deficits, problems in everyday life functioning, and difficulties in interpersonal interaction; and
3. augment the process of formulating intervention strategies.

Training on the ORM procedures was found to result in consistent and substantial improvement on all tasks in the sequence, with evidenced carryover to certain psychometric tests which contain a strong attentional component. Where assessed, the effect of training tended to remain stable over time (up to 6 months). Furthermore, in those instances where an in-depth analysis was undertaken (see the case of M.S.), it was revealed that improvement in remedial training was mirrored by positive changes in functional life behaviors. Our clinical experience has been that over the course of ORM training patients do tend to exhibit an improvement in the quality of their participation in other aspects of our program.

Several qualifications are, however, in order. First, the magnitude of functional changes was found to vary considerably from patient to patient. Second, because of the holistic nature of our program, the source of the improvements cannot be exclusively attributed to the ORM training. Third, clinical observations suggest that patients differ with respect to the course of improvement on individual training tasks, as well as with respect to the carryover effects of the training. While such differences need to be further explored, they are likely to be influenced by factors relating to the underlying nature and the extent of the brain injuries sustained.

A final comment is in place regarding the computerized version of the ORM battery. As mentioned earlier, our computerized version incorporates the graded cuing system of the original battery (Piasetsky et al, 1983). It also contains several recent modifications which effectively raise the upper range of the training capabilities of this remedial series. Our experience in using this upgraded version, over the past 2 years, suggests that it is at least as effective as was the original training system. Moreover, possession of such a uniform assessment and training tool, and its availability on a large scale, will enable us to undertake, simultaneously in many places, collaborative clinical research in a significant area of rehabilitation of the head-injured.

## ACKNOWLEDGMENTS

The authors wish to thank Phyllis Lakin, Ph.D, Barbara Ross, Ph.D., Ora Ezrachi, M.A., and Saralyn Silver, M.S. for their significant contributions to this study. This study was supported in part by NIHR grant No. G00-8300-39 and a grant from the Transitional Learning Community, Galveston, Texas.

## REFERENCES

Ben-Yishay Y 1976 Setting up a therapeutic community for comprehensive rehabilitation of Israeli out-patient war casualties with severe head injuries: Structure and remedial systems. Invited panelist on 'Meet the Expert' workshop. The 13th World Congress of Rehabilitation, Israel

Ben-Yishay Y, Diller L 1983 Cognitive rehabilitation. In: Rosenthal M, Griffith E R, Bond M R, Miller J D (eds) Rehabilitation of the head injured adult. F A Davis, Philadelphia, ch. 26, pp. 367–378

Ben-Yishay Y, Ben-Nachum Z, Cohen A, Gross Y, Hoofien D, Rattok J, Diller L 1978 Digest of a two-year comprehensive clinical rehabilitation research program for out patient head injured Israeli veterans. In: Ben-Yishay Y (ed) Working approaches to remediation of cognitive deficits in brain damaged persons. NYU Medical Center, Rehabilitation Monograph No. 59, pp. 1–62

Ben-Yishay Y, Rattok J, Diller L 1979a A clinical strategy for the systematic amelioration of attentional disturbances in severe head trauma patients. In: Ben-Yishay Y (ed) Working approaches to remediation of cognitive deficits in brain damaged persons. NYU Medical Center, Rehabilitation Monograph No. 60, pp. 1–27

Ben-Yishay Y, Diller L, Rattok J, Ross B, Schaier A 1979b Rehabilitation of cognitive and perceptual defects in people with traumatic brain damage: a five year clinical research study (HEW, RSW, Project RT-93). In: Ben-Yishay Y (ed) Working approaches to remediation of cognitive deficits in brain damaged persons. NYU Medical Center, Rehabilitation Monograph No. 60, pp. 28–37

Ben-Yishay Y, Rattok J, Ross B, Schaier A, Scherzer P, Diller L 1979c Rehabilitation of cognitive and perceptual defects in people with traumatic brain damage. Implementation: Seven case studies. In: Ben-Yishay Y (ed) Working approaches to remediation of cognitive deficits in brain damaged persons. NYU Medical Center, Rehabilitation Monograph No. 60, pp. 88–203

Ben-Yishay Y, Rattok J, Ross B, Lakin P, Cohen J, Diller L 1980 A remedial module for the systematic amelioration of basic attentional disturbances in head trauma patients. In: Ben-Yishay Y (ed) Working approaches to remediation of cognitive deficits in brain damaged persons. NYU Medical Center, Rehabilitation Monograph No. 61, pp. 70–127

Ben-Yishay Y, Rattok J, Lakin P, Piasetsky E, Ross B, Silver S, Ezrachi O, Zide E 1986 Neuropsychological rehabilitation: the quest for a holistic approach. Seminars in Neurology. (In press)

Ezrachi O, Ben-Yishay Y, Rattok J, Ross B, Lakin P, Piasetsky E, Diller L 1983 Rehabilitation of cognitive and perceptual defects in people with traumatic brain damage: a five year clinical research study. In: Ben Yishay Y (ed) Working approaches to remedation of cognitive deficits in brain damaged persons. NYU Medical Center, Rehabilitation Monograph No. 66, pp. 53–78

Joynt R J, Benton A L, Fogel N L 1962 Behavioral and pathologic correlates of motor impersistence. Neurology 12: 876–884

Piasetsky E B, Rattok J, Ben-Yishay Y, Lakin P, Ross B, Diller L 1983 Computerized ORM: a manual for clinical and research uses. In: Ben-Yishay Y (ed) Working approaches to remediation of cognitive deficits in brain damaged persons. NYU Medical Center, Rehabilitation Monograph No. 66, pp. 1–40

Rattok J, Ben-Yishay Y, Ross B, Lakin P, Silver S, Thomas L, Diller L 1982 A diagnostic remedial system for basic attentional disorders in head trauma patients undergoing rehabilitation: A preliminary report. In: Ben-Yishay Y (ed.) Working approaches to remediation of cognitive deficits in brain damaged persons. NYU Medical Center, Rehabilitation Monograph No. 64, pp. 177–187

Strub R L, Black F W 1977 The mental status examination in neurology. F A Davis, Philadelphia

9 *Michael I. Posner and Robert D. Rafal*

# Cognitive theories of attention and the rehabilitation of attentional deficits

## INTRODUCTION

Problems with attention are frequently the chief disability in brain-injured individuals. Consider the following hypothetical patients who have normal hearing, vision, speech, comprehension, and motor capacity, but who have attentional deficits. The first patient has recovered from a head injury except for post-traumatic seizures. He is failing in school because he is drowsy from anticonvulsant medications. The second is an intelligent, articulate gentleman with a right parietal stroke who is embarrassed because left-sided neglect leads him into the wrong restroom when he fails to see the 'wo . . . ' in 'women'. Finally, consider a patient who has suffered bilateral contusions of the frontal lobes. To the casual observer he appears normal. Given a task which requires flexibility in concept manipulation and mental concentration, he fails because, stuck in a mental rut, he perseverates on the same idea and is sidetracked from his goal.

All three individuals have a problem with 'attention,' but the problem in each case is very different. A therapeutic intervention designed to help one is unlikely to help all. If the remediation of attentional deficits is to proceed rationally, we must know more about what attention is, and how it relates to other cognitive functions such as memory, object recognition, motor control, language, and propositional reasoning. Finally, we must be able to identify and isolate different components of attention which may be differentially affected by brain injury. Thus, for our three patients, we must be prepared to differentiate disorders of general arousal (as in our first patient) from more selective aspects of attention such as neglect of part of the sensory world (as in our second patient).

Cognitive rehabilitation is best guided by a sophisticated knowledge of the underlying mechanisms involved in the process of attention. With this in mind we first review three general senses of attention. Next we present a framework for relating the mental operations involved in attention to underlying neural systems that support those operations. Third, we review the application of this framework to spatial attention. Finally we discuss potential implications of a framework for understanding normal attention to future approaches in the development of rehabilitation.

## SENSES OF ATTENTION

Although there is no generally agreed-upon definition of attention, three senses of the term are predominant in the literatures of psychology and biology (Posner & Boies, 1971). While these definitions are neither mutually exclusive nor exhaustive, there is good reason to believe that they depend upon different neural substrates which, together, form a common system. The first sense in which the term attention is used is that of general alertness or arousal. A second sense of the term refers to selection from available, competing environmental and internal stimuli, of specific information for conscious processing. The third sense in which the term attention has been used refers to sustained concentration or vigilance (Table 9.1).

**Table 9.1** Senses of attention

| Component | Function |
|---|---|
| I. Alertness | |
| A. Tonic arousal | Diurnal fluctuation in wakefulness and performance. |
| B. Phasic arousal | Instantaneous generalized facilitation of performance induced by warning signal. |
| II. Selective attention | |
| A. Pre-conscious | Facilitation of selected information. Parallel processing of multiple-input codes and simultaneous pathway activation. |
| B. Conscious | Voluntary allocation of attention. Sequential processing. Limited capacity. |

### Alertness

Alertness refers to a generalized physical and mental state of arousal preparedness to respond. Alertness, in turn, can be subdivided into two different types: *tonic arousal*, which refers to how awake the organism is from one time of day to the other; and *phasic arousal*, the sudden increased attentiveness which immediately follows a warning signal which the organism knows will soon require a quick response. Tonic arousal incorporates not only the sleep–waking cycle, but other neurochemical and behavioral diurnal rhythms as well. For example, we tend to be more efficient early in the day than late in the afternoon and evening; these slow fluctuations in performance tend to coincide with fluctuations in serum cortisol, body temperature, and other physiologic measures. In contrast to these slow tonic modulators of alertness, *phasic* changes in general processing efficiency can be produced within a few hundred milliseconds by a warning signal. For example, if I were to throw a ball to you while you were daydreaming, you would be much more likely to catch it if I first warn you to 'Look out!'. Interest in these phasic changes in alertness dominated the physiology of attention 30 years ago as an understanding of the brainstem ascending reticular formation (ARF) emerged. This neural system deploys a complex mental and physiological response to a warning signal:

speeding of reaction times to any subsequent stimulus; cardiac deceleration; changes in organic galvanic skin resistance (GSR); and dilatation of the pupil. This general psychophysiological alerting complex is one component of the 'orienting reflex' (Sokolov, 1963).

## Selective attention

Another component of the orienting response is the *selective* biasing of neural function which facilitates the processing of specific information for special treatment, while tuning out other available signals. Selective attention differs from phasic alerting, as discussed above, in that it does not prepare the organism to respond to any and all signals. Instead, it improves responsiveness to selected information. If I add to my 'Look out!' the specific information 'Catch the tennis ball!' your preparation will be more specific; and may not be helpful if I toss you something else – you're likely to drop a shot put or a whiffle ball. A warning signal, then, can affect performance by general alerting, and also by providing relevant information about the upcoming signal. The effect of these two components of attention, alerting and selection, can be separated and isolated for study (Posner & Boies, 1971).

Selective attention can facilitate the processing either of information arising at the sensory surface, or of information stored in memory. Thus, we can attend selectively to a location in space in order to better detect a signal expected there; for example, turning in the direction of a loud noise to see what made it. Or we can attend to semantic attributes of a signal; for example, preparing to stop when a traffic light turns yellow. When selection is determined by a single physical property of a stimulus, such as the location of a noise, the selection is said to involve a 'stimulus set.' If selection requires the extraction of semantic information about the signal from memory, such as knowing the symbolic meaning of a yellow light, the term 'response set' is applied. Selective attention to an expected sensory event can be summoned by an exogenous signal, e.g., a sudden movement seen out of the corner of the eye; or endogenously from a central command, e.g., a decision to look both ways before crossing the street.

Whether our attention is triggered exogenously or endogenously, and regardless of whether it is based on a stimulus set or a response set, we can dissect the resulting orienting response into its several components (Table 9.2): a general arousal effect (phasic alerting), and a selective orienting of attention to the source of information. When the orienting of attention is to a spatial location, the orienting response will include not just a general arousal, but also a selective turning of the head and eyes toward the point of interest – overt spatial orienting. In addition to these overt shifts of attention involving head, eye, and body movements, there is also, as we shall see later, a covert orienting of attention which involves the shifting of a mental attention mechanism to the source of interest. As we shall see further, this covert orienting of attention can be further subdivided into several more basic operations (Table 9.2).

To a considerable degree the process of selective attention proceeds

**Table 9.2** Spatial orienting response

I. Phasic arousal
   Generalized speeding of reaction time.
   Physiologic indices: heart rate, GSR, pupillary changes

II. Selective orienting
   A. Overt orienting – movement of head, eyes and body to target.
   B. Covert orienting – mental shifting of attention to target.
      1. Facilitory component with three elementary operations:
         (a) Disengage (parietal lobe)
         (b) Move (midbrain)
         (c) Engage
      2. Inhibition of return (midbrain).

automatically and unconsciously such that a great deal of information about a signal is processed simultaneously. For example, when we see the word 'orange' in the sentence, 'The ball is orange' we automatically and simultaneously activate input codes for: physical (graphemic) properties, i.e., how it looks; phonologic properties, i.e., how it sounds; and semantic properties, i.e., what it means (Posner, 1978). Furthermore, at the same time that we activate the semantic meaning of the color orange, we also activate related semantic pathways, e.g., the fruit orange. Experimentally, the activation of a psychologic pathway by a signal can be inferred by facilitations or inhibitions in responding to subsequent information. For example, if we are presented the single word 'orange' we can read it faster if it is immediately preceded by the word 'apple' than if it is preceded by 'house' (Meyer & Schvaneveldt, 1976). In this kind of experiment, the processing of the second word can be facilitated even if the first word is presented so briefly that the subject is never consciously aware of it (Marcel, 1983).

## Vigilance

A third sense in which the term 'attention' has been used refers to the amount of conscious mental effort invested in a given act. As we have seen, much selective attention seems to proceed automatically and unconsciously. However, further selection of information for decision-making and response execution requires the commitment of a separate attention system which is under the control of conscious volition. The amount of information reaching consciousness that we can voluntarily select to 'pay attention' to is quite limited. The limitations of this conscious attention system are evident in the cocktail party situation; it just isn't possible to 'hear' more than one conversation at a time. The limitations of conscious mental capacity also account for the fact that telephone numbers are seven digits, since this is the upper limit of digit span for most people. Experimentally, the degree to which the conscious attention mechanism is committed to a given task can be measured in terms of the time required to disengage from the task to respond to an unrelated signal. For example, you will probably respond to me quicker if I call you while you are reciting the alphabet than you would if you were doing long division in your head. The amount of attention required may vary widely, even for the same task. For example, learning to drive a car requires a great deal of concentration. On the other hand, the experienced driver may be able to drive from home to work while thinking about something entirely different. Since brain-injury victims must cope with greater limitations of the conscious attention mechanism, they commonly report that everyday tasks which they formerly 'did without thinking,' now demand effortful concentration.

In addition to its limitations in simultaneous processing, the conscious attention system is limited in the degree in which it can be sustained. The term vigilance refers to the ability to sustain conscious attention over long periods. Its problems are illustrated by the example of a radar operator who must attend for long periods of time in order to detect a signal appearing against background environmental 'noise.'

The availability and capacity of this limited attention system is strongly influenced by other components of attention. The radar operator who didn't get any sleep the night before, and who falls asleep on the job, demonstrates how sustained concentration of the central attention mechanism is dependent upon maintaining levels of tonic arousal. Our first hypothetical patient who is overmedicated on anticonvulsant medications, and falls asleep in class, also illustrates this problem. Information selected for conscious attention is more likely to affect our awareness, behavior, and subsequent memory. For 'carryover' to occur in a cognitive retraining program, it will be important to optimize the degree to which the patient is able to commit the limited capacity, conscious attention system.

These three components of attention – alerting, selection and conscious attention – relate quite well to the remedial devices which Ben-Yishay (see Chapter 8) employs in his studies of attentional rehabilitation. For example, Ben-Yishay attempts to improve alertness by the introduction of warning signals, he attempts to improve selectivity by training subjects to attend to an area of the visual world, and he attempts to improve concentration by training the subjects to sustain their efforts over time. A major challenge is to determine, for each individual, what components of the attention system are disordered, and then to formulate a remediation program rationally designed to specifically help that problem.

## FRAMEWORK FOR RELATING COGNITIVE TO NEURAL SYSTEMS

For both theoretical and practical reasons, our goal must be to identify fundamental cognitive systems, isolate and characterize their component mental operations, and, finally, to link these components to the neural mechanisms which mediate them. A cognitive system is similar to what is known in physiology as an organ system – a set of component functions performed in pursuit of a common goal by several specialized organs. Thus, the process of nutrition involves swallowing by the pharynx, digestion by the stomach, absorption by the intestines, and metabolic processing by the liver. Similarly, a cognitive system is a set of mental operations performed in pursuit of common processing goals that are carried out by a common neural system. Taking attention as an example of a cognitive system, some components, such as alertness, may require subcortical mechanisms (the reticular formation), while others, like conscious attention, require cerebral cortex. Other putative examples of cognitive systems include object recognition, spatial localization, language processing, motor control, emotional regulation, and memory.

We have been working with both normal individuals and brain-injured patients to develop a better understanding of one particular cognitive system, *viz*. the orienting of attention in the visual field. This relatively simple cognitive act was selected as a model for testing certain hypotheses about how cognitive systems in general might act and interact with one another. Our goal has been to identify the individual components involved in this model cognitive system, to characterize the properties of these components, and to understand the elementary mental operations which produce them.

An elementary operation, as we use the term, is an internal computation which transforms information in some way. The operation can be specified logically in terms of the input to the operation and the output of the operation. For example, if one is scanning a list of digits to determine if there is an 8 in the list, the following three mental operations may be involved: A *disengage* operation (to leave digit N); a *move* operation (to go to the next digit); and a *compare* operation (matching the digit to the 8). These operations are the logical computations that would have to be specified in performing the task. During the past 20 years computer simulations have been developed to try to better understand the mental procedures which might be required to perform certain tasks. This work in artificial intelligence research has formulated putative mental operations which can be sought, experimentally, in human subjects.

Over the past 15 years, many such operations have been studied experimentally to determine the component facilitations and inhibitions of performance that occur when people execute specific mental operations (Posner, 1978). These component facilitations and inhibitions in processing efficiency, when time-locked experimentally to the occurrence of signals, can provide us with signs of the execution of the mental operation. In this chapter we will examine such operations in one simple cognitive act, namely spatial attention.

In the case of spatial attention it has been possible to identify elementary operations, to show how they are affected by brain injury, and thus to link them to neural systems and to the operations of individual cells. This has been possible because spatial attention is a cognitive act that we share with other animals, and thus a great deal of work has been done with brain injury cases, electrical recording of evoked potentials from humans, and single cell recording from alert monkeys. There are no animal models for many complex operations people perform. On the other hand, once clinicians understand an impairment in terms of the elementary operations involved, it may be possible to predict strategies which might usefully aid patients in understanding, adapting to, or overcoming their deficits.

It is too early to be certain of the degree to which any given elementary operation is localized within the brain. We do not know the extent to which, for example, the neural systems related to the 'disengage' operation, discussed above, may be common to different contents (e.g., disengage from a visual location, from a hand location or from thinking about a word). However, cognitive systems themselves must be highly distributed in the brain requiring the integration of many operations at different levels of the nervous system. The general framework that we have developed – namely specifying cognitive tasks in terms of elementary operations, studying their facilitory and inhibitory components in performance, and linking such components to neural systems – may eventually deepen understanding of how operations relate to cognitive systems.

Luria (1966) has emphasized the importance of interpreting a given symptom complex produced by a brain lesion in terms of the dysfunction of some common 'mental action' underlying the disordered functions. This view predicts what is often seen in clinical experience: that similar symptoms can be produced by lesions at different levels of the nervous system; and secondly, that certain functional deficits after localized brain injury tend to cluster together.

For example, the syndrome of hemi-neglect can be produced by lesions of parietal, frontal, or cingulate cortex, and even by lesions of the mesencephalic tegmentum (Mesulam, 1981). Conversely, a lesion in a single brain center may produce impairment in several apparently unrelated functions by depriving them of some common, underlying elementary operation which all require. It is known, for example, that with left frontal lesions a cluster of symptoms occurs with associated impairment for both speech production (aphasia) and manual motor control (apraxia) (Kimura, 1982). Our framework would incline the investigator to think about this clinical association as resulting from a dysfunction in an elementary operation for processing sequences. This putative processor, assumed to operate on information from either linguistic or motor codes, is not specifically part of either motor or language systems, but is required by both.

To illustrate this approach we will proceed with our analysis of one cognitive act, spatial orienting, as a model cognitive system.

## SPATIAL ATTENTION AS A MODEL SYSTEM FOR LINKING COGNITIVE AND NEURAL SYSTEMS

Since shifts in visual attention are usually accompanied by observable motor behavior (the orienting response), this cognitive act has been widely studied in animals as a model of attention, and much has been learned about its underlying physiology. Orienting in humans is a relatively simple cognitive act which can be objectively measured and related to rich experimental literature in animals.

Orienting behavior is a complex process with several components: there is a general alerting with associated physiological changes; there are overt movements of the head and eyes to align the fovea with the spatial locus of interest; and finally, there are mental shifts of attention, covert orienting, to the locus of interest.

The first part of this work documented the existence of a separate mental process for covert orienting, which could be dissociated from the eye movement system. In other words, to prove that people in general (not just quarterbacks) can 'look out of the corner of the eye.'

## Covert components of spatial orienting

One method of studying covert orienting is to demonstrate that attention can move through the visual field independent of overt action (Posner, 1980). Our basic experiment involved a simple detection task requiring that a subject keep the eyes fixed in the center of a cathode ray tube (CRT) screen and press a key (with the index finger of the dominant hand) whenever a large, bright target appears. The targets typically occur equidistant to the left or right of fixation with equal probability. The dependent variable is simple reaction time for detection of the target. Prior to the appearance of the target, however, a cue is presented to attract attention to one of two locations. For example, a box brightening 10° to left or right, or an arrow appearing at fixation pointing either to left or right. The preliminary cue may either be valid, i.e., correctly prepare the subject to detect a target, or invalid, i.e., it brings the subject's attention to the opposite visual field. Or the cue may be neutral, i.e., brightening of a central box, which produces a general alerting but gives no spatial information to bias selection. Note that in this paradigm there are no movements of the eyes (overt orienting) and the simple motor response remains the same in all cue conditions. Any difference in reaction time for different cue conditions must therefore index movements of attention - a purely mental operation.

The results of such experiments were quicker reaction times (RTs) for valid cues, slower RTs for invalid cues, and intermediate RTs for neural cues (Posner, 1980; Posner & Cohen, 1984). Since the response was always the same, the difference in reaction time for different cue conditions could be attributed to the psychological effects of performing the mental operation activated by the cue. The results indicate that the mental act of shifting attention (covert orienting) to one locus in the visual field does facilitate the selection and detection of information arising there, while inhibiting the processing of information in the contralateral visual field in comparison to a neutral cue. This method permits the time-locking of mental events to presented information. By varying the time between cue and target, it is possible to time how long it takes the nervous system to perform the attention shift. Using a variation of this covert orienting paradigm in which spatial relationships between cue and target were varied systematically across the visual field, it was estimated that attention moves in an analog manner through the visual field at a rate of about 8 milliseconds per degree (Shulman et al, 1979; Tsal, 1983).

The properties of covert spatial orienting have been further characterized in other experiments which have shown that covert orienting may be produced both automatically by exogenous sensory signals, or by endogenous mechanism operating probabilistically on the basis of expectation. Let us look, for example, at a version of this experiment in which a central arrow pointing to left or right is presented as the cue. When the arrow correctly predicts where a target will appear (i.e., it is valid 80% of the time at least), then attention shifts are produced with reaction time to invalid cues being slower than those to valid cues. If a central cue is used which does not predict target location (the arrow is valid only 50% of the time), there is no difference in reaction time between the two fields. If a cue is an exogenous sensory signal which requires no symbolic processing, *viz.* a box brightening in the periphery, it was found that this kind of cue facilitates detection of information occurring at the locus, even when it is not predictive (i.e., occurs with a 50% probability). In other words, even though the cue provides no information about where to expect the target, the sensory signal appears to summon attention to its spatial location.

Another experiment showed the separation between automatic, exogenous orienting and endogenously generated orienting (Posner et al, 1982). In this experiment the cue was a peripheral box brightening 10° to left or right of fixation. However, the cue was valid only 20% of the time. That is, the cue instructed the subjects to expect the target to appear in the *opposite* visual field. For short warning intervals reaction times were quicker on the side that the cue appeared. With warning intervals of more than 150 milliseconds the reaction times were quicker to targets appearing opposite the cue. In other words, during the first 100 milliseconds or so, a sensory event produces an automatic orienting of attention which facilitates processing of information subsequently presented there, even if the sensory information inaccurately predicts where the target is likely to appear.

Further experiments elucidated some of the further properties of this automatic facilitation produced by exogenous sensory signals. In experiments where the subject's attention was moved to one area of the visual field, and then the eyes to another, it was found that this facilitory effect operates and moves in retinotopic coordinates (i.e., based on eye position) (Posner & Cohen, 1984).

## Covert orienting: elementary mental operations

The act of orienting attention toward a target may be considered in terms of three more elementary mental operations: disengaging from the current focus of attention; moving attention to the location of the target; and engaging the target. Consider a person facing a blank visual display as in the experiments we have described here. If a cue is given to expect a target at some location, and sufficient time is also given to orient attention there, then the only remaining operation required when the target appears is to engage it. If the person facing the blank screen is given no cue, when the target appears attention must first be moved to the target, and then the target can be engaged. Finally, if a cue is first given, and a target subsequently appears at a location other than the cued one, the person must first disengage attention from the cued location, next move it to the target location, and finally, engage the target. We have been seeking to determine whether control of any of these three putative elementary operations – disengage, move, engage – involved in covert orienting could be linked to a given level of the nervous system. Our studies have involved patients with impaired spatial orienting due to lesions at different levels of the nervous system, and proceeded from a viewpoint which considered covert orienting as a distributed system with both cortical and subcortical mechanisms. We have found evidence in these studies that the 'disengage' component of spatial orienting requires intact parietal lobe cortex, while lesions at the midbrain level produce deficits in the 'move' component of covert orienting.

## Parietal lobe contributions to covert spatial orienting

A covert orienting experiment was performed on 13 patients with parietal lobe lesions (Posner et al, 1984). In the basic experiment, the cue was the brightening of a peripheral box which was valid on 80% of the trials. The major result was relatively normal reaction times except when a cue was presented to the ipsilateral field followed by a contralateral target. In this case, reaction times were greatly lengthened at all cue-to-target intervals. There was a relatively small difference in reaction time between the two visual fields when the subjects were first correctly cued to either field (valid trials). (In fact, in several subjects valid cuing into the neglected field resulted in detections which were just as quick as in the non-neglected field.) There was also a steady drop in reaction time in the neglected as well as the non-neglected field when subjects were first cued there. In other words, if parietal lobe patients are presented a cue, they seem to be able to move their attention as well to the neglected as to the non-neglected field. Compare this with what happens to performance when subjects are first presented a cue in the wrong visual field. In this case they must first disengage from the cue before they can then move their attention to the target. In this case subsequent targets in the contralateral (neglected) visual field result in dramatic inhibition of detection. The cost of disengaging from a target in order to move attention into the neglected field is very large. These results suggest that parietal lobe lesions may selectively interfere with the 'disengage' elementary operation of covert spatial orienting without affecting the 'move' component. The same basic results were obtained when the cue was a central arrow pointing to left or right indicating that the difficulties with disengaging in parietal lobe patients occurred whether the cue produced orienting through either exogenous or endogenous mechanisms.

A modification of this experiment used a neutral cue (brightening of a central box) which gave no information about where to expect the target. The results of this experiment indicated that the neutral cue had the same effect as on an invalid cue in the ipsilateral field. In other words, even when a signal provides no information about where the target will appear, the subject must still disengage from it before he or she can move attention to the target. When the target appears in the visual field contralateral to the lesion subjects are much slower to disengage from fixation than when they have to move their attention in the ipsilateral direction.

This finding suggested to us that the elementary operation of disengaging attention performed by parietal lobe was coded on the basis of the direction of movement of attention rather than on the basis of either visual field *per se* or hemispace (Bowers et al, 1981). Kinsbourne (1973) had previously suggested that each hemisphere controls the operations which orient covert attention in the contralateral direction, irrespective of specific spatial location.

To test this hypothesis, a modification of the covert orienting paradigm was used to test parietal lobe patients (Posner et al, 1983). In addition to the cuing of either the left or right visual field, in this experiment cues were introduced at different locations within each visual field to measure the time to disengage attention to move from one part of each visual field to another part of that same field. Right parietal lesion patients with left-sided neglect were found to be slower in moving from right to left than from left to right: this effect was present in both visual fields.

To summarize, we have found that at least one of our putative elementary mental operations involved in covert orienting (i.e., the disengagement mechanism) can be selectively affected by localized brain injury. The impairment in disengagement of attention was selective for patients with cortical lesions in the parietal lobe and did not occur with lesions of the temporal or frontal lobes. There was also evidence that lesions affecting the non-dominant parietal lobe produce greater effects on the disengagement mechanism than did comparable lesions of the dominant hemisphere; and that lesions of the superior parietal region were more likely to affect disengagement than were lesions of the inferior parietal region (Posner et al, 1984).

We must now turn to the critical clinical question: does this selective impairment in an elementary mental operation for disengaging attention account for the clinical phenomenon of neglect? Our best guess is that this deficit in disengaging attention is only part of the story. There is evidence that the parietal cortex, in addition to its role in shifting attention in the visual field, also supports the neural mechanism for visual imagery. Bisiach et al (1919) found that parietal lesion patients failed to report buildings on the left side of a mental image when asked to 'take a mental walk' down a familiar street; but subsequently reported these same buildings when asked to take a mental walk down the same street coming from the other direction such that the previously unreported buildings were now in their non-neglected side. It seems likely to us that the neglect syndrome as it occurs clinically is based on two (at least) separable deficits: (1) inability to generate or sustain a visual image on the non-neglected side; and (2) an inability to mentally scan the visual field (or visual image) because of a defect in the disengage mechanism required for shifting attention.

At this point we have identified at least one elementary operation which is affected by parietal lobe injuries. We don't yet know how, or how much, this basic deficit accounts for or contributes to the clinical symptom complex underlying visual neglect. Much less are we in a position to say whether the difficulty in disengaging attention to move it through the visual field might also in some way be related to the other components of the parietal lobe symptom complex. However, we can at least begin to ask whether a deficit in disengaging attention for visual orienting might also cause difficulties with disengaging from one idea to the next in a way which might account for the illogicality of thought seen in many parietal lobe patients (Lezak, 1983).

## Midbrain contributions to the control of orienting behavior and spatial attention

One of the most interesting areas to be attacked by neuroscience concerns the role of the midbrain in visual perception and in the elaboration of visually guided behavior. The superior colliculus of the midbrain tectum has been of special interest because this neural structure has served throughout most of vertebrate evolution as the primary visual center of the brain. Only with the appearance of mammals did the encephalization of vision occur with the development of primary visual cortex in the occipital lobes. So now, what role does this phylogenetically old visual center play in humans and other mammals? How does the newer geniculostriate visual apparatus interact with the extrageniculate system of the midbrain?

Over the past few decades a two-visual system hypothesis has emerged (Schneider, 1969): The geniculostriate system is believed to subserve fine visual discrimination in object recognition, i.e., knowing what; while the extrageniculate subserves 'ambient' (Trevarthan, 1970), or 'panoramic' (Denny-Brown & Fischer, 1976) vision for processing salient features in the periphery, i.e., 'knowing where.'

According to this model, the midbrain plays an important role in orienting behavior (at least orienting triggered by exogenous stimuli). When I 'see' something large moving in the jungle out of the corner of my eye, my midbrain gets very busy localizing it and initiating orienting movements of the head and eyes to look at my attacker. Then the occipital lobes of the geniculostriate system take over to discriminate and identify my target. Of course, our visual experience in real life is a unified one and must result from the interaction of the two visual systems as an integrated whole. Through the visual association cortex, the geniculostriate system communicates with the midbrain extra-geniculate visuomotor centers through relays in the pulvinar of the thalamus.

This process of foveation – (aligning of the fovea for discriminating objects) – is only one role of the optic tectum. In addition, it has a more primitive and general role in stabilizing the organism's visual world (Ingle & Sprague,

1972). It is the colliculus which integrates sensory and motor information for the fish, allowing it to hover in one place over a stream bed with a stable orientation whatever the current may do. To give another example which makes this point, let me ask you to imagine standing next to a wall facing parallel to it. If that wall were suddenly to move, you would certainly turn to see what was going on. On the other hand, what if you started to walk along the wall? The wall would be moving relative to you; but since your motor system initiated the movement, some corollary message would, according to our model, be sent to your colliculus inhibiting it from initiating an inappropriate orienting response. What if you oriented toward it anyway? If, as you started to walk, some reflex orienting response turned you toward the wall at the same time, you would probably fall on your face.

An uncommon neurological disorder called progressive supranuclear palsy (PSP) (Steele et al, 1964) is of special interest to students of attention because of its unique tendency to produce degeneration in the superior colliculus and related mesencephalic visuomotor centers. This lesion results in the distinguishing clinical feature of the disease, a paralysis of voluntary gaze accompanied by a global derangement of orienting and other visually guided behaviors. Clinical and experimental observations in patients with PSP have begun to converge with evidence from animal research to tell us a great deal about what role the midbrain plays in human visuomotor function.

Before proceeding with that story, however, we must put it in the context of the disease as a whole. This degenerative disorder involves not just the midbrain tectum, but also many subcortical nuclei. The substantia nigra degenerates just as in Parkinson's disease, with the resulting decrease in dopamine and parkinsonian symptoms. Other basal ganglia are also degenerated including the globus pallidus, red nucleus, and subthalamic nucleus. In addition, there is extensive degeneration of the ascending reticular formation including the midline raphe nuclei of the reticular formation deploying the neurotransmitter serotonin. The locus ceruleus, which projects noradrenalin to the rest of the brain, also is frequently involved. Thus, at least three ascending neurotransmitter systems are affected by this disease: dopamine, serotonin, and noradrenalin. It is not surprising, therefore, that one of the clinical components of this disorder is a severe disruption of tonic arousal. All spontaneous behavior is impoverished and slowed (Albert et al, 1974; Rafal & Grimm, 1981), and the sleep–waking cycle is disorganized (Gross et al, 1978).

If we wish to define the effect of one limited part of the pathology (the superior colliculus) on selective attention, we must proceed with caution. Lesions of the basal ganglia will impair motor behavior from which attention is inferred, and the disease of the reticular formation affects attention at the more general level of alertness. In using PSP as a model for understanding human extrageniculate visuomotor capabilities, it has become conventional to contrast the syndrome with Parkinson's disease. Both diseases show many of the same clinical and pathological features. PSP differs from Parkinson's disease because of the voluntary ophthalmoplegia and collicular degeneration. Therefore, visuomotor defects found in PSP patients which are not present in Parkinson's disease can be ascribed, at least tentatively, to the peritectal lesion including the colliculus.

The ophthalmoplegia of PSP is considered to be the distinguishing clinical feature of the disease. Reflex eye movements, specifically the vestibulo-ocular reflex which stabilizes the eyes while the head is turned, are spared and actually disinhibited. So when the examiner turns the patient's head, the eyes remain fixed in space as they rotate in the eye sockets. We know, therefore, that the oculomotor nuclei, nerves, and muscles must be intact. Yet supranuclear control of eye movements is lost. Typically, vertical eye movements are more affected first and affected earlier in the disease.

The impairment of ocular motility, however, is only one component of a more global impairment of visually guided behavior. Although visual acuity *per se* is unaffected by the disease, these patients often *behave as if they were blind*. Rafal & Grimm (1981) called attention to a unique deficit in orienting behavior in these patients. Even before the eyes become paralyzed, these patients fail to turn to face people who approach them, don't make or sustain eye contact during conversation, and often don't look down at their plates when eating, even though they can do so on request. Fisk et al (1982) showed quantitatively that PSP patients were more impaired than Parkinson's disease controls in visual search and scanning. Rafal & Grimm (1981) also speculated on some more general consequences of deranged orienting behaviour for PSP patients. Not only do these individuals fail to orient when they should; they often orient when they should not have. When walking down a hall they often *did* turn toward a doorway they were passing and *did* fall. When drug therapy was begun in some patients they became very distractible for several days, turning toward anything that moved.

In describing the behavioral effects of drug therapy with methysergide (a serotonin antagonist) and antiparkinsonian drugs, Rafal & Grimm (1981) observed that patients who responded to therapy were more alert, more active, and more animated. They slept more soundly at night and were less drowsy during the day. They noted that, although ocular motility *per se* did not improve greatly, orienting behavior improved dramatically in some patients. These observations raise an interesting question which can't be answered at this point. Does orienting behavior improve in treated patients because the drug affects selective attention? Or is improved orienting a by-product of a general improvement in arousal? In PSP we find a disorder in which several components of attention appear to be affected by lesions at different levels of the brainstem. Disease in the reticular formation of the lower brainstem produces a disorder of tonic arousal, while disease at the level of the midbrain tectum seems to produce a disorder of selective attention, at least as far as selective attention can be inferred from orienting behavior.

Using the chronometric techniques for measuring covert orienting as described previously, we have been able to ask whether this disorder of orienting behavior, i.e., overt orienting, in PSP is accompanied or caused by a deficit in covert orienting. In other words, do patients with collicular damage have trouble mentally shifting their attention in the visual fields? We found not only that PSP patients were impaired in covert spatial orienting, but also that a different elementary mental operation appears to be impaired than that produced by parietal lobe cortical lesions. In conducting this experiment we exploited one of the clinical peculiarities of this disease. Namely, that vertical gaze is affected more than horizontal eye movements. In studying covert orienting in these patients, therefore, we measured how well these patients were able to shift their attention in the horizontal plane as compared to their ability to do so vertically. Posner et al (1982) found that PSP patients could shift their attention in the vertical dimension, even when eye movements were entirely paralyzed in this plane. However, we also found that they were *slower* to move their attention in the vertical than in the horizontal plane for both valid and invalid trials. No such asymmetry between vertical and horizontal attention shifts was found in parkinsonian control subjects.

This result contrasts with that found in parietal lobe patients. As you will recall, parietal lobe patients were able to move their attention equally well into either field in response to a valid cue. On the other had, if they had to disengage from a cue to respond to a contralateral target, a dramatic slowing of reaction time occurred. To summarize this contrast, it appears that parietal lobe patients are able to move their attention but the disengage operation is impaired. Conversely, PSP patients appeared to have a disturbance in the 'move' operation such that they are slow to orient their attention, but do not have any difficulty in the disengage operation.

This kind of experimental evidence in humans converges with animal experimental studies which have implicated the midbrain in visual attention and spatial orienting. Goldberg & Wurtz (1972) have described single units in the optic layers of the superior colliculus in behaving primates which discharge 50 milliseconds before the eye movement begins. The response properties of these neurons were affected by the behavioral stimulus, i.e., whether the animal attended to it. Small tectal lesions did not affect the speed or accuracy of eye movements into the receptor field of these units, but the *latency* for the saccade increased. This and subsequent work (Wurtz & Mohler, 1976) has provided strong evidence that the superior colliculus is involved, not in the initiation of eye movements *per se*, but in the selective shifting of intention in the visual field in preparation for eye movement. The clinical and experimental observations in PSP patients provide further evidence that the phylogenetically ancient midbrain visuomotor structures continue to play an important role in selective spatial attention and in regulating a whole range of visually guided behavior. The challenge now will be to consider how this visual system interacts with corticovisual operations in normal and brain-injured patients.

## Inhibitory effects of covert spatial orienting

We will ask now what happens to information arriving at an area of the visual field immediately after it has been attended, when attention is withdrawn from that locus. Take the experimental paradigm described earlier and modify it as follows: a peripheral cue lights up summoning attention to left or right. After the cue disappears, a second cue lights up at fixation bringing attention back to the center. Then a target appears either at the previously cued location, or, with equal probability, somewhere else in the visual field. Posner & Cohen (1984) have shown, using this paradigm, that once attention has been withdrawn from a locus in the visual field, reaction times to detect a target there are inhibited relative to other areas of the visual field. Thus, it appears that covert spatial orienting has both a facilitory and an inhibitory component. The inhibitory effect is only produced by exogenous cues. This inhibitory effect, which we call the inhibition of return, appears to be related to a reduced tendency to move the attention or the eyes to a visual location which has recently been inspected. Unlike the facilitory effect, if the eyes move after attention has been shifted to a locus, the inhibition of return remains in the same environmental location (Posner & Cohen, 1984).

We have used this same experimental paradigm in patients with neurological disease to try to determine the neuroanatomic substrates for this inhibitory component of covert spatial orienting (Posner et al, 1984). When six patients with PSP were studied in this paradigm (again comparing attention shifts in the vertical and the horizontal planes), it was found that, in the vertical direction, there was no inhibition of return, whereas it was present in the horizontal direction. Parkinsonian control subjects showed no such asymmetry between vertical and horizontal inhibition. Patients with cortical lesions involving frontal, temporal, or parietal lobe all showed the presence of an inhibition of return (even the parietal patients who, as we discussed earlier, had great impairment in the disengage operation of the facilitory component).

Let us summarize what we have learned about attention impairments in PSP:

1. Spontaneous orienting behavior – for example, social orienting – is impoverished and orienting movements (overt orienting) are slowed. We also have evidence that the covert movement of mental attention is slowed and that this selective impairment in the *move* component of covert spatial orienting may account for at least part of the behavioral dysfunction observed clinically.
2. When orienting behavior does occur in these patients, it is often inappropriate. Orienting responses that should be inhibited are not. We now have evidence that midbrain lesions impair the inhibitory component of covert spatial orienting, and we can speculate that this deficit may account for the distractibility sometimes seen in these patients and possibly for some of the reasons that they fall.
3. Finally, we know that tonic arousal is deranged in these patients. How does this deficiency in general alertness related to the impairment in selective attention (covert orienting) that we have described? If we consider, together, the slowness in moving covert attention, accompanied by a deficiency in inhibiting orienting, we are left with the impression of a car

> being driven with the accelerator and the brake simultaneously. In patients who respond to medication, alertness tends to improve. As it does, orienting responses increase and become brisker; but at the same time, inappropriate orienting also may increase. Thus, in this syndrome, we can isolate several components of attention which are impaired, and synthesize from this knowledge an understanding of the symptom complex as it occurs in everyday life.

Unfortunately, PSP is a malignant, degenerative disease, and it is unlikely that our new understanding will lead us to a successful rehabilitation program.

We will now return to disabilities of attention caused by cortical lesions. These are often caused by static disease processes which allow patients to live for many years, and oblige us to provide rehabilitation which will optimize their independence and quality of life.

## POTENTIAL APPLICATIONS OF ATTENTION THEORY TO THE REHABILITATION OF UNILATERAL SPATIAL NEGLECT

Can we apply cognitive methods and the theory of the interaction between cortical and subcortical mechanisms of attention to problems of cognitive rehabilitation? On the methodological end there seems little doubt that cognitive psychology can and is making a contribution. Our reaction time technique for the study of spatial attention as one example provides a sensitive assay of the tendency toward neglect of one side of space. We can pick up deficits in patients who would not be diagnosed as having any residual neglect or extinction. This sensitivity can be useful in conjunction with any rehabilitation program in assessing the success of various methods.

We believe that the general framework and language of cognitive systems and mental operations also will contribute to rehabilitation. A deficit can be described both in terms of the cognitive system involved and in terms of the operations within that system which are affected. The same operations may be involved in different cognitive systems (e.g., in spatial cognition and language). It is not yet known the extent to which a lesion affecting the operations in one system will also affect another. However, the clinician who is aware of these potential connections can use the knowledge of the operations involved in different tasks to calculate the areas that might present problems for the patient. This ability to think about a deficit as it might affect different cognitive domains (what we tend to call calculation in the performance domain) should be an asset in trying to discover and provide systematic links between brain injury and real life cognitive performance.

Perhaps the theory we have provided can suggest specific procedures. One example is in the area of ways of remediating neglect.

Sprague (1966) found that combined lesions of the visual cortex and the superior colliculus did interact to affect the organism's visual capacity. Animals that had large lesions of the visual cortex developed an hemianopia which subsequently partially recovered. If a lesion was then placed in the superior colliculus on the same side, the animal lost its previously recovered abilities and again had a dense visual field loss. Conversely, when cortical and collicular lesions were placed sequentially on opposite sides, the clinical results did not summate but instead were opposed. Animals in whom visual field impairment was produced by cortical lesions were found to regain considerable visual function in the impaired field if a lesion was made in the contralateral superior colliculus. Of course, the improvement in the previously impaired visual field from collicular lesions was produced at the cost of a new impairment in visually guided behavior in the opposite, previously normal, visual field.

In discussing these observations, Sprague postulated that the cortex and colliculus on each side acted as a unit. Cortical lesions on one side, he proposed, resulted in the colliculus on that side being inhibited by the contralateral colliculus whose visual cortex was intact. By removing the superior colliculus on the 'good' side, the opposite colliculus was released from its inhibition and was able to subserve some visual function in a previously densely hemianopic field. Support for this concept of collicular inhibition was obtained by producing the same results simply by placing a section in the posterior commissure region such that the two superior colliculi were separated from one another.

Sprague's findings give support for the idea that the cortical and subcortical visual centers operate in concert in the control of visual perception and spatial attention. Can we exploit these cortical–subcortical interactions therapeutically? Obviously we cannot treat patients with cortical parietal lesions by placing lesions in their opposite midbrains. However, we have reason to believe that it might be possible to functionally produce a similar effect by monocular patching of one eye on the side ipsilateral to the parietal lesion. Unlike the geniculostriate cortical visual system, the collicular midbrain system is mainly crossed. The predominant visual imput to the left superior colliculus comes from the right eye. Therefore, by patching the right eye, it might be possible to functionally deafferent the left superior colliculus and thereby, hopefully, to decrease visual neglect in the left visual field in patients with right parietal lesions. Shulman (1984) studied orienting biases in normal individuals when they were presented with bilateral visual targets under conditions of unilateral eye occlusion. Under these conditions he found out there was a strong bias for subjects to make eye movements toward the target in the temporal direction. That is, when the right eye was patched and normal subjects were presented bilateral targets and asked to make an eye movement in either direction they chose, they were much more likely to make saccade to the target on the left side. This effect was presumed to be mediated by mechanism of a unilateral activation of the right superior colliculus producing an orienting bias toward the left side. This orienting bias was present only for overt orienting and did not occur for covert shifts of attention using a paradigm similar to that discussed earlier in this chapter.

Based on Sprague's work in experimental animals, and Shulman's findings in normal subjects, could we anticipate that monocular patching of the right eye in patients with right parietal lesions might improve visual neglect on the left side? Any improvement in the left-sided neglect which might occur with right eye patching would likely be small relative to the loss of visual capacity in the previously normal part of the field. Therefore, patching the right eye is unlikely to improve the individual's functional capacity in everyday life and, on balance, might well result in even greater overall visual impairment. We would like to propose, however, that patching the right eye might be helpful in laboratory training exercises as part of a cognitive remediation program.

## SUMMARY

We began this paper with a general view of attention, and have worked our way to a specific proposal for remediation of one form of attentional deficit. While we believe that deficits of spatial attention are in some ways a model of how psychological theory, brain function, and cognitive rehabilitation can be linked, we understand that there are many disorders of attention for which little is known at the neural level. We believe that a detailed analysis of these deficits in terms of impairments of mental operations may allow for better rehabilitation techniques and may also increase our ability to discover the neural systems which relate to them.

## ACKNOWLEDGMENT

This research was supported by NIMH Grant No. MH 38503-01

### REFERENCES

Albert M L, Feldman R G, Willis A L 1974 The subcortical dementia of progressive supranuclear palsy. Journal of Neurology, Neurosurgery and Psychiatry 37: 121–130

Bisiach E, Luzzatti C, Perani D 1979 Unilateral neglect representational schema and consciousness. Brain 10: 609–618

Bowers D, Heilman K F, Van Den Abell T 1981 Hemispace-VHF compatibility. Neuropsychologica 19: 757–765

Denny-Brown D, Fischer E G 1976 Physiological aspects of visual perception: the subcortical visual direction of behavior. Archives of Neurology 33: 228–243

Fisk J D, Goodak M A, Burkhart G, Barnett H J M 1982 Progressive supranuclear palsy: the relationship between ocular motor dysfunction and psychological test performance. Neurology 32: 698–705

Goldberg M E, Wurtz R H 1972 Activity of superior colliculus neurons in behaving monkeys. Journal of Neurophysiology 35: 542–560

Gross R A, Spehlmann R, Daniels J C 1978 Sleep disturbances in progressive supranuclear palsy. EEG and Clinical Neurophysiology 4: 16–25

Ingle D, Sprague J M 1973 Sensorimotor function of the midbrain tectum. Neuroscientific Research Bulletin 13

Kimura D 1982 Left hemisphere control of oral and brachial movements and their relation to communication. Philosophical Transactions of the Royal Society of London B298

Kinsbourne M 1973 Hemi-neglect and hemispheric rivalry. In: Weinstein E D, Friedland R L (eds) Hemi-inattention and hemisphere specialization. Advances in Neurology 18. Raven Press, New York, 41–52

Lezak M 1983 Neuropsychological assessment. Oxford University Press, Oxford
Luria A R 1966 Higher cortical functions in man. Basic Books, New York
Marcel A J 1983 Conscious and unconscious perception: an approach to the relations between phenomenal experience and perceptual processes. Cognitive Psychology 238–300
Mesulam M M 1981 A cortical network for directed attention and unilateral neglect. Annals of Neurology 10: 309–325
Meyer D E, Schvaneveldt R W 1976 Managing memory structure and mental processes. Science 192: 27–33
Posner M I 1978 Chronometric explorations of mind. Lawrence Erlbaum, Hillsdale, NJ
Posner M I 1980 Orienting of attention. The VIIth Sir Frederick Bartlett Lecture. Quarterly Journal of Experimental Psychology 32: 3–5
Posner M I, Boies S W 1971 Components of attention. Psychological Review 78: 391–408
Posner M I, Cohen Y 1984 Components of visual orienting. In: Bouma X H, Bowhuis D (eds) Attention and performance. Erlbaum, Hillsdale, NJ
Posner M I, Cohen Y, Rafal R D 1982 Neural systems control of spatial orienting. Philosophical Transactions of the Royal Society of London B298: 187–198
Posner M I, Friedrich F J, Walker J, Rafal R D 1983 Neural control of the direction of covert visual orienting. Paper given to the Psychonomics Society, San Diego, November
Posner M I, Walker J, Freidrich F J, Rafal R D 1984 Effects of parietal injury on covert orienting of visual attention. Journal of Neuroscience 4: 1863–1874
Rafal R D, Grimm R J 1981 Progressive supranuclear palsy functional analysis of the response to methysergide and anti-Parkinsonism agents. Neurology 31: 1507–1518
Schneider G E 1969 Two visual systems. Science 163: 895–902
Shulman G L 1984 An asymmetry in the control of eye movements and shifts of attention. Acta Psychologica 55: 53–69
Shulman G L, Remington R W, McLean J 1979 Moving attention through visual space. Journal of Experimental Psychology: Human Perception and Performance 5: 522–526
Sokolov Y N 1963 Perception and the conditioned reflex. Macmillan, New York
Sprague J M 1966 Interaction of cortex and superior colliculus in mediation of visually guided behavior in the cat. Science 123: 1544–1546
Steele J C 1964 Progressive supranuclear palsy. Archives of Neurology 10: 333–359
Trevarthan C 1970 Experimental evidence for a brain stem contribution to visual perception in man. Brain Behavior and Evolution 33: 338–345
Tsal Y 1983 Movements of attention across the visual field. Journal of Experimental Psychology: Human Perception and Performance 9: 523–530
Wurtz R H, Mohler C W 1976 Organization of monkey superior colliculus enhanced visual response of superficial layer cells. Journal of Neurophysiology 39: 745–765

10 *Rosamond Gianutsos and Pauline Matheson*

# The rehabilitation of visual perceptual disorders attributable to brain injury

This chapter critically reviews the current state of the art and offers a conceptual framework of visual perception for the development of effective rehabilitation protocols. In this field, diagnostic issues must first be fully explored in relation to this conceptual framework. An apt diagnosis provides the necessary foundation for the design of effective individualized rehabilitation planning. Our ultimate concern is with rehabilitation.

Visual imperception can occur with a variety of visual system pathologies, but the concern here is largely with the forms of visual imperception which are associated with acute-onset brain injury (including cerebrovascular accident). We have used an umbrella term, *visual imperception* because experience has convinced us that all visual system pathologies must be investigated and taken into account in planning rehabilitation with survivors of brain injury. Visual sensory dysfunction, if present, will be translated through the remainder of the information processing system. What appears to be hemi-inattention or confusion may in fact be a normal response to abnormally processed input. As Sergent (1984) puts it: 'the disorganization of the interactive process of the lesioned brain at the sensory level creates a state unlike that of the normal brain and complicates the interpretation of behavioral deficits' (p. 106).

## DEFINITION

*Visual imperception* refers to a disorder in the reception or the processing of information using the visual modality. Visual imperception from brain injury is a significant problem for rehabilitation. A variety of behavioral sydromes is subsumed under this category, including oculomotor disorders and unilateral deficits (*hemi-imperception*). Hemi-imperception can occur in either the *ambient* (i.e., peripheral field) or *focal* (i.e., central field or foveal) visual systems (to borrow terms from Belleza et al, 1979). To understand the phenomena of visual imperception, it will be useful to differentiate at least three major underlying behavioral factors: *spatial (peripheral field) hemi-imperception*, *focal (central field) hemi-imperception* and *scanning (oculomotor) dysfunction* (Gianutsos et al, 1983). This multi-factor view of visual imperceptive behavior will be elaborated on later.

## SENSORY (VISUAL) SYSTEM EVALUATION: AN ESSENTIAL PRELIMINARY

Before one can interpret visual imperception, the status of the sensory inputs must be carefully assessed. This assessment must take into account the premorbid status of the visual system. For example, if the patient was suffering from glaucoma prior to the brain injury, there may be visual field defects relating to this condition. Careful visual system screening in rehabilitation facilities is essential, and in many, if not all, cases optometric consultation is useful. The major parameters of vision which must be examined are:

1. acuity, in each eye at both near and far point;
2. field of vision;
3. binocular incapacities, including problems of diplopia (double vision), accommodation, and suppression;
4. oculomotor function.

### Acuity

Clarity of vision is obviously essential, no matter what the cause. Impaired acuity can be a direct result of head trauma, especially when intracranial pressure causes damage to the optic tract, including the retina. In clinical practice there are may patients whose acuity has declined for other reasons, for example, uncorrected refractive error, including presbyopia in the middle-aged, or as a complication of diabetes. If examination shows that it is not possible to achieve a clear image, this information will be critical for treatment planning.

Acuity can be tested by conventional letter eye charts, or variations such as 'Tumbling E' or symbols to accommodate the non-verbal patient. Near point (40 cm or 16″) acuity should be measured as well as distant (20 ft) acuity. For non-ambulatory brain-injured patients, in particular, distant acuity is of reduced importance. Many therapeutic activities are conducted at near point. Yet near point acuity was reported in only one of the studies we reviewed (Torjussen, 1978).

In the brain-injured patient, measuring acuity can be time-consuming. An alternative is to use plates designed to yield a contrast sensitivity function where some values can easily be translated into conventional acuity measures (Tyler, 1985). Clinically, the simplicity of the task (indicating the direction of tilt of bar gratings, see Fig. 10.1) makes it ideal for use with the brain-injured. Indeed, because of the simplicity of assessment, and the fact that it offers additional information, it is likely that contrast sensitivity measurement will replace conventional acuity measurement. These plates and the meaning of the contrast sensitivity function for rehabilitation will be discussed later.

### Visual field

Visual field assessment is important because partial losses of vision ('field cuts') are often a direct result of brain injury. Usually, these losses are associated with cortical, or at least post-chiasmic, injury, as suggested by the fact that most losses are *homonymous*, involving congruent areas in both eyes. In our ongoing research with brain-injured persons undergoing rehabilitation at NYU Medical Center, Bellevue, we are fortunate to have one of the finest quantitative perimeters, the Oculus Tubinger, which has made it possible for detailed visual field examinations to be done. The full potential of this device is shown in the work of Zihl and his colleagues, who have used it in their research on restitution of the visual function by perimetric stimulation (Zihl & Von Cramon, 1979) and 'blindsight' (Zihl, 1980; Zihl & Werth, 1984). An exquisitely detailed perimetric examination is reported by Zihl et al (1983).

We have found it necessary to modify the standard method of kinetic perimetry (Tate and Lynn, 1977) to accommodate the needs of brain-injured patients, who respond more consistently in a discrete trial, forced-choice mode. On careful examination, we rarely find cases of homonymous hemianopia (where half-fields are totally lost). The locus of the loss, particularly if it includes the central 10 degrees (e.g., if there is *macular splitting*), is significant for both function and awareness of the loss. The contour of the boundary of the loss relates to the ability to compensate for peripheral losses: if it is abrupt (that is, the boundary between seeing and non-seeing areas is sudden), spontaneous compensation is not likely to occur. Also, areas of reduced sensitivity (relative loss), called *depressions* of the visual field, have significance for visual perception and functioning. For example, depressions of the left central field have proved to be associated with left paralexic reading errors, such as 'FIGHT' for EIGHT or 'RANK' for BANK. Suffice it to say that these findings have convinced us that there is much to be gained from a thorough, quantitative examination of the visual field. Unfortunately, the testing time (4 hours) and equipment cost (over $20,000) make the use of this equipment prohibitive for all but research applications.

However, screening devices exist, e.g., the periometer of the Keystone Ophthalmic Telebinocular, or the Keystone VS-II Vision Screener which allow controlled assessment of peripheral points along the horizontal plane. With such findings, one can then refer the patient to a vision specialist for quantitative field measurement.

The traditional method of screening for visual field losses, visual confrontation, has been demonstrated to be insensitive, missing as many as half the cases where other methods demonstrate a loss (Trobe et al, 1981). This insensitivity makes it particularly unsuited for screening, where one should err in the direction of false positives, rather than misses.

## Binocularity

Binocularity, the coordinated use of both eyes, is a major problem area for the head-injured; yet this problem is rarely evaluated and treated. The type of problems which result include double vision (sometimes experienced as blurring), eye strain, reduced depth perception, or inability to adjust focus easily between distant and near targets. Often these problems are exacerbated in close work. Stereoscopic testing devices, such as those available from Keystone, allow one to test for the functions which are associated with these problems: vertical and lateral *phoria* (alignment of the eyes), *diplopia* (double vision), *fusion capability, stereopsis* (the ability to perceive depth based on binocular cues), and *suppression* (the tendency for one macula not to function when the other macula is working). These problems are assessed at both near and far points. *Accommodative range* (the ability to adjust focus between near and far) is also assessed, because frequently this range is limited following brain injury.

*Depth perception*, another understudied topic in rehabilitation, is essential for patient mobility, particularly driving. While assessment traditionally has focused on depth perception at close range, e.g., with measures of three-dimensional constructional praxis, depth perception at a distance would seem to be more relevant in activities of daily living. Customarily, cues for depth are distinguished as being monocular or binocular. Binocular cues are especially important in the perception of distances in low-light situations, as, for example, driving a car at night. Monocular cues for depth perception include size, superposition, texture gradients, motion parallax, interpretation of shadows and linear perspective. Clearly, these latter cues depend on other aspects of visual perception, such as acuity (to appreciate texture gradients), form perception, etc. More work is needed in this area.

## Oculomotor function

Oculomotor function can be impaired directly by injury to the systems of the brain controlling eye movements (e.g., injury to the cranial nerves) as well as indirectly through losses in the other domains, e.g., scanning into a non-seeing field is slowed and often halting. Simple observation of the eyes is helpful. Do the eyes move smoothly? Do they move in all directions? Can they sustain a fixation? Do they converge on a near stimulus?

In studies which have measured the eye movements of brain-injured persons (including Belleza et al, 1979; Chedru and Leblanc, 1972; Girotti et al, 1983; Holmes, 1938) gross abnormalities were found on several measures, including fixation duration, number of fixations, search time for targets on the left and right, and the quadrant of the screen to which the gaze is first directed. The eye movements of the brain-injured may be erratic and fail to identify critical elements. Locher and Bigelow (1983) reported no asymmetry in visual exploration in hemiplegic stroke patients, some of whom were hemianopic. Unfortunately, the measurement of direct eye movement remains a specialized technology suitable only for research. For clinical purposes, therefore, the researcher must observe what the eyes are doing while the individual is performing a task. The simple expedient of a mirrored wall serving as a backdrop for a computer monitor makes it possible to observe the viewer's eyes and the task display at the same time.

## Other visual phenomena of potential significance

Contrast sensitivity is a new approach to acuity measurement based on spatial frequency analysis, a theoretical introduction to which is contained in Chapter 9 of the Levine and Shefner (1981) text. Practically speaking, a contrast sensitivity function can be attained using the Vistech plates (VCTS, Vistech Consultants Inc., 1372 North Fairfield Road, Dayton, Ohio 45432). Each Vistech plate contains disks with a 'grating' consisting of dark bars on gray backgrounds, as illustrated in Figure 10.1.

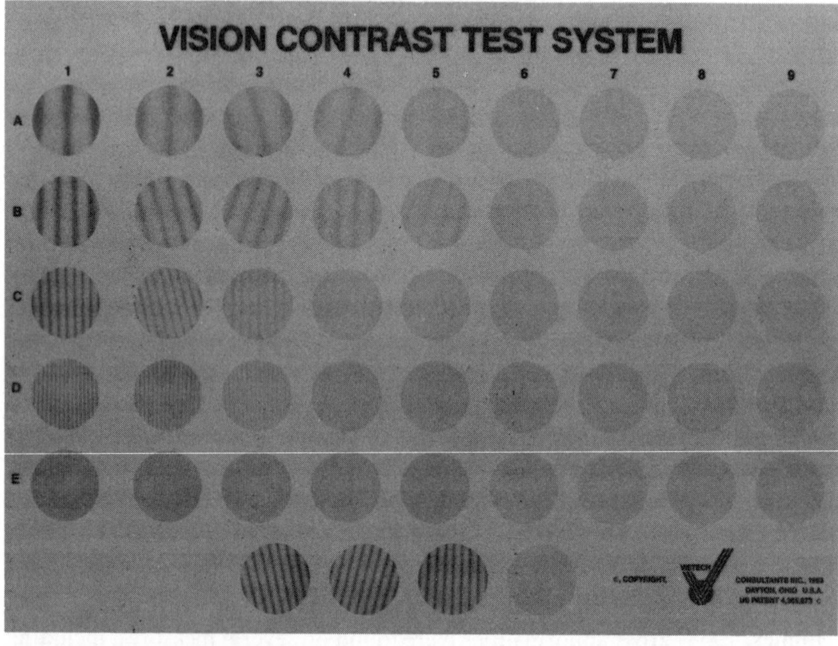


**Fig. 10.1** Contrast sensitivity plates (Vistech) with disks bearing a 'grating' of dark bars on gray backgrounds. The examinee indicates the orientation of the bars in each disk. (Reproduced by kind permission of Vistech Inc.)

At high spatial frequencies these bars are narrow and close together. They appear well-defined. At low spatial frequencies the bars are broad and there is a gradual transition from bar to bar. For each disk the examinee indicates the orientation of the grating. The information yielded by this procedure pertains to the individual's vision in low and intermediate contrast situations, where boundaries are graduated, as is typical of daily living situations.

An alternative visual system mediated through upper brainstem structures, most notably the superior colliculus (or tectum), appears to be sensitive to motion and gross shapes with low spatial frequencies. Current thinking (Levine & Shefner, 1981) is that this system is important in orienting, visual tracking, eye movements, and localization of objects in the visual world. The individual does not have any subjective awareness of the operation of this system, but performs better than chance in a force-choice paradigm. The result for the brain-injured is a phenomenon dubbed 'blindsight' (Weiskrantz et al, 1974), where perimetrically unresponsive individuals (who do not report seeing test lights in controlled perimetric testing), demonstrate some responsivity to light stimuli.

Zihl et al (1983) also present evidence for this phenomenon in a case study in which a bilateral posterior stroke patient showed a selective disturbance of movement perception. Other visual functions were intact. The patient's reported experience of moving objects was as if they were frozen in one position, then suddenly in another position with no in-between. This report, together with similar ones reviewed by Pizzamiglio et al (1984), constitute evidence that this alternate visual pathway, i.e., through the colliculus, mediates some types of vision. Although these new findings and ideas are still in the research phase, clinicians should bear in mind that the ability to perceive movement may be impaired in an otherwise intact patient. Conversely, patients with pronounced hemianopic losses may have sensitivity to movement in their perimetrically impaired fields, which may account for why some seem to 'compensate' relatively well.

## Findings

The rehabilitation specialist concerned with visual imperception should screen for these sensory functions. My colleague and I (R.G.) at the Head Injury Recovery Center at Woodmere sought to discover the result of following this recommendation thoroughly. In a retrospective clinical study (Perlin et al, 1985) of our practices we found that of the 39 patients screened as part of the routine cognitive intake evaluation, 19 warranted the services of a rehabilitative optometrist specializing in 'low vision'. A therapist always accompanied the patient, which proved to facilitate communication between the doctor and both the patient and therapist. The optometric evaluation typically required two 2-hour sessions. Treatments included: refraction (new glasses), different glasses for near and distant viewing (for those with accommodative insufficiency), occlusion of one lens (sometimes only in reading glasses), prism lenses, and fusion training. All but one patient derived significant gain, which enhanced their ability to participate in the rehabilitation program as a whole. These findings dramatically underscore the value of rigorous visual system (optometric) evaluation because many of the problems it uncovers are easily treatable. Indeed, we are inclined to agree with our colleague Dr. Ethel Tobach (personal communication) who says that each patient should be given 'a complete sensory psychophysical'.

## WHY A COMPREHENSIVE EVALUATION OF VISUAL PERCEPTUAL FUNCTION IS IMPORTANT

Comprehensive evaluation of visual perceptual function is important for at least two reasons: first, the nature of the perceptual deficit is such that it is hidden, both to the casual observer and, often, to the patients themselves. There is an excellent way to demonstrate that a substantial loss may not be experienced as such by the subject. Consider one's own blind spot. Close one eye and try to locate the blind spot, which occurs where the optic nerve leaves the retina. Is it on the nasal (inside) or temporal (outside) side? How far off center is it? At arm's length, how large an area is without vision? Most people cannot answer these questions based on subjective experience. The answers are that the blind spot is on the temporal side about one-fifth of the way from midline to the side. It is larger than a golf ball (2.5 $cm^2$) at arm's length. Some forms of visual imperception are based on similar partial losses of the visual field. Why then should we expect our patients to be any more aware of their losses than we are of our own physiological blind spot? In general, persons with neurologically based losses of vision do not behave as if they experience an obstruction of vision. Unlike individuals with cataracts or glaucoma, they rarely seem to be peering around their blind spots.

Second, and not unrelated to the first point, visual perceptual function is essential for effectiveness and safety in activities of daily living. This point has been documented in the now-classic paper by Diller and Weinberg (1970) and more recently for driving by Booher (1978) and by Sivak et al (1981). In our experience we have seen the importance of visual perception for two main categories of activities: (1) the so-called academic functions, reading, studying and clerical work; and (2) finding one's way around in public places, including operation of a motor vehicle. Frequently, the visual imperceptive individual functions worse than individuals with no vision at all, a phenomenon which is attributable to diminished awareness or acknowledgment. In other words, a partial loss, of which one is not aware, is sometimes worse than a total loss.

For these reasons we recommend a comprehensive evaluation of visual perception for all brain-injured persons. Unlike motor deficits, which are directly observable, perceptual deficits may go undetected since patients are often unable to articulate the difficulty they are having. Nevertheless, the consequences of an undiagnosed deficit are serious.

## A MULTI-FACTOR VIEW OF VISUAL IMPERCEPTIVE BEHAVIOR

Before reviewing the many approaches to measurement and treatment of visual imperception, we should like to set out a multi-factor view of visual imperception. This conceptual analysis helps to organize an understanding of the underlying components of assessment tasks and to guide strategies for rehabilitation. This view evolved empirically from observing the perceptual performance of brain-injured persons. It took little formal analysis to see that imperception can take a variety of forms, and that difficulties on one measure were not necessarily correlated with difficulties on another. To pursue this observation formally, Gianutsos et al (1983a) conducted a factor analytic study of perceptual performance in a group of 98 patients. The group was drawn from an acute medical rehabilitation population, including both brain-injured and non-brain-injured people. (For example, had we only included stroke patients, we might not have found evidence of an oculomotor factor, since stroke patients are not prone to this type of disorder.) Three independent (uncorrelated) behavioral patterns (factors) emerged from the study. Patients could be found who had deficits in any one or more of these factors, and a deficit on one factor did not imply a deficit on another.

### Behavioral pattern I: spatial (peripheral field) hemi-imperception

This is a *unilateral spatial deficit*, (Battersby et al, 1956). This deficit was manifest in difficulty processing information in the field contralateral to the brain injury, particularly in the periphery. It interfered with localization tasks, including finding the margin at the beginning of a line of print. It would affect an appreciation of any supra-span form or display, which requires multiple fixations to examine. Visual search of the affected side was retarded. Finally, spatial hemi-imperception led to deficits in monitoring events in the periphery, including stimuli which ordinarily provoke an orienting response.

### Behavioral pattern II: lateral scanning disorder

This factor was manifest in impaired reading of lines of print as distinguished from words presented singly in the center of a screen. Presumably the saccadic eye movements, which were not directly measured, were impaired. Also affected were localizing movements to stimuli on either side. Visual search would be slower overall. This deficit is bilateral. This pattern can also be associated with central field defects. Such individuals may experience problems with eccentric viewing as a compensatory strategy.

### Behavioral pattern III: focal (central field) hemi-imperception

This deficit is unilateral and within the span of fixation, or what Belleza et al (1979) call the *focal*, as opposed to the *ambient*, system. A typical focal hemi-imperceptive would consistently misread the beginnings (or ends) of words presented in a central location, which, indeed, we observe in a computerized tachistoscopic reading task, FASTREAD (Gianutsos et al, 1984), to be discussed later. They also have trouble with matching complex shapes and with written arithmetic. Proofreading and bookkeeping are not ideal occupations for them. While they may be able to read text that is redundant, their difficulty will come out on technical material. Gianutsos et al (1983c) designed a proofreading task (ERROR DETECT) in which errors involve either the first (e.g., 'fongue' for tongue) or last letters (e.g., 'Americs' for America) of words. Errors were also distributed on both sides of the page. This task has proven itself sensitive to focal hemi-imperception, with individuals showing disproportionate failures to detect errors at the beginnings or the ends of words. The practical and articulatory demands of this task are also minimal.

In our clinical experience we have found several cases in which the imperception was exclusively focal. Generally these individuals were not recognized as imperceptive by any other members of the rehabilitation team. In the usual inpatient rehabilitation activities of daily living (which are largely domestic) focal hemi-imperception seems to have little opportunity to show itself. We believe that when neuropsychologists are mindful of the focal hemi-imperception syndrome, they will be able to understand and better treat the performance of some patients who might otherwise be regarded as alexic, confused, or unable to self-monitor.

This three-factor behavioral view of imperception parallels what is known about the neurological organization of the visual system. The oculomotor system is distinct from the receptive system. Within the receptive system there is a basic difference between central (focal) and peripheral (ambient) vision. In the retina, cone receptors and one-to-one innervation are characteristic of the central (foveal) area. Rod receptors and many-to-one innervation are characteristic of the periphery. In the brain, foveal (focal) vision is served by a pathway which goes to the striate cortex by way of the lateral geniculate body; whereas some peripheral vision reaches the visual association areas by way of the superior colliculus.

In the intact individual these systems interact in complex ways which result in such functions as attention and recognition. Attention, for example, many develop from an orienting response in the following way. A stimulus excites the ambient system, eliciting a localizing eye movement which brings the stimulus into the purview of the focal system. An alternative to this data-driven ('bottom-up') scenario is a conceptually driven one in which an idea or hypothesis leads to the eye movement. Both of these modes normally occur; part of the rehabilitation process may be to build up the conceptually driven ('top-down') mode when the data-driven one is disabled by losses in the ambient system.

To summarize, our purpose in elaborating this multi-factor view of imperception has been to provide a framework within which to understand better the approaches to assessment and rehabilitation which we shall now describe. With this information before us, we shall discuss issues and conclude with some suggestions for future directions in this field.

## MEASUREMENT

Measurement is important for two reasons: (1) it operationally defines the entity under study and (2) in the case of visual imperception where diminished or distorted awareness is often a significant problem, measurement is the beginning of the rehabilitative process. To expand this last point, many of the diagnostic procedures can be structured as demonstrations of the deficit to the patient. Permitting practice and attempts to compensate are sometimes the only ways in which patients can convince themselves of the existence of a problem. Until there is some recognition and understanding of the problem rehabilitation will be difficult.

### Current approaches

Turning now to the measures themselves, Table 10.1 is a listing of all the procedures used in all the articles we surveyed. This survey was based on a computer search of the Medlars (Medline) database for all articles written on 'vision' or 'perception' and 'brain injury' or 'brain damage' between 1978 and 1984. From a listing of the titles we selected those articles which we judged to be relevant to our topic. We were then able to review the vast majority of the selected articles, and we believe our sample to be comprehensive and representative of practices in the field. We also included procedures which we have developed. Overall 94 articles were included.

Matching and copying were the clear favorites, reported in 16 and 15 of the articles, respectively. Delayed matching (a multiple choice version of the Benton Visual Retention Test) was used in another 5 articles, adding to the lead already enjoyed by matching. The next cluster of popular procedures, each used in about 10 of the articles, contained: object naming, visual search, variations of the Gottschaldt Hidden Figures Test, overlapping or embedded figures, so-called figure-ground tasks, and reading. Used in about 5 articles were: cancellation, identification of what is missing, abstract figural reasoning, form assembly/construction, line bisection and drawing.

What are some of the limitations of the use of these tasks? First, the vast majority of the tasks in current use do not incorporate the temporal dimension. They involve static displays and do not measure perception (response) time. Second, most are two-dimensional. Third, many involve a substantial motor/practic component. Fourth, and perhaps most problematic, is that the most widely used tasks are poorly understood, either in terms of underlying cognitive processes or in terms of applicability to the demands of daily living. For example, after a thoughtful discussion and investigation, Suzanne Corkin (1979) concludes 'The nature of the deficit revealed by the Hidden Figures Test remains a puzzle (p. 594).' Such forthrightness is refreshing. The state of the art will advance only when we recognize that traditional tasks are often complex

**Table 10.1** Measures of visual perception currently represented in the literature

| Task | Study |
|---|---|
| Line Bisection | Colombo et al (1976) |
| | Gianutsos et al (1983c) |
| | Heilman & Howell (1980) |
| | Paterson & Zangwill (1944) |
| | Schenkenberg et al (1980) |
| | Weinberg et al (1979) |
| | Zarit & Kahn (1974) |
| Line Bisection by Matching | Rosenberger (1974) |
| Discrimination | Mack & Levine (1981) |
| Length | Bisiach et al (1976b) |
| | Mack & Levine (1981) |
| | Paterson & Zangwill (1944) |
| Slope | Bisiach et al (1976b) |
| Form | Bisiach et al (1976b) |
| Area | Bisiach et al (1976b) |
| Brightness | Bisiach et al (1976b) |
| Angle Size | Mack & Levine (1981) |
| T-scope Threshold to Detect | Golding (1981) |
| Dot Stimulus | Paterson & Zangwill (1944) |
| | Warrington & Rabin (1970b) |
| Novel Stimulus | Salmaso & Denes (1982) |
| Visual Reaction Time | DeRenzi & Spinnler (1966) |
| | Gianutsos & Klitzner (1981) |
| Single and Double Simultaneous Stimulation | Gianutsos et al (1983c) |
| | Paterson & Zangwill (1944) |
| | Zarit & Kahn (1974) |
| Detect Grating or Spots | Perenin & Jeannerod (1978) |
| of Light in 'blindfield' | Ratcliff & Davies-Jones (1972) |
| Monitoring 3×3 Array (T-scope) | Holtzman et al (1981) |
| Monitor Horizontal Lights | Dimond (1976) |
| Localization of Peripheral Point | Ratcliff & Davies-Jones (1972) |
| | Riddoch (1935) |
| | Weiskrantz et al (1974) |
| Lateral Saccadic Scanning ('Jump') | Gianutsos et al (1983c) |
| Light-Sequence Pattern Test | Carmon & Nachshon (1971) |
| | Carmon (1978) |
| Light Pattern Delayed Matching | Bentin & Gordon (1979) |
| Eye Pursuits (Ayers) | Taylor et al (1971) |
| Copying Tasks: | |
| Name and address | Weinberg et al (1977) |
| | Weinberg et al (1979) |
| Geometric designs | Battersby et al (1956) |
| | Gainotti (1968) |
| | Paterson & Zangwill (1944) |
| | Zarit & Kahn (1974) |
| Drawings | Colombo et al (1976) |
| | Colombo et al (1982) |
| | Lawson (1962) |
| | McFie et al (1950) |
| | Miceli et al (1981) |
| | Paterson & Zangwill (1944) |
| | Zarit & Kahn (1974) |
| Benton Visual Retention (Admin. C) | Arena & Gainotti (1978) |
| | Dee (1970) |
| | Dee & Benton (1970) |

**Table 10.1** Contd.

| Task | Study |
|---|---|
| Minnesota Percepto-Diagnostic Test | Putnam (1981) |
| Bender Gestalt Visual Motor Test | Belleza et al (1979) |
| | Diller & Weinberg (1965) |
| Rey-Osterrieth | Pillon (1981) |
| Graphic Skills (Ayers) | Taylor et al (1971) |
| Drawing Task | Battersby et al (1956) |
| | Gasparrini et al (1980) |
| | Heilman & Howell (1980) |
| | Lawson (1962) |
| | McFie et al (1950) |
| | McFie et al (1950) |
| | Paterson & Zangwill (1944) |
| | Schenkenberg et al (1980) |
| | Zarit & Kahn (1974) |
| Memory for Designs | McFie et al (1950) |
| | Schenkenberg et al (1980) |
| | Zarit & Kahn (1974) |
| Ball and Hole Test | Colombo et al (1976) |
| Cross Copying | Gainotti (1968) |
| | Tartaglione et al (1981) |
| Counting Faces/Objects | McFie et al (1950) |
| | Paterson & Zangwill (1944) |
| | Weinberg et al (1977) |
| | Weinberg et al (1979) |
| Pick out Specific Designs or Objects | Colombo et al (1982) |
| | Colombo et al (1982) |
| | Zarit & Kahn (1974) |
| | Zarit & Kahn (1974) |
| Cancellation Tasks | Diller & Weinberg (1970) |
| | Diller & Weinberg (1972) |
| | Weinberg et al (1977) |
| | Weinberg et al (1979) |
| Crossing out lines | Albert (1973) |
| | Heilman & Howell (1980) |
| Striking Keys on Keyboard | Chedru (1976) |
| Matching Tasks | Bentin & Gordon (1979) |
| | Bentin & Gordon (1979) |
| | Bentin & Gordon (1979) |
| | Bisiach et al (1979) |
| | Capitani et al (1978) |
| | Faglioni et al (1969) |
| | Harness et al (1977) |
| | Kertesz (1979) |
| | Kirshner & Webb (1982) |
| | Mandleberg (1972) |
| | Miceli et al (1981) |
| | Varney (1981) |
| | Weinberg et al (1977) |
| | Weinberg et al (1979) |
| Same/Different | Bisiach et al (1976b) |
| | Gianutsos et al (1983c) |
| | Warrington & Rabin (1970a) |
| | Warrington & Rabin (1970b) |
| Benton Visual Retention Test (Multiple Choice) | Arena & Gainotti (1978) |
| | Belleza et al (1979) |
| | Dee (1970) |

**Table 10.1** Contd.

| Task | Study |
|---|---|
| | Dee & Benton (1970) |
| | Varney (1981) |
| Symbol Digit Modalities Test | Sivak et al (1981) |
| Motor Free Visual Perception Test | Sivak et al (1981) |
| Naming Tasks | Bradshaw & Gates (1978) |
| | DeRenzi & Spinnler (1966) |
| | Golding (1981) |
| | Kertesz (1979) |
| | Kertesz (1979) |
| | Kirshner & Webb (1982) |
| | McKeever et al (1981) |
| | Newcombe & Russell (1969) |
| | Warrington & James (1967) |
| | Warrington & Rabin (1970b) |
| Incomplete Shapes | Golding (1981) |
| | DeRenzi & Spinnler (1966) |
| | Newcombe & Russell (1969) |
| | Warrington & James (1967) |
| | Warrington & Rabin (1970b) |
| Completion of Drawings | McFie et al (1950) |
| | Paterson & Zangwill (1944) |
| | Semenza et al (1978) |
| WAIS - Picture Completion | Sivak et al (1981) |
| | Weinberg et al (1977) |
| | Weinberg et al (1979) |
| Form Constancy | Paterson & Zangwill (1944) |
| | Taylor et al (1971) |
| Description of After Image | Torjussen (1978) |
| Reading Tasks | Battersby et al (1956) |
| | Colombo et al (1982) |
| (speeded) | Gianutsos & Klitzner (1981) |
| | Kertesz (1979) |
| | Kirshner & Webb (1982) |
| | Lawson (1962) |
| | McFie et al (1950) |
| | McKeever et al (1981) |
| | Paterson & Zangwill (1944) |
| | Poppel & Shattuck (1974) |
| | Warrington & Shallice (1980) |
| Oral | Weinberg et al (1977) |
| | Weinberg et al (1979) |
| Trigrams | Hannay et al (1982) |
| Words - horizontal | Friedman (1982) |
| vertical | Friedman (1982) |
| | Paterson & Zangwill (1944) |
| | Weinberg et al (1977) |
| | Weinberg et al (1979) |
| Clock | Paterson & Zangwill (1944) |
| Error Detection Task | Gianutsos et al (1983) |
| Visual Searching | Battersby et al (1956) |
| | Belleza et al (1979) |
| | Chedru & LeBlanc (1972) |
| | Ehrenstein et al (1982) |
| | Gainotti (1968) |
| | Gianutsos (1981) |
| | Gianutsos & Klitzner (1981) |

**Table 10.1** Contd.

| Task | Study |
|---|---|
| | Gianutsos et al (1983c) |
| | Kertesz (1979) |
| | Turbiner & Derman (1980) |
| | Zarit & Kahn (1974) |
| Maze – Porteus | Sivak et al (1981) |
| Guided | Newcombe & Russell (1969) |
| Trailmaking Test (Form A) | Ehrenstein et al (1982) |
| Locations on US Map | Battersby et al (1956) |
| Gottschaldt Figure/Ground | Battersby et al (1956) |
| | Corkin (1979) |
| | Ehrenstein et al (1982) |
| | Lawson (1962) |
| Overlapping Figures – | Bisiach et al (1976a) |
| (Poppelreuter/Ghent/Ayers) | DeRenzi & Spinnler (1966) |
| | Sivak et al (1981) |
| | Taylor et al (1971) |
| | Hamsher (1978) |
| Rod and Frame | Sivak et al (1981) |
| Verticality Perception | Taylor et al (1971) |
| Right–Left Orientation | McFie et al (1950) |
| | Ratcliff (1979) |
| Arithmetic Tasks | Weinberg et al (1977) |
| | Weinberg et al (1979) |
| WAIS – Picture Arrangement | Battersby et al (1956) |
| | Sivak et al (1981) |
| Abstract Reasoning | Dahmen et al (1982) |
| DAT | Sivak et al (1981) |
| Ravens Progressive Matrices | Colombo et al (1976) |
| | Denes et al (1978) |
| | Denes et al (1978) |
| | DeRenzi & Spinnler (1966) |
| | Gainotti (1968) |
| | McFie et al (1950) |
| | Miceli et al (1981) |
| | Paterson & Zangwill (1944) |
| Form Board Test (Minnesota) | Dee (1970) |
| | Dee & Benton (1970) |
| Ayres Space Test | Sivak et al (1981) |
| | Taylor et al (1971) |
| Form Assembly/Construction | Dahmen et al (1982) |
| | Lawson (1962) |
| | Mack & Levine (1981) |
| WAIS – Object Assembly | Battersby et al (1956) |
| | Bentin & Gordon (1979) |
| | McFie et al (1950) |
| | Weinberg et al (1977) |
| | Weinberg et al (1979) |
| WAIS – Block Design | Battersby et al (1956) |
| | Bentin & Gordon (1979) |
| | Paterson & Zangwill (1944) |
| Kohs | McFie et al (1950) |
| Stereopsis – Random Letter | Hamsher (1978) |
| Shapes | Hamsher (1978) |
| 3D Shapes – Counting | Dahmen et al (1982) |
| | Lawson (1962) |

**Table 10.1** Cont.

| Task | Study |
|---|---|
| | McFie et al (1950) |
| | Paterson & Zangwill (1944) |
| | Warrington & Rabin (1970b) |
| Praxis Tests | Dee (1970) |
| | Taylor et al (1971) |
| Construction | Dahmen et al (1982) |
| Preview Tracking | Jones & Donaldson (1981) |
| | Greene & Tager (1981) |
| Visual Reproductions | Veroff (1980) |
| Estimation of Distance | McFie et al (1950) |
| | Paterson & Zangwill (1944) |
| | Riddoch (1935) |

and themselves require explanation. All too often they are used for clinical assessment and then offered as explanations.

How does the neurosensory view of visual imperceptive behavior, articulated earlier, change the way we would approach the measurement of visual imperception? First, it causes us to distinguish tasks which involve the appreciation of objects in space (spatial imperception) from those which involve the careful examination of objects (focal imperception). In the former category would be tasks such as cancellation and visual search (although these usually have a significant matching component). In the latter category would be matching and word reading. The contrast can be seen in reading: locating the words on the page represents the spatial component; while reading them accurately represents the focal component. Finally, oculomotor function and scanning must be evaluated explicitly, a grievous omission in the studies we surveyed which can easily be remedied using dynamic computerized displays.

Tasks such as drawing, copying, and object assembly should be reserved for use in evaluating practic and motor factors, once perceptual function has been clearly understood. Similarly, naming tasks should be used not to assess perception, but to assess for agnosia or anomia, once perception is well understood.

## The impact of computerization on the measurement of visual perception

The advent of small computers has already begun to change things, however. Dynamic displays are easily produced with computers which offer precise temporal and spatial control of stimuli. The importance of the temporal factor was demonstrated over 15 years ago in a study by Levin et al (1969). On visual discrimination tasks (e.g., size of angles, line length and degree of curvature), patients with occipital lesions showed elevated thresholds compared to individuals with non-occipital cerebral lesions *only when stimulus exposure was limited to 0.2 or 0.5 second.* Hannay et al (1982) showed that tachistoscopic thresholds for trigram recognition were elevated in all degrees of severity of head injury, as compared to non-brain-injured controls. Similarly, Harness et al (1977) found that response latency was of special differential significance. These findings concur with our own overwhelming impression that visual perceptual tasks involving rapid computer displays are distinctly more sensitive than unspeeded tasks.

The preview tracking tasks of Jones and Donaldson (1981) and Greene and Tager (1981) were implemented on laboratory computers. The senior author has developed and used several such computer-presented tasks using popular 'personal' computers, e.g., Apple II family; TRS-80 models I, III, and IV; and IBM-PC.

In Reaction Time Measure of Visual Field (REACT, Gianutsos & Klitzner, 1981) one must make a switch-closing response, such as a key press, as soon as one detects rapidly incrementing digits which appear after a random interval in an unpredictable location on the screen of the computer. Speeded Reading of Word Lists, SRWL, in the same collection, involves tachistoscopic displays of words in several formats. In Single and Double Simultaneous Stimulation (SDSST, Gianutsos et al, 1983c) one must identify stimuli flashed on one or both sides of the screen. A lateral scanning exercise in this series, 'JUMP' requires an individual to make increasingly rapid lateral scanning movements in order to decide whether two stimuli presented on opposite sides of the screen were the same or different. This program exploits the interactive capabilities of the computer by adjusting the speed of the display based on the correctness of the person's response.

A good contrast between the old and the new approaches is found in the computerized version of the Poppelreuter/Teuber search task (SEARCH, Gianutsos & Klitzner, 1981). The computerized SEARCH displays an array of nonsense shapes. In the center is the target shape. As soon as it is displayed, the individual must find its match, which will be in one location in the display. Different test locations are sampled in different trials. In each trial the test matrix and the location of the match are randomized. The response time for each location is automatically measured and displayed as part of the results in a corresponding location.

Two further programs were created to separate out the scanning (i.e., Behavioral patterns I and II, Spatial (peripheral field) Hemi-imperception and Lateral Scanning Disorder), and the shape inspection/matching component (i.e., Behavioral pattern III, Focal (central field) Hemi-imperception) of successful performance on SEARCH. In Search for the Odd Shape, SOSH, the individual scans an array, much as is done in the SEARCH task, to locate one shape which differs slightly from the rest. As in the SEARCH task, the response times are presented in locations corresponding to the test stimuli. If an individual is slow to respond in a particular area of the display, it is evident in the displayed results.

To measure focal (central field) hemi-imperception (Behavioral pattern III): two other computer tasks were designed. In MATCH, two complex but similar shapes are displayed, one above the other, in the center of the screen. The individual makes a same/difference judgment as soon as possible. The time to make this judgment is automatically recorded and the results include both accuracy and response times for different types of matches, e.g., whether the stimulus pair differs on the left side, the right side, both sides or not at all.

FASTREAD (Gianutsos et al, 1984) is a tachistoscopic reading task which is sensitive to focal (central-field) imperception. On this task, individuals with focal hemi-imperception show a consistent pattern of misreading, involving either the beginnings or ends of the words.

The advantages of computer-controlled tasks are several, and we should expect to see much more of them in the future. In addition to offering precise control of the duration of stimulus displays and convenient measurement of response time, how else will the advent of computrization change neuropsychological assessment of visual perception? We expect that it is also likely to reduce the practic/motoric demands on the examinee. The reason for this prediction is that the keyboard and binary switches will remain the most convenient way to enter information into the computer. For example, in a computerized line bisection task (BISECT, Gianutsos et al, 1983c), one adjusts a gap in a line by pressing keys representing the direction of the adjustment. In the paper-and-pencil version one must actually place a mark in the middle of the line.

Finally, computerization is likely to increase our reliance on two-dimensional displays because of the convenience of the flat computer screen. Increased assessment of three-dimensional objects and space is not likely to occur with computerization as we now have it, and will continue to be lacking in many of our assessment techniques. With computer-generated holographic images, we will one day have the practical potential to incorporate the third dimension.

Improved high-resolution graphics and associated programming aids are the wave of the future in computer technology. Recently a set of 'Visual/Perceptual Diagnostic Testing and Training Programs' has been published with outstanding graphics (Greenberg & Chamoff, 1984) based on the use of the Gibson light pen. These routines include several of the most popular procedures alluded to earlier, e.g., matching, copying embedded figures, cancellation, and mazes. Because a light pen is used for most responses, a distinct practic component is inherent in these procedures. They are faithful representations of conventional tasks.

### A diagnostic strategy

By way of summarizing, we offer the following approach to diagnostic evaluation: in visual perception, diagnosis assumes increased importance because deficits are hidden, subjective awareness may be poor or lacking altogether, and the long-run consequences of undiagnosed deficits are great. We begin our assessment with gross screening procedures, usually the computerized Reaction Time Measure of Visual Field (REACT, Gianutsos & Klitzner, 1981), simple tests of visual acuity and reading. Screening for visual problems is essential and the stereoscopic devices, such as those mentioned earlier, can be useful in identifying cases for referral to an optometric specialist. The visual perception evaluation should be repeated when (or deferred until) the optometric evaluation and treatment are complete.

With this preliminary information, if the person shows no apparent deficits, we will use one or two perceptually challenging procedures which we consider 'definitive'. For this purpose we use the computerized Single and Double Simultaneous Stimulation (SDSST, Gianutsos et al, 1983c) and Speeded Reading of Word Lists (SRWL, Gianutsos & Klitzner, 1981) tasks. SDSST is a dynamic task sensitive to spatial hemi-imperception. SRWL is excellent because it is both difficult and measures all three of the behavioral factors in our neurosensory model. However, it is often impossible to conduct because it requires oral reading, and the examinee must be neither dysarthric nor dysphasic. As an alternative, we can use the paper-and-pencil proofreading task, ERROR DETECT (Gianutsos et al, 1983c), because it is sensitive to foveal hemi-imperception. If the individual does well on these procedures, the remainder of the visual perceptual evaluation can be bypassed.

The following clinical example illustrates this procedure. A young woman (B.M.), who had survived a serious head trauma from a motor vehicle accident, was just beginning to come out of coma. She was completely non-vocal, but seemed to comprehend well and was not aphasic. Her motoric functions were severely limited, allowing her to make only gross indications with one hand. Because of the combination of her multiple disabilities and her limited endurance, there was a great premium on her availability for assessment and treatment. Our assessment was therefore limited to the procedures described; namely: sensory screening and Reaction Time Measure of Visual Field. The results of the sensory evaluation confirmed a diplopia but otherwise adequate vision for most table-top rehabilitation tasks. Because of the diplopia, subsequent testing was done monocularly.

With the Reaction Time procedure, the results were slowed overall because of her motoric problems. However, there was no pattern suggestive of any partial visual field deficits. Unambiguous confirmation of this conclusion occurred when we tested her on Single and Double Simultaneous Stimulation (SDSST), where she made four errors in 45 trials, essentially a normal performance. Based on these findings, we decided to turn our focus to other cognitive problems, especially memory, judging that her visual perception was at least adequate for the moment. An optometrist managed her diplopia and provided her with prism glasses for near point viewing and another pair for far point. This resulted in a significant improvement in her acuity.

In contrast, a neuropsychological evaluation indicated visual perceptual problems. We believe this may have been because no steps (e.g., patching one eye during testing) were taken to alleviate the diplopia nor were the acuity problems recognized.

If, however, there are deficits, an assessment should evaluate which of the underlying systems is affected. Our own approach is detailed in the *Handbook to Computer Programs for Cognitive Rehabilitation (Vol. 2): Further Procedures for Visual Imperception* (Gianutsos et al, 1983c) and in Gianutsos (1984). We use the multi-factor model, detailed earlier, to guide our assessment. Visual perception is not a singular entity, but rather a product of subsystems, any one of which, and any combination of which, may be impaired by brain injury. The deficits suggested by a pattern of performance on one test should always be confirmed by different tests of the same factor.

Because visual perceptual problems become most evident when time is at a premium (e.g., Harness et al, 1977; Levin et al, 1969), it is important to use dynamic tasks in the assessment. Computerized procedures are, therefore, ideal.

## REHABILITATION

### Review of previous research

First we shall review studies of how visual perception recovers without treatment. Following that, we shall focus on studies in which groups of patients were given perceptual retraining protocols. Finally, we shall consider intervention studies in which individual cases have been pursued intensively.

#### *Recovery studies*

Several studies have been published on the recovery of visual perception, mostly in stroke patients. Initial testing was within the first month post-onset and follow-up was 6 months to a year later. These reports (Campbell & Oxbury, 1976; Colombo et al, 1982; Meerwaldt, 1983) show an overall trend of improvement, but they are not specific on treatment. Colombo and his colleagues reported on 20 patients who were followed up a year later. Five, the most severely impaired to begin with, remained unchanged in the degree of severity of 'neglect.' All other persons improved considerably and a significant subgroup had no remaining perceptual problems. Campbell and Oxbury found that visual perceptual deficits persisted on some measures from the first to the sixth month post-onset. Improvement depended on which measure was used. In the Meerwaldt study the individuals were tested with the Rod and Line Orientation Test and, on these measures, improvement occurred in virtually all cases by about 6 months.

The general conclusion of the recovery studies is that, if left untreated, a majority of individuals with perceptual problems will recover, at least from the gross manifestations of hemi-imperception. Further, these individuals tend to be ones whose deficits were not severe as measured within the first month post-onset. However, in a significant subgroup, severe deficits do persist beyond the first year.

In evaluating intervention research, then, one must be mindful of a substantial 'spontaneous' recovery factor for visual perception, which operates within the first 6 months.

With regard to visual fields, we have been unable to locate any longitudinal studies, although our experience and general impression is that visual field losses persist. Compensation may develop, but the actual field losses persist. Longitudinal studies of the visual fields are needed. Perhaps with the new automated projection perimeters, these types of studies will become feasible, and hopefully, therefore, begin to appear in the literature.

Eye movements in three persons recovering from occipital lesions were studied by Meienberg et al, 1980. Individuals were assessed early in recovery and at a point later on. An interesting finding with one patient, retested at 7½ months post-onset, was a qualitative change in lateral eye movements which were made into hemianopic fields. Early on in recovery the eye movements tended to have a 'staircase' pattern; that is, the initial move into the hemianopic field would be a short eye movement with further short saccades made until the target was localized. Later in recovery the patient learned to make 'overshoots,' that is a lengthy swing into the non-seeing field, and then to come back to the target point. The overshoot method is much quicker than the staircase approach. The small number of subjects involved in this study does not permit any general statements about the probability of recovery of eye movements. However, the qualitative changes described do suggest an approach which could be developed through training if it does not occur spontaneously.

These long, compensatory overshoot eye movements may not generalize to daily living situations, where it seems that the preponderance of eye movements are evoked by peripheral stimulation. In the hemianopic individual, in the absence of such peripheral stimulation, there would be no occasion for these eye movements. In the training setting the individual was given an indication of when it was appropriate to make an eye movement. In real life these indications often come from stimulation to the peripheral field.

### *Perceptual retraining studies*

The major, and by far the best designed and executed, research on perceptual retraining is from the Rusk Institute at NYU Medical Center by Joseph Weinberg, Leonard Diller and their team, e.g., Weinberg et al, 1977, 1979 and Gordon et al, 1985. These reports are supplemented by descriptive materials which give complete details on the rationale and procedures for such interventions (Diller & Weinberg, 1977; Diller & Gordon, 1981).

In the two Weinberg et al research reports, groups of 25 and 30 'right brain-damaged' stroke patients were compared to conventionally treated controls on a variety of visual perceptual measures. The first study was predicated on a view that the problem was largely a failure to properly scan the environment and focused on reading-related tasks, e.g., word reading, simple arithmetic, oral reading, and copying.

Treatment consisted of 20 1-hour sessions, including practice with a 'scanning' machine and methods of self-cuing, such as a vertical anchor line at the margin with sequential line numbers. The authors identified the critical elements:

1. compelling the patient to turn into the affected field;
2. providing an *anchoring* stimulus (e.g., vertical line at the margin);
3. decreasing the *density* of stimuli (e.g., isolating lines of print; and
4. *pacing* so as to slow the patient's scanning.

Statistically significant gains for the treatment group were found. The severely impaired patients improved most. These gains were maintained in a 1-year follow-up. In view of the recovery studies, which were least optimistic for the severely involved cases, this finding is especially compelling evidence for the efficacy of the intervention.

The second Weinberg et al study added training in (non-visual) sensory awareness and spatial organization (size estimation training) to the perceptual training program. Treatment effects were enhanced and, again, were most noticeable in the severe subgroup. The study by Gordon et al examined the effect of a series of perceptual remediation interventions on a large group of right brain-injured patients. Compared with a conventionally treated group, their perceptual recovery was faster.

A comparable methodology was used by Young et al (1983), who added training on the Wechsler Adult Intelligence Scale block design task to the visual scanning practice. Again, 20 1-hour sessions were conducted with right hemisphere ('left hemiplegic') stroke patients. The 27 subjects were subdivided into matched subgroups. The control group received 'conventional occupational therapy.' The results replicate the efficacy of scanning training, as found by Weinberg et al, and suggest that block design training may also be helpful.

Taylor et al's (1971) study is usually interpreted as lack of support for the efficacy of perceptual retraining. They studied 26 'experimental' cases and 20 'conventionally treated controls'. Although all improved with the 20 individualized treatment sessions, the controls improved as much as the experimentals. However, the authors note that 'all of the improved variables had some relation to vision or visual concept ... visual problems were most susceptible to training and relearning or spontaneous recovery' (p. 168).

In other words, of the five studies involving a total of about 150 treated patients, all but one found consistent effects of visual perceptual training for groups of patients, over and above conventional treatment. Ironically, the study which had the least effect did use individualized training protocols, which the others did not. It was not clear, however, on what basis subtypes of imperception were divided, and consequently, why each person was given a particular treatment.

It is noteworthy that these studies succeeded in demonstrating statistically significant intervention effects over and above conventional treatment (not an untreated control).

This group design research is complemented by a series of case studies which illustrate individualization and a variety of approaches. One of the earliest and most forward-looking publications on perceptual remediation was that of Lawson (1962). Two post-stroke patients received individualized sessions which focused on problems with reading. The results were favorable.

A case report on an individual with an early childhood onset of traumatic brain injury (Mikula, 1982) used a dynamic computerized response time measurement procedure. This author emphasized the importance of rehabilitating visual perception with timed procedures, such as is possible with the computer. Again, the results were that training was 'very effective.' Rao and Bieliauskas (1983) reported successful intervention with a tumor removal case, with treatment *beginning* 2½ years after onset. They emphasize the role of the clinician to promote insight and generalization to advanced activities of daily living.

Taken together, these studies do support the value of rehabilitative interventions for visual perception. The bottom line is that the individuals (groups) who received these treatments ended up doing well.

In our opinion future research in this area will be enhanced if the sensory systems are rigorously evaluated and treated. Also, subtypes of imperception should be differentiated, based on a theoretical model, as outlined earlier in this chapter.

*Intensive studies of individuals*

Some interesting studies have come out of the laboratory of Josef Zihl in Germany. These studies have made extensive use of the Tubinger projection perimeter and are impressive for the precision and detail with which the visual fields are measured. A report by Zihl and Von Cramon (1979) made bold claims of restitution of the visual fields through perimetric stimulation. In the projection perimeter, the individual is asked to fixate a central target in an otherwise white sphere which extends a full 180 degrees. After identifying the boundaries of the visual field the examiner initiates perimetric stimulation (repeated stimulation) at the boundary of the affected field. This procedure was used with 12 patients who had visual field losses due to postchiasmatic lesions, mostly due to stroke. In half of the group there was a substantial gain (37% to 60%) in spatial resolution. In all but two cases there was a moderate increase in temporal resolution. They found that their procedures worked best in individuals whose loss of vision was not abrupt. Furthermore, these gains were reported in relatively short intervals of time. These results underscore the need for longitudinal baseline studies of visual field recovery.

A concern with the Zihl and Von Cramon perimetric stimulation procedure appears to be replication. In our own facility at NYU-Bellevue, inspired by their findings, we obtained a Tubinger projection perimeter. Although the device yielded much fruitful diagnostic information, we were unable to find any patients who would tolerate further perimetric stimulation after the diagnostic sessions. The problem was that patients were insufficiently aware of the problem to justify to themselves the tedious procedure involved in perimetry. Because of the dramatic nature of the gains and enormous clinical potential of this procedure, we believe that any successful replication would have been published by now.

Zihl (1980) and Zihl and Werth (1984) have also reported studies, predicated on the presence of the alternate visual pathway mediated through the superior colliculus (Levine & Shefner, 1981) which is sensitive to movement and low-contrast shapes. This system, discussed earlier, is one which the individual reports no awareness. The idea is that there is potential visual sensitivity which is unused or underused, especially since the individual is unaware, which might come into greater use through feedback and training. Three patients with post-geniculate brain injury were included in each Zihl study. The interventions required 10 to 16 sessions of practice making localizing eye movements to stimuli exposed perimetrically in the 'blind' hemi-field. All performed well above chance (guessing) level. The Zihl and Werth report describes a similar intervention – namely, forced-choice localization trials, again using the perimeter. Blank items were used for control purposes. The conclusion: 'Forcing the patient to frequently choose between different locations within his perimetrically blind hemi-field may help him to use his spared localization ability even though he can never see the target' (p. 13).

Zihl's findings are definitely exciting. However, because of the technology involved, studies need to be replicated if only to demonstrate the generalizability of the findings beyond his laboratory. This, by the way, is by no means to cast any doubt on the integrity of Zihl's work. Indeed, as individuals who have also become intimate with the precision apparatus with which he works, we can only respect his methodological sophistication.

## A clinical strategy

In this section we will describe the distillation of our own experience in attempting to rehabilitate visual perception in the survivors of brain injury.

### *Step 1: diagnostic evaluation*

The beginning of the process, of course, is the diagnostic evaluation previously mentioned.

### *Step 2: education*

The second step in our rehabilitative strategy is educational. To teach the patient what is wrong, a detailed, but simple, verbal explanation is given, ideally backed up in writing. This requires more than informing and counseling the patient about the problems identified in the diagnostic testing because of a disparity between the individual's subjective experience and the objective findings. As is typified by the expression, 'I'll believe it when I see it,' people invariably trust their senses over other sources of information, including expert advice. In the situation where neurological injury has impaired the functioning of the sensory system, the individual can become confused, especially when the sensory system does not inform the individual of its misbehavior.

Therefore, in these cases, the best method is to repeat the most revealing diagnostic procedures in the guise of allowing the person to practice overcoming the problem. (Indeed, if they do overcome the problem, so much the better.) Next, other procedures may be used to demonstrate the fact that the problem is not task-specific.

The strategy is to have the individual experience the consequences of the imperception. This experience is not to be confused with verbal confrontation. No amount of convincing or arguing will be as effective as the individual seeing the result of the reliance on the impaired sensory system. In effect, patients need to discover for themselves that their senses are no longer reliable. The clinician's job is to offer the individual the opportunity to be exposed to the feedback. A few well-placed observations on the part of the therapist may be in order, especially if the individual does not seem to be attending to the feedback. Time is also necessary. Clinicians must remember that they are trying to break down a very fundamental correspondence on which the individual has relied for a lifetime.

To illustrate this process, consider a gentleman (T.J.) who was recovering from multiple strokes and was close to being discharged home from the acute medical rehabilitation unit at Bellevue Hospital. Initial evaluation revealed that this individual was having difficulty with stimuli which occurred in a portion of the lower left visual field. On the Reaction Time Measure of Visual Field he would miss, or be extremely delayed in identifying, targets in the lower left (but not the extreme periphery) of the display, as shown in the sample output of REACT in Figure 10.2. On the Speeded Reading of Word List task, he missed some of the words which were displaced suddenly to the left side. Figure 10.3 shows a typical transcript of his performance. Perimetric assessment revealed a scotoma (large blind spot) in the lower left quadrant which, however, did not extend into the central field. This loss of vision was in corresponding locations in each eye, suggesting a postchiasmatic neurological problem. Figure 10.4 shows the visual fields.

Naturally, we discussed our findings with the individual, who reported that he really did not recognize a problem. In fact, neither did most of the other members of the rehabilitation team except the referring occupational therapist, who had noticed that he had difficulty doing puzzles in the lower left part. Since this gentleman was uninterested in making puzzles, he tended to discount the significance of the problem, especially because he did not feel that he lacked any

```
COMPUTER PROGRAMS FOR COGNITIVE REHABILITATION
COPYRIGHT (C) 1982 LIFE SCIENCE ASSOCIATES
==============================================================
   >>>>>>>>>>>>>>>>>>> REACTION TIME <<<<<<<<<<<<<<<<<<<
==============================================================

NAME:  ...."TJ"..........          DATE ..................

TESTED WITH EYES FREE TO MOVE (BINOCULAR)  GLASSES: YES/NO

  .4                       .                         .3
                           .
  .4           .3          .          .3             .3
                           .
  .5           .4          .          .3             .5
                           .
 2.5           .4          .          .4             .3

 1.5                                                 .3

             LEFT                  RIGHT

 MEDIAN (SEC)   .4                      .3
```

**Fig. 10.2** A sample of patient T.J.'s performance on the Reaction Time Measure of Visual Field (REACT) task. The numbers represent the response times in seconds for stimuli which appeared in corresponding locations during the test. These times are within the normal range, except for the two in the lower left of the display.

vision. Since he was a sophisticated individual, even after his strokes, we introduced the issue in an intellectual way. We explained that there was a disparity between the functioning of his senses and his sensory experience and that this was a natural concomitant of brain injury. He was respectful but made it clear that he still relied on his sensory experience.

The next step was to allow him to practice with the computerized Reaction Time procedure, which can be used with and without fixation. He asked to practice without fixation so that he could compensate. While he brought his times down a little, it was still clear that he was very slow in the area corresponding to his loss of vision. For a few months we interspersed counseling and information with practice on the Reaction Time procedure. When it became apparent there was no progress on the task, the individual became increasingly aware of what we were trying to communicate to him.

We had been particularly concerned because he had expressed an intention to resume driving an automobile. We believe that the experience with the Reaction Time procedure at least caused him to delay this plan. Certainly, while he was doing the Reaction Time task, we would occasionally observe when he missed a stimulus that 'That object looked awfully much like a young child darting into the street,' facetiously drawing the analogy between the monitoring of items appearing suddenly on the screen to the visual monitoring required when driving a car.

-----)SINGLE WORDS DISPLACED............................PROTOCOL 1 , PAGE 4

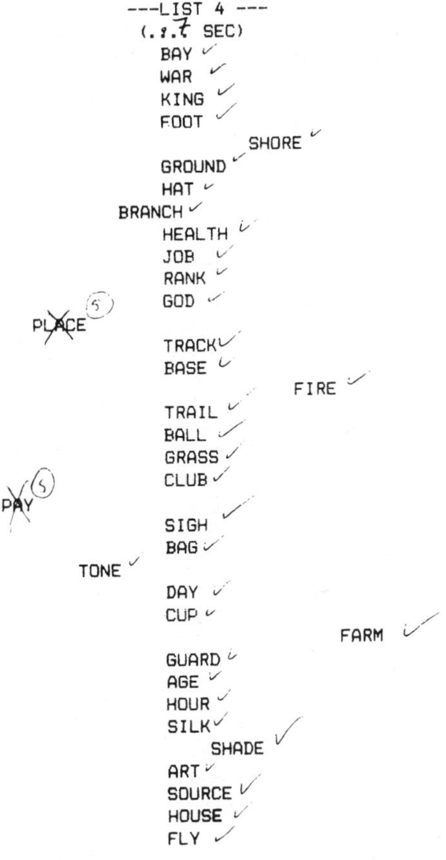

---LIST 4 ---
(.?.7 SEC)
BAY
WAR
KING
FOOT
SHORE
GROUND
HAT
BRANCH
HEALTH
JOB
RANK
GOD
PLACE
TRACK
BASE
FIRE
TRAIL
BALL
GRASS
CLUB
PAY
SIGH
BAG
TONE
DAY
CUP
FARM
GUARD
AGE
HOUR
SILK
SHADE
ART
SOURCE
HOUSE
FLY

.........................................................................
COMPUTER PROGRAMS FOR COGNITIVE REHABILITATION (TRS-80 MODELS I & III)
COPYRIGHT (C) 1981 BY ROSAMOND gIANUTSOS

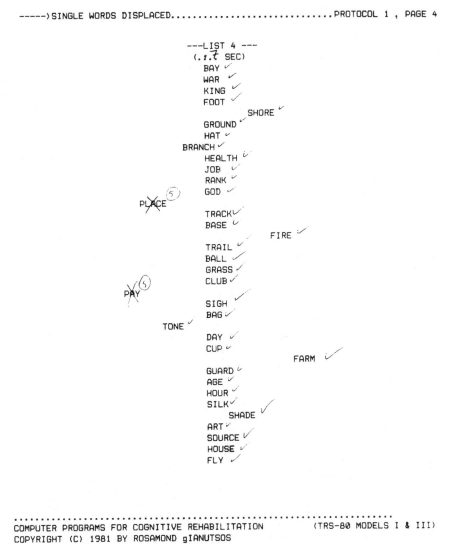

**Fig. 10.3** A typical transcript of T.J.'s performance on the Speeded Reading of Word Lists task in which single words were displaced unexpectedly to the side of the computer screen. On this and many other trials, T.J. missed items displaced to the extreme left side.

Incidentally, we offered this individual the opportunity to undergo perimetric stimulation on a research basis, in an attempt to reduce the scotoma. However, he felt he had other priorities, a judgment which was undoubtedly reinforced by his lack of subjective experience of the problem (despite our educative interventions).

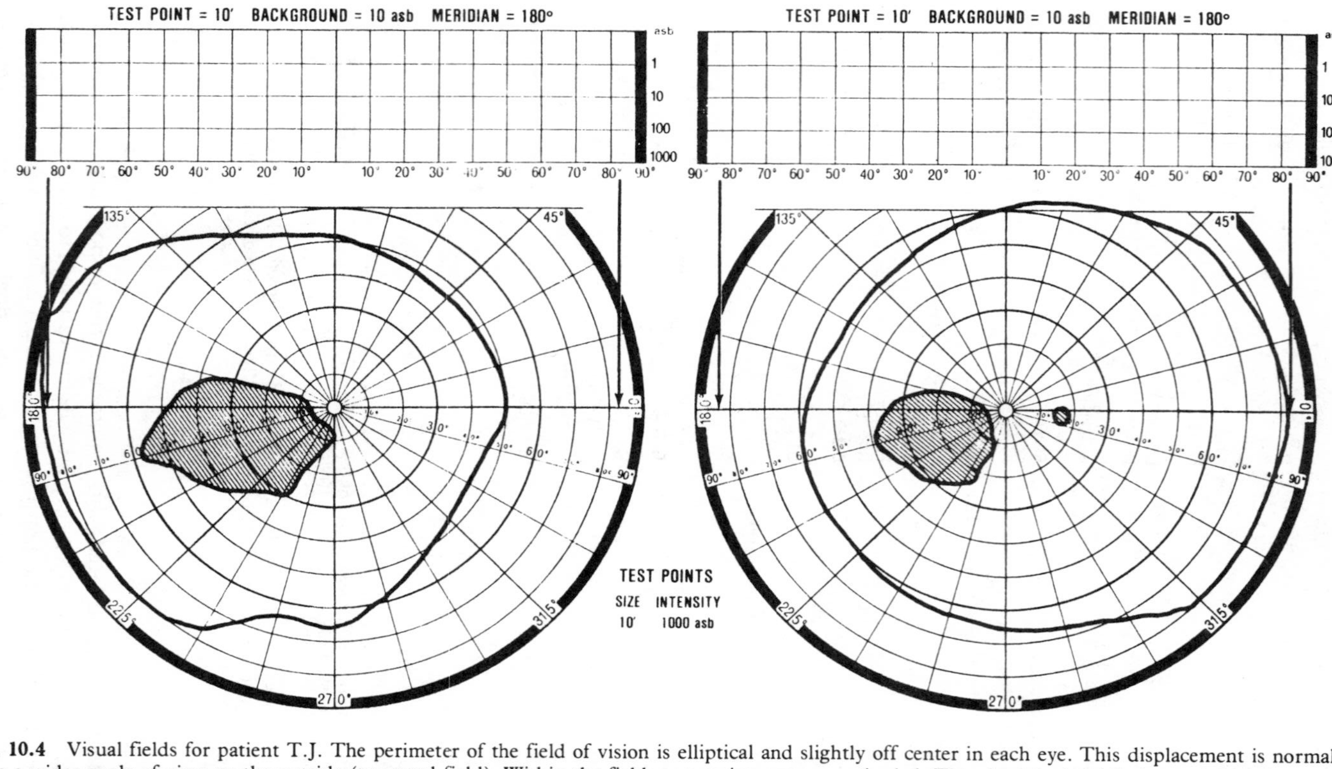


**Fig. 10.4** Visual fields for patient T.J. The perimeter of the field of vision is elliptical and slightly off center in each eye. This displacement is normal and gives a wider angle of view on the outside (temporal field). Within the field, non-seeing areas are stippled. The physiological blind spot (which is normal) is represented in the small spot to the right of the center (fixation point) of the right eye's field. As in the present case, it is normally located 12 to 18 degrees from the center and is a landmark which is mapped to confirm fixation. The large scotomata (non-seeing areas) in the left fields of each eye are attributable to post chiasmal central nervous system damage, because they were found in corresponding (homonymous) halves of the fields of each eye (hemianopia). Because of the scotoma, the physiological blind spot could not be mapped in the left eye.

*Step 3: exercise and retraining*

The third step involves the use of exercises on a repeated basis with the hope of producing improved function. In some situations this might be accompanied by specific instructions or training in compensatory methods.

For example, on Speeded Reading of Word Lists (SRWL, Gianutsos & Klitzner, 1981), in the lines of single words, if the individual does not consistently find the margin on one side of the page, one might train the person by practicing this task and offering feedback. As part of the process, solicit information on the individual's subjective awareness of the problem. Here, one would begin by asking patients if they thought they had missed any words at the margin, before telling them how many they missed. If feedback at the end of the trial does not lead to consistent anchoring to the margin, immediate feedback (while the individual is reading) may help.

We have also used Tachistoscopic Reading (the computerized FASTREAD, Gianutsos et al, 1984) for training. In this procedure the computer automatically speeds up as the person succeeds. For focal hemi-imperceptives, special vocabularies specifically pressure the affected side. For example, a right hemianopic may have a vocabulary that includes words such as *rehabilitate, rehabilitating, rehabilitated*, and *rehabilitation*, as well as other words with multiple endings. Typically, these individuals do show some improvement but do not achieve the level of a neurologically intact person, especially on these vocabularies which stress the affected side.

One of our patients (K.R.) was a proofreader before multiple strokes left her with several disabilities including a left focal hemi-imperception with sparing of the periphery. Her central visual field, which we measured at the beginning of training and at the end, showed no change. At both times she had a depression of the left central fields; that is, her visual acuity was reduced in the central field in both cases. More accurately, her acuity dropped off much more rapidly on the left side than the right. On proofreading tasks she would fail to detect words that had similar appearing first letter, as, for instance, 'gognitive' for cognitive. With this individual we created numerous materials for proofreading and gave her feedback explaining the pattern of deficit which she was showing. We made the materials very challenging, including bibliographic material which had minimal redundancy. Her performance improved noticeably with this practice.

Incidentally, to our knowledge, this pattern of visual field defect, with or without the peripheral loss, has not been reported in the literature. However, we have observed it in virtually every focal hemi-imperceptive whom we have been able to examine perimetrically.

We have found, for severe spatial hemi-imperceptives, that practice with tasks which involve large body movements into the affected space may be helpful. We have therefore designed a version of the computerized Reaction Time task using a light pen. The individual reaches with the light pen to touch a spot as soon as it appears on the screen. Reaction times are recorded as in the standard diagnostic (non-practic) version of the REACT task. Systematic research is under way to confirm this clinical impression.

Frequently the improvements appear to be specific to the exercises which the individual has practiced. Therefore new procedures should be introduced in order to generalize the perceptual gains. It is especially helpful to travel with the individual outside of the clinical setting into the home and/or work situation. A common problem in these environments is that the perceptual problems interact with the informational demands on the individual.

One young head-injured man (M.A.), who has a complete (macular splitting) right homonymous hemianopia and attendant right hemi-imperception, does fairly well in situations he has practiced. When going out for a walk, however, he not only has to pay attention to his ambulation because of a right hemiparesis, but, in addition, he finds his head turned, literally, towards any female that comes his way. Under these circumstances, curbs and broken pavement become hazardous. Compensation techniques which one must consciously implement are particularly vulnerable to the pressure of simultaneous information.

Alternatively, if generalization does not occur, the individuals may learn to be suspicious of their visual system or their visual functioning in new situations. This suspicion can be the basis for rationalizing improved self-management techniques.

To summarize, as the exercise process continues, one may increase the demands of the tasks until performance is within the normal range. If improvement does not occur, then one's therapeutic strategy shifts towards improved self-management.

*Step 4: promoting compensation and self-management*

The general strategy in promoting compensation is to assist the individual in maximizing 'top-down' processing given that 'bottom-up' processing is impaired. Sometimes we call this 'developing an intellectual override.' Individuals need to know as much as possible about how their visual–perceptual system is operating and how it is failing to function. They can then learn to plan for situations in which they will need to compensate, for instance, to adjust their timing or to make orienting responses in the absence of peripheral stimulation.

The implementation of this approach, however, will be difficult in individuals who have generally reduced cognitive function including memory impairment. Under these circumstances some external cues may assist, provided the individual sees them. Instead of simply prompting the individual to look to their affected side, one might try to develop an appropriate pattern of response to a question such as 'When you are having difficulty finding something, where do you think it is?' The next step is to gradually fade the prompt so that the individual begins to self-prompt.

Finally, wherever possible, surmount problems with devices. For individuals who have difficulty reading a conventional watch, rather than spending a great deal of time teaching them to read a conventional watch, it may be simpler to get them a digital watch.

## Specific problems involving visual perception

The two areas of daily living functioning most affected by visual perceptual problems are reading and operating a motor vehicle. Walking in city traffic presents similar problems, but not the risks to others.

### *Reading*

Reading is, of course, fundamental for individuals in school and for individuals with a vocational or avocational relevance. In severe spatial hemi-imperceptives reading is simply impossible, because they are unable to anchor their reading at the beginning of lines of print. Consequently, what they read makes no sense. In these situations, procedures such as those described in the articles by Weinberg et al (1977) and Lawson (1962) are relevant.

Frequently, however, we have observed individuals with more subtle but also disabling deficits that are often missed by conventional methods. These individuals typically have a focal hemi-imperception.

A good example is a lawyer (R.D.), who had a large meningioma removed. His primary complaint was that he was 'no longer able to read', a serious problem for a lawyer. Although he had no difficulty with a newspaper heading, he explained that he would fall asleep when he read. As it turned out, clearly on the Error Detection task, he consistently failed to perceive the left-most letters of words accurately, e.g., he missed 50 out of 60 words in which the first letter was incorrect, as compared to 10 of the 60 words in which the last letter was wrong. When we read some textual material together, he read rapidly, as he had always done. He was observed to make substitutions that were plausible, such as a 'when' for a 'then' and 'incidently' for 'consequently,' a 'she' for a 'he.' With his superior higher verbal intellectual functions intact, he would catch any misperceptions that grossly changed the meaning of the sentence. As a result, each sentence would make sense. Confusion mounted as he attempted to integrate the sentences.

This lawyer had been totally unaware of this perceptual problem and consequent pattern of error. The first step, then, was to explain the pattern to him clearly and how it was affecting his reading. Second, our interpretation of the problem was that his form perception was no longer able to operate quickly and therefore was not keeping up either with his scanning or with his ability to comprehend meaning. We therefore advised him to slow his reading down to allow these systems to operate in synchrony. He seemed to be better able to monitor his reading and catch his imperception under these circumstances. The individual was able to utilize this advice and resume productive, if slower, reading.

*Driving*

Operation of a motor vehicle is a particular challenge because it involves the processing of visual information at high speeds and requires much simultaneous information processing. Most important, unlike many other behaviors, this behavior involves the safety of others. A special dilemma arises when the brain-injured person is physically limited and, therefore, stands to gain more than most people from the use of an automobile.

The goal of rehabilitation where the individual's performance strongly indicates that driving is not safe should be to convince the individual of this by demonstrating current functioning. This was described earlier with T.J. who had multiple strokes and lower left quadrant scotomata. As he practised with the Reaction Time task, we made explicit the implications of missing information for driving. Laws vary, but often there is no way legally to prevent an individual driving.

In all cases, however, the ultimate decision should be made in an on-the-road evaluation by an evaluator experienced with the problems of recovering survivors of brain-injury. If such an evaluator is not available, it is possible that the neuropsychologist could educate an experienced driving instructor/evaluator as to the issues, i.e., defects of partial losses of vision, distractibility, and/or reduced performance with increased attentional demands. (Incidentally, the computerized Reaction Time procedure may be conducted with distraction, such as engaging the individual in conversation. In some patients, reaction times increase dramatically. Under these circumstances it is easy to generalize this problem to the driving situation and thereby to demonstrate to the individual that, because of this vulnerability to distraction, he or she would not be able to drive safely.)

An on-the-road evaluation should be the ultimate basis for a decision about driving, to provide reassurance for a seemingly good candidate. However, in the doubtful individual this procedure is still, we believe, the proper one. For instance, some hemianopic individuals may be able to drive safely with the appropriate training. Although logic would suggest this is unlikely, there may be poorly understood and therefore overlooked factors which permit the individual to have adequate vision. One such factor is 'blindsight', mediated through the superior colliculus pathway, which gives responsivity to motion and gross shapes in a perimetrically unresponsive field. Perhaps this is sufficient vision to produce an orienting response in the driving situation adequate for safe driving. The only way to evaluate this is to test the individual extensively behind the wheel with an experienced evaluator (equipped, of course, with dual controls and other safety devices). Perhaps such an individual would be able to drive safely augmented by appropriate mirror systems. As clinicians, then, our role should be to insist on this type of evaluation rather than to make specific recommendations about driving in borderline cases.

This view should not be construed as to discourage neuropsychologists from developing tasks which have apparent validity for driving. Indeed, these types of tasks can be very useful in rehabilitation. Computerized tasks are especially valuable because they are dynamic in nature, naturally incorporating time, both in speed of displays and measurements of response time. Time, of course, is a critical part of the information processing requirements of driving. Further, many tasks have already been developed using graphic simulations of speedways and roadraces. These are entertaining and can be useful in giving the individual practice in a realistic and, therefore, motivating context.

One additional point relating to driving: we have observed that many individuals confuse the ability to operate a car mechanically with the ability to drive safely in traffic. The neuropsychologist needs to assist the individual in recognizing this difference, and in being realistic about the individual's ability to meet the demands of driving in traffic.

## ANALYSIS AND COMMENT

This chapter has described the current state-of-the-art in the evaluation and treatment of visual imperception as well as our own, somewhat different view. This section will present an analysis. Critical differences can be demonstrated in the framework of the distinction between *bottom-up* and *top-down processing* of visual information.

### Implications of bottom-up and top-down models of visual information processing

In experimental cognitive psychology (e.g., Matlin, 1983; Reed, 1982) a distinction is made between data-driven (bottom-up) and conceptually-driven (top-down) views of information processing. The data-driven approach begins with the sensory input, which is then interpreted, integrated, and stored. For example, in a data-driven interpretation of reading, one first sees letters, which are combined into words, which in turn are integrated into statements and expressed ideas. The conceptually driven model, in contrast, emphasizes the hypotheses about what one is reading. Reading is simply a matter of confirming hypotheses. This view is supported by findings such as the word superiority effect, in which letters are perceived faster if they are part of a word rather than part of a nonsense syllable (Matlin, 1983). Apparently, one perceives the whole word before the letters in the word.

Each view is recognized as an extreme, however, and most psychologists acknowledge that visual information processing is an interactive product of both approaches. Our contention is that in neuropsychology the prevailing view of visual imperception represents a top-down model, which ought to be balanced by a bottom-up approach.

For example, most writers would have used the term *neglect* rather than *visual imperception*. Some, like Weinberg et al (1977), use the term even though their definition seems identical to what we call *visual hemi-imperception*. We object to the use of *neglect*, including its narrow focus, pejorative tone, and especially the implication of a cognitive (rather than a sensory) basis for the disorder. For example, Locher and Bigelow (1983) equate *neglect* with 'a lack of exploration of stimuli on the side opposite the patient's lesion' (p. 91). Why not use a neutral term which embodies no presumptions about the basis (cognitive or sensory) of the disorder. In the Locher and Bigelow study the behavior in question, eye movements, was well defined and the findings were clear. Nothing was gained by using the term *neglect*. If anything, it may distract from the important questions: What are the reasons people ordinarily initiate exploratory eye movements? What enables them to execute eye movements to a target location? How may these processes be disrupted by central nervous system injury? And, of course, what are the best strategies for rehabilitative intervention?

*Neglect* should be reserved for situations where sensory loss has been ruled out. However, in practice this principle is routinely violated (e.g., Colombo et al, 1976; Locher and Bigelow, 1984). The use of the term *neglect* implies that the negligent person has a deficit in the control and allocation of attention in the visual information processing system. Yet, if a sightless person were to fall into a utility hole because the utility workers had forgotten to replace the cover, one would not accuse the sightless person of neglect! Why then apply this terminology to the brain-injured person who has a partial loss of sight?

The top-down approach is manifest in other ways in the literature. One is the neglect (here the term is warranted!) of the sensory examination. Most of the papers on visual perceptual disorders report no sensory information at all. A few report a minimum standard of acuity for participation in the study; however, near acuity was mentioned only in Torjussen, 1978 even though it would be more relevant than distant acuity for most perceptual assessment tasks. If there was any visual field information, all too often it was based on the method of confrontation, which is notoriously insensitive. As mentioned earlier in this chapter, according to Trobe et al (1981) this method fails to detect as many cases as it finds.

Further, most of the studies reporting visual field deficits did so in a binary way (i.e., present or absent), totally overlooking the fact that partial losses of vision come in many shapes, sizes, locations, and gradients – factors we found significant for perceptual function. A sensory examination can offer useful information. Likewise it is also useful if it uncovers nothing wrong and rules out sensory loss.

The most important thing is to know for each imperceptive person whether the sensory system is operating properly. If it is, then one must look further along in the visual information processing system for such cognitive factors as inattention, agnosia, and confusion. If the sensory system is not operating properly, then one must be aware that the effects of sensory dysfunction will be referred through the system. What appears to be hemi-inattention or confusion may in fact be a normal response to abnormal inputs.

For example, our assessment showed that patient T.J.'s left hemi-imperception was accompanied by a lower left quadrant scotoma. Despite this objective evidence of deficit, his description of his subjective experience was that he had no problems with visual perception. Tempting as it might have been to call this denial, it would not have been appropriate. Denial implies that at some level the person can subjectively experience the problem but fails to acknowledge it. However, without help T.J. was not able to experience his problem and his reaction was a normal response – indeed just as we would respond if someone started telling us that we had a similar deficit. He was being true to his senses, which were not being true to him.

It strikes us, as it did the empiricist philosophers centuries ago, that this reliance on the senses is fundamental to human functioning. When the sensory system does not offer direct feedback of its dysfunction, then it may be necessary to arrange indirect feedback.

Our job was to expose T.J. to experiences which enabled him to see the effects of his dysfunctional visual system. He had to see that his subjective experience was not trustworthy. Only then was he prepared to accept the need for a cognitive override in his visual system. Knowing of T.J.'s sensory deficit was essential to our approach to treatment, because we could see that his reaction was not 'denial.'

Our emphasis on the value of the sensory examination should not be construed as anti-cognitive; far from it. We are arguing for accurate diagnosis and balance, not for an abrupt shift to the sensory end of the spectrum.

The final manifestation, which we should like to discuss, of the prevailing top-down view of visual information processing in neuropsychology is the predilection for terms like *agnosia, alexia*, and *inattention*. About 30 years ago, Battersby et al (1956) presented cogent data and arguments against the use of these interpretive terms. The thrust of their case was that *unilateral spatial deficits* (note the use of descriptive terminology) can be accounted for by a combination of sensory deficits (homonymous hemianopia) and mental confusion. They argued that it is unnecessary to postulate higher-order cognitive/interpretive processes which have been affected by brain injury. However, no one should come to the conclusion that they ended the debate. For example, Benson and Geschwind (1969), taking the opposite view in a chapter on The Alexias, say that *alexia* is the more modern term, replacing the older term, *word blindness*. In our opinion both terms are prejudicial: the former presumes a cognitive (top-down) basis for the disorder, while the latter presumes a sensory (bottom-up) basis. In general the cognitive terminology prevails. We would have no objection if cognitive terms were adopted after sensory deficits have been ruled out; but this is not the ordinary sequence of events.

Once again, we are arguing for objectivity and accuracy. Our contention is that neutral descriptive terminology would better serve the diagnosticians and rehabilitation planners because it would underscore the need to identify the locus of the deficit.

However, if there must be any bias, better that it be sensory, which is amenable to observation and test. For this reason it seems ironic to us that neuropsychologists shun sensory factors which are accessible to measurement in favor of gnostic and other cognitive factors which must be inferred from indirect measurement.

In a thought-provoking review article, Justine Sergent (1984) identifies much evidence from basic vision, neuroanatomical, and neuropsychological research which strengthens our convictions about the importance of clear and comprehensive assessment of sensory functions. For instance, she cites numerous studies which show that sensory losses are associated with injury to many areas of the brain, not just the striate area of the cortex (conventionally viewed as the primary visual area). She reviews the literature on contrast sensitivity measurement, discussed earlier in this chapter as a new dimension to the measurement of visual acuity. She cites studies by Bay and Ettlinger in which all but one of 39 brain-damaged patients were found to have deficiencies in elementary visual functions, upon careful examination – including spatio-*temporal* characteristics. This chapter concludes with a discussion of hemisphere-specific effects. The Sergent article is recommended for readers who wish to pursue these topics.

### Restitution 'versus' substitution

Attempts to restore function in rehabilitation usually emphasize strengthening through exercise. Although this premise may be correct for muscles, the brain is not a muscle. Some would therefore argue against exercise (strengthening) for perceptual rehabilitation. While exercise may not necessarily strengthen, as it does with muscles, the possibility should not be automatically ruled out.

In our opinion, restitution does have a clinical priority. First of all, it will obviate the need for later stages in rehabilitation. Even if it is not likely, the potential payoff is great. Second, when they are aware of deficits, patients give restitution a priority. Most patients seek not to learn to manage their problems but to overcome their problems. Therefore, for these two reasons we feel strongly that restitution should be a goal initially in the rehabilitation of visual perception as in other aspects of cognitive rehabilitation.

On the other hand, our zeal for restitution does have limits. We certainly would provide an individual with glasses rather than attempt to train them to overcome a myopia (nearsightedness). As is already clear, we believe strongly in optimizing the sensory inputs with whatever devices and management strategies the optometric community has to offer.

The issue is not really restitution versus substitution but, rather, one of timing and priorities. We believe restitution should be included in the objectives early in the treatment program. If success is not forthcoming, the individual will be more receptive to approaches that are substitutive in nature.

## SUMMARY AND CONCLUSIONS

In this chapter we defined *visual hemi-imperception* as difficulty in processing information through the visual modality. We focused our attention on those forms of imperception attributable to brain injury. Alternative tasks, many of which use personal computers for displays and data collection, were described. These tasks have the particular advantage of incorporating the temporal dimension, i.e., speeded displays and convenient measure of response time.

In the rehabilitation of visual perception, an emphasis must be placed on diagnosis and in educating the patient as to the findings. Education must be stressed because the individual's subjective awareness of visual-perceptual deficits is impaired by the neurological injury. There is a discrepancy between subjective experience and objective reality. Research is needed on individualized treatment protocols, i.e., based on identification of the underlying systems that have been impaired by the brain injury. The prevalent view in the field is that visual imperception is 'neglect,' i.e., an attentional problem. Our view is that attention is not the problem but an important part of the solution.

## ACKNOWLEDGMENT

We are grateful to Megan Willis, MA, Elizabeth Willis, MA, and Robert Perlin, OD, for their thorough perusal and constructive comments on the manuscript. Michele Blouin, BA, and Gloria Ramsey, BA, of the Head Injury Recovery Center at Woodmere kindly supplied the findings from the study of vision screening and optometric intervention. Finally, our appreciation goes out to Becky Nielsen, OTR, for her diligent word processing and, especially, for the inspiration of her interest even in the wee hours.

Arthur Ginsberg, PhD, of Vistech Inc. generously provided Figure 10.1.

### REFERENCES

Albert M 1973 A simple test of visual neglect. Neurology 23: 658–664

Arena R, Gainotti G 1978 Constructional apraxia and visuoperceptive disabilities in relation to laterality of cerebral lesions. Cortex 14: 463–73

Battersby W S, Bender M B, Pollack M, Kahn R L 1956 Unilateral 'spatial agnosia' ('inattention') in patients with cerebral lesions. Brain 79: 68–92

Belleza T, Rappaport M, Hopkins H K, Hall K 1979 Visual scanning and matching dysfunction in brain-damaged patients with drawing impairment. Cortex 15: 19–36

Benson D F, Geschwind N 1969 The alexias. In: Vinken P J, Bruyn G W (eds) Handbook of clinical neurology, Vol 4: Disorders of speech, perception, and symbolic behavior. Wiley, New York, pp 112–140

Bentin S, Gordon D H 1979 Assessment of cognitive asymmetries in brain-damaged and normal subjects: validation of a test battery. Journal of Neurology, Neurosurgery and Psychiatry 42: 715–723

Bisiach E, Capitani E, Nichelli P, Spinnler H 1976a Recognition of overlapping patterns and focal hemisphere damage. Neuropsychologia 14: 375–379

Bisiach E, Nichelli P, Spinnler H 1976b Hemispheric functional asymmetry in visual discrimination between univariate stimuli: an analysis of sensitivity and response criterion. Neuropsychologia 14: 343–325

Bisiach E, Nichelli P, Sala C 1979 Recognition of random shapes in unilateral brain damaged patients: a reappraisal. Cortex 15: 491–499

Booher H R 1978 Effects of visual and auditory impairment in driving performance. Human Factors 20: 307–320

Bradshaw J L, Gates E A 1978 Visual field differences in verbal tasks: Effects of task familiarity and sex of subject. Brain and Language 5: 166–187

Campbell D C, Oxbury J M 1976 Recovery from unilateral visuo-spatial neglect. Cortex 12: 303–312

Capitani E, DiCostanzo M, Spinnler H 1978 Do focal neocortical lesions hamper short-term recognition of visual spatial patterns? Archives Suisses de Neurologie, Neurochirurgie et de Psychiatrie 123: 207–221

Carmon A 1978 Spatial and temporal factors in visual perception of patients with unilateral cerebral lesions. In: Kinsbourne M (ed) Asymmetrical function of the brain. Cambridge University Press, Cambridge, ch. 4, pp. 86–98

Carmon A, Nachson I 1971 Effect of unilateral brain damage on perception of temporal order. Cortex 7: 410–418

Chedru F 1976 Space representation in unilateral spatial neglect. Journal of Neurology, Neurosurgery and Psychiatry 39: 1057–1061

Chedru F, LeBlanc M 1972 Application of a visual searching test to the study of unilateral inattention (UI). International Journal of Mental Health 1: 55–64

Colombo A, DeRenzi E, Faglioni P 1976 The occurrence of visual neglect in patients with unilateral cerebral disease. Cortex 12: 221–231

Colombo A, DeRenzi E, Gentilini M 1982 The time course of visual hemi-inattention. Archiv für Psychiatrie und Nervenkrnkheiten (Archives of Psychiatry and Neurological Sciences) 231: 539–546

Corkin S 1979 Hidden-figures test performance: lasting effects of unilateral penetrating head injury and transient effects of bilateral cingulotomy. Neuropsychologia 17: 585–605

Dahmen W, Hartje W, Bussing A, Sturm W 1982 Disorders of calculation in asphasic patients – spatial and verbal components. Neuropsychologia 20: 145–153

Dee H L 1970 Visuoconstructive and visuoperceptive deficit in patients with unilateral cerebral lesions. Neuropsychologia 8: 305–314

Dee H L, Benton A L 1970 A cross-modal investigation of spatial performances in patients with unilateral cerebral disease. Cortex 6: 261–272

Denes F, Semenza C, Stoppa E 1978 Selective improvement by unilateral brain-damaged patients on Ravens Coloured Progressive Matrices. Neuropsychologia 16: 749–752

DeRenzi E, Spinnler H 1966 Visual recognition in patients with unilateral cerebral disease. International Journal of Nervous and Mental Disease 142: 515–525

DeRenzi E, Colombo A, Faglioni P, Gibertoni M 1982 Conjugate gaze paresis in stroke patients with unilateral damage. Archives of Neurology 39: 482–486

Diller L, Gordon W A 1981 Rehabilitation and clinical neuropsychology. In: Filskov S, Boll T (eds) Handbook of Clinical Neuropsychology. Wiley, New York, ch. 22, pp. 702–733

Diller L, Weinberg J 1965 Bender Gestalt test distortions in hemiplegia. Perceptual and Motor Skills 20: 1313–1323

Diller L, Weinberg J 1968 Attention in brain-damaged people. Journal of Education, Boston University, School of Education 150: 20–21

Diller L, Weinberg J 1970 Evidence of accident-prone behavior in hemiplegic patients. Archives of Physical Medicine and Rehabilitation 51: 358–363

Diller L, Weinberg J 1972 Differential aspects of attention in brain-damaged persons. Perceptual and Motor Skills 35: 71–81

Diller L, Weinberg J 1977 Hemi-attention in rehabilitation: the evolution of a rational remediation program. In: Weinstein E, Friedland R (eds) Advances in Neurology, vol. 18, Raven Press, New York, pp. 63–82

Dimond S J 1976 Depletion of attentional capacity after total commissurotomy in man. Brain 99: 347–356

Ehrenstein W H, Heister G, Cohen R 1982 Trail making test and visual search. Archiv für Psychiatrie und Nervenkrankheiten (Archives of Psychiatry and Neurological Sciences) 231: 333–338

Faglioni P, Scotti G, Spinnler H 1969 Impaired recognition of written letters following unilateral hemispheric damage. Cortex 56: 120–133

Friedman R 1982 Mechanisms of reading and spelling in a case of alexia without agraphia. Neuropsychologia 20: 533–545

Gainotti G 1968 Les manifestations de negligence et d'inattention pour l'hemispace. Cortex 4: 64–91

Gasparrini B, Shealy C, Walters D 1980 Differences in size and spatial placement of drawings of left versus right hemisphere brain-damaged patients. Journal of Consulting and Clinical Psychology 48: 670–672

Gianutsos R 1984 The use of personal computers for the rehabilitation of visual perception. Presented to the American Academy of Optometry, St Louis, Mo., 10 December

Gianutsos R, Klitzner C 1981 Computer programs for cognitive rehabilitation. Life Science Associates, Bayport, NY

Gianutsos R, Glosser D, Elbaum J, Vroman G M 1983a Visual imperception in brain-injured adults: multifaceted measures. Archives of Physical Medicine and Rehabilitation 64: 456–461

Gianutsos R, Vroman G M, Bottomley S 1983b Visual perceptual factors in reading disability in non-aphasic brain-injured adults. Based on a presentation to the New York Academy of Sciences

Gianutsos R, Vroman G M, Matheson P 1983c Computer programs for cognitive rehabilitation, vol. II: Further procedures for visual imperception. Life Science Associates, Bayport, NY

Gianutsos R, Cochran E E, Blouin M 1984 Computer programs for cognitive rehabilitation (vol. III): Therapeutic memory exercises for independent use. Life Science Associates, Bayport, NY

Girotti F, Casazza M, Musicco M, Avanzini G 1983 Oculomotor disorders in cortical lesions in man: the role of unilateral neglect. Neuropsychologia 21: 543–553

Golding E 1981 The effect of unilateral brain lesion on reasoning. Cortex 17: 31–40

Gordon W, Hibbard M R, Egelko S, et al 1985 Perceptual remediation in patients with right brain damage: a comprehensive program. Archives of Physical Medicine and Rehabilitation 66: 353–359

Greenberg H R, Chamoff C 1984 Visual/perceptual diagnostic testing and training programs. Educational Electronic Techniques, Ltd, Wantagh, NY

Greene E, Tager R M 1981 The influence of stroke on visual gestalt operations. International Journal of Neuroscience 14: 47–60

Hamsher K D 1978 Stereopsis and the perception of anomalous contours. Neuropsycholgia 16: 453–459

Hannay H J, Levin H S, Kay M 1982 Tachistoscopic visual perception after closed head injury. Journal of Clinical Neuropsychology 4: 117–129

Harness B Z, Bental E, Carmon A 1977 Comparison of cognition and performance in patients with organic brain damage and psychiatric patients. Acta Psychiatrica Belgica 77: 339–347

Heilman K M, Howell G J 1980 Seizure-induced neglect. Journal of Neurology, Neurosurgery and Psychiatry 43: 1035–1040

Holmes G 1938 The cerebral integration of the ocular movements. British Medical Journal 2: 107–112

Holtzman J D, Sidtis J J, Volpe B T, Wilson D H, Gazzaniga M S 1981 Dissociation of spatial information for stimulus localization and the control of attention. Brain 104: 861–872

Jones R, Donaldson I M 1981 Measurement of integrated sensory-motor function following brain damage by a computerized preview tracking task. International Rehabilitation Medicine 3: 71–83

Jones R, Giddens H, Croft D 1983 Assessment and training of brain-damaged drivers. American Journal of Occupational Therapy 37: 754–760

Kertesz A 1979 Visual agnosia: the dual deficit of perception and recognition. Cortex 15: 403–419

Kirshner H S, Webb W G 1982 Word and letter reading and the mechanism of the third alexia. Archives of Neurology 39: 84–87

Lawson I R 1962 Visual-spatial neglect in lesions of the right cerebral hemisphere: a study in recovery. Neurology 2: 23–33

Levin G Z, Meerson Y A, Tonkonogii I M 1969 Visual perception of the elements of form in focal cerebrovascular lesions. Zhurnal Nevropatologii i Psikhiatrii 69: 1794–1799 (English summary)

Levine M W, Shefner J M 1981 Fundamentals of sensation and perception. Addison-Wesley, Reading, Mass

Locher P J, Bigelow D L 1983 Visual exploratory activity of hemiplegic patients viewing the motor free visual perception test. Perceptual and Motor Skills 57: 91–100

McFie J, Piercy M F, Zangwill O L 1950 Visual-spatial agnosia associated with lesions of the right cerebral hemisphere. Brain 73: 167–190

Mack J L, Levine R N 1981 The basis of visual constructional disability in patients with unilateral cerebral lesions. Cortex 17: 515–532

Mandleberg I A 1972 Visual matching as a function of stimulus complexity in normal and brain-injured persons. Perceptual and Motor Skills 34: 859–866

Matlin M 1983 Cognition. Holt, Rinehart & Winston, New York

McKeever W F, Sullivan K F, Ferguson S M, Rayport M 1981 Typical cerebral hemisphere disconnection deficits following corpus callosum section despite sparing of the anterior commissure. Neuropsychologia 19: 745–755

Meerwaldt J D 1983 Spatial disorientation in right-hemisphere infarction: a study of the speed of recovery. Journal of Neurology, Neurosurgery and Psychiatry 46: 426–429

Meienberg O, Zangemeister W H, Rosenberg M, Hoyt W F, Stark L 1980 Saccadic eye movement strategies in patients with homonymous hemianopia. Annals of Neurology 9: 537–544

Miceli G, Caltagirone C, Gainotti G, Masullo C, Silveri M C 1981 Neuropsychological correlates of localized cerebral lesions in non-aphasic brain-damaged patients. Journal of Clinical Neuropsychology 3: 53–63

Mikula J A 1982 Perceptual retraining for left sided visual neglect in a head injured patient. Presented to the American Congress of Rehabilitation Medicine, Houston, Texas

Newcombe F, Russell W R 1969 Associated visual perceptual and spatial deficits in focal lesions of the right hemisphere. Journal of Neurology, Neurosurgery and Psychiatry 32: 73–81

Paterson A, Zangwill O L 1944 Disorders of visual space perception associated with lesions of the right cerebral hemisphere. Brain 67: 331–358

Perenin M T, Jeannerod M 1978 Visual function within the hemianopic field following early cerebral hemidecortication in man – I: Spatial localization. Neuropsychologia 16: 1–13

Perlin R R, Ramsey G, Blouin M, Gianutsos R 1985 Rehabilitative optometry for survivors of brain injury. Presented to the American Academy of Optometry Atlanta, Georgia, 10 December

Pillon B 1981 Negligence de l'hemi-espace gauche dans des epreuves visuo-constructives (Influence de la complexite spatiale et de la methode de compensation). Neuropsychologia 19: 317–320

Pizzamiglio L, Antonucci G, Francia A 1984 Response of the cortically blind hemifields to a moving visual scene. Cortex 20: 89–99

Poppel E, Shattuck S 1974 Reading in patients with brain wounds involving the central visual pathways. Cortex 10: 84–88

Putnam L R 1981 Minnesota percepto-diagnostic test and reading achievement. Perceptual and Motor Skills 53: 235–238

Rao S M, Bieliauskas L A 1983 Cognitive rehabilitation two and one-half years post right temporal lobectomy. Journal of Clinical Neuropsychology 5: 313–320

Ratcliff G 1979 Spatial thought, mental rotation and the right cerebral hemisphere. Neuropsychologia 17: 49–54

Ratcliff G, Davies-Jones G A B 1972 Defective visual localization in focal brain wounds. Brain 95: 49–60

Reed S K 1982 Cognition: theory and applications. Brooks/Cole, Monterey, California

Riddoch G 1935 Visual disorientation in homonymous half-fields. Brain 58: 376–382

Rosenberger P 1974 Discriminative aspects of visual hemi-inattention. Neurology 17: 17–23

Salmaso D, Denes G 1982 Role of the frontal lobes on an attention task: a signal detection analysis. Perceptual and Motor Skills 54: 1147–1150

Savir H, Michelson I, David C, Mendelson L, Najenson T 1977 Homonymous hemianopsia and rehabilitation in fifteen cases of C.C.I. Scandinavian Journal of Rehabilitation Medicine 9: 151–153

Schenkenberg T, Bradford D C, Ajax E T 1980 Line bisection and unilateral visual neglect in patients with neurologic impairment. Neurology 30: 509–517

Semenza C, Denes G, D'Urso V, Ramano O, Montorsi T 1978 Analytic and global strategies in copying designs by unilaterally brain-damaged patients. Cortex 14: 404–410

Sergent J 1984 Inferences from unilateral brain damage about normal hemispheric functions in visual pattern recognition. Psychological Bulletin 96: 99–115

Shallice T, Coughlan A K 1980 Modality specific word comprehension deficits in deep dyslexia. Journal of Neurology, Neurosurgery and Psychiatry 43: 866–872

Siev E, Freishat B 1976 Perceptual dysfunction in the adult stroke patient. Charles B. Slack, New York

Sivak M, Olson P L, Kewman D G, Won H, Henson D L 1981 Driving and perceptual/cognitive skills: behavioral consequences of brain damage. Archives of Physical Rehabilitation Medicine 62: 476–483

Tartaglione A, Benton A, Cocito L, Bino G, Favale E 1981 Point localisation in patients with unilateral brain damage. Journal of Neurology, Neurosurgery, and Psychiatry 44: 935–941

Tate G, Lynn J R 1977 Principles of quantitative perimetry: testing and interpreting the visual field. Grune & Stratton, New York

Taylor M M, Schaeffer J N, Blumenthal F S, Grisell J L 1971 Perceptual training in patients with left hemiplegia. Archives of Physical Medicine and Rehabilitation 52: 163–169

Torjussen T 1978 Visual processing in cortically blind hemifields. Neuropsychologia 16: 15–21

Trobe J D, Acosta P C, Krischer J P, Trick G L 1981 Confrontation visual field techniques in detection of anterior visual pathway lesions. Annals of Neurology 10: 28–34

Turbiner M, Derman R M 1980 Assessment of brain damage in a geriatric population through use of a visual searching task. Perceptual and Motor Skills 50: 371–375

Tyler A 1985 Vistech introduces eyechart based on contrast sensitivity. Ophthalmology Times 10 (1 March), No. 5

Varney N R 1981 Letter recognition and visual form discrimination in aphasic alexia. Neuropsychologia 19: 795–800

Veroff A E 1980 The neuropsychology of aging. Qualitative analysis of visual reproductions. Psychological Research 41: 2590–2668

Warrington E K, James M 1967 Disorders of visual perception in patients with localised cerebral lesions. Neuropsychologia 5: 253–266

Warrington E K, Rabin P 1970a A preliminary investigation of the relation between visual perception and visual memory. Cortex 6: 87–96

Warrington E K, Rabin P 1970b Perceptual matching in patients with cerebral lesions. Neuropsychologia 8: 475–487

Warrington E K, Shallice T 1980 Word-form dyslexia. Brain 103: 99–112

Weinberg J, Diller L, Gordon W A, Gerstman L J, Lieberman A, Lakin P, Hodges G, Ezrachi O 1977 Visual scanning training effect on reading-related tasks in acquired right brain damage. Archives of Physical Medicine and Rehabilitation 58: 479–486

Weinberg J, Diller L, Gordon W A, Gerstman L J, Lieberman A, Lakin P, Hodges G, Ezrachi O 1979 Training sensory awareness and spatial organization in people with right brain damage. Archives of Physical Medicine and Rehabilitation 60: 491–496

Weiskrantz L, Warrington E K, Sanders M D, Marshall J 1974 Visual capacity in the hemianopic field following a restricted occipital ablation. Brain 97: 709–728

Young G C, Collins D, Hren M 1983 Effect of pairing scanning training with block design training in the remediation of perceptual problems in left hemiplegics. Journal of Clinical Neuropsychology 5: 201–212

Zarit S H, Kahn R L 1974 Impairment and adaptation in chronic disabilities: spatial inattention. Journal of Nervous and Mental Disease 159: 63–74

Zihl J 1980 'Blindsight': improvement of visually guided eye movements by systematic practice in patients with cerebral blindness. Neuropsychologia 18: 71–77

Zihl J, Von Cramon D 1979 Restitution of visual function in patients with cerebral blindness. Journal of Neurology, Neurosurgery, and Psychiatry 42: 312–322

Zihl J, Werth R 1984 Contributions to the study of 'blindsight' – II. The role of specific practice for saccadic localization in patients with postgeniculate visual field defects. Neuropsychologia 22: 13–22

Zihl J, Von Cramon D, Mai N 1983 Selective disturbance of movement vision after bilateral brain damage. Brain 106: 313–340

# 11 *Graham Ratcliff*

# Perception and complex visual processes

Coming to work in a rehabilitation center can be a shock to the neuropsychologist accustomed to an academic setting where theory and scientific rigor are highly valued, or to acute care where assessment and diagnosis receive priority. In rehabilitation, some form of treatment (or, at the very least, prognosis) is the end and, in most cases, assessment and theory are regarded as little more than a means to that end. One is, therefore, confronted at an early stage to justify one's work by showing its immediate practical significance.

While I appreciate this point of view, I do not regard practical treatment suggestions as the only justification for my clinical work or the main aim of this chapter. Instead, I would argue that the better one understands a patient's problem, the more likely one is to be able to treat that patient effectively, and that some knowledge of the neuropsychology of perceptual and spatial disorders is basic to the understanding of the patient's problems. As Baddeley pointed out when discussing the relevance of theory to therapy in the area of memory disorders (Baddeley, 1984) a theory is like a map that can help you discover where you are, and help you navigate from one place to another.

Similarly an understanding of perception and its neural basis provides a general orientation for the therapist and a conceptual framework within which to consider perceptual disorders. It alerts one to the range of possibilities, helps one to recognize and distinguish different forms of disorder, guides one's analysis of the factors potentially limiting performance in perceptual and spatial tasks, and enables one to specify the nature and extent of the deficit more precisely. Some of the bizarre manifestations of perceptual disorder become more believable if one understands, even vaguely, how they might occur. Hopefully, in the hands of a good and creative therapist, these products of understanding will, in turn, lead to the design of better and more rational ways of treating or managing perceptual disorder.

The goal of this chapter, then, is to help the reader to recognize and understand perception and some of those behavioral disorders which seem to have a perceptual component. There is an enormous and bewildering literature on the subject, particularly on the physiological basis of perception, and my strategy is to draw attention to those findings and points of view which I have found most helpful, rather than attempting a detailed review. In doing so we will pass from anatomy and physiology, through psychophysics and clinical description to the more abstract and rarefied concepts of cognitive psychology and artificial intelligence.

## VISUAL ANALYSIS

The most important single step is to begin thinking of perception as an active process rather than as the passive transmission of a picture from the eye along a neural cable to a sort of projection screen spread out on the occipital lobe of the brain. In fact an extraordinarily complex series of neural mechanisms is involved and the conventional textbook diagram of the visual pathway from the retina to the lateral geniculate nucleus of the thalamus and then to the primary visual cortex in the calcarine fissure does scant justice to the sophistication of the system. Three examples of this oversimplification may illustrate the point.

### The visual pathway and contrast sensitivity

First, the individual nerve fibers which collectively form the 'neural cable' differ not only in terms of the part of the visual field from which they arise but also in the information which they transmit. The evidence suggests that analysis, as opposed to simple reception, of the visual stimulus begins at a very early stage. The retina contains at least two types of ganglion cell, originally called X and Y cells (Enroth-Cugell & Robson, 1966), which give rise to distinct types of optic nerve fiber with different destinations and different functions. X cells tend to be concentrated in the center of the retina and seem to be sensitive to stationary detail, while Y cells are more evenly distributed across the retina, respond best to coarser or moving features of the stimulus and project to the superior colliculus as well as to the lateral geniculate nucleus (see Ikeda & Wright, 1972; Rowe and Stone, 1977; Lennie, 1980 for reviews).

The X and Y systems have been studied mainly in the cat and may not be as clearly differentiated as was at first supposed, but similar systems sensitive to different spatial and temporal components of visual stimuli almost certainly exist in man and can probably be differentially damaged in disease. When visual acuity is tested by the conventional clinical method the subject is confronted with very high contrast stimuli (black on white) and asked how small the detail has to be before he can no longer resolve it. The operation of a system maximally sensitive to coarser or moving stimuli is therefore not being assessed and dysfunction in that system may be missed.

It can, however, be detected by other means. In these more sophisticated visual tests a grating is exposed on an oscilloscope or television screen in which the distribution of luminance across the screen varies sinusoidally. Such a sine-wave grating appears as a pattern of light and dark gray fuzzy-edged stripes and both the width of the stripes and the contrast – i.e., the difference in 'lightness' between the light and dark gray components – can be varied. Sensitivity to stimuli of different sizes can then be tested by selecting a particular width of stripe, turning the contrast down so that the screen appears an even gray and gradually increasing contrast until the subject reports seeing faint stripes. When this is done for a variety of stripe sizes a contrast sensitivity function can be plotted which resembles an audiogram. The human eye is maximally sensitive to medium-size stripes whereas more contrast is required before relatively large or very small stripes can be detected (Blakemore & Campbell, 1969; Campbell & Maffei, 1974). The pattern can also be drifted across the screen to explore the ability to detect movement. Measurements of contrast sensitivity conducted in this way have revealed hidden visual loss which was not reflected in reduced Snellen acuity in several disease states including cerebral lesions (Bodis-Wollner & Diamond, 1976) and multiple sclerosis (Regan et al, 1977, 1981; Bodis-Wollner et al, 1979).

The significance of these findings for rehabilitation is probably remote at present but they illustrate the point that conventional testing of visual acuity and visual fields is not an exhaustive examination of visual sensory status, let alone of perception. Reduced contrast sensitivity is the first of several potential explanations to be mentioned in this chapter for the patient who insists that his vision is 'blurred,' 'not right,' 'different,' or 'not coming in strong enough' in the presence of apparently normal acuity.

### The 'second' visual system

The second point is that the retina sends information to several other brain structures which play a role in vision as well as to the lateral geniculate nucleus and the visual cortex. The importance of these other brain structures, notably the superior colliculi, was emphasized by Schneider (1969), who suggested that they could be regarded as a second visual system in the mammalian brain. In man the colliculi form a pair of bulges on the dorsal aspect of the midbrain and correspond to the optic tectum which is the main visual center of lower vertebrates. The anatomy and physiology of the colliculi suggest that they are equipped to contribute to several aspects of visual function (see Goldberg & Robinson, 1978 for a review) and the visual role of structures outside the traditional visual system has been demonstrated by lesion studies in primates, including man.

A monkey with almost total destruction of striate cortex (the traditional primary visual cortex or Brodmann's area 17, destruction of which should cause cortical blindness) was found by Humphrey (1974) to be able to avoid obstacles and to pick up small objects. At first glance the monkey appeared to be almost normal although she suffered from a condition similar to visual agnosia in that she seemed unable to discriminate and recognize objects that she could clearly detect and locate. Human patients with restricted occipital lobe damage have also been shown to be able to reach accurately and discriminate between the shapes and orientations of stimuli presented in perimetrically blind areas of their visual fields in which they cannot consciously 'see' (Weiskrantz et al, 1974; Weiskrantz, 1980). It even seems that the acuity of this 'blindsight' can be almost as good as that of conventional vision in the preserved parts of the visual field although actual training rather than passive experience may be needed to develop it (Weiskrantz et al, 1974; Zihl, 1980).

This evidence and other similar data suggest that, even in man, the superior colliculi and other structures outside the retino-geniculo-striate system are involved in noticing, locating, and shifting the gaze to peripheral visual stimuli though probably not in recognizing or identifying them. Further support for this view comes from studies of patients with damage to these structures. Progressive supranuclear palsy, for example, a condition in which the damage includes the colliculi but is not limited to them, causes poor performance on tasks requiring complex scanning and visual search (Kimura et al, 1981) and more restricted damage to the colliculus (Heywood & Ratcliff, 1975) and pulvinar (Zihl & von Cramon, 1979) is associated with a reduction in the frequency of saccadic eye movements to the contralateral side and with symptoms of unilateral neglect (see also Chapter 9 of this volume). The difficulty with visual search in these cases may be due to deficient feedback about the eye movements the patient is making, and consequent confusion about where he is looking relative to previous fixations (Heywood & Ratcliff, 1975). This in turn causes a difficulty in organizing and monitoring a search of the environment.

These findings are potentially significant for rehabilitation in two ways. First, it is conceivable that the residual vision or 'blindsight' might be exploited to compensate in part for visual field defects. There is preliminary evidence that scotoma may, in some circumstances, be made to shrink (Zihl & Von Cramon, 1982) by appropriate training. The practical significance of this observation is yet to be demonstrated and may not apply to large lesions which cause extensive cortical damage. Second, they suggest another possible explanation for some of the patients' visual complaints who have near-normal acuity, full visual fields, and no evidence of damage to traditionally visual parts of the brain.

Collicular lesions are not common, but when they occur they are often associated with paralysis of upward gaze which should alert the therapist to the possibility of more subtle disorders of oculomotor function and visual attention. I recently saw a patient with paralysis of upward gaze and probable progressive supranuclear palsy who complained that (amongst other things) she could not watch television because the picture 'got confused.' On the chance that this was the result of disorganized and inaccurate eye movements around the television screen it was suggested that she substitute a small portable set for the larger model in her living room and place it on the floor below eye level. She derived some relief from this procedure, presumably because upward gaze was not required and the smaller picture elicited smaller or fewer saccades, although the 'treatment' would seem paradoxical if one thinks of vision purely in terms of acuity.

## Visual processing beyond striate cortex

Finally, and probably most important, the visual system certainly does not stop at the primary visual cortex (also known as striate cortex, Brodmann's area 17 or

V1, an abbreviation of visual area 1) in the calcarine fissure. As the term visual area 1 implies, there are now known to be at least six more cortical visual areas (V2, V3, etc.) the first few of which contain a topological map of the visual field and form a belt around the anterior aspect of V1 corresponding to the traditional visual association cortex (Zeki, 1978). They are multiply interconnected but in general can be seen as a cortical continuation of the visual pathway which projects forward from striate cortex towards temporal and parietal areas.

The function of these visual areas would probably be better described collectively as visual analysis rather than visual association because, although new findings which blur the distinction between them are appearing with depressing (or exciting, depending on one's point of view) regularity, it seems that these different groups of neurons are tuned to respond to different properties of the visual stimulus – e.g. color or depth. They can be conceptualized as specialized visual analyzers responsible for reporting on the presence of that particular property of the stimulus situation which they are equipped to recognize (Cowey, 1979).

If the cortical component of the visual system includes these relatively discrete and specialized visual analyzers, then one would expect that cortical lesions would occasionally cause selective impairment of one aspect of visual processing leaving vision intact in other respects. This turns out to be the case. Isolated impairment of the ability to discriminate color (Meadows, 1974), depth (Danta et al, 1978), and movement (Zihl et al, 1983) have all been reported after cerebral lesions although such impairments are rare, presumably because it is unusual for a cerebral lesion to be so precisely placed as to affect only one of these visual areas. Ratcliff & Cowey (1979) described these deficits as 'disorders of sensory analysis' and, while thinking of them in this way may be an oversimplification, it does emphasize the point that vision is not an all-or-none process.

One other disorder which can conveniently be grouped in this category deserves mention because it is more common and has functional implications. This is defective visual localization, which is one element of Balint's syndrome (Balint, 1909) or the syndrome of visual disorientation (Holmes, 1918) and which is manifested most obviously by inaccurate visually guided reaching. The patient with classical visual disorientation following a bilateral parietal lesion will misreach for objects anywhere in the visual field, including those upon which he is fixating. The disorder is dramatically obvious and the patient is seriously disabled, feeling his way almost as though he were blind. Yet he may be able to identify objects which he cannot locate or pick up, name their color, and be able to reach accurately for stimuli whose position can be specified through some other sensory modality (e.g., a point on his own body) indicating that the disorder is one of visual localization rather than of reaching *per se*. Visual disorientation can thus be distinguished from ataxia on finger–nose testing as the patient will reach accurately for his nose but inaccurately for the examiner's finger. The picture is the reverse of that described previously as 'blindsight,' in which identification but not localization of visual stimuli is preserved.

Such a disorder is unlikely to be overlooked, but defective localization confined to the half-field contralateral to a unilateral parietal lesion is less obvious and more frequent. It can conveniently be detected after confrontation testing of the visual fields by asking the patient to maintain central fixation on the examiner's face and asking him tc reach for a peripheral stimulus (e.g., the examiner's outstretched hand) which he has indicated he can detect. The patient with defective localization will typically miss on the side of the fixation point (i.e., reach for a point between the examiner's hand and his face) with either hand in the contralateral half-field but reach accurately with both hands in the ipsilateral half-field. The disorder is common enough that assessment of visual localization should be a routine part of the examination of the visual field. Although the patient may be unaware of his difficulty, it may cause him to misplace objects while his attention is directed elsewhere (e.g., place a cup from which he has been drinking off the edge of the table while talking to someone sitting opposite) and has obvious implications for driving. This disorder may follow damage to the posterior part of the parietal lobe in either hemisphere (Ratcliff & Davies-Jones, 1972), a part of the brain which includes Brodmann's area 7 where neurophysiological studies suggest that the neurons are involved in the direction of attention to peripheral visual stimuli and the coordination of eye and hand (Mountcastle, 1975; Robinson et al, 1978; Lynch, 1980; Hyvarinen, 1982). While the cortical control of visually guided reaching is undoubtedly complex (Humphrey, 1979) it seems that posterior parietal cortex is part of the neural circuit involved.

## PERCEPTUAL INTEGRATION

The moral of the story so far is that a considerable number of neural mechanisms each make their own distinct contribution to the analysis of the visual stimulus. However, just as the leader of a rehabilitation team must integrate the reports of all the team members in order to get a total picture of the patient, so the visual system must put together all the information provided by the diverse neural mechanisms contributing to vision in order to obtain a coherent percept. Precisely how this is done is not known, but it seems to be a function of still more anterior brain areas and, in man, particularly of specialized mechanisms in the right cerebral hemisphere which seem to be brought into play at later, integrative and more abstract stages of perceptual processing (Moscovitch, 1979). Again there are several converging lines of evidence to suggest that more than one mechanism is involved.

### Object recognition, Gestalt formation, figure-ground perception

Ungerleider and Mishkin (Ungerleider & Mishkin, 1982; Ungerleider, 1985) have shown that the cortical continuation of the visual pathway which we have been discussing can be separated into two distinct anatomical pathways, one leading into the parietal lobe and subserving spatial aspects of vision and one towards the temporal lobe which is chiefly responsible for object recognition. Lesion studies in both monkeys and man support this view. Monkeys with parietal lesions have difficulty with tasks such as learning to go to the foodwell nearest to a landmark, a spatial task, but have no difficulty with object discrimination, while monkeys with temporal lesions exhibit the reverse pattern of impairment (Pohl, 1973). A similar double dissociation has been shown in man: patients with focal parietal lesions have difficulty with spatial tasks like learning a visually guided stylus maze but may perform normally on other perceptual tasks such as extracting the face from degraded pictures (Fig. 11.1) while patients with lesions near the temporo-parieto-occipital junction learn the maze normally but have difficulty 'seeing' the faces (Newcombe & Russell, 1969).

The function of the object recognition system is illustrated in Figure 11.2, an item from the Street Completion Test, which presents a problem to the visual system similar to that posed by the degraded faces used in Newcombe and Russell's study. The drawing is quite clear in that the contrast is high and the contours are clearly visible. Most readers would probably have little difficulty in copying it accurately with pen and ink – certainly less difficulty than in drawing a picture of an animal from life. Yet many will not immediately recognize it as a rabbit (of the kind favored by manufacturers of cuddly toys,

**Fig. 11.1** An item from Mooney's visual closure test (Mooney and Ferguson, 1951). The reader should see a face.

**Fig. 11.2** An item from the Street completion test (Street, 1931). Most people need a clue (see text) to aid in identification of the stimulus.

seen from the side, crouching down, facing to the right and with ears laid back almost flat against the body) a feat which would seem so trivial as to require no explanation if one were looking at a real rabbit.

The difficulty that normal observers sometimes experience in recognizing the rabbit in Figure 11.2 without cuing is probably similar in kind, though not in degree, to the difficulty that patients with temporo-parieto-occipital lesions have in seeing the face in Figure 11.1. Patients who have this difficulty are another group who persistently complain of something wrong with their vision in spite of 'normal' vision as assessed by most tests. The disorder does not actually handicap them in most circumstances but they find it disturbing. Patients with even more severe and usually bilateral disruption of the object recognition system have difficulty identifying real objects or realistic drawings which they can copy recognizably but without recognition (Ratcliff & Newcombe, 1982). In other words this is a simulation of one form of visual agnosia (see Rubens, 1979 for a review of the agnosias). The lines are perceived clearly but the information provided by the cortical visual analyzers is insufficient to enable the object recognition system to form a hypothesis about the three-dimensional structure whose two-dimensional image is projected onto the retina. When a hypothesis is suggested the object recognition system is able to fit the information arriving at the eye to the hypothesis provided and the rabbit appears.

This view of the later stages of visual object recognition as being an attempt to fit the information provided by the feature detecting mechanisms of the visual system to a hypothesis about the identity of the stimulus causing them helps one to understand some of the geometric visual illusions (see e.g. Gregory, 1966, 1973; Frisby, 1979) in which deliberately misleading information is provided. It may also help to explain the visual hallucinations which sometimes result when the visual system is damaged and information is distorted or lost in transit. In both cases the object recognition system struggles to make sense of the situation, the wrong hypothesis is accepted and one 'sees' something not actually there. This is, however, a personal interpretation of the way the system works and is a large leap from what we know of the physiology to this account of its function. The aim is to be helpful rather than necessarily correct.

## Spatial integration

Contrast the function of the object recognition system, putatively posterior temporal lobe in man, and the disorders of figure-ground discrimination, difficulty in recognizing degraded or overlapping figures and visual agnosias which occur when it is damaged with the role of the, putatively parietal, spatial system and visuo-spatial disorders. More than any other aspect of perception, our understanding of spatial orientation, such as it is, comes from the study of patients with cerebral lesions and can best be illustrated by describing the disorders from which they suffer. Reviews of the topic (Benton, 1969, 1979; De Renzi, 1982; Ratcliff, 1982) will be briefly mentioned here.

The term 'visual–spatial agnosia,' which has been applied to the clinical picture of spatial disorder associated with right hemisphere damage, is at first sight misleading because it is not an agnosia in the sense that something clearly definable is not recognized. However, on reflection the term seems more appropriate as there is a sense in which the patients suffering from these disorders do not recognize spatial relationships. In Benton's (1979) words, they have 'a faulty appreciation of the spatial aspects of visual experience'.

As an example consider the three copies of the Rey Figure shown in Figures 11.3–11.5. Figure 11.3 is a fairly good copy of the original and is included to show what the stimulus looks like and to prove that it can be drawn accurately by patients with cerebral lesions and visual field defects. Figure 11.4 drawn by a 57-year-old man about 10 weeks after a right hemisphere stroke, contains some of the individual components of the original figure but the drawing is disorganized, the elements are inappropriately placed, and the left side is neglected. The final drawing is the work of a highly intelligent man in full-time employment over 20 years after he sustained a right parietal missile wound. He also exhibits some left-sided neglect, but one can also see that he has difficulty with spatial relationships on the right side of the drawing – the horizontal line which bisects the main part of the figure is discernible on the left side, but seems to turn into the bottom of the triangle to the right and the bottom of the

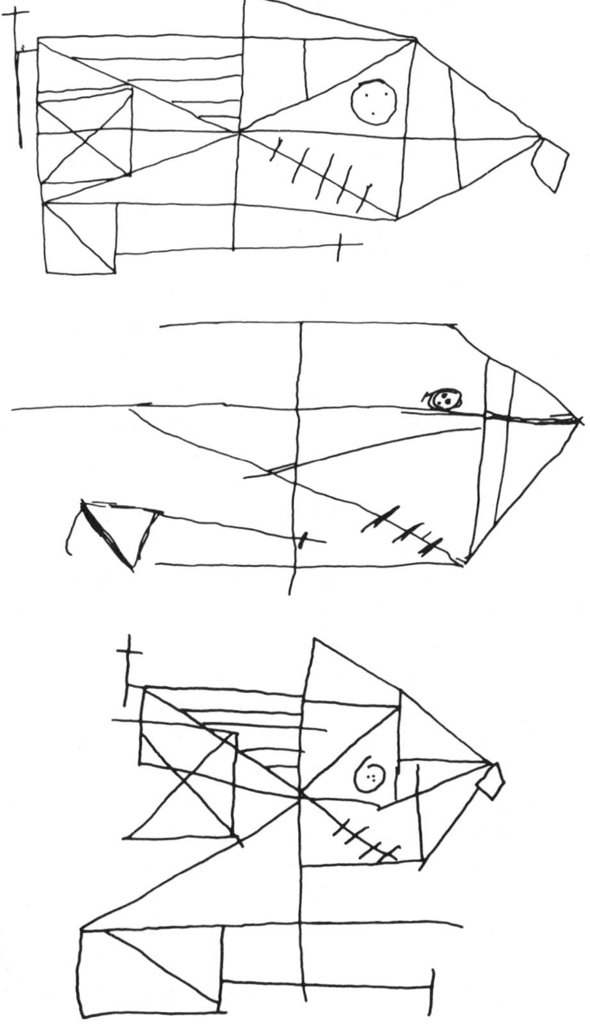

**Figs. 11.3–11.5** Copies of the Rey figure. See text for details (Reproduced from Ratcliff, 1980).

main rectangle is represented by different lines on the left- and right-hand sides of the drawing. The patient seems to perceive the individual components but cannot integrate them into a coherent spatial framework. Incidentally, this patient in whose drawing the neglect of the left side is quite apparent is the only one of the three who does not have a hemianopsia. Although the two usually go together, probably because of the proximity of the optic radiation to the parietal lobe mechanisms involved in the redirection of attention and their common blood supply, they are not identical and neglect can result from damage to many different parts of the brain (Heilman, 1979).

## COGNITIVE CONSIDERATIONS

Our increasing knowledge of the anatomy and physiology of the visual system – the hardware dedicated to visual perception – has increased our understanding of those perceptual disorders which seem to result from damage at earlier stages of perceptual processing. However, beyond showing that two anatomically separate cortical mechanisms seem to be involved, anatomy and physiology are not yet able to tell us much about the way in which the products of visual analysis are turned into a coherent percept of an object or integrated into a coherent spatial framework. Consequently, they cannot tell us much about the perceptual disorders which result from dysfunction at these later stages of processing. We are, therefore, forced to take a different approach, basically the approach of the cognitive psychologist, and attempt to deduce from the patient's behavior and test results what cognitive processes are involved in tasks that the patient cannot perform and which of these processes is defective in the patient under consideration. This approach uses logic, what little information is available about the cognitive processes involved in perception and spatial orientation, and the empirical information in the neuropsychological literature which lists the manifestations of these disorders. Guided by this information, one forms a hypothesis about the nature of the patient's deficit, and checks this hypothesis by further testing or observation, essentially treating the evaluation of every patient as a mini-experiment or single case study.

The drawings in Figures 11.4 and 11.5 are examples of a rather general and intuitive application of this approach. The difficulty of these two patients could be subsumed under the heading 'constructional apraxia' but labeling it as such is less useful than looking critically at their drawings and attempting to identify the underlying problem which causes them to perform poorly. Constructional apraxia may be the result of apraxia in the sense of motor planning difficulty, and patients with these difficulties may perform relatively well if tested on non-constructional spatial tasks like finding their way around or in matching tasks. Performance may even depend on the type of constructional task used (Benton, 1967; Dee, 1970) or the scale of space in which they are required to operate (Ratcliff & Newcombe, 1973). A thorough analysis of the patient's deficit would investigate the effects of all these variables by comparing performance on a variety of tasks, but usually the problem seems to result either from unilateral neglect or a difficulty in integrating individually well-perceived elements into a coherent spatial framework, or both. Performance on all tasks which involve these abilities will be affected and complex drawing tests are just a convenient and sensitive way of detecting them.

Figure 11.6, on the other hand, seems to reflect a different problem. This is also a copy of the Rey figure, and does not show any obvious neglect or disarticulation of the parts. The problem is that it bears only the most general resemblance to the original and would be more acceptable as a variation on a theme than as a copy. Bizarre performances like this are sometimes seen after frontal lobe damage and this patient, with a closed head injury, exhibited the

**Fig. 11.6** Copy of the Rey figure suggesting non-perceptual disorder.

poor problem-solving skills and lack of initiative which frequently occur after damage in this area. While we cannot yet specify the patient's problem in precise cognitive terms it is clearly different from the spatial difficulty evident in the other drawings. This illustrates the very important point that there is more than one reason for failing any given test, and that the way in which it is failed is frequently more important than the actual score. The cookbook approach which implies that poor performance on Test A indicates disorder B and requires treatment C is simply not valid in most cases. There is no test which cannot be failed for more than one reason, and which potential reason was the cause of failure in a given patient must be determined. Whatever additional tests may be needed to determine this should also be performed.

Several authors (including Posner & Rafal in this volume) have applied the cognitive approach to perceptual disorders in a much more rigorous form. Farah (1984) has considered neurological impairments of mental imagery and related disorders in the light of Kosslyn's (1980) model, Warrington (1975), Ratcliff & Newcombe (1982) and Humphreys & Riddoch (1984) have attempted analyses of the cognitive processes involved in visual agnosia; Morrow et al (1985) have studied the 'cognitive maps' of patients with right hemisphere lesions, and Bisiach and his colleagues (Bisiach & Luzzatti, 1978; Bisiach et al, 1981) demonstrated that unilateral neglect includes a component which could better be described as cognitive than perceptual.

The general point emerging from this work is that one needs to think in terms of internal, mental representations as well as the external stimulus. In Bisiach & Luzzatti's (1978) study, patients with left-sided neglect following a stroke were asked to imagine that they were standing in a familiar square in Milan facing the cathedral and to describe what they saw in their mind's eye. The patients described predominantly the right side of the square, neglecting the left just as they might have been expected to do in real life. When they were asked to take a different perspective, imagining themselves with their backs to the cathedral, they again neglected that part of the square now on their left side.

These patients had not forgotten the environment in which they were being asked to imagine themselves – putting their descriptions from the two viewpoints together gives a description of the whole square. Nor could their neglect be attributed to a peripheral visual or oculomotor difficulty in any ordinary sense as they could not see any of the square from their hospital beds. Bisiach and Luzzati described the disorder as 'neglect of representational space' and what seems to have been happening is that their patients were extracting information about the contents of the square from their preserved long-term memory and attempting to generate a mental picture incorporating that information. Mental pictures generated in this way are apparently subject to the same sort of neglect as scenes which one actually inspects.

This may seem to take us back full circle to the internal 'projection screen' mentioned earlier rather disparagingly. Some similar concept is part of several cognitive models – e.g., the 'visual buffer' of Kosslyn (1980) and Farah (1985) and the 'visuospatial sketch pad' of Baddeley's (1983) model of working memory. The difference is that the image represented in the visual buffer or on the visuospatial sketch pad is not to be regarded as a photograph of the stimulus but as the product of all the visual information processing which we have discussed plus some form of image generation process or control mechanism.

Patients with right hemisphere lesions tend to have more difficulty in tasks in which they are required to draw a visual stimulus or construct it in some other way than when they simply have to pick an identical stimulus from an array in a simultaneous matching to sample task. Indeed this difference between constructional and matching tasks led LeDoux et al (1977) to suggest that the essence of right hemisphere specialization was its capacity to handle the 'manipulo-spatial' element of these tasks. However an alternative explanation would be that constructional tasks require more sophisticated analysis and manipulation of internal representations than do matching tasks. The patient must internally generate and represent a picture which he is about to draw as well as one which remains in the mind's eye. Some support for the view that internal representations and mental operations are important comes from the finding that patients with right posterior lesions are selectively impaired on a task which involves no drawing but in which they are required to mentally rotate visual stimuli (Ratcliff, 1979).

Construction of an internal spatial representation – a sketch on the mental pad – will also be required in short-term visual memory tasks and tasks in which the patient is required to draw a map of a familiar environment such as the layout of his house. Patients with visuospatial disorders have difficulty in such tasks (a particularly good example is provided by McFie et al, 1950 and reproduced in Ratcliff, 1982). While in some cases this may reflect memory impairment or an executive difficulty, it may also reflect a failure to create or sustain an internal representation to be read out in the form of a copy. In these cases too it is difficult to see how the deficit can be sensorily based as the patient is trying to represent information in the form of a map which he holds in memory rather than information presented to his eyes. Spatial difficulties are typically supramodal, affecting performance on visual and tactile spatial tasks, which suggests that there is a common spatial representation system for both modalities although the separation of the spatial and object recognition systems may be maintained even at this level (Martin, 1985; Levine et al, 1985).

This has been a brief, speculative, and selective review which has attempted to alert the reader to some of the complexities of visual perception and to suggest ways of thinking about perception and perceputal disorder. Theoretically interesting perceptual disorders (e.g., prosopagnosia, the inability to recognize familiar faces) and clinically important variables (e.g., oculomotor function) have been almost totally ignored. Description, definition, and classification have taken second place to analysis, explanation, and interpretation because descriptions, definitions, and classifications are available elsewhere and the author takes the view that the evaluation and management of perceptual disorder requires that the therapist has a conceptual framework in which to form and test hypotheses about the patient's problem as well as a repertoire of tests to give and labels to assign. However some more concrete but very general guidelines may help the reader to apply this framework in practice.

## ASSESSMENT

Assuming that facilities for measuring contrast sensitivity are not available to most rehabilitation professionals, the first steps will be measurement of visual acuity, assessment of the visual fields including testing for extinction on bilateral simultaneous stimulation, and checking oculomotor function. If these are impaired, adequate information may not reach the cortex for further analysis and the patient may not be able to bring the cerebral mechanism of perception into full operation. Particularly in cases of head injury where involvement of the third, fourth, and sixth cranial nerves is common, it is always worth checking whether performance in visually guided tasks improves with one eye patched as diplopia may be hampering the patient even if he does not complain of double vision. Diplopia and other visual disturbances can also occur secondary to the bitemporal visual field cuts associated with chiasmal lesions (Kirkham, 1972) but these are rarely encountered in a rehabilitation setting.

Small scotomata or visual field cuts which are not always detected on initial confrontation testing may impair functioning in specific situations. I recently encountered a patient who complained that he had been unable to shoot a basketball accurately since surgery for an arteriovenous malformation in the right temporal lobe, and who casually mentioned that he seemed to be misjudging distances when driving, twice bumping the car in front of him when it stopped unexpectedly. Examination revealed a small sector defect adjacent to the vertical meridian in the left upper quadrant of the visual field, typical of temporal lobe lesions and readily demonstrable to confrontation if one looks in the right place. This part of the visual field, above and to the left of fixation, is precisely where a traffic light usually occurs in North America, and his accidents were probably caused by failure to notice the red light signaling the car ahead to stop rather than by faulty depth perception. His trouble in shooting baskets was cured by tilting his head to the left prior to shooting, thereby placing the basket in the right visual field, although no such simple solution was available for driving.

Having checked the afferent visual pathway and established whether or not binocular single vision can be achieved in all directions of gaze, the next logical step is to look for disorders of sensory analysis. Assessment of visual localization via visually guided reaching has already been described, and color and depth perception can usually be checked informally unless they are of special interest, perhaps because of the patient's occupation. Some care needs to be taken to distinguish between disorders resulting from faulty perception as opposed to those which reflect the patient's inability to respond adequately. Difficulty naming colors, for example, may reflect a word-finding difficulty or visual verbal disconnection syndrome (Oxbury et al, 1969) rather than faulty color perception.

Unilateral neglect needs to be assessed independently of the visual fields as neglect may occur without hemianopsia and vice-versa. This can conveniently be achieved by drawing tests, letter cancellation tasks, visual search tasks, or by noticing a response bias in multiple-choice visual matching tasks. If a drawing test like the Rey figure is used, it may also provide evidence of higher-level visuospatial deficits and this can be supplemented by block designs and non-constructional spatial tasks. Finally, object naming can rule out gross visual agnosia though again failure may be attributable to dysphasia, disconnection, or dementia rather than perceptual disorder and tests of figure-ground discrimination or measures using degraded stimuli are required to detect more subtle recognition disorders.

Many of these observations can be made as a by-product of testing which is not primarily designed as a perceptual evaluation. The Luria Nebraska Neuropsychological Battery includes degraded pictures of objects and a form of mental rotation test, while the Trail Making Test and Tactual Performance Test of the Halstead–Reitan Battery involve visual scanning, search, and appreciation of spatial relationships. The results must always be considered within the broader picture of the patient's general cognitive status and in association with evaluation of the patient's behavior in functional tasks. This is a two-way street. The observation that the patient has difficulty dressing may alert one to the presence of a difficulty with spatial thinking (anyone who has observed a young child attempting to orient a coat appropriately before inserting his arms will appreciate the complexity of the spatial task involved) and, conversely, the knowledge that a patient has difficulty with mental rotation or three-dimensional block designs may suggest an explanation for his difficulty in dressing. This in turn should lead to a treatment strategy which is predicated on a working hypothesis about the factor which is limiting his performance.

The reader will note that no prescription has been offered for the evaluation or treatment of perceptual disorders. Returning to the comments with which this chapter began, I would justify this lack by saying that the most important weapon in the armament of those who work with perceptually disordered patients is a working knowledge of the neuropsychology of vision. Certainly this is a prerequisite for the interpretation of any test results. If this chapter has provided useful information or given the reader a different perspective on any patient, it will have served its purpose.

## REFERENCES

Baddeley A D 1983 Working memory. Philosophical Transactions of the Royal Society of London, Series B 302: 311–324

Baddeley A D 1984 Memory theory and memory therapy. In: Wilson B A, Moffat N (eds) Clinical management of memory problems. Croom Helm, London

Balint R 1909 Seelenlahmung des 'Schavens', optische Ataxie, raumliche Storung der Aufmerksamkeit. Monatschrift fur Psychiatrie and Neurologie 25: 51–81

Benton A L 1967 Constructional apraxia and the minor hemisphere. Confinia Neurologica (Basle) 29: 1–16

Benton A L 1969 Disorders of spatial orientation. In: Vinken P J, Bruyn G W (eds) Handbook of clinical neurology, vol. III. North Holland, Amsterdam

Benton A L 1979 Visuoperceptive, visuospatial and visuoconstructive disorders. In: Heilman K E, Valenstein E (eds) Clinical neuropsychology. Oxford University Press, New York

Bisiach E, Luzzatti C 1978 Unilateral neglect of representational space. Cortex 14: 129–133

Bisiach E, Capitani E, Luzzatti C, Perani D 1981 Brain and conscious representation of outside reality. Neuropsychologia 19: 543–551

Blakemore C, Campbell F W 1969 On the existence of neurons in the human visual system selectively sensitive to the orientation and size of retinal images. Journal of Physiology 203: 237–260

Bodis-Wollner I, Diamond S P 1976 The measurement of spatial contrast sensitivity in cases of blurred vision associated with cerebral lesions. Brain 99: 695–710

Bodis-Wollner I, Hendley C D, Mylin L H, Thornton J 1979 Visual evoked potentials and the visuogram in multiple sclerosis. Annals of Neurology 5: 40–47

Campbell F W, Maffei L 1974 Contrast and spatial frequency. Scientific American 231: 106–114

Cowey A 1979 Cortical maps and visual perception. Quarterly Journal of Experimental Psychology 31: 1–17

Danta G, Hilton R C, O'Boyle D J 1978 Hemisphere function and binocular depth perception. Brain 101: 569–590

Dee H L 1970 Visuoconstructive and visuoperceptive deficit in patients with unilateral cerebral disease. Cortex 6: 261–272

DeRenzi E 1982 Disorders of space exploration and cognition. Wiley, New York

Enroth-Cugell, Robson J A 1966 The contrast sensitivity and retinal ganglion cells of the cat. Journal of Physiology 187: 517–552

Farah M 1984 The neurological basis of mental imagery. Cognition 18: 245–272

Frisby J P 1979 Seeing. Oxford University Press, New York

Goldberg M E, Robinson D L 1978 Visual system: superior colliculus. In: Masterton R B (ed) Handbook of behavioral neurology, vol. I: Sensory integration. Plenum, New York

Gregory R L 1966 Eye and brain. Weidenfeld & Nicolson, London

Gregory R L 1968 Visual illusions. Scientific American 219: 66–76

Heilman K M 1979 Neglect and related disorders. In: Heilman K M, Valenstein E (eds) Clinical neuropsychology. Oxford University Press, New York

Heywood S P, Ratcliff G 1975 Long-term oculomotor consequences of unilateral colliculectomy in man. In: Lennerstrand G and Bach-y-Rita P (eds) Basic mechanisms of ocular motility and their clinical implications. Pergamon, Oxford

Holmes G 1918 Disturbances of visual orientation. British Journal of Ophthalmology 2: 449–468, 506–518

Humphrey D R 1979 On the cortical control of visually-directed reaching: contributions by non-precentral motor areas. In: Talbot R B, Humphrey D R (eds) Posture and movement. Raven, New York

Humphrey N K 1974 Vision in a monkey without striate cortex: a case study. Perception 3: 241–255

Humphreys G W, Riddoch M J 1984 Routes to object constancy: implications from neurological impairments of object constancy. Quarterly Journal of Experimental Psychology 36A: 385–415

Hyvarinen J 1982 The parietal cortex of monkey and man. Springer-Verlag, Berlin

Ikeda H, Wright M J 1972 Receptive field organization of 'sustained' and 'transient' ganglion cells which subserve different functional roles. Journal of Physiology 262: 265–284

Kimura D, Barnet H J M, Burkhart G 1981 The psychological test pattern in progressive supranuclear palsy. Neuropsychologia 19: 301–306

Kirkham T H 1972 The ocular symptomatology of pituitary tumors. Proceedings of the Royal Society of Medicine 65: 517–518

Kosslyn S M 1980 Image and mind. Harvard University Press, Cambridge, MA

LeDoux J E, Wilson D H, Gazzaniga M S 1977 Manipulo-spatial aspects of cerebral lateralization: clues to the origin of lateralization. Neuropsychologia 15: 743–750

Lennie P 1980 Parallel visual pathways: a review. Vision Research 20: 561–594

Levine D N, Warach J, Farah M 1985 Two visual systems in mental imagery. Neurology 35: 1010–1018

Lynch J C 1980 The functional organization of posterior parietal cortex. Behavioral and Brain Sciences 3: 485–534

McFie J, Piercy M F, Zangwill O L 1950 Visual–spatial agnosia associated with lesions of the right cerebral hemisphere. Brain 73: 167–190

Martin A 1985 Preserved memory in patients with Alzheimer's disease. Paper presented to the thirteenth annual meeting of the International Neuropsychological Society. San Diego, California, 6–9 February

Meadows J C 1974 Disturbed perception of colours associated with localized cerebral lesions. Brain 97: 615–632

Mooney C M, Ferguson G A 1951 A new closure test. Canadian Journal of Psychology 5: 129–133

Morrow L, Ratcliff G, Johnston C S 1985 Externalizing spatial knowledge in patients with right hemispheric lesions. Cognitive Neuropsychology (in press)

Moscovitch M 1979 Information processing and the cerebral hemispheres. In Gazzaniga M S (ed) Handbook of behavioral neurobiology, vol. II: Neuropsychology. Plenum, New York

Mountcastle V B 1975 The view from within: pathways to the study of perception. Johns Hopkins Medical Journal 136: 109–135

Newcombe F, Russell W R 1969 Dissociated visual perceptual and spatial deficits in focal lesions of the right hemisphere. Journal of Neurology, Neurosurgery and Psychiatry 32: 73–81

Oxbury J M, Oxbury S M, Humphrey N K 1969 Varieties of colour anomia. Brain 92: 847–860

Pohl W 1973 Dissociation of spatial discrimination deficits following frontal and parietal lesions in monkeys. Journal of Comparative and Physiological Psychology 82: 227–239

Ratcliff G 1979 Spatial thought, mental rotation and the right cerebral hemisphere. Neuropsychologia 17: 49–54

Ratcliff G 1980 The clinical significance of disorders of visuospatial perception. Geriatric Medicine 10: 71–74

Ratcliff G 1982 Disturbances of spatial orientation associated with cerebral lesions. In: Potegal M (ed) Spatial abilities: development physiological foundation. Academic Press, New York

Ratcliff G, Cowey A 1979 Disturbances of visual perception following cerebral lesions. In: Osborne D J, Gruneberg M M, Eiser J R (eds) Research in psychology and medicine, vol. 1. Academic Press, London

Ratcliff G, Davies-Jones G A B 1972 Defective visual localization in focal brain wounds. Brain 95: 46–60

Ratcliff G, Newcombe F 1973 Spatial orientation in man: effects of left, right, and bilateral posterior cerebral lesions. Journal of Neurology, Neurosurgery and Psychiatry 36: 448–454

Ratcliff G, Newcombe F 1982 Object recognition: some deductions from the clinical evidence. In Ellis A E (ed) Normality and pathology in cognitive function. Academic Press, London

Regan D, Raymond J, Ginsburg A P, Murray T J 1981 Contrast sensitivity, visual acuity and the discrimination of Snellen letters in multiple sclerosis. Brain 104: 333–350

Regan D, Silver R, Murray T V 1977 Visual acuity and contrast sensitivity in multiple sclerosis – hidden visual loss. Brain 100: 563–579

Robinson D L, Goldberg M E, Stanton G B 1978 Parietal association cortex in primates: sensory mechanisms and behavioral modifications. Journal of Neuropsychology 41: 910–932

Rowe M H, Stone J 1977 Naming neurons. Brain, Behavior and Evolution 14: 185–216

Rubens A B 1979 Agnosia. In: Heilman K M, Valenstein E (eds) Clinical neuropsychology. Oxford University Press, New York

Schneider G E 1969 Two visual systems. Science 163: 895–902

Street R F 1931 A Gestalt completion test. Contributions to Education, No. 481. Columbia University, New York

Ungerleider L 1985 The corticocortical pathways for object recognition and spatial perception. Chagas C, Gattas R, Gren C (eds) Pattern recognition mechanisms. Pontifical Academy of Sciences, Vatican City

Ungerleider L, Mishkin M 1982 Two cortical visual systems. In: Ingle D J, Mansfield R J W, Goodale M S (eds) The analysis of visual behavior. MIT Press, Cambridge, MA

Warrington E K 1975 The selective impairment of semantic memory. Quarterley Journal of Experimental Psychology 27: 635–657

Weiskrantz L, Warrington E K, Sanders M D, Marsall J 1974 Visual capacity in the hemianopsic field following a restricted occipital ablation. Brain 97: 709–728

Weiskrantz L 1980 Varieties of residual experience. Quarterly Journal of Experimental Psychology 32: 365–386

Zeki S M 1978 Uniformity and diversity of structure and function in rhesus monkey prestriate visual cortex. Journal of Physiology 277: 273–290

Zihl J 1980 'Blindsight'; improvement of visually guided eye movements by systematic practice in cerebral blindness. Neuropsychologia 18: 71–77

Zihl J, von Cramon D 1979 The contributions of the 'second' visual system to directed visual attention in man. Brain 102: 835–856

Zihl J, von Cramon D 1982 Restitution of visual field in patients with damage to the geniculostriate visual pathway. Human Neurobiology 1: 5–8

Zihl J, von Cramon D, Mai N 1983 Selective disturbance of movement vision after bilateral brain damage. Brain 106: 313–340

# 12

*Margaret O'Connor and Laird S. Cermak*

# Rehabilitation of organic memory disorders

Memory rehabilitation has always seemed to hold a great deal of promise. For decades stage entertainers have captivated audiences with memory feats suggesting that their accomplishments could be mastered by anyone. The implication is that we humans do not use our full or even a small portion of our cognitive capacities. Why we fail so miserably or are so lazy as to neglect these untapped reserves is never explained, yet somehow we are made to feel guilty for the waste of such inherent potential.

Some therapists working with memory-impaired patients are enthusiastic about the prospects of 'tapping' these hidden reservoirs. Their expectations have spawned many new ideas about memory retraining. Although there is a high level of interest, surprisingly the field of memory rehabilitation has developed slowly. Perhaps its growth has been stunted because current retraining methods rely on patients' ability to learn techniques they had not employed prior to injury. Another drawback is the complexity of these techniques, since they are often too difficult for individuals with 'normal' brains to use.

The apparent potential of memory aids turns out to be a mirage when applied to everyday situations. While they may be useful in experimental list learning, they pale in the face of learning a philosophical point of view, words for a spelling test, or even items to buy at a store. We just don't find mnemonics useful and consequently fail to develop them. This is not a result of an unwillingness to use all of our brain, but simply a decision concerning the economical allocation of its resources.

In light of these considerations, one can foresee difficulties in attempts at teaching mnemonics to brain-injured patients. Nevertheless, many researchers have attempted to do so and some have been marginally successful. In this chapter we will review and criticize these attempts, describing them and suggesting what we ought to have learned from them. Before doing so, however, it is important to discuss the recovery of memory functions from a biological perspective since this will provide insight into the mechanisms upon which therapeutic measures might capitalize.

## BIOLOGICAL ASPECTS OF RECOVERY FROM AMNESIA

Although memory problems are linked to a variety of neuropathologic conditions, damage to the medial temporal or diencephalic regions of the brain is most often implicated in severe cases of global amnesia. In particular, structures such as the hippocampus, the mammillary bodies, and the dorsal medial nucleus of the thalamus are the proposed sites of amnesic problems. Intuitively, an appreciation of the neuroanatomy of amnesia would beget an understanding of the biological processes involved in recovery, yet there are reasons why this is not so. Spontaneous and/or therapeutically induced recoveries from severe forms of organic amnesia are rare. To the extent that memory restoration does occur, it probably involves a complex network of biological and psychological substrates which we do not fully understand. Consequently, our overview of the biological factors involved in the recovery of memory functions must be broadened to general considerations pertaining to recovery of function in the CNS which may or may not have direct bearing on memory.

### Theoretical models of recovery in the CNS

Biological models of recovery include both static and dynamic formulations (Laurence & Stein, 1978). Static theories attribute the recovery of function to various types of cortical sparing. A function's survival depends on whether it is represented in cerebral areas other than the damaged one. Redundancy static theories advocate that these areas are anatomically distinct but functionally homogeneous. Multiple control static theories emphasize the resiliency of the organism and the preservation of function. The difference between the models is that redundancy depicts the duplicate functions as being nested within each other while multiple control refers to independent centers of functional localization.

There are a number of problems with static theories of recovery. First, they assume that recovery is dependent upon the anatomical organization of the brain. This assumption makes recovery seem like an all-or-none phenomenon leaving little room for the gradual clearing of deficits which so often follows brain injury. Static explanations also are difficult to verify experimentally. The manifestation of a 'regained' function may appear to indicate the activation of another brain region when, in fact, the individual may have merely learned to use an alternative response strategy.

Dynamic explanations of recovery focus on sequences of biological changes involved in the restoration of particular functions. A concept often associated with these theories is cerebral plasticity. This refers to the reorganization of neural tissue occurring during normal CNS development and possibly during the post-trauma adaptation period. Evidence of morphological plasticity in the CNS exists (see Cotman, 1978; Finger & Stein, 1982 for reviews), but the functional meaning of these neural developments is controversial. LeVere

(1975) argues strongly against notions of functional reorganization and 'design plasticity'. He admits that the damaged neuron is capable of new growth and even functional restitution, but he maintains that the pre-and post-lesion functions of a particular region are consistent. In other words he believes that mature biological systems do not possess the ability of immature systems to alter their fundamental modes of operation.

The notion of 'functional substitution' has also been introduced as an explanation of recovery. This refers to the ability of an intact system serving an unrelated function to take on the function of a damaged system. A particular subsystem may undergo transformations allowing it to perform the function of another (Kennard, 1938) or an entirely new subsystem may emerge to take on the functions of a damaged one (Horel et al, 1966; Meyer, 1973). The major tenet of these proposals is that the nervous system is composed of flexible subsystems which may either adopt novel programs or modify old routines.

## Physiological responses to brain injury

Most of the above theoretical models do not offer explicit descriptions of the physiological processes involved in recovery. Nevertheless, a physiological level of analysis is essential to a comprehensive understanding of cerebral recovery. The following is a brief outline of some popular physiological explanations of recovery. These include: regenerative and collateral sprouting; denervation supersensitivity; the activation of inefficient synapses; and diaschisis.

Some physiological explanations link recovery to new growth in the nervous system. Regenerative sprouting refers to the emergence of new axons from the distal end of the injured neuron. Collateral sprouting focuses on auxiliary growth from the intact portion of an axon. Denervation supersensitivity attributes the restoration of function to increased synaptic activity – a possible consequence of an increased number of receptor sites.

Other physiological approaches to recovery do not assume that new growth has occurred in the CNS. For instance, some theorists believe that the post-lesion activation of otherwise 'inefficient' synapses (Wall, 1976) facilitates recovery. In this instance 'back-up' pathways are used while the normal circuits remain obstructed. Last of all is the diaschisis model (von Monakow, 1914) which explains recovery as the spontaneous reduction of metabolic depression in cerebral areas remote to the lesion.

## Biological discoveries relevant to memory recovery

As noted initially, there have been few biological investigations directly related to memory recovery. Those reported have generally addressed the role of memory in the restoration of preoperatively learned behavior. For instance, LeVere & Davis (1977) replicated Lashley's original demonstration that the removal of a rat's visual cortex would not permanently affect its ability to perform a brightness discrimination task. Like Lashley, they found that rats were initially unable to perform the task but that they eventually recovered this behavior even though the neural tissue thought to be associated with brightness discrimination had been destroyed. Curious as to whether this regained capacity represented old memory or new learning, Davis & LeVere (1979) administered a drug, specifically known to prevent new learning from taking place, to those rats with visual cortex ablations. They found that the animals receiving this anti-learning drug were even better than their counterparts (a normal saline group) in their performance of the preoperatively learned brightness discrimination task. This supported LeVere's belief that recovery from brain injury is related to spared memory rather than to new learning.

Davis and LeVere's emphasis on the importance of spared memory in the recovery of pre-lesion behaviour is reminiscent of Meyer's (1972) earlier thoughts on this subject. Meyer specifically focused on disturbances in 'accessing engrams' (memory traces) as the primary source of behavioral deficits following brain damage. His animal studies pointed to the possible benefits of promoting one's access to previously formed engrams. For example, the recovery of learned tasks such as a cat's placing behavior or a rat's visual discrimination ability was enhanced by facilitating access to spared neural traces through amphetamine administration and septal lesions.

Exploring the recovery of memory functions through the restoration of learned behaviors is a meritable enterprise when a dissociation between memory and new learning can be revealed, as in the studies noted above. Another way of investigating memory recovery involves the more direct approach of examining the neuroanatomical areas associated with memory functions. Although the localization of memory is nearly an impossible undertaking, a few of the locations typically associated with memory functions (the temporal lobes and the hippocampus) have been in the limelight of physiological research on recovery. Several studies (e.g. Lynch, 1974; Cotman et al, 1973) have demonstrated regenerative sprouting in the entorhinal cortex of the temporal lobe (an area with connections to the ipsilateral hippocampal dentate gyrus). These data revealed that the unilateral destruction of this region of the temporal lobe was followed by regenerative sprouting from the opposite entorhinal cortex to the hippocampal dentate gyrus on the side of the lesion.

Of paramount concern to our interests is the fact that the contralateral sprouting between these areas has been shown to take place 8–12 days post-lesion (Loesche & Steward, 1977), correlating temporally with the reappearance of evoked potentials and, more important, with the recovery of a function (alternation performance) thought to be subserved by these structures. The association of behavioral recovery with the reinnervation of the hippocampus by the entorhinal cortex provides some evidence for functional sprouting in the mature CNS. Furthermore, this research points to a possible connection between physiological recovery and restored memory functions.

Among the latest developments in the area of recovery have been studies involving the transplantation of fetal tissue and its effect on behavioral recuperation. Using fetal tissue, which is known for its rich supply of nerve growth factors, Labbe et al (1983) transplanted the frontal and cerebellar cortex from rat embryos directly into ablated areas in the medial frontal cortex of mature rats. They found that transplanted frontal, but not cerebellar, tissue was able to establish afferent neural connections with host cells. More significantly, these researchers reported functional recovery as indexed by improved performance on an alternation behavioral task in the animals receiving the frontal cortex transplants. This research, and that of others (Dunnett et al, 1982), points to a promising future for biological approaches to the recovery of function.

As mentioned earlier, a biological perspective on the recovery of cerebral functions complements the psychological point of view. Unfortunately, research in these separate domains is difficult to integrate. To date, predicting the psychological outcome of a biological event and inducing biological change using psychological tactics has not been possible. Hopefully, the gulf between the biological and psychological approaches to recovery will narrow in the near future. Certainly the studies cited above offer a promising entrée. Unfortunately, most studies of recovery adhere to the traditional dichotomy between biology and psychology. Consequently, this literature review now turns to an entirely different perspective – the psychological variables associated with recovery of memory function.

## PSYCHOLOGICAL VARIABLES OF RECOVERY FROM AMNESIA

Two models of normal memory have greatly influenced amnesia research during the past decade. These are the duplex theory proposed by Atkinson & Shiffrin (1967) and the levels of processing hypothesis proposed by Craik & Lockhart (1972). The former proclaims that memory consists of short- and long-term storehouses which differ along several dimensions, including storage capacities, life spans and codes. Adherents of this theory tend to view memory problems as a failure in the transfer of information from the short- to the long-term store. The levels of processing model, a more dynamic explanation, holds that memory is a consequence of the way to-be-remembered information is analyzed. Deep or semantic analysis is said to result in better retention than shallow (acoustic or orthographic) encoding. Memory deficits are in turn attributed to shallow processing of information. A third theory, the retrieval deficit hypothesis, has been developed by researchers in the field of amnesia (Warrington & Weiskrantz, 1970). They believe that memory deficits are due to an inability to retrieve that which is stored in memory.

These models have also been used to describe mechanisms of memory recovery. The duplex theory defines clinical recovery as improvements in transfer from short- to long-term memory; the levels hypothesis characterizes recovery as the regained capacity to engage in elaborative or deep analysis of information; and the retrieval deficits theory proposes that recovery is premised on a renewed ability to retrieve information. Evidence supporting and negating these models is voluminous and beyond the scope of this chapter (but see Cermak, 1982 for a review). They are mentioned here simply to note that different cognitive hypotheses regarding memory recovery have been entertained.

More germane to our review of recovery are the various forms of psychological intervention that have been employed to remediate memory problems. These will be presented, but first it is important to clarify some of the issues which could obscure their evaluation. The chances for spontaneous recovery should always be evaluated alongside any claims of therapeutically induced change. In other words, all claims of success should be carefully scrutinized to determine whether the appropriate control groups are included. Secondly, it seems that the cause of amnesia should also be considered since therapeutic maneuvers may be useful only with specific types of amnesia. The importance of making etiological distinctions is not clear, however. Some investigators, such as Butters and Cermak, go to great lengths to group patients according to etiology. Others, such as Warrington and Weiskrantz, are less inclined to do so. They prefer to include patients with amnesia of divergent origins within an umbrella group of primary amnesia.

Baddeley (1982), who has tended more towards the primary amnesia approach, has addressed this methodological discrepancy by advocating a symptomatic categorization of amnesia patients. He highlighted the classical features of amnesia within a 'minimal model' whereby amnesia was described as a deficit in episodic (experientially based) long-term memory. The patient with classical amnesia was described as manifesting an inability to learn but was not otherwise cognitively impaired. Baddeley believed that patients with damage to the temporal lobe, the hippocampus, and the mammillary bodies fall within this category of classical amnesia. Hirst (1982) has also promoted the idea of a homogeneous 'core' amnesia noting that across the board, amnesics exhibit rapid forgetting, increased sensitivity to proactive interference, normal short-term storage, normal skill acquisition, and responsiveness to retrieval cues.

The argument for a 'core' amnesia is a strong one, but so is the evidence for neuropsychological diversity between groups of amnesics (see Butters & Miliotis, 1983). For instance, performance on the Brown–Peterson distractor memory paradigm seems to vary with the population of amnesics being examined (Butters & Cermak, 1980; Butters et al, 1979). Likewise, the anterograde/retrograde memory profile varies according to patient population. These investigations and others lend credence to the notion of cognitive heterogeneity in amnesia. Furthermore, they underscore the importance of making etiological distinctions before evaluating the success or failure of any therapeutic endeavors. By considering etiology one would be able to assess a program's true merits and, hopefully, prescribe therapeutic measures which would capitalize upon an individual's intact functions.

Listed below are various psychological techniques which have been used to improve memory. So far, visual imagery represents the most thoroughly researched method of mitigating memory problems. Consequently, the discussion will begin with a review of studies focusing on the use of imagery with memory-impaired individuals. Subsequently, it will turn to cognitive programs, computer techniques, and some other interesting approaches to memory rehabilitation.

## Imagery as a therapeutic mnemonic

The facilitating effect of visual imagery on human recall has been recognized since the Greek poet Simonides was called upon to identify the unrecognizable bodies of banquet guests who had been crushed to death when a building caved in upon them (Yates, 1966). Simonides, who had performed at the banquet earlier that day, relied upon his memory of the banquet's seating arrangement to identify the victims. His ability to employ this strategy as a way of naming the guests lead Simonides to appreciate the significance of organization and imagery in human memory.

Recently, cognitive researchers such as Pavio (1969), Bower (1970), and Atwood (1971) and professional mnemonists such as Furst (1944), Lorayne & Lucas (1974) have stressed the utility of imagery as a way of organizing information for subsequent recall. Their evidence comes from experimental investigations demonstrating that an individual's memory capacity can be increased dramatically when to-be-remembered items are linked with an image. The application of imagery techniques in enhancing the memory of normal individuals has grown in popularity as indicated by the increased number of books, magazine articles, and commercial schools devoted to this topic. Less popular, though no less important, is the application of imaging techniques in the facilitation of the memory of cognitively impaired people. In this area the number of investigations is far fewer and the nature of the results more controversial.

Pioneers in the use of imagery with brain-injured patients were primarily interested in the remediation of focal deficits. For instance, Patten (1972) employed the 'peg system' of memorization with patients who had verbal learning deficits associated with dominant (usually left) hemisphere lesions. Patten's technique required that the subject visually couple a list of objects (e.g., a teacup or a radio) with the numbers one through ten. Then each subject was presented with the to-be-remembered items which were to be connected with the peg list by imagining them in an interactive relationship. Patten reported remarkable success with four clients who were able to use their preserved visual memory skills in order to boost their poor verbal memories. One of the patients, however, showed a concurrent clearing of his expressive aphasia, suggesting a spontaneous recovery of memory functions. Three patients tested by Patten who did not benefit from the peg system were unable to form vivid visual images. In addition, these patients were not aware of their memory problems and consequently were unmotivated to change. These patients all had lesions in the midline structures of the brain, and therefore, their amnesia was probably more severe than the patients with left hemisphere lesions.

Jones (1974) attempted to use imagery to ameliorate the memory deficits of patients who had undergone right and left unilateral temporal lobe excisions. She taught these patients to visualize a list of paired associates in order to facilitate their verbal recall. Jones' hypothesis was that left temporal lobectomy patients would benefit from imagery since they would be able to enlist the visual skills of their preserved right hemisphere. She expected that patients with right temporal lobectomies would not be able to do the same. Consonant with these predictions, and Patten's previously reported results, patients with left temporal lobectomies did benefit from the use of imagery. Contrary to Jones' expectations, however, patients with right temporal lobectomies also improved their verbal recall when using imagery. They were, in fact, able to employ imagery as efficiently as normal control subjects. Jones explained this unexpected result by saying that the memory task she had chosen might have been too easy for the right lobectomy group and that a more difficult list would allow group differences to emerge with more clarity.

Jones also examined the effects of imagery on the memory of two patients (H.M. and H.B.) with bilateral mesial temporal lobectomies. She found that they performed similarly to Patten's amnesics with midline lesions in that they were unable to recall the to-be-remembered items under any condition. Unlike Patten's patients, however, Jones reported that H.M. and H.B. were both able to form vivid visual images as per instructions. Their difficulty lay in their inability to utilize the newly formed images. They uniformly forgot that they had previously formed a visual association linking the to-be-remembered items. Furthermore, even when reminded that he had done so, H.M. was unable to retrieve his prior image and would instead conjure up an entirely new one.

The puzzling ability of patients with right temporal lobe excisions to profit from the use of imagery even though they lack the supposed anatomical 'site' involved in visual memory led Jones to explore this phenomenon further several years later (Jones-Gotman & Milner, 1978). This time she increased task difficulty by using a list of 60 paired associates which were presented only one time. As expected, the left temporal lobectomy group did derive some benefits from the use of imagery but performed well below the normals. In contrast to her previous results, the right lobectomy patients were found to be impaired on both immediate and delayed recall of high imagery information. This finding supported the supposition that this group would manifest visual memory deficits with these increased experimental demands. Quite significantly, this group's abysmal performance was correlated with the amount of hippocampus removed during surgery, thereby implicating the right hippocampus in imagery-mediated verbal learning. These findings take on added significance when contrasted with the groups' performance on a subsequent task requiring *verbal* mediation between abstract paired associates. In this instance, right lobectomy patients performed normally and no correlation could be found between the size of the hippocampal excision and memory performance.

Baddeley & Warrington (1973) performed one of the first imagery studies using a more heterogeneous group of amnesics. They investigated these patients' ability to utilize taxonomic or imagery clustering in their recall of a list of words. Their findings revealed that taxonomic clustering proved to be beneficial for the facilitation of the amnesics' memory while imagery was not. They suggested that the amnesics' failure to profit from visual imagery was due to an inability to generate a novel interactive relationship between two items. Like Jones-Gotman and Milner, Baddeley and Warrington believed that the amnesics were proficient at forming single visual images, but that they could not form an image in which the two images interacted.

Lewinsohn et al (1977) also explored the application of imagery in the remediation of memory deficits in a heterogeneous group of brain-injured patients. They trained patients in visual imagery techniques for both paired associates and a face–name learning task. The success of his training was most conspicuous in an amnesic group's facilitated acquisition of the paired associates. They reported that 33% of the patients in the non-imagery control condition were unable to learn the list of paired associates within the allotted ten trials while all of those trained in imagery were able to do so. The effects of imagery-facilitated recall only persisted to a 30-minute retention interval, however, and they were barely noticeable after 1 week. Equally disappointing, imagery did not facilitate the brain-injured participants' memories on the face–name task at all. Lewinsohn attributed this result to the ineffective operationalization of Lorayne & Lucas' (1974) and Furst's (1944) mnemonic programs.

Lewinsohn's conclusion that the face–name mnemonic technique advocated by Lorayne and Lucas and by Furst might not be appropriate for use with brain-injured patients was borne out in several other investigations. Glasgow et al (1977) also failed in their attempt to help a brain-injured client (Mr T.) remember to associate names and faces. Although imagery was useful when the face–name list was restricted to a small number of easily imageable names, Mr T.'s performance declined with increased task complexity. Mr T. was unable to utilize the four-step procedure in which he had to translate a person's name into a concrete noun and then associate this image with one of the person's prominent facial features. Perhaps the cognitive manipulations of this task are too complicated for a brain-injured person to use effectively.

The inefficiency of using popular face–name mnemonics with brain-injured clients was underscored by the success of Glasgow et al (1977) with a simple rehearsal program for the improvement of Mr T.'s face–name recognition. Jaffe & Katz (1975) also achieved success in this area using a technique other than imagery. They taught their patients cues for each name (initials) and presented these cues at the time of input as well as recall. Gradually they were able to fade the cues until the patients were able to recall the names spontaneously. One Korsakoff patient was taught the names of people on his hospital ward in just 2 weeks, even though he had lived there for 5 years without learning them.

Crovitz (1979) has stressed the importance of retrieval cues when trying to apply imagery techniques. He read a chain-type of mnemonic, the so-called 'Airplane List' to a Korsakoff and a closed head injury patient, both of whom were experiencing memory difficulties. Crovitz found that neither of these individuals were able to freely recall the list unless provided with retrieval cues. This procedure, like that of Jaffe and Katz, focused on both encoding and retrieval aspects of information processing by encouraging elaborate organization of incoming information and a concentrated search at time of recall.

In a detailed series of case studies, Crovitz (1979) described several variable affecting the efficacy of imagery mnemonics with three brain-injured patients. He emphasized the importance of giving brain-injured individuals sufficient processing time when instructing them in a mnemonic technique. In addition he found that the traditional reverence for the formation of *bizarre* images was counterproductive when used with brain-injured individuals since these people tend to be concrete thinkers and might need more plausible forms of mnemonics. Crovitz also cited the differential impact of experimenter-provided vs. subject-generated images, stressing the superiority of the latter for brain-injured patients. Finally, based on the significant improvement of one of his patients who had read parts of a memory improvement book during the time he was tested, Crovitz recommended that selected readings might increase the patient's chances of being able to utilize imagery.

The bulk of the studies concerning the use of imagery with brain-injured individuals have focused on patients with heterogeneous sorts of memory problems. In many ways this diversity limits interpretations of their predominantly negative findings since some positive results may be population-dependent. The consistency of Jones-Gotman and Milner and of Patten's patients with dominant hemisphere lesions would seem to suggest a certain heuristic value in concentrating on a homogeneous population of amnesics. Unfortunately, studies limited to select populations of amnesics, such as Korsakoff patients, have attained results which are as puzzling as the aforementioned ones.

Cutting (1978) explored certain aspects of meaningfulness in relation to the verbal memory of Korsakoff patients. He concluded that imagery was a meaningful variable to which Korsakoff patients were not sensitive. Cutting compared subject-generated and experimenter-provided imagery conditions with a non-imagery condition and found that the Korsakoff patients were deficient in both conditions. He attributed their failure to use imagery to a deficit in enacting active operations and stated that Korsakoff patients were adept only at tasks which measured passive forms of meaningfulness.

Cermak (1976) used a shorter list of items and found that Korsakoff patients could benefit from imagery in both recognition and free recall tasks. This was indicated by the fact that their imagery-aided retrival was superior to both rote and cued learning. He qualified this success by noting that the advantages of imagery were much greater for normal subjects. In addition he pointed out that the Korsakoff patients had to be provided with imagery instructions at both the time of encoding and retrieval, a point noted as well by Crovitz (1979) and by Jaffe & Katz (1975).

Undoubtedly the most optimistic report on the use of imagery with brain injured individuals is by Kovner et al (1983) who taught patients with severe anterograde amnesias of mixed etiology to utilize ridiculously imaged stories as a way of enhancing their free recall of a list of words. By the eighth week of training all five amnesics (two of whom were Korsakoff patients) demonstrated superior free recall (although still below normal). This contrasted with their ability to improve when using a selective reminding procedure (Buschke, 1973). Kovner and his associates ascribed this positive effect of the visually imaged stories to the possibility that they provided 'artificial chunks' of information. The authors maintained that this explanation was consistent with the idea that the cortical processes necessary for clustering items were preserved in amnesia, and that the failure of amnesic patients to encode information properly might be due to impairment in their subcortical arousal mechanism. Along these lines, imagery might be viewed as a sort of metaphorical prosthesis - enabling patients to organize information despite their natural tendency not to do so. Spurred on by this success, Kovner et al attempted to explore the learning potential of other amnesics using the ridiculously imaged stories. Remarkably, they were able to teach two amnesics up to 120 words using their method.

Despite this optimism, it should be reiterated that the practical applications of imagery have been largely overlooked. Morris (1978) believed that imagery was only advantageous in the retention of meaningless information. This would limit the value of any therapeutic application. Another limitation of imagery and related mnemonics (e.g., verbal mediation, rhymes, and first-letter memorization schemes) is their narrow focus on tasks irrelevant to everyday memory needs. Finally, the fact that most memory aids concentrate on encoding operations (while failing to address the retrieval component of memory deficits) diminishes their applicability even more. This flaw is a serious one since elaborate encoding requires vigilance and planning, which are often beyond the capabilities of the brain-injured individual. Research has shown that individuals with normal memories most often elect to use retrieval mnemonics such as the mental retracing of events and alphabetical search (Harris, 1978), which in itself is an argument against the exclusive study of encoding mnemonics.

## Cognitive retraining programs

Other psychological methods for memory improvement emphasize effective ways to minimize cognitive deficits. Some of these have been loosely referred to as 'cognitive retraining programs' since they attempt to provide the brain-injured person with new cognitive strategies to circumvent those no longer available. Luria, a pioneer in retraining theory, recommended that restorative therapy be individually tailored to the neuropsychological assets and liabilities of the brain-injured person. In addition, he suggested that restorative programs adhere to the ontogenesis of the disturbed function. Accordingly, the design of treatment to reinstate a behavior should conform to the mode of its original acquistion.

Of particular significance to retraining strategies are Luria's ideas on the role of speech in cognition. He placed critical importance on the cognitive mediation of behavior and believed that a disruption in covert mediation or private speech is often a consequence of brain injury. Luria (1982) suggested that attentional disturbances were precipitated by disruptions in covert mediation. He reasoned that external mediation in the form of self-instruction could offset the attentional difficulties of his patients. In practice, however, Luria found that this technique was effective only with certain types of patients.

A more recent and successful attempt to use self-instruction with brain-injured patients was that of Webster & Scott (1983), who focused on remediation of the attentional and memory skills of a 24-year-old patient who was 2 years post-closed head injury. These authors borrowed some of the procedures which Meichenbaum formerly used to mitigate the problem-solving difficulties of the elderly (Meichenbaum, 1974), schizophrenic adults (Meichenbaum & Cameron, 1973) and impulsive children (Meichenbaum & Goodman, 1971). In Meichenbaum's technique self-instruction is achieved through a shaping process which originates with the subject observing the experimenter perform a task and ends with the subject self-instructing via covert mediation. Meichenbaum (1974) referred to this method as the 'functional interiorization' of private speech.

Webster and Scott were able to enhance the retention and attention capacities of their brain-injured patients by using a variant of Meichenbaum's program. They speculated that verbally guiding behavior would facilitate the organization of incoming information by providing the patient with moment-by-moment cognitive structure. Structuring cognition in this way was thought to lessen the frequency of thought intrusions, poor inhibition, and perseverative tendencies which often precipitate the memory problems.

Another memory rehabilitation program was devised by Grafman & Matthews (1978) at the University of Wisconsin. Their target population consisted of 75 head-injury patients who had been shown to have memory deficits on the Wisconsin Neuro-Memory Battery. Employing various mnemonic techniques, imagery, and organizational strategies, the researchers trained their patients during three 1-hour training sessions each week over a 3-month period. At the end of the training program, and again 3 months later, the patients were tested on the memory exams. Results indicated that 40% of the patients increased their memory performance by 50%. This notable achievement merits further exploration.

## Behavioral techniques

Behavioral methods have been used occasionally by those attempting to improve the deficient memory skills of the brain-injured. Whereas the analysis of cognitive processes is integral to cognitive programs, the environmental influences on retention are the focus of behavioral programs. Research in this area is in a preliminary stage, and opinion concerning the absolute merits of behaviorally based programs must await further investigations. In the meantime some interesting studies have been conducted.

Reinforcement techniques were shown to be effective when used to enhance the memorial skills of a mixed group of brain-injured adults. Dolan & Norton (1977) successfully employed an operant reinforcement schedule as a way of facilitating the memory abilities of patients. This success underscores the therapeutic possibilities of behavioral intervention, yet the study itself did not clearly indicate whether any other systematic regimen would have been equally beneficial in enhancing the memory capacities of these patients.

Seidel & Hodgkinson (1979) designed a program to help a Korsakoff patient (Mr T.) change his maladaptive smoking habits. Reportedly Mr T. tended to hoard cigarettes and to leave half-lit ones strewn about in ashtrays on the hospital ward. With the cooperation of the nursing staff the investigators instituted a strict smoking regimen whereby cigarettes were allocated on an hourly basis and smoking behavior was closely supervised. Happily, within 45 days Mr T. was able to responsibly manage his own cigarette intake. This success is noteworthy, yet one wonders whether it represents a true cognitive achievement or merely reflects the Korsakoffs' well-documented facility at skill acquisition. In other words, the behavioral enterprise might have only facilitated the articulation of an intact ability (skill acquisition) rather than improving a dysfunctional one (memory).

A behavioral regimen with Korsakoff patients has also been studied by Oscar-Berman and her colleagues (1980), who reveal far less promising outcomes than those mentioned above. These researchers showed that the response rate of the patients did not coincide with the reinforcement schedules in the same way that the normal individuals' did. Oscar-Berman et al (1980) surmised that Korsakoff patients were basically insensitive to differences in reinforcement contingencies. Such a limitation would certainly render them unlikely candidates for extensive behavioral training.

## External memory aids

Other aids for memory improvement are directly linked to the environment. Harris (1978) has given the name 'external memory aids' to this category. Included in this group are shopping lists, diaries, timers, and activities such as writing on one's hand, relying on another person, and leaving something in a special place. Harris highlighted several features he believed were essential for an optimal memory aid. He noted that active cues were preferable to passive ones and that the specificity, temporal contiguity, and accessibility of the cue were important.

One device described recently in the memory rehabilitation literature which meets these criteria is the digital alarm chronograph. Gouvier and his associates (1982) have found this instrument efficient for brain-injured clients when supplemented by a personal appointment calendar. In effect, the chronograph is set to beep hourly reminding the person to consult her/his daily schedule book. This device is both convenient for amnesics to use and allows them to be more independent in their daily routines.

### Computerized rehabilitation of amnesia

Computer technology has recently been used to meet the needs of brain-injury victims. Both the efficacy of this approach and its practical utility make it a promising resource for rehabilitative interventions. Neuropsychologists such as Bracy, a prominent advocate of computer-based rehabilitation, give glowing accounts of its successful clinical applications. Bracy (1983) recently reported two case studies in which remarkable cognitive recovery was demonstrated when computer programs were used with brain-injured people. Both of his clients were evaluated 3 years post-injury, at which time Bracy initiated a regimen of approximately 25 hours per week of home-based computer work in conjunction with weekly meetings with a neuropsychologist. These therapy sessions served as times to review the patients' progress and provide emotional support. Over a period of 2 years Bracy's patients gained 23 and 28 points in their IQ scores.

Computer-based rehabilitation methods mechanically simulate programs which a behavioral analyst would prescribe. More specifically they address the isolated operations involved in cognition including selective attention, vigilance, discrimination, inhibition and generalization of responses. These tasks, referred to as 'foundation skills,' are inherent components of higher cognitive functions. Improvement in each area is thus important in enabling the patient to perform more complex operations.

The orientation towards the hierarchical attainment of adaptational skills is a definite advantage of this type of intervention. Other advantages include its pragmatic value for the patient and therapist. Therapy can be conducted at home with the computer serving as an extension of, or supplement to, the psychologist. In addition, the patient receives prompt and accurate feedback. Finally, it seems that computer intervention might provide patients with a sense of autonomy they might not achieve when learning is constantly supervised by another person.

As with so many other aspects of computer technology, however, the potential applications seem to outstrip the practical applications. Software packages written for the computer have generally been nothing more than simplistic variations of testing procedures already used with brain-injured patients, and thus merely provide a mechanized vehicle for repetitive presentation of material. Another problem is that many of the programs are written solely for a particular microprocessor, thereby mandating the purchase of an expensive device.

Two things are needed before computers can truly play a role in rehabilitation of the brain-injured patient. First, evidence must be provided to show that rehabilitation occurs more rapidly than that obtained in normal memory therapy. Second, a training schedule should be initiated which is more than simple repetition of randomly selected, otherwise available, test instruments. The potential for the use of computers is tremendous, but the history of rehabilitation has shown that no mnemonic has been very effective. To assume that the addition of computerization to our armament of failures will result in success is ludicrous. Application of computers ought to be viewed skeptically so long as the software remains based within the domain of the mnemonic failures we have outlined here.

## INDIVIDUAL THERAPEUTIC ATTEMPTS

Over the years researchers at the Boston VA Medical Center have been involved in the development of several individualized memory retraining programs. Most of these were designed for alcoholic Korsakoff patients and, as might be expected, these attempts were not very successful. Their failure has been attributed to a variety of sources. One problem was that the majority of patients were not aware of their own memory deficits. This resulted in their lack of motivation to participate in the remedial programs. Another problem was that the severity of the patients' information processing deficits often made the use of mnemonics seem futile. The greatest disappointment, however, was that even those patients who were able to learn the memory aids did not employ them spontaneously.

Other patients with amnesia of differing etiologies have also entered extensive individualized programs of memory retraining. Most notable was a post-encephalitic patient with a dense anterograde and retrograde amnesia. Our attempts to retrain this patient have been documented elsewhere (Cermak, 1976; Cermak & O'Connor, 1983) so they will simply be synthesized here. After many months of participating in a program focused on the use of imagery, verbal mediation, and rote memorization, it was found that the patient could be trained to memorize information but that he could not incorporate it into his knowledge base in any comprehensible fashion. For instance, he was taught to answer the question 'Who broke Babe Ruth's record for lifetime runs?' by replying 'Henry Aaron.' But he could not apply this knowledge in a practical way. When asked who held the record for the most home runs hit in a career he would reply, 'Babe Ruth.'

Because of the parrot-like nature of his responses we believed that this patient could not profit from memory aids since any learning would remain insulated from his comprehension of the information. In short, his memory seemed beyond hope of recovery. This patient clearly exemplified a problem which recurrently undermines memory retraining endeavors. Specific information can be readily taught via mnemonic devices, but this information rarely is integrated into a patient's true comprehension of material.

One patient who was somewhat adept at employing mnemonic strategies came to our facility after suffering an aneurysm of the anterior communicating artery. Following surgical intervention he displayed a dense anterograde amnesia with a retrograde amnesia extending back several years. The patient's memory (MQ = 97) seemed quite impaired, especially in light of his preserved intellectual functions (IQ = 141). Clinically, his memory deficits were manifested in his confusion concerning his whereabouts and his difficulty learning people's names.

The major difference between this patient and the one described previously was his ability to use mnemonics. He had, in fact, learned a series of memory aids prior to his disability – an advantage which allowed him to rely on old knowledge in order to gain access to new information. Unfortunately, the mnemonics did not affect the patient's memory in any dramatic way since he was never able to incorporate new learning into his semantic memory.

The last patient we shall describe was a head-injury victim who was afflicted with chronic intermittent seizures. Her memory problems were secondary to other neuropsychological disorders. These 'secondary memory problems' afford the greatest potential for therapy because certain cognitive functions (e.g., attention and sequencing) lend themselves to therapy more than others (i.e., memory). This patient's memory deficit (MQ = 64) was superimposed upon perceptual difficulties such as an inability to sequence properly, and difficulties distinguishing a portion of a stimulus from the whole. As a result, she was impaired in many daily operations (spelling, reading, arithmetic, etc.), especially those premised upon intact perceptual organization.

Obviously these impairments confounded any attempts to measure her intelligence. We suspected that she was a very bright person due to her former profession and various indices of her premorbid intellect. In her more lucid moments (most of the time) she came across as a literary and knowledgeable woman as well as an entertaining and interesting conversant. At less propitious times she would become overwhelmed and confused by environmental stimuli which seemed to bombard her sensorium. This patient was aware of her disorder, however, and was quite determined to learn compensatory techniques as a way of mitigating her handicaps.

Most of these compensatory techniques provided the patient with ways of overcoming her perceptual and sequencing problems. For instance, instructions which seemed too complicated for the patient to spontaneously carry out (such as which medication to take, when to take it, and the appropriate quantity) were simplified by placing the appropriate amounts in individual containers on a large spice rack labeled by days of the week and hours. The patient's house keys were color-coded with the locks and arrows placed above the lock to provide direction for locking/unlocking. Another daily routine, the operation of the stove, was broken down into a series of steps which were written in bold print and tacked above the stove with directional arrows all around. Memory for information that did not have to be sequenced, or that was not perceptually confusable (such as people's names) proved to be amenable to mediating. The patient enjoyed these games and, in fact, proved to be remarkably good at them. Nevertheless, her ability to put these pieces together in a comprehensive way remained poor.

This patient's success in memory retraining might be due to the fact that her memory difficulties were secondary to other neuropsychological deficits (sequencing and perception). Her ability to grasp the nature of her difficulties was also essential to her successful outcome. Most important, the patient's deficit was not ultimately overcome, but merely bypassed via environmental restructuring.

## CONCLUSIONS

In our discussion the biological and psychological approaches to recovery were examined separately. This clearly reflects the dualistic nature of the recovery literature which historically has distinguished between these perspectives. Hopefully, future work in memory rehabilitation will embody a more integrative point of view so that areas of overlap between psychological and biological domains will become part of an eclectic approach to memory recovery. This eclectic approach must also incorporate well-known clinical observations with research findings. This combination would allow investigators to scrutinize individual patients' functional abilities, to document any changes that take place, and to formulate hypotheses accordingly.

At present, rehabilitative techniques have not successfully met the needs of the memory-impaired individual. Memory improvement strategies such as the use of imagery, mnemonic devices, and external memory aids provide limited relief for memory problems. They do not, however, effect dramatic or generalized changes in memory. Furthermore, they are myopic in their goals in that they only grant the amnesic patient temporary access to a limited set of to-be-remembered items. These limited gains may reflect the irrecoverable aspects of brain injury but such pessimism should not be entertained until integrated research and clinical findings advance our knowledge of recovery further.

One way of achieving a broader and more integrated perspective on memory recovery lies in facilitating communication between various health care professionals. The occupational therapist, nurse, neuropsychologist, neurologist, and social worker all play different roles in promoting the patients' post-injury adaptation. A team effort by these individuals would enhance their ability to view the patient in a holistic fashion. The family of the brain-injured person should also be included in this enterprise since these people are often most sensitive to the patient's needs and abilities and are the most knowledgeable about her/his pre-injury personality and mental status.

Over and above all other considerations it should be emphasized that when assessing a patient's recovery the most useful perspective to take is the patient's own perspective. The cases reviewed in the last section of this chapter provided substantial evidence for the utility of focusing on individual differences. Each person, whether brain-injured or not, has skills, deficits, feelings and needs peculiar to her/his own range of experiences. Individual differences should thus weigh heavily on the evaluation of the memory capacities of the brain-injured.

## REFERENCES

Atkinson R C, Shiffrin R M 1967 Human memory: a proposed system and its control processes. Technical Report No. 110, Stanford University

Atwood G 1971 An experimental study of visual imagination and memory. Cognitive Psychology 2: 290–299

Baddeley A 1982 Amnesia: a minimal model. In: Cermak L (ed) Human memory and amnesia. Lawrence Erlbaum, Hillsdale, NJ

Baddeley A D, Warrington E K 1973 Memory coding and amnesia. Neuropsychologia 11: 159–165

Bower G H 1970 Analysis of a mnemonic device. American Scientist 58: 496–510

Bracy O 1983 Computer based cognitive rehabilitation. Cognitive Rehabilitation, 1(1): 7

Buschke H 1973 Selective reminding for analysis of memory and learning. Journal of Verbal Learning and Verbal Behavior 12: 543–550

Butters N, Cermak L S 1980 Alcoholic Korsakoff's syndrome: an information-processing approach to amnesia. Academic Press, New York

Butters N, Miliotis P 1983 Memory assessment: evidence of the heterogeneity of amnesic symptoms. In: Goldstein G (ed) Advances in clinical neuropsychology. Plenum, New York

Butters N, Albert M, Sax D 1979 Investigations of the memory disorders of patients with Huntington's disease. In: Chax T, Wexler N, Barbeau A (eds) Advances in neurology, vol. 23: Huntington's disease. Raven, New York

Cajal S R 1928 Degeneration and regeneration of the nervous system. Oxford University Press, London

Cermak L S 1976 The encoding capacity of a patient with amnesia due to encephalitis. Neuropsychologia 19: 311–326

Cermak L S 1982 The long and the short of it in amnesia. In: Cermak L (ed) Human memory and amnesia. Lawrence Erlbaum, Hillsdale, NJ

Cermak L S, O'Connor M 1983 The anterograde and retrograde retrieval ability of a patient with amnesia due to encephalitis. Neuropsychologia 21(3): 213–234

Clemente C D 1964 Regeneration in the vertebrate central nervous system. International Review of Neurobiology 6: 257–301

Cotman C W 1978 Neuronal plasticity. Raven, New York

Cotman C, Matthews D, Taylor D, Lynch G 1973 Synaptic rearrangement in the dentate gyrus: Histochemical evidence of adjustments after lesions in immature and adult rats. Proceedings of the National Academy of Sciences 70: 3473–3477

Craik F I M, Lockhart R 1972 Levels of processing: a framework for memory research. Journal of Verbal Learning and Verbal Behavior 11: 671–684

Crovitz H F 1979 Memory retraining in brain-damaged patients: the airplane list. Cortex 15: 131–134

Crovitz H F, Harvey M T, Horn R W 1929 Problems in the acquisition of imagery mnemonics: three brain-damaged cases. Cortex 15: 225–234

Cutting J 1978 A cognitive approach to Korsakoff's syndrome. Cortex 14: 485–495

Davis N, LeVere T E 1979 Recovery of function after brain damage: different processes and the facilitation of one. Physiological Psychology 7: 233–240

Dolan M, Norton J 1977 A programmed training technique that uses reinforcement to facilitate acquisition and retention in brain-damaged patients. Journal of Clinical Psychology 33: 496–501

Dunnett S B, Law W C, Iversen S D, Steiner U, Bjorklund A 1982 Septal transplants restore maze learning in rats with fornix-fimbria lesions. Brain Research 251: 335

Finger S 1978 Recovery from brain damage. Plenum, New York

Finger S, Stein D 1982 Brain damage and recovery. Academic Press, New York

Furst B 1944 The practical way to a better memory. Goose & Dunlap, New York

Glasgow R E, Zeiss R A, Barrera M, Lewinsohn P M 1977 Case studies on remediating memory deficits in brain damaged individuals. Journal of Clinical Psychology 33(4): 1049–1054

Goldman P, Lewis M 1978 Development biology of brain damage and experience. In: Cotman C W (ed) Neuronal plasticity. Cavin, New York

Gouvier W 1982 Using the digital alarm chronograph in memory retraining. Behavioral Engineering 7(4): 134

Grafman J, Matthews C (1978) Assessment and remediation of memory deficits in brain-injured patients. In: Gruneberg M, Morris P, Sykes R (eds) Practical aspects of memory. Academic Press, London, pp. 720–728

Harris J 1978 External memory aids. In: Gruneberg M, Morris P, Sykes R (eds) Practical aspects of memory. Academic Press, London, pp. 172–179

Hirst W 1982 The amnesic syndrome: descriptions and explanations. Psychological Bulletin 91: 435–460

Horel J A, Bettinger L A, Royce G J, Meyer D R 1966 Role of neocortex in the learning and relearning of two visual habits by the rat. Journal of Comparative and Physiological Psychology 61: 66–78

Jaffe P G, Katz A N 1975 Attenuating anterograde amnesia in Korsakoff's psychosis. Journal of Abnormal Psychology 84: 559–562

Jones M K 1974 Imagery as a mnemonic aid after left temporal lobectomy: contrast between material specific and generalized memory disorders. Neuropsychologia 12: 21–30

Jones-Gotman M K, Milner B 1978 Right temporal lobe contribution to image mediated verbal learning. Neuropsychologia 16: 61–71

Kennard M A 1938 Reorganization of motor function in the cerebral cortex of monkeys deprived of motor and premotor areas in infancy. Journal of Neurophysiology 1: 477–496

Kovner R, Mattis S, Goldmeier E 1983 Journal of Clinical Neuropsychology, 5(1): 65–71

Kovner R, Mattis S, Pass K 1983 Some amnesic patients can freely recall large amounts of information in new contexts. Meeting of the International Neuropsychological Society, Mexico City

Labbe R, Firl A, Mufson E, Stein D 1983 Fetal transplants: reduction of cognitive deficits in rats with frontal cortex lesions. Science 221: 470–472

Lahey B, Drabman R 1974 Facilitation of the acquisition and retention of sight-word vocabulary through token reinforcement. Journal of Applied Behavior Analysis 7: 307–312

Laurence S, Stein D 1978 Recovery after brain damage and the concept of localization of function. In Finger S (ed) Recovery from brain damage. Plenum, New York

LeVere T E 1975 Neural stability, sparing and behavioral recovery following brain damage. Psychological Review 82(5): 344–358

LeVere T E, Davis N 1977 Recovery of functions after brain damage: the motivational specificity of spared neural traces. Experimental Neurology 57: 883–899

Lewinsohn P M, Danaher B G, Kikel S 1977 Visual imagery as a mnemonic aid for brain-injured persons. Journal of Consulting and Clinical Psychology 45: 717–723

Loesche J, Steward O 1977 Behavioral correlates of denervation and reinnervation of the hippocampal formation of the rat: recovery of alternation performance following unilateral entorhinal cortex lesions. Brain Research Bulletin 2: 31–39

Lorayne H, Lucas J 1974 The memory book. Stein & Day, New York

Luria A R 1961 The role of speech in the regulation of normal and abnormal behavior. Livingston, New York

Luria A R 1982 Language and cognition. Wiley, New York

Lynch G 1974 The formation of new synaptic connections after brain damage and their possible role in recovery of function. Neuroscience Research Progress Bulletin 12: 226

Meichenbaum D 1974 Self-instructional strategy training: a cognitive prosthesis for the aged. Human Development 17: 273–280

Meichenbaum D, Cameron R 1973 Training schizophrenics to talk to themselves: a means of developing attentional controls. Behavior Therapy 4: 515–534

Meichenbaum D, Goodman J 1971 Training impulsive children to talk to themselves: a means of developing self control. Journal of Abnormal Psychology 77: 115–126

Meyer D R 1972 Access to engrams. American Psychologist 27: 124–133
Meyer P M 1973 Recovery from neocortical damage. In: French G (ed) Cortical functioning in behavior. Scott, Foresman, Illinois
Monakow C von 1914 Die lokalisation in grosshirnride und der abbau der funktion durch korticale herde. Bergmann, Weisbaden
Moore R Y, Central regeneration and recovery of function: the problem of collateral reinnervation. In: Stein D G, Rosen J J, Butters N (eds) Plasticity and recovery of function in the central nervous system. Academic Press, New York
Morris P E 1978 Sense and nonsense in classical memories. In: Gruneberg M, Morris P, Sykes R (eds) Practical aspects of memory. Academic Press, London, pp. 155–163
Oscar-Berman M, Heyman G, Bonner R, Ryder J 1980 Human neuropsychology: some differences between Korsakoff and normal operant performance. Psychological Research 41: 235–247
Patten B M 1972 The ancient art of memory – usefulness in treatment. Archives of Neurology 26: 28–31
Pavio A 1969 Mental imagery in associative learning and memory. Psychological Review 76(3): 241–263
Ramon y Cajal S 1928 Degeneration and regeneration of the nervous system (R M May, trans.). Hafner, New York
Seidel H A, Hodgkinson P E 1979 Behavior modification and long-term learning in Korsakoff's psychosis. Nursing Times 75: 1855–1857
Stein D G, Rosen J J, Butters N (eds) 1974 Plasticity and recovery of function in the central nervous system. Academic Press, New York
Tulving E, Thomson D M 1973 Encoding specificity and retrieval processes in episodic memory. Psychological Review 80: 352–373
Wall P D 1976 Plasticity in the adult mammalian central nervous system. Unpublished manuscript.
Warrington E K, Weiskrantz L 1970 Amnesic syndrome: consolidation or retrieval? Nature 228: 628–630
Webster J, Scott R 1983 The effects of self-instructional training on attentional deficits following head injury. Clinical Neuropsychology 4: 69–74
Yates F A 1966 The art of memory. Routledge & Kegan Paul, London

13 *David P. Salmon and Nelson Butters*

# Recent developments in learning and memory: implications for the rehabilitation of the amnesic patient

Theoretical developments in the study of human learning and memory have occurred for the most part in relative isolation from the study of amnesia (see Schacter & Tulving, 1982). Fortunately, this trend has changed recently (e.g., Cermak, 1982) and our understanding of both normal and abnormal memory processes has profited from the new synthesis. For example, careful examination of the memory deficits of amnesic patients has led to the discovery of potential structural bases for several of the theoretical constructs often applied in memory research, such as the short-term, long-term memory dichotomy (Atkinson & Shiffrin, 1968; Warrington, 1982) and the distinction between procedural and declarative knowledge (Winograd, 1975; Cohen & Squire, 1980). In turn, students of amnesia have been provided with an impressive array of experimental techniques for characterizing memory deficits, as well as theoretical frameworks within which these deficits can be conceptualized. By characterizing normal memory processes and developing methods to enhance memory through their conscious control, researchers have set the stage for rehabilitative efforts with the amnesic patient.

The ensuing chapter will briefly review some of the recent theoretical developments in the study of human learning and memory, discuss their contribution to the study of amnesia, and, where possible, describe some of the implications they may have for memory rehabilitation. In order to facilitate the discussion we will address different aspects of memory, beginning with encoding processes, followed by organization and storage, and ending with retrieval processes. It should be emphasized here, and will be noted throughout the chapter, that these stages of memory are not isolated processes, but are closely related and interdependent.

## ENCODING PROCESSES IN MEMORY

Encoding refers to the process by which an organism converts a perceived experience into an engram, a physical memory representation. As will be discussed, the manner in which information is encoded can greatly influence its subsequent retrieval. Several theories of memory focus centrally upon encoding processes and how they influence overall memory performance. The most extensively investigated of these is the levels-of-processing framework originally proposed by Craik & Lockhart (1972). A second approach that will be discussed is the encoding–specificity hypothesis of Tulving & Thomson (1973).

Within Craik & Lockhart's (1972) levels-of-processing framework the durability of a memory trace is held to be a function of the degree of processing that the to-be-remembered information undergoes. A hierarchical relationship is presumed to operate such that orthographic or acoustic (shallow) processing of information leads to a less durable trace than phonemic processing which, in turn, leads to a weaker trace than a more meaningful semantic (deep) analysis. Though not without its critics (e.g., Baddeley, 1978), the levels-of-processing proposal has generated a considerable body of research since its inception, most of which compares semantic and non-semantic orienting tasks in incidental learning paradigms. Although empirical results are generally consistent with the levels view (i.e., better memory following semantic than non-semantic processing), experimental procedures have been devised to demonstrate that semantic is not always superior to non-semantic encoding. Non-semantic processing has also been shown to sometimes lead to a more durable memory trace than predicted by the levels-of-processing view (see Horton & Mills, 1984).

As more data have become available the levels-of-processing framework has been modified by the concepts of elaboration and distinctiveness of encoding. Several recent studies have shown that memory for sentences can be substantially improved by meaningful elaboration of the target material at the time of encoding (Stevenson, 1981; Bradshaw & Anderson, 1982). For example, the sentence 'The fat man read the sign' can be better remembered if the subject elaborates on the sentence creating 'The fat man read the sign warning of thin ice.' Similarly, the distinctiveness of a given memory trace, which can be developed by requiring more difficult semantic decisions regarding the target material, can influence subsequent retrieval (Jacoby et al, 1979). The concept of elaboration, of course, is not new to memory research. Many of the mnemonic strategies proposed over the years involve the elaboration of target material at the time of encoding in terms of visual images or integration of new information with old (Bower, 1970; Miller et al, 1960).

The memory disorder exhibited by certain amnesics has been interpreted within the levels-of-processing framework. Butters & Cermak (1975, 1980) have suggested that the memory deficits of alcoholic Korsakoff patients arise from their failure to fully encode all of the attributes of the to-be-remembered stimulus. According to these investigators the Korsakoff patient fully analyzes verbal material at the phonemic level but does not carry out a semantic analysis sufficient to produce a durable memory trace. Since the information is thus stored in a somewhat degraded manner, it may be more susceptible to interference. Considerable evidence for the encoding deficit hypothesis of Korsakoff amnesia has been gathered over the past decade. For example, phonemic, but not semantic, cues aid the retrieval of verbal information in Korsakoff amnesics (Cermak & Butters, 1972). Korsakoff patients fail to show an improvement in memory performance when categorically organized word lists are to be learned, presumably because of their failure to employ a rehearsal strategy that uses the semantic associations among words (Cermak et al, 1976). Also, these patients fail to demonstrate a release from proactive interference (PI) when a taxonomic (semantic) shift occurs in a list of to-be-remembered word triads, but release normally after an alphanumeric (non-semantic) shift (Cermak et al, 1974).

The model applies to non-verbal as well as to verbal material. That is, Korsakoff patients may not sufficiently analyze all of the attributes of complex visual stimuli, such as geometric forms or faces. Evidence supporting this view was recently provided by Biber and her associates (Biber et al, 1981) who demonstrated that the ability of Korsakoff patients to recognize faces can be improved by administering a 'high-level' orientation task (i.e., a likeability judgment) at the time of encoding. Presumably, the orienting task leads to a thorough analysis of facial features, which, in turn, results in improved recognition.

An important prediction from the encoding deficit hypothesis is that the memory impairment of the Korsakoff amnesic could be greatly ameliorated if the patient were somehow able to produce a deep, semantic analysis of the stimulus material. Several investigators have attempted to verify this prediction, with limited success. In general these experiments employed orientation tasks that required either an orthographic, phonemic, or semantic analysis of the target material followed by an unexpected retention test. Though the degree of retention demonstrated by the Korsakoff patients improves when a semantic rather than a lower-level analysis occurs, their performance does not reach a normal level, and the benefit they derive from the deeper analysis is not different from that derived by non-Korsakoff control subjects (Cermak & Reale, 1978; McDowall, 1979; Mayes et al, 1980). In any event, the memory deficit of Korsakoff amnesics can apparently be somewhat attenuated if they engage in semantic processing of stimulus material. While theoretically interesting, this conclusion may be of little practical value to the professional in the field of memory rehabilitation because of the relatively small gain in memory performance realized, and because of the difficulty encountered in Korsakoff patients consistently performing a semantic analysis of all material potentially important to be remembered. In regard to this latter point, however, the performance of a semantic analysis may be a cognitive 'skill' (see below) that can be made easier with practice and thus more likely to be applied by the patient. Furthermore, the likelihood of the Korsakoff patient applying the deeper analysis could possibly be increased through behavioral training techniques (cf. O'Connor & Cermak, Chapter 12 in this volume).

As mentioned previously, certain empirical results have proven troublesome for the levels-of-processing framework; namely, that deep processing does not always produce optimal memory performance, nor does it invariably lead to better retention than shallow processing. Tulving and his colleagues (Tulving, 1979; Tulving & Thomson, 1973) have developed the encoding–specificity hypothesis of memory which takes these anomalous findings into account. The encoding–specificity view holds that there is an interaction between the encoding processes employed at input and the particular circumstances present at retrieval, such that better retention is evident when input and retrieval conditions are the same. Thus, the semantic encoding of information is only beneficial, according to this view, when semantic cues are present at the time of retrieval, and may even be debilitating if phonemic or orthographic retrieval cues are employed. In support of this position, Fisher & Craik (1977) demonstrated that retention levels are highest in normal subjects when the type of information provided by a retrieval cue is the same as the type of processing elicited by an input question during an incidental learning task. For example, when subjects were presented with the input question 'Is this word a form of transport?' a semantic retrieval cue produced better recall than a phonemic cue. On the other hand, if the input question generated phonemic processing as in 'Does the word rhyme with brain?' a phonemic rhyming cue was superior to a semantic cue in a subsequent recall test.

The performance of Korsakoff amnesics on cued recall tests does not neatly conform to the predictions of the encoding–specificity hypothesis. Although these patients do benefit when a strongly associated cue word is presented at the time of encoding and as a retrieval cue at recall, they benefit little when a weakly associated cue word is provided at input and retrieval (Cermak et al, 1980). Cermak et al (1980) suggest that this result demonstrates that Korsakoff amnesics are not so much affected by encoding–specificity as they are by the presence of a strong semantic associate. In any case, the encoding–specificity hypothesis implies that if the Korsakoff amnesics' memory deficits are to be ameliorated by training them to analyze information at a semantic level, care must be taken to ensure that the available cues at the time of retrieval are congruent with that level of encoding.

A distinction has recently been made between those encoding processes that occur with and without cognitive effort (Shiffrin & Schneider, 1977; Hasher & Zacks, 1979). Automatic encoding, which occurs without effort, has been defined by Hasher & Zacks (1979) in terms of the following set of converging criteria. First, the instructional set should have no influence on memory for automatically encoded information. That is, memory performance should be at the same level whether instructions to remember the information are presented or not. Second, there should be no interference between concurrent automatic and effortful encoding processes. Third, automatic encoding should not be affected by the attentional capacity available to the subject. Fourth, no developmental trend should be evident in automatic encoding processes. Fifth, automatic encoding should not improve as a function of practice. A number of types of information have been suggested by Hasher & Zacks (1979) as candidates for automatic encoding. Among these are temporal order, frequency of occurrence, and spatial location of an event. Thus, according to Hasher & Zacks, effortful encoding is necessary to remember a particular event, while its spatial–temporal context is encoded automatically.

Hirst (1982) has recently suggested that at least a portion of an amnesic's memory deficit may result from a breakdown in the automatic encoding of spatial–temporal context. What comes effortlessly to a normal person may require cognitive effort on the part of the amnesic, taking away processing capacity that is normally used in encoding the event itself. If such is the case, either the contextual cues surrounding the event that usually aid in its retrieval are not properly encoded, the event itself is not encoded to a normal degree because of the divided processing capacity, or some combination of the two. The result is an attenuated memory for the event. Though tentative, this hypothesis is supported by preliminary evidence demonstrating that one type of information that is automatically encoded in normals, spatial location, requires effort on the part of amnesics (Hirst & Volpe, 1985). Further support is provided by recent demonstrations of markedly impaired memory for event frequency in Korsakoff amnesics (Weingartner et al, 1983).

The breakdown of automatic encoding processes in amnesia would have several important implications for rehabilitative efforts with the disorder. First, types of processing taken for granted by normals would have to come under conscious control in the amnesic. Active processing of contextual information would have to be performed. For example, upon meeting several people the amnesic would have to encode not only the event but something on the order of 'I met Mr X after I met Mr Y' or 'I met Mr X in my room and Mr Y in the library.' Second, since all types of encoding would be effortful, longer processing of information would be required by amnesics than by normals in order to obtain the same level of memory performance (e.g., Huppert & Piercy, 1977).

## ORGANIZATION AND STORAGE IN MEMORY

The manner in which information is organized in memory has become the focus of considerable theoretical interest. Several recent views suggest that memories are organized dichotomously, based upon the type of information that is stored. Two such theoretical positions that have important implications for students of amnesia are the episodic–semantic distinction, and the distinction between procedural and declarative knowledge.

The distinction between episodic and semantic memory was originally proposed by Tulving (1972). According to this position, episodic memory is autobiographical in nature, concerning events that are tied to a specific temporal and spatial context. Semantic memory, on the other hand, contains context-independent general knowledge, such as knowledge of language, facts, concepts, and rules. Considerable evidence for the semantic–episodic distinction has been garnered over the years, primarily in the form of experimental dissociations of the two types of knowledge (e.g., Shoben et al, 1978; Jacoby & Dallas, 1981; see review by Tulving, 1983). An interesting experiment illustrating the semantic–episodic distinction was performed by Kihlstrom (1980). Subjects learned a list of unrelated words while under hypnosis, and were subsequently given a post-hypnotic suggestion that they would not remember having learned the list until a particular signal was presented. When awakened from hypnosis seven of the ten most hypnotizable subjects did not remember having learned the list and were unable to recall the words, demonstrating a deficit in episodic memory. In contrast, subjects that were least hypnotizable performed quite well on the free-recall task. Semantic memory performance was next assessed by presenting the subjects with a free association test in which associations were elicited for words that were strong associates of the list words. On this task the highly hypnotizable subjects generated as many words from the learned list as did the least hypnotizable subjects. The fact that free-association performance was not influenced by the post-hypnotic amnesia while episodic free-recall performance was, provides support for the episodic–semantic memory distinction.

A number of investigators have analyzed the memory deficits of amnesic patients in terms of episodic and semantic memory (Tulving, 1983; Schacter & Tulving, 1982; Wood et al, 1982). That amnesics generally have preserved general intelligence, language, and perceptual and social skills, while simultaneously demonstrating profound memory deficits for day-to-day events, suggests that amnesia is a disorder of episodic, and not semantic, memory. Wood et al (1982) have presented considerable clinical and experimental evidence that points to this conclusion. One of their most compelling pieces of evidence comes from a case study of a young girl who was left densely amnesic following an acute attack of herpes simplex encephalitis. This young patient eventually recovered to the point where she was able to return to public school though she remained quite amnesic, exhibiting extreme difficulty in learning the way to her classes. Despite her dense amnesia, this patient was able to learn many traditional academic skills as evidenced by her performance on standardized achievement tests, even though she could not describe the circumstances under which any of this new knowledge was acquired. Wood et al conclude that this case provides a clear and unambiguous example of the dissociation between episodic and semantic memory in amnesic patients.

In contrast to this position, a number of investigators have recently concluded that the memory deficit of amnesic patients is unlikely to be limited to episodic information. Several observations have fostered this disparate view. In the first case amnesic patients have difficulty acquiring new semantic memory, such as new names or vocabulary words, in addition to their episodic deficits. Secondly, and more importantly, retrograde amnesia seems to apply to both semantic and episodic memory as evidenced by the amnesic's difficulty in recalling non-autobiographical general information about past public events or famous public figures (Albert et al, 1979; Cohen & Squire, 1981). A particularly striking instance of retrograde amnesia for both episodic and semantic information is revealed in the case study of the alcoholic Korsakoff patient P.Z. (Butters, 1984; Butters & Cermak, in press). P.Z. (fictitious initials), an eminent scientist and university professor who developed alcoholic Korsakoff's syndrome at age 65, exhibited severe anterograde and retrograde amnesia as assessed by both clinical and psychometric techniques. During his career patient P.Z. had published over 300 papers, books, and book chapters, including an autobiography published 2 years prior to the onset of his disorder. To assess P.Z.'s episodic and semantic memory, Butters & Cermak constructed a test of autobiographical memory based upon episodes and information taken from P.Z.'s autobiography and a test of scientific terms from P.Z.'s area of expertise. On the test of autobiographical memory, P.Z. exhibited no memory for major life and career events that had occurred during the past 20 years (i.e., a loss of episodic memory). When P.Z. and an appropriate control subject were administered the test of scientific definitions, most of which had been discussed in one or more of P.Z.'s textbooks, P.Z. proved to be remarkably impaired in his knowledge of his profession (i.e., a deficit in semantic memory). Butters & Cermak (in press) conclude that alcoholic Korsakoff patients have endured a loss of semantic as well as of episodic memory, although impairments in the latter are more apparent and severe.

In light of these and similar observations, Squire and his colleagues (Cohen & Squire, 1980; Squire, 1982) have proposed that both semantic and episodic information are instances of the more inclusive class of declarative knowledge, which is subject to amnestic disturbance. Declarative knowledge in their view is information that encompasses specific facts, data, and episodes. Procedural knowledge, on the other hand, is information that encompasses procedures and skills, and is usually spared in amnesia. One way in which these types of knowledge have been characterized is 'knowing how' versus 'knowing that'.

The preserved capacity of amnesics to learn and remember perceptual-motor skills has been known for some time (e.g., Corkin, 1968). Cohen & Squire (1980) have recently extended the domain of preserved procedural knowledge in amnesics to the acquisition of a 'cognitive' skill, reading mirror-reversed text. In this latter study, amnesic patients increased their mirror-reading skills at a normal rate over three training sessions, and retained the ability over a 3-month period, despite amnesia for the testing situation and the specific words read (Cohen & Squire, 1980). A recent study (Martone et al, 1984) comparing the mirror-reading and recognition memory capacities of alcoholic Korsakoff patients and dementing patients with Huntington's disease (HD) has provided further confirmation of the dissociation between procedural and declarative memory. While Korsakoff patients again demonstrated an intact rate of acquisition of mirror-reading (i.e., procedural knowledge) and impaired recognition of verbal stimuli (i.e., declarative knowledge), the HD patients showed an opposite pattern of results. These demented patients with basal ganglia lesions were retarded in their acquisition of the mirror-reading skill despite normal recognition of the words employed in the task. Besides emphasizing the special roles of the diencephalon and basal ganglia in cognitive and memory processes, these latter findings provide the double dissociation necessary for establishing the conceptual and heuristic value of the procedural–declarative distinction.

The demonstrations of preserved learning and memory capacities in amnesics, be it for semantic or procedural knowledge, should be of considerable interest to those concerned with memory rehabilitation. The profoundly amnesic patient's ability to acquire procedural knowledge in a normal manner can be incorporated into rehabilitative strategies in at least two ways. First, preserved skill learning may allow amnesics to acquire and apply complex mnemonic strategies (i.e., skills) such as those described by O'Connor & Cermak (Chapter 12 of this volume). Second, it may be possible to teach amnesic patients vocational skills which, when applied with other mnemonic strategies in controlled settings, may enhance the quality of their day-to-day life.

Another topic of growing theoretical interest concerning organizational processes in memory is the integration of newly acquired information with prior knowledge. An important theoretical construct in this regard is *schemata*. Schemata, or *scripts* as they are known in research concerning memory for stories, are clusters of structural knowledge that are concerned with particular events or routines. For example, a script of going to the movies may include waiting in line to purchase a ticket, entering the theater and handing the ticket to the usher, buying refreshments, choosing a seat, and so on. These are generic components of attending a movie that are uniquely experienced at each actual event. When a particular experience of attending a movie occurs, or a story about attending a movie is heard, the actual events are imprinted on the script that is represented in memory. In attempting to recall the event after a delay, the script can be used as a guide from which the particular instances can be recalled. As the delay between the input and recall of the event is lengthened the script becomes more important in guiding retrieval (Smith & Graesser, 1981).

The employment of scripts in memory retrieval have been demonstrated in a number of ways. Bower et al (1979) observed that subjects tend to provide information during recall of a script-based story that was not actually presented in the story but is consistent with their script. Subjects also tend to reorder events in the story toward their appropriate location in the script when action is displaced in the story (e.g., choosing a seat before buying a theater ticket). The degree of prior knowledge, or the complexity of a script, in a particular area can influence recall of new information. For example, Chiesi et al (1979) found that particular events in a baseball game are better remembered by individuals high in baseball knowledge than by those low in baseball knowledge. According to Chiesi et al this occurs because the highly knowledgeable individual can more easily integrate the new information with their prior knowledge, and because they have a more complex script than the low-knowledge individual.

As a new area of research in human memory, schema theory has at this time had little impact on amnesia research. Presumably amnesic patients retain scripts as evidenced by their appropriate performance of events such as dining in a cafeteria or going through a morning grooming routine. Whether their script is less complex than normal, or can be employed with abstract information such as a story, are empirical questions. Squire (1982) has recently suggested that the development of scripts may proceed in the amnesic patient so that information that they seem unable to retain may nonetheless influence their behavior by becoming incorporated into their schemata. Undoubtedly, these and other important issues will become the focus of research as the development of schema and script theory continues. The potential importance of this line of research for the rehabilitation of amnesic patients is illustrated by O'Connor & Cermak (Chapter 12 of this volume). The failure of their postencephalitic amnesic patient (S.S.) to integrate new information with his prior knowledge base virtually eliminated any hope of meaningful improvement in his memory performance. Although patient S.S. can acquire some new knowledge with considerable difficulty, the application or utilization of that knowledge may be extremely limited because of S.S.'s inability to store it in terms of a schemata. The guidance provided by a schemata in the memory processes of an unimpaired person may permit related information to be retrieved in an integrated fashion.

## RECOGNITION MEMORY

The nature of the recognition process is a topic of growing interest in the area of human memory research. Although recognition has often been viewed as involving simplified retrieval processes, some investigators have now provided impressive evidence that the recognition process may be composed of two cognitive components. Mandler (1980), one of the major advocates of this dual process view of recognition, has proposed that a judgment of familiarity occurs concurrently with a search of memory (retrieval) in attempting to recognize a stimulus. Familiarity results from the integration of sensory and perceptual elements of an event through repeated exposure, and occurs independently, but in parallel with the search (i.e., retrieval) process. When an event occurs in a recognition memory task both familiarity and retrieval processes operate, but a judgment of prior occurrence based on familiarity is assumed to occur faster than a judgment based on retrieval. If the event is not identified on the basis of familiarity, it may still be recognized on the basis of recalled (retrieved) information.

Jacoby & Dallas (1981) have recently proposed a similar dual process model in which relative perceptual fluency and retrieval of contextual information are proposed as the components of the recognition process. Relative perceptual fluency refers to the ease with which subjects process items that have been previously presented. For example, Jacoby (1982) reports that 'subjects in recognition experiments often report that "*old*" items seem to "*jump out*" from the page.' Subjects correctly attribute this perceptual fluency, according to Jacoby (1982), to their previous experience with the stimulus. The second component of the recognition process, retrieval of contextual information, allows the subject to recognize a stimulus based upon the context that uniquely characterized the item when it was encoded. This active retrieval process provides a more reliable basis for a recognition judgment but requires greater cognitive effort. Perceptual fluency, on the other hand, requires little or no effort but can lead to less reliable recognition judgments because it can be influenced by factors (e.g., frequency of usage for verbal materials) other than the prior presentation of an item in the current experimental situation. Jacoby also notes that the use of perceptual fluency alone would lead to incomplete recognition since the item would appear familiar, whereas the context in which it appeared would remain unknown.

Both Mandler (1980) and Jacoby (1982) have suggested that demonstrations of intact cued recall in amnesic patients who exhibit retrieval deficits can be interpreted in terms of their dual process models. In the cued recall paradigm a subject is first shown a list of words in the guise of some non-memory task (e.g., rating the words for likeability). In the second phase of the procedure the subject is shown a set of word stems (e.g., first two letters) and asked to produce the first word that comes to mind beginning with each stem. Warrington & Weiskrantz (1974, 1978) have demonstrated that amnesic patients are as likely as normal controls to complete these partial cues (word stems) with the previously seen words despite a failure to recall or recognize the words as test items. For example, if shown a list that contains the word *TABLE*, amnesics are subsequently unable to either recall or recognize *TABLE* as being from the list, but are as likely as normals to complete the stem *TA* with the letters *BLE*. Mandler (1980) has noted that this stem completion performance, which occurs without reference to the previously presented list or to a memory task, may be considered a more or less 'pure' familiarity phenomenon since episodic input (retrieval) is not required. According to this notion, the prior presentation of the word *TABLE* increases the familiarity of the word, making the *BLE* response more likely to the *TA* cue than some other equally appropriate response such as *SK*.

Manipulation of the instructional set presented to the subject can greatly influence performance on such stem completion tasks. Graf et al (1984) demonstrated that presenting the task as a stem completion problem in which the subject was to create the first word that came to mind led to normal performance by amnesic patients. However, if the amnesic subjects were told to use the stems as recall aids for words from the previously presented list, their performance remained well below that of normal controls. Presumably, the former situation leads amnesic subjects to base their word completion on familiarity, while in the latter case retrieval processes are unsuccessfully employed. From a theoretical standpoint, the ability to produce the specific words presented in a study list under these circumstances suggests that representations of the words exist in the brain but are inaccessible. Alternatively, representations may be formed at the time of encoding by the amnesic that are sufficient to support perceptual fluency, but are insufficient to permit a successful retrieval process.

The preserved ability of amnesic patients to employ the perceptual fluency (familiarity) component of the recognition process adds to the growing list of capacities that are spared in the disorder. Like the procedural skills described earlier, perceptual fluency may prove useful in efforts to rehabilitate the amnesic patient. A previously noted difficulty encountered by the patient with a severe memory impairment is an inability to correctly discriminate items presented in the current experimental situation from other items represented in memory that were not presented, presumably because of the impaired manner in which the experimental context of the items is encoded (Jacoby, 1982). The lack of this additional information not only results in the failure of amnesics to recognize items from a previously presented list, but also leads amnesic patients to have little confidence in their judgment of whether a word they correctly produce through cued recall is from the previously presented list (Mayes & Meudell, 1981). The detrimental effects of the incomplete memory representation may be attenuated if amnesic patients can be trained to use those aspects of the representation that are spared to form fine-grained discriminations between currently relevant and irrelevant information. In a sense, amnesics may possibly be taught to become better 'signal detectors' recognizing an item on the basis of less information than is available to the normal person. Whether this function is beyond the cognitive capabilities of amnesic patients has yet to be determined.

## SUMMARY AND CONCLUSIONS

Our brief review attests that recent developments in the study of normal human learning and memory bear greatly upon our understanding of the amnesic syndrome. In the past, theorists have tried to characterize amnesia as a deficit in either the encoding, consolidation, or retrieval process. The dynamic and interdependent nature of these processes as described in current conceptions of memory makes it unlikely that amnesia can be explained in such simple terms. The encoding-specificity hypothesis of memory exemplifies this view, with its emphasis on the relationship between encoding and retrieval contexts in memory performance. Similarly, the importance of contextual information throughout the memory process has recently been discussed in a number of theoretical positions including the distinction between automatic and effortful encoding (Hasher & Zacks, 1979) and the perceptual fluency position of Jacoby & Dallas (1981). The role of contextual information in the memory deficits of amnesics during encoding, storage, and retrieval, has been subsequently emphasized in several theories of amnesia (Hirst, 1982; Jacoby, 1982).

Unfortunately, memory rehabilitation efforts in the past have, more often than not, resulted in little success (see O'Connor and Cermak, Chapter 12 in this volume). The inability of amnesic patients to employ complex mnemonic strategies to overcome their deficits has been described numerous times, and may be at least partially due to concomitant loss of other cognitive capacities such as the ability to generalize from one situation to another or to easily elaborate on to-be-remembered information. This being the case, a more fruitful approach may be to identify and characterize the preserved memory capacities of amnesics, and to build rehabilitative strategies around them.

A further complicating factor in the development of effective memory rehabilitation strategies is the recent demonstration of qualitatively distinct characteristics of the amnesia arising from various etiologies and lesion sites. For example, patients with diencephalic and hippocampal lesions may differ from patients with basal ganglia lesions in the nature of their memory problems. Amnesia following diencephalic–limbic damage is characterized by normal procedural and impaired declarative memory systems, whereas the opposite relationship may typify the memory deficits of some dementias associated with atrophy of the basal ganglia. These findings suggest that before a rehabilitation strategy is developed, the nature of the patient's impairment, including any preserved memory capacities, should be carefully evaluated so that remedial efforts can be maximized.

## ACKNOWLEDGMENT

The preparation of this manuscript was supported by funds from the VA Medical Research Service and by NIAAA grant AA-00187 to Boston University.

### REFERENCES

Albert M S, Butters N, Levin J 1979 Evidence for separate neural circuits underlying anterograde and retrograde amnesia. Paper presented at the Annual Society Meeting, New York, February

Atkinson R C, Shiffrin R M 1968 Human memory: a proposed system and its control processes. In: Spence K, Spence J (eds) The psychology of learning and motivation vol. 2. Academic Press, New York

Baddeley A D 1978 The trouble with levels: a reexamination of Craik and Lockhart's framework for memory research. Psychological Review 85: 139–152

Biber C, Butters N, Rosen J, Gerstman L, Mattis S 1981 Encoding strategies and recognition of faces by alcoholic Korsakoff and other brain-damaged patients. Journal of Clinical Neuropsychology 3: 315–330

Bower G H 1970 Analysis of a mnemonic device. American Scientist 58: 496–510

Bower G H, Black J B, Turner T J 1979 Scripts in memory for text. Cognitive Psychology 11: 177–220

Bradshaw G L, Anderson J R 1982 Elaborative encoding as an explanation of levels of processing. Journal of Verbal Learning and Verbal Behavior, 21: 165–174

Butters N 1984 Alcoholic Korsakoff's syndrome: an update. Seminars in Neurology 4: 226–244

Butters N, Cermak L S 1975 Some analyses of amnesic syndromes in brain damaged patients. In: Pribram K, Isaacson R (eds) The hippocampus. Plenum, New York

Butters N, Cermak L S 1980 Alcoholic Korsakoff's syndrome: an information-processing approach to amnesia. Academic Press, New York

Butters N, Cermak L S in press A case study of the forgetting of autobiographical knowledge: implications for the study of retrograde amnesia. In: Rubin D (ed) Autobiographical memory. Cambridge University Press, New York

Cermak L S 1982 Human memory and amnesia. Erlbaum, Hillsdale, NJ

Cermak L S, Butters N 1972 The role of interference and encoding in the short-term memory deficits of Korsakoff patients. Neuropsychologia 10: 89–96

Cermak L S, Reale L 1978 Depth of processing and retention of words by alcoholic Korsakoff patients. Journal of Experimental Psychology: Human Learning and Memory 4: 165–174

Cermak L S, Butters N, Moreines J 1974 Some analyses of the verbal encoding deficit of alcoholic Korsakoff patients. Brain and Language 1: 141–150
Cermak L S, Naus M J, Reale L 1976 Rehearsal and organizational strategies of alcoholic Korsakoff patients. Brain and Language 3: 375–385
Cermak L S, Uhly B, Reale L 1980 Encoding specificity in the alcoholic Korsakoff patient. Brain and Language 11: 119–127
Chiesi H L, Spilich G J, Voss J F 1979 Acquisition of domain-related information in relation to high and low domain knowledge. Journal of Verbal Learning and Verbal Behavior 18: 257–273
Cohen N J, Squire L R 1980 Preserved learning and retention of pattern analyzing skill in amnesia: dissociation of knowing how and knowing that. Science 210: 207–209
Cohen N J, Squire L R 1981 Retrograde amnesia and remote memory impairment. Neuropsychologia 19: 337–356
Corkin S 1968 Acquisition of motor skill after bilateral medial temporal lobe excision. Neuropsychologia 6: 225–265
Craik F I M, Lockhart R S 1972 Levels of processing: A framework for memory research. Journal of Verbal Learning and Verbal Behavior 11: 671–684
Fisher R P, Craik F I M 1977 The interactions between encoding and retrieval operations in cued recall. Journal of Experimental Psychology: Human Learning and Memory 3: 701–711
Graf P, Squire L R, Mandler G 1984 The information that amnesic patients do not forget. Journal of Experimental Psychology: Learning, Memory, and Cognition 10: 164–178
Hasher L, Zacks R T 1979 Automatic and effortful processes in memory. Journal of Experimental Psychology: General 108: 356–388
Hirst W 1982 The amnesic syndrome: descriptions and explanations. Psychological Bulletin 91: 435–460
Hirst W, Volpe B J 1985 Encoding of spatial relations with amnesia. Neuropsychologia 22: 631–634
Horton D L, Mills C B 1984 Human learning and memory. Annual Review of Psychology 35: 361–394
Huppert F A, Piercy M 1977 Recognition memory in amnesic patients: a defect of acquisition? Neuropsychologia 15: 643–652
Jacoby L L 1982 Knowing and remembering: some parallels in the behavior of Korsakoff patients and normals. In: Cermak L S (ed) Human memory and amnesia. Erlbaum, Hillsdale, NJ
Jacoby L L, Dallas M 1981 On the relationship between autobiographical memory and perceptual learning. Journal of Experimental Psychology: General 110: 306–340
Jacoby L L, Craik F I M, Begg I 1979 Effects of decision difficulty on recognition and recall. Journal of Verbal Learning and Verbal Behavior 18: 585–600
Kihlstrom J F 1980 Posthypnotic amnesia for recently learned material: interactions with 'episodic' and 'semantic' memory. Cognitive Psychology 12: 227–251
Mandler G 1980 Recognizing: the judgement of previous occurrence. Psychological Review 87: 252–271
Martone M, Butters N, Payne M, Becker J, Sax D S 1984 Dissociations between skill learning and verbal recognition in amnesia and dementia. Archives of Neurology 41: 965–970
Mayes A R, Meudell P R 1981 How similar is immediate memory in amnesic patients to delayed memory in normal subjects? A replication, extension and measurement of the amnesic cueing effect. Neuropsychologia 19: 647–654
Mayes A R, Meudell P R, Neary D 1980 Do amnesics adopt inefficient encoding strategies with faces and random shapes? Neuropsychologia 18: 527–540
McDowall J 1979 Effects of encoding instructions and retrieval cuing on recall in Korsakoff patients. Memory and Cognition 7: 232–239
Miller G A, Galanter E, Pribram K 1960 Plans and the structure of behavior. Holt, Rinehart & Winston, New York
Schacter D L, Tulving E 1982 Amnesia and memory research. In: Cermak L S (ed) Human memory and amnesia. Erlbaum, Hillsdale, NJ
Shiffrin R M, Schneider W 1977 Controlled and automatic human information processing. II: perceptual learning, automatic attending, and a general theory. Psychological Review 84: 127–190
Shoben E J, Westcourt K T, Smith E E 1978 Sentence verification, sentence recognition,

and the semantic–episodic distinction. Journal of Experimental Psychology: Human Learning and Memory 4: 304–317

Smith D A, Graesser A C 1981 Memory for actions in scripted activities as a function of typicality, retention interval, and retrieval task. Memory and Cognition 9: 550–559

Squire L R 1982 The neuropsychology of human memory. Annual Review of Neuroscience 5: 241–273

Stevenson R J 1981 Depth of comprehension, effective elaboration, and memory for sentences. Memory and Cognition 9: 169–176

Tulving E 1972 Episodic and semantic memory. In: Tulving E, Donaldson W (eds) Organization of memory. Academic Press, New York

Tulving E 1979 Relations between encoding and levels of processing. In: Cermak L S, Craik F I M (eds) Levels of processing in human memory. Erlbaum, Hillsdale, NJ

Tulving E 1983 Elements of episodic memory. Oxford University Press, New York

Tulving E, Thomson D M 1973 Encoding specificity and retrieval processes in episodic memory. Psychological Review 80: 352–373

Warrington E K 1982 The double dissociation of short-term and long-term memory deficits. In: Cermak L S (ed) Human memory and amnesia. Erlbaum, Hillsdale, NJ

Warrington E K, Weiskrantz L 1974 The effect of prior learning on subsequent retention in amnesic patients. Neuropsychologia 12: 419–428

Warrington E K, Weiskrantz L 1978 Further analysis of the prior learning effect in amnesic patients. Neuropsychologia 16: 169–177

Weingartner H, Grafman J, Boutelle W, Kaye W, Martin P R 1983 Forms of memory failure. Science 221: 380–382

Winograd R 1975 Frame representations and the declarative–procedural controversy. In: Bobrow D, Collins A (eds) Representation and understanding. Academic Press, New York

Wood F, Ebert V, Kinsbourne M 1982 The episodic–semantic memory distinction in memory and amnesia: Clinical and experimental observations. In: Cermak L S (ed) Human memory and amnesia. Erlbaum, Hillsdale, NJ

# Approaches to neuropsychological rehabilitation: language disorders

In the literature on aphasia rehabilitation, more has been written about such various, albeit important, peripheral questions as the efficacy of aphasia rehabilitation than about the rehabilitation techniques themselves. One reason for this could be the still widespread belief that recovery from aphasia is largely a matter of chance, self-determined, and that aphasia therapy has purely non-specific effects.

In their classical work, *Aphasia: a clinical and psychological study*, Weisenburg & McBride (1935) summed up the then current views about the efficacy of aphasia rehabilitation: 'Opinions are divided as to whether improvement can be aided or prolonged by training, and there has been comparatively little decisive evidence either one way or the other.' Nevertheless, much attention was given to aphasia rehabilitation after the Second World War, mainly because of the practical problem of re-educating many thousands of young people aphasic as a result of war wounds. This problem, rather than a critical evaluation of the techniques available, dictated for a long time the form of aphasia therapy. The reasons underlying the choice of a particular method are not always clearly stated.

For the adult subject, widely different language intervention strategies that can tentatively be grouped into four main categories have been elaborated in different countries under the influence of various psychological doctrines. This chapter will briefly outline the main approaches to aphasia therapy and will discuss how therapy is generally conducted. The factors influencing recovery and the patterns of recovery of the various language behaviours will be considered. A brief description of dysarthria closes the chapter.

## THE CLASSIC OR STIMULATION APPROACH

This approach includes many different techniques (see for example Chapey, 1981) based on two general assumptions. The first is that aphasia is a central language deficit, which thus affects all language modalities (e.g., comprehension, production) in ways which may differ somewhat, but always within the bounds of a certain overall pattern.

According to Wepman (Wepman & Jones, 1964) the various aphasic syndromes represent different levels of language dissolution, and thus present in reverse order the process by which a child acquires language. The different syndromes are not seen as differing qualitatively from each other, but only quantitatively. For Schuell (Schuell et al, 1964) too, there is just one all-embracing aphasia, though the presence of other deficits can make it appear more or less severe in an individual patient.

This assumption heavily affects aphasia rehabilitation. If, as these authors assume, aphasia is due to the breakdown of one single mechanism, re-education of each modality in turn and by different techniques is not necessary. Improvement, like the deficit, will manifest itself simultaneously in all the behaviors. Schuell's re-education technique, for example, is basically nothing other than intense auditory stimulation, quantitatively controlled by the therapist so that the severely aphasic patient is required to process less information than the less impaired. Wepman, however, like the French authors, does in fact distinguish in practice between re-education of comprehension and re-education of expression, though the same exercises (naming and pointing to objects, for instance) are recommended for both.

Concentration on oral language is a characteristic common to the therapeutic principles expounded by the authors of this school, directly deriving from the interpretation of aphasia as a central language disorder. If both written and spoken language are affected in both their facets, that is to say in both comprehension and production, all the more reason to utilize oral language that allows a quicker and more direct exchange between therapist and patient, with results – if results there are to be – extending also to those verbal behaviors which were not specifically rehabilitated.

The second assumption is that aphasia is characterized by reduced efficiency in gaining access to language knowledge. Aphasia therapy is approached in this case from the viewpoint of levels of language availability. Certainly this is not a novel approach, for Jackson's analysis of aphasia in the last century is based on observation of the dissociation between automatic usage (conserved) and intentional or propositional usage of language, which is particularly defective (Jackson, 1958). Thus, in everyday language there is not always the same degree of intention, used in this context to mean part and parcel of the informative value or the originality of the thought content to be expressed. If what you want to say is an original and informative thought, its originality can only express itself by an unforeseeable ordering of the units (*words*) that go to make up the message. Therefore, in this case the choice of words and their order call for a high degree of intention. If, on the other hand, the thought is not original, and one that others in the same position might well express, the choice and ordering of the words would be foreseeable, calling for less intention on the part of the speaker.

In other terms, we can say that language which is intentional and without any specific relationship with the actual circumstances has informative content, whereas automatic language, in that it is in part determined by external factors, lacks informative content. It is natural to all of us to alternate between the intentional and the automatic in our speech. This is not a clear-cut dichotomy, automatic and intentional language, but rather two extremes of a continuum.

We can add others to the three levels of intention in speech (oaths, lower, and real) described by Jackson. At the top of the scale there is metalinguistic language, used to describe language itself. This is the level at which the linguist works. Any attempt to classify these levels is only speculative at present. However, it will be helpful to analyze the circumstances in which aphasic patients employ language.

In aphasia, selective loss of the levels of highest intention has highly significant connotations for rehabilitation treatment. As mentioned earlier, from this point of view aphasia would consist of a restriction of language availability, rather than an actual loss of language itself. The speech therapist should not teach naming or other specific responses to particular stimuli, but should stimulate patients to improve their accessing strategies.

## THE SOVIET APPROACH

Luria's research and highly developed aphasia rehabilitation scheme made him one of the foremost and most widely known scholars in the field of aphasia therapy. According to Luria's theory (1973), any functional system may be deranged by lesions in diverse parts of the cortex, but the quality of the impediment is dependent on the localization of the lesion.

Luria theorized that in acquiring a psychological function, such as language, man passes through successive stages: the function is first effectuated by explicit external operations that gradually become more internalized, to end up as automatized implicit mental acts. The majority of habits and functions in adults are so hermetic that it is nearly impossible to analyze the underlying operations. Yet, when there is a cortical lesion, automatic execution is lost and the patient is forced to follow the different links step by step. This enables us to study the psychological components of the various higher cortical functions, such as reading, calculating, and solving problems.

Recovery is achieved through reorganization of the functional system under treatment in such a way as to transfer affected function to a new structure, replacing the defective link with a new one, so that the function can re-establish itself. This is perfectly possible, since the functional systems in the human brain are extremely adaptable: there is scarcely any part of the cortex that cannot take on a new functional role and become part of almost any functional system. Functional reorganization can be either intrasystemic or intersystemic. When the missing link is replaced by one coming from a different functional system, the reorganization is intersystemic. Intrasystemic reorganization involves the damaged function alone. Here either a primitive or low-level reorganization can be effected, or else there can be reorganization at a more intentional level. Luria described this latter situation in great detail. The patient should, according to Luria, be made to understand the nature of his impediment and to learn to do intentionally things which previously were automatic.

A rehabilitation program, to be effectual, should observe two fundamental rules. It must be rigorously differentiated, i.e., be based on an accurate analysis of the deficit, and it must start out by requiring external operations for each of the different links composing the function that must then be progressively internalized. Only at the very end of the treatment is it possible to cut out some of the steps. In Luria's scheme each deficit calls for its own rehabilitative program based on a qualitative analysis of the impairment. Everything depends on the theoretical interpretation of the deficit. The potential strength of this form of therapy is that the treatment will be appropriate and efficacious if the theoretical analysis is detailed and correct. Yet its very specificity will render it inefficacious if the analysis is incomplete.

## THE OPERANT CONDITIONING APPROACH

This approach is based on the theoretical principles of operant conditioning, a theory of learning developed by Skinner (1972) in the sphere of behaviorism. Behaviorism holds that only what can be strictly observed and subjected to scientific investigation should be studied, while explanatory mechanisms are to be shunned. Thus causality is considered to be a principle of association or contiguity. In operant conditioning the stimulus is not important and can even be ignored. Greater emphasis is placed on consequences, which are considered to be the primary modifiers of behavior. By manipulating the consequences (reinforcement) it is possible to condition behavior, relating it to a previous situation which triggers it off.

Principles of operant conditioning have often been described in detail and some of their application to aphasia therapy can be found in Brookshire (1969), Holland and colleagues (Holland, 1970; Holland & Harris, 1968; Holland & Sonderman, 1974) and Goldfarb (1981). Baseline data must be collected, criteria for success must be defined, and steps within the program planned. To achieve this last, one must know what is easy and what is difficult for the aphasic patient, but the grounds for judging the difficulty of an exercise vary considerably. The criterion most commonly employed is based on structural analysis of the impaired behavior and takes for granted, for example, that comprehension of a single word is easier than comprehension of a long and syntactically complex sentence. Otherwise, what is correctly achieved by a larger number of aphasics might be considered easier, and what is achieved by a smaller number more difficult.

I strongly believe that when the reasons why an aphasic patient cannot do a given task are known, i.e., what the primary deficit is, more pertinent and efficacious exercises can be programmed and scaled. Thus to construct an adequate therapeutic program for aphasia it is not enough to observe the patient's behavior; it is also necessary to understand precisely the underlying mechanisms of the impaired behavior. Operant conditioning (along with programmed instruction and behavior modulation which are based on the same principles) is, in reality, a pure methodology. How a program must be applied is accurately and rigorously described (for instance, how and when the reinforcement should be given). What, however, it does not tell us much about is the content of the program. In fact, operant conditioning is a very useful tool in the systematic implementation of any rehabilitation approach.

## THE PSYCHOLINGUISTIC APPROACH

Classification of different approaches is arbitrary. For example, the Melodic Intonation Therapy (Sparks & Holland, 1976) has been classified as a neurolinguistic approach by Seron (1979), and as an operant conditioning approach by Goldfarb (1981) but also as a way to identify the aspects emphasized in the different therapeutic techniques. This is particularly true for the psycholinguistic approach. Linguistic criteria have always played a part in aphasia rehabilitation. The linguist who influenced aphasia therapy most strongly was probably Jakobson (1964) with his selection–combination dichotomy in language use. Chomsky's (1965) competence-performance dichotomy also had a direct effect on aphasia therapy, as can be seen, for instance, in Weigl's (1961) deblocking technique that presupposes a breakdown of performance (the speaker's actual use of language) without breakdown of competence (his underlying knowledge of the language) (Weigl & Bierwisch, 1970).

These dichotomies, however, are extremely general and can hardly be used to formulate specific therapeutic exercises. Only recently have highly detailed and specific submodels, generally applicable, however, to only one particular verbal behavior, been described and therapists are now trying to design some specific therapy programs based on these. At present the psycholinguistic approach is more a hope for better planned aphasia therapy than a reality.

### Two considerations

These approaches are not mutually exclusive but are focused differently. Yet some considerations seem to be relevant to all of them, with relation to two general topics: the rapport between rehabilitation of comprehension and rehabilitation of expression, and the importance given to syntax in aphasia therapy.

Communication requires both comprehension and production but the former was long considered to be a purely passive process, asking for no active participation on the part of the listener. Both production and comprehension in language are active processes which, though not entirely similar, do have much in common. The intrinsic characteristics of speech and understanding, however, vary somewhat – the memory factor in language usage, for instance, probably plays a stronger part in message decodification – while other components are the same in both production and comprehension. Vocabulary could well be classed as one of these latter.

Some studies show that expression and comprehension are impaired in similar ways in aphasia. Gainotti (1976) found that in aphasic patients semantic disintegration can be observed at the expressive and the receptive level of verbal communication. The syntactic deficit suffered by Broca's aphasics is assumed by Berndt & Caramazza (1981) to involve a central component of the linguistic system. This seems to confirm the fact that production and comprehension involve the same linguistic structures. The abstract syntactic or phonological rules needed to understand a sentence are also needed to produce it, but only at an abstract level. Even though they exploit the same structural information, the same components are not involved in the actual processes of comprehension and production.

In rehabilitation, then, one must take care to distinguish between, and to re-educate, production and comprehension separately. Comprehension, in matters of verbal intercourse at least, is easier than expression, as well shown by a child's ability to understand words which he cannot use or by the experience of learning a second language. In aphasia therapy, comprehension, sharing much with production but being easier, should always be the first target of rehabilitation. Schuell et al (1964) suggest that aphasia rehabilitation should essentially be based on auditory stimulation. While rehabilitation of expression generally gets described in detail, only a few lines are devoted to comprehension rehabilitation. My feeling is that this proportion should be reversed, and comprehension trained more than production. A study in our Aphasia Unit (Basso et al, 1982b) provides some evidence that a rehabilitation program like ours, which emphasizes comprehension over expression exercises, does not impede recovery of expression.

The second comment concerns the kind of syntactic language frequently used and what verbal exchanges between patient and therapist accomplish in aphasia therapy.

By '*syntax*' we mean the rules for interrelation of words. For instance, in the two phrases 'the boy is chasing the girl' and 'the girl is chasing the boy' the words are the same, and it is only by syntactical analysis that we know who is chasing whom in each case. For years aphasia therapy has focused on syntax, using exercises requiring the patient to say or understand a single sentence, i.e., the meaning of the words and their respective relationships. One of the most truly important steps forward in present-day psycholinguistics has been the realization that understanding is not limited to the literal meaning. To really grasp the full meaning of the sentence 'it has rained hard and the meadow is flooded' one must appreciate that the meadow is flooded *because* it has rained hard; that is to say, to be aware of a connection between the two events. Sometimes these connections are made explicit by a linguistic signal (like a pronoun or a *because*) which shows the hearer how to interpret the information. Yet in seizing upon the connectors (verbally explicit or not) in a sentence, the hearer can only fall back on his own ability to reason and to draw inferences. At this point it becomes extremely hard to distinguish between linguistic competence and cognitive processes as a vehicle of comprehension.

To understand a sentence, in addition to what has been said so far, we also need information about the speaker's situation at the actual moment, and about his knowledge of the world. The latter is usually called '*encyclopaedic*,' the former '*contextual*,' information. In contextual information there are two facets: the linguistic – details drawn from what has previously been said, for example, 'it has rained heavily' – and the extralinguistic, referring to the situation in which the sentence is spoken. Another aspect of comprehension that should be considered in aphasia therapy, is the purpose for which a sentence is formed. Indeed a sentence, quite apart from its content, relays the purpose for which that content has been expressed, as when giving an order or asking for information. The speaker's purpose may be verbally explicit, for example, 'tell me if you want to go back,' in which the aim of asking something is verbalized in 'tell me,' while the content of the question is the other's inclination to return – or the purpose can also be inexplicit. Often a sentence seeks more than to merely communicate the information it contains. If someone says 'it's late,' the speaker probably does not mean just to say that it is late, but he wants the hearer to understand that 'it's time to go home' or 'we'll miss the train,' etc. To understand the ulterior motives of a sentence and not to limit oneself to the literal meaning is a basic aspect of linguistic comprehension, which is usually only possible through an understanding of context. This specific aspect of comprehension, however, does not seem to pose particular problems to aphasic patients, who have been shown (Wilcox et al, 1978; Kadzielawa et al, 1981) to comprehend better those utterances whose correct interpretation is not literal, but rather an indirect request, than they do standard comprehension tasks.

Aphasia therapy has often limited itself to stimulating the patient to produce and comprehend single sentences. The assumption was that longer texts could be understood or produced simply by putting one sentence after the other. This is certainly not so, and the emphasis given to single sentence usage might be the basis of some of the limitations of current aphasia rehabilitation techniques. On the one hand it is difficult to find in the literature any recommendations for the rehabilitation of only slightly affected aphasics. When a patient is able to say and to understand isolated sentences, he is dismissed and therapy discontinued. On the other hand, the syntactic language used in aphasia therapy is different from everyday language which is not always syntactically correct. In addition, the language of aphasia therapy has too often lost its function of communication, for the therapist seeks to find out whether the patient is or is not capable of saying something (e.g., naming exercises), and it is often used for pure description (as with the description of complex scenes so often used in aphasia therapy) in a way which does not require the presence of a hearer, and seldom in a conversational way.

## Factors influencing recovery

Much has been written about recovery from aphasia and the variables considered to be particularly relevant. There are still some factors that have not yet been considered. This could be one reason why it is so difficult to render an exact prognosis for a case of aphasia. The factor far most closely studied in relation to recovery is treatment, i.e., whether language rehabilitation has any effect on recovery of specific language skills or not. One of the reasons why there is no clear-cut answer to the question is that language rehabilitation does not entail any clearly specified therapeutic approach.

Studies of the different factors that influence recovery will not be reviewed here in detail (for a review see Sarno, 1981). In the literature there is agreement about the effects of some factors, while others are more controversial, and there are still other factors whose supposed effects are based on nothing but clinical impressions.

The first group includes handedness, etiology, severity, and time since onset. More left-handers and right-handers with familial left-handedness recover than pure right-handers (Subirana, 1958; Luria, 1970). More patients with post-traumatic aphasia improve than patients with aphasia following stroke (Butfield & Zangwill, 1946; Wepman, 1951; Luria, 1970; Marks et al, 1957; Kertesz & McCabe, 1977; Basso et al, 1982a). The initial severity of aphasia also has prognostic value: those with the more severe aphasias do not recover as well as those with the milder forms (Sands et al, 1969; Kertesz & McCabe, 1977; Basso et al, 1979). Finally, there is considerable agreement about the time-course of recovery in aphasia, the most dramatic changes being seen in the first 2 or 3 weeks after stroke (Kohlmeyer, 1976). Remarkable recovery can still take place in the next 2 months and decreases considerably after 6 months (Vignolo, 1964; Culton, 1969; Sarno & Levita, 1971; Kertesz & McCabe, 1977; Basso et al, 1979).

Age and type of aphasia belong to the second group. The influence of age on recovery is controversial; aphasiologists generally consider age an important variable, but evaluations of the effects of age are not consistent. Age has been reported both as having no effect on recovery (Culton, 1971; Sarno, 1980) or as being an important factor in that fewer older patients recover than younger ones (Marshall et al, 1982). The effect of type of aphasia is difficult to study because, in addition to problems of classification, the type of aphasia is closely tied to the severity, some aphasic syndromes being by definition milder than others. Problems of classification could be one of the reasons for the variability of the conclusions about the effect of aphasia type on recovery. There have been reports that there is no difference in outcome between fluent and non-fluent aphasics (Basso et al, 1975, 1979) and that there is a better prognosis for Broca's or expressive aphasics (Butfield & Zangwill, 1946; Messerli et al, 1976; Kertesz & McCabe, 1977) or for receptive aphasics (Vignolo, 1964).

Other factors that have been considered prognostic for an aphasic patient include education, social milieu, general health, occupational status, and intelligence, but very few of these have been specifically investigated (Sarno et al, 1970b; Smith, 1971; Keenan & Brassell, 1974; Marshall et al, 1982). The effects of three factors on recovery i.e., sex, intelligence and rehabilitation, will be considered in detail.

*Sex*

Sex differences in brain organization have recently been suggested (for a review see McGlone, 1980). A number of studies of normal and brain-damaged subjects indicate a more bilateral representation of language and visuo-spatial functions in women than in men. This would seem to predict better recovery in women, though this does not unambiguously mean a more bilateral representation of language in women. For this it would be necessary to postulate that recovery from aphasia depends on the taking over of language by the right hemisphere.

Two studies designed to test the different specialization hypotheses have specifically examined recovery from aphasia in men and women. Basso et al, (1982a) studied the recovery of auditory comprehension and oral expression separately in 264 male and 121 female aphasic patients, controlling for factors that might significantly influence recovery. A second examination was made at least 6 months after the first. There was no significant difference in comprehension between men and women, but oral expression of women recovered significantly better than that of men. Pizzamiglio et al (1985) studied recovery in different language tasks in 48 male and 21 female aphasic patients, first tested within 3 months after the stroke. All patients undertook language rehabilitation programs and were retested 3 months later. The authors found no sex difference in recovery in the naming task. Yet global women recovered significantly more than global men in three comprehension tasks (phonemic discrimination, semantic discrimination, and syntactic comprehension) but not in the Token Test. These two studies provide some evidence that sex has a significant effect on recovery, although the results are inconsistent for the verbal behavior which recovered more, comprehension in Pizzamiglio et al's study, and production in Basso et al's study.

*Intelligence*

From time to time intelligence is quoted as a factor that influences recovery from aphasia (Darley, 1975), but there are few supporting data. This question was examined in the hope of selecting good candidates for aphasia therapy. In a retrospective study (Basso and Capitani, unpublished data) we investigated whether the improvement in the Token Test score can be predicted by the level of performance in Raven's Colored Progressive Matrices on first examination. This question requires a careful approach (1) because subjects with a high Token Test score on first examination may be considered to have a smaller chance of achieving considerable improvement because of the upper limit of the score itself, and (2) because the same improvement (in terms of score difference) in different regions of the scale might not reflect strictly corresponding degrees of improvement. We therefore selected patients seen at the Aphasia Unit in Milan from February 1977 to September 1982, all right-handed, left-hemisphere brain-damaged vascular aphasic patients who were first examined less than 6 months post-onset and who had scored less than 25 on the Token Test on first examination. One hundred and one subjects (29 women and 72 men) fulfilled these conditions: 52 were fluent and 49 non-fluent aphasics. The relation between improvement in the Token Test at the second examination and the Progressive Matrices score was estimated by means of the Pearson's product moment coefficient, which yielded a value of –0.17. This outcome could, indeed, be due to the fact that the scale of the Token Test has an upper limit, i.e., that moderately aphasic patients (with higher Token Test scores) had a limited scope for improvement. We therefore calculated the correlation coefficients separately for very severe patients (scoring 0 to 5 in the Token Test in the first examination; $n$=20) and for moderate aphasics (scoring 14 to 22 in the Token Test in the first examination; $n$=36). For the severe group the correlation was –0.06, and for the moderate sample it was –0.36. On this basis we are fairly confident that the lack of positive correlation between the initial Progressive Matrices scores and improvement in the Token Test is not an artifact of the method. This result is not in line with the hypothesis of a negative influence of a low intelligence level on recovery of verbal comprehension, as examined by the Token Test.

### *Effect of therapy*

As stated earlier, the question of whether language rehabilitation accomplishes measurable gains beyond what can be expected from spontaneous recovery has been much debated. Studies aimed at verifying the efficacy of treatment can be grouped according to the methodology employed. The earliest studies generally comprised only treated aphasics and considered whether recovery was good after treatment. Conditions, however, varied considerably from one patient to another in the same study. Therapy sessions varied, from one to 110 in the study by Marks, et al (1957) and from 5 to 290 in Butfield & Zangwill's study (1946). Time post-onset also varied (from 2 weeks to 48 months in Sands et al's study, 1969). Wepman (1951), however, tried to take these variables into consideration and studied 68 young soldiers with traumatic injuries who did not receive language rehabilitation until 6 months post-onset and were then retrained for approximately 18 months. He thought that recovery in such cases could be ascribed to treatment, since spontaneous recovery occurs primarily within the first month and it does not occur after 6 months.

All these studies, while firmly stating that aphasia therapy is effectual, are unfortunately beset with methodological weaknesses, of which the most important is probably lack of a control group. Later studies compared improvement of treated and untreated patients. Vignolo (1964) did not find any difference in recovery between 42 treated and 17 untreated patients. Sarno et al (1970b) compared three groups of global aphasics who were at least 3 months post-stroke. The groups were comparable in age, time post-onset, education, and sex distribution. One group was given programmed instruction therapy, the second traditional speech therapy, and the third no treatment. At the end of treatment, tests were again administered. The authors did not find any significant differences in outcome after the three treatments. Hagen (1973) studied the effects of treatment in 10 treated and 10 untreated males. Both groups showed improvement in the first 3 months and after that period only the treated patients continued to improve. In a study by Basso et al (1975) recovery of expression was compared in 94 untreated patients and 91 patients treated for at least 6 months. Results of the statistical analysis showed a significantly greater recovery in treated than in untreated patients. There was no difference in the Functional Communication Profile (Sarno, 1969) results for 18 untreated and 17 treated patients (Levita, 1978), examined at 4 and 12 weeks post-onset. The influence of specific aphasia rehabilitation on recovery of expression and comprehension of oral and written language was investigated in 162 re-educated and 119 not re-educated aphasic patients (Basso et al, 1979). Patients were further subdivided according to type (fluent/non-fluent) and severity (severe/moderate) of aphasia and time post-onset. It was found that rehabilitation had a significant positive effect on improvement in all four verbal behaviors investigated. Time lapse between onset and first examination, and severity of aphasia, were negatively correlated with improvement, and type of aphasia was not significantly correlated to recovery.

At first sight the results of the studies comparing treated and untreated patients are contradictory, aphasia therapy was reported to have a significant effect in some, but not in all of them. However, this approach to the study of efficacy of language therapy also has weak points: the control group is seldom perfectly comparable to the group under study, and the assignment to treatment or non-treatment groups is not random. For the two Milan studies (Basso et al, 1975, 1979), the treated and untreated groups were fairly comparable. In Italy, aphasia therapy is in its early days and until a few years ago it was practised only in Milan. This fact, however lamentable, has made it possible to find patients who had not undergone rehabilitation because they lived far from Milan, but were not otherwise different from the treated patients. Moreover, when the studies were started in 1965 we had no clear-cut ideas about which patients would benefit more from rehabilitation, and we were willing to re-educate all-comers. Conditions have now changed and aphasia therapy is carried out in many different places. Ethical considerations forbid the withholding of treatment, and new methods of studying the old question of whether aphasia therapy is efficacious or not have been devised.

In the past few years a certain number of studies comparing different treatments have appeared. The study of Sarno et al (1970b) has already been mentioned. Meikle et al (1979) compared recovery of aphasic patients treated by qualified speech therapists and by non-professional volunteers who were aware of their patients' specific communication disorders and given guidelines for treatment. The two groups received the same amount of therapy. There were no major differences in the results obtained by speech therapists and by volunteers trained in speech therapy methods. In a multi-center study, individual treatment and group treatment were compared (Wertz et al, 1981).

The individually treated group fared better, but with only a few significant differences.

Speech therapy has been compared to both operant training and to non-specific treatment by Lincoln et al (1982). Twelve patients received speech therapy for 4 weeks – either before or after – four weeks of non-specific treatment. Twelve more patients received 4 weeks' speech therapy and 4 weeks' operant conditioning. All groups improved significantly in 31 of the 38 variables assessed, but there was no significant difference between the treatments. In a recent study (David et al, 1982) volunteers and speech therapists have again been compared. Patients re-educated by both improved equally.

With the exception of Sarno et al's study (1970b), these studies suggest that treatment is indeed effective but need not be specific: recovery could be a non-specific effect of receiving attention, independent of the kind of treatment. This conclusion seems, however, to be rather extreme and warrants some comment. Only Sarno et al's study (1970b) described the patients studied. In the other studies they were generally qualified as being aphasic and their Porch Index of Communicative Ability (Porch, 1967) or Functional Communication Profile (Sarno, 1969) scores (or mean score) were given. Some patients may benefit more from a specifically designed therapy while others, probably the less severely affected, are helped by any verbal intercourse. There are, however, two rather more important objections to the conclusion stated above. In the study of David et al (1982), all but nine patients started therapy less than 2 months after onset, and recovery had nearly reached a plateau by the end of the third month. Spontaneous recovery rather than therapy could well have caused the improvement. For their late group they do not state when they started therapy, only the range (12–125 weeks post-onset) and the median interval (20 weeks). Moreover, they do not say whether these patients were trained by speech therapists or volunteers, making it difficult to draw any conclusions about these nine patients.

The second objection concerns the duration of therapy. In one study the patients received 8 weeks (Lincoln et al, 1982) and in another 30 therapy sessions over a period of 15–20 weeks (David et al, 1982). As can be inferred from the data in the literature, these periods are probably too short to show any effects of therapy. Vignolo (1964) also compared patients treated with a minimum of 20 therapy sessions with untreated patients, and did not find any difference in the outcome. A comparison between patients re-educated for more than 6 months and untreated patients showed a much higher frequency of improvement in the re-educated group. Sarno & Levita (1981) systematically studied seven global aphasics, still classified as global 3 months post-onset. The study patients received intensive speech therapy for 1 year. The authors note that the most dramatic improvement took place during the last 6 months. Marshall et al (1982) investigated the effects of selected prognostic factors, including the number of treatment sessions, on improvement in aphasic patients. Unfortunately the impact of the investigation is diminished by the absence of some crucial details regarding the experimental design (e.g., on what basis the patients were treated for different lengths of time and to what extent factors found to affect the prognosis were interrelated). Nevertheless, the results of the step-wise regression analysis are impressive because the number of treatment sessions is the main explaining variable within a model that comprises the whole set of candidate factors.

In a retrospective study (Basso & Capitani, unpublished data) we investigated the effect of length of treatment on improvement of oral comprehension and expression. From the patients examined at the Aphasia Unit in Milan from 1962 to 1975, we studied 174 patients who fulfilled the following criteria: they were right-handed, had finished at least primary school, had left hemisphere lesions, and had had at least two complete aphasia examinations, the first having been given at least 2 months post-onset. Etiology was vascular for 87%, traumatic for 11%, and 2% had tumors, without any difference between the groups. We considered two factors: (1) presence or absence of, and (2) duration of, aphasia therapy. For the definition of improvement and severity of aphasia see Basso et al (1979). Separate analyses for expression and comprehension were carried out. The analysis of expression yielded a $\chi^2$=17.239, with 2 df, $p$<0.001. Partitioning the degrees of freedom, comparison of the non-rehabilitated with the two groups of rehabilitated patients yielded a $\chi^2$=11.073, with 1 df, $p$<0.001. Comparison between the two groups of patients rehabilitated for different periods yielded a $\chi^2$=6.166, with df, $p$=0.013. Length of rehabilitation had a significant effect on improvement of expression. This result cannot be traced back to any differences in initial severity of aphasia in the two groups (9 of 21 patients were classified as severe among patients rehabilitated for less than 3 months, and 30 of 58 patients rehabilitated for more than 6 months), the $\chi^2$ being =0.169, with 1 df, $p$=ns. Rehabilitated patients generally had their second examination just after therapy was discontinued; the time interval for the two groups of rehabilitated patients is thus different, being longer for patients rehabilitated for 6 months. Nevertheless, we do not think that this biased the results because even patients rehabilitated for only 3 months had had their second examination at least 5 months post-onset, when spontaneous recovery is unlikely to occur in such a way that their performance would have improved had they been examined again 3 months later. Data for comprehension yield a different result. Patients scoring 3 or 4 in comprehension on first examination were excluded from the study (Basso et al, 1979). The general $\chi^2$ was =6.752, with 2 df, $p$=0.034. Partitioning the degrees of freedom, comparison of non-rehabilitated with rehabilitated patients yielded a $\chi^2$=6.587, with 1 df, $p$=0.010, and comparison of patients rehabilitated for different lengths of time yielded a $\chi^2$=0.165, with 1 df, $p$=ns. Forty-one per cent of patients rehabilitated for 3 months or less and 53% of patients rehabilitated for more than 6 months had been classified as severe on first examination. From this analysis it can be concluded that rehabilitation of 3 or 6 months' length has significantly different effects on improvement of expression but not of comprehension. Other studies have confirmed that comprehension recovers more quickly and to a greater extent than expression in non-re-educated patients, too, although it only exceptionally reaches the premorbid level. It is certainly possible that specific rehabilitation aimed at the most subtle aspects of comprehension is necessary for maximal recovery. However, no such therapy has as yet been described. In conclusion, the evidence from those studies that have compared different therapeutic techniques (Meikle et al, 1979; Wertz et al, 1981; David et al, 1982; Lincoln et al, 1982; Marshall et al, 1982) is not conclusive because all the patients were re-educated for too short periods. The factors that influence outcome of aphasia therapy can be recapitulated by sketching the ideal patient. This would be a young left-handed woman in good general health apart from a moderate traumatic aphasia that occurred only a short time before, and who will undergo a long period of aphasia rehabilitation.

As for the negative factors, the influence of no single factor can negatively influence recovery that can not be counterbalanced by the positive effects of rehabilitation. Only a combination of several factors would justify excluding a patient from aphasia therapy.

## PATTERN OF RECOVERY

Another important aspect of recovery that has been studied with groups of treated and untreated patients is the pattern of recovery itself. Recoveries of the different language modalities (particularly expression and comprehension) have been investigated separately and the percentages of patients improved in one or the other have been compared. Results of the various investigations (Kenin & Swisher, 1972; Kertesz & McCabe, 1977; Hanson & Cicciarelli, 1978; Lomas & Kertesz, 1978; Prins et al, 1978) concur fairly well. There is a certain degree of recovery, and comprehension recovers more quickly and more completely than expression.

These studies, however, are only concerned with groups of patients, and one is left wondering how and why and in what areas improvement comes about in a single patient. In a recent study (Basso et al, 1982b), we addressed ourselves to the question of whether improvement in one language modality is associated with a higher probability of improvement in another. In 388 aphasics we studied the relationship in individual patients between improvement in oral and written expression and comprehension. One hundred and thirty-eight patients had not been treated, and 250 had been rehabilitated for at least 6 months. Aphasia therapy emphasized oral language most, and within oral language, comprehension more than production. Improvements of all pairs of modalities were found to be significantly associated in rehabilitated patients. In non-rehabilitated patients, improvement of oral comprehension was not significantly associated with improvement of any of the other three modalities. When we considered, however, the percentage of patients in the two groups improved in each modality, there were no differences in the recovery patterns of rehabilitated and non-rehabilitated patients: comprehension improved more than expression and oral language improved more than written language. The reason for the lack of agreement in the non-rehabilitated group between improvement of oral comprehension and of the other verbal behaviors studied seems to be that too many non-rehabilitated patients recovered only in oral comprehension. Comprehension seems to be easier than expression and improves even without specific treatment; one reason for this is that the aphasic patient, unless so severely affected as not to understand anything, is more frequently stimulated in everyday life to understand than to express himself. Be this as it may there is now evidence that comprehension improves more and with greater speed than any other verbal behavior, in both treated and untreated patients. For expression, things are different: patients need to be re-educated to demonstrate improvement in many subjects. Spontaneous recovery of expression seems to be rather aleatory.

The main result of this study is that language therapy centered on oral rather than written language brought about uniform improvement in written as well as oral verbal behaviors. Thus it seems partly justified for aphasia therapy, to deal globally with the aphasic impairment, rather than specifically. Only when the underlying linguistic structures presumed to be involved in both comprehension and production, as well as in both the auditory-verbal and visual channels, are intact is it justifiable to re-educate all the impaired verbal behaviors separately. Yet, even with a unique underlying central language deficit, the deficit will not manifest itself in exactly the same way in different modalities, as each modality has its own distinct characteristics and the processes involved in understanding and speaking are dissimilar. According to Caramazza et al (1981), a deficit of the auditory-verbal STM, for instance, could explain asyntactic comprehension co-occurring with normal syntactic production, because comprehension but not production of sentences requires the storing of parts of the sentence in the working memory, while syntactic and semantic analyses are performed.

## DYSARTHRIAS

A motor disorder resulting from a central and/or peripheral nervous system lesion that causes weakness, paralysis, incoordination or alterations in tone of the speech musculature gives rise to dysarthria. The term dysarthria does not designate a unitary deficit; neurologists and speech pathologists use it as a collective name and recognize different forms of dysarthria, each with its specific characteristics. The deficit is not exclusively articulatory; all processes of motor speech are involved. Impairment of the articulatory system is, however, probably responsible for the most prominent acoustic features that affect intelligibility of speech, but deficits of respiration, phonation, and resonation can all be present and contribute to the characteristics of the speech of the dysarthric patient.

Lesions that cause dysarthria affect the control of the vocal tract muscles for all gestures – voluntary or involuntary, articulatory or otherwise – in a generally uniform way. For speech, the deficit concerns exclusively the realization or actualization of the phonological component of language; the dysarthric patient cannot properly move the vocal tract muscles and will thus produce distorted consonants and vowels, sometimes atypical of his native language. Darley et al (1969a,b, 1975) describe six types of dysarthria which differ in site of the lesion (lower motor neuron, upper motor neuron, cerebellar or extrapyramidal lesion) and in the particular grouping of disorders according to the 38 factors considered, including respiration, phonation, resonation, articulation, and prosody. These types will be briefly outlined below. In '*spastic*' dysarthria there is a diffuse reduction, weakening or loss of motor speech movement activity; speech is usually slow with short utterances. Articulation is very imprecise, pitch is low, and the voice harsh and strained-strangled. *Hyperkinetic* dysarthria is well exemplified in Huntington's chorea; movements are irregular, random, unpatterned, and rapid. Respiration, phonation, and articulation are often involved, producing many speech difficulties. Highly variable patterns of articulation, sudden variations in loudness, and rhythmic hypernasality are the most distinctive speech deviations in hyperkinetic dysarthria. Parkinson's disease causes *hypokinetic* dysarthria marked by slowness of articulatory movements, accompanied by limitations in range, direction, and force of muscular contraction. There is monopitch and monoloudness and a cluster of prosodic insufficiencies. Errors in timing, speed, range, and force of vocal tract muscles which result in dysrhythmia of speech, syllable repetition, phoneme and interval prolongation, and a slow rate are peculiar to '*ataxic*' dysarthria speech. The most common speech difficulties in '*flaccid*' dysarthria are marked hypernasality, imprecise consonant production, breathy voice, and audible inspiration. Finally, '*mixed*' dysarthrias occur when there is impairment of two neurologic levels, as in amyotrophic lateral sclerosis, which results in a spastic and flaccid mixed dysarthria.

Diagnosis of dysarthria can be made on medical grounds which identify the cause of the deficit (e.g., Parkinson's disease, multiple sclerosis). Examination of the structure of the motor speech mechanism is, however, an important part of the speech-language diagnostic process. Diagnosis should lead to the recommendation of specific procedures for speech rehabilitation. The clinical examination of the motor speech mechanism must be systematic, accurate, and thorough. Respiration, phonation, resonation, articulation, and prosody must be evaluated separately, by specific tests, by a trained speech pathologist (Dworkin, 1978). Acoustic analysis is also possible, and probably more accurate and consistent than perceptual evaluation; however, instrumentation is required to obtain a visual representation of the speech signals and this instrumentation is not always available.

Many of the causes of dysarthria are not static and there is no starting point from which to predict the future. Prognosis, for all that it takes into account the cause of the disease, is generally tentative and cannot be very exact. Some prognostic signs are influenced by the patient's speech and speech-related symptoms. If primary functions (breathing, for instance, or swallowing) are impaired, the prognosis is poor; the same is true if the dysarthria is severe. A patient who can use the therapeutic techniques outside the hospital has a better prognosis than a patient incapable of doing so. In any case, prognosis for improvement in speech symptoms in dysarthria is generally bleak.

Dysarthria therapy can be approached from three different points of view. First, although medical care of the basic disorder cannot consistently reduce the motor speech impairment, it can keep the level from deteriorating. Second, prosthetic and surgical management is sometimes advisable, such as a palatal-lift prosthesis for velopharyngeal incompetency, thus reducing hypernasality and improving intelligibility. Finally there is the therapeutic approach of the speech pathologist, which is behavioral but utilizes some instrumental aids when available. Only extremely rarely does dysarthria disappear and dysarthria therapy is symptomatic, supportive (having the patient perform as well as possible at his present level), and compensatory. Some general rules must not be forgotten when caring for the dysarthric patient: reasons for his speech errors must always be given to the patient, who must train his ear to control his output if what has been drilled into him in the clinical setting is to be used outside, and he must be made aware of the results. For a detailed description of treatment for dysarthria see Rosenbeck & La Pointe (1978). One of the goals of dysarthria therapy is to improve articulation. The reason for articulation errors (e.g., weakness or incoordination of articulatory muscles) must first be determined and then carefully constructed hierarchies of exercises must be given starting with those sounds that are sometimes correct and ending with those most seriously involved. The length and complexity of the utterance can then be increased and prosody also taken into account. The patient should be asked to produce the same short sentence in response to the speech pathologist's questions, in such a way that he has to stress different parts of the sentence according to the question asked ('Who went to Glasgow?' '*John* went to Glasgow'. 'Where did John go?' 'John went to *Glasgow*').

Respiration, phonation, and resonance are all involved in the speech motor act and improvement of any of these would make speech more intelligible. Reduction of hypernasality is generally obtained, improving resonance. For example, this can be achieved by asking the patient to produce oral and nasal sounds alternately (/pa-ma-pa-ma/)and strengthening the palatin vault with exercises such as sucking and blowing. Laryngeal valve exercises (for instance, production of /i-i-i/ or rapid pitch changes) improve phonation. When respiration is inadequate, muscles must be strengthened (possibly with the help of the physical therapist) and the patient taught to make the best use of his respiration. Exercises which have proved useful include blowing up balloons, counting aloud during expiration, or increasing loudness rapidly and dramatically. Sometimes respiration is adequate for speech but air is wasted by an inefficient valve at some point in the vocal tract. Valve exercises (/ta-ta-ta/ for linguoalveolar valves, /pa-pa-pa/ for bilabial valves, for example) can thus be appropriate.

In recent years speech pathologists have shown an increasing interest in dysarthria. Yet rehabilitation problems have been the last to be dealt with, much as in the field of aphasia. On the basis of these more comprehensive and exhaustive analyses of the dysarthrias, however, therapy has become more detailed and more appropriately planned for the specific patient. How successful dysarthria therapy will be is difficult to determine, mainly because of the often degenerative nature of the primary deficit. The hope is that many more patients will undergo rehabilitation and thus gain better intelligibility and maintain it longer.

## CONCLUDING REMARKS

The aim of this chapter was not to exhaustively describe any specific therapeutic approaches but to present a critical analysis of the state-of-the-art in aphasia rehabilitation. The more widely-used approaches to the aphasic patient have been delineated. At the moment it is not possible to tell whether any of these are more effective than the others. However, they need not be alternative and could be profitably combined. A therapeutic program based on a sound psycholinguistic analysis which might identify the primary deficit, a program that would not ignore the basic principles of the classic approach and that would be rigorously applied, would combine the advantages of the different approaches.

Ideas about the treatment of aphasia abound. What I feel is needed for language rehabilitation to progress is to structure more closely the various techniques and relate scattered thoughts on intervention to each other and make them more accessible to everybody. Yet, even detailed handbooks on aphasia rehabilitation will always lack an important aspect of aphasia therapy, which is in part a creative act. Each patient brings to rehabilitation his individual problems and characteristics. Two patients can present nearly the same language disorder, but one lives alone and the other with a supportive family: their premorbid usage of language and their jobs are different; one is able to accept his new condition and speech therapy, and the other is not, and defends himself against anxiety by refusing speech therapy and denying his problems. Language therapy must be different for these two cases, even when the language deficits are similar.

Language intervention is a complex, flexible, dynamic process that can lose its efficacy if it is excessively stereotyped. More dangerous, however, is the opposite position; aphasia therapy is not a continuous and total invention.

> There are now substantial data to guide us in our efforts to improve the patient's comprehension and language output .... We know that there are systematic things we can do in a carefully programmed, graduated manner that lead him comfortably from success to success. And we know that there are better and worse ways to go about it (Darley, 1982, p. 69).

Most important of all, language rehabilitation does not any longer need to demonstrate its usefulness. To quote Darley (1982, p. 57) again:

> No single study has proved to be so comprehensive and so rigorously designed and executed as to provide by itself one unequivocal answer to questions about efficacy of aphasia treatment. But the studies taken together provide a series of answers and satisfactorily lay to rest our doubts about the efficacy of therapy.

The effects of single factors on recovery of individual patients must be better understood. Much still needs to be done in the realms of recovery and rehabilitation in aphasia, but much has been done already and we can confidently draw some conclusions. Aphasia therapy is effective if protracted for a long enough period of time. Not all rehabilitated aphasic patients improve but as yet no one factor has been proved to completely prevent recovery; only a combination of factors negatively influencing recovery would probably have such an effect.

Many different therapeutic approaches that overlap only in part are currently employed in aphasia therapy. Whichever approach one chooses, we should always remember that we are trying to help the aphasic patient to communicate better; not only to speak but also to understand what people tell him and to say something not already known to the hearer.

## REFERENCES

Basso A, Faglioni P, Vignolo L A 1975 Etude controlée de la rééducation du langage dans l'aphasie: comparaison entre aphasiques traités et non-traités. Revue Neurologique 131: 607–614

Basso A, Capitani E, Vignolo L A 1979 Influence of rehabilitation on language skills in aphasic patients. A controlled study. Archives of Neurology 36: 190–196

Basso A, Capitani E, Moraschini S 1982a Sex differences in recovery from aphasia. Cortex 18: 469–475

Basso A, Capitani E, Zanobio M E 1982b Pattern of recovery of oral and written expression and comprehension in aphasic patients. Behavioural Brain Research 6: 115–128

Berndt R S, Caramazza A 1981 Syntactic aspects of aphasia. In: Sarno M T (ed) Acquired aphasia. Academic Press, New York

Brookshire R 1969 Probability learning by aphasic subjects. Journal of Speech and Hearing Research 12: 857–864

Butfield E, Zangwill O L 1946 Re-education in aphasia: a review of 70 cases. Journal of Neurology, Neurosurgery and Psychiatry 9: 75–79

Caramazza A, Basili A G, Koller J J, Berndt R S 1981 An investigation of repetition of language processing in a case of conduction aphasia. Brain and Language 14: 235–271

Chapey R 1981 Language intervention strategies in adult aphasia. Williams & Wilkins, Baltimore

Chomsky N 1965 Aspects of the theory of syntax. MIT Press, Cambridge

Culton G L 1969 Spontaneous recovery from aphasia. Journal of Speech and Hearing Research 12: 825–832

Culton G L 1971 Reaction to age as a factor in chronic aphasia in stroke patients. Journal of Speech and Hearing Disorders 36: 563–564

Darley F L 1975 Treatment of acquired aphasia. In: Friedlander W J (ed) Advances in neurology, vol. 7. Raven, New York

Darley F L 1982 The treatment of aphasia. In: de Montfort Supple M (ed) Language disability – congenital and acquired. Boole Press, Dublin

Darley F L, Aronson A E, Brown J R 1969a Differential diagnostic patterns of dysarthria. Journal of Speech and Hearing Research 12: 246–269

Darley F L, Aronson A E, Brown J R 1969b Clusters of deviant speech dimensions in the dysarthrias. Journal of Speech and Hearing Research 12: 462–496

Darley F L, Aronson A E, Brown J R 1975 Motor speech disorders. Saunders, Philadelphia

David R. Enderby P, Bainton D 1982 Treatment of acquired aphasia: speech therapists and volunteers compared. Journal of Neurology, Neurosurgery and Psychiatry 45: 957–961

Dworkin J P 1978 Differential diagnosis of motor speech disorders: the clinical examination of the speech mechanism. Journal of National Student Speech and Hearing Association: 37–62

Gainotti G 1976 The relationship between semantic impairment in comprehension and naming in aphasic patients. British Journal of Disorders of Communication 11: 57–61

Goldfarb R 1981 Operant conditioning and programmed instruction in aphasia rehabilitation. In: Chapey R (ed) Language intervention strategies in adult aphasia. Williams & Wilkins, Baltimore

Hagen C 1973 Communication abilities in hemiplegia: effect of speech therapy. Archives of Physical Medicine and Rehabilitation 54: 454–463

Hanson W R, Cicciarelli A W 1978 The time, amount and pattern of language improvement in adult aphasics. British Journal of Disorders of Communication 13: 59–63

Holland A 1970 Case studies in aphasia rehabilitation using programmed instruction. Journal of Speech and Hearing Research 35: 377–390

Holland A, Harris B 1968 Aphasia rehabilitation using programmed instruction: an intensive case history. In: Sloane H, MacAuley B (eds) Operant procedures in remedial speech and language training. Houghton Mifflin, Boston

Holland A, Sonderman J 1974 Effect of a program based on the Token Test for teaching comprehension skills to aphasic. Journal of Speech and Hearing Research 17: 589–598

Jackson J H 1958 Selected writings of John Hughlings Jackson. Basic Books, New York

Jakobson R 1964 Towards a linguistic typology of aphasic impairments. In: de Reuck A V S, O'Connor M (eds) Disorders of language. Churchill, London

Kadzielawa D, Dabrowska A, Nowakowska M T, Seniow J 1981 Literal and conveyed meaning as interpreted by aphasics and non-aphasics. Polish Psychological Bulletin 12: 57–62

Keenan J, Brassell E 1974 A study of factors related to prognosis for individual aphasic patients. Journal of Speech and Hearing Disorders 39: 257–269

Kenin M, Swisher L P 1972 A study of pattern of recovery in aphasia. Cortex 8, 56–68

Kertesz A, McCabe P 1977 Recovery patterns and prognosis in aphasia. Brain 100: 1–18

Kohlmeyer K 1976 Aphasia due to focal disorders of cerebral circulation: some aspects of localization and of spontaneous recovery. In: Lebrun Y, Hoops R (eds) Recovery in aphasics. Swets & Zeitlinger, Amsterdam

Levita E 1978 Effects of speech therapy on aphasics' responses to the Functional Communication Profile. Perceptual and Motor Skills 47: 151–154

Lincoln N B, Pickersgill M J, Hankey A I, Hilton C R 1982 An evaluation of operant training and speech therapy in the language rehabilitation of moderate aphasics. Behavioural Psychotherapy 10: 162–178

Lomas J, Kertesz A 1978 Patterns of spontaneous recovery in aphasic groups: a study of adult stroke patients. Brain and Language 5: 388–401

Luria A R 1970 Traumatic aphasia. Mouton, Le Hague

Luria A R 1973 The working brain, an introduction to neuropsychology. Penguin, Harmondsworth

Marks M, Taylor M L, Rusk H A 1957 Rehabilitation of the aphasic patient: a survey of three years experience in a rehabilitation setting. Neurology 7: 837–843

Marshall R C, Tompkins C A, Phillips D S 1982 Improvement in treated aphasia: examination of selected prognostic factors. Folia Phoniatrica 34: 305–315

McGlone J 1980 Sex differences in human brain asymmetry: a critical review. Behavioural and Brain Sciences 3: 215–263

Meikle M, Wechsler E, Tupper A M, Benenson M, Butler J, Mulhall D, Stern G 1979 Comparative trial of volunteer and professional treatments of dysphasia after stroke. British Medical Journal 2: 87–89

Messerli P, Tissot R, Rodriguez J 1976 Recovery from aphasia: some factors of prognosis. In: Lebrun Y, Hoops R (eds) Recovery in aphasics. Swets & Zeitlinger, Amsterdam

Pizzamiglio L, Mammucari A, Razzano C 1985 Evidence for sex differences in brain organization from recovery in aphasia. Brain and Language 25: 213–222

Porch B E 1967 The Porch Index of Communicative Ability. Consulting Psychologists Press, Palo Alto

Prins R S, Snow C E, Wagenaar E 1978 Recovery from aphasia: spontaneous speech versus language comprehension. Brain and Language 6: 192–211

Rosenbeck J C, La Pointe L L 1978 The dysarthrias: description, diagnosis and treatment. In: Johns D F (ed) Clinical management of neurogenic communicative disorders. Little, Brown, Boston

Sands E, Sarno M T, Shankweiler D 1969 Long-term assessment of language function in aphasia due to stroke. Archives of Physical Medicine and Rehabilitation 50: 203–207

Sarno M T 1969 The functional communication profile: manual of directions. Institute of Rehabilitation Medicine, New York University Medical Center, New York

Sarno M T 1980 Language rehabilitation outcome in the elderly aphasic patient. In: Obler L K, Albert M L (eds) Language and communication in the elderly: clinical, therapeutic and experimental issues. D C Heath, Lexington

Sarno M T 1981 Acquired aphasia. Academic Press, New York

Sarno M T, Levita E 1971 Natural course of recovery in severe aphasia. Archives of Physical Medicine and Rehabilitation 52: 175–179

Sarno M T, Levita E 1981 Some observations on the nature of recovery in global aphasia. Brain and Language 13: 1–12

Sarno M T, Silverman M, Levita E 1970a Psychosocial factors and recovery in geriatric patients with severe aphasia. Journal of the American Geriatrics Society 18: 405–409

Sarno M T, Silverman M, Sands E 1970b Speech therapy and language recovery in severe aphasia. Journal of Speech and Hearing Research 13: 607–623

Schuell H, Jenkins J, Jiménez-Pabòn E 1964 Aphasia in adults. Harper, New York

Seron X 1979 Aphasie et neuropsychologie. Pierre Mardaga, Bruxelles

Skinner B F 1972 Cumulative records: a selection of papers. Appleton-Century-Crofts, New York

Smith A 1971 Objective indices of severity of chronic aphasia in stroke patients. Journal of Speech and Hearing Disorders 26: 167–207

Sparks R, Holland A 1976 Method: melodic intonation therapy for aphasia. Journal of Speech and Hearing Disorders 41: 287–297

Subirana A 1958 The prognosis in aphasia in relation to the factor of cerebral dominance and handedness. Brain 81: 415–425

Vignolo L A 1964 Evolution of aphasia and language rehabilitation: a retrospective exploratory study. Cortex 1: 344–367

Weigl E 1961 The phenomenon of temporary deblocking in aphasia. Zeitschrift für Phonetik und Kommunikations-forschung 14: 337–364

Weigl E, Bierwisch M 1970 Neuropsychology and linguistics: topics of common research. Foundations of Language 6: 1–18

Weisenburg T, McBride K 1935 Aphasia: a clinical and psychological study. Commonwealth Fund, New York (2 edn, 1964, Hafner, New York)

Wepman J 1951 Recovery from aphasia. Ronald, New York

Wepman J, Jones L V 1964 Five aphasias: a commentary on aphasia as a regressive linguistic phenomenon. In: Rioch D, Weinstein E A (eds) Disorders of communication. Williams & Wilkins, Baltimore

Wertz R T, Collins M J, Weiss D, Kurtzke J F et al 1981 Veterans administration cooperative study on aphasia: a comparison of individual and group treatment. Journal of Speech and Hearing Research 24: 580–595

Wilcox M J, Davis G A, Leonard L B 1978 Aphasics' comprehension of contextually conveyed meaning. Brain and Language 6: 362–377

*Harold Goodglass*

# Neurolinguistic principles and aphasia therapy

## INTRODUCTION

It is axiomatic in the rehabilitation of a functional deficit that prerequisites for treatment lie in a sound understanding of the processes at work in normal performance and in an analysis of the patient's deficit and residual ability. If we take sensory deficits, such as deafness, as an example the application of this axiom is very transparent. In the absence of auditory input it is necessary to develop another sensory channel capable of processing information about the speaker's production. With training, the deaf speaker may become sufficiently adept at rapidly processing the subtle cues from lip reading gained through an intact visual channel to make him a functional communicator.

The assumption in this model is that, with sufficient repeated practice, it is possible either to restore functional efficiency to the defective capacity or bring an alternative route to a level of voluntary and eventual automatic skill. The strengthening of an impaired function is exemplified by the determination of which muscles have been weakened by disease or disuse, and design exercises to progressively build up the strength of the target muscle. The chief practical task of the therapist is to devise the most efficient teaching strategy for building up skill, either in the weakened function or in the new, substitute operation.

With some important exceptions, most approaches to the rehabilitation of neuropsychological deficit, including language retraining in aphasia, follow one of these two models, which will be referred to as the substitute skill model and the direct treatment model. I propose to consider the reasons for the successes and failures of these approaches, as well as of alternative approaches, in the light of theoretical analyses of language processes.

## ASSUMPTIONS UNDERLYING THE DIRECT TREATMENT AND THE SUBSTITUTE SKILL MODEL IN NEUROPSYCHOLOGY

There are at least two major assumptions in these two approaches to retraining. One is that the impairment involves only the instrumentalities by which a central cognitive capacity is accessed or by which it gains expression. The second is that once we have identified an alternative mode of producing the desired result, it takes only practice to bring it to voluntary control and eventual functional skill. In the case of aphasia there are instances in which the first assumption appears justified; others in which it may be questioned or rejected.

Examples of positive instances are those forms of aphasia in which language comprehension is demonstrably preserved, via the auditory or the graphic modality or both, and in which the major impairment is in motor articulatory control or in impaired auditory but not reading comprehension. In such cases it is clear from the patient's spared linguistic abilities that the basic capacity to attach meaning to language symbols and to interpret syntactic relationships between lexical elements is preserved. A range of techniques for approaching articulatory problems is within the repertory of speech pathologists. They may involve the use of voluntary strategies, such as self-cuing with familiar segments already under voluntary control, the use of auxiliary sensory channels (e.g., a mirror) to enhance impaired sensory-motor control, and imitation of the examiner. In the case of impaired auditory language comprehension, an effort is generally made to increase the patient's function in this area by direct attack, i.e., by exercises in listening to words and sentences. Profound difficulty, as in pure word deafness, may lead to the decision to test the facilitating value of lip reading or abandon formal efforts to regain comprehension of speech and have the patient solicit written communication from others.

The foregoing illustrate only a few of the applications of a direct attack and of substitute skills in language output or input channels. Even in these few instances it is evident that the therapist has a wide scope of possibilities for devising strategies for cuing, for testing the patient's ability to develop voluntary control and eventual automatization of substitute skills, and for devising means of grading the difficulty of retraining exercises by initially providing contextual support, then withdrawing it. The details of these teaching strategies constitute a part of the repertory of the skills of the language therapist. They are both empirical and derived from well-known learning principles, including applications of shaping techniques and programmed teaching, as developed by Skinner and his students (Holland, 1970; see also Chapter 7 by Seron, in this volume.) A detailed diagnostic study of the patient's deficits and residual capacities must precede a rational choice of a retraining program.

The relevance of retraining focused on exercising reduced functions or substituting for a deficient language skill comes into question when we are faced with disorders at a more central conceptual level and with the problem of impaired initiation. Among these problems are:

1. Profound impairment in word retrieval and in language comprehension via both speech and writing, as seen in global aphasia and in severe Wernicke's aphasia.
2. Profound anomia, manifested by the inability to retrieve vocabulary items

in speech or writing or to retain them more than momentarily when they are provided by the therapist.

3. Severe agrammatism, manifested by the loss of capacity to enter lexical items into syntactic frames or to use grammatical morphemes.
4. Severe impairment in initiating or formulating an utterance, as seen in transcortical motor aphasia, where repetition may be intact as to both articulation and syntax and when short factual responses may be elicited by highly structured questions.
5. Severe alexia in which written symbols have lost all significance.

It is around these symptoms that the major unresolved theoretical questions remain in aphasia – questions which bear on the nature of language, its organization, and its cerebral representation.

Even at the level of gross clinical observation, however, there are a number of features which have influenced thinking about the nature of language therapy. One of these is the fact that, although a patient may initially be profoundly impaired in all language functions, spontaneous recovery follows the path of a return of old knowledge and in no way resembles the relearning of a child. This is true also for protracted recovery, in which articulatory, syntactic, and word retrieval functions return slowly over a year or more.

Alongside this observation is the one that some patients respond with a remarkable improvement both in comprehension and speech output when engaged in a topic of strong emotional value to them – their children, their hobby, or their favorite sports. These have led some therapists to view their role primarily as catalysts to facilitate the reawakening of latent language knowledge. This position was developed explicitly by Wepman (Wepman & Jones, 1966; Wepman & Morency, 1963) with the three key words 'stimulation, facilitation, and motivation.' Wepman's view was that the complex integrative activity of the brain in recovering language is not under the control of the therapist, and that the best therapeutic results were obtained when the therapist assisted the patients to converse, write, and read in totally free improvisation, on topics which engaged their interest. This position is particularly striking when one recalls that Wepman was a pioneer in the psycholinguistic analysis of aphasia, and in the application of these psycholinguistic principles to evaluation and classification. He represents, to an extreme degree, the dissociation between psycholinguistic research and therapeutic applications. While Wepman's positions may appear somewhat rejecting toward systematic intervention, a similar note is detected in Lesser's (1978) careful review of psycholinguistic research in aphasia. Lesser points out that the applications of this research have had their major impact on diagnosis and classification, while provision of answers for the daily work of the language therapists has been extremely limited and disappointing.

In considering the problems in moving from theory and research to therapeutic application let us return to the list of 'central' cognitive operations which may be affected in aphasia.

## Global impairment in communication through natural language

While some writers (e.g., Finkelnberg, 1870; Head, 1926; Bay, 1962) see all forms of aphasia as representing an impairment in symbolic capacity, it is hard for anyone to escape this interpretation in the face of global aphasics, who represent the largest single diagnostic subgroup. The same applies in the case of severe Wernicke's aphasics who are left with phonologically intact output and relatively well-preserved syntactic forms, but who neither receive nor convey information through language. Since the attachment of meaning to spoken or written symbols is the major component of natural language, a severe impairment in this capacity poses a special challenge for rehabilitation. Persistent efforts to re-educate global aphasics by conventional methods have produced disappointing results (Sarno et al, 1970).

These cases illustrate most forcefully the role of the assumption pointed out earlier, as underlying the direct attack and the substitute skills models of rehabilitation. This is the assumption that there remains intact a central capacity to process linguistically encoded information in some form and to originate a linguistically encoded output of some form. A number of researchers have risen to the challenge of dealing with the deficit in this capacity, modeling their approaches on work done with primates, who also appear to have rudimentary symbol-forming capacity (Premack, 1971; Savage-Rumbaugh, 1981). These will be discussed below.

## Anomia

The process by which the phonological form of a word is recovered for production has been resistant to direct attack, although the clinical varieties of word-finding failure suggest that the breakdown may occur at different stages of an unfolding process (Goodglass, 1980). For example, Whitehouse et al (1978) report that the conceptual representation of the word itself may be impaired in anomic patients. Kohn (1984) has presented evidence that in conduction aphasia, the phonological representation may be partly or wholly accessed, but that this representation does not adequately control the speech output mechanism. As in other forms of aphasic difficulty, these defective processes may partially reconstitute themselves with time and practice, but the means of reconstructing alternative channels or hastening the process of recovery are still obscure.

## Agrammatism

While the clinical manifestations of agrammatism are well known in the Western languages, the underlying deficit has been a topic of great controversy in the recent neurolinguistic literature. Some writers view it as a disorder defined in terms of omissions of morphological forms and simplifications of grammatical structure in speech production. Others view it as an underlying impairment of the representation of syntactic knowledge in all modalities of language. These alternative views are well represented in the new volume by Kean (1985). Since at least reduction of symptoms can be achieved by practice of specific sentence patterns (Beyn & Shokhor-Trotskaya, 1966) some therapeutic efforts are possible without solution of the underlying theoretical problem.

### Initiation

One of the most intractable problems following head trauma involving the frontal lobes is the patients' loss of initiative to carry out the most mundane of plans, though these may be verbalized quite convincingly. An analogous deficit, specific to language, is seen in a subgroup of aphasic patients who have transcortical motor (dynamic) aphasia. In fact, some of these individuals show no linguistic disturbance at all, except for their inability to initiate an utterance (Von Stockert, 1974). More commonly, the difficulty in initiation is compounded by inability to formulate an idea, and is dramatized by the patients' superb repetition and ability to name and to supply short factual answers to specific questions. Here again is an aspect of language which seems to defy treatment by either the direct or substitute skills model. At least, the therapist may seek to manipulate the environment to provide the external structure on which the patient has become totally dependent.

## CURRENT APPROACHES

Perhaps the most articulated and reasoned presentation of the substitute skills model is that of Luria (1970), which is summarized by Basso in Chapter 14 of this volume. Luria, in fact, proposes techniques for dealing not only with disorders of such instrumentalities as articulation, but with impairments of central cognitive processes such as syntactic production and comprehension, anomia, and loss of speech formulation ability in dynamic aphasia. The only problem which he does not touch upon is global aphasia. Luria's illustrations of step-by-step attacks on each of the problems cited earlier as intractable, convey a boundless optimism in the capacity of the aphasic patient to carry out, with the therapist's aid, a conscious analysis of speech and thought processes, and to bring under his voluntary control the capacity to call on his preserved abilities as self-cuing devices. The step-by-step reconstruction of a functional language operation which he proposes is in direct contrast with Wepman's conclusion that such analytically grounded therapy is of dubious value. A few illustrations of Luria's approach will illustrate the rationale involved, and the relation of the therapeutic method to the therapist's model of the disorder.

A patient suffering from severe agrammatism enters a therapeutic program. As viewed by Luria, his disorder takes the form of restriction of speech to single uninflected nouns and verbs, and results from a total inability to deal with predication in the expressive language. Luria proposed to build on the patient's preserved syntactic comprehension, holding that 'As a rule, patients in this group are able to comprehend relatively complex logico-grammatical relationships.'

The first step in therapy was to substitute external frameworks of subject–verb–object relationships, by pictures, to take the place of 'missing inner dynamic schemata.' By requiring the patient to write the word for each object or person and for each action depicted, the therapist made him aware of the incompleteness of his own holophrastic utterances and led him to appreciate the value of complete sentences. With practice, the patient reached the stage where he could compose sentences containing noun, verb, and noun, but no grammatical morphemes; i.e., he spoke telegraphically.

The next stage of training involved specific instructions as to the function of locative prepositions, with the aid of diagrams. When this had been mastered, the more subtle problem of sensitizing him to the significance of case endings and verb inflections was undertaken, again with the aid of concrete diagrams and instruction in sentence analysis. At each stage the patient was initially dependent on the pictures and diagrams, but eventually internalized the depicted relationships.

An interesting 'preventive' approach to anticipate and avoid the emergence of an agrammatic speech pattern in Broca's aphasics was described by two of Luria's collaborators, Beyn & Shokhor-Trotskaya (1966). Their method is solidly grounded in Luria's theoretical view of agrammatism, i.e., that it represents a recourse to almost exclusively nominative use of nouns because of the inability to deal with predication.

These authors essentially excluded all use of nouns in the early stages of language therapy, both in their presentations to the patients and in what they permitted the patient to say. Instead, they began with grammatically acceptable one- or two-word sentences consisting of interjections, verbs in the imperative, and adverbs.

As nouns appeared in the patient's speech, they were guided into non-initial positions in the sentence frame where they did not appear as subject, while the use of pronoun subjects was encouraged. The authors report these patients developed better-organized speech than those treated by the conventional means of vocabulary building.

It is interesting to note the congruence of this approach with the views recently presented by Heeschen (1985) and by Kolk (1985). Both of these authors present evidence that agrammatic and telegraphic speech represent strategies adopted by aphasic speakers to compensate for their difficulties in syntax. Their speech pattern is a reflection of an underlying deficit, but not a one-to-one definition of the disorder.

Luria's suggestions for dealing with anomia cite the observation that it is easier to learn a series of words (e.g., bed–blanket–towel–soap–brush) than to retrieve a word individually. Word lists and words learned in sentence frames are proposed as a crutch to assist in word retrieval. This method has also been suggested by Goldstein (1948). Reinforcement of picture-vocabulary drill by writing is also suggested.

Difficult as the problem of lack of speech initiation and formulation may appear, Luria offered suggestions for dealing with these as well. Here, however, his rationale and procedures are rather abstract and unconvincing:

> One approach is to substitute a series of external stimuli to elicit successive steps in thought patterns whose inner dynamic schemata have been disrupted. The patient can learn to apply the stimuli which are initially presented by the therapist. Once he can respond to and communicate with other people, corresponding processes can be transformed into inner mental activity. In other words, through the use of special retraining techniques, we can give the patient the means whereby he can carry through continuous thought processes (1970, p. 453).

Luria's case illustration is of a patient with dynamic aphasia following injury in the left cerebral parasagittal pre-motor area. The extended spontaneous explanation by the patient of his subjective difficulty, however, marks him as a relatively mild and atypical candidate. His difficulties in organizing a narrative were treated by giving him lists of phrases, representing elements of a narrative, which he was required to place in proper sequence and then organize into a connected story. Elsewhere, Luria has reported that the initiation problems of dynamic aphasics may be aided by motor reinforcement of the speech act, as in pounding on the table.

A reading of Luria's methods suggests that they depend to a high degree on conscious, analytic efforts by the patient and on the belief that external crutches in the form of pictures and diagrams of relationships, or retrieval of mnemonic devices, will eventually be internalized and automatized. He qualifies his optimism by stating that not all cases will respond to treatment. In the case of anomia, specifically, he acknowledges that this is a very difficult problem which requires many training sessions before results are apparent. The reader who has struggled for small gains with severely aphasic and cognitively impaired patients may regard Luria's prescriptions as applicable to a small number of ideal subjects. Though this may be the case, Luria's account is the most coherent theoretically based presentation of a rationale for dealing with a wide range of problems in aphasia.

## SUBSTITUTE SYMBOL SYSTEMS

If a patient appears incapable of dealing either expressively or receptively with the words of natural language, as in the case of global aphasia, can he learn to communicate through a substitute symbol system, such as those used in the investigation of the language capacities of the great apes (Premack, 1971; Savage-Rumbaugh, 1981)? Several efforts have been made (Velletri-Glass et al, 1973; Gardner et al, 1976), to teach aphasics a limited set of symbols on cards, which represent people, objects, actions, and prepositions and which may be combined in a simple word-order grammar. These efforts have had limited success, with a limited number of subjects. Some patients simply failed either at the level of learning the symbols or combining them. With those who succeeded, it was not clear whether they ever saw the procedure as more than an exercise with a specific set of possible combinations, but rather as a potentially productive means of communication. Amerind sign language (Skelly et al, 1974) is reported to have had some success with patients who have severe expressive problems.

At the Boston VA Medical Center, Helm-Estabrooks found that some patients who had been through Gardner and Zurif's Visual Communication Program appeared to have acquired a greater readiness to interact, using objects with communicative intent. Her Visual Action Therapy (1982) was introduced as a bridge to prepare severe global aphasics for conventional therapy by beginning with interactive pantomime and then introducing oral language.

Deblocking is a term that was introduced by Weigl (1961) for the temporary facilitation of performance in an impaired modality through production of the same items in a more intact modality. For example a patient who failed almost completely in auditory recognition of a series of object names was allowed to copy the names of those objects in writing. On retesting after copying, he was able to point correctly in response to auditory presentations. A large number of illustrations of these temporary effects, both at the word and the sentence level, are described. Deblocking appears to call on a different mechanism from that which operates in the many varieties of cuing which are familiar to speech pathologists, as it operates through another modality from the one to be deblocked and is effective over a time interval which is considerably longer. Weigl's observations emphasize that there may be considerable latent performance capabilities which are hidden in the usual testing procedures. Deblocking phenomena must be looked for. They are not to be found in every patient, but when they are found, they represent an additional therapeutic device which, in some cases, may be brought under the patient's control.

The common observation that improvement brought about by retraining in one modality may be accompanied by corresponding improvement in untrained skills may be related to the phenomenon of deblocking. This is a promising area for study which has been insufficiently explored.

Melodic Intonation Therapy (MIT) (Sparks et al, 1974) and its variant Melodic Rhythm Therapy (TMR) (Van Eeckhout et al, 1983) are unique, among therapeutic procedures, in that they utilize a device for facilitating speech output whose mechanism is unknown and which is not obviously related to the content of the message. In the MIT method of Sparks et al, the patient is induced to chant a target phrase along with the examiner, to an improvised melody which is created to approximate the normal sentential intonational contour of the phrase. Emphasizing the rhythm, by beating time with the patient's hand, appears to be helpful. In its most dramatic successes this procedure has 'deblocked' voluntary speech production in patients who had plateaued at a point where they could only produce a stereotyped utterance and had failed to benefit from all other efforts to get them to model the production of words or phrases. The patients with the best results were Brocas aphasics with fair to good comprehension. They could be permanently weaned from dependence on melodic facilitation and progressed to a stage of useful telegraphic speech.

The procedure of Van Eeckhout et al is more adapted to French, which does not resemble English in its intonational contour, but can be represented as having two pitch levels, the higher one corresponding to points of stress and rising intonation both within and at the end of sentences. This feature makes TMR for French easy to represent as a visual pattern, which provides another modality of cuing and reinforcement.

The suggestion that MIT mobilizes the right hemisphere to activate the left is based on the simplistic notion that all aspects of musical expression are lateralized in the right hemisphere. It is sufficient to recognize that the organization of musical abilities – whatever their lateral representation – is autonomous from speech. The fact that melody and rhythm may be mobilized to produce dramatic and lasting facilitation of speech production is one of the most important discoveries in aphasia therapeutics and challenges us to understand the mechanism of the linkage.

## APPLICATIONS FROM PSYCHOLINGUISTIC RESEARCH

Psycholinguistic research on the nature of language pathology in aphasia may be classified as bearing on the level of phonology, of lexical semantics and lexical production, of syntax, and of pragmatics. Each of these levels has its receptive and productive aspects and, of course, there are fuzzy boundaries both between levels and between their receptive and productive aspects.

How psycholinguistic principles may be exploited in treatment depends heavily on the theory which is espoused by the therapist. The examples that we had seen of Luria's applications of his theoretical view may be used to illustrate this dependence. Luria is quite explicit in viewing agrammatism as a disorder of language output in which the basic defect is an inability to use the operation of predication, while the ability to name is relatively preserved. Hence, his therapy exploits the supposedly intact ability of the patient to understand syntactic relations and to use this understanding to analyze his intended sentences.

This view is at variance with concepts of agrammatism proposed by other investigators (Kean, 1977; Saffran et al, 1980; Zurif et al, 1972) who have presented data to support the view that agrammatism is a central disorder, affecting the appreciation of syntactic relations in all modalities. Other recent contributors have provided well-studied cases in which syntactic comprehension and written production are intact (Miceli et al, 1983). By now, it appears clear that the concept of agrammatism is sufficiently loose that its specific psycholinguistic manifestations differ from case to case. While the common 'family resemblance' feature of impoverished syntax, short utterances, and the tendency to delete inflections and other grammatical morphemes is always noted, the reduction of this syndrome to a single underlying principle has not succeeded.

The lesson to be derived for therapy is that a psycholinguistically motivated approach requires a case-by-case analysis of the patient's unique pattern of deficits and a custom-designed therapeutic program. Yet it is possible to compromise between this idea and a practice which is more reasonable in terms of expert man-hours, to say nothing of the stress on the patient of probing tests. This compromise entails the treatment of the most apparent deficits, using a combination of symptomatic and theoretically motivated techniques, which are relevant for a large number of patients.

For example, (Kolk, unpublished) showed that agrammatic patients can benefit by practice with a particular sentence frame, so that the effects generalize to similar constructions using other vocabulary. The approach of Beyn and Shokhor-Trotskaya, described earlier, also contains features which are applicable to agrammatic patients of any language, such as encouraging verb–object phrases and discouraging naming and initiating sentences with nouns.

Looking at the level of phonology, the theoretical position of the therapist also has its influence. If, as some writers (e.g., Luria, 1970) suggest, auditory comprehension is impaired in aphasia because of inaccurate 'phonemic hearing,' practice in discrimination speech sounds should be a fundamental therapy for disorders of comprehension. Alternatively, therapy ought to focus at the level of semantic interpretation, where the functional failures are apparent.

While, as Lesser points out, psycholinguistic analyses of language processes do not necessarily lead to prescriptions for remediation, they do suggest hypotheses which may guide therapeutic procedures. These hypotheses are, to a considerable degree, incorporated as assumptions in the thinking of neuropsychologists and speech pathologists. One class of assumptions bears on the order of complexity of linguistic operations. Naive assumptions that single words are necessarily simpler than sentences, or that isolated sounds are easier than words, have largely disappeared from the field. The recognition that language in context is easier to deal with than words or phrases isolated from immediate experience is now a universal guiding principle.

The problem to be surmounted in establishing the effectiveness of theoretically motivated rehabilitation techniques is that of assessing the contribution of the therapy to recovery.

This is particularly true for treatment which is geared to the individual patient's deficits. Not only is it difficult to rule out the effects of spontaneous recovery, but the differences between patients make large-group studies of questionable value. Single-case techniques, applied to patients who have become stabilized prior to intervention, would seem to be the method of choice.

## CONCLUSIONS

In this discussion emphasis has been placed on the fact that language rehabilitation remains largely an empirical field, in which the major assumption is that the representation of language in the brain is rarely totally abolished by a brain lesion, and that therapy serves to elicit and strengthen prior patterns. Repeated practice as a means of re-establishing language skills is a primary tool.

Little space has been devoted in this discussion to enumerating the great repertory of techniques which have been devised to help recall and reinforce language skills. In this category we can place the use of cues, reinforcement with auxiliary modes of input or output, efforts to bring sporadic spontaneous production under voluntary control, and many others. Similarly, the use of behavioral reinforcement techniques, programmed teaching, and role-playing, can be considered to be strategies for teaching, rather than theoretically derived efforts to develop in the patient alternative communicative mechanisms.

The neuropsychologist and speech pathologist can work collaboratively in the design of new experimental therapeutic procedures and the measurement of their effectiveness. As resistant as aphasia has been to major breakthroughs, the possibility for theoretically based progress is encouraging.

## ACKNOWLEDGMENT

This work was supported in part by the Medical Research Service of the Veterans Administration and in part by USPHS Grant NS 06209.

### REFERENCES

Bay E 1962 Aphasia and non-verbal disorders of language. Brain 85: 411–426

Beyn E S, Shokhor-Trotskaya M K 1966 The preventive method of speech rehabilitation in aphasia. Cortex 2: 96–108

Finkelnberg R 1870 Vortrag in der Niederrheinische Gesellschaft der Aerzte. Berliner Klinische Wochenschrift 7: 449–450, 460–462

Gardner H, Zurif E, Berry T, Baker E 1976 Visual communication in aphasia. Neuropsychologia 14: 275–292

Goldstein K 1948 Language and language disorders. Grune & Stratton, New York

Goodglass H 1980 Disorders of naming following brain injury. American Scientist 68: 647–655

Head H 1926 Aphasia and kindred disorders of speech. Cambridge University Press, Cambridge

Heeschen K 1985 Conventionality of expression in cross-linguistic research in aphasia. Conference on 'Grammatical processing in aphasia: cross-linguistic studies.' Royaumont, France. 11–14 March

Helm-Estabrooks N, Fitzpatrick P, Barresi B 1982 Visual action therapy for global aphasia. Journal of Speech and Hearing Disorders 47: 385–389

Holland A 1970 Case studies in aphasia rehabilitation, using programmed instruction. Journal of Speech and Hearing Research 35: 377–390

Kean M-L 1977 The linguistic interpretation of aphasic syndromes. In: Walker E (ed) Explorations in the biology of language. Bradford, Montgomery, Vermont

Kean M-L 1985 Agrammatism. Academic Press, San Diego

Kohn S 1984 The nature of the phonological deficit in conduction aphasia. Brain and Language 23: 97–115

Kolk H 1985 Telegraphic speech and ellipsis. Presented at Conference on 'Grammatical processing in aphasia: cross-linguistic studies.' Royaumont, France, 11–14 March

Lesser R 1978 Linguistic investigations of aphasia. Edward Arnold, London

Luria A R 1970 Traumatic aphasia. Mouton, The Hague

Miceli G, Mazzuchi A, Menn L, Goodglass H 1983 Contrasting cases of Italian agrammatic aphasia without comprehension disorder. Brain and Language 19: 65–97

Premack D 1971 Language in chimpanzee? Science 172: 808–822

Saffran E M, Schwartz M F, Marin O S M 1980 The word-order problem in agrammatism. II: Production. Brain and Language 10: 263–280

Sarno M T, Silverman M, Sands E 1970 Speech therapy and language recovery in severe aphasia. Journal of Speech and Hearing Research 13: 607–623

Savage-Rumbaugh E S 1981 Can apes use symbols to represent their world? Annals of the New York Academy of Sciences 364: 35–59

Skelly M, Schinsky L, Smith R, Fust R 1974 American Indian sign (AMERIND) as a facilitator of verbalization for the oral verbal apraxic. Journal of Speech and Hearing Disorders 39: 445–456

Sparks R, Albert M L, Helm N 1974 Aphasia rehabilitation resulting from melodic intonation therapy. Cortex 10: 303–316

Van Eeckhout P, Honrado C, Bhatt P, Deblais J-C 1983 De la T.M.R. et de sa pratique. Réeducation Orthophonique 21: 305–316

Velletri-Glass A, Gazzaniga M, Premack D 1973 Artificial language training in global aphasics. Neuropsychologia 11: 95–103

Von Stockert T 1974 Aphasia sine aphasia. Brain and Language 1: 277–283

Weigl E 1961 The phenomenon of temporary deblocking in aphasia. Zeitschrift für Phonetik, Sprachwissen-schaft, und Kommunikationsforschung 14: 337–364

Wepman J, Jones L V 1966 Aphasia: diagnostic description and therapy. In Proceedings of Conference on Research Needs of Patients with Strokes

Wepman J M, Morency A S 1963 Filmstrips as an adjunct to language therapy for aphasia. Journal of Speech and Hearing Disorders 28: 191–199

Whitehouse P J, Caramazza A, Zurif E B 1978 Naming in aphasia: interactive effects of form and function. Brain and Language 6: 63–74

Zurif E B, Caramazza A, Myerson R 1972 Grammatical judgments of agrammatic aphasics. Neuropsychologia 10: 405–417

*Felicia C. Goldstein and Harvey S. Levin*

# Disorders of reasoning and problem-solving ability

## INTRODUCTION

Reasoning and problem-solving behaviors are generally conceptualized as the most complex of all intellectual functions. They require a number of intact emotional and cognitive prerequisites such as adequate levels of motivation and attention; the restraint of impulsive tendencies; the ability to organize, categorize, and shift responses; the use of feedback to modify behavior; and the capacity to evaluate final performance (Ben-Yishay & Diller, 1983b; Lezak, 1983; Luria, 1973). Disorders can occur in conjunction with other neuropsychologic conditions such as aphasia or hemispatial neglect or they may appear in relative isolation (e.g., secondary to frontal lobe damage), while other functions remain unimpaired (Luria, 1973).

One can conceive of a myriad of situations in which the breakdown of problem-solving behavior can hamper daily performance. Individuals could encounter difficulty in carrying out such basic activities as sequencing the steps needed for dressing, organizing the task of preparing meals, scheduling and keeping appointments, and prioritizing and paying bills. Surprisingly, there is a dearth of published remediational studies in this area despite evidence for the impact of impairments in intellectual functioning for psychological and vocational outcome of head injury (Levin et al, 1979) as well as the encouraging finding that rehabilitation may facilitate the recovery process both in animals (Yu, 1976) and humans (Cope & Hall, 1982).

Comparatively more remediational effort has been devoted to deficits involving language, memory, attention, and visual–spatial processing. In the memory area, for example, there are specific mnemonic strategies for improving performance such as imagery (Gasparrini & Satz, 1979; Jones, 1974) and verbal elaboration (Gianutsos & Gianutsos, 1979). Despite the relatively meager theoretical and empirical contributions to this area of rehabilitation, investigators have recently proposed some frameworks for conceptualizing the processes involved in problem-solving abilities, and they have described (albeit mostly in clinical case reports) remediational techniques.

This chapter will present the state of the art regarding the understanding and remediation of these disorders. Neurological mechanisms will be briefly reviewed, followed by a description of models of reasoning/problem-solving. Next, particular deficits identified in the models will be examined. The approach of this review is process-oriented in that it is organized by global behaviors such as motivation or ability to shift response sets as they affect problem-solving and reasoning as opposed to specific disorders such as the inability to perform calculations. This approach is felt to be more consonant with the goal of rehabilitation in attempting to understand the nature of the underlying deficit in functional terms. In addition, the population will include individuals with closed head injuries or strokes. The ways in which these two groups differ in cognitive performance and the implications for designing remediation programs will be discussed. Finally, a number of conceptual and methodological issues will be raised with suggestions for future directions.

## Neurological mechanisms

Attempts to implicate a localization of cerebral lesion for deficits in reasoning and problem-solving have been complicated by the contribution of diffuse (or multifocal) cerebral trauma. The degree of impairment in cognition may depend to an equal degree on lesion size as compared to its location (Goodglass & Kaplan, 1979). While most work in this area has focused on frontal lobe disorders, damage to other regions such as the temporal lobes may also produce problem-solving impairments (cf. Rausch, 1977). This section will briefly review some neuroanatomical considerations of the frontal lobe syndrome. Although we recognize the contribution of other regions of the brain to problem-solving, both the human neuropsychology literature and ablation studies in animals have emphasized the role of the frontal lobes. For a more detailed discussion, the reader is referred to excellent reviews by Jouandet & Gazzaniga (1979), Nauta (1971), and Stuss & Benson (1984).

The prefrontal region communicates through reciprocally organized afferent and efferent connections with association areas of the parietal, temporal, and occipital lobes as well as the telecephalic limbic system and subcortical areas such as the hypothalamus (involved in emotionality) and the medial dorsal nucleus of the thalamus (Nauta, 1971). Perhaps due to its rich connections with other areas, the frontal lobes have been most implicated in disorders of reasoning and problem-solving. Jouandet & Gazzaniga (1979) have postulated that the frontal lobes represent the external world after it has been first integrated in diverse cortical regions. Damage to the frontal areas will therefore alter the interpretation of information gained from other cortical areas, even if these regions remain neurologically intact. Figure 16.1 shows the integration of sensory information onto the anterior frontal lobe which is located anterior to the Rolandic fissure and above the Sylvian fissure.

Milner (1982) has suggested that participation of the left frontal lobe is important on tasks requiring voluntary planning and self-monitoring, whereas the right lobe is critical on tasks requiring temporal monitoring of external events. The lobes are further subdivided into dorsolateral, basiliar-orbital, and

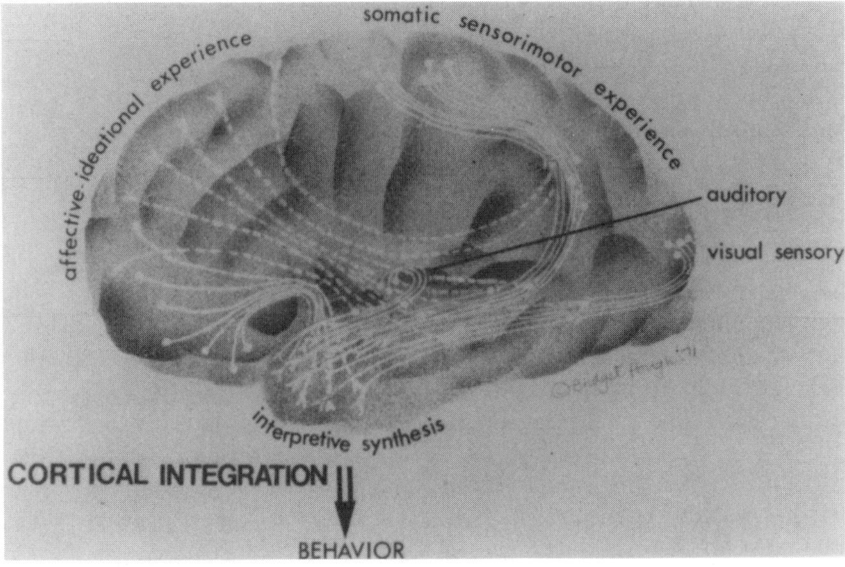


**Fig. 16.1** Convergence of sensory information onto the convexity of the anterior frontal lobe. (Adapted from Powell, 1972. From Livingston K E, 1977. Reproduced with permission of Powell and publisher.)

medial areas. The orbital and medial frontal regions are involved in the modulation of arousal and tone through connections with the brainstem reticular formation. The dorsolateral areas are important for functions such as visual control (e.g., ability to shift gaze) and response initiation (e.g., verbal fluency, fluency in creating designs) (Jouandet & Gazzaniga, 1979; Milner, 1982; Stuss & Benson, 1984). Milner (1963) demonstrated that dorsolateral as opposed to orbital lesions produce an inability to shift responses. However, studies of patients with frontal lobe lesions have not supported strict specialization of function of these regions.

Damage to the frontal lobes has been shown to lead to a variety of cognitive disturbances. Sensory-perceptual and attentional functions may be impaired as in the inertia of gaze seen in patients who focus on one aspect of the visual field or in the unilateral neglect syndrome in which patients fail to respond, report, or orient to stimuli presented to the side opposite a lesion (Heilman, 1979). The frontal-limbic-reticular loop has been implicated in this latter disturbance. Lesions in the premotor regions may produce problems in executing and alternating two responses or yield stereotypic responses. Drewe (1957b) found that medial frontal lesions produced poor performance on a go/no go learning task. Perseveration is a frequently cited occurrence of frontal lobe damage but may occur from damage to other regions as well (Stuss & Benson, 1984). Damage to the frontal lobes may also produce a variety of emotional disturbances such as apathy and hyperemotionality as well as memory disorders such as the inability to retain new information following interference (Stuss & Benson, 1984).

Any of these disorders will interact with problem-solving and reasoning processes and hamper performance. In the following section some behavioral manifestations and models will be presented.

## Models of reasoning/problem-solving

Models of the reasoning/problem-solving process agree on the basic substages required for intact functioning. At the simplest level, problem-solving is said to involve orientation and analysis of the task, generation of alternative hypothetical solutions, the formulation of motor programs for each solution, and evaluation of the end result through a feedback system (Lhermitte et al, 1972, cited in Jouandet & Gazzaniga, 1979). Problem-solving is described as an active process which can deteriorate at any particular substage. Reasoning can be considered the level of analysis which the performer applies to any of these substages. Thus, such reasoning skills as the ability to organize or to categorize concepts can determine the quality of the manner in which a problem will be formulated and the tactics applied for solution.

Luria (1963, 1966, 1973) contributed immensely to the experimental analysis of disturbed processes in thought resulting from brain injury. In an excellent chapter on the psychological structure of thinking, Luria (1973) synthesized the literature and outlined six stages involved in thought. These include:

1. a motive to perform a task for which there is no inborn or habitual solution;
2. an ability to restrain impulsivity, to investigate the problem, and to analyze/correlate its features;
3. the selection of one of many possible alternatives and creation of a general scheme;
4. the choice of appropriate methods and operations for placing the scheme into action;
5. the solution of the problem or discovery of the answer to the question; and
6. the comparison of obtained results with the original task conditions.

Luria demonstrated how different core deficits could interfere with problem-solving on an identical task. For example, patients with parieto-occipital lesions evidenced disorders in spatial synthesis on a constructive task (Koh's blocks) and yet had both the intention and the principle to solve the problem. On the other hand, patients with frontal lobe lesions could find the necessary spatial relationships but did not analyze the problem or break it into units. Luria (1973) thus emphasized the relationships between specific and integrative cortical functions on problem-solving ability and offered a process analysis of the stages at which performance could fail.

Luria's concepts of hierarchical functions and the stages in problem-solving are utilized in the remediational program at New York University's (NYU) Institute of Rehabilitation Medicine. Ben-Yishay and his associates (Ben-

Yishay et al, 1978; Ben-Yishay & Diller, 1983a,b) have evolved a model to explain the post-traumatic behavioral deficits resulting from severe head injury. They hypothesize a lower tier of five basic deficit areas (arousal/attention; memory; impairments in underlying skill structures; language/thought; feeling tone) and two higher domains of problem-solving/rational processes and emotive, imaginative, and empathetic processes (Ben-Yishay & Diller, 1983a). In this model (see Fig. 16.2), disorders in the higher domains can be produced by the core deficits, and the appearance of normal or disturbed behavior will depend upon the interaction between the two domains. One component of the NYU remediation program includes the administration of retraining techniques in each core area such as tasks designed to increase arousal and orientation, psychomotor, and visual information-processing skills.

The elaboration of the problem-solving process based on Luria's conceptualization includes eight stages which are organized into a chain of connected behaviors (see Fig. 16.3) (Ben-Yishay & Diller, 1983b). Some of the links are 'convergent' (aimed at arriving at a central idea), some are 'divergent' (aimed at generating alternative approaches and choosing the most relevant one), and some are 'executive' (aimed at placing thoughts and plans into action). An additional component of the NYU program includes cognitive retraining in convergent reasoning, flexibility of thought needed for divergent reasoning, evaluative–integrative skills, and the executive functions (Ben-Yishay & Diller, 1983b).

The executive functions are perhaps the most intriguing of the processes involved in problem-solving. Luria (1963, 1973; Luria & Homskaya, 1964) devoted a great deal of his career to studying disturbances resulting from frontal lobe lesions in which

> patients can remain without marked disturbances of motor activity or sensitivity, gnosis, or praxis, or defects of speech or even 'formal intellectual functions,' but at the same time meaningful, directed behavior can be severely disturbed as a whole (Luria & Homskaya, 1964, p. 353).

Thus, even if cognitive abilities such as memory, attention, and reasoning are intact, individuals can experience difficulty in generating hypotheses and goals during problem-solving or even in knowing where to begin. Lezak (1983) divides the executive functions into four stages:

1. Goal Formulation (realization and statement of an objective – 'What do I want or need?');
2. Planning (analysis of the situation – 'How will I get what I need?');
3. Carrying Out Activities (actual behavior – 'Am I doing things to obtain my objective?'); and
4. Effective Performance (feedback and self-correction – 'Are my activities fulfilling my objective?').

Lezak (1983) notes a conceptual paradox in attempting to assess the executive functions through standardized neuropsychological measures due to the fact

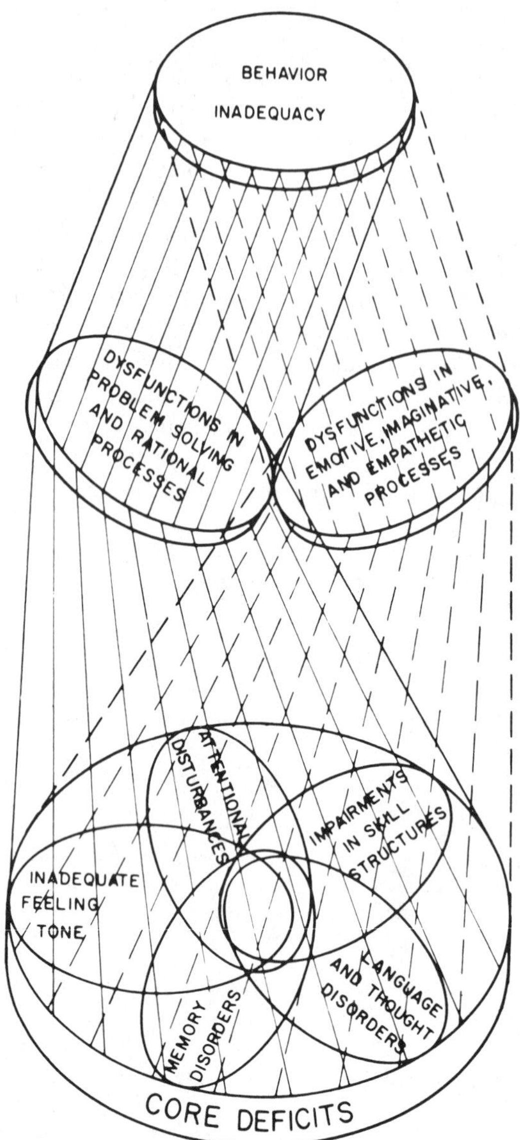


**Fig. 16.2** A schematic presentation of a hypothesis concerning the cause–effect relationship between generic deficits and behavior dysfunctions in severe head injuries. (From Ben-Yishay & Diller (1983a). Reproduced with permission of the author and publisher.)

that most testing situations are structured, and deficits in initiation and goal-directed behavior may not appear. She advocates the use of unstructured tasks such as those requiring the patient to perform a construction without guidance from the examiner on what to make (for example, giving the patient Tinkertoys and asking for a model of the patient's own choosing). The

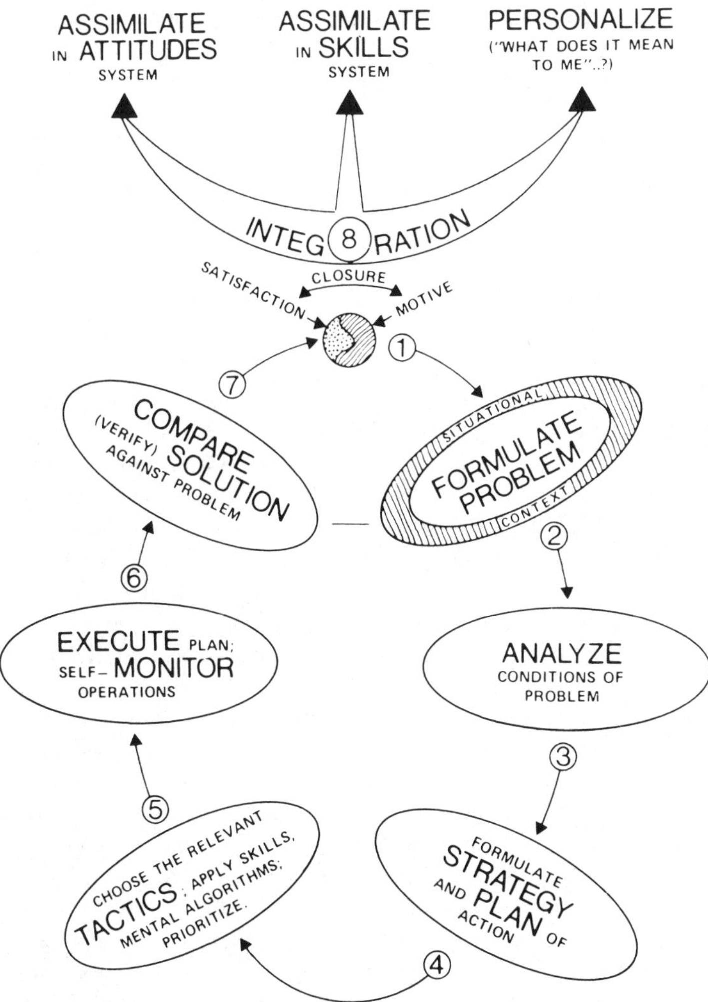


**Fig. 16.3** Stages of the problem-solving process. (From Ben-Yishay & Diller (1983b). Reproduced with permission of the author and publisher.)

construction can be scored for such aspects as the number of pieces used and its complexity (including whether it is three-dimensional, the number of moving parts, symmetry, and misfit of pieces). Utilizing the Tinkertoy task, Lezak examined the performance of 35 patients with cerebral pathology who were classified as dependent or independent (could perform daily routines on their own, drive or use transportation) and a control group of 10 subjects. As seen in Table 16.1, the dependent group used fewer pieces (NP) and had lower complexity scores than the other two groups. The usefulness of unstructured assessment of problem-solving for rehabilitation beyond the results obtained with structured tests awaits further study.

**Table 16.1** Comparisons between groups on number of pieces and complexity scores

| | Patients | | Control | |
|---|---|---|---|---|
| Group | Dependent | Non-dependent | | |
| Measure | | | | F |
| Number of pieces | | | | |
| Mean ± SD | 13.5 ± 9.46 | 30.24 ± 11.32 | 42.2 ± 10.03 | 26.91* |
| Range | 0–42 | 9–50 | 23–50 | |
| Complexity | | | | |
| Mean ± SD | 2.22 ± 2.10 | 5.47 ± 1.77 | 7.8 ± 1.99 | 28.27* |
| Range | -1–8 | 2–9 | 5–12 | |

*One-way ANOVA, $p<0.001$.
(From Lezak (1983). Reproduced with permission of the author and the publisher.)

A major theme emerging from the previous discussion is the concept of *levels* of impairment in problem-solving ability. Deficits in problem-solving behavior can occur due to processing difficulties in 'lower' functioning areas such as memory or attention, they may appear in the absence of core deficits, and finally, reasoning and general intellectual functioning may be intact but the overseer or executive functions (as in the frontal lobe syndrome) are impaired. From a remediation standpoint it is critical to conduct a detailed process analysis to determine where performance is breaking down, and then to design programs which focus on the level of impairment. For example, is failure to solve a problem attributable to a short-term memory deficit, a basic reasoning difficulty, or a disorder in carrying out the arrived-at solution? A second theme is the concept of problem-solving as a complex process involving many stages. Deficits in reasoning, such as the inability to think in abstract terms, to comprehend relationships, or to make practical judgments, can affect the quality of performance. This breakdown of problem-solving into concrete behaviors may help to guide remediation attempts in the design of procedures.

In the following section, remediation efforts in problem-solving/reasoning disorders will be discussed. Using the framework synthesized from the literature, deficits will be organized under the stages seen as critical to problem-solving behavior. These include motivation, formulation of a problem, strategy, and plan (involving reasoning and abstraction), executing a plan (production), and comparison of the solution against the problem (cue utilization and flexibility).

## REMEDIATION OF REASONING/PROBLEM-SOLVING DISORDERS

### Motivational disturbances

#### *Description/formulation*

Motivational disturbances following brain injury can affect both the perception of a problem and whether a solution is attempted. Anergia (decreased or absent motivation) may express itself as a lack of interest in problem-solving and the failure to use active strategies. The demonstration of the impact of motivation on performance is vividly illustrated by Luria (1963), who plotted the learning curves of subjects instructed to recall a list of 10 words over a series of repeated trials. Subjects with brain lesions outside the frontal lobes (see Fig. 16.4) showed a tendency to learn words, but performance fell off after capacity was reached or fatigue set in. In contrast, subjects with frontal lobe lesions retained two to five words on every trial with no attempt to retrieve words from memory.

Difficulties in maintaining an appropriate level of motivation in problem-solving can stem from a number of underlying reasons. First, brain-injured persons may deny that they have any deficits, or they may tend to minimize the importance of their cognitive problems for daily living, i.e., exhibit inaccurate self-appraisal. Levin et al (1979) studied cognitive and psychological

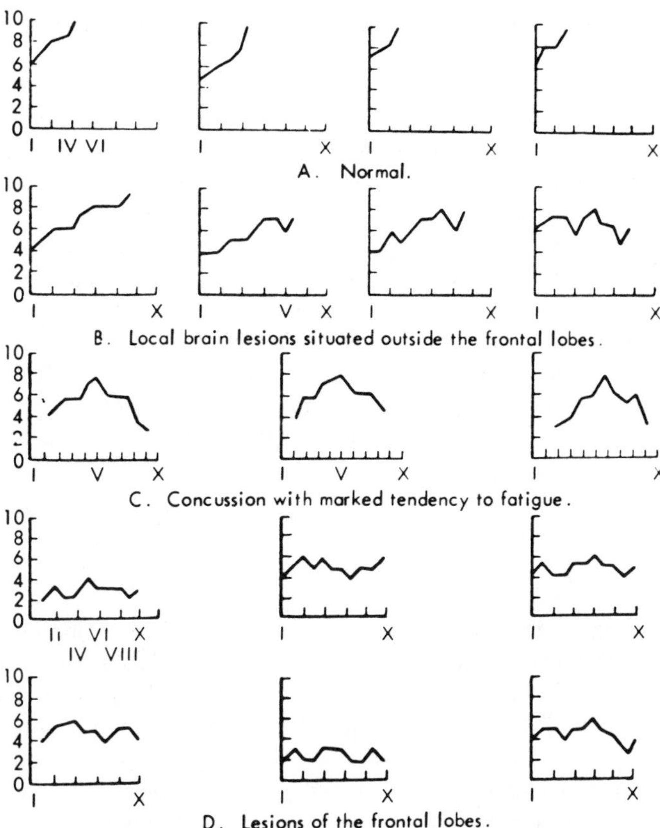


**Fig. 16.4** Memorizing curves in normal subjects and in patients with lesions of the frontal lobes and of other parts of the brain. The X axis refers to number of trials while the Y axis refers to the number of words recalled. (From Luria (1963). Reproduced with permission of the publisher.)

adjustment in individuals who had sustained severe closed head injuries. On long-term follow-up it was found that patients with moderate or severe disabilities evidenced thinking disturbances (characterized by such qualities as conceptual disorganization with intrusion of irrelevant material and fragmented speech) and tended to deny cognitive deficits or focused on minor symptoms. This apparent failure to appreciate deficits may reflect an inability to profit from cues and to analyze settings.

Another correlate of a motivational problem may involve depression following brain injury. Lezak (1983) notes that personality changes often occur as a result of the experience of loss, frustration, and life difficulties, and depression is perhaps the most common emotional characteristic of brain-injured patients. Finally, a third variable influencing motivation entails the individual's responsivity to environmental reinforcement. Yu (1976) reports rehabilitation efforts with animals who were motivated to learn through the use of food reward during training. The time course of recovery in movements was slower for animals who refused to eat in the first few days or to take food from the observer's hand for the first 2 weeks.

Most assessment techniques for motivational disturbances are informal. On current neuropsychological measures it is difficult to separate poor performance resulting from a lack of motivation versus other factors such as low arousal or conceptual difficulties. Perhaps more unstructured tests, such as projective techniques, may be useful in ascertaining the individual's responsiveness to the environment as well as attitudes and ambitions (Lezak, 1983). Deficiencies in motivation are often detected through naturalistic observations and family ratings (Caplan, 1982). Manipulation of the reward for correct answers in a problem-solving task might also be a useful technique for assessing the patient's capacity for greater effort. A detailed clinical interview can also be a valuable diagnostic tool, provided that the examiner verifies that the brain-injured patient can implement plans and demonstrate strategies which he or she verbalizes.

### *Remediation techniques*

There is a growing realization of the importance of including motivational training in cognitive remediation programs. An example of such an effort is the Neuropsychological Rehabilitation Program (NRP) at Presbyterian Hospital in Oklahoma City (Prigatano et al, 1984). This program includes treatment aimed at increased awareness/acceptance of deficits, cognitive retraining, the development of compensatory skills, and understanding of emotional/motivational disturbances. Prigatano et al compared the neuropsychological outcome of 18 closed head-injured patients who had been in the NRP versus 17 control patients who had sustained non-missile head injuries of comparable severity but were unable to attend the NRP for various reasons. The authors found significant differences in favor of the treated patients on WAIS Performance

IQ, WAIS Block Design, and Wechsler Memory Quotient. Perhaps even more striking, though, were personality findings as assessed by relatives' ratings on the Katz Adjustment Scale. NRP patients received lower (in the direction of normality) ratings on helplessness, withdrawal, general psychopathology, and restlessness/hyperactivity. In addition, NRP patients who were working were compared with NRP patients who were unemployed. While there were no differences in neuropsychological indices, the employed patients were rated as more emotionally and motivationally adjusted.

Prigatano et al (1984) concluded that patients can be taught awareness and acceptance of their compromised capacities, and that these individuals show a greater willingness to use compensatory strategies to overcome their deficits. As the authors note, however, longitudinal evaluation of the maintenance of these improvements is needed.

Behavior modification techniques have been used to enhance motivation in patients who might otherwise not benefit from rehabilitation. Newcombe (1982) describes the approach of the Kemsley Unit at St Andrews Hospital in England. This program admits patients with reduced drive, apathy, lack of pleasurable responses, and social indifference who are unable to participate in traditional programs. Behavior modification techniques, including positive reinforcement, time out, and a token economy system, are employed to diminish inappropriate behavior and to shape more appropriate responses such as goal setting.

Luria (1963) recognized the vital importance of motivation on goal-directed action, the restraint of impulsivity, and the ability to self-correct. He suggested that the way to overcome the deficit was to replace the disturbed internal regulation of behavior with external control. Luria thus advocated the creation of conditions in which behavior was directed by the supervision of another person, or was so simple that it required no internal control (as in work on a mass-production line). Interestingly, Luria's strategy of remediation is most consistent with a behavioral approach which attempts to bring behavior under external control.

Craine (1982) similarly reports that the problem of motivation is frequently encountered in patients with frontal lobe lesions. He recommends the use of environmental stimuli to act as motivators so that training can be achieved. In the absence of strong motivators it may be important to structure activities and gradually reduce these as the patient becomes capable of self-regulation. In a rehabilitation setting the patient's day is typically scheduled on an hourly basis (including meals). When the patient returns home that structure may be missing, and the patient may end up spending the entire day in solitary, unconstructive activities.

From the previous discussion it is clear that motivational disturbances can impede rehabilitation efforts. Attempts to remediate problem-solving deficits must focus on these issues. Several techniques, including counseling and behavior modification, have been introduced into the literature, but the success of these endeavors requires more rigorous investigation.

## Impairments in reasoning and concept formation

### *Description/formulation*

Impairments in reasoning and concept formation can occur at various stages of cognitive functioning, including formulation of a problem, strategy, and plan for solution. Reasoning involves the ability to understand relationships, identify essential parts, synthesize them, and arrive at a common theme. Individuals with impaired reasoning may examine an isolated portion of a picture and thus fail to grasp its meaning or focus on one fragment of a story and arrive at an erroneous conclusion concerning its theme (Hagen, 1984; Luria, 1966). Tests of reasoning include the Raven's Progressive Matrices (Raven, 1960), Arithmetic, Picture Completion, and Picture Arrangement on the WAIS-R (Wechsler, 1981), and Problem Situations, Problems of Fact, Verbal Absurdities, and Picture Absurdities on the Stanford-Binet (Terman & Merrill, 1973). Many of these tests tap the individual's ability to process visual and auditory information and, as such, are not 'pure' measures of reasoning but may reflect deficits in other areas such as visual–spatial or auditory receptive difficulties.

Concept formation requires the capacity to analyze the relationships between objects and their properties. Deficits in concept formation are manifested by the adoption of a stimulus-bound or 'concrete' solution and the inability to form and utilize abstract superordinate categories (Goldstein et al, 1968; Goodglass & Kaplan, 1979). Examples of assessment measures for conceptual functions are the Category Test (Halstead, 1947), the Color Sorting Test (Goldstein & Scheerer, 1953), the Wisconsin (Grant & Berg, 1948) and Modified (Nelson, 1976) Card Sorting Tests, Similarities on the WAIS-R, and the Proverbs Test (Gorham, 1956).

Kurt Goldstein (1942; Goldstein & Scheerer, 1941) originally conceived of concrete and abstract thought as two fundamentally different qualitative dimensions rather than as quantitative aspects of the same process. A concrete attitude toward problem-solving encompassed such attributes as the lack of conscious activity in reasoning and self-awareness as well as a tendency to be bound to the stimulus properties of a task and the inability to detach oneself from the immediate surroundings. An abstract attitude, on the other hand, entailed the ability to consciously transcend the here and now, shift to different aspects of the problem, simultaneously reflect upon several aspects at one time, and categorize/think symbolically. According to Goldstein (1942), a non-impaired individual could adopt either a concrete *or* an abstract attitude, and, in fact, certain problem-solving situations lent themselves more readily to one or the other ways of thinking. The author inferred that brain damage led to a loss of the 'abstract attitude,' i.e., the individual could function only at a concrete level.

Goldstein & Scheerer (1941) devised numerous sorting tests (e.g., the Gelb–Goldstein–Weigl–Scheerer Object Sorting Test, the Goldstein–Scheerer Cube Test, the Goldstein–Scheerer Stick Test) which demonstrated the loss of the abstract attitude in neurologically impaired populations (see Fig. 16.5). Perhaps one of Goldstein's most significant contributions was his insistence that task performance be analyzed qualitatively. Thus, he argued that one needed to delve further into the process by which problems were solved. To illustrate this the researchers showed that patients and non-brain-damaged individuals could both sort objects according to color or use. However, only unimpaired individuals could verbalize the reason for their sorts or actively shift from one principle to another. The patients were bound by the immediate perceptual qualities of the stimuli, were unreflective, and demonstrated a lack of conscious activity.

The view that ability to abstract is an all-or-none phenomenon has since been revised. Gerald Goldstein et al (1968) examined the performance of 30 brain-damaged patients on a concept identification task requiring them to discover the principle uniting a series of visually presented stimuli. According to an all-or-none view of abstract thought, the brain-injured population would not be expected to be able to pass this task or to show signs of learning over trials. However, Goldstein and his colleagues showed that while some patients were unable to solve the task even with repeated exposure, a number of patients evidenced abstract ability. Neuringer et al (1973) later demonstrated that age may be an important factor in the type of deficit one sees. Utilizing the same concept identification task in the 1968 study, Neuringer et al found that a qualitative deficit occurred with greater frequency in older individuals coupled with an increase in the severity of a quantitative deficit (i.e., more trials to reach criterion).

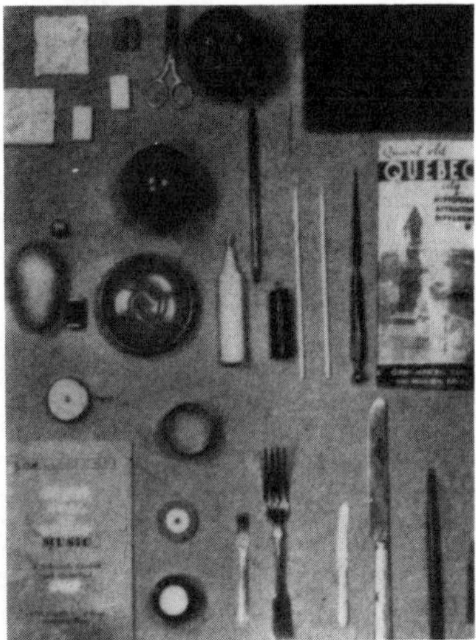

**Fig. 16.5** Gelb–Goldstein–Weigl–Scheerer Object Sorting Test. Two sets of objects are used, one for males (left) and one for females (right). (Reprinted from Goldstein & Scheerer 1941.)

The type of impairment seen in concrete/abstract ability has implications for cognitive retraining. It has been suggested that patients who cannot abstract at all should be taught to make greater use of their concrete skills (e.g., Goldstein et al, 1968) in problem-solving. In contrast, when there is evidence for some residual abstract ability, patients could be instructed in ways of raising their level of abstraction (Neuringer et al, 1973). Goldstein & Reuthen (1983) suggest that direct training in categorization and sorting tasks which provide the patient with cues concerning concept formation may be useful techniques in this area. However, there are no specific remediation procedures offered by these authors for how this approach might be implemented.

*Remediation techniques*

The remediational program developed at the Institute for Rehabilitation Medicine includes exercises designed to develop abstract reasoning skills (Ben-Yishay et al, 1978). One procedure, similar to the WAIS-R Similarities subtest, requires the individual to deduce properties which relate two items. One item is presented first, its most obvious extrinsic qualities are defined (e.g., automobile – can be any color, shape, size, it is large and heavy, etc.), and the individual takes the items through a number of graduated steps including its distinguishing properties, origin, function, definition, and category (e.g., motorized vehicle, means of transportation). A second item is then presented, the steps are repeated, and the shared properties between the items are revealed. The answers are removed, and the individual goes through the process from memory before the next item pairs are presented. If transfer to the new pair does not occur, the process is repeated.

Another procedure is designed to develop the ability to extract concise information. The individual is given the task of sending, for example, a two-word telegram. The facts, circumstances, and assumptions are given, and the individual must generate a series of questions such as 'What does the sender want to get across?' and 'What should the receiver understand to do?' (Ben-Yishay et al, 1978). There are no data presented on the success of these two remediational strategies with which to evaluate their efficacy.

Craine (1982) describes concept formation remediation with a patient who sustained left frontal brain injury. The patient was unable to extract information from a paragraph even though he could read and understand what he had read. The intervention involved having the patient write out the information in a paragraph as he was led by such questions as how many people were there in the story, what were their names, etc. When left on his own, however, he was still unable to spontaneously break down the problem because he had not appreciated the importance of using this strategy. Through repeated feedback, Craine (1982) reports that the patient became motivated to actively engage in the task. The finding that the individual must be made aware of a deficit in order to facilitate the utilization of strategies emphasizes again the important role of motivation in problem solving.

Leftoff (1983) has hypothesized an interesting relationship between disorders of concept formation and psychopathology (the development of paranoid thinking). She argues that paranoid processes may evolve in some cases as a restitutive attempt to impose order on the interpersonal relationships disturbed by concrete and self-referential thought. The patient she describes had a stroke which resulted in unilateral left cerebral brain damage. Although he returned to work and his linguistic defects were confined to a mild anomia, he experienced difficulty due to an inability to understand financial reports, prepare written reports, follow conversations involving more than two people, or recall information provided at meetings. His responses on the Vocabulary subtest of the WAIS were concrete and egocentric, he evidenced poor performance on the logical Memory passages of the Wechsler Memory Test, his Raven Progressive Matrices score disclosed a disorder of abstraction, and he was totally unable to perform the Wisconsin Card Sorting Test. In addition, he focused on only a single aspect of the cards presented in the Thematic Apperception Test. The patient was seen for psychotherapy by Leftoff and for cognitive retraining at NYU. Psychotherapeutic remediation included teaching the patient to become aware of his inability to shift perspective, skill training in adopting another person's point of view, and hypothesis testing about the other's behavior in relation to himself. Leftoff's approach demonstrates the potential use of cognitive retraining methods as applied to psychotherapy.

Research from the more intensively studied area of language disorders may be useful in guiding remediation efforts in problem-solving. Although the left hemisphere is most often studied in relation to linguistic deficits (e.g., aphasia), individuals with right hemisphere damage also develop communication disorders which frequently interfere with their ability to solve problems. It has been noted that as a task becomes less concrete and more complex, right hemisphere-damaged patients evidence difficulty in organizing information efficiently, tend to produce impulsive, tangential answers, have problems in assimilating and using contextual cues, and overpersonalize external events (Myers, 1984).

## Impairments in the productive aspect of thought

### *Description/formulation*

A particularly disabling effect of brain injury on problem-solving behavior entails what Luria (1963) described as breakdowns in productive activity and active thought. These deficits can impact all components of the problem-solving process including the formulation of a plan and analysis of task conditions. However, a deficiency in productive thought may be most pronounced in the execution stages because even if motivational and conceptual/reasoning difficulties are resolved, the individual will have difficulty in implementing a plan into action.

Two fundamental levels of impairment contributing to deficits in the productive aspect of thought can be identified. One concerns a deficiency in knowing where to begin a problem and actually executing a plan. Luria (1963) described patients with frontal lobe disorders as unable to produce a complete line of reasoning. One patient commented, 'My thoughts will not flow . . . . My head is empty . . . . When I begin to write a letter, I don't know where to begin, and it takes me all day to write one letter' (p. 211). Deficits tend to appear in unstructured tasks such as the previously described Tinkertoy Test where an individual must show initiative and planning (Lezak, 1983).

Another level of impairment interfering with productive thought may be the decreased speed of information-processing and decision-making which frequently accompanies brain injury. The Paced Auditory Serial Addition Task (Gronwall & Wrightson, 1981) provides a measure of information-processing capacity which is related to an attentional/concentration factor. A series of auditorily presented digits are given at progressively more rapid rates, and the subject is instructed to add each number to the one immediately preceding it. The level of performance declines as the interval between digits is decreased. The test is a good predictor of ability to return to work, and may be most useful in evaluating return to those positions requiring rapid decision-making and concentration (Levin et al, 1982). Fluency tasks such as the Controlled Oral Word Association Test (Benton & Hamsher, 1978) are useful techniques for examining the productive aspects of thought when language functions (e.g., anomia, aphasia) are unimpaired. Reduced fluency is a prominent feature of left frontal injury even in nonaphasic patients (Benton, 1968). Diminished capacity to invent novel designs under timed conditions, i.e., reduced 'design fluency,' is a relatively specific finding in patients with right frontal injury, whereas verbal fluency may be intact (Jones-Gotman & Milner, 1977).

### *Remediation techniques*

Luria (1963) outlined a treatment regimen for a patient with frontal lobe damage who was unable to tell a story unless he was aided by external questions. The method consisted of 'transition formulae' which were written on a card and included words such as 'although,' 'then,' 'since,' and 'however.' After having a story read to him, the patient referred to the card and found the appropriate transition formulae in order to continue to a new component. Luria reported success with this method and generalization to other tasks such as the spontaneous description of a picture. He noted, though, that such a method was useless in unstructured tasks where the patient had to produce his own flow of thought unguided by external cues. To remediate this situation, Luria had the patient write down fragments of his story in any order, arrange them in sequence, and then use this plan to relate the elements.

Jenning & Lubinski (1981) instituted a cognitive remediation program with a 66-year-old male who had cerebral cortical atrophy of the frontal and temporal cortex and subsequently developed communication difficulties. Training included concept awareness in which the client was asked to express verbally or non-verbally as many attributes as he could about an object and classify two objects according to their similarities or differences. At first, the objects were concrete, but they were eventually replaced by pictures or words. The goal of their program was to increase the number of expressed ideas. At first the therapist provided a lot of cues to the client, but these were gradually reduced. The number of ideas expressed by the patient and the number of cues provided by the therapist were the performance measures. There was a 200% increase in the number of ideas from baseline to the final evaluation and a 150% increase in the number of different ideas produced (non-redundant).

Craine (1982) used a strategy to increase verbal fluency in a patient who demonstrated an inability to verbalize the steps he took in problem-solving. Training consisted of instructing the patient to produce 30 words beginning with a particular letter in 2 minutes. Craine reported that the patient eventually reached this criterion through his discovery of strategies and compliance with the examiner's insistence that he move on if he got stuck. The description of the procedure is anecdotal, and no data are presented.

## Impairments in cue utilization and ability to shift response sets

### *Description/formulation*

The culmination of successful problem-solving performance entails the capacity to evaluate one's behavior by comparing it with the original task conditions and goals. Many views of the concept learning process are built on a 'win–stay, lose–shift' model in which the individual selects one hypothesis, responds according to that hypothesis, and shifts only when information suggests that it is no longer correct or relevant (Oscar-Berman, 1973). Brain-injured individuals frequently display deficits in profiting from feedback, modifying their behavior to meet current task demands, and shifting response sets. At a mild level this deficit can be observed as a slowness to reorient, alternate, and respond to another step in the problem-solving process. At a more impaired level a total breakdown in performance may occur as in perseveration, defined as the continuation of a response which is no longer relevant to a new stimulus (Goodglass & Kaplan, 1979).

There is ample documentation for difficulties in cue utilization and response shifting resulting from brain injury (Drewe, 1974; Helmick & Berg, 1976; Johnson & Diller, 1983; Nelson, 1976; Rausch, 1977; Robinson et al, 1980). Johnson & Diller (1983), for example, employed a number cancellation task with right hemisphere-damaged patients. At the completion of a trial, patients rated how they thought they had performed and were provided with feedback. They were then given additional instructions and feedback for a series of trials until perfect performance was achieved or levels of feedback were completely used up. Patients tended to overestimate their performance and required at least three attempts to achieve perfect scores, with one subject completely failing the task. Similarly, Cicerone & Lazar (1983) have demonstrated that patients with frontal lobe lesions make more 'lose–stay' errors than patients with lateralized anterior or posterior lesions. As seen in Table 16.2, they tend to stay with an incorrect hypothesis after negative input, thus indicating an inability to eliminate irrelevant cognitive strategies.

Milner (1982) has also described a loss in the ability of patients with massive frontal lobe lesions to control their behavior differentially according to changes in external stimuli. In one study, patients were taught a series of different hand postures (e.g., hand flat, palm up; hand flat, palm vertical, etc.). They then had to learn to associate these hand positions with various colored lights. Compared with a control group, the patients with frontal lobe lesions were significantly impaired in learning the task. A similar finding reported by Luria & Homskaya (1964) showed that patients with frontal lobe tumors were unable to learn to pair motor behavior with external signals even though they could repeat the instructions, thus demonstrating that they understood the task.

The usefulness of sorting procedures in the assessment of concept formation is illustrated by the description of a head injured patient on our service. Figure 16.6 depicts improvement in concept formation and shifting responses on the Modified Card Sorting Test (Nelson, 1976) in a 17-year-old student who sustained a severe non-missile head injury complicated by bilateral frontal intracerebral hematomas (the right hematoma was small and therefore it is not seen here) after he was struck by a car. As shown in Fig. 16.6, both his perseverative and non-perseverative errors markedly declined between 3 and 6 months after injury. This improvement in concept formation on formal testing was paralleled by more accurate self-appraisal, realistic planning, and more appropriate socialization skills.

**Table 16.2** Mean number of appropriate hypotheses (maximum four) on H1, H2, and H3 following either positive or negative outcome trials (two-tailed *t* tests following ANOVA)

| | | Positive Outcome | | | Negative Outcome | | |
|---|---|---|---|---|---|---|---|
| | | H1 | H2 | H3 | H1 | H2 | H3 |
| Frontal | $\overline{X}$ | 3.20 | 3.05 | 1.95** | 2.35** | 1.05** | 0.50* |
| | s.d. | (0.70) | (0.76) | (0.76) | (1.23) | (0.94) | (0.76) |
| Posterior | $\overline{X}$ | 3.25 | 3.50 | 3.00 | 3.25 | 2.33 | 1.17 |
| | s.d. | (0.87) | (0.67) | (1.04) | (0.75) | (1.15) | (0.94) |

An appropriate hypothesis was defined by the use of an hypothesis consistent with all prior feedback.
Difference between groups significant at: $^{*}p<0.05$; $^{**}p<0.01$.
(From Cicerone & Lezar (1983). Reproduced with permission of the authors and publisher.)

### *Remediation techniques*

Most of the research on perseveration has focused on describing the phenomenon and finding measures which can be used to detect its occurrence and discriminate among groups of patients (Drewe, 1974; Helmick & Berg, 1976; Robinson et al, 1980). Although there have been few active attempts to

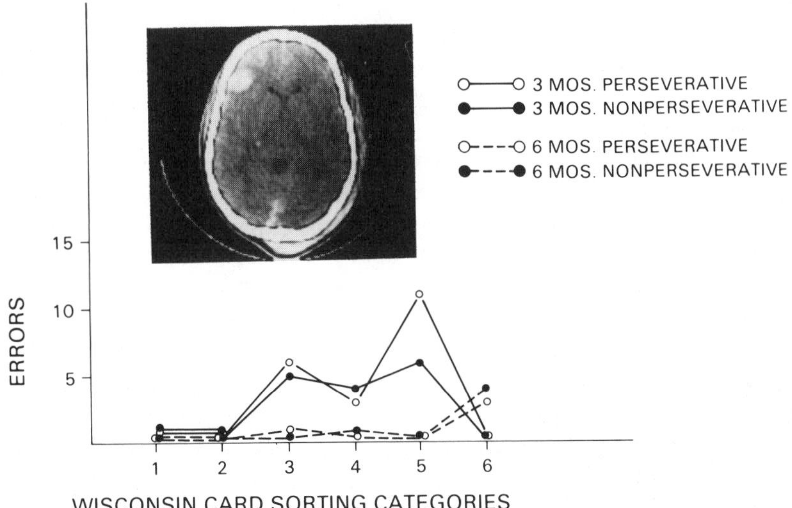


**Fig. 16.6** Improvement in concept formation and shifting responses in a patient with severe closed head injury complicated by bilateral frontal intracerebral hematomas.

remediate deficits, there are suggestions in the research literature that such factors as automaticity of a task and time intervals between responses may be important variables. Pietro & Rigrodsky (1982) reported that speech pathologists have frequently tried to reduce perseverative tendencies in aphasic patients by giving them more time to make responses. The researchers obtained experimental support for this strategy in their study of perseveration in patients who were at least 1 year post-left hemisphere stroke and who exhibited a variety of aphasic disorders. Subjects were required to complete sentences, name objects, and read single words. The interval between a subject's response and the next stimulus presentation was either 1 or 10 seconds. Each task also contained semantically easy and difficult stimuli. The most strikingly consistent finding was that perseveration decreased as the interval between a response and the subsequent stimulus increased. Pending more experimental verification of this phenomenon, perhaps rehabilitation efforts might be directed toward teaching patients with perseverative tendencies to slow their response rates.

Helmick & Berg (1976) utilized a variety of tasks to measure perseverative responses in patients with predominantly left-sided CVAs. The authors noted that tasks which were least automatic (e.g., counting backwards, writing sentences and a letter, drawing designs from memory) produced greater perseveration than more automatic tasks (counting forwards or naming objects). While their criteria for judging a task as automatic were not well defined, 'effort' may be an important component of perseverative behavior.

Researchers could examine those conditions which aid automaticity such as practice and apply these to situations in which perseveration is most likely to occur.

Craine (1982) has attempted to train intellectual flexibility through exercises which require rapid shifting of response sets. Tasks such as 'add–subtract' and 'odd–even' engage the individual in one mode of processing (e.g., addition) and then require a change to another contrasting process (subtraction). Craine works on promoting faster change rates in the patient. Tasks which make use of competing response tendencies and require the individual to inhibit one response (e.g., as in the Stroop Color Word test) might also prove fruitful in remediation.

Luria (Luria & Homskaya, 1964) described the frontal lobe patient as demonstrating a loss of 'critical attitude' which he conceptualized as resulting from the absence of a feedback mechanism. He felt that disturbances in the ability to modify responses represented the loss of verbal control over motor behavior. 'If a verbal program involves the arrest of a former action or an association it loses its controlling function, and the action turns into an unselective, impulsive 'field reaction' or 'perseveration' (Luria & Homskaya, 1964, p. 360).

The suggestion from Luria's work might be to train verbal control over behavior in patients with perseveration. However, Drewe (1975a) has challenged the generality of Luria's hypothesis and has obtained some experimental support against his position in a variety of task situations which required subjects to inhibit responses to particular stimuli and to respond according to certain stimulus characteristics. Drewe instructed subjects on some trial blocks to pair a verbal response with a motor response (e.g., say 'yes' and push red light key; say 'no' and do not push blue light key). Drewe found that on only one task did verbalization correlate with poor motor responses, and that the inability to use verbalization to control motor performance was not as pervasive as predicted by Luria's position. Milner (1982) similarly reported that frontal lobe lesions produced impairments on spatial (non-verbal) as well as non-spatial tasks, thus arguing against the notion of a selective impairment in verbal control of behavior.

As seen from the previous discussion, remediation attempts in cue utilization and response set shifting are at a rudimentary level. The findings from the literature need to be applied to these very commonplace deficits in brain-injured individuals.

## CONCLUSIONS

### Conceptual/methodological issues

A review of the literature reveals a paucity of theoretical and empirical rigor applied to the remediation of problem-solving and reasoning disorders. Most attempts are descriptive, lack experimental designs for measuring treatment effectiveness, and have not elucidated the nature of the deficit by analyzing total neuropsychological functioning. In this section some major issues which treatment providers must address will be highlighted.

*Conceptualization of the deficit*

Noticeably lacking in studies attempting remediation is a detailed process analysis of the underlying deficit before beginning training. We have noted in the foregoing sections that apparent problem-solving/reasoning disorders can arise from deficits in other areas such as language, attention, memory, and visual–spatial processing, or can occur in relative isolation while other functions remain intact. Within problem-solving, for example, an individual might either lack the capacity to abstract or be unable to carry out the arrived at solution. Researchers in the field (cf. Ben-Yishay & Diller, 1983a,b; Caplan, 1982) have acknowledged the importance of conducting what Luria (1966) referred to as a 'syndrome analysis' in order to understand information-processing difficulties. This approach is critical because remediational strategies which are effective in one patient may fail with another due to differences in the core process (Caplan, 1982).

There is no easy solution to pinpointing the underlying deficit or deciding which measures should be used to examine the functions in need of remediation. Newcombe (1982) notes that intelligence tests measure 'crystallized' knowledge but may fail to examine 'fluid' capacity to solve new problems or learn novel material. For this reason subtle deficits in problem-solving may not show up on standardized materials. In addition, rehabilitation is typically directed toward 'real-world' behaviors which are not currently emphasized in neuropsychological tests. A rehabilitation approach requires that functional measures of problem-solving and reasoning be obtained as well (Ben-Yishay & Diller, 1983a). Finally, Lezak (1983) contends that problems in carrying out activities (the executive functions) tend to appear in unstructured settings for which there are very few assessment techniques. Heaton & Pendleton (1981) have noted that research has focused on whether neuropsychological tests can be used to predict general categories of behaviors (e.g., self-care, academic achievement, vocational functioning), and has often failed to sample more specific functional activities such as the ability to handle finances or to drive a car. The researchers demonstrate how test results can be interpreted to obtain information and to make recommendations about more discrete forms of day-to-day activities.

The evaluation of reasoning and problem-solving disorders can be facilitated by utilizing a variety of traditional and non-traditional measures as well as a detailed process analysis of the underlying deficit. Figure 16.7 presents a hierarchical framework for how assessment/remediation might proceed. The approach suggested here encompasses a series of stages arranged in the form of a decision tree which incorporates the three types of problem-solving and reasoning disorders outlined earlier. As seen in Fig. 16.7, initial assessment

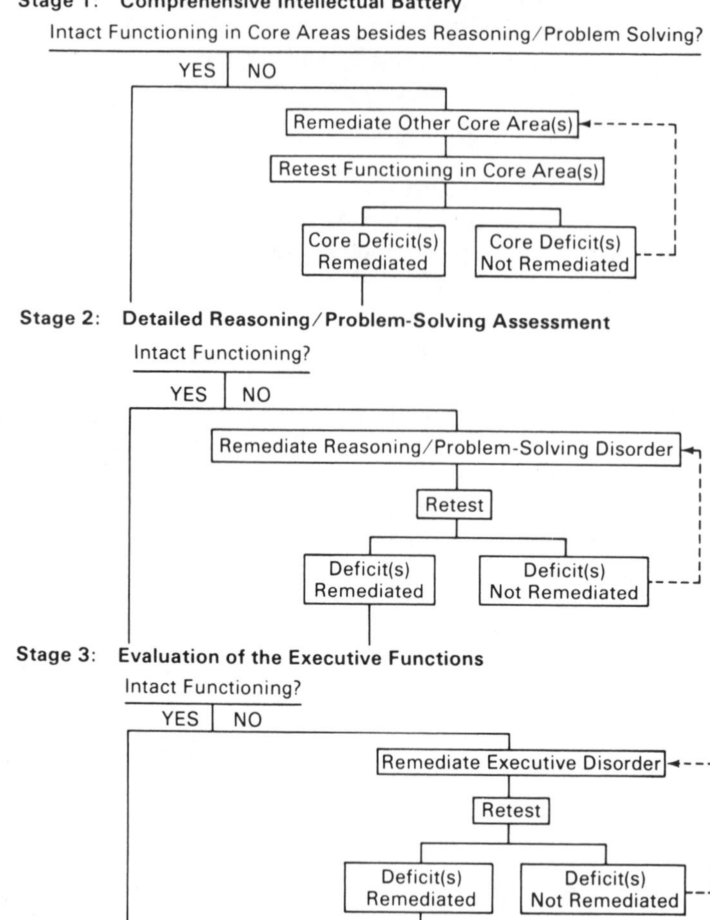


**Fig. 16.7** Decision Tree for Assessment and Remediation of Reasoning/Problem Solving Disorders. Stage 1 consists of a comprehensive intellectual battery in which deficits in other core areas such as memory and attention are evaluated. If deficits are detected, remediation and retesting occurs. All individuals ultimately proceed to Stage 2 in which a detailed evaluation of such reasoning/problem-solving functions as abstraction and perseveration takes place. Deficits here are remediated, and retesting occurs. Finally, all individuals pass to Stage 3 in which the executive functions such as goal formulation and planning are evaluated. Remediation and retesting are implemented if deficits are detected.

might entail a comprehensive battery which examines functioning in a number of areas such as language, memory, visual–spatial processing, and attention. If a deficit(s) was detected, remediation would be implemented and the function(s) re-evaluated. Two outcomes are possible. First, the deficit(s) might not be remediated, and reformulation/retraining would need to be undertaken again. Second, the function(s) could be restored, and evaluation would now proceed to a more detailed analysis of such reasoning/problem-solving processes as abstraction, perseveration, and cue utilization. If deficits were demonstrated, remediation would be implemented and retesting would occur. Finally, all individuals would pass to an evaluation of the executive functions. The tests here would most likely incorporate both unstructured and functional measures. If deficits were still demonstrated, remediation would take place.

Admittedly, this approach to assessment and remediation is highly detailed and individualized. The treatment strategy differs from other models in which the individual passes through all training modules, regardless of whether a deficit is demonstrated (e.g., Ben-Yishay & Diller, 1983b). Regardless of the framework one adopts, however, it is necessary that researchers conceptualize their understanding of problem-solving deficits before remediation is undertaken.

*Generalization of teaching to 'real-life' skills and the view of the recovery process*

A second issue which needs to be addressed concerns the relationship between the training experience and generalization to the patient's environment, i.e., 'ecologic validity' of cognitive remediation. At present, studies in the field use materials and train skills which are removed from the individual's day-to-day activities. Researchers must consider whether laboratory tasks and skills can be extrapolated to naturalistic settings. The NYU team (Ben-Yishay & Diller, 1983a) has adopted the position that tasks employed in remediation should not necessarily use real-world examples. First, it is argued that it is impractical to devise such tasks due to the complex nature of deficits, and second, such everyday materials may frustrate the patient. In their model the therapist's role is to relate the laboratory tasks to the patient's life. It has not yet been demonstrated whether this approach is effective, but we suggest that remediational attempts should focus on both laboratory and real-world teaching. Thus, one might train cognitive flexibility by having the patient alternate between processes requiring addition and subtraction and then link this learning to an everyday event of counting change with money. Or one might teach the patient to organize a list of words and pictures into taxonomic categories and then have the patient apply this learning towards organizing a grocery list. Motivation could be increased by such an approach because the individual learns the relevance of these skills to daily living.

In addition, there is an absence of a clear-cut rationale for many of the procedures utilized in the literature. More attention needs to be paid to formulating a model of the individual's deficit, outlining a plan for how recovery might be facilitated, and then designing procedures which encompass this scheme. Two views of neurobehavioral recovery are restitution which emphasizes recovery or reorganization of function in the damaged area of the brain versus a substitution position which states that other areas of the brain take over functions of the impaired site. An implication of the restitution position is that remediation should focus on stimulation techniques of the impaired function such as gradually increasing a patient's auditory short-term memory span by aurally presenting longer sequences of digits. A substitution view would aim at finding alternative intact strategies for arriving at the same end result, such as using visual imagery to promote memory (Rothi & Horner, 1983). A restitution approach is currently utilized in many rehabilitation settings (e.g., the use of music therapy to stimulate language in aphasics). Gianutsos (1980) and Rothi & Horner (1983) have suggested that rehabilitation techniques should include both types of training, but there is a lack of data to support this position.

### *Measurement of recovery*

A third issue confronting the field concerns the length of time and amount of evidence needed to demonstrate that treatment is effective. The measurement of problem-solving and reasoning is extremely complicated. It has been suggested (Brooks et al, 1984) that more complex cognitive processes may recover over longer periods of time, and therefore, extended follow-up examinations may be necessary. An implication is that training of higher-level functions might be confounded with 'spontaneous' recovery, or that there is an interaction between the effects of remediation and time since injury, i.e., the training is most effective if it is introduced early after the period of initial medical treatment. Thus, for example, a rehabilitation specialist might introduce a problem-solving remediational program too soon after an injury and erroneously conclude that the program itself was largely responsible for the improvements shown. Conversely, a remediation technique might be misinterpreted as ineffective because its application is too early in the patient's course of recovery. At this embryonic stage of cognitive rehabilitation, researchers need to demonstrate the effectiveness of techniques *per se* and must be careful to consider the time since injury and include appropriate control groups. Apart from remediation, the non-specific effects of additional stimulation should be considered.

Perhaps another implication of extended recovery periods for problem-solving and reasoning disorders is the importance of incorporating long-term follow-ups for evaluating treatment effectiveness. It is conceivable that an individual might not show immediate benefit but demonstrate improvement 1 year later in comparison with a control group. Currently, the majority of studies do not assess functioning past the training period. It is also critical that individuals receive a sufficient amount of time in a program before a training strategy is abandoned. Miller (1980), for example, has observed that head-injured patients typically have slow start-up rates, much like the mentally handicapped population, but they do benefit from training. In this connection, employment of a cross-sequential design might be an efficient strategy for collecting longitudinal data in cohorts of patients who are entered in the study at different intervals after head injury or stroke.

Researchers also need to consider the kinds of data they will utilize to demonstrate efficacy of training. Is improvement on neuropsychological tests sufficient evidence of efficacy to implement a widespread program? Or are more functional measures needed? One might even conceive of utilizing physiological data such as electrophysiologic changes indicative of frontal lobe activation following specific training on a card-sorting task.

### *Differences in the treatment population*

Finally, innovators in cognitive rehabilitation must devise treatment strategies which accommodate the heterogeneity of the population they serve. Deficits resulting from stroke and head injury, for example, are typically different especially in the relative prominence of impairment secondary to focal cortical injury (Levin et al, 1982; Newcombe, 1982). Stroke tends to produce well-defined, focal lesions and specific, lateralized deficits whereas non-missile head injury frequently results in diffuse cerebral insult and relatively nonlateralized cognitive and behavioral dysfunction. Thomas & Trexler (1982) have obtained experimental support for this dichotomy through a factor analytic study comparing neuropsychological functioning in stroke and closed head-injured patients. The factor analysis of the stroke group yielded focal or lateralized functions while the analysis of the closed head-injured group produced factors related to bilateral brain processes.

Thomas & Trexler (1982) offer two recommendations for cognitive remediation. First, they suggest that tasks used with a closed head-injured population should be more holistic and train a variety of functions along an interdisciplinary approach. Tasks utilized with stroke patients might focus on more specific deficits such as unilateral neglect. Second, they argue that closed head injury tends to produce a general decline in information processing capacity and that remediation should restore both capacity and flexibility. Clearly researchers need to coordinate rehabilitation programs to address the pattern of deficits associated with the pathological entity under treatment.

## GENERAL CONCLUSIONS

At present, the literature on remediating problem-solving and reasoning disorders is fragmented. The field has come a long way in designing assessment techniques and in describing the nature of deficits. However, there is a lack of theoretical cohesion and an absence of rationales for many of the techniques currently in use. Researchers might consider applying the paradigms and theories from the cognitive literature to guide their attempts. For example, the specific information-processing models of problem-solving derived from the field of artificial intelligence could be applied to remediation programs. Shallice (1982) has recently illustrated how one such model (the Supervisory Attentional System) may be used to explain planning disorders in patients with left anterior frontal lobe lesions. This research could be adapted further to the design of specific techniques.

Brain-injured individuals and their families often experience tremendous distress surrounding their cognitive impairments and the uncertainties of neurorehabilitation. Consequently, remediation programs should be theoretically and empirically sound. In describing the field of cognitive remediation, Diller & Gordon (1981) commented that

> Indeed, providers of intervention programs find themselves in a situation analogous to that of developers of the airplane in the early part of the 20th century. The first concerns of those in aviation were not speed, safety, or cost, but whether the contraption could get off the ground and stay in the air (p. 822).

Perhaps we need to return to some of these other questions before we attempt to fly.

## ACKNOWLEDGMENT

This work was supported in part by the National Institute of Neurological and Communicative Diseases and Stroke, Javits Neuroscience Investigator Award NS 21889 and grant NS 07377, A Center for the Study of Nervous System Injury. We thank Beverly White for her help in manuscript preparation.

### REFERENCES

Benton A L 1968 Differential behavioral effects in frontal lobe disease. Neuropsychologia 12: 557–563

Benton A L, Hamsher K deS 1978 Multilingual aphasia examination. University of Iowa, Iowa City

Ben-Yishay Y, Diller L 1983a Cognitive deficits. In: Griffith E A, Bond M, Miller J (eds) Rehabilitation of the head injured adult. Davis, Philadelphia, ch. 12, pp. 167–183

Ben-Yishay Y, Diller L 1983b Cognitive remediation. In: Griffith E A, Bond M, Miller J (eds) Rehabilitation of the head injured adult. Davis, Philadelphia, ch. 26, pp. 367–380

Ben-Yishay Y, Piasetsky E, Diller L 1978 A modular approach to training (verbal) abstract thinking in brain injured people. In: Ben-Yishay, Y (ed) Working approaches to remediation of cognitive deficits in brain damaged persons. NYU Monographs (59), New York, ch. 5, pp. 133–153

Brooks D N, Deelman B G, Zomeren A H, Dongen H, Harskamp F, Aughton M E 1984 Problems in measuring cognitive recovery after acute brain injury. Journal of Clinical Neuropsychology 6: 71–85

Caplan B 1982 Neuropsychology in rehabilitation: its role in evaluation and intervention. Archives of Physical Medicine and Rehabilitation 63: 362–366

Cicerone K D, Lazar R M 1983 Effects of frontal lobe lesions on hypothesis sampling during concept formation. Neuropsychologia 21: 513–524

Cope N, Hall K 1982 Head injury rehabilitation: benefit of early intervention. Archives of Physical Medicine and Rehabilitation 63: 433–437

Craine J F 1982 The retraining of frontal lobe dysfunction. In: Trexler L E (ed) Cognitive rehabilitation: conceptualization and intervention. Plenum, New York, ch. 13, pp. 239–262

Diller L, Gordon W A 1981 Interventions for cognitive deficits in brain-injured adults. Journal of Consulting and Clinical Psychology 49: 822–834

Drewe E A 1974 The effect of type and area of brain lesion on Wisconsin Card Sorting Test performance. Cortex 10: 159–170

Drewe E A 1975a An experimental investigation of Luria's theory on the effects of frontal lobe lesions in man. Neuropsychologia 13: 421–429

Drewe E A 1975b Go–no go learning after frontal lobe lesions in humans. Cortex 11: 8–16
Gasparrini B, Satz P 1979 A treatment for memory problems in left hemisphere CVA patients. Journal of Clinical Neuropsychology 1: 137–150
Gianutsos R 1980 What is cognitive rehabilitation? Journal of Rehabilitation 13: 36–40
Gianutsos R, Gianutsos J 1979 Rehabilitating the verbal recall of brain-injured patients by mnemonic training: an experimental demonstration using single-case methodology. Journal of Clinical Neuropsychology 1: 117–135
Goldstein G, Reuthen L 1983 Rehabilitation of the brain-damaged adult. Plenum, New York
Goldstein G, Neuringer C, Olson J 1968 Impairment of abstract reasoning in the brain-damaged: qualitative or quantitative? Cortex 4: 372–388
Goldstein K 1942 Aftereffects of brain injuries in war. Grune & Stratton, New York
Goldstein K, Scheerer M 1941 Abstract and concrete behavior: An experimental study with special tests. Psychological Monographs 53: 1–151
Goldstein K, Scheerer M 1953 Tests of abstract and concrete behavior. In: Weider A (ed) Contributions to medical psychology, vol. 2. Ronald, New York
Goodglass H, Kaplan E 1979 Assessment of cognitive deficit in the brain-injured patient. In: Gazzaniga M S (ed.) Handbook of behavioral neurobiology, vol. 2: Neuropsychology. Plenum, New York, ch. 1, pp. 3–22
Gorham D R 1956 A proverbs test for clinical and experimental use. Psychological Reports 1: 1–12
Grant D A, Berg E A 1948 A behavioral analysis of degree of reinforcement and ease of shifting to new responses in a Weighl-type card-sorting problem. Journal of Experimental Psychology 38: 404–411
Gronwall D, Wrightson P 1981 Memory and information processing capacity after closed head injury. Journal of Neurology, Neurosurgery and Psychiatry 44: 889–895
Hagen C 1984 Language disorders in head trauma. In: Holland A L (ed) Language disorders in adults. College-Hill Press, San Diego, ch. 8, pp. 245–281
Halstead W C 1947 Brain and intelligence. University of Chicago Press, Chicago
Heaton R K, Pendleton M G 1981 Use of neuropsychological tests to predict adult patients' everyday functioning. Journal of Consulting and Clinical Psychology 49: 807–821
Heilman K M 1979 Neglect and related disorders. In: Heilman K M, Valenstein E (eds) Clinical neuropsychology. Oxford University Press, New York, ch. 10, pp. 268–307
Helmick J W, Berg C B 1976 Perseveration in brain-injured adults. Journal of Communication Disorders 9: 143–156
Jenning E A, Lubinski R B 1981 Strategies for improving productive thinking in the language impaired adult. Journal of Communication Disorders 4: 255–271
Johnson C W, Diller L 1983 Error evaluation ability of right-hemisphere brain-lesioned patients who have had perceptual–cognitive retraining. Journal of Clinical Neuropsychology 5: 401–402
Jones M K 1974 Imagery as a mnemonic aid after left temporal lobe lobectomy: contrast between material-specific and generalized memory disorders. Neuropsychologia 12: 21–30
Jones-Gotman M, Milner B 1977 Design fluency: the invention of nonsense drawings after focal cortical lesions. Neuropsychologia 15: 653–674
Jouandet M, Gazzaniga M S 1979 The frontal lobes. In: Gazzaniga M S (ed) Handbook of behavioral neurobiology, vol. 2: Neuropsychology. Plenum, New York, ch. 2, pp. 25–59
Leftoff S 1983 Psychopathology in the light of brain injury: a case study. Journal of Clinical Neuropsychology 5: 51–63
Levin H S, Benton A L, Grossman R G 1982 Neurobehavioral consequences of closed head injury. Oxford University Press, New York
Levin H S, Grossman R G, Rose J E, Teasdale G 1979 Long-term neuropsychological outcome of closed head injury. Journal of Neurosurgery 50: 412–422
Lezak M D 1983 Neuropsychological assessment. Oxford University Press, New York
Livingston K E 1977 Limbic system dysfunction induced by 'kindling': its significance for psychiatry. In: Sweet W., Obrador S, Martin-Rodriguez J G (eds) Neurosurgical treatment in psychiatry, pain, and epilepsy. University Park, Baltimore, pp. 63–75
Luria A R 1963 Restoration of function after brain injury. Pergamon, New York
Luria A R 1966 Higher cortical functions in man. Basic Books, New York
Luria A R 1973 The working brain. Basic Books, New York
Luria A R, Homskaya E D 1964 Disturbances in the regulative role of speech with frontal

lobe lesions. In: Warren J M, Ahert K A (eds) The frontal granular cortex and behavior. McGraw-Hill, New York, ch. 17, pp. 353-371

Miller E 1980 The training characteristics of severely head-injured patients: a preliminary study. Journal of Neurology, Neurosurgery and Psychiatry 43: 525-528

Milner B 1963 Effects of different brain lesions on card sorting. Archives of Neurology 9: 100-110

Milner B 1982 Some cognitive effects of frontal-lobe lesions in man. Philosophical Transactions of the Royal Society of London 298: 211-229

Myers P S 1984 Right hemisphere impairment. In: Holland A L (ed) Language disorders in adults. College-Hill, San Diego, ch. 6, pp. 177-208

Nauta W J H 1971 The problem of the frontal lobe: a reinterpretation. Journal of Psychiatric Research 8: 167-187

Nelson H E 1976 A modified card sorting test sensitive to frontal lobe defects. Cortex 12: 313-324

Neuringer C, Goldstein G, Jannes D T 1973 The relationship between age and qualitative or quantitative impairment of abstract reasoning in the brain damaged. Journal of Genetic Psychology 123: 195-200

Newcombe F 1982 The psychological consequences of closed head injury: assessment and rehabilitation. Injury: The British Journal of Accident Surgery 14: 111-136

Oscar-Berman M 1973 Hypothesis testing and focusing behavior during concept formation by amnesic Korsakoff patients. Neuropsychologia 11: 191-198

Pietro M J, Rigrodsky S 1982 The effects of temporal and semantic conditions on the occurrence of the error response of perseveration in adult aphasics. Journal of Speech and Hearing Research 25: 184-192

Powell T P S 1972 Sensory convergence in the cerebral cortex. In: Laitinen L V, Livingston K E (eds) Surgical approaches in psychiatry. Proceedings of the Third International Congress of Psychosurgery. University Park, Baltimore, pp. 266-281

Prigatano G P, Fordyce D J, Zeiner H K, Roueche J R, Pepping M, Wood B C 1984 Neuropsychological rehabilitation after closed head injury in young adults. Journal of Neurology, Neurosurgery and Psychiatry 47: 505-513

Rausch R 1977 Cognitive strategies in patients with unilateral temporal lobe excisions. Neuropsychologia 15: 385-395

Raven J C 1960 Guide to the standard progressive matrices. H K Lewis, London and Psychological Corporation, New York

Robinson A L, Heaton R K, Lehman R A, Stilson D W 1980 The utility of the Wisconsin Card Sorting Test in detecting and localizing frontal lobe lesions. Journal of Consulting and Clinical Psychology 48: 605-614

Rothi L J, Horner J 1983 Restitution and substitution: two theories of recovery with application to neurobehavioral treatment. Journal of Clinical Neuropsychology 5: 73-81

Shallice T 1982 Specific impairments of planning. Philosophical Transactions of the Royal Society of London 298: 199-209

Stuss D T, Benson D F 1984 Neuropsychological studies of the frontal lobes. Psychological Bulletin 95: 3-28

Terman L M, Merrill M A 1973 Stanford-Binet intelligence scale. Manual form the third revision, Form L-M. Houghton Mifflin, Boston

Thomas J D, Trexler L E 1982 Behavioral and cognitive deficits in cerebrovascular accident and closed head injury: implications for cognitive rehabilitation. In: Trexler L E (ed) Cognitive rehabilitation: conceptualization and intervention. Plenum, New York, ch. 3, pp. 27-81

Wechsler D 1981 WAIS-R manual. Psychological Corporation, New York

Yu J 1976 Functional recovery with and without training following brain damage in experimental animals: a review. Archives of Physical Medicine and Rehabilitation 57: 38-41

# Personality and psychosocial consequences after brain injury

## INTRODUCTION

Brain lesions of various types produce alterations in personality, but they are frequently 'overlooked' because they lack neurologic diagnostic utility (i.e., lesion localization) and are difficult to measure objectively. Moreover, pre-existing personality characteristics of a patient interact with neuropathologically mediated changes in cognition and affect to yield variable patterns of personality disturbances. Thus, descriptions such as 'frontal lobe personality' syndrome are doomed to be oversimplifications (Blumer & Benson, 1975) and confusing both to clinicians and researchers. As the connecting neural circuitry between limbic structures and the cerebral hemispheres is identified, greater understanding of personality changes after brain injury will occur and a true 'neurology of emotion' will be possible (see Bear, 1983).

The importance of personality disturbances following brain injury is obvious to rehabilitation therapists and family members of the patient. Having to deal with these patients on a day-to-day basis is difficult, and their personality characteristics either lessen or substantially increase the work-load. Patients who seem depressed and 'unmotivated' often frustrate therapists and receive minimal therapy or inappropriate therapy. Those who are paranoid and have trouble controlling temper may simply be eliminated from rehabilitation programs on the basis of their being 'management problems.' Yet, these affective disturbances are frequently as neurologically based as aphasia and hemiplegia. Additionally, there are also affective problems which are part of the reaction patients experience when attempting to cope with their disabilities, as Goldstein (1942) pointed out years ago. These later disturbances are potentially amenable to change if the rehabilitation therapist can teach the patient more efficient means of coping. This has been one major goal of an intensive neuropsychological rehabilitation program for young adult brain-injured patients at Presbyterian Hospital, in Oklahoma City, Oklahoma (Prigatano & Fordyce, in press).

While various models of personality have generated interesting concepts concerning the nature of psychopathology (see Freedman et al, 1976), these models often do not directly relate to what is known about brain function.

When attempts have been made to do this (Pribram & Gill, 1976), the result is often more theoretical in nature than clinically useful.

This chapter will present, therefore, a neuropsychology-oriented definition of personality. A review of the common personality disturbances following brain injury will then be considered. A brief discussion of personality disturbances after brain injury in children will be presented, followed by a discussion of the psychosocial consequences of brain injury and principles of therapeutic intervention. Since this chapter is intended for the clinical psychologist and neuropsychologist working in rehabilitation, the emphasis will be on information important to clinical management of patients. Detailed discussion of the neuroanatomical and neuropathological correlates of personality disturbances are available elsewhere (see Bear, 1983; Valenstein & Heilman, 1979; Poeck, 1969).

## PERSONALITY AND NEUROPSYCHOLOGICAL CONSIDERATIONS

### Personality defined

Personality is defined as patterns of emotional and motivational responses which develop over the life of the organism; are highly influenced by early life experiences; are modifiable, but not easily changed, by behavioral or teaching methods; and greatly influence (and are influenced by) cognitive processes. In humans, these patterns of emotional and motivational responses are, in part, self-recognized, but may remain outside of the individual's realm of conscious awareness. Other people, familiar with the individual's daily behavioral characteristics, may recognize emotional and motivational responses that the person may not be fully aware of or able to subjectively report. Finally, the form of a given emotional and/or motivational response is highly dependent on the environmental consequences, as well as the biological state of the organism. This definition draws heavily from the work of Pribram (1971), Freud (1924), Jung (1964), various 'social biologists' (e.g. Timbergen, 1953 and Lorenz, 1966), Simon (1967), Goldstein (1942), and Sullivan (1953). As such, biological, psychological, and psychosocial constructs are inevitably involved in defining personality.

Neuropsychology, however, can aid in defining what emotions and motivations are, and the neural structures involved in sustaining them. Also, understanding the disturbing effects of various brain lesions on the balance between affect and cognition is possible through the study of neuropsychologic mechanisms (e.g., Prigatano & Pribram, 1981). Eventually, a neuropsychological model of the underlying structures and dynamics involved in personality should become a reality.

### Feelings, emotions, and motivations

Feelings are the most rudimentary, generalized, and differentiated perceptions of internal bodily states. By nature they have an intensity or an arousal dimension to them (Lindsley, 1970). Core brain receptors involved in the central nervous system's regulation of the organism's metabolic and endocrine functions are probably responsible for the initial or 'crude sensation' of feeling states. These core brain receptors for temperature, thirst, hunger, pain, and respiration are localized in the brainstem and are near the midline ventricular system involving hypothalamic and midline thalamic nuclei (see Pribram, 1971).

If feelings can be considered the basic representation for homeostatic states of the organism, the terms emotion and motivation can be used to refer to more complex and refined feeling states which incorporate basic homeostasis but also go beyond it. Motivation refers to the complex feeling states that parallel hierarchical goal-seeking behavior (Simon, 1967). As such, it can be described as the arousal component of behavior which regulates the development and execution of a plan of action. In Simon's (1967) information processing model, motivation controls attention and thereby influences learning by influencing which program will be followed. A program here is defined simply as a series of steps that are taken in order to achieve a goal (Miller et al, 1960).

Using Simon's (1967) model, emotion, on the other hand, refers to the complex feeling states that parallel an interruption of whatever ongoing goal-seeking behaviors or programs are engaged. Emotion interrupts an ongoing process according to Simon (1967), particularly when stimuli entering the perceptual world must be addressed for survival value. In humans, attention to the activities of other humans is especially important for survival, and thus emotion is crucial and indispensable in human social interaction. While there are certainly other models of motivation and emotion, this system has appeal for the neuropsychologically oriented clinician.

Schacter & Singer (1962) have also eloquently shown the cognitive appraisal of an induced arousal state determines the name humans ascribe to a feeling state. Thus, whether one feels angry, sad, fearful, or happy depends to a large extent on what the person's cognitive appraisal is of these perceived changes in arousal. Lazarus' (1977) work also suggests that only those perceptions which have 'emotional' meaning effect change or are 'attended to.'

These considerations have two important corollaries for the rehabilitation neuropsychologist. Disturbances in brainstem and related structures may influence basic arousal and/or attentional mechanisms. As such, goal-seeking (motivational behaviors) and the interruption of ongoing behaviors for biological–social (emotional) reasons may be altered because basic arousal and attentional dimensions of behavior have been impaired. In severe cases, unless this can be altered by medications and/or environmental stimuli, little can help the patient learn and socially adapt. Even months or years post-traumic brain injury, some patients' 'personality' difficulties may be secondary to brain arousal and attentional deficits.

Secondly, disturbances of higher 'cerebral' or 'cortical' centers may influence the ability of the person to correctly perceive and interpret feelings in self and others. These emotional and motivational disturbances do not flow from a lack of sustained or modulated arousal, but rather from an inability to cognitively deal with arousal-producing stimuli. Therapies aimed at the cognitive underpinnings of these types of personality disturbances are vital. Conversely, in cases where there is diffuse cerebral dysfunction and associated impairment in abstract reasoning skills (see Luria, 1966), traditional forms of psychotherapy or the so-called cognitive behavior therapies may be relatively ineffective. However, in cases of localized cerebral injury or where abstract reasoning and memory skills are greatly preserved, such therapies may be quite effective and desperately needed by certain patients.

### *Pertinent animal literature*

A consistently demonstrated finding, in the animal literature, has been that general visceral regulation and control of feelings is performed by highly complicated and differentiated mechanisms of the hypothalamus and the amygdaloid complex. Pribram (1971) reviewed available evidence that the amygdala, with its ventral medial hypothalamic connections, seems to play a key role in 'emotional feeling' states. Damage to the amygdala in animals, by surgical intervention or electrical stimulation, fails to influence basic appetitive behaviors once they start. Thus, disturbances have been noted in animals who cannot stop eating, fighting, or engaging in sexual activities. Moreover, there is some evidence in humans, who have had unilateral surgical removal of the amygdala, hypothalamus, and part of the temporal lobe, of a dissociation between subjective reported feeling states and publicly observable appetitive behavior (see Pribram, 1971).

Amygdaloid monkeys also show disruption of their basic visceral, autonomic functioning as measured by habituation studies (see Pribram & Luria, 1973; Pribram & McGuinness, 1975). Finally, some patients given stereotaxic amygdalotomies show reduced rage reactions even when there is a history of rather severe aggressive behavior. Taken together, one can indirectly surmise that the intact amygdala may be very important in the normal stop or interrupt functions of appetitive or emotional behavior (see Pribram, 1971, for a detailed description).

Pribram (1971, 1977) has also suggested that the basal ganglia and the connecting fiber tracts to the far lateral hypothalamic region play an important role in motivation. Neurochemically, this far lateral region appears to be replete with nigral striatal fibers which carry dopaminergic substances. These substances seem to be quite important for carrying out complex animated movements and the performance of what we often describe as purposeful or motivated behaviors. Thus, damage to the limbic system and basal ganglia may lead to very important disturbances in motivation. This is especially important when considering the fact that lesions to these areas frequently occur following traumatic head injury (Graham et al, 1978).

### *A note on anatomical correlates*

Given the importance of emotion and motivation for survival, the role cognition plays in interpreting feeling states, and the variable learning histories, it is highly unlikely that a specific brain lesion will produce a specific personality deficit. However, different lesions may influence the neurophysiological substrates of emotion and motivation in predictable ways. This is in keeping with Luria's concept of functional systems and interrelated subsystems which underlie all adaptive complex behaviors. Valenstein & Heilman (1979) have reviewed in some detail various affective disturbances associated with lesions of the central nervous system. Sackheim et al (1982) and Bear (1983) have recently reviewed the literature on hemispheric asymmetry and the expression of emotions. The reader is referred to those sources for a comprehensive review of this topic. However, specific correlations which may be helpful for the rehabilitation neuropsychologist are considered next in light of the common personality disturbances seen after brain injury.

## COMMON PERSONALITY DISTURBANCES AFTER BRAIN INJURY

Common personality changes associated with brain injury often include descriptions of patients as irritable, impulsive, socially inappropriate, unaware of their personal impact on others, less motivated, and more emotional. These latter problems typically include poorer tolerance for frustration, greater dependence on others, insensitivity to others, and generally a more demanding attitude (e.g., increased helplessness). A scheme for classifying these and other common personality changes after brain injury has not yet appeared. However, Goldstein (1942) suggests that these problems may flow directly from the cognitive confusion (i.e., loss of abstract attitude) and increased fatigability commonly found in brain-injured patients. Some personality changes after brain injury truly reflect the struggle of the damaged organism to adapt to an environment which no longer takes into consideration limited cognitive skills and physical disabilities.

While some clinicians are clearly impressed with the notion that premorbid personality influences postmorbid personality changes (Schilder, 1934), it is difficult to demonstrate this empirically. Kozol (1945, 1946), for example, was unable to show that pre-trauma personality characteristics correlated with post-trauma 'neurotic' symptomatology. Despite premorbid functioning, most trauma patients were described as 'irritable' and easily frustrated following injury. These data and others suggest that affective disturbances post-brain injury may be greatly influenced by the type and extent of neural damage. Yet, in cases of particularly mild head injury, pre-existing psychiatric disturbances may be correlated with later presence of general psychiatric disturbance. McLean et al (1983) found no significant differences between closed head injury (CHI) patients and peer groups (i.e., friends or matched relatives of CHI patients) on psychiatric symptomatology. They suggest that others have found psychiatric differences between groups due to using inadequate (cross-sectional) control groups (Weddell et al, 1980). Their study provides indirect evidence that CHI patients do not represent a typical cross-section of the population, but may be more representative of people who were previously maladjusted or risk-takers. This to some degree, has been documented in children (Brown et al, 1981).

In more severe brain injuries the role of the pre-existing personality for latter post-injury personality disorders may be considerably lessened. There is rather strong evidence, for example, that the severity of brain injury is directly related to certain, but not all, psychiatric or behavioral disorders (e.g., Lishman, 1968, 1973; Levin & Grossman, 1978; Levin et al, 1979).

Personality disturbances following brain injury, particularly traumatic head injury, appear to fall into four broad 'classes' of behavioral phenomena that seem especially important for neuropsychological rehabilitation. They are: (1) anxiety and the catastrophic reaction; (2) denial of illness or anosognosia; (3) paranoia and psychomotor agitation; and (4) depression, social withdrawal, and the so-called amotivational states. While some of these phenomena may occur more frequently with right versus left brain injuries (e.g., anosognosia) or with temporal lobe dysfunction (i.e., paranoid ideation), they are so common in brain-damaged patients that they will be discussed without extensive detailed reference to possible neuroanatomical correlates.

## Anxiety and the catastrophic reaction

> A patient may look animated, calm, in a good mood, well-poised, collected and cooperative when he is confronted with tasks he can fulfill; the same patient may appear dazed, become agitated, change color, start to fumble, become unfriendly, evasive and even aggressive when he is not able to fulfill the task. His overt behavior appears very much the same as a person in the state of anxiety, and I have called the state of the patient in the situation of success, *ordered condition*; the state in the situation of failure, *disordered* or *catastrophic condition* (Goldstein, 1952, p. 255).

Goldstein (1942, 1952) has eloquently described the plight of brain-injured adults and has provided classical insights into why they may appear so emotionally labile. Unable to deal with their cognitive confusion (or decreased abstract reasoning skills), brain-injured patients can be easily threatened and experience an associated anxiety about life. Goldstein (1952) pointed out that many brain-injured patients have a strong need to discharge this tension or anxiety and frequently do so without the social amenities. This results in them being described as impulsive, inappropriate, and psychologically unsophisticated. He points out that these patients experience a release of tension by such actions, but do not necessarily feel a sense of enjoyment or freedom over their actions. Consequently, they are in a situation in which impulsive or inappropriate responses have a reinforcing quality (i.e., reduction of tension), but also bring punitive social reactions from the environment. This may simply add to the patient's confusion and hopelessness.

Studies which have assessed anxiety after brain injury typically do not report a strong relationship between the degree of anxiety and the degree of brain damage. Lishman (1968) investigated the relationship between psychiatric disability and indices of brain damage. Anxiety was not particularly related to estimates of post-traumatic amnesia or degree of brain tissue destroyed. In contrast, signs of intellectual and memory impairment were related to these latter measures. Levin & Grossman (1978) report a statistical relationship between grade of head injury and anxiety, but again the relationship was not clinically impressive. Prigatano (1983) classified 48 consecutive head injury patients as 'restless' or 'not restless,' based on their relatives' rating on the KATZ Adjustment Scale. Patients did not differ in age, education, length of coma, or chronicity of injury. Yet the restless patients were described by relatives as notably more emotionally distressed. These data are in keeping with Goldstein's (1952) assertions that anxiety after brain injury may reflect more the patient's struggle to adapt than the degree or extent of brain injury and associated neuropsychological impairment.

Research on the catastrophic reaction has been primarily limited to whether the phenomenon is more common in patients with right versus left brain injury. Gainotti (1972) compared patients with right versus left vascular and neoplastic lesions. On various emotional indices, left hemisphere patients were considered to show more signs of anxiety, tears, abusive language, and uncooperativeness. Yet there were no differences between the groups on aggressive behavior or depressive reactions. Also, there were some patients in each group that showed all the signs of the catastrophic reaction. Gainotti (1972) further pointed out, however, that patients with Broca's aphasia were especially prone to show emotional outbursts. While this, at first glance, might be taken as a reflection of some specific relationship between anterior left hemisphere disturbance and the catastrophic reaction, a more parsimonious explanation is possible. These patients may have simply lost the linguistic and cognitive resources for dealing with their anxiety and consequently, appear more emotional (see Dikmen & Reitan, 1977). At this point it appears that the catastrophic reaction is a common occurrence following brain injury, and more associated with failures in coping rather than a specific type of lesion.

The natural course of development of the catastrophic reaction over time is only starting to be investigated. Fordyce et al (1983) report that the more chronic head-injury patients frequently experience greater emotional distress than acute patients. This was based on self-report and relatives' ratings of the patient's emotional and motivational behavior. These data suggest that with cumulative experiences of failure in the environment, patients can become more, not less, disturbed in their personality functioning. Prigatano (1981) reported that during the early phases following brain injury, when cognitive confusion is perhaps greatest, the patient may experience relatively little emotional distress. During the first year following traumatic brain injury, however, the patient may be more emotionally distressed. He or she, at this time, tends to misjudge the degree of the cognitive deficit and attempts to return to work and social activities. The patient soon becomes frustrated and unable to cope. Family members typically now see the patient as more belligerent, negativistic, and generally using poor judgment. After failing in the environment, the patient then tends to withdraw and generally becomes more suspicious of others. The catastrophic reaction may change its form as the patient's cognitive confusion lessens and the degree of contact with the environment changes. One coping strategy for many brain-injured patients may be simply to withdraw from the environment after repeated failures in dealing with it. Certainly, neuropsychological rehabilitation needs to directly address the problem of social withdrawal and interpersonal isolation following brain injury.

## Denial of illness or anosognosia

The phenomenon of frank denial of a neurologic deficit or disease has been recognized for many years. Weinstein and Kahn (1955) have provided a comprehensive overview of this phenomenon as well as a method of classifying the types of denial that are clinically seen. They note that the phenomenon is more frequent with non-dominant (usually right) hemispheric lesions and is associated with alterations in mood, disorientation for time and place, and/or non-aphasic misnaming errors. Patients with a right hemisphere stroke and left hemiplegia can demonstrate striking examples of this phenomenon, particularly during the acute phase of their neurological illness. When asked to move both arms, for example, the patient may move only the right hand and say that the left is either 'tired' or not wanting to move. If asked if the left hand can move, the patient may state that it can and persist with this misbelief despite evidence to the contrary. As the acute period resolves, this denial phenomenon may diminish or even disappear. Yet, in many traumatic head injury patients with bilateral and deep brain lesions, denial of the severity of residual neuropsychological deficits may persist for many years post-trauma.

An interesting clinical example, which demonstrates the denial phenomenon, and which connects it with the catastrophic reaction is the following: A 23-year-old severe head injury patient who remained grossly amnestic with cognitive confusion 14 months post-traumatic head injury was given a neuropsychological examination. The patient was asked if he had any memory difficulties since his accident. He smiled and in a very congenial manner, said 'no'. The patient was then asked to listen and later recall the first story of the Logical Memory subtest of the Wechsler Memory Scale. After hearing the story, the patient tried to recall it but could give only one bit out of a possible 22 bits of information. He immediately swore at the examiner and the test, stated that he wanted the testing stopped, and would not participate in any form of rehabilitation. This example is repeated thousands of times in the course of neuropsychological evaluation of traumatic head injury patients, although frequently in a less dramatic fashion. Such patients often insist that their residual neuropsychological deficits following head injury are mild or minimal. This is in contrast to relatives' reports that their deficits are significant and greatly disturb their day-to-day function. When confronted with this evidence, patients frequently become agitated and angry or withdraw.

This phenomenon suggests that denial is motivated by the need to keep out of awareness the harsh reality of cognitive, perceptual and motor deficits. When these deficits are made obvious to the patient the catastrophic reaction can and often does occur. Dealing with the problem of denial of illness and the catastrophic reaction are two major tasks of intensive neuropsychological rehabilitation. Unless these personality disturbances are dealt with, improvement in psychosocial adjustment seldom occurs. Awareness allows the individual to experience a normal grief reaction and to readjust to lost skills and associated changes in body usage.

Research on denial of illness phenomena has centered on its frequency in right versus left hemisphere patients (Gainotti, 1972). Its natural course is not well understood and methods for dealing with it are inadequately outlined. Labaw's (1969) retrospective analysis of his own anosognosia following closed head injury is especially insightful. He reminds clinicians that as a head injury patient, who previously practiced as a physician, he was honestly convinced that the impact of his brain injury was not that significant. Whether this reflects a psychological reaction to the painful realities of life following brain trauma (i.e., he was motivated not to recognize the threatening information about how he had changed) or true neurologic disturbance in awareness and attention needs to be more thoroughly evaluated in future research (see Heilman, 1979). The work of Morrow et al (1981) strongly suggests that disturbances of the right hemisphere may affect arousal level, and consequently the capacity to respond to emotional stimuli. Their creative work suggests that the phenomenon of denial of illness may represent a neurophysiologic disturbance as well as a psychological reaction to painful and emotional stimuli. Figure 17.1 shows that after right or left hemisphere brain injury, there is a decrease in autonomic nervous system responsiveness to 'emotional' stimuli. However, right hemisphere patients show less arousal to 'emotional' and 'non-emotional' stimuli. Thus, right hemisphere disease may specifically alter arousal and attentional mechanisms and thereby decrease the capacity for self awareness.

In the clinical arena, both neurologic and psychologic mechanisms appear to be frequently involved in the denial of illness phenomenon. For example, the author has seen patients with primarily left hemisphere injury who have insisted that they have had no residual neuropsychological deficits despite repeated evidence to the contrary. In these patients there is often evidence of premorbid problems in psychological functioning and social adaptation. Other patients seem to have fragmented cognitive and perceptual experiences and do not appreciate their deficits because of an organically mediated disturbance in self-perception. The interaction between locus of lesion, neuropsychological

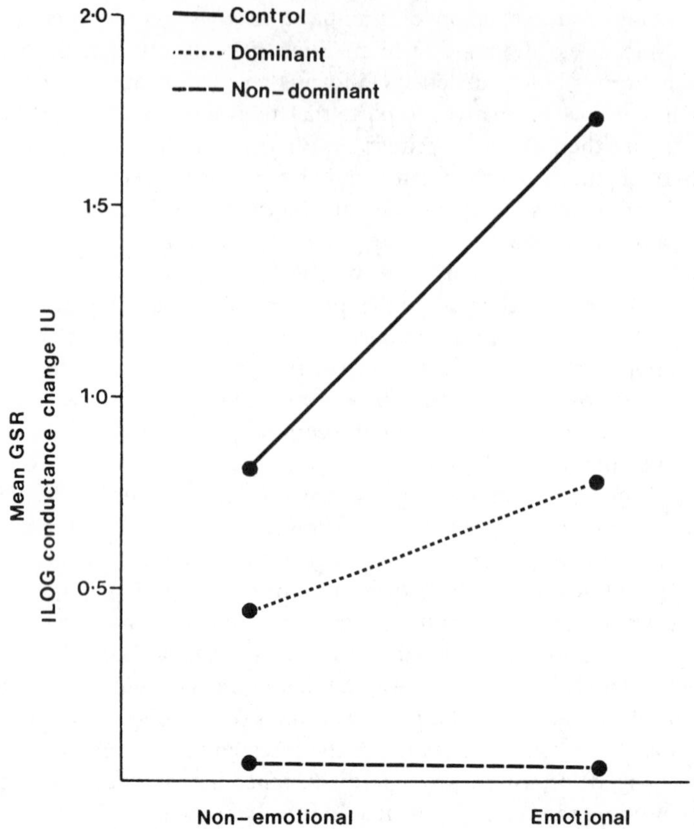


**Fig. 17.1** Means of the galvanic skin response to emotional and non-emotional stimuli for the three groups, demonstrating source of the significant interaction. (Morrow et al, 1981)

deficits, and premorbid personality in producing various forms of denial of illness is worthy of further scientific exploration.

## Paranoia and psychomotor agitation

During the acute period following post-traumatic head injury, many patients are restless, agitated, combative, and disoriented. They are easily confused and show signs of paranoid ideation. Antipsychotic medications are frequently administered to reduce psychomotor agitation. Many of these drugs seem to block postsynaptic dopamine receptors in the brain. In contrast, amphetamines are assumed to release dopamine and can, at high dosages, produce a similar series of behaviors known as amphetamine psychosis (Lipton et al, 1978). Therefore, either increases in dopamine or supersensitivity to dopamine immediately after traumatic brain injury may cause psychomotor agitation and associated cognitive confusion. One case report even suggests that dextroamphetamine may, in fact, decrease confusion and paranoia following craniocerebral trauma (Lipper & Tuchman, 1976). Theoretically, this alters dopamine levels in the brain.

Case reports with schizophrenic patients indicate that neuroleptic medications can exacerbate psychotic symptoms in some patients. Increases of plasma levels of haloperidol (one antipsychotic medication known to increase dopamine levels) has been suggested as accounting for this paradoxical effect (Tornatore et al, 1981). The author has also seen two traumatic head injury patients who, upon receiving haloperidol, showed increased restlessness, agitation, and paranoid ideation. Stopping the medication greatly reduced these symptoms. Apparently, obtaining the right 'balance' of dopamine and related neurotransmitters after traumatic head injury may be necessary to reduce psychomotor agitation and paranoid thinking.

Several weeks or months past the acute phase of trauma, some patients continue to be restless and have thought disorders similar to functional psychosis. Schilder (1934) was one of the first clinicians to note this. Later, Lishman (1968) cited earlier work that suggested a special frequency of 'schizophreniform' psychosis associated with left temporal lobe disorder. Lishman (1968) also cited work which linked violent behavior to lesions of the medial temporal lobe. Damage to this region frequently includes impairment of amygdala. As the earlier discussion indicated, such damage may produce problems in controlling the appetitive behaviors, particularly fighting.

Convex and inferior temporal lobe structures are known to be important for visual discrimination (Pribram, 1971). Lesions to this region may literally interfere with the interpretation of visual inputs from the environment, and this could enhance or mediate paranoid interpretations of the world. Ferguson et al (1969), for example, found notable paranoid tendencies in the interpretation of visual cartoons by temporal lobe epileptic patients. Thus, paranoid ideation, in some brain-injured patients, may literally flow from neuropsychologically based perceptual and cognitive disturbances. Leftoff (1983) provides a recent case study which argues that paranoia after brain damage is linked to disordered cognition.

Pre-existing personality difficulties also appear to contribute to paranoid ideation. It is a well-accepted principle that failure to establish basic trust and confidence in parental figures during early childhood is commonly found in paranoid individuals (Freedman et al, 1976, p. 489). For example, one closed head injury patient with severe memory disorder (Memory Quotient = 76 over 5 years, post-injury) insisted that others did not talk to her, actively avoided her, and despised her. This was in contrast to overwhelming evidence that relatives and friends were willing to work and live with her despite her paranoid tendencies and memory disturbance. This patient's history, as corroborated by relatives, suggested that early in life she developed a strong feeling of unworthiness and associated self-hatred. Before her accident she was able to compensate for these problems by keeping socially active and doing 'good works' for others. After the accident she was unable to carry out her social activities, and this seemed to precipitate the development of paranoid ideation, which did not decline as her cognitive functioning improved. It is noteworthy that another patient who had equally poor memory, but no premorbid history of distrust in the environment, showed none of these paranoid ideations.

Frank paranoid ideation and psychomotor agitation are extremely complex phenomena and may reflect disturbances in neurotransmitters, alterations in the perceptual and cognitive systems following neural damage, as well as being related to pre-existing personality difficulties. The treatment of this class of behavioral problem requires a true team approach. The patient should be tried on psychopharmacological medications, should undergo a thorough neuropsychological analysis to see how perceptual and cognitive impairments may influence paranoid ideation, and be treated by an experienced psychotherapeutic clinician aware of how early childhood experiences influence later (paranoid) perceptions of the world. This class of personality disturbance appears to be one of the most difficult problems to treat after brain injury, and if not substantially modified makes psychosocial adjustment an impossibility.

## Depression, social withdrawal, and amotivational states

The fourth class of personality disturbance that is seen after acquired brain injury in adults is a mixture of affective problems that result in an apparent lack of commitment to the rehabilitation process by the patient. While caused by different factors, three clinically identifiable problems can be classified under this dimension. They include depression, social withdrawal, and the so-called amotivational states.

Depression covers a broad scope of affective disorders (Freedman et al, 1976). As applied to patients who have suffered damage to the brain, it typically includes feelings of worthlessness, helplessness, guilt, loss of interest in work and family activities, and decreased libido. Depression also includes a sense of catastrophic loss over abilities that at times truly overwhelms individuals and immobilizes them. It can be distinguished from normal sadness over loss of cerebral function, social status, and employment in the following way. Sadness over loss of function is, of course, a normal response to 'bad news.' When patients receive 'good news,' as reflected by improvement in their function, increased social acceptance, etc., the sadness typically lessens or disappears. In depression, such 'good news' is met with no shift in the affective state. Patients appear to hang on to their cognitive structures which perpetuate feeling bad, helpless, and maintaining a non-productive approach to life. Depression is extremely common after brain injury, but again, it does not seem to be especially related to the actual severity of the brain injury (Lishman, 1968; Levin & Grossman, 1978) or level of neuropsychological impairment (Prigatano, 1983). It also appears to be as common in right hemisphere patients as left (Gainotti, 1972). However, in patients who have frank denial of illness, which is more frequently associated with non-dominant hemisphere injury, depression certainly is less common. Depression is also more common in acute left hemisphere stroke patients (see Finkelstein et al, 1982). Earlier psychometric studies have shown that depression is the single most common affective complaint of brain-injured patients several months after injury, as measured by the MMPI (Reitan, 1952).

Social withdrawal, which may be a part of a depressive syndrome, can also exist without accompanying depression. After repeated failures in coping with the environment, many brain-injured patients simply withdraw to a safer milieu. This typically includes less social contact with others. Degree of social withdrawal has been related to severity of injury (Levin & Grossman, 1978) and residual neuropsychologic impairment (Prigatano, 1983). Unlike depression, therefore, social withdrawal may be indirectly related to the severity of brain dysfunction and consequent failures in coping with the environment.

As the discussion on catastrophic reaction suggested, many brain-injured patients initially do not expect to meet with as much failure in the environment as they do. Once they become aware of their failures, social withdrawal may be part of their natural tendencies to avoid anxiety and the catastrophic situations. Working with patients in a group can be of great help in dealing with the problem of social withdrawal and isolation, since such group work by its nature reduces social isolation and places the patient in an environment in which he or she can more easily relate and cope. Group work, however, does not necessarily help depression. Changing the patient's cognitions about self, either by group or individual methods, is needed in order for psychotherapeutic work to substantially change depression. The depressed patient can remain depressed even though social isolation is reduced.

Finally, there exists the so-called amotivational states that are frequently attributed to bilateral frontal lobe dysfunction. Benson et al (1981) describe schizophrenic patients who received prefrontal leucotomies and show severe apathy several years post-operation. Yet, as they note, this affective problem was common even in the non-operated schizophrenics. Fuster (1980), in his excellent analysis of frontal lobe function, described patients with severe frontal lobe pathology as lacking perspective with respect to past and future events. This cognitive deficit, coupled with the well-known disorders of attention manifested by easy distractibility, helps explain why frontal lobe patients often appear amotivational. It is hard for these patients to develop a plan of action (i.e., be motivated) and to follow through on such a plan because of difficulties in sustaining attention. Information processing theories (Simon, 1967), and the basic model of emotional and motivational disturbances presented earlier, would suggest that such amotivational states may in fact be a result of cognitive difficulties and not a disturbance in basic feeling states *per se*. A case example highlights this point.

A young adult traumatic head-injury patient with bilateral frontal lobe injury was noted to be very slow in his thinking and actions. It was assumed that he had a paucity of feelings and decreased drive state. The patient was involved in intensive neuropsychological rehabilitation for 1 year. During that time the patient reported having feelings but often would report them in a slow and easily distractible manner. When this patient was given a plan of action by others (as opposed to being asked to self-generate the plan), he proved to be one of the most motivated patients. Given external structure, he would practice on tasks repetitively, often fatiguing those involved in his care. He worked very diligently and was eventually able to become employed, albeit in a sheltered setting. This patient's performance raises the question of whether the amotivational symptomatology associated with frontal lobes is truly a problem of reduced drive or a secondary problem related to cognitive (i.e., planning) difficulties. This case also demonstrates the dissociation of reported feelings (by the patient) from actual behavior. Slow, easily distracted patients may not be unmotivated: they are often just confused.

In summary, problems encountered by the rehabilitation neuropsychologist which seem to undercut the patient's commitment or drive to work at rehabilitation are frequently reflections of depression, social withdrawal as an attempt to avoid the catastrophic condition and inability to self-generate a plan of action (so-called amotivational states). These problems can and must be separated from one another in order to develop an appropriate treatment plan.

## PERSONALITY DISTURBANCES IN BRAIN-INJURED CHILDREN

Developmental changes of the central nervous system during the prenatal and early postnatal period are exceedingly rapid and complex (Curtis et al, 1972). Injury to the brain during this period is known to carry severe consequences for intellectual development in some children (Woods, 1980). Injuries during the fifth to fourteenth year period also have definite effects on problem-solving ability and memory, and are related to the severity of brain injury (Chadwick et al, 1981; Rutter, 1981). What impact, however, do early cortical and subcortical lesions have on personality development? This question has been extremely difficult to answer for a number of reasons, as Rutter (1981) has reviewed.

In clinical practice one is often impressed with parents who insist that their child's behavior was normal, if not above average, prior to the brain injury. They can list in exquisite detail a myriad of behavioral problems that the child has had post-injury. This point of view is eloquently described by Taylor (1959) in describing the personality of a boy who suffered a severe head injury at age 7. The work of Rutter and his associates, however, suggests a different story (Rutter et al, 1980; Chadwick et al, 1981; Brown et al, 1981; Rutter, 1981). In reviewing their work Rutter states:

> Findings were striking in showing a strong relationship between the children's pre-injury behavior and their psychiatric state at the one year follow-up. Of the children with no behavior difficulties before the accident, half were psychiatrically normal one year later, whereas this was so for none of those who showed mild behavioral problems before the head injury. Pre-injury behavior was a strong predictor of children's psychiatric problems after severe head injury (Rutter, 1981, pp. 1539–1540).

These data suggest that the incidence of new psychiatric disturbances after brain injury may be high (i.e., 50%), but pre-existing behavioral disturbance, plus acquired brain injury, ensures subsequent behavioral problems. Obviously it is quite important to document, from more than one source, the child's behavioral characteristics prior to injury in order to evaluate the emotional and motivational problems post-injury. Behavioral scales such as the Child Behavioral Checklist (Achenback & Edelbrock, 1981) may be especially helpful in this regard.

The personality problems of brain-injured children are often classified under the rubric of social inappropriateness (see Ruttger, 1981; Brown et al, 1981). The child often says embarrassing things, reflecting poor judgment of the social situation. In addition, the child may be overly talkative, impulsive, careless in his dress or manner, and forgetful of school and social responsibilities. Interestingly, impulsivity and hyperactivity were not considered by Rutter and his colleagues to be the *sine qua non* of brain damage. Also, problems such as lying and stealing were as common in orthopedic control patients as in brain-injured patients (Brown et al, 1981). The same could be said for general responses to affective distress such as nail-biting, eneuresis, and phobias.

The family situation appears to greatly influence these behavioral problems. Rutter's recent work, as well as that of Shaffer et al (1975), suggested that adverse social and family situations increased the likelihood of psychiatric disturbance in brain-injured children. In fact, a measure of psychosocial disadvantage correlated more with psychiatric disturbance in brain-injured children than the extent of coma. It appears that brain-injured children, like adults, show symptoms that are as much a function of the environment as is a function of neural damage *per se*. This must constantly be kept in mind when evaluating and treating such patients.

The emotional and motivational disturbances in brain-injured children have generally received very little attention. Such problems have been reported to be frequent in children supratentorial lesions or cranial irradiation (Kun et al, 1983). Periodic clinical reports suggest that hydrocephalic children may be hyperverbal and disinhibited (see Prigatano & Zeiner, in press). Yet, systematic studies are lacking which look at type and locus of brain pathology and different environmental conditions which interact to produce emotional and motivational disturbances during childhood and their subsequent effect on personality development.

## PSYCHOSOCIAL CONSEQUENCES

Brain-injured patients frequently describe themselves as 'out of step' with the rest of the world. They are often confused as to why others are upset with them and progressively withdraw. Common psychosocial problems after brain injury include inability to maintain gainful employment, loss of pre-traumatic friendships and relationships, impaired sense of body image, reduced self-esteem, and enhanced dependency on family and welfare systems.

Papers on psychosocial outcome often fail to communicate the impact of brain injury on people's lives, although there are some exceptions (Lezak, 1978). In this context, Jenett (1978) made an interesting comment when describing what he would do, as a neurosurgeon, if his son were to suffer a traumatic head injury. After attending to the medical and surgical considerations he, his wife, and his son would need sound psychotherapeutic help in facing the frustrations and personal crises associated with coping with the problems produced by brain injury. This 'family need' is frequently overlooked in studies on psychosocial outcome after brain injury.

Assessing the psychosocial consequences of brain injury must ultimately include external, community criteria (e.g., the ability to return to work or drive a car), as well as personal or subjective criteria (e.g., quality of interpersonal relationships between a husband and wife or degree of stress experienced by the parent of a brain-injured child). In the course of intensive neuropsychological rehabilitation work at Presbyterian Hospital with brain-injured young adults, a relatively simplified model of psychosocial adjustment has evolved.

When asked what does it mean to be psychologically normal, Freud purportedly responded to one interviewer with this statement: to work and to love. Translated into the rehabilitation arena, this might be stated as the ability to be productive (which often, but not always, includes gainful employment) and the ability to maintain interpersonal relationships. Buss (1966) has suggested three other dimensions which serve as qualifiers to these two broad classes of outcome behavior. They are: discomfort, bizarreness, and inefficiency. Table 17.1 presents a scheme for evaluating psychosocial outcome in both objective and subjective terms for these two broad classes of behavior. Specific examples of what types of behavior would fall within each cell of this 'grid' are presented.

In assessing a patient's ability 'to work,' researchers have typically assessed the inefficiency dimension. For example, Bond (1975) inquired as to whether a patient was able to return to a previous job or had to return to a lower form of work, versus no work at all. Using this type of criteria, the present best estimates are that approximately one-third of severe head injury patients, who walk and talk, return to gainful employment (Weddell et al, 1980; Gilchrist & Wilkinson, 1979; Bruckner & Randle, 1972).

Predictors of returning or not returning to work are numerous. Emotional lability and post-psychotic states are clearly related to reduced work capacity (Bruckner & Randle, 1972) and so are memory deficits (Bruckner & Randle, 1972; Weddell et al, 1980) and severity of communication disorders (Dresser et al, 1973).

While often not reported, subjective discomfort on the part of the patient returning to a particular work setting is common. Patients with previously high-level jobs and localized cerebral deficits may return to their old position, only to be greatly stressed by it. Frequently these patients have relatively isolated neuropsychological deficits (e.g., a visual-spatial deficit or a modality-specific memory deficit) and have a difficult time efficiently

**Table 17.1** Model for assessing psychosocial outcome after brain injury

| | To work (be productive) | To love (maintain interpersonal relations) |
|---|---|---|
| Discomfort | e.g. unhappy with job performance and needing to work long hours to keep up previous productivity levels; decreased loss of self-confidence and enjoyment in work. | e.g. unwillingness to attend gatherings, progressive social isolation, and withdrawal from others. |
| Bizarreness | e.g. excessive note-taking, repetition of questions already asked co-workers. | e.g. inappropriate social comments to spouse or children in public. |
| Inefficiency | e.g. unable to be gainfully employed, too slow in carrying out work activities, needing more structured supervision than the job normally requires. | e.g. spouse having to manage most of the family affairs, children feeling very uncomfortable in the presence of a brain-injured parent and avoiding contact with him or her. |

performing. Progressively, they become very upset and disillusioned. Many eventually take a lower level of employment or seek psychiatric consultation. Weddell et al (1980) reported, for example, a significant correlation between residual memory disturbance and personality disturbance after brain injury.

A non-experienced neuropsychological clinician may inadvertently assume that a mild head injury patient's complaints are purely psychiatric in nature. If the patient is given standard clinical psychological tests of intelligence, memory, and personality, specific neuropsychological deficits may not emerge. The patient may then be placed into long-term insight psychotherapy which is not needed and, in fact, may serve to upset the patient more because the subtle underlying neuropsychological deficits are not understood and dealt with.

The dimension of interpersonal relationship of psychosocial outcome is perhaps the most difficult to assess scientifically, but is of major importance to the family. Walker (1972) eloquently listed how wives describe the personality changes in the head injury husbands that substantially interfered with the degree of comfort and efficiency in their relationships. In keeping with the problem of self-awareness after brain injury, many traumatic head-injury patients (and stroke patients for that matter) describe their residual difficulties only in terms of physical factors such as weakness or problems in walking. In contrast, spouses describe *both* physical and mental changes following brain injury. Notably, wives describe their husbands as quick-tempered, fearful, easily fatigued, showing loss of interest in life and family activities, and prone to 'fits of anger.' Several wives mentioned in letters that husbands were impotent, but frequently failed to state this during clinical interviews for fear of hurting their spouse's 'feelings.'

Thus, in terms of the degree of comfort in interpersonal relationships, most, if not all families, experienced increased disharmony in relationship to their brain-injured relative. If the patient is not working or being productive at home, there is certainly an inefficiency (i.e., lack of reciprocity) in the interpersonal relationships. Many family members can't comprehend personality disturbances following brain injury and frequently avoid the patient or assume that they 'aren't trying.' Weddell et al (1980) noted, for example, that personality changes after trauma resulted in a significant loss of pre-accident friendships.

While family members can often tolerate a brain-injured young adult who cannot be gainfully employed, they have an extremely difficult time handling the breakdown of interpersonal relationships. Paranoid, depressed, and belligerent brain-injured patients, by far, put the most stress on family members. While the divorce statistics for head-injury patients versus non-head-injury patients are unknown, based on clinical experience, termination of the marriage or long-term separation from the spouse and family is common. Increased dependency on other family members and public welfare systems thus becomes a common psychosocial problem.

A final psychosocial outcome worthy of further investigation is the incidence of psychiatric illness in spouse and children of brain-injured adults. While Rutter's (1981) work implicates the parents' psychiatric state as a precursor for mild head injury in children, that is only half of the story. The problems of brain injury can enhance psychiatric distress in parents and spouse. Mash & Johnston (1983) report, for example, decreased self-esteem and enhanced stress levels in mothers of hyperactive children.

## PSYCHOTHERAPEUTIC INTERVENTIONS

Psychosocial adjustment problems can be substantially helped in many brain-injured patients. Patients with relatively mild or specific neuropsychological deficits often require a combination of cognitive retraining and psychotherapy. These patients need to understand their neuropsychological impairments, recognize how these impairments influence their ability to perform different types of work, and deal with their personal reaction to their deficits.

Insight-oriented psychodynamic forms of psychotherapy may be especially helpful to patients understanding how their pre-trauma personality has influenced their ability to cope or not cope with existing neuropsychological deficits. Various forms of behavioral therapy may be helpful in setting realistic goals and taking the necessary steps to meet them. Structuring the environment, planning successes, and charting these successes can combat the emergence of the catastrophic reaction. Finally, group psychotherapy can help deal with the problem of social withdrawal and depression frequently experienced by these individuals.

Helping patients express, in words and art form, their state in life fosters the process of adaptation and can also reduce the catastrophic reaction. The following poem was written by a woman physician who suffered a rupture of an arteriovenous malformation in the right occipital–parietal region. It was composed as she was struggling with the expression of her feelings within the context of group psychotherapy. Her poem presents a very powerful commentary of what such patients experience when undergoing psychotherapy. The patient wrote the following:

*Group psychotherapy*

In group psychotherapy we sit
Wondering where in life we can fit,
Which of our feelings should we admit?
And which whole with bridle and bit?
Once some of us on the head were hit.
Sometimes we feel we were hit by shit.
Some of us had good jobs that we quit;
Are we able to do more than knit?
When we fail again, our teeth we grit,
Sometimes words are hard to spit,
Is there more to life than this big pit?

Exploration of her feelings of anger over suffering an arteriovenous malformation rupture and her pre-trauma personality and post-trauma fears of inadequacy helped her come to grips with major issues of identity. Dream material was helpful in clarifying her understanding of the feeling that 'something had died inside of her.' Dream images symbolized both the arteriovenous malformation and the associated brain injury. Coming to grips with lost professional hopes and aspirations was vital to her rehabilitation. Such grief reactions are frequently necessary if patients are going to live with their residual deficits and approach life in a productive manner.

Patients with diffuse cerebral injuries and brainstem involvement also need a combination of cognitive retraining and psychotherapeutic intervention, although the form for both usually differs from those individuals who have mild and/or specific neuropsychological deficits. The former patients need very simple, repetitive, and arousal-producing training activities. They need to decrease their cognitive confusion and learn to express their ideas in a clear and concise way, particularly in groups. Psychotherapy for these individuals frequently focuses on helping them simply become aware of what is wrong without 'digging' into psychodynamic issues. Insight into their brain pathology and associated neuropsychological deficits, however, is vital. As they are able to progressively understand why they are having problems in thinking, perception, motor functions, etc., they can then learn behavioral methods for compensating for those deficits. Thus, use of compensation techniques, as opposed to purely cognitive retraining, often seems most appropriate for this group of patients. They also seem to respond more to the structure and simplicity of behavioral techniques, provided that the clinician is sensitive to their confused and tragic world.

The psychotherapy of brain-injured patients must, at some level, confront the existential realities of life. Once patients become aware of their confusion, they need help adjusting to this tragedy. Figure 17.2 is a drawing by a young adult male who suffered a severe craniocerebral trauma with a resultant dysphasia and right hemiparesis. Approximately 3 years post-injury he was seen in an intensive neuropsychological rehabilitation program. At that time he insisted that 'all he needed' was bigger and better speech and language therapy. Progressively, through the use of cognitive group therapy and individual counseling by a speech and language pathologist, he was able to become aware of the fact that his disturbances were not just in the motor and speech area. He began to recognize that his thoughts were as confused as was his language. This painful realization eventually helped him to accept his situation in life. He turned toward religion as a means of personal strength during this time, as his drawing indicates. He became committed to helping others recognize their own problems of unawareness after brain injury and eventually was able to work in a sheltered workshop.

Thus, dealing with the personality problems of brain-injured patients requires the therapist to have an understanding of the nature of personality

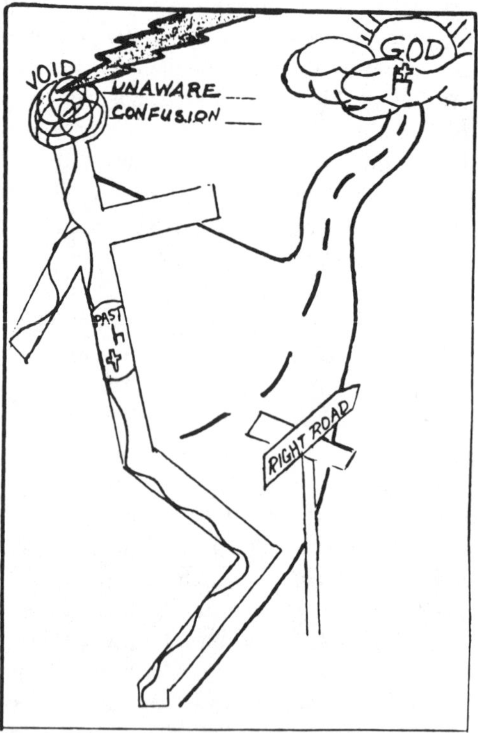


**Fig. 17.2** Spontaneous drawing by a traumatic head-injury patient at the completion of a rehabilitation program.

disturbances as well as cognitive deficits. Therapists must be able to explain, in concrete and simple terms, the various personality and cognitive deficits that the patient experiences. Of particular importance is the ability of the therapist to explain the catastrophic reaction. The patient needs to be repetitively taught behavioral methods for avoiding situations which stimulate this reaction, while still remaining socially active and appropriate. This is especially important when attempting cognitive retraining. Cognitive retraining, by itself, can stimulate the catastrophic reaction. If this happens the patient will avoid needed re-educational experiences. Preparing the patient for this reaction and teaching him or her to work at a cognitive task while keeping tension or anxiety low is essential. If this does not occur, the patient often appears 'unmotivated' and/or 'belligerent.' At such times the patient may simply be frightened or upset with a given task because it is not within his/her realm of personal competence. Working with patients in groups can facilitate a greater understanding of the catastrophic reaction and undercuts the problem of social withdrawal and isolation. It can also, however, stimulate misperceptions and thereby spark interpersonal conflict in the rehabilitation setting. The clinicians conducting such groups must be able to modify misperceptions and help patients improve and handle interpersonal conflicts within the group setting. This is a major undertaking, but one that is vital for ultimate psychosocial adjustment.

Finally, psychotherapeutic work with families of brain-injured patients is frequently needed. Unless the family has a realistic understanding of the patient's strengths and weaknesses, and comes to grips with these realities, changes which are obtained in a rehabilitation setting may not be reinforced in the home environment. Families can often be seen in small groups. A 'relatives group' is one means of giving information as well as supporting family members. Families can compare notes and learn from each other regarding the practical steps in managing a brain-injured patient. They can feel supported, not isolated in their struggles. If this latter dimension is not achieved, families frequently disintegrate and feel quite guilty over this.

## CONCLUSIONS

Disturbances in personality are common after acquired brain injury in adults and children. They are frequently overlooked because they lack diagnostic utility, but they are crucial for rehabilitation planning. Since there is no universally agreed definition of personality and most theories of personality are not related to models of brain function, neuropsychologists have not systematically studied emotional and motivational problems after brain injury. Yet there are clusters of common personality disturbances after brain injury in adults which should be recognized, particularly by the clinical neuropsychologist involved in rehabilitation.

It is unlikely that a specific (i.e., focal) brain lesion will produce a specific personality disturbance. Yet different lesions may influence various neurophysiological and neuropsychological substrates of emotion and motivation in predictable manners. Some lesions will influence arousal and attentional mechanisms, while others will influence the cognitive appraisal of feeling states and the manner in which feelings are expressed. Premorbid personality and present social situations also greatly influence the form of affective response after brain injury.

Personality disturbances after brain injury have been shown to greatly influence psychosocial adjustment. Neither work nor inter-personal relationships can be adequately maintained unless these affective problems are modified. Methods of personality assessment and therapeutic intervention are greatly needed for the rehabilitation of brain-injured adults and children. Cognitive remediation, in and of itself, is not adequate.

## REFERENCES


Achenbach T M, Edelbrock C S 1981 Behavioral problems and competencies reported by parents of normal and disturbed children aged four through sixteen. Monographs of the Society for Research in Child Development 46(1): 1–82

Bear, D M 1983 Hemispheric specialization and the neurology of emotion. Archives of Neurology 40: 195–202

Benson D F, Stuss D T, Maeser M A, Weir W S, Kaplan E F, Levin H L 1981 The long-term effects of prefrontal leukotomy. Archives of Neurology 38: 165–169

Blumer D, Benson D F 1975 Personality changes with frontal and temporal lobe lesions. In: Benson D F, Blumer D (eds) Psychiatric aspects of neurologic disease. Grune & Stratton, New York, pp. 151–170

Bond M R 1975 Assessment of the psychosocial outcome after severe head injury. In: Ciba Foundation (ed) Outcome of severe damage to the nervous system. Elsevier/Excerpta Medica, North-Holland, Amsterdam

Brown G, Chadwick O, Shaffer D, Rutter M, Traub M 1981 A prospective study of children with head injuries. III: Psychiatric sequelae. Psychological Medicine 11: 63–78

Bruckner F E, Randle P H 1972 Return to work after severe head injuries. Rheumatology and Physical Medicine 11: 344–348

Buss A H 1966 Psychopathology. Wiley, New York

Chadwick O, Rutter M, Brown G, Shaffer D, Traub M 1981 A prospective study of children with head injuries. II: Cognitive sequelae. Psychological Medicine 11: 49–61

Curtis B A, Jacobson S, Marcus E M 1972 An introduction to the neurosciences. Saunders, Philadelphia

Dikmen S, Reitan R M 1977b MMPI correlates of adaptive ability deficits in patients with brain lesions. Journal of Nervous and Mental Disease 165: 247–253

Dresser A C, Meirowsky A M, Weiss G H, McNeel M L, Simon G A, Caveness W F 1973 Gainful employment following head injury. Archives of Neurology 29: 111–116

Ferguson S M, Schwartz M C, Rayport M 1969 Perception of humor in patients with temporal lobe epilepsy. Archives of General Psychiatry 21: 363–367

Finkelstein S, Benowitz L, Baldessarini R et al 1982 Mood, vegetative disturbance and dexamethasone suppression test after stroke. Annals of Neurology 12: 463–468

Fordyce D J, Roueche J R, Prigatano G P 1983 Enhanced emotional reactions in chronic head trauma patients. Journal of Neurology, Neurosurgery and Psychiatry 46: 620–624

Freedman A M, Kaplan H I, Sadock B J 1976 Modern synopsis of comprehensive textbook of psychiatry/II. 2nd edn. Williams & Wilkins, Baltimore

Freud S, 1924 A general introduction to psychoanalysis, 24th edn. Pocket Book, Simon & Schuster, New York

Fuster J M 1980 The prefrontal cortex. Raven, New York

Gainotti G 1972 Emotional behavior and hemispheric side of lesion. Cortex 8: 41–55

Gilchrist E, Wilkinson M 1979 Some factors determining prognosis in young people with severe head injuries. Archives of Neurology 36: 355–358
Goldstein H 1942 After effects of brain injuries in war. Grune & Stratton, New York
Goldstein H 1952 The effect of brain damage on the personality. Psychiatry 15: 245–260
Graham D I, Adams J H, Doyle D 1978 Ischemic brain damage in fatal nonmissile head injuries. Journal of Neurological Sciences 39: 213–234
Heilman K M 1979 Neglect and related disorders. In: Heilman K M, Valenstein E (eds) Clinical neuropsychology. Oxford University Press, New York
Jenett B 1978 If my son had a head injury. British Medical Journal 1: 1601–1603
Jung C G 1964 Man and his symbols. Doubleday/Windfall, Garden City
Kozol H L 1945 Pretraumatic personality and psychiatric sequelae of head injury. Archives of Neurology and Psychiatry 53: 358–364
Kozol H L 1946 Pretraumatic personality and psychiatric sequelae of head injury. Archives of Neurology and Psychiatry 56: 245–275
Kun L E, Mulhern R K, Crisco J J 1983 Quality of life in children treated for brain tumors. Journal of Neurosurgery 58: 1–6
Labaw W 1969 Denial inside out: subjective experiences with anosognosia in closed head injury. Psychiatry 32: 174–191
Lazarus R S 1977 Psychological stress and coping in adaptation and illness. In: Lipowski Z J, Lipsitt D R, Whyleron P C (eds) Psychosomatic medicine: current trends and applications. Oxford University Press, New York
Leftoff S 1983 Psychopathology in the light of brain injury: a case study. Journal of Clinical Neuropsychology 5(1): 51–63
Levin H S, Grossman R G 1978 Behavioral sequelae of closed head injury. Archives of Neurology 35: 720–727
Levin H S, Grossman R G, Rose J E, Teasdale G 1979 Long-term neuropsychological outcome of closed head injury. Journal of Neurosurgery 50: 412–422
Lezak M D 1978 Living with the characterologically altered brain injured patient. Journal of Clinical Psychiatry 39(7): 592–598
Lindsley D B 1970 The role of nonspecific reticulo-thalamocortical systems in emotion. In: Black P (ed) Physiological correlates of emotion. Academic Press, New York
Lipper S, Tuchman M M 1976 Treatment of chronic post-traumatic organic brain syndrome with dextroamphetamine: first reported case. Journal of Nervous and Mental Disease 162(5): 366–371
Lipton M A, Dimascio A, Killam K F (eds) 1978 Psychopharmacology: a generation of progress. Raven, New York
Lishman W A 1968 Brain damage in relation to psychiatric disability after head injury. British Journal of Psychiatry 114: 373–410
Lishman W A 1973 The psychiatric sequelae of head injury: a review. Psychological Medicine 3: 304–318
Lorenz K 1966 On aggression. Harcourt, Brace & World, New York
Luria A S 1966 Higher cortical functions in man. Consultants Bureau Enterprises/Basic Books, New York
Mash E J, Johnston C 1983 Parental perceptions of child behavior problems, parenting self-esteem, and mothers' reported stress in younger and older hyperactive and normal children. Journal of Consulting and Clinical Psychology 51(1): 86–99
McLean A, Temkin N R, Dikmen S, Wyler A R 1983 The behavioral sequelae of head injury. Journal of Clinical Neuropsychology 5(4): 361–376
Miller G A, Galanter E, Pribram K H 1960 Plans and the structure of behavior. Holt, Rinehart & Winston, New York
Morrow L, Vrtunski K, Kim Y, Boller F 1981 Arousal responses to emotional stimuli and laterality of lesion. Neuropsychologia 19: 65–71
Poeck K 1969 Pathophysiology of emotional disorders associated with brain damage. In: Vinken P J, Bruyn A W (eds) Handbook of clinical neurology. North-Holland, Amsterdam, vol. 3, pp. 343–376
Pribram K H 1971 Languages of the brain: experimental paradoxes and principles in neuropsychology, 2nd edn. Prentice-Hall, Englewood Cliffs
Pribram K H 1977 New dimensions in the function of basal ganglia. In: Shagass C, Gershen S, Friedhoff A J (eds) Psychopathology and brain dysfunction. Raven, New York
Pribram K H, Gill M M 1976 Freud's 'project' reassessed. Basic Books, New York

Pribram K H, Luria A R (eds) 1973 Psychophysiology of the frontal lobes. Academic Press, New York

Pribram K H, McGuinness D 1975 Arousal, activation and effect in the control of attention. Psychological Review 82: 116–149

Prigatano G P 1981 Rehabilitation of post traumatic brain damaged patients. Paper presented at 89th Annual Convention, American Psychological Association, Los Angeles

Prigatano G P 1983 The role of cognition as it affects psychosocial adjustment. Paper presented at Models and Techniques of Cognitive Rehabilitation Third International Symposium 25–30 March, Indianapolis

Prigatano G P, Fordyce D J In press Neuropsychological Rehabilitation Program, Presbyterian Hospital, Oklahoma City. Caplan B, Bray G (eds) Handbook of contemporary rehabilitation psychology. Charles C Thomas, Springfield

Prigatano G P, Pribram K H 1981 Humor and episodic memory following frontal versus posterior brain lesion. Perceptual and Motor Skills 53: 999–1006

Prigatano G P, Zeiner H K In press Information processing and reading competencies in hydrocephalic and letter reversal children. In: Peng F C C (ed) Neurology of languages: a first approximation. LEA of London

Reitan R M 1952 Affective disturbances in brain damaged patients. Archives of Neurology and Psychiatry 73: 530–532

Rutter M 1981 Psychological sequelae of brain damage in children. American Journal of Psychiatry 138(12): 1533–1544

Rutter M, Chadwick O, Shaffer D, Brown G 1980 A prospective study of children with head injuries. I: Design and methods. Psychological Medicine 11: 49–61

Sackheim H A, Greenberg M S, Weiman A L, Gur R C, Hungerbuhler J P, Geschwind N 1982 Hemispheric asymmetry in the expression of positive and negative emotions. Archives of Neurology 39: 210–218

Schacter S, Singer T E 1962 Cognitive, social and physiological determinants of emotional state. Psychological Review 69: 379–397

Schilder P 1934 Psychic disturbances after head injuries. American Journal of Psychiatry 91: 155–188

Shaffer D, Chadwick O, Rutter M 1975 Psychiatric outcome of localized head injury in children. In: Ciba Foundation (ed) Outcome of severe damage to the nervous system. Elsevier/Excerpta Medica, North-Holland, Amsterdam

Simon H A 1967 Motivation and emotional controls of cognition. Psychological Review 74: 29–39

Sullivan H S 1953 The interpersonal theory of psychiatry. Norton, New York

Taylor E M 1959 Psychological appraisal of children with cerebral defects. Harvard University Press, Cambridge

Timbergen N 1953 Social behavior in animals. Methuen, London

Tornatore F L, Lee D, Sramek J J 1981 Psychotic exacerbation with haloperidol. Drug Intelligence and Clinical Pharmacy 15: 209–213

Valenstein E, Heilman K M 1979 Emotional disorders resulting from lesions of the central nervous system. In: Heilman K M, Valenstein E (eds) Clinical neuropsychology. Oxford University Press, New York

Walker A E 1972 Long-term evaluation of the social and family adjustment to head injuries. Scandinavian Journal of Rehabilitative Medicine 4: 5–8

Weddell R, Oddy M, Jenkins D 1980 Social adjustment after rehabilitation: a two-year follow-up of patients with severe head injury. Psychological Medicine 10: 257–263

Weinstein E A, Kahn R L 1955 Denial of illness. Charles C Thomas, Springfield

Woods B T 1980 The restrictive effects of right hemisphere lesions. Neuropsychologia 18: 65–70

# **Part three:** International Neuropsychological Rehabilitation Programs

# 18 *Anne-Lise Christensen and Ulla Tarp Danielsen*

# Neuropsychological rehabilitation in Denmark

Neuropsychology in Denmark has its roots in psychology as well as in psychiatry and neurology. During the Gestalt period in psychology, research was stimulated in two major areas: perception and learning. At the same time psychiatry and neurology were concerned with studies of brain dysfunction, primarily in tumor and stroke patients. The influence of clinical psychology was first felt in psychiatry and then some years later in both neurology and neurosurgery. The Second World War had no particular influence on the direction of either neuropsychology or rehabilitation since Denmark's attention and energies were involved in underground warfare.

The first approach to neuropsychology in Denmark was diagnostic and did not immediately imply rehabilitation. Rehabilitative efforts were mainly directed by physiatrists. In the three Danish rehabilitation hospitals, physiatric treatment was combined with occupational therapy. Aphasic patients were treated primarily with speech therapy, as exemplified by the work of Thomsen (1980) in the follow-up studies of head trauma patients. In later years neuropsychologists began to work as consultants, primarily in the area of assessment.

A more recent development is a day program in neuropsychological rehabilitation at the University of Copenhagen utilizing the approach of Luria's method of investigation and an eclectic approach from the USA based on the work of Ben-Yishay, Prigitano and Trexler (see Chapter 25, this volume).

## LURIA'S METHOD

The rehabilitative work performed in the clinical psychological department at the University Hospital of Aarhus was based upon A. R. Luria's theory as exemplified in *Higher Cortical Functions in Man* (1980). The problem encountered in clinical work of making a differential diagnosis between depression and dementia led to a series of visits to Luria's laboratory at the Burdenko Hospital in Moscow which in turn resulted in the publication of *Luria's Neuropsychological Investigation* (Christensen, 1979a, 2nd edition). It soon became clear that Luria's examination not only served diagnostic purposes, but also opened possibilities for restoration via qualitative elucidation of functions. Disclosure of the inner structure of the defect, and of the intact functions in cases of destruction of cortical tissue, had led to a scientifically founded theory of diagnostics which proved applicable to the needs of rehabilitation.

Due to restricted resources the research was centered around giving optimal treatment to individual patients. The methods applied, and the results obtained, have been presented as papers at conferences, and published in books as case histories (Christensen, 1979b, 1984).

The majority of patients are outpatients since referrals are accepted 2–6 months after brain injury; however, some are occasionally hospitalized as inpatients. The policy of early referrals is in accordance with practice in Tsvetkova's Department at the Neurological University Rehabilitation Hospital in Moscow. The intention is to support the patient's own compensatory efforts and to prevent the development of behavior reactions which in the long run may inhibit the processes of adaption and learning (Christensen, 1984, 1986).

Characteristic of the program is the individualized approach. The training is divided into stages that may vary in time for the single patient, but not in sequence. The first stage is the assessment period. The Luria assessment procedure is flexible. Attention is given to the great variety of individual differences in brain organization. It is not the tasks used that are most essential; rather, it is the skills, abilities, and inventiveness, within the framework of general psychology, of the neuropsychologist. The aim is to get as precise a knowledge of the specific functional systems of the patient as possible. The social and emotional characteristics of the patient also have to be taken into consideration. In this respect the assessment is extended to include personality tests, e.g. the Rorschach.

When the results of the assessment have been reviewed and integrated, the individual program is determined by the team collaborating around the patient. The team, headed by the neuropsychologist, can include an occupational therapist, a physiotherapist, and/or a speech therapist, and for inpatients, a physician and one or two nurses. A social worker may also become an important member of the team. The patient participates as early as possible. His/her attendance is considered important on the basis of the principle stressed by Luria: continuous feedback from therapist to patient about disturbed functions and the effect of training is necessary for rehabilitation progress. The structure of treatment is thus adapted to the patient's situation. His/her family members are included as early and as often as possible.

The second stage in the program has two aims: first, disinhibition or deblocking of temporarily reduced secondary areas of the brain, and second, reorganization of disturbed functions. The disinhibition period is necessary due to the acuteness of early referrals. Time is spent facilitating and practicing preserved automatic functions which are usually lower-level hierarchical functions, such as singing well-known songs, playing games, doing simple arithmetic, or performing practical daily tasks. The purpose is to support the patient emotionally and to stimulate and challenge his/her motivation. It is important to emphasize involuntary fluent reactions, by way of tasks such as drawing, reporting news, or writing notes. The activities are chosen in accordance with the individual patient's habits and experiences. This period is usually rather short. If it is successful, the patient will have developed a realistic understanding of his/her situation and will be able to collaborate in further planning.

The retraining of lost functions follows. The reorganization can be either intrasystemic or intersystemic. Intrasystemic reorganization occurs when behaviors are integrated to a lower level, i.e., become automatic, or when they are integrated to a higher level, i.e., made more conscious by introducing language. Intersystemic reorganization occurs when an entirely different functional system has to be created. In this case specific cognitive tasks are planned so that elements from the intact functions are coordinated in a way, e.g., if a patient has articulatory difficulties due to a sensorimotor deficit, intact visual functions are available for the planning of expressive speech. The training is never directed toward the deficits. The same steps are followed in daily exercises with the final goal of creating an automatized process that eventually can reach full integration. The program is continued to the point of overlearning. The process is discussed continuously with the patient, who receives feedback after every session. The training periods for patients who have been through the program are at least 6 months. The patients are then discharged to their homes for a period of readaptation. Contact is maintained with the neuropsychologist to watch development, to make new assessments when required, and to initiate new training periods when needed.

A neuropsychological and therapeutic intervention has recently been attempted at the University Department of Psychiatry, Rigshospitalet Copenhagen. These patients primarily have temporal lobe epilepsy which has proved untreatable by other means. Neuropsychologically oriented cognitive training, together with insight therapy, appears to open new possibilities for these patients.

## THE ECLECTIC APPROACH

The second direction which rehabilitation has taken in Denmark is an eclectic approach. In the Copenhagen County Hospitals, neuropsychological rehabilitation has grown out of a tradition of close cooperation between psychologists and neurologists both in research and in daily work. In the early 1970s, psychologists' study of theories and practices was inspired by Luria's work. However, a second orientation toward rehabilitation, a comparison between different theoretical viewpoints resulting in a more eclectic approach to rehabilitation, has emerged. General and applied psychology is integrated within the neuropsychological approach. The Danish teaching tradition based on phenomological psychological viewpoints placed emphasis upon the patients' own experiences in elucidating symptoms and in guiding goals and means of rehabilitation. In addition to cognitive deficits, other relevant factors present both in the patient and the patient's environment are stressed (Angelsoe, 1977; Danielsen, 1977; Smed, 1977).

In this eclectic approach, symptoms are believed to reflect the interplay between damaged and intact brain structures, and are seen as the patient's individualized compensatory efforts. Early rehabilitation measures are for this reason considered important to prevent fixation on inadequate compensation mechanisms. Since patients are preferably seen in a rather acute phase, assessment of symptoms provides a broad and rather gross evaluation. The purposes of this evaluation are (1) to deduce main problems and their practical consequences on the ward, and (2) to give a starting point to rehabilitation, refinement of analysis being integrated in treatment (Angelsoe & Smed, 1977, 1980a).

This neuropsychological rehabilitation grew into a holistic approach based on thorough analysis of brain damage symptomatology. As stressed by Busch-Jensen (1981)

> 'Rehabilitational training must take an active interest in the broader aspects of personal development because these inevitably are bound to be deeply affected by the oranic injury. The intellectual and the emotional/social sides of rehabilitational training can hardly be separated and hence must be treated as interwoven as they are.'

There are three equally important aspects in neuropsychological rehabilitation. First, reorganization of function by applying preserved functions in new ways is stressed continuously during diagnostic treatment. Integrated within this purpose is assisting the patient to acknowledge his/her actual level of function, and the implications this has for different situations. Secondly, emotional support is given and personality-restoring efforts are made. It is necessary to differentiate between emotional change and emotional reaction. Restoring premorbid, currently disturbed personality characteristics can be essential in restoring cognitive function (Danielsen, 1981). The third aspect of rehabilitation is integrating activities within the person's social surroundings. Exchange of information with the team, ward personnel, and family members about the patient's actual level of function and rehabilitation treatment measures is essential. Sometimes considerable effort must be made to change patients' attitudes, some of which have damaging impact and mitigate against social reintegration (Angelsoe, 1981). Lack of guidance and coordination can be disastrous (Smed, 1981).

The eclectic approach uses a general conceptual framework to help the therapist in handling and utilizing vital aspects of individual differences in training. Five levels of function, each with associated rehabilitation measures, are accordingly differentiated. These levels focus on spontaneous strategies whereby the person transforms his perception of the world into subsequent action, cognitive style, and conception of social context. All these are given central consideration.

> A favorable result in the readjustment process after brain injury is very dependent on the possibility the person has for taking action, and the flexibility he exhibits in constructively accepting his altered situation. The neuropsychological training program must endeavor to encourage and strengthen suitable strategies. The consequence of this is that therapy cannot simply be based on specific symptoms but must likewise be individualized according to the functional level of the person (Angelsoe & Busch-Jensen, 1983).

Coordinated professional team-work based upon shared knowledge has resulted in an emphasis by the team upon the mediation and understanding of specific symptomatologies. Efforts not only include the coordination of ward activities but also seminars and papers for the staff (Anderson et al, 1976; Danielsen & Angelsoe, 1979; Angelsoe & Smed, 1980b; Smed et al, 1982).

The two approaches described have much in common. The first has been developed in a clinical psychological department in a psychiatric hospital. The other was developed as a result of the eclectic approach to serve the needs of patients in a neurological ward. Due to the growing interest in neuropsychological rehabilitation in hospitals and social welfare centers throughout the country the future development of the field seems to be assured.

## REFERENCES


Andersen R, Smed A, Angelsoe B 1976 Plejeproblemer i forbindelse med patienter med afasi Sygeplejersken 28: 10–13; 29: 8–11

Angelsoe B 1977 Neuropsykologisk behandling af en afatisk patient. Nordisk Psykiatrisk Tidsskrift 31: 155–163

Angelsoe B 1981 Effects of aphasia rehabilitation? A case review. Platform paper, 4th International Neuropsychological Society European Conference, Bergen

Angelsoe B, Busch-Jensen L 1983 The spontaneous work strategies of brain-damaged patients. How can rehabilitation benefit and improve these? Platform paper, 6th International Neuropsychological Society European Conference, Lisbon

Angelsoe B, Smed A 1977 Aphasia and treatment of aphasia. Platform paper, 1st International Neuropsychological Society Conference, Oxford

Angelsoe B, Smed A 1980a Behandling af afatiske patienter i et somatisk sygehus. Nordisk Psykiatrisk Tidsskrift 34: 51–61

Angelsoe B, Smed A 1980b Behandling af afatiske patienter. Ugeskr Laeger 142: 12–15

Busch-Jensen L 1981 Brain injury and personal development – a case review. Platform paper, 4th International Neuropsychological Society European Conference, Bergen

Christensen A-L 1979a Luria's neuropsychological investigation, 2nd ed. Munksgaard, Copenhagen

Christensen A-L 1979b A practical application of the Luria methodology. Journal of Clinical Neuropsychology 1: 241–247

Christensen A-L 1984 The Luria method of examination of the brain-impaired patient. In: Logue P E, Schear J M (eds) Clinical neuropsychology — a multidisciplinary approach. Charles C Thomas, Springfield

Christensen A-L 1986 Applying Luria's theory to the rehabilitation process of brain damage. In: Uzzell B, Gross Y (eds) Clinical neuropsychology of intervention. Martinus Nihoff, Boston

Danielsen U T 1977 Neuropsykologers genoptraening/behandling af afatiske patienter, et udviklingsarbejde. Nordisk Psykiatrisk Tidsskrift 31: 147–154

Danielsen U T 1981 Neuropsychological rehabilitation based on personality characteristics. Platform paper, 4th International Neuropsychological Society European Conference. Bergen

Danielsen U T, Angelsoe B 1979 Afatiske patienter og integreret behandling. Danske Fysioterapeuten 14: 4–9

Danielsen U T, Angelsoe B 1982 Hemiplegi-patienten: Symptomer og behandling ud fra neuropsykologisk synsvinkel Ergoterapeuten 12: 418–423

Luria A R 1980 Higher cortical functions in Man, 2nd edn. Basic Books, New York

Smed A 1977 Neuropsykologisk behandling og genoptraening efter apoplektisk attack. En forlobsbeskrivelse. Nordisk Psykiatrisk Tidsskrift 31: 164–170

Smed A 1981 The impact of social surroundings on rehabilitation. Platform paper, 4th International Neuropsychological Society European Conference, Bergen

Smed A, Angelsoe B, Andersen R 1980 Hjerneskadens psykosociale konsekvenser. Sygeplejersken 44: 5–10

Thomsen I V 1980 Evaluation, outcome and treatment of aphasia in patients with severe head injuries. In: Sarno M T, Hook O (eds) Aphasia, assessment and treatment. Almqvist & Wiksell, Uppsala

*Ritva Laaksonen*

# Neuropsychological rehabilitation in Finland

## INTRODUCTION

Reconstruction and rehabilitation of higher cortical functions of brain dysfunctional patients has been established as part of the clinical practice of Finnish neuropsychologists only during the past 10 years. The historical roots of rehabilitation of mental functions after head injuries, however, date back to the 1940s. The pioneering work was done by Professor Niilo Mäki (1902–1968) at the Finnish War Veterans Hospital in Helsinki. Mäki had studied psychology in Frankfurt-am-Main in Germany in the 1920s and was well acquainted with the work of Kurt Goldstein and Adhémar Gelb, long before his colleagues in many European countries.

Mäki was particularly concerned with aphasic patients and their overall rehabilitation and social readjustment. His approach was partly based on the psychological–pedagogical principles of the German school, and partly developed by himself to suit the particular needs and demands of the national circumstance in Finland. His objective in rehabilitation was to treat the whole person, not just a limited handicap, and at times he found it difficult to draw lines between medical treatment, educational progams and work therapy (Mäki, 1944). His writings emphasized the importance of individually designed rehabilitation tasks and programs, which he thought should be personally meaningful and of interest to the patients.

Despite the remarkable and internationally known work of Mäki, and later his follower Risto Lehtonen, there was a gap in the development of rehabilitation programs for civilian patients. The origins of the present trend go back to the late 1960s, when the University clinics in Helsinki and Turku established positions for clinical neuropsychologists. The clinical psychologists Anna-Riitta Putkonen and Raija Portin, who were then engaged for those new positions, saw the importance of starting anew a neuropsychological tradition suited for modern demands of neurological diagnosis and rehabilitation.

Today there is a school of neuropsychologists in Finland whose work has been inspired and influenced by a number of international authorities in the field, among them Arthur L. Benton, Lubov S. Tsvetkov, Anne-Lise Christensen, Byron B. Rourke, Louis Costa, Kenneth Adams, and the late

Mariusz Maruszewski, who first (in 1971) acquainted Finnish neuropsychologists with the clinical application of the theory and methods of A. R. Luria.

## PRESENT PROGRAM GOALS AND OBJECTIVES

At present most neuropsychological rehabilitation programs are being developed at the neurological clinics or units of University hospitals and other central hospitals in Finland, as well as some private rehabilitation centers such as The Käpylä Rehabilitation Institute in Helsinki. Since 1979 The Helsinki University Hospital has had a special outpatient/rehabilitation clinic for stroke patients.

In Finland neuropsychological rehabilitation is most often considered as part of medical rehabilitation programs for acutely disabled patients with central nervous system disorders such as cerebrovascular insults, post-traumatic and postoperative conditions, and toxic or inflammatory neurological etiologies. However, there is increasing interest in applying neuropsychological expertise to specific learning disabilities, particularly with young adults, with whom the school system and special education have failed, and also with mentally retarded young people who have finished their formal educational requirements. In recent years there has been government support available for the latter groups from special rehabilitation funds in individual cases. The future trend seems promising in this respect, since in 1983 neuropsychological rehabilitation was officially included in the treatment methods to be financially supported.

The practical purposes of neuropsychological treatment programs in general can be classified under the following goals for individual patients:

1. to regain the functional capacity of going back to work;
2. to gain capabilities for further educational or occupational rehabilitation progams, some intermediate form of rehabilitation or sheltered work, if previous work is not within reach;
3. to gain sufficient independence for dealing with everyday life situations in a home environment or at an institute.

In most cases neuropsychological rehabilitation is planned as an integrated part of a medical rehabilitation program in which the professional teams of speech, physical, and occupational therapists, as well as medical doctors and nurses, share the responsibility of working towards the goals with the patient. At times, however, neuropsychological treatment may be the only therapeutic management for the patient.

The cognitive functions to be rehabilitated or reconstructed may vary from specific perceptual, motor or aphasic disturbances to impairment of memory and the more complex intellectual functions as well as attentional difficulties or problems of behavioral control, motivation and altered personality. The cognitive defects to be rehabilitated are never separated from the patient's whole personality, premorbid interests and orientations.

In this approach the Finnish tradition follows Mäki's early conceptions. The rehabilitation goals and treatment strategies are designed according to the patient's personal needs, and the treatment procedures are carried out taking into consideration the emotional crisis that most patients undergo after sudden and crippling illness. Special attention is also paid to counseling. As Muriel Lezak (1976) points out:

> the patient must have factual information about his functioning to be able to set realistic goals. The concerned family also needs to know the patient's psychological condition, in order to deal with him appropriately, understand his adjustment problems and readjust to his changes.

To make the counseling more intensive and systematic an audiovisual slide program for stroke patients was prepared by the neurological rehabilitation team of the Helsinki University Central Hospital Department of Neurology with financial support from the Finnish Heart Association, distributed to other central hospitals in Finland and shown regularly at the hospital wards. Also a booklet was published in 1978 for the patients and their family to gain better understanding of the psychologically and physiologically altered life situation.

This material was also meant to facilitate questions and openness in the patients and their families to discuss even the emotionally painful problems, which so often appear to be obstacles for all rehabilitation unless faced and worked at.

## THEORETICAL FRAMEWORK, PROCEDURES, AND METHODS OF NEUROPSYCHOLOGICAL REHABILITATION

The influence of Maruzewski's application of Luria's methods of rehabilitation and neuropsychological analysis of basic defects and their underlying mechanisms has been very deep-rooted in Finnish neuropsychology although today the practical work has been integrated with eclectic strategies particularly from modern learning theories.

The following features are most descriptive of the neuropsychological approaches in Finland from the 1970s to the 1980s:

1. The approach toward reconstruction of higher cortical functions is based on Luria's conception of dynamic 'systemic' localization of higher cortical functions (Luria, 1963, 1970, 1973, 1976; Maruszewski, 1968, 1969, 1972; Tsvetkova, 1972).
2. Rehabilitation is planned on the basis of detailed qualitative neuropsychological analysis of the basic defects, differentiation between primary and secondary disturbances and qualifying the mechanisms or disturbed links underlying the defects, as well as evaluation of the preserved abilities and psychogenic reactions that may influence the symptoms.

3. The rehabilitation strategies and methods are designed individually using the unimpaired and accessible functional properties of the patient's preserved capacity in neuropsychological reorganization.
4. The reconstruction methods can be divided into two types:
   a. direct methods, which include the more mechanical training procedures and stimulations;
   b. indirect ('compensatory') methods which aim at neuropsychological reorganization of functional systems and the prophylaxis of wrong compensations.
5. The central mechanism of recovery worked toward is the reorganization of impaired functional systems that form the psychophysiological basis of man's higher mental processess.

Even though the general framework for therapy is relatively uniform, the clinical rehabilitation methods are usually individually tailored and thus dependent on the therapist's creative insight, ingenuity and familiarity with the dynamic localization theory, and overall knowledge of present scientific brain and behavior research. General difficulties in planning the therapy arise from inadequate knowledge of the cerebral organization of complex forms of mental activity and the interaction of various factors and individual properties that influence the outcomes of therapy, as also outlined by Powell (1981).

Most of the practical work is based on 'self-made' programs with the exception of rehabilitation of aphasic disturbances which follows more closely the treatment methodology and specific programs created by Luria and his collaborators. The group treatment methods for aphasics developed by L. S. Tsvetkova and her team (Glozman et al, 1980) in Moscow, have been adopted and developed for Finnish purposes by Ritva Hänninen and her group at the North Carelian Central Hospital since 1980.

At the Helsinki University Central Hospital (HUCH) we have a tradition of neuropsychological rehabilitation practices since 1967. The main emphasis of neuropsychological work has, however, been in diagnostic work as in all acute hospitals. Recently, rehabilitation activities have gained more ground and since 1979 the new rehabilitation unit has opened new vistas for future development.

According to the yearly statistics, the most common combination of disturbances treated in 108 patients with 1055 therapy sessions has been impairment of memory combined with defects in abstract thinking, some specific cognitive deficits, attentional difficulties, behavioral alterations, and emotional problems mostly due to cerebrovascular etiology. Isolated memory defects and unilateral visuo-spatial neglect with associated disturbances have also been rehabilitated as well as aphasic syndromes, which form about 30–40% of all cases.

In planning the treatment Luria's Neuropsychological Investigation by Anne-Lise Christensen (1974) is used as the basis for qualitative analysis, together with Maruszewski's Luria Method and some specific tests developed at the HUCH Neurological Clinic. Psychometric tests are also used whenever possible for treatment evaluation and assessment of the patient's initial capacity as compared with that of the peer groups. The most commonly used traditional methods are the Wechsler Adult Intelligence Scale, the Wechsler Memory Scale, the Benton Visual Retention Test, and Raven Progressive Matrices.

Even though the rehabilitation procedures are based mainly on the results of qualitative testing, the use of psychometric methods has proved indispensable in evaluating the functional recovery for work or readiness for further social rehabilitation programs. Of interest is the transfer effects of certain rehabilitation procedures on the more complex intellectual functions, measured by the WAIS.

As for the testing procedures the psychometric tests are also analyzed qualitatively, and each response to subtest items is analyzed separately and interpreted in accordance with the general theoretical conceptions. The scores on some subtests and the quality of individual answers may also give important information about the patient's premorbid capacity, which would not otherwise be detected objectively through the altered overall behavior. Qualitative analysis of individual subtests of psychometric methods is also advocated by Lezak (1976) and Golden (1979). The general treatment principles for individual disorders or combinations of disorders depend on and vary according to the mechanisms underlying the defects, the nature of primary and secondary disturbances, and the practical meaning of the disability.

## ILLUSTRATION OF TREATMENT PLANNING

To illustrate the diagnostic thinking in planning treatment programs, reconstruction of memory disturbances is used as an example. The central issues in Luria's theory are that mental functions are viewed as

> 'complex functional systems, which cannot be localized in narrow zones of the cortex or isolated cell groups, but must be organized in systems of concertedly working zones, each of which performs its role in the complex functional system, and which may be located in completely different and often distant areas of the brain.'

Luria also maintains that localization of higher mental processes is never static, but changing during the development of the child and at subsequent stages of training. Another important issue is Luria's distinction between the three principal functional units: a unit of regulating tone or waking (structures in the subcortex and the brainstem); a unit for obtaining, processing, and storing information arriving from the outside world (postcentral cortical areas in the parietal, occipital, and temporal lobes); and a unit for programming, regulating, and verifying mental activity (anterior or prefrontal areas of the hemispheres) (Luria, 1973).

As for the cerebral organization of complex forms of mnestic activity, Luria's approach is based on analysis of the various aspects of mnemonic process, which form the basis for integrated memory function, and associating these somewhat different aspects or memory mechanisms to the three functional units.

Let us consider the type of memory disturbance in a patient with localized lesion in the first functional unit.

Case M.A.

Patient M.A. was a 50-year-old-male with professional education and a high executive position at work, who had two consecutive operations for an aneurysm, shown in the vertebral angiography at the basilar bifurcation, quite separate from the posterior cerebral arteries. After the second operation a small local infarction was to be seen by computed axial tomography, located in the left anterior thalamus. The neurological status was normal except for observed initial confusion, memory defects, and strange psychotic-like behavior.

Neuropsychological examinations were performed only a month after the operations, when the patient was transferred to the Helsinki University Central Hospital. The detailed investigation of neuropsychological functions indicated a relatively well preserved overall intellectual capacity (superior/very superior WAIS IQ), with some selective impairment of verbal intellectual functions involved with recall of previous information and abstract concept formation, as well as some deficiency in the ability to differentiate essential from non-essential details (the WAIS PC). Arithmetic Reasoning and Block Design were very superior as for the level of performance. Qualitative assessment methods indicated no specific gnostic, practic or aphasic disturbances at the time of testing, although anamnestic data indicated word-finding difficulties and paraphasic features for some time after the operations. At the examinations the patient was generally oriented to time, place, and recent life events, being only partially aware of his memory difficulties, which appeared quite striking at the formal testing.

The detailed qualification of the mnestic functions revealed the following features: intact memory span for words and digits, preserved ability to repeat moderately difficult and long sentences, but a marked deficiency in retaining stories with semantic context. A tendency for contamination and also some confabulation was to be noted, indicating the inhabitability of memory traces by interfering irrelevant images. However the simple tests of heterogeneous and homogeneous inhibition did not pick out this feature. Frequent repetition did not improve recall nor eliminate contamination, which manifested as extremely poor performance at the WMS paired associates. The most depressing experience for the patient was the fact that he could not recall three names after 2 minutes delay. This, however gave him insight as to the need of rehabilitation. The pictogram method indicated a fairly good use of the ability to profit from cues even though there were problems with the accuracy of recall. On the whole the memory disturbances were modally non-specific in nature. However the reproduction of visual memory images was to recover sooner, and the deficiency of verbal-semantic memory was clearly more persistent. Behaviorally the patient was easily frustrated, prone to fatigue and showed exaggeration of certain premorbid personality characteristics. The illness had also brought about interpersonal problems in the family and counseling and supportive discussions were to be an essential part of rehabilitation.

Even though the theoretical conceptions of memory mechanisms concerning the first functional unit, which according to Luria give rise to modality non-specific disturbances of mnestic activity, with the central mechanism of increased inhabitability of memory traces by interfering actions both in recall and other memorizing activity, are somewhat vague for practical work, the qualification of various aspects of neuropsychological deficits, together with this understanding, form a basis for individual treatment.

In the case of M.A. the treatment plan was first to strengthen the relatively well-preserved formal–logical intellectual ability and its use in structuring the material to be used in memory training. Pieces of current news were used as contextual material, because this was of particular interest to the patient and also helped to keep him updated with current events. Since the process of active recall was more difficult for the patient than the more elementary and passive form of recall by recognition, the latter was used at the initial stages to facilitate recall of learned material. Emphasis was put on the conscious differentiation of essential features from the non-essential. The use of memorizing aids by visual and also semantic cues was introduced to the patient, and though slow and inaccurate at first, the patient was able to learn new conscious ways of assisting active recall. After the patient was able to recall small passages modified and worked by himself from news material, a memory-enrichment program, developed at the neurological clinic by the author, was used as a functional aid for relearning ways to deal with accumulated knowledge met with in everyday life. This method includes personal histories of six men (in this case only three could be used) to be memorized so that at each therapy session a certain amount of new material is presented, to be repeated with all previous material at the following session.

The process of recovery was slow, and at times the patient was extremely depressed. Return to work was long a distant, and insecure goal, both for the patient and the therapist. When it appeared that it was the only possibility for the patient for psychic reasons, and that the achieved improvement gave support to this goal, it was decided that the last stage of training would be based on material connected with the patient's work.

After 6 months of rehabilitation the patient was able to attempt his former job and manage there, even though troubled by fatigue and relative slowness at work. The therapy sessions had been twice a week, but the rest of the time had been filled with homework. A therapeutic follow-up was arranged after return to work. The control examinations indicated marked improvement also in psychometric tests; the WMS MQ had risen from initial 92 to 120 showing still some residual defect. The WAIS subtest scores were likewise improved.

A different training program would be designed for the modally specific memory disturbances as well as for memory dysfunction due to frontal or combined lesions.

For visual perceptual and constructional disturbances, as well as for other specific cognitive defects, the same general theoretical principles apply in planning the treatment. However, resort to eclectic knowledge has also been the guide for practical work due to the theoretical ambiguity of the basic nature of the deficits. The use of direct and indirect methods varies, but in general mechanical training is avoided as of little use, except for certain attentional difficulties and milder forms of certain defects. Control and feedback are also used very carefully.

The evaluation of rehabilitation outcomes and efficiency of methods has so far been mainly based on repeated testings in individual cases, and the practical experience gained through the years. Systematic and large-scale rehabilitation research is very limited. An experiment of adjustment training for aphasics with video-feedback was carried out in 1972 (Putkonen et al, 1978), and there are some present ongoing research projects at the university hospitals of Helsinki and Turku and the North Carelian Central Hospital.

The present trend in rehabilitation practices is toward inclusion of neuropsychological rehabilitation as a form of remediating specific learning disabilities of congenital etiology. There is some evidence of individual case studies (Laaksonen, 1982), which indicate the potentialities of using neuropsychological orientation as the basis for this.

A case report with combined neuropsychological (analytic) and cognitive behavioral procedures and treatment methods indicated improvement of complex intellectual functions as well as reconstruction of congenitally defective writing skills, in a 25-year-old female. The program included 125 therapy sessions during 3 years. Evaluation at the end of the treatment period indicated a WAIS Verbal Scale IQ rise from initial 103 to 113, with respective Performance Scale rise from 100 to 119. The WMS MQ-values rose from 86 to 103, as measured by parallel forms of the WMS. The most significant rise was to be seen in Digit Span, originally the most deficient subtest, which had improved 6 scale score points. No direct exercises of digit memory were used, nor any other tasks analogous to the WAIS subtests. The specific methods used were based on qualitative neuropsychological investigation.

A follow up 1 year and 8 months after the treatment period confirmed the persistence of the gained improvement. As for personal and social competence and overall well-being, the patient had become more active and confident, had had further training and was promoted at work.

Fully aware of the shortcomings of available programs and the limits of any single theory at the present stage of knowledge, to provide all the answers for methodological problems, in such a demanding task as reconstruction of man's higher cortical functions, the application of the analytic approach has proved a fruitful starting point and work-orientation for future developments.

## REFERENCES

Christensen, A-L 1974 Luria's neuropsychological investigation. Munksgaard, Copenhagen

Glotzman, I M, Kalitex W G, Tsyganok A A 1980. On one system of methods of aphasics group rehabilitation. International Journal of Rehabilitation Research 3(4): 519–526

Golden C J 1979 Clinical interpretation of objective tests. Grune & Stratton, New York

Laaksonen R 1982 Improvement of complex intellectual functions, personality adjustment and congenitallv defective writing skills after cognitive rehabilitation based on cognitive-behavioral and neuropsychological procedures. 12th European Congress of Behavior Therapy, Rome, 5–8 September (Book of abstracts)

Lezak M 1976 Neuropsychological assessment. Oxford University Press, New York

Luria A R 1963 Restoration of function after brain injury. Pergamon, Oxford

Luria A R 1970 Traumatic aphasia. Mouton, New York

Luria A R 1973 The working brain. An introduction to neuropsychology. Allen Lane/Penguin, Harmondsworth

Luria A R 1976 The neuropsychology of memory. Winston, Washington, D C

Mäki N 1944 Koulu sotasairaalassa. Aivosairaalan opetustoimintaa. Suomen Punainen Risti 7: 124–140

Maruszewski M 1968 A Polish–Soviet neuropsychological symposium. International Journal of Psychology 3(4): 313–315

Maruszewski M 1969 Neuropsychology in neuropsychological rehabilitation. International Journal of Psychology 4(1): 73–75

Maruszewski M 1972 Johdatus Kliiniseen neuropsykologiaan. (Toim) A-R Putkonen, Psykologien Kustannus Oy, Helsinki

Powell G 1981 Brain function therapy. Gover, London

Putkonen A-R, Kalimo R, Laaksonen R, Tenkku M, Jarho L 1978, Afasiapotilaiden sopeutumisvalmennuksen kehittäminen. Ryhmäkeskustelu kokeilu. Sos lääket. Aikak. 1(15): 124–134

20

*Xavier Seron*

# Neuropsychological rehabilitation in European French-language countries

## HISTORICAL BACKGROUND

In the European French-language countries, Blanche Ducarne was an influential pioneer in aphasia therapy. Working initially at le Centre du Langage at La Salpêtrière Hospital, first with Theophile Alajouanine and later with François Lhermitte, she developed numerous original methods for the re-education of aphasics. Although little has been published on her work (Lhermitte and Ducarne, 1962, 1965), for many years anyone who wanted to work on aphasia therapy spent several months apprenticeship at La Salpêtrière Hospital. The influence of Ducarne's work in the French-language countries may be thus compared to that of Schuell and Wepman in the US. But in the absence of sufficient publications, it is not easy to specify the originality and the merits or the shortcomings of Ducarne's approach, and we may only offer here some general observations.

As regards general therapeutic principles the main points are the following:

1. Ducarne's therapy was clearly adapted to the nature of the disorder, different methods being used depending on the type and semiology of the aphasia.
2. Therapy was not viewed as a learning enterprise and thus was not administered with a pedagogical orientation. The French founders stressed that aphasic patients were able to speak before their accident, and thus the intervention must be oriented to the reactivation of preserved knowledge. Their interpretation was thus close to what Sarno (1981) calls the 'loss of access' theory, and the therapeutic strategy may be considered as a stimultion–facilitation approach.
3. For the most part, with the exception of apraxia of speech, the therapy was not finely programmed as learning approaches are. Ducarne insisted on the necessity of adapting exercises and progressions to the individual patient's evolution.
4. Other general recommendations were to emphasize multi-stimulation, to use residual intact functions, to stress oral repetition, and to establish hierarchies of exercises but without rigid *a priori* programming.

Similar to Schuell's school, Ducarne's French school thus employed a stimulation–facilitation approach without the stress on auditory stimulation or fine-grated progressions in cues and prompts. Similar to Luria's school, there was an attempt to adapt the re-education to the nature of the disorder and, in some cases, the objective was to reorganize behavior. However, the therapeutic practice was not so clearly linked as in Luria's school with precise theoretical framework.

In summary, Ducarne's therapies were semiologically motivated, adapted to individual cases, and did not insist on a strict programming of exercises. Furthermore, no special attention was given to the social and familial environment of the patients. The most important limitation of her pioneering work was its lack of empirical validation. Nevertheless the influence of Ducarne's work has been of primary importance and is still felt in the present renewal of contemporary French therapeutic approaches (Seron, 1979; Seron & Laterre, 1982).

## NEW APPROACHES IN LANGUAGE REHABILITATION

Since the early 1970s, the climate has changed in clinical rehabilitative practice, largely due to a modification of attitude of neuropsychologists toward the plasticity of brain structures and functions after cerebral lesions (Jeannerod & Hécaen, 1979). Other influences were the development of new forms of therapy in the US, notably those derived from learning principles (the work of Sarno and Holland, for example) and Luria's work in the Soviet Union. But the relatively late evolution in the French-language countries is extremely difficult to discern since French-speaking clinicians publish very little and and there is little scientific literature devoted to re-education in neuropsychology. Our review of present practices is thus necessarily limited and is based largely on our personal contacts with French, Belgian, and Swiss centers. It certainly is not exhaustive.

## ADAPTION OF MELODIC INTONATION THERAPY IN FRENCH LANGUAGE

Philippe Van Eeckhout introduced Melodic Intonation Therapy at La Salpêtrière Hospital (Van Eeckhout & Allichon, 1978; Van Eeckhout et al, 1979, 1981, 1982). It was retitled Thérapie Mélodique et Rythmée, and some important modifications of Sparks' original method were made. The major problem with the original Melodic Intonation Therapy is that, in contrast to English, it is not possible to identify in French a stable natural prosodic pattern for a given sentence in order to stress this basis pattern for Melodic Therapy. Van Eeckhout was therefore obliged to create arbitrary melodic patterns and to adapt them to patients' idiosyncratic preferences. He also introduced some modifications in Sparks' standard methodology. However, on the whole, he followed the original hierarchy and the Thérapie Mélodique et Rythmée is globally applied according to the Sparks' criteria. For patients presenting atypical disorders in rhythm production, a pretherapeutic program employing a microcomputer-controlled device has been developed in collaboration with Gérard Deloche of the Salpêtrière in Paris and Xavier Seron of St Luc Hospital in Brussels to train patients to reproduce rhythmic patterns before entering the Thérapie Mélodique et Rythmée. Currently Gérard Deloche, Isabelle Wendling, and Philippe Van Eeckhout are developing a program using a microcomputer biofeedback device to train the patients to produce high and low contrasted sounds in different rhythmic patterns. Both these programs are intended to train patients who would otherwise not be able to participate in Thérapie Mélodique et Rythmée therapy. These programs are still in their infancy and more empirical evidence must be assembled to evaluate fully their efficiency (Deloche et al, 1983). At present the French adaption of Melodic Intonation Therapy is being used in several places and particularly at Lausanne (Buttet and Aubert, 1980).

## THERAPY OF COMMUNICATIVE BEHAVIOR AND USE OF NON-VERBAL SYSTEMS

Several experimental studies on non-verbal behavior in aphasia have been constructed in French-language countries (Goldblum, 1978; Labourel, 1982; Feyereisen & Seron, 1982a,b; Feyereisen & Lignian, 1981; Feyereisen et al, 1981; Seron et al, 1979b). However, until recently they have not had much influence on therapeutic approaches, which remain focused solely on verbal behavior. Nevertheless, Premack's approach in aphasia therapy (Glass et al, 1973) and other non-verbal therapeutic systems (Visual Communication–VIC: Gardner et al, 1976; Bliss: Ross, 1979; Amerind: Skelly et al, 1974; and Visual Action Therapy - VAT: Helm-Estabrooks et al, 1982) have had an impact on clinical practice. Dominique Rectem at St Luc Hospital in Brussels has adapted Premack's method with a single case of global aphasia. The originality of Rectem's program is that while it respects the errorless procedure of the programmed therapy of Glass et al (1973), it uses pictographic and ideographic symbols. This approach is thus very close to that of Gardner et al (Rectem et al, 1980). Recently Davis' PACE method (Davis & Wilcox, 1981) was tested and further developed in Brussels by Nadine Clerebaut and colleagues (Clerebaut et al, 1983). The PACE method was not viewed as an alternative to other language-oriented therapeutic methods but as complementary to them. New interactive situations were introduced into the method such as scenery with mobile elements, and the multiple scale for rating the patient's communicative effectiveness differed from the original American scale. The Bliss method has also begun to appear in various places, but there have been no publications on the results obtained. Finally, Pillon et al (1980) have described the successful therapeutic use of drawing activity and captions as an augmentative and deblocking system with an aphasic who was a cartoonist. This patient, in collaboration with his speech and medical therapists, has written an interesting history of his aphasic condition and recovery, and illustrated it with very illuminating caricatures (Fig. 20.1) (Sabadel, 1980).

## APHASIC SOCIAL ADJUSTMENT

During the past 5 years another noteworthy evolution in French-language countries has been the appearance of more global care approaches to the patient from the psychoaffective and sociological points of view. In Lyon and Lausanne, therapy and post-therapy groups of aphasics have been formed in which the stress is not only on functional verbal behavior but also on familial integration and social adjustment. Currently, several other places have also introduced group therapy. Unfortunately, very little has been published on this development (Buttet & Hirnsbrunner, 1982). Dominique Labourel at Lyon has written an information booklet for the aphasic's family explaining stroke and aphasia conditions. The publication, (*On a du mal à se comprendre*, 1981) was the result of collaboration between eight different centers in Switzerland, France, and Belgium. In Brussels, language therapy is followed or accompanied by ergotherapeutic and preprofessional teaching; but with few exceptions the therapy in French-language countries is too restrictive, often limited to the neuropsychological instrumental disorders (Boehringer, 1982).

## EVOLUTION TOWARD MORE PRECISE COGNITIVE APPROACHES

The idea that re-education is a reorganizational enterprise and that in order to be effective, it is necessary to understand the nature of the disorders, has been frequently underlined by Alexandre R. Luria (Luria et al, 1969). In the French-language countries, Luria has had little influence on therapeutic practice (see however, Derouesné et al, 1975). The development of therapy conducted in a cognitive perspective seems to be a direct result of fundamental research on agraphic/alexic syndromes at La Salpêtrière (Andreewsky & Seron, 1975; Beauvois & Derouesné, 1979, 1981; Deloche et al, 1982) and at St Anne's in Paris (Goldblum, 1979; Kremin, 1980). A link between these studies and clinical practice has been forged in France by Marie-France Beauvois and Jacqueline Derouesné (1982), who have presented four very promising single-case studies of the re-education of disorders that are well documented on the theoretical level. These present four reorganizational strategies for different very specific and well-isolated syndroms: a case of bilateral tactile aphasia, a case of total alexia without agraphia, a case of phonological alexia, and a case of dynamic aphasia. Their approach in each case is as follows: first, they used a theoretically oriented approach to the syndrome to produce an information processing model both for normal processing and for the disorder; second, they either taught the patient an alternative new strategy or reinforced a pre-existing but not frequently used strategy. For example, in the case of bilateral tactile aphasia, the patient was able to recognize objects after tactile inspection but was

**Figure 20.1**
I have a door in my brain
which is half open,
I have synonyms which
do not come out,
antonyms which *do not come out*
words which *do not*
*come out*
Damn, damn, damn!
when a word wants to come out
it wants to come
out
it can COME OUT

From 'L'homme qui ne savait plus parler,' 1980.

unable to name them correctly. Nevertheless, his visual naming performance had been preserved. The strategy consisted of teaching the patient first to inhibit his spontaneous tactile naming (which was consistently wrong), then to construct, by careful palpation, a visual mental representation of the object, and finally to name this visual representation. The positive effects of such a compensatory strategy were obvious, and after the therapy the patient was able to name correctly all objects presented for palpation if they were visible by using a visual mental relay. Other re-educational attempts in a reorganizational spirit have been made with the frontal lobe syndrome by Derouesné et al (1975) and by Seron et al (1979a) for naming disorders. The study by Derouesné et al shows that it is possible, using Luria's concept of frontal disorders of planning, to help frontally damaged patients with external cues to plan actions, then through exercises to provoke at least a partial internalization of such learned plans.

In the work of Seron et al (1979a) on naming disorders, the approach concerned two groups of patients: one group received therapy focused on the restoration of specific lexical items, the other on the restoration of the access processes (whatever they are). It was found to be more efficient to restore process access than to learn specific lexical items. But, as noted by Shallice (1979), the evolution of studies with an information-processing approach is hampered by the wide variety of interindividual differences. Currently Noëlle Bachy in Brussels is developing, therapeutic methods for naming disorders with single-case paradigms. Her first results indicate that the strategies used by patients to compensate for their deficits are far more numerous than was previously thought (Seron & Bachy, in press). In summary, work from a cognitive perspective will probably continue to be single-case studies.

## MICROCOMPUTER TECHNOLOGY IN NEUROPSYCHOLOGICAL THERAPY

Microcomputer technology in therapy is used at La Salpêtrière Hospital in Paris and at St Luc Hospital in Brussels. Seron and Deloche have studied the effectiveness of computer-based therapy in the treatment of aphasic subjects with writing disorders. The task they use is writing from dictation. Reinforcement is differential in that a correct response appears immediately on the screen; for incorrect responses, two different situations are taken into account: if the letter belongs to the word but was produced in a wrong position (serial ordering error) the computer displays the letter in dots in the correct position; if the erroneous letter does not belong to the word, it is simply not displayed on the screen. Thus the procedure avoids visual reinforcement of false choices and aids the correction to serial ordering disorders. This method has proved efficient for typewriting, and some transfer to handwriting has also been observed (Seron et al, 1980). First implemented on a PDP 10, the procedure has been adapted to a microcomputer and extended to written naming tasks (Deloche et al, 1983).

In collaboration with Marie-Thérèse Hirnbrunner, Françoise Coyette and Isabelle Wendling, Gerard Deloche and Xavier Seron have also developed a four-task battery for hemineglect and hemianopsia rehabilitation, which is currently being tested empirically for validation. For example, the first task is detecting on the screen unpredictable stops of a moving horizontal target, and the second is comparing two vertical moving lines displayed in the right and the left visual hemifields and indicating by pressing a key when the extremities are on the same horizontal line.

## THERAPIES OF OTHERS NEUROPSYCHOLOGICAL DISORDERS

Other therapeutic programs are being developed for disorders of attention, memory, praxis and gnosis, but apart from specific studies on the hemineglect syndrome (Seron & Tissot, 1973) and on memory re-education (Seron et al, 1981; Bruyer, 1981), the only detailed progam is that of Marie-Anne Vanderkaa and Martial Vanderlinden (1983 a and b) from the University of Liège, which focused on memory disorders. In their first program, these authors designed a very detailed progression of exercises to teach residual aphasic patients to use mental imagery as aids for verbal memory. Their programs contain clearly hierarchicalized levels going from visual discriminative attention to systematic use of a mental file. The second program, derived from Kintch's analysis of discourse structure, teaches aphasic patients to organize varying and long sequences of verbal written information by discovering their structures. This enables them to memorize long texts. These programs are still in development stage but the initial results are very promising.

## SUMMARY

Although as early as 1865 Broca had briefly described one of the first examples of lexical re-education of an aphemic patient (Broca, 1865), neuropsychological re-education has not been well developed in the French-language countries of Europe. The reasons for the present retardation are legion, among them being inadequate speech therapy training, the current economic difficulties in most care institutions of these countries, and insufficient awareness of other scientific traditions. Nevertheless, there are signs of renewal. Among the most promising are cognitive therapeutic approaches to single-case subjects, theoretically oriented work with microprocessor technology, and the broadening of rehabilitation programs beyond the neuropsychological disorder. The creation in December 1976 of 'La Société de Neuropsychologie de Langue Française' has provided considerable motivation for clinical activities and research. The future will surely be better than the past.[1]

[1]For additional information on the centers mentioned here the reader may write either to the secretariat of La Société de Neuropsychologie de Langue Française at the following address: B. Pillon, Inserm U 84, Hôpital de la Salpêtrière, 47 Boulevard de l'Hôpital, F-75651, Paris Cedex 13 (France); or to the author: X. Seron, Centre de Revalidation Neuropsychologique, Cliniques Universitaires St Luc, Avenue Hippocrate, 10/1350, B-1200 Bruxelles (Belgium).

## REFERENCES

Andreewsky E, Seron X 1975 Implicit processing of grammatical rules in a classical case of agrammatism. Cortex 11: 379–390

Beauvois M F, Derouesné J 1979 Phonological alexia: three dissociations. Journal of Neurology, Neurosurgery and Psychiatry 42: 1115–1124

Beauvois M F, Derouesné J 1981 Lexical or orthographic agraphia. Brain 104:21–49

Beauvois M F, Derouesné J 1982 Recherche en neuropsychologie et rééducation: quels rapports? In: Seron X, Laterre C (eds) Rééduquer le cerveau, logopédie, psychologie, neurologie. Mardaga, Brussels. ch. 11, pp. 163–189

Boehringer C 1982 Rendements et séquelles neuropsychologiques: la remise au travail du patient cérébrolésé. In: Seron X, Laterre C (eds) Rééduquer le cerveau, logopédie, psychologie, neurologie. Mardaga, Brussels, ch. 15, pp. 243–254

Broca P 1865 Sur la faculté du langage articulé. Bulletin de Société d'Anthropologie Paris 6: 337–393

Bruyer R 1981 Approche opérante des atteintes traumatiques de la mémoire, effet de la connaissance des résultats sur la performance. Journal de Thérapie Comportemantale III: 3–42

Buttet J, Aubert C 1980 La thérapie par l'intonation mélodique: apport de la réflexion neuropsychologique à la clinique. La Revue Médicale Suisse Romande 100: 195–199

Buttet J, Hirnsbrunner M T 1982 Rééducation des aphasiques: le travail en groupes. In: Seron X, Laterre C (eds) Rééduquer le cerveau, logopédie, psychologie, neurologie. Mardaga, Brussels, ch. 10, pp. 157–160

Clerebaut N, Coyette F, Seron X, Feyereisen P 1983 Rééducation de la communication chez des patients aphasiques, présentation d'une méthode: la PACE. Réunion de la Société de Neuropsychologie de langue française, Marseille, 13–14 May

Davis G A, Wilcox M J 1981 Incorporating parameters of natural conversation in aphasia treatment. In: Chapey R (ed) Language intervention strategies in adult aphasia. Williams & Wilkins, Baltimore, ch. 8, pp. 169–193

Deloche G, Andreewsky E, Desi M 1982 Surface dyslexia: a case report and some theoretical implications to reading models. Brain and Language 15: 11–32

Deloche G, Seron X, Coyette F, Wendling I, Hirnsbrunner T, Van Eeckhout P 1983 Microcomputer-assisted rehabilitation programs for patients with aphasia or visual neglect. Sixth annual meeting International Neuropsychological Society European Conference, Lisboa, 14–17 June

Derouesné J, Seron X, Lhermitte F 1975 Rééducation de patients atteints de lésions frontales. La Revue Neurologique 131: 677–689

Feyereisen P 1983 Manual activity during speaking in aphasic subjects. International Journal of Psyhology 18: 545–556

Feyereisen P, Lignian A 1981 La direction du regard chez les aphasiques en conversation: une observation pilote. Cahiers de Psychologie Cognitive 1: 287–298

Feyereisen P, Seron X 1982a Non verbal communication and aphasia: Part I: comprehension. Brain and Language 16: 191–212

Feyereisen P, Seron X 1982b Non verbal communication and aphasia: Part II: reception. Brain andLanguage 16: 213–236

Feyereisen P, Seron X, Macar de M 1981 L'interprétation de différentes catégories de gestes chez des sujets aphasiques. Neuropsychologia 19: 515–521

Gardner H, Zurif E B, Berry Th, Bakker E 1976 Visual communication in aphasia. Neuropsychologia 14: 275–292

Glass A V, Gazzaniga M S, Premack P 1973 Artificial language training in global aphasics. Neuropsychologia 11: 95–103

Goldblum M C 1978 Les troubles des gestes d'accompagnement du langage au cours des lésions corticales unilatérales. In: Hecaen H, JeannerodM (eds) Du contrôle moteur á l'organisationdu geste. Masson, Paris,pp. 383–395

Goldblum M C 1979 Auditory analogue of deep dyslexia. In: Creutzfeld O, Schneich H, Schreiner Ch (eds) Hearing mechanism and speech. Springer Verlag, Berlin

Helm-Estabrooks N, Fitzpatrick P M, Barresi B 1982 Visual action therapy for global aphasia. Journal of Speech and Hearing Disorders 47: 385–389

Jeannerod M, Hécaen H 1979 Adaptations et restaurations des fonctions nerveuses. Simep, Lyon

Kremin H 1980 Deux stratégies de lecture dissociables par la pathologie: description d'un cas de dyslexie profonde et d'un cas de dyslexie de surface. In: Etudes Neurolinguistiques. Université de Toulouse-le Mirail, pp. 131–156

Laboratoire de Neuropsychologie de Lyon (ed) 1981 On a du mal à se comprendre. Sandoz Editions

Labourel D 1982 Communication non verbal et aphasie. In: Seron X, Laterre C (eds) Rééduquer le cerveau, logopédie, psychologie, neurologie. Mardaga, Brussels, ch. 6, pp. 93–108

Lhermitte F, Ducarne B 1962 La rééducation des aphasiques. Flammarion, Paris

Lhermitte F, Ducarne B 1965 La rééducation des aphasiques. La reveu du Praticien 15: 2345–2363

Luria A R, Naydin V L, Tsvetkova L S, Vinarskaya E N 1969 Restoration of higher cortical function following local brain damage. In: Vinken P J, Bruyn G W (eds) Handbook of Clinical Neurology. Vol. III. North Holland Publishing Company, Netherlands, p. 368–433

Pillon B, Signoret J L, Van Eeckhout P, Lhermitte F 1980 Le dessin chez un aphasique, Incidence possible sur le langage et sa rééducation. La Revue Neurologique 136: 699–710

Rectem D, Bruyer R, Seron X, Stroot-Dieryck M 1980 Rééducation programmée et aphasie globale: apprentissage d'un système arbitraire de communication visuelle et transfert au code écrit naturel. Journal de Thérapie Comportementale II: 19–32

Ross A J 1979 A study of the application of Blissymbolics as a means of communication for a young brain damaged adult. British Journal of Disorders of Communiction 14: 103–109

Sabadel 1980 L'homme qui ne savait plus parler. Nouvelles éditions Baudinière, Paris

Sarno M T 1981 Recovery and rehabilitation in aphasia. In: Sarno M T (ed) Acquired aphasia. Academic Press, New York, ch. 17, pp.485–521

Seron X 1979 Aphasie et neuropsychologie, approches thérapeutiques. Mardaga, Brussels

Seron X, Tissot R 1973 Essai de reéducation d'une agnosie spatiale unilatérale gauche. Acta Psychiatrica Belgica 73: 448–457

Seron X, Deloche G, Bastard V, Chassin G, Hermand N 1979a Word-finding difficulties and learning transfer in aphasic patients. Cortex 15: 149–155

Seron X, Van der Kaa M A, Remits A, Vanderlinden M 1979b Pantomime interpretation and aphasia. Neuropsychologia 17: 661–668

Seron X, Deloche G, Moulard G, Roussell M 1980 Computer-based therapy for the treatment of aphasic subjects with writing disorders. Journal of Speech and Hearing Disorders 45: 45–48

Seron X, Bruyer R, Rectem D, Lepoivre H 1981 Essais de revalidation des troubles post-traumatiques de la mémoire. Monographie non publiée, Brussels

Seron X, Laterre C (eds) 1982 Rééduquer le cerveau, logopédie, psychologie, neurologie. Mardaga, Brussels

Seron X, Bachy N In press Remarques sur la rééducation du manque du mot chez les patients aphasiques

Shallice T 1979 Case study approach in neuropsychological research. Journal of Clinical Neuropsychology 1: 183–211

Skelly M, Schinsky L, Smith R W, Fust R S 1974 American indian sign (Amerind) as a facilitator of verbalization of the oral verbal apraxic. Journal of Speech and Hearing Disorders 39: 445–456

VanderKaa M A, Vanderlinden M 1983a La prise d'information dans les textes: élaboration d'un programme de rééducation adapté à des sujets aphasiques. Réunion de la Société de Neuropsychologie de langue française, Marseille, 13–14 May

VanderKaa M A, Vanderlinden M 1983b Programme de rééducation de la mémoire auditive verbale par le biais de la médiation imagée. Réunion de la Société de neuropsychologie de langue française, Marseille, 13–14 May

Van Eeckhout P, Allichon J 1978 Rééducation par la mélodie des sujets atteints d'aphasie. La Rééducation Orthophonique 16: 25–32

Van Eeckhout P, Meillet-Haberer C, Pillon B 1979 Apport de la therapie mélodique et du rythme dans quelques cas de réductions sévères du langage. La Rééducation Orthophonique 17: 353–369

Van Eeckhout P, Meillet-Haberer C, Pillon B 1981 Utilisation de la mélodie et du rythme dans les mutismes et les stéréotypies. La Rééducation Orthophonique 19: 109–124

Van Eeckhout P, Pillon B, Signoret J L, Deloche G, Seron X 1982 Rééducation des réductions sévères de l'expression orale: la'thérapie mélodique et rythmée'. In: Seron X, Laterre C (eds) Rééduquer le cerveau, logopédie, psychologie, neurologie. Mardaga, Brussels, ch. 7, pp. 109–121

# 21

*Maria Ester Zanobio*

# Representative neuropsychological rehabilitation programs: Italy

In Italy neurological clinics and the major hospitals began in the 1950s to train medical and paramedical staff specifically for the task of rehabilitation and the specialty of Physical Medicine and Rehabilitation came into being. This specialty is still generally considered a poor relation among the specialties, a view which detracts from the professional standing of the physiatrist and contributes to the neglect of conditions which require rehabilitation. What is more, the pathology of superior cortical function resulting from cerebral damage has so far been studied only by neuropsychologists, whose discipline was, in fact, also not officially recognized in Italian universities until 1983, and whose interest is mainly theoretical, seldom addressed to problems of rehabilitation. Neuropsychological rehabilitation is therefore a union of two disciplines which have not had a vigorous development in Italy.

In 1971 a speech therapist for aphasic patients was employed in Milan, a speech therapist with no previous adequate preparation, not because of any personal lack of interest but because the first and only school for speech therapists interested in aphasia began operation in the same year. The creation of the first aphasia unit and school in Milan, however, and the rising demand for research in the pathology of superior cortical function, have encouraged other groups to extend their efforts to other neuropsychological deficits such as apraxia, agnosia, and attention and memory deficits, which often follow cerebral damage. Today the main obstacles in the path of neuropsychological rehabilitation are practical, the most important being the lack of standardized neuropsychological tests to provide data on normal controls and the lack of specialized clinics for the diagnosis and treatment of neuropsychological impairments. Neuropsychological rehabilitation has, nonetheless, developed in three roughly different clinical settings: (1) aphasia services (2) physiotherapy departments and (3) head injury departments. These are, however, seldom identifiable, since they are not independent and autonomous departments. They are generally included in widely different clinical settings and sometimes consist of a single person. This is one of the reasons why – regrettably – this note is certainly not very exhaustive.

In the aphasia rehabilitation services, speech pathologists with specific preparation in the field of aphasia and neuropsychological disorders provide rehabilitation treatment for the neuropsychological consequences of lesions in the language-dominant hemisphere. Acalculia is, next to aphasia, the language-dominant hemisphere lesion pathology most accessible to rehabilitation.

Among the different types identified by Hécaen et al (1961), the disorder called anarithmetia, i.e, the inability to carry out either mental or written calculations without spatial organization disorders, is generally considered for rehabilitation. A standard written test, based on addition, subtraction, multiplication, and division, has been developed to assess the severity of impairment in these cases (Basso & Capitani, 1979). A large number of aphasics, whatever the type, and a certain percentage of non-aphasic left brain-damaged patients suffer from acalculia. Subjects whose deficits are disproportionately severe compared to their language disturbances, and who do not have alexia and/or agraphia for digits and numbers, go on to rehabilitation programs. The re-education of acalculia is specifically directed at overcoming the deficit itself and is organized into various stages of difficulty according to the type and severity of impairment. In cases where the calculation test points to severe impairment, the first rehabilitation exercises deal with basic concepts (e.g., equal–unequal, greater–lesser, even–uneven). At this stage the difficulty of the exercise can be adjusted through the number of alternatives and the length of the interval between the parts of the test. The next step is a series of exercises in counting up and down, or mental two-phase sums. Next, sums requiring decoding of a statement (e.g., how much is twice a quarter of eight, or how many couples are there in a dozen) instead of a straight figure calculation can be employed, and one can progress from those to problems embracing all forms of common measurement that may be encountered in everyday life.

Oral apraxia, often found with non-fluent aphasia, is the other pathology ensuing from language-dominant hemisphere focal damage that is frequently re-educated. In these patients oral apraxia is not, however, a deficit that prevents the patient from leading a normal life and it comes to light only with adequate tests. Hence re-education of oral apraxia is not an end in itself, but is undertaken only when associated with severe articulatory difficulties, thus rendering it very difficult to re-educate speech articulation movements. Since these exercises are not aimed at re-educating the deficit itself but are simply a means of tackling articulation problems, they are interrupted as soon as the patient is able to reproduce the buccofacial movements required for rehabilitation of articulatory difficulties. Exercises for oral apraxia are initially composed of a series of situation-stimulated movements (blowing, chewing, licking, kissing, etc.) which the patient can watch in a mirror, leading up to the execution of isolated movements carried out without the mirror.

Re-education of acalculia and of oral apraxia have different purposes: re-education of calculation deficits aims at recovery of the impaired skills, which must in this case be specifically stimulated; oral apraxia re-education is a sideline program that seeks to obviate a fundamental obstacle to treatment of aphasic impairment.

Another deficit frequently associated with a left hemisphere lesion that sometimes interferes with normal everyday life is ideomótór apraxia. To the best of my knowledge, however, ideomótór apraxia is not currently treated, even though speech therapists do in fact take it into account when it is severe enough to interfere with those gestures a patient may be required to make during a therapy session, such as intentionally pointing to an object named by the therapist.

Re-education of impairments of praxis and attention is sometimes attempted in general rehabilitation settings. Physiotherapists treat these conditions if they hamper treatment of the defective activity which is the specific object of the treatment. In a case, for instance, of severe hemiplegia in which the subject has symptoms of unilateral neglect and/or apraxia of the limbs, the neuropsychological deficit must be re-educated or it would interfere with the specific motor re-education program.

In Italy there is as yet no fully accepted re-education program for these pathologies, but the preliminary evidence available shows quite clearly that inclusion of treatment of these pathologies in the treatment program has either improved re-education techniques for adult brain-damaged patients or provided keys to their inadequacies.

Neuropsychological rehabilitation of pathologies caused by severe head trauma is quite new in Italy and still in the experimental phase. It differs from aphasia rehabilitation of adults in both the nature of the lesion - usually multifocal and sometimes involving the diencephalic and mesencephalic structures - and the fact that most subjects are young people, often of school age. Studies of 117 patients at the Neurological Clinic in Parma (Mazzucchi et al, 1984) have shown that memory deficits and damage to reasoning processes account for most neuropsychological symptoms, followed by language impediments (aphasia and/or dysarthria), calculation deficits, and unilateral neglect.

A few years ago they started a rehabilitation program for severely injured patients. Their rehabilitation program is not directed to overcoming specific deficits, such as ideomotor apraxia, but involves different types of stimuli and activities. The first step is to concentrate the subject's attention on one stimulus, and then they apply other stimuli so that the patient's attention to one or another requires swift and apposite choice of priorities. Video-games have proved ideal - stimulating, as they do, attention on different fronts simultaneously, without affecting the relationship between patient and therapist, but, rather, enlivening it with an atmosphere of competition.

These preliminary steps set the stage for what follows. They make the subject aware of his problems and the value of therapy, and thus a willing collaborator in the program. When the subject has learned to exploit his propensity for concentration, the focus of the re-education program becomes more specific, with exercises for individual neuropsychological deficits, such as deficits of reasoning or memory. Learning an episodic story (for memory impairment), word-acquisition exercises, exercises in word usage with tendency away from common contexts and mathematical or logic problems are all recommended.

At this stage the severity of the deficit and the educational and social background are the deciding factors for the level of difficulty of the exercises: a rehabilitation program can be based only on pre-illness knowledge and is not a scholastic course. At a later stage verbal logic problems can be employed along with motor–praxic and task-concentration exercises, so the patient must process information for the logic problem while simultaneously maintaining performance in the praxic task. Today only a few patients have been admitted to the rehabilitation program and it is thus impossible to say whether it is effective.

## SUMMARY

To sum up the information gathered, we conclude that aphasia, oral apraxia, and acalculia are the only neuropsychological deficits to be regularly treated. Rehabilitation of head-injury patients is new and enjoying a burst of interest. Rehabilitation of other neuropsychological impairments, such as unilateral neglect and ideomotor apraxia, is still wanting.

Notwithstanding this apparently distressing situation, the interest in rehabilitation problems is now lively in Italy, and we hope that the joint efforts of therapists, psychologists, neurologists and physiatrists will soon transform the current tentative and *ad casum* lines of approach into set programs for each specific categorized form of neuropsychological complaint, and thus make rehabilitation a formal and recognized discipline.

### REFERENCES

Basso A, Capitani E 1979 Un test standardizzato per la diagnosi di acalculia: descrizione e valori normativi. Rivista di Applicazioni psicologiche 1: 551–564

Hécaen H, Angelergues R, Houillier S 1961 Les variétés cliniques des acalculies au cours des lésions retrorolandiques: approche satistique du problème. Revue Neurologique 105: 85–103

Mazzucchi A et al 1984 I postumi neuropsicologici e comportamentali dei traumi cranici: osservazioni sulla classificazione, sulla diagnostica e sulle correlazioni con le variabili del trauma. Rivista di Neurologia 46: 1–51

# Neuropsychological rehabilitation of aphasia in Japan

## HISTORICAL BACKGROUND

Although neuropsychological research on aphasia in Japan dates from 1893, only in the past 20 years have studies incorporated the remedial aspect of aphasic impairment. The past decade has witnessed an increasing interest in the issue of the therapeutic applications of neuropsychologic knowledge in aphasia rehabilitation.

## CLINICAL PROCEDURES CURRENTLY IN USE

Clinical procedures for aphasia rehabilittion are generally conceived as consisting of a series of dynamically interacting steps:

1. gathering necessary information about language and communication disorders as well as the related problems by testing and observational methods;
2. framing hypotheses about the nature and cause of the problem based on the critical analysis of the data gathered in Step 1; and
3. testing these hypotheses through therapeutic intervention.
   Procedures in Step 1 and Step 2 amount to assessment or evaluational–diagnostic work-up, which is crucially important for the adequate programming and execution of remedial procedures in Step 3.

### Assessment

For an optimal description of language deficits, most clinics administer a comprehensive, sandardized language test. In some clinics the findings from this formal test are supplemented by the administration of a set of additional (often experimental) tests for the detailed assessment of specific areas of dysfunctions. Non-verbal tests for cognitive abilities, such as the Raven Progressive Matrices, Koh's Block Designs, the Visual Retention Test (Benton, 1974) and Three-Dimensional Block Construction (Benton et al, 1983), are also given to gain a more complete picture of the patients' mental status (Benton, 1982).

*Standardized language tests*

Two standardized language tests are currently in use in most clinics: Roken (a Japanese abbreviation for Tokyo Metropolitan Institute of Gerontology) Test of Differential Diagnosis of Aphasia (RTDDA) (Sasanuma, 1978) and the Standard Language Test of Aphasia (Hasegawa, 1975). Since the two tests are similar, only the former will be described.

The RTDDA is a comprehensive examination designed to sample a wide variety of language behavior at different levels of difficulty. It was standardized on a representative sample of 100 aphasic patients, and is used at the intake as well as at regular re-evaluations.

The goals of the RTDDA include:

1. arriving at a differential diagnosis of aphasia distinguishing it from nonaphasic language disturbances due to dementia (general intellectual impairment), memory loss, or confusional state;
2. identifying the type and severity of aphasia;
3. establishing a prognosis for recovery of language skills;
4. identifying realistic treatment goals and appropriate treatment tasks; and finally
5. evaluating recovery from aphasia following therapeutic intervention.

The current version of the RTDDA is the result of several systematic revisions of the original experimental version of 1965, incorporating the results of a series of factor analyses with data from a large number of aphasic patients (Sasanuma, 1972; Fukusako, 1974). The battery is composed of 48 subtests grouped into five broad areas: auditory comprehension, oral expression, reading, writing, and arithmetic functions. The nature and kind of subtests included are comparable to comprehensive tests currently in use in other parts of the world, except that a fair number of subtests for processing kana (phonetic symbols for syllables) and kanji (logographic symbols representing morphemes) are included in the battery. The reason is that the relative performance levels in kana and kanji processing provide important diagnostic implications. Responses are scored as either correct or incorrect for 46 subtests and on a rating scale for two subtests, which then are arranged as a z-score profile. The z-score conversions for the RTDDA subtests are based upon data obtained from a representative sample of 100 aphasic patients. These profiles are useful not only for classifying patients with respect to type and severity of aphasia, but also for charting recovery over time in individual patients. The time requirement for the RTDDA is 2–3 hours. Thus the test is administered in portions over several days.

In interpreting the test results, emphasis is placed on critical analyses of the obtained data in such a way that the neuropsychological mechanism(s) underlying the symptom complex, or the core deficit(s), can be identified as well as the five test objectives (specified above) attained.

*Experimental tests for specific functions*

To supplement the information gained by the standard test battery, a variety of tests aimed at probing into specific aspects of linguistic dysfunctions have been developed. The following are some examples.

*The Token Test:* The Japanese version of a short form (Spellacy & Spreen, 1969) is used to examine subtle auditory comprehension deficits.

*Syntax Test of Aphasia* (Fujita & Miyake, 1983): This test consists of a 44-item sentence comprehension subtest and a 17-item sentence production subtest. The sentences used represent a wide range of syntactic complexity carefully controlled in terms of variables: (1) word order, (2) reversibility of the semantic functions of the content words, (3) the case relation in the deep structure, and (4) the grammatical relation of the surface structure to the deep structure. In the comprehension section of the Syntax Test the patient's task is to listen to each sentence read by the examiner and point to an appropriate picture out of a display of four, while in the production part the patient is required to describe a series of pictures shown to him.

*Phonemic Segmentation Test* (Monoi & Sasanuma, 1975): This test is designed to identify candidates for the specific kana retraining program to be described in the following section. The test assesses the patient's ability to analyze speech into its component moras (or syllables) as well as singling out a given mora from its surrounding context. It consists of two parts. In part I, patients are given a spoken list of three-mora words and asked whether they hear the /ka/ mora in each word. In part II they are given a spoken list of words which contain a /ka/ mora either in the initial, the middle, or the final position of the words, and asked to identify the position of the /ka/ by pointing to one of the three circles shown.

*Kana/Kanji Reading Test* (Sasanuma, 1980b): This test was developed to examine the patient's reading comprehension, oral reading of kana and kanji, and related abilities. The stimulus words (n = 238) are controlled in terms of part of speech, frequency of usage, abstractness, word length, and configurational complexity (the number of strokes per character).

*Test for Functional Communication Abilities:* This test might be considered a Japanese version of Holland's (1980a) *Communicative Abilities in Daily Living*. The test consists of 22 items incorporating everyday communication activities and is presented in a natural style and sequence approximating normal communication. Responses are scored on a 5-point scoring system. Results yield information about the functional communication skills of individual patients.

## TREATMENT PROGRAMS

The two major methodologies which have been widely used are the 'stimulation approach' (Wepman, 1951; Schuell et al, 1964) and the 'programmed instruction approach' (Sarno et al, 1970; Holland, 1970). The 'stimulation approach' is characterized by an organized presentation of controlled, intensive and adequate stimuli to the patient for the purpose of eliciting target responses from him, which are selectively reinforced, so as to facilitate the reorganization of functions within the brain necessary for linguistic operations. The deblocking method described by Weigl (1968) is used quite often, too, as a variant of the stimulation approach. The 'programmed instruction approach,' on the other hand, rigorously applies operant conditioning principles drawn from learning theory and draws heavily on psycholinguistic data to guide the content and order of presentation of the linguistic materials presented to the patient. Between these two there is a wide spectrum of approaches which differ mainly in the relative amount of structure employed. Common to all these approaches, however, is the use of a stimulus–response situation in which the therapist's role is to manipulate stimulus conditions so as to elicit optimum responses from the patient and to determine contingencies of reinforcement.

The components or levels of language which can be selected for direct application of the specific methodologies include auditory discrimination, retention and comprehension of various units of speech; word retrieval or lexical processing; syntax (comprehension and production of various types of grammatical constructions); articulation and prosody; reading and writing; etc. In order to guarantee the specificity and effectiveness of the therapy programs used, it is imperative that the target areas be selected based on critical analyses of symptom patterns of individual patients, in such a way that an appropriate hypothesis about the underlying neuropsychological mechanisms can be formulated.

The candidates for these direct language therapy approaches are the majority of patients with moderately severe to mild aphasia. For severely impaired patients the major share of time is spent managing the communication environment of individual patients so as to optimize their communication potential (e.g., development of individualized non-verbal communication systems of various kinds). With patients whose aphasia is very mild or subtle, on the other hand, it is often necessary to devise a highly individualized high-level program focusing on specific problems, such as vocational problems, that might arise as a result of the communiction disorder. The compensatory communication strategies (Aten et al, 1982) are also useful in handling difficult communication tasks in these patients.

### *The effect of multi-modality treatment programs*

Standard procedures to document the effect of these multi-modality direct treatment programs consist of administering a comprehensive formal test pre- and post-treatment and comparing the two evaluations. In general, re-evaluation procedures using the comprehensive battery take place once every 3 months. Parallel with these procedures, somewhat less formal procedures monitoring progress are used in daily clinical sessions by maintaining careful records of the patient's responses to treatment tasks so as to identify subtle changes in performance.

It is difficult, however, to provide comprehensive, definitive data showing that a given treatment approach has brought about a significant change in the language behavior of the patient beyond what is expected to occur as a result of spontaneous recovery, chiefly because of the large number and complexity of the variables involved (e.g., etiologies, types, severities, and duration of aphasia; sites and extent of lesions; age, health, and background of patients; types, intensity, and duration of treatment programs, etc.). Nevertheless there has been an increasing number of studies in recent years which have succeeded in controlling some of the important variables, thus gaining more quantifiable information on the behavioral change obtained. Some of these are large group studies without control (non-treatment) groups (studies with control groups are yet to be done); others are so called single-subject-time-series (subject-as-his-own-control) studies. A few examples of these will be given.

### *Studies without control groups*

Takeuchi et al (1975) studied the effect of language therapy on 200 predominantly post-stroke aphasics examined between 1970 and 1974 at Nanasawa Hospital. The mean age of the patients was 51.6 years (26 years to 76 years) and the mean time elapsed since the onset of aphasia was 7.2 months (1 month to 19 months). All patients were right-handed and right hemiplegic (or hemiparetic), and received language therapy using the stimulation approach for at least 3 months (a mean of 4.2 sessions per week). The evaluation of language functions by means of a shortened version of a comprehensive aphasia examination was made pre- and post-treatment with a minimum time interval of 3 months. The difference in the scores between the two evaluations was then calculated. Fifty-two patients (26%) achieved excellent recovery (difference scores of 16 to 42, the total score being 80) and 94 patients (47%) moderate recovery (difference scores of 4 to 15), while 54 patients (27%) showed no recovery at all (difference scores of –11 to 3). Factors significantly related to improvement were:

1. the severity of aphasia (the mild and moderate aphasic patients showed better improvement);
2. the age of the patients at the onset of aphasia (the patients who showed excellent recovery were found more frequently in younger age groups, while those who showed no improvement were found more frequently in older age groups); and
3. the time elapsed since the onset of aphasia (only a few patients in the early training group – within the first 3 months – showed no recovery, indicating the effect of spontaneous recovery, but for the rest of the patients who began therapy later than 3 months post-onset there was no significant relation between the amount of recovery and the time elapsed).

Fukusako and Monoi (1983) investigated the recovery processes of 303 predominantly post-stroke aphasic patients examined and treated between 1972 and 1981 at the Tokyo Metropolitan Geriatric Hospital. The age of the patients ranged from 18 years to 87 years (a mean of 59.7 years), 53% of the patients being over 60 years old ('geriatric' aphasics) and 47% being under 59 years old ('adult' aphasics). The time elapsed since the onset of aphasia for the majority of the patients was from 1 to 18 months. In terms of types of aphasia exhibited by these patients there was a striking difference between the geriatric and the adult groups. In the geriatric group the incidence of global aphasia was significantly higher, while the incidence of Broca's aphasia was significantly lower as compared to the adult group. Wernicke's aphasia was extremely rare before age 39 but appeared at a moderate rate after age 40, while the peak for the incidence of amnestic aphasia was under age 39. All patients received language therapy, essentially of a stimulation approach type, two to six sessions per week, for at least 2 months. Improvement was defined in terms of the gain in the percentage of the total score of the RTDDA administered pre- and post-treatment. A patient was judged 'improved' if his gain after therapy was over 20% when his initial score was lower than 50% in the RTDDA. When his initial score was over 50%, 10% was the minimum gain judged 'improved.'

The results indicated that improvement was shown by 46% of the patients and was related to the following three variables.

1. The type and severity of aphasia: incidence of improvement was higher for conduction aphasia and mild Broca's aphasia (with minimal comprehension deficits), followed by amnestic aphasia, moderate to severe Broca's aphasia (with comprehension deficits,) Wernicke's aphasia and global aphasia.
2. The age of the patients: only 35% of the geriatric aphasics showed improvement as against 58% of the adult aphasics.
3. Time elapsed since onset: incidence of improvement was significantly higher for patients with early initiation of therapy (within 3 months post-onset) than patients with a later start, apparently indicating the effect of spontaneous recovery.

Three distinctive recovery patterns identified were: Pattern 1, shown by 80% of the patients, where a plateau of improvement was reached at about 12 months after the initiation of language therapy; Pattern 2, shown by 10% of the patients, where improvement continued well beyond the twelve month after the initiation of therapy; and Pattern 3, shown by the rest of the patients, where little or no improvement was observed. The final level of performance reached post-treatment was significantly lower in the geriatric aphasics than in the adult aphasics. Less than one-fourth of the geriatric patients reached the level of 80% or over in the RTDDA (which is considered to be the minimum level of functional language) against one half of the adult aphasics reaching that level.

### *Single-subject studies*

Watamori and Sasanuma (1978) investigated the recovery processes of two English–Japanese bilingual aphasics, one with Broca's aphasia and the other with Wernicke's aphasia, with special emphasis on the effect of language therapy. The degree of impairment initially manifested in English and Japanese was almost equivalent in each case, the pattern of impairment corresponding to the respective types of aphasia. In both cases therapy consisted of intensive multi-modality stimulation of the type described by Schuell and co-workers (1964). Parallel English and Japanese subtests from the RTDDA were administered at the initial evaluation (2 months post-onset for the patient with Broca's aphasia and 3 months post-onset for the patient with Wernicke's aphasia) as well as during and/or at termination of therapy (14, 26, and 49 months post-onset for the Broca's aphasic patient and 9 months post-onset for the Wernicke's aphasic patient).

Analyses of the recovery courses revealed that in both of the patients all the language modalities recovered, by and large, in the language under therapy. Improvement in the non-treated language, on the other hand, was confined to certain modalities predicted by the specific types of aphasia, and the amount of improvement even in these modalities tended to be less than that for the treated language. Auditory comprehension was the modality in which similar improvement was observed in the treated and the non-treated languages, regardless of type of aphasia. Writing ability, on the other hand, seemed to improve as a function of a language therapy in both languages. As for reading, the Broca's aphasic patient showed a similar recovery rate in both the treated and the non-treated languages, while the Wernicke's aphasic patient showed a selective recovery only in the treated language. In the oral production modality, differential recovery patterns were observed between the two types of aphasias: the Wernicke's aphasic patient showed improvement not only in the treated but in the non-treated language as well, though to a lesser degree; while the Broca's aphasic patient showed improvement only in the treated language until therapy in the other language was initiated.

On the basis of these findings the authors concluded that systematic, controlled language therapy is one decisive variable affecting the relative degree of recovery in a bilingual aphasic's two languages.

### *Treatment programs for specific functions*

As an adjunct to the multi-modality treatment approaches described above, a variety of programs aimed at working on specific functions, modalities, or components of language have been developed and their effects evaluated. These modality-specific treatment programs have some advantages over the more traditional multi-modality approaches in that they are amenable to more precise description of step-by-step retraining procedures and consequently to more rigorous evaluations of their effects. The following are only a few examples of these programs.

*Kana retraining program* (Monoi, 1976; Sasanuma, 1980a). The underlying hypothesis of the program is that the impairment of phonological processing (segmentation into phonological units of Japanese CV syllables or moras, in particular) constitutes the common core of disorders of kana processing and of articulation in some aphasic patients (Sasanuma & Fujimura, 1971), and thus, aimed at working directly upon the phonological processes (e.g., phonemic identification, segmentation, and synthesis) of the patient. The program consists of five steps of graded difficulty and is best suited for patients with moderate to severe Broca's aphasia exhibiting defective performance in the phonemic segmentation test described in the previous section.

In step 1 the patient is made thoroughly familiar with a small number of key words in kana, in order to recognize, repeat, read and write them freely and with ease. In step 2 the patient is trained to become aware of the fact that each word is made up of component moras, and to be able to analyze each word into these moras. For this purpose various activities that help the patient identify each mora in a word and single it out from its context (or sound sequence) are used, e.g., tapping the desk or placing a marble for each mora of the word spoken by the therapist. In step 3 the patient is introduced to the one-to-one correspondence that exists between a mora and a kana character. In order to help the patient grasp this mora–grapheme relationship and strengthen the association between the two, various activities, such as locating kana symbols spoken by the therapist in a word or in a non-word kana sequence, etc., are used again. Step 4 is devoted to synthesizing isolated moras into a meaningful sequence such as a word. The patient is asked to construct a word with a set of kana symbols presented randomly. Throughout these steps full use is made of the key words, starting with them at every step and then gradually expanding this core to incorporate other, more difficult, words. Step 5 is a graded application of these skills mastered in the previous steps to practical situations, such as reading and writing phrases, simple sentences, and paragraphs in a variety of real life situations.

This program has been widely in use in Japan because a relatively large proportion of aphasic patients exhibit kana processing impairments, and the program has proved effective with most of them. One such example is illustrated by a case study of a 37-year-old housewife whose aphasia was of vascular etiology (Monoi, 1976). On the linguistic evaluation made 3 months post-onset, she showed a profile typical of Broca's aphasia accompanied by severe impairment of kana processing, and at 6 months post-onset was assigned to the five-step kana therapy program on a 1-hour, three-session/week basis. Therapy continued for 22 months with a 2½-month period of temporary discontinuation starting at 8 months post-onset. The month-by-month improvements in her performance levels were charted on three tasks (repetition of syllables, reading individual kana characters aloud and writing individual kana characters to dictation), all of which involve some kind of phonological processing.

Analyses of the results showed that the performance levels of the patient on all three tasks improved parallel to each other throughout the training period. This is exactly what was predicted from the nature of the program; i.e., since the program is intended to work directly upon the phonological system, it should bring about an improvement not only in kana processing, but also in phoneme production/reception. Another finding of interest was that during the 2½-month discontinuation of the therapy the improvement came to a complete stop for all three tasks, while performance on other types of tasks such as 'naming' and 'describing pictures' continued to improve during the same period of non-training. This finding was interpreted to indicate not only the efficacy of the program but also that an intensive training program is indispensable in a certain critical period in the recovery to improve kana processing in severely impaired patients.

*Visual communication in use of kanji for severely impaired patients.* This program grew out of the empirical observation that a large proportion of patients with global aphasia can match a few high-frequency kanji (logographic symbols) with corresponding pictures or objects. Details of the program are still in the process of being developed at the present moment. The program is analogous to Visual Communication Therapy (VIC) (Gardner et al, 1976) in many respects. For instance both VIC and our program make use of an index card system of symbols, but the nature of the symbols used is partially different in the two programs: i.e., we use kanji for lexical items, and arbitrary symbols only for syntactic items. At the time of this writing, three patients with global aphasia are being treated under this program, but the final outcome of the efficacy of the program is yet to be determined.

*Retraining program for syntactic processing* (Fujita, 1979). This experimental program is based on data on the syntactic abilities of a large group of aphasic patients examined using the Syntax Test of Aphasia (Fujita & Miyake, 1983). The step-by-step procedures are arranged according to the hierarchy of difficulty (or syntactic complexity), and the patient is helped to progress through this hierarchy by means of appropriate strategies, i.e., from stage 1: the stage of processing irreversible simple sentences by means of decoding semantic features of the content words through Stage 5: the stage of processing relative clause constructions by decoding particles. Selected patients treated with this program have achieved significant progress in their syntactic abilities.

*Therapy program for lexical processing* (Fujita, 1978). This program has been developed in the course of a detailed analysis of some variables affecting word usage ability in an anomic patient. It focuses on the semantic relations of nouns to verbs (case relations), and consists of three-step procedures: step 1: using verbs and nouns to express a specific referent; step 2: comprehending the semantic relations of nouns to verbs and then using these verbs or nouns in a variety of structured tasks; step 3: using the verbs or nouns learned in steps 1 and 2 in daily-life situations. The program is still in the process of being modified and expanded, but it has proved to be effective in a limited number of patients with anomic aphasia.

## FUTURE DIRECTIONS

The population of the aged (65 years old and over) during the past two decades in Japan has increased to a degree that no other country has ever experienced. This increase will continue at an even greater pace for the next two decades. As a consequence of this trend Japan will face an increased incidence of age-related diseases involving higher brain functions, such as aphasia and dementia.

The need for the development of neuropsychological remedial strategies specifically tailored for the aged is obvious. However, in order to meet this need it is first essential to obtain a comprehensive knowledge of the impact of normal aging on higher cortical functions – knowledge which is surprisingly scarce at this moment. In view of this general lack of information, the Tokyo Metropolitan Institute of Gerontology recently initiated a longitudinal study for elucidating neuropsychological changes in old age. Thus far, a comprehensive test battery for both linguistic and cognitive functions has been constructed and is being administered to aged normal volunteers. It is expected that the findings gleaned from this study will form the database against which to evaluate pathological conditions such as aphasia and dementia. Furthermore, the findings will have crucial implications for issues of impending importance, such as the elucidation of characteristics of aphasia and dementia.

### Characteristics of aphasia in the aged

Data are accumulating indicating that aphasia in the aged is qualitatively different from that in younger age groups; patients with Wernicke's aphasia tend to be older than patients with Broca's aphasia (Obler et al, 1978; Harashymiw et al, 1981; Holland, 1980b; De Renzi et al, 1980; Kertesz & Sheppard, 1981; and Fukusako & Monoi, 1983); the incidence of global aphasic patients increases significantly in older age groups while the incidence of improvement decreases significantly with age (Fukusako & Monoi, 1983). Further evidence on the qualitative difference between older and younger aphasics comes from Watamori's report (1982). In a study investigating the effect of age at onset on the outome of linguistic and non-linguistic functions of aphasic patients, she compared the results of the comprehensive test in six adult aphasics (onset between 20 and 59) and geriatric aphasics (onset over 60). While no statistically significant differences were found between the two groups on linguistic tests, half of the geriatric patients showed defective scores on the two tests of visuoperceptual abilities, i.e., Facial Recognition (Japanese version) and Judgement of Line Orientation (Benton et al, 1983). Furthermore, while the adult aphasics demonstrated good correspondence between the type of aphasia and the lesion site as indicated by the CT scan, geriatric aphasics' symptom patterns did not always correspond to the lesion sites. Taken together these findings suggest the need for more systematic research on the nature of interactive variables operating in aphasia in old age. Comprehensive evaluation of linguistics, as well as non-linguistic cognitive performances (Benton, 1982), should be of crucial importance for such research in arriving at a deeper understanding of the functional status of the brain in the elderly aphasics, which in turn will lead us to the development of more appropriate and meaningful therapeutic procedures.

## Early detection and differential diagnosis of senile dementia

Closely related to aphasia in old age is the problem of senile dementia. Incidence of early signs of dementia accompanying aphasia clearly increases with age, posing a difficult question of differential diagnosis. The need for the development of a sensitive means for early detection of senile dementia is obvious.

Considerable evidence now suggests that behavioral decline in dementia is not a unitary or general process, but that differential patterns of deterioration in non-linguistic as well as linguistic functions tend to be identified. In the sphere of linguistic functions, selective vulnerability of semantic processing as compared to syntactic or phonological processing has been reported (Watamori et al, 1983). In the domain of non-linguistic cognitive functions, on the other hand, dissociations in performance between different visuoperceptual tasks have been reported for dementia patients in mild to moderate stages, e.g., between judgment of line orientation and facial discrimination (Eslinger & Benton, 1983) and between three-dimentional block construction and facial discrimination (Watamori & Etoh, 1983). It is yet to be determined, however, whether these specific patterns of dissociations differ from patient to patient according to different stages of behavioral deterioration and/or to different types of dementia. Comprehensive and longitudinal research is imperative to elucidate differential processes of decline in both the linguistic and non-linguistic functions with different subgroups of subjects (including the patients with borderline or very mild decline of functions, as well as the patients with different types of dementia with different etiologies). Such investigation will yield information that is crucial for the identification of early signs of dementing conditions and for the differential diagnosis thereof, which will eventually contribute to the development of a more appropriate means of treatment and management for the patient and his or her family.

REFERENCES

Aten J L, Caligiuri M P, Holland A 1982 The efficacy of functional communication therapy for chronic aphasic patients. Journal of Speech and Hearing Disorders 47: 93–96

Benton A L 1974 The Revised Visual Retention Test. University of Iowa Press, Iowa City (translated into Japanese by Takahashi)

Benton A L 1982 Significance of nonverbal cognitive abilities in aphasic patients. Japanese Journal of Stroke 4: 153–161

Benton A L, Hamsher K, Varney N R, Spreen O 1983 Contributions to neuropsychological assessment. A clinical manual. Oxford University Press, New York

De Renzi E, Faglioni P, Ferrari P 1980 Note: The influence of sex and age on the incidence and type of aphasia. Cortex 16: 627–630

Eslinger P J, Benton A L 1983 Visuoperceptual performances in aging and dementia: clinical and theoretical implications. Journal of Clinical Neuropsychology 5: 213–220
Fujita I 1978 The nature of lexical impairment in anomia: a therapeutic approach based on the semantic relations of nouns to verbs. Japan Journal of Logopedics and Phoniatrics 19: 274–284 (in Japanese)
Fujita I 1979 Reacquisition processes of syntax: a case study. Transcriptions of Committee on Speech Research, Acoustic Society of Japan, pp. 78–70: 523–531 (in Japanese)
Fujita I, Miyake T et al 1983 Syntax test of aphasia: experimental version I. Japanese Speech and Hearing Association Bulletin 25: 2–14 (in Japanese)
Fukusako Y 1974 A factorial study of aphasic symptoms. Japanese Journal of Otolaryngology 77: 31–47 (in Japanese)
Fukusako Y, Monoi H 1983 Recovery patterns and prognosis in aphasic patients. Japan Journal of Logopedics and Phoniatrics 24: 49 (in Japanese)
Gardner H, Zurif E, Berry T, Baker E 1976 Visual communication in aphasia. Neuropsychologia 14: 275–292
Harasymiw S, Halper A, Sutherland B 1981 Sex, age and aphasia type. Brain and Language 12: 190–198
Hasegawa T 1975 Manual for standard language test of aphasia. Homeido, Tokyo (in Japanese)
Holland A L 1970 Case studies in aphasia rehabilitation using programmed instruction. Journal of Speech and Hearing Research 35: 377–390
Holland A L 1980a Communicative abilities in daily living. University Park Press, Baltimore
Holland A L 1980b Working with the aging aphasic patient; Some clinical implications. In: Obler L K, Alber M L (eds) Language and communication in the elderly. Lexington Books, Lexington
Kertesz A, Sheppard A 1981 The epidemiology of aphasic and cognitive impairment in stroke; age, sex, aphasia type and laterality differences. Brain 104: 117–128
Monoi H 1976 A kana training program for a patient with Broca's aphasia: a case report. Communication Disorder Research 5: 105–117 (in Japanese)
Monoi H, Sasanuma S 1975 Phonemic segmentation and kana processing in aphasic patients. Japan Journal of Logopedics and Phoniatrics 16: 169–170 (in Japanese)
Obler L, Albert M, Goodglass H, Benson D F 1978 Aphasia type and aging. Brain and Language 6: 318–322
Sarno M T, Silverman M, Sands E 1970 Speech therapy and language recovery in severe aphasia. Journal of Speech and Hearing Research 13: 607–623
Sasanuma S 1972 A factorial study of language impairment of 269 poststroke aphasic patients: Part I: The factorial structure of aphasic impairment. Japanese Journal of Rehabilitation Medicine 9: 20–33 (in Japanese)
Sasanuma S 1978 Roken Test of Differential Diagnosis of Aphasia. Yaesu Rehabilitation Ltd Tokyo (in Japanese)
Sasanuma S 1980a A therapy program for impairment of the use of the kana-syllabary of Japanese aphasic patients. In: Sarno M T, Hook O (eds) Aphasia: assessment and treatment. Almqvist & Wiksell, Stockholm, pp. 170–180
Sasanuma S 1980b Acquired dyslexia in Japanese: clinical features and underlying mechanisms. In: Coltheart M, Patterson K, Marshall J C (eds) Deep dyslexia. Routledge & Kegan Paul, London, ch. 3, pp. 48–90
Sasanuma S, Fujimura O 1971 Selective impairment of phonetic and non-phonetic transcription of words in Japanese aphasic patients: kana vs. kanji in visual recognition and writing. Cortex 7: 1–18
Schuell A, Jenkins J J, Jimenez-Pabon 1964 Aphasia in adults: diagnosis, prognosis, and treatment. Harper & Row, New York
Spellacy F J, Spreen O 1969 A short form of the Token Test. Cortex 5: 390–397
Takeuchi A, Kawachi J, Ishii Y 1975 Language rehabilitation in aphasia: some factors related to the improvement of language functions. Kanagawa-ken General Rehabilitation Center Bulletin 2: 47–68 (in Japanese)
Watamori T S 1982 Prognosis for acquired aphasia and significance of age at onset: the long-term outcome of linguistic and nonlinguistic functions. Japan Journal of Logopedics and Phoniatrics 23: 227–243 (in Japanese)
Watamori T S, Etoh F 1983 A longitudinal study of linguistic and nonlinguistic functions in

a patient with Alzheimer's disease. Japanese Journal of Clinical Psychiatry 12: 1153–1168 (in Japanese)

Watamori T S, Murakami S, Itoh M, Sasanuma S (1983) Language disorders in senile dementia; a review of recent findings. Clinical Psychiatry 25: 914–922 (in Japanese)

Watamori T, Sasanuma S 1978 The recovery processes of two English-Japanese bilingual aphasics. Brain and Language 6: 127–140

Weigl E 1968 On the problem of cortical syndromes. In: Simmel M L (ed) The reach of mind. Springer, New York

Wepman J M 1951 Recovery from aphasia. Ronald, New York

*Ivar Reinvang*

# Neuropsychological rehabilitation in Norway and Sweden

The range and quality of neuropsychological rehabilitaion must be evaluated in relation to several background factors, the most important of which are the existence of academic or professional training programs in clinical neuropsychology and the resources allotted to rehabilitation in national health planning. By neuropsychological rehabilitation is meant programs focused on memory, communicative functions, attention, sensorimotor integration, visuospatial skills, and intellectual functions in individuals with acquired brain lesions. Disorders of emotional function are becoming candidates for inclusion on the list in light of research relating them to location of injury (for review see Finset & Robinson 1985). This review will focus on work with adults suffering from strokes or head injuries. School-age children are educated in schools of special education as soon as the need for acute medical treatment is satisfied, and are not included in this review.

## SWEDEN

An academic degree in psychology is offered at six universities. No training program in clinical neuropsychology is offered, either by the universities or by the national psychological association, which organizes postgraduate clinical training. The only course offered in clinical neuropsychology is at the University of Gothenburg.

The system of rehabilitation in Sweden is described by Høøk (1969). The country is divided into seven regions and one department of general rehabilitation planned for each region. This plan has not yet been fulfilled. In the most developed regions (Stockholm and Gothenburg) there are neurological rehabilitation clinics. These are for mixed neurological cases, and the specialization goes in the direction of paraplegia.

In listing the types of treatment offered at a rehabilitation clinic Høøk (1973) notes that the contribution of the psychologist comprises counselling and relaxation therapy. A separate item on the list is language therapy for aphasics. Both in Sweden and Norway speech therapists are responsible for this treatment.

### Neuropsychological treatment programs

A treatment package for neuropsychological functions, the Intellectual Function Training (IFT) has been developed by Søderback (1982), an occupational therapist affiliated to one of the larger Stockholm hospitals. The program consists of an assessment part and a training part, with materials gathered in a workbook. The tasks are mainly of the pencil-and-paper type, and the areas of function covered are visual perception, spatial analysis, language, calculation, memory, and logical reasoning. The program is intended for use conjointly with functional training in activities of daily living (ADL) and has been used with stroke patients. Recently, observation and training in the context of housework have been added to the program.

The neuropsychological basis of the program is said to be the theories of Luria, and the treatment strategy contains options for focusing on reorganization, reintegration or compensation of functions. In addition to neuropsychology, the treatment approach builds on pedagogical principles. Studies of training effects are based on group designs, and a first study reports positive effects of treatment in 13 brain injured subjects who were compared with 15 controls (Normell & Søderback, 1985; Søderback & Norwell, 1985). A larger scale investigation is in progress.

## NORWAY

Two universities have programs leading to an academic degree in psychology, which qualifies for certification as a psychologist. Postgraduate training leading to certification as a specialist is organized by the national psychological association.

The universities offer courses in neuropsychology, but no full training program. The possibility of a training program leading to a specialist certificate in clinical neuropsychology has been discussed by the psychological association, but the issue is unresolved.

Norway is divided into five regions for health planning. A government commissioned report recommends that each region should have one department of general rehabilitation. No national policy on rehabilitation has yet been adopted. There are three departments of rehabilitation with recognized specialty status. Sunnaas Hospital is the only department with patient beds (Kristiansen, 1979).

At present there are in all three positions for psychologists at these departments, all at Sunnaas Hospital. This does not give a complete picture since rehabilitative work is also done in other hospital departments and at vocational training institutes (Kristiansen, 1974). The general conclusion still must be that there is no national plan on organization of rehabilitation and that the resources are very limited.

## Neuropsychological treatment programs

For several years psychologists at the Institute of Clinical Neuropsychology, University of Bergen, have been working with children with developmental dysfunctions in which abnormalities of psychophysiological activation and arousal are central. As a parallel to this work Kløve (1982) has studied two patients with head injury and markedly reduced psychophysiological activation. Administration of Ritalin improved both activation and general behavior. The effect is stable over time and dependent on continuation of medication.

The group at Sunnaas Hospital has performed a series of studies on aphasics in order to establish assessment methods and prognostic criteria (Reinvang, 1985). As a preliminary to treatment the importance of test findings in relation to naturalistic functioning has been studied for communicative functions (Sundet & Reinvang 1982) and for self care skills (Bjørneby & Reinvang, 1985) (Sundet et al, 1985). The results confirm the close relationship between neuropsychological deficit and functional impairment. The severity of neuropsychological deficits as a whole seems more significant than deficits in limited functional areas.

Finset has studied depression in right hemisphere patients (Finset, 1982, 1983a, 1985; Finset & Robinson, 1985). He found that depression in left hemiplegics seems dependent on the intra-hemispheric location of the lesion, with a higher probability of depression when the lesion is mainly posterior, and effects cortical as well as subcortical structures.

Finset has suggested that a traditional psychotherapeutic approach may not be indicated in these patients. Rather, a reattribution approach should be applied, giving the patient a better understanding of depressive affect as an integrated part of the disease (Finset, 1984b). Antidepressive medication should also be considered. Finset, (1983c) reported a double-blind medication study, giving seven depressed left hemiplegics doxepin, and seven placebo. Patients receiving the active drug had significantly better relief of depression over a 6-week period than did placebo patients.

Finset et al have reported on out-patient treatment of two stroke patients (Finset, 1983b; Gundhus & Meier, 1984; Finset, 1984b). Although both patients were independent in primary ADL and had finished physical rehabilitation, they were both extremely passive and took little initiative in the family or community. Treatment included cognitive behavioral techniques, such as self-monitoring, self-instruction, self-reinforcement etc. over a 10-week treatment period. The behavior of the patients was recorded by their respective wives, based on an observation checklist specially designed for this study. One of the patients showed significant progress.

On the basis of the above mentioned psychometric studies and our experience with diverse treatment approaches, the development of a more comprehensive neuropsychological treatment program was started in 1983. This program has developed along two parallel, but interacting, lines. One is a broadly conceived treatment program for head injured patients; the other is a laboratory-based package of specific training programs for focal neuropsychological deficits.

The only unit for head-injury rehabilitation in Norway is at Sunnaas Rehabilitation Hospital, where head-injury patients have been trained since the early 1960s (Gjone et al, 1972). However, little systematic evaluation has been conducted.

Recently an interdisciplinary program for the moderately head-injured patient has been undertaken. The program is designed for five or six patients at a time, who stay as inpatients for a 6–8 week period. There is strong emphasis on group treatment, with daily group sessions including occupational therapy, physical therapy and group psychotherapy. Each patient is also given an individual psychological training program, specially designed on the basis of individual neuropsychological profiles. An individual training program, inspired by cognitive behavioral therapy strategies (Meichenbaum, 1974), is aimed at treating lack of initiative, inappropriate behavior, deficits in structuring daily activities, changes in emotional behavior etc. The approach has been described as cognitive–affective reintegration (Finset, 1984a,b).

Considerable emphasis in the program is given to the development of adequate assessment procedures. The behavioral deficits characteristic of these patients are often subtle and hard to measure by traditional neuropsychological tests. A description of the program and data on the first 15 patients is forthcoming (Finset & Landrø, 1985).

The laboratory-based program is called the Neurocognitive Training Module (NCTM) and is directed at specific cognitive deficits. The content areas and main types of method are summarized in Table 23.1. Tasks for training have partly been taken from other sources. The microcomputer tasks are mostly

**Table 23.1** Content of the neurocognitive training module (NCTM)

| Area | Criterion performance | Training tasks |
|---|---|---|
| Attention | Reading of two-column newspaper article | Tachistoscopic letter detection<br>Microcomputer tasks |
| Motor skills | Handwriting | Stylus maze tasks<br>Microcomputer tasks<br>Games of skill |
| Spatial orientation | Following a marked route in map of the psychology laboratory | Pencil and paper<br>Feedback box<br>Microcomputer tasks |
| Word memory | Shopping list recall | Word lists, word associations with instructions in mnemonics |
| Text memory | Story recall | Newspaper clippings with exercises in story analysis |

**Table 23.2** Multiple baseline single-case design for NCTM

| | Time(week) | | | | | |
|---|---|---|---|---|---|---|
| | 1 | 2 | 3 | 4 | 5 | 6 |
| Event | Neuropsychological test<br>Criterion test 1 | Criterion test 2<br>Treatment type 1 | Treatment type 1 | Criterion test 3<br>Treatment type 2 | Treatment type 2 | Criterion test 4<br>Neuropsychological test |
| Phase | Pre-treatment test<br>Baseline | Baseline | Treatment phase 1 | Evaluation | Treatment phase 2 | Evaluation<br>Post-treatment test |

American software from the laboratories of Gianutsos et al (1983) and Bracy (1985). We have also used standard neuropsychological laboratory equipment for presenting training tasks (The Halstead Category Test apparatus is called in this context the feedback box).

The concepts of criterion performances are special to this program, and it attempts to specify concrete goals that are meaningful for the patient as well as reasonably functionally specific.

The model for training is eclectic. It emphasizes two stages of acquisition: the strategy stage and the skill stage. The patient must have an adequate strategy for solving the task in hand, and the strategy must function with sufficient speed and accuracy. If the patient has no strategy the experimenter gives suggestions. Feedback is emphasized, both in terms of immediate responses and weekly summaries of performance. Finally, training in small groups is preferred when possible, in which the patient performs, observes, and interacts with another patient and the experimenter.

The overall design of the program is shown in Table 23.2. It is a single-case multiple-baseline design. Attempts to evaluate effects of treatment are based on statistical randomization models (Hart et al, 1984). About 10 patients have completed the program, but so far the results have not been evaluated.

## CONCLUSIONS

The situation both in terms of availability of adequately trained psychologists and of resources available for rehabilitation of neuropsychologically impaired individuals is not favourable in either Sweden or Norway. Still, development of clinical neuropsychological training programs is in progress, and attempts at clinical research are made. This work is expected to grow in the future. However, special rehabilitation clinics or programs for patients with acquired brain injury are not part of official health planning. Hence there is risk that any program developed will remain experimental.

## REFERENCES


Bjørneby E, Reinvang I 1985 Acquiring and maintaining self care skills after stroke. Scandinavian Journal of Rehabilitation Medicine 17: 75–80

Bracy O 1985 Programs for cognitive rehabilitation. Psychological Software Services, Indianapolis, Indiana

Finset A 1982 Depressive behavior, outbursts of crying, and emotional indifference in left hemiplegics. Paper presented at 2nd International Symposium on Models and Techniques of Cognitive Rehabilitation, Indianapolis, Indiana

Finset A 1983a Emotional dysfunction after brain damage: cerebral interaction effects and their implications for treatment strategy. Paper presented at 3rd International Symposium on Models and Techniques of Cognitive Rehabilitation, Indianapolis, Indiana

Finset A 1983b Single case studies in rehabilitation of stroke: an example. Paper presented at Norwegian Research Council meeting on Somatic Psychology, Ustaoset, Norway

Finset A 1983c Antidepressant drug therapy for stroke patients with left hemiplegia: results from a medication trial. Unpublished

Finset A 1984a Reintegrering av reguleringsfunksjoner som nevropsykologisk behandlingsstrategi (with summary in English). Journal of the Norwegian Psychological Association 21: 127–135

Finset A 1984b Cognitive-affective reintegration of function: an approach to the treatment of emotional disorders in the brain damaged. Paper presented at 4th International Symposium on Models and Techniques of Cognitive Rehabilitation, Indianapolis, Indiana

Finset A 1985 Depression in patients with right hemisphere CVA. Paper presented at 8th European Conference of the INS, Copenhagen

Finset A, Landrø N I 1985 Sørfløy prosjektet: et nevropsykologisk behandlingsprogram for pasienter med moderate hodeskader. Unpublished

Finset A, Robinson R G 1985 A diagonal pattern of emotional symptoms and pathological correlation after brain damage: an interaction theory approach. Submitted for publication

Gianutsos R, Vroman G, Matheson P 1983 Cognitive rehabilitation. Vol 2. Life Science Associates, New York

Gjone R. Kristiansen K, Sponheim N 1972 Rehabilitation in severe head injuries. Scandinavian Journal of Rehabilitation Medicine 4: 2–4

Gundhus T, Meier N 1984 Utvikling av psykologiske metoder for rehabilitering i hjemmesituasjonen av hjerneslagpasienter med svikt i reguleringsfunksjonene. Psychology Thesis, University of Oslo

Hart T. Carbonnari J P, Sheer D E 1984 A new single-case methodology for evaluation of cognitive remediation techniques. Paper presented at 12th Annual Meeting of the INS, Houston

Høøk O 1969 Comments on rehabilitation of the brain injured. In: Walker A E, Caveness W F, Critchley M (eds) Late effects of head injury. Charles C Thomas, Springfield, Illinois

Høøk O 1973 Panel discussion. In: Samordnad rehabilitering efter olycksfall. Skandia International Symposia, Stockholm, p. 40–44

Kløve H 1982 Central activating mechanisms: hyperactivity and traumatic brain injury. Paper presented to the 2nd International Symposium on Models and Techniques of Cognitive Rehabilitation, Indianapolis, Indiana

Kristiansen K 1974 Rehabilitation after central nervous trauma. Coordination efforts in Norway. In: Rehabilitation after central nervous trauma. Skandia International Symposia, Stockholm

Kristiansen K 1979 Sunnaas Hospital 25 years. The story of a rehabilitation centre. Journal of the Oslo City Hospitals 29: 24–34

Meichenbaum D 1974 Cognitive behavior modification. General Learning Press, Morristown, New Jersey

Normell L, Søderback I 1985 Intellectual function training in adults with acquired brain damage. I: An occupational therapy approach. Submitted for publication

Reinvang I 1985 Aphasia and brain organization. Plenum Publishing Corporation, New York

Søderback I 1982 Intellektuell funkstionstrening. Psykologførlaget, Stockholm

Søderback I, Normell L 1985 Intellectual function training in adults with acquired brain damage. II: Evaluation. Submitted for publication

Sundet K, Reinvang I 1982 Aphasia and communication. Paper presented at 5th European Meeting of the INS, Deauville

Sundet K, Finset A, Reinvang I 1985 Neuropsychological predictors in stroke rehabilitation. Submitted for publication

# 24

*Barbara Wilson*

# Neuropsychological rehabilitation in Britain

## INTRODUCTION

While it would be generally accepted that neuropsychologists in Britain, as elsewhere, have long been involved in the assessment and diagnosis of the neurologically impaired, it would also be true that most of them do not participate in the rehabilitative treatment of such patients. Clinical psychologists, on the other hand, are treatment oriented but frequently lack sufficient training in neuropsychology that would perhaps encourage greater participation in assessment and diagnosis. A group of clinical psychologists in Britain, however, are now specializing in the treatment of adults with neuropsychological deficits and work in all areas of assessment, diagnosis, and treatment. The programs offered by this group tend to share certain characteristics which will be described in this chapter, together with representative examples of treatment programs carried out at Rivermead, Oxford, a rehabilitation centre for adults with acquired, non-progressive brain damage.

## ASSESSMENT FOR TREATMENT

Before planning any treatment information from neuropsychological and behavioral assessments is usually considered necessary. A neuropsychological assessment can answer questions about a person's current intellectual functioning, probable pre-morbid level, areas of cognitive strengths and weaknesses, and possible localization of lesions. It does not, however, provide detailed information about the nature, frequency, or severity of problems faced by the neurologically impaired in their everyday lives. We do not know, for example, if there is a correlation between impaired performance on verbal fluency tests and impaired performance at work. One of the Rivermead patients, for example, with a very low verbal fluency test score, successfully completed a degree in chemistry at Oxford University.

Everyday problems can be assessed more directly by observation, rating scales, interviews or analog studies in which a situation similar to that encountered in real life is set up and the person's behavior assessed. The case of

Mr B (Wilson, 1982) provides an example of a program in which neuropsychological and behavioral assessments are combined. Mr B exhibited a classical amnesic syndrome. Formal neuropsychological assessment showed him to have an IQ in the very superior range of ability and normal or superior performance on all tests of language, perception, and reading provided he was not required to retain information for longer than 2 minutes. On tests of delayed memory he was severely impaired, although on the Wechsler memory scale his MQ was 92, i.e. in the average range. These results did not convey, however, the extent of Mr B's devastating handicap. He was totally unable to lead anything resembling a normal life despite his high intelligence. The behavioral assessment in this case consisted of asking him

1. about his daily timetable, e.g. 'Where do you go when you leave the ward in the morning?' and 'What time does your session end?'
2. the names of various people with whom he came into regular contact at the rehabilitation centre;
3. to remember a shopping list: and
4. to find his way from one part of the centre to another

Points were given for each correct response, baselines were taken, and a clearer picture emerged of the severity of his handicap. Treatment was planned on the basis of this behavioral assessment but his neurological status also influenced the strategies chosen.

## DESIGNING TREATMENT

Treatment techniques used in Britain are, broadly speaking, behavioral but with due recognition being given to limitations imposed by the neurological findings. Thus a person whose fear of walking stems from impaired depth perception would require a different treatment strategy from one whose fear stemmed from one bad fall several weeks previously. In keeping with the behavioral approach, programs are individually designed. The goals of treatment, as well as the particular techniques used, vary according to the needs of each patient. Even for cognitive deficits the steps followed in designing a behavior modification program are frequently found to be useful guidelines. The following example illustrates this approach, used with J.R., an 18-year old head-injured girl with agnosic alexia (Wilson & Baddeley, 1983).

### J.R.'s reading remediation program

| | |
|---|---|
| 1. Specify the problem | Inability to name letters of the alphabet |
| 2. State goals of treatment | Long term: to teach J.R. to read again.<br>First sub-goal: to teach J.R. to name all letters in both upper and lower case. |

| | |
|---|---|
| 3. Obtain baseline | All letters presented in four different sizes for both upper and lower case (208 letters in total). J.R. asked to name them. Letter effect and size effect noted |
| 4. Select appropriate strategy | Teaching techniques used were: (a) practice, (b) feedback, (c) visual and verbal associations, (d) rewards in the form of books about horses and visits to see horses. |
| 5. Plan treatment | (a) Ten most difficult letters selected<br>(b) One to be taught at a time<br>(c) Multiple baseline design used to evaluate the treatment<br>(d) J.R. seen three times a week for 15 minute reading sessions.[1] |
| 6. Begin treatment | Started program in July 1982 |
| 7. Monitor and evaluate progress | Ten letters learned by March 1983 |
| 8. Change procedure if necessary | Treatment extended to cover sound combinations, e.g. 'oa' and 'ur'. |

A more detailed description of the eight stages may be found in Wilson (1984). This structure can be adapted for a wide range of neurological deficits and has, for example, been successfully used in the treatment of memory, language, and concentration disorders.

## Amelioration of deficits or restoration of function?

In some cases, such as that described above, rehabilitation attempts to restore lost function. The aim with J.R. was to teach her to read again. Often, however, it is unrealistic to expect a full return of lost function so emphasis must then be placed on amelioration of deficits. This is the point of view put forward by Miller (1978) for the treatment of amnesia. There is, to date, no evidence that treatment can restore lost memory functioning in severely amnesic patients. For those with milder impairments, such as those following certain head injuries, the picture may be more promising. A recent study at Rivermead looked at improvement in memory functioning following group treatment. A crossover design was used in which some patients received 3 weeks of daily treatment in a memory group followed by 3 weeks in another group not concerned with memory skills. The remaining patients received training in the non-memory group first and then the memory group. Preliminary findings suggest that more people improved in general memory functioning following the memory group than following the non-memory group (Wilson, 1983). In the majority of cases, however, it would seem that better results can be achieved

[1]J.R. was also being treated for memory difficulties and visual object agnosia.

in the rehabilitation of memory-impaired people if alternative solutions are found which bypass the poor memory, and if attempts are made to reduce the problems caused by the memory deficit rather than attempting to improve memory *per se* (Wilson & Moffat, 1984a, 1984b).

Perceptual and language impairments may also require an ameliorative approach. For some globally aphasic patients, perhaps several years post-stroke, it may be possible to teach some simple alternative communication system. While such a system would not be anywhere near as efficient as speech it would nevertheless increase communication and thus reduce stress and frustration caused by an inability to communicate needs or understand other people. B.H. was one such person. Three years post-stroke he remained totally without speech and had severely impaired comprehension. He was seen twice a week and taught a visual symbol card system adapted from that described by Gardner et al (1976). Initially progress was slow but after 3 months it was possible to convey to him changes in his routine. After 9 months he began using his cards to express his own needs. However, even after 2 years he rarely used the cards as expressive communication unless prompted. Nevertheless, it should be noted that the cards proved to be a useful aid towards comprehension.

## USING STRATEGIES FROM OTHER FIELDS WITHIN PSYCHOLOGY

This is a common feature in neurological rehabilitation in Britain. Reality orientation therapy (Brook et al, 1975), originally designed for geriatric patients, is sometimes used for younger disorientated patients. Teaching techniques such as shaping, prompting, and modelling, frequently used with the mentally handicapped (Yule & Carr, 1980), can be employed with aphasic and amnesic people. Social skills training, normally associated with the treatment of psychiatric patients (Marzillier & Winter, 1978), has a place in the treatment of head-injured patients who talk too much or conversely become passive and withdrawn. One approach developed for pre-school mentally handicapped children and known as 'Portage' (Weber, 1975) has also proved useful. Named after the town of Portage in Wisconsin, USA, it is both an assessment and treatment technique. The assessment consists of five developmental checklists (language, self-help, motor, cognitive, and socialization skills) ranging from zero months to 6 years of age. The treatment consists of teaching those skills in which the child is deficient. Portage may be employed with some brain-damaged adults. I was once asked to assess a woman who had suffered an anesthetic accident which left her blind, dysphasic, and dyspraxic. The rehabilitation staff wanted to know her intelligence status. Although there are neuropsychological tests for people who cannot see, or who cannot talk, or who have motor problems, there are no tests, as far as I know, for people who can do none of these things. In this particular case developmental checklists or rating scales such as the Vineland Social Maturity Scale (Doll, 1965) are probably the most objective and reliable measures to be found. Both Portage and the Vineland were used with the woman and each scale showed her mental age to be below 2 years. The physiotherapists, occupational therapists, and nurses could therefore see where the gaps in her functioning lay, and were consequently able to plan appropriate treatment.

## REHABILITATION IS NOT RESTRICTED TO COGNITIVE DEFICITS

Besides treating cognitive deficits clinical psychologists working in neuropsychological rehabilitation are frequently called upon to deal with numerous other symptomatic problems which arise amongst patients. These include:

1. behavior problems such as frequent swearing or refusal to attend occupational therapy;
2. emotional problems such as depression or suicidal tendencies;
3. fears and anxieties, e.g. fear of walking unaided or fear of the hydrotherapy pool;
4. social skills problems like talking too much or too little;
5. self-control problems such as obesity or chain smoking; and
6. motor problems, e.g., limb apraxia or pressure sores resulting from a patient's refusal to lift his buttocks from the wheelchair.

An example of the last-mentioned problem can be found in Carr & Wilson (in press). A man with a spinal injury and mild head injury developed pressure sores because he would not push himself up from his wheelchair often enough. Nurses, physiotherapists, and doctors had explained the importance of this procedure, argued with the patient and cajoled him, but all to no avail. The psychologist then introduced a piece of equipment which was attached to the wheelchair and once in this position it recorded the number of lifts made. A lift was defined as the man's buttocks leaving the seat of the wheelchair for at least 4 seconds. Six lifts per hour was considered a desirable target figure. The equipment was designed to emit a loud noise if 10 minutes passed without a lift being made. This is similar to the device used by Malament et al (1975). A multiple baseline across settings (see Hersen & Barlow, 1976) was used, the equipment being first introduced during the man's daily woodwork session. Subsequently the equipment was introduced during lunch break, then tea break, and finally on the ward. The rate of lifting increased dramatically and his pressure sores healed. Interestingly, the loud noise (aversive stimulus) was never needed: feedback on the number of lifts recorded each session was sufficient inducement for lifting to occur.

## AN INTERDISCIPLINARY APPROACH IS CONSIDERED ESSENTIAL

In Britain today there is growing recognition among those concerned with rehabilitation that increased collaboration between the different therapy professions will achieve greater advances in our understanding of the broad range of problems faced by patients. Furthermore, such collaboration between physiotherapists and occupational therapists, nurses, clinical psychologists, and speech therapists will encourage the development of better treatment programs characterized by the width of their vision, the speed at which they can alter course, and their stronger appreciation of the individual patient's variety of difficulties set in the context of everyday living. Undoubtedly, the skills of the different disciplines can be usefully combined in order to rehabilitate the whole person. The role of the psychologist is crucial in the encouragement of more efficient ways of learning, through, for instance, such procedures as shaping and reinforcement. In addition, psychologists are skilled in specifying the nature and extent of a particular deficit, whether it be cognitive or otherwise.

## CONCLUSION

Not every psychologist involved in neuropsychological rehabilitation in Britain will agree with all of the points made in this section. Amongst those who do agree, some may be constrained by factors beyond their control to such an extent that they are unable to put their beliefs and theories into practice. Nevertheless, it is hoped that the general trends in the thinking of psychologists working in neuropsychological rehabilitation in Britain today are fairly represented in this chapter. Certainly the examples provided in support of the arguments are truly representative of the actual work that goes on in an establishment committed to collaborative teamwork.

### REFERENCES

Brook P, Degun G, Mather M 1975 Reality orientation, a therapy for psychogeriatric patients: a controlled study. British Journal of Psychiatry 127:42–45

Carr S, Wilson B (In press) promotion of pressure relief exercising in a spinal injury patient: a multiple baseline across settings design. Behavioural Psychotherapy

Doll E A 1965 Vineland social maturity scale: manual of directions, rev. edn. American Guidance Service, Minneapolis

Gardner H, Zurif E B, Berry T, Baker E 1976 Visual communication in aphasia. Neuropsychologia 14: 275–292

Hersen M, Barlow D H 1976 Single case experimental designs: strategies for studying behaviour change. Pergamon, New York

Malament I B, Dunn M E, Davis R 1975 Pressure sores: an operant conditioning approach to prevention. Archives of Physical and Medical Rehabilitation 56: 161–165

Marzillier J, Winter K 1978 Success and failure in social skills training: individual differences. Behaviour Research and Therapy 16: 67–84

Miller E 1978 Is amnesia remediable? In: Gruneberg MM, Morris P, Sykes R (eds) Practical aspect of memory. Academic Press, London

Weber S et al 1975 The Portage guide to home teaching. CESA, Portage, Wisconsin

Wilson B 1982 Success and failure in memory training following a cerebral vascular accident. Cortex 18: 581–594

Wilson B 1983 Memory rehabilitation: treatment for individuals and groups. Paper presented at the Sixth Annual European Conference of the International Neuropsychological Society. Lisbon, Portugal

Wilson B (1984) Memory therapy in practice. In: Wilson B, Moffat N (eds) The clinical management of memory problems. Croom Helm, London

Wilson B, Baddeley A D 1983 Single case methodology and the remediation of acquired dyslexia. Paper presented at the Second World Congress on Dyslexia. Halkidiki, Greece

Wilson B, Moffat N 1984a Rehabilitation of memory for everyday life. In: Harris J, Morris P (eds) Everyday memory: actions and absent mindedness. Academic Press, London

Wilson B, Moffat N (1984b) The clinical management of memory problems. Croom Helm, London

Yule W, Carr J (eds) 1980 Behaviour modification for the mentally handicapped. Croom Helm, London

Yule W, Hemsley D 1977 Single case methodology. In: Rachman S (ed) Contributions to medical psychology 1: 211–229. Pergamon, Oxford.

25 *Lance E. Trexler*

# Neuropsychological rehabilitation in the United States

## INTRODUCTION AND EVOLUTION

Over the past 10 years in the United States there has been a steadily increasing interest in the rehabilitation of patients with brain lesions. This development follows from a variety of interrelated factors, which include professional, social and programmatic developments. A brief review of these evolutionary factors will supply the background for a subsequent examination of evolving philosophies and a survey of the current status of American neuropsychological rehabilitation.

### Professional factors

The growing involvement of neuropsychologists in rehabilitation is, in part, representative of a more general trend; namely, that of increasing participation of psychologists and other behavioral scientists in health care. (McNamara, 1979, p.2). Part of the armamentarium psychologists brought to health care was clinical neuropsychology. Simultaneously, increases in the number of physicians in training in behavioral neurology and physiatry brought greater awareness of brain–behavior phenomena to medical practice. Presentations, meetings and publications in relevant journals have mirrored the swift growth in the number of neuropsychologists in health care settings and a shift in the focus of such presentations towards more applied topics. The emerging awareness of the role of behavioral and psychological factors in medical disorders has generated more attention to behavioral preventive measures with medical applications (e.g, smoking cessation, hypertension and weight control). Such interventions have simultaneously led to the development of more adequate clinical follow-up procedures. This trend is exemplified by one particular rehabilitation project, which illustrates the clinical need for follow-up after discharge. The 1982 report of the Santa Clara Valley Medical Center Head Injury Rehabilitation Project concluded that in the case of traumatic brain injury 'the psychological distress of patients and families is significantly more limiting than the physical ... ' following discharge from the hospital (Cope, 1982, p. 8). In addition, studies of this nature have shown that recovery from brain injury may not be as time-limited as previously thought.

One salient reason why neuropsychologists are becoming more involved in rehabilitation is the shift in the clinical utilization of neuropsychological evaluation. The great bulk of research in clinical neuropsychology in the United States has historically been concerned with the diagnostic validity and reliability of defined test batteries (e.g., Reitan, 1974; Golden, 1981; Lezak, 1983). However, advances in neurodiagnostic techniques, such as computerized tomography, often eliminate the need for the neuropsychological examination as an aid to neurologic diagnosis (Caplan, 1982). Neuropsychological examination has begun to focus more on a quantification and qualification of brain *function*, as opposed to *structure*. The principal application of neuropsychological testing in rehabilitation today may be considered to

1. establish the existence of any cognitive deficits related to the insult.
2. establish the relative magnitude of the insult
3. estimate the patient's ability to return to his previous life-style, and
4. suggest remediation programs (Crockett et al, 1981, p. 2).

In other words, clinical neuropsychological investigation is now required to say more about brain-based psychological *functions* and how these functions relate to behavioral adaptation than previously required. Heaton and Pendleton (1981) examined the relationship between neuropsychological test performance and everyday functioning. They found that certain composite scores, derived from various measures of global neuropsychological test performance, are significantly predictive of success in daily functional adaptation, when considered in a statistical, actuarial manner. These latter investigators point out that, when making case-by-case recommendations, a variety of individual factors must be considered and each patient's unique clinical picture must be examined. Neuropsychological examination in some rehabilitation settings, which is concerned with the quantification and qualification of function, has moved beyond conventional neuropsychological approaches to be more sensitive to rehabilitation questions. This broader functionally-oriented model of the neuropsychological examination represents a significant trend in American clinical neuropsychology.

Thus, clinical neuropsychologists involved in rehabilitation must be concerned with a broader and more functional set of variables then required for diagnostic actuarial clinical neuropsychology. Gross (1982) has suggested that neuropsychologists should 'intervene ... and produce abilities and behavioral repertoire not predictable on the basis of diagnosis along (p. 100). He points out that 'interventive cognitive neuropsychology' requires the inclusion of environmental treatment variables into predictive statements about the patient's potential re-adaptation. Further, while treatment approaches derived from behavior therapy, psychotherapy, occupational therapy, and speech therapy can be integrated into the repertoire of the clinical neuropsychologist, the existing correspondence between these domains of knowledge is minimal. More specifically, the kinds of analysis performed by neuropsychologists, clinical psychologists, and rehabilitation therapists suffer limitations: clinical neuropsychologists have sometimes been unable to provide meaningful, practical translations of voluminous data, clinical psychologists frequently view brain functions on a unitary dimension (i.e. 'damaged' or 'not damaged'), and rehabilitation therapists often proceed with treatment without an understanding of the correspondence between behavioral and brain function. Diller (1984) has pointed out that there are significant language differences between neuropsychologists and rehabilitation professionals, which have evolved from diverging traditions, and impact on not only methods but goals in rehabilitation. The intent of neuropsychology has historically been to determine brain–behavior diagnoses where, in contrast, rehabilitation professionals intend to facilitate adaptation by the way of overcoming specific deficits. Neuropsychologists typically speak of deficits whereas rehabilitation professionals emphasize functional skills. Finally, the neuropsychologist's traditional environment is the laboratory, but for the rehabilitation staff it is the patient's natural environment. Systematic interventive collaboration between disciplines has been rare, but recent attempts at such are very promising (cf. Stanton et al, 1983). The historical lack of common perspective has made obvious the need to derive a new paradigm for intervention, often referred to as cognitive or neuropsychological rehabilitation, or cognitive remediation.

## Social factors

Professional evolution is inexorably related to social phenomena. Probably the most significant social factor fostering neuropsychological input into the rehabilitation process is the steady increase in the number of traumatic brain injuries in the United States. While neuropsychological rehabilitation is certainly not restricted to traumatic brain injury patients, the alarming increase in incidence has brought about a certain clinical need. Anderson and McLaurin (1980) reported approximately 422 000 cases of head injury in 1974 in the United States. Further, Jennett and Teasdale (1981) have suggested that there is an increase in survival rates which is attributable to improvements in emergency medical care. Further, the traumatic brain injury patient and the family require long-term psychological management and treatment following medical stabilization. These factors, when solely considering traumatic brain injury, necessitate neuropsychological intervention in rehabilitation.

The remarkable increase in incidence of traumatic brain injury has brought about a need for advocacy on behalf of patients and their families. The National Head Injury Foundation (NHIF) has taken on such a role. Established in 1980, NHIF has grown quickly in terms of membership and has worked to promote refinement in neuropsychological examination and rehabilitation of patients with traumatic brain injury. This influence has been expressed through advocacy for research priorities with the National Institute of Handicapped Research and with the National Institute of Neurologic and Communicative Disorders and Stroke of the US Public Health Service. Furthermore, NHIF has worked to promote standards of rehabilitation care through the professional members of NHIF. It is clear that the profession of neuropsychology is being influenced by these social and epidemiological forces to develop new required paradigms.

One certain danger that follows from any social trend which has the momentum characteristic of neuropsychological or cognitive rehabilitation is the 'bandwagon' effect. Thomas and Trexler (1982) observed that one 'impediment to the coherent development of effective treatment strategies lies in the lack of a comprehensive theoretical base concerning the nature of cognitive dysfunction associated with brain injury'. In the absence of any substantive brain-based, empirically derived theory of cognitive function and cognitive dysfunction, two potentially serious errors are possible. The first is a propensity to utilize certain psychological tests to define cognitive functions, rather than as a means to sample certain aspects of behavior which depend upon cognition. The absence of a predictive theory of cognitive dysfunction following brain injury makes test-based definitions tantalizing, albeit atheoretical. Similarly, over-utilization of technology, particularly micro-computers, for cognitive rehabilitation promotes a technology-based definition of intervention. While technology can serve as a tool to the neuropsychologist, it seems that what micro-computers offer in terms of training is no more than a test offers when sampling behavior; a specific case of a very multi-dimensional function. Stated simply, neuropsychological tests and *in vitro* rehabilitation techniques do not deal directly with *in vivo* human performance, which is the goal of rehabilitation. The mere acquisition of test protocols or computer programs does not constitute a program of neuropsychological rehabilitation, although the social and the professional forces in the United States have in some cases fostered this behavior. Neuropsychological rehabilitation is still too new a paradigm for such an atheoretical approach. Doing so seems analogous to conducting an experiment, with a methodology and dependent measures (tests), but without hypotheses.

## Programs in neuropsychological rehabilitation

Several pioneering programs have greatly influenced the emerging paradigm of neuropsychological rehabilitation. The brief description of these programs is not commensurate with the size of the contribution each of them have made to the current state of knowledge about neuropsychological rehabilitation. It is nonetheless important that a basic description of these programs be included, as well as some indication of their unique contributions.

The Brain Injury Rehabilitation Unit (BIRU) of the Palo Alto Veteran's Administration Medical Center was established in 1970. Originally, the service was primarily diagnostically oriented, but the evolution of BIRU has led to a decided treatment focus. The BIRU has three phases of treatment: basic, advanced, and transitional. Cognitive abilities and functional adaptive skills are the focus of rehabilitation throughout all three phases. The average length of stay for patients is 10–12 months. One of the most significant contributions of the BIRU program has been the explicit incorporation of a focus on practical activities of daily living in both assessment and treatment. The use of practical problem lists and goal attainment scaling serves these purposes. Further, the BIRU pioneered the use of video-games and microcomputers for the restoration of neuropsychological function.

The Neuropsychological Rehabilitation Program (NRP) at Presbyterian Hospital of Oklahoma City, which began admitting patients early in 1980, focuses on both the cognitive and personality disturbanes which follow brain injury. NRP is particularly known for its emphasis on psychotherapeutic intervention with the emotional sequalae and psychosocial adjustment following brain injury (see Chapter 17 of the present volume). Prigatano and his colleagues have also recently completed an outcome study which includes an untreated group of matched neurologic patients (Prigatano et al, 1984), which is an important advance for neuropsychological rehabilitation.

The Cognitive Rehabilitation Program (CRP) at the Robert Wood Johnson, Jr, Lifestyle Institute, developed by Dr Yigal Gross, began in March 1981. Dr Gross and his staff are best known for their efforts in the derivation of a theoretical framework for cognitive and emotional processes (Gross, 1982) and the translation of this framework into integrated and converging cognitive rehabilitation techniques (Gross et al, 1982). These efforts are important to the field, given, as mentioned earlier, the relative paucity of such theory and knowledge base for 'interventive cognitive neuropsychology'. Organizationally, the program is an affiliate of the John F Kennedy Medical Center, Edison, New Jersey. Staff of the CRP includes one part-time and five full-time neuropsychologists, three occupational therapists, three therapeutic recreation counselors, two speech pathologists, two physical therapists, three vocational counselors, two social workers, and one counselor. The staff is organized into teams (headed by neuropsychologists) with a designated case load of 12 outpatients. Patients attend CRP 5 hours a day, although when clinically indicated patients attend on a part-time basis, and receive a variety of group and individual therapies.

## PHILOSOPHY OF NEUROPSYCHOLOGICAL SCIENCES AS APPLICABLE TO REHABILITATION

This section examines the philosophical assumptions which appear to be framing an emerging neuropsychological rehabilitation paradigm in the United States. Following a review of diverging approaches to defining neuropsychological defects, corresponding perspectives on neuropsychological rehabilitation in the United States will be presented.

### Defining neuropsychological defects: what are we rehabilitating?

The historical emphasis on actuarial clinical neuropsychology in the United States has not laid a fully adequate foundation for rehabilitation efforts. As has been previously mentioned, the focus of research in American clinical neuropsychology has been the diagnostic validity and reliability of specific tests and test batteries. Reitan (1974a) stated that 'the validity of neuropsychological assessment ... depends upon the validity with which inferences can be made regarding the brain'. The development of this approach to neuropsychological examination was decidedly inherited from American psychometric theory with a focus on predictions about the presence of a brain lesion, its nature and site in the brain (Wheeler and Reitan, 1963). Given that accuracy and prediction was the hallmark of neuropsychological examination, interpretation of clinical data was highly dependent upon comparison to normative data, matched on potentially influential variables such as demographic characteristics, handedness, etc., relative to the individual patient in question. Such statistical comparisons therefore mandated highly standardized approaches in the administration of test protocols to all individuals. Further, such comparisons required the delineation of cut-off scores of criteria which were indicative of pathology. One prominent school of neuropsychology further argued that data gleaned from standardized administration of test protocols had to be interpreted 'blind', without knowledge of the individual's history, presenting medical complaints and other individual variables. Neuropsychological data were then interpreted by way of four methods of inference, which included level of performance, specific deficits of pathognomonic significance, differential scores, and comparisons of the efficiency of the two sides of the body (Reitan, 1974b).

This approach to neuropsychological assessment was developed for the purpose of making predictions about the structure of the central nervous system. As pointed out earlier, however, rehabilitation necessitates a psychological description of brain-based functions; the structural status of the brain is typically sufficiently known. Traditional American neuropsychological techniques were not derived to describe cerebral functions, or *how* specific brain functions were disturbed, or the way in which these disruptions affect other psychological processes dependent upon the impaired functions (Luria & Majovski, 1977). This approach to neuropsychological examination leads to what can be referred to as a psychometric or statistical definition of neuropsychological function.

The process of determining 'what are we rehabilitating?' depends in part upon the neuropsychologist's philosophical assumptions about the nature and definition of neuropsychological defects, and how these neuropathologically induced defects affect a given person. At a neuropsychological level of analysis an over-simplified example would be the case of a lowered score on the Block Design subtest of the Wechsler Adult Intelligence Scale (Wechsler, 1955). One rehabilitation recommendation might be that the patient is offered some type of visuospatial training. Considerable research would support the assumption that the Block Design is a good measure of visuospatial functions (Lezak, 1983). Consequently, a test (e.g. Block Design) could be used to *define* the status of a given brain-based function (visuospatial functions). Further, given this definition, a rehabilitation program could be designed to theoretically improve this function. This strategy assumes a test-based definition of brain function philosophy. However, Lezak (1983) describes how a variety of impaired brain functions may be manifested behaviorally as impaired on Block Design. This point serves to underscore the view of neuropsychological function as multi-dimensional phenomena requiring multi-dimensional neuropsychological examination procedures (Goodglass & Kaplan, 1979), and hence multi-dimensional rehabilitation techniques. Neuropsychological test performances cannot necessarily be viewed as having a one-to-one correspondence with brain functions, and psychological test(s) cannot be 'based on a preconceived classification of "function" (Luria, 1966). This concept suggests that a single or perhaps multiple tests cannot define a neuropsychological function any more than a single test can define 'organicity'. This would appear to contraindicate the mere tabulation of unidimensional test deficits, based on psychometric theory, to define a patient's neuropsychological status. Improving upon test-based definitions of neuropsychological functions necessitates a more thorough understanding of cerebral mechanisms and a more observant, non-actuarial approach to examination. However, it should be noted that these include examiner as well as test variables.

The methodology utilized in making observations on human behavior, and the philosophical assumptions inherent in a given methodology, clearly influence the resulting view of the phenomena. The methods used in the fields of cognitive psychology, experimental neurophysiology, and neuropsychology are potentially helpful in answering our question: what are we treating? The problem with these potentially converging lines of investigation has historically been diverging terminology, but more importantly, diverging measurement techniques: reaction times, evoked potential latency, psychometric test results, etc. Experimental and clinical methodologies are obviously used for different reasons. With regard to a statistical and psychometric approach in neuropsychological examination, the cautions of Eysenck (1967), with regard to intelligence testing, that 'the psychometric approach has become almost completely divorced from both psychological theory and experiment' are cogent.

Filskov and Goldstein (1974) have suggested that 'accuracy and prediction' were the most important criteria of what constitutes a good test. The danger inherent in this philosophy is that statistically defined approaches result in atheoretical views of brain–behavior relationships. Neuropsychological tests designed, constructed, and validated for purposes of prediction may provide only a very limited and contextually bound view of human neuropsychological function. Since the task of neuropsychological examination in a rehabilitation setting is to *describe* accurately the functional neuropsychological status of the patient in the context of a theory which will permit the generation of rehabilitation strategies, one might not want to limit oneself to tests which were designed solely for the purpose of 'accuracy and predicition'. An alternative would be to rely on experimental approaches to the definition of neuropsychological function. This would at least provide theoretical referents from which to view the results. Moscovitch (1979), on the other hand, points out that, while 'artificial experimental procedures ... do indeed help isolate components' of human neuropsychological function, everyday functional behavior involves more continuous and dynamic processes. Answering 'what are we treating?' depends on both how we conceptualize neuropsychological function and how we evaluate it.

Views derived from experience in rehabilitation settings have resulted in an enlargement in perspectives from which neuropsychological examination must be conducted. Ben-Yishay and Diller (1983a) have suggested that assessment be performed from psychometric, neurological, remedial and functional perspectives. These authors' view of psychometric assessment of the patient is broader than just a statistical, normative comparison, but also includes comparison of the patient's performance with what could be theoretically assumed, given neurological and 'interventive' variables. The neurologic aspects of assessment refer to a neurobehavioral analysis of cerebral mechanisms mediating psychological processes. These authors' view of remedial assessment refers to observing patients' responses to intervention, which generally refers to their ability to learn and modify their behavior as a function of their rehabilitation experiences. Functional assessment includes the *in vivo* assessment of daily functional competencies.

It is obvious that broader models of neuropsychological assessment can be developed because more observations are possible in the rehabilitation setting. Rather than having the patient in the laboratory for a circumscribed period of time, the neuropsychologist in the rehabilitation setting can make multiple observations of the patient in different settings. Such 'methodologies' are likely to provide better information about the correspondence between neurogical levels of performance to functional and naturalistic aspects of the patient's behavior. Furthermore, incorporation of a variety of methodologies into neuropsychological assessment provides information about the importance, or lack thereof, of a given neuropsychological defect, the extent to which this defect functionally impairs the patient, and many ideas about the possibilities for rehabilitation.

The way in which one proceeds with approaches to neuropsychological rehabilitation is then dependent upon assumptions about the nature of the neuropsychological defect, which is a theoretical issue, and the way in which one goes about defining this defect. There appear to be two traditions for this definitional process: a psychometric–statistical and a theoretical–clinical definitional process. The former is decidely American in origin and, as has been discussed, based on metric and actuarial methodologies with the goal of defining the structure of the central nervous system. The latter is focused on qualitatively describing function dependent upon cerebral processes and originates from Soviet psychology (Luria, 1966). The theoretical–clinical definitional process suggests that 'each patient analysis is a theoretically based dynamic experiment on the behavioral effects accrued from a disturbance in the brain' (Luria & Majoviski, 1977). Both, as well as combined, approaches can be found among neuropsychologists in the United States.

A general model for assessment in neuropsychological rehabilitation, developed by Trexler and Zappala (1985), bears some similarities to that advanced by Ben-Yishay and Diller (1983), but is somewhat more global. This model is schematically presented in Figure 25.1. It was derived from experience in the rehabilitation setting with differing levels of human functioning that all influence the patient's neuropsychological course of recovery and outcome. A description of the patient, along these lines, before and after neurologic disease, makes possible a comparison of the major ways in which his or her life has changed. It is assumed that the results of careful neuroradiological examination are an integral component of the patient's total evaluation. Specific aspects of each consideration can be found in Table 25.1.

These levels of functioning are not viewed as static human states, but rather as changing and interacting within and between levels. Consequently, the assessment of the patient's memory functioning, for example, may include an analysis of what the patient believed was important to remember, as determined by or influenced by personal characteristics, how anxiety resultant from conflict in a significant interpersonal relationship affected memory functions, as well as how the patient's language difficulties interacted with memory functions, depending upon the clinical situation. The relevance of this hypothetical memory disorder to the patient's total life can be made explicit using this approach to assessment. The relevance and meaningfulness together represent a crucial factor in determining not only the significance of rehabilitation to the patient and his or her motivation, but also the extent to which gains obtained from rehabilitation efforts can be functionally expressed

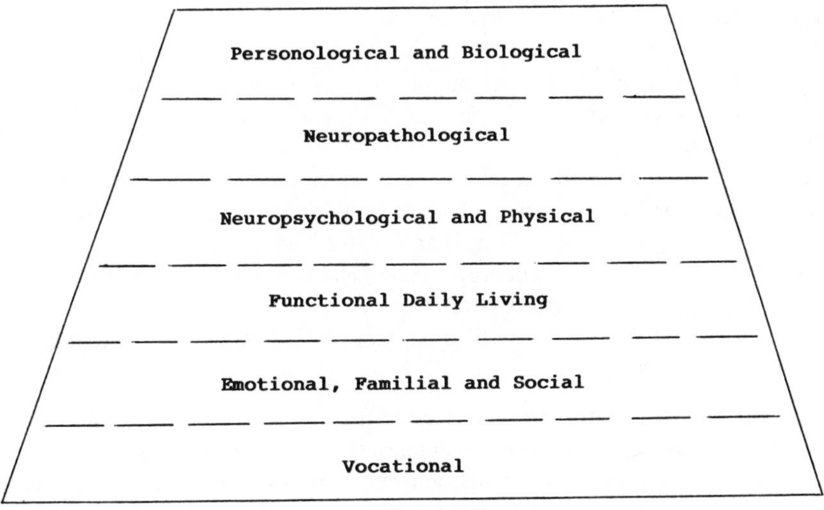


**Fig. 25.1** Considerations affecting outcome following brain injury.

**Table 25.1** Description of considerations affecting outcome following brain injury

| | |
|---|---|
| Personological and Biological | |
| — | Education, age and cerebral dominance |
| — | Emotional, family and vocational stability |
| — | Alcohol and drug usage |
| — | Personality |
| Neuropathological | |
| — | Severity: length of coma, post-traumatic amnesia and degree of motor residuals |
| — | Presence or absence of skull fracture and extent of diffuse-local injury |
| — | Presence or absence of normotensive hydrocephalus |
| Neuropsychological and Physical | |
| — | Type and severity of general functions, e.g. memory and attention processes and behavioral disturbance |
| — | Type and severity of specific functions, e.g. spatial or linguistic abilities |
| — | Type and severity of motor and sensory sequalae |
| Functional Daily Living | |
| — | Degree of independence in and initiation of daily living activities, including self-care, management of finances and transportation |
| Emotional, Familial and Social | |
| — | Emotional reactive response to situation |
| — | Strength and maintenance of interpersonal relationships |
| — | Cohesion and awareness of family |
| — | Degree of social isolation of interaction |
| Vocational | |
| — | Interest and motivation to return to work or the presence of disincentives |
| — | Interest and commitment of employer |

and generalized. In this example, the memory disorder may be quantified metrically, but is interpreted in the context of the presented schema. Rehabilitation efforts may at times modify or alter the interaction between these levels, as much as they lessen the difficulties characteristic of one particular level.

In summary, it has been proposed that there is a psychometric–statistical and a theoretical–clinical definitional approach to neuropsychological functions. It has also been suggested that the application of neuropsychology to rehabilitation requires analysis of *function*, as opposed to structure, of the central nervous system. A relevant question, aptly stated by Caplan (1982), is 'Does "function" equal the processor or its consummation?' If neuropsychological sciences in the rehabilitation setting must describe function, the neuropsychological definition of function must include not only what neuropsychological functions appear involved as a consequence of neuropathology, but also *how* a neuropsychological function has been affected by neuropathology. Defining the latter requires *in vivo* as well as *in vitro* methods of observation as well as careful qualification. It has been the intent of this section to suggest:

1. that methods of observations derived for purposes of statistical prediction are generally not adequate vehicles through which to define relevant neuropsychological functions, and are certainly not adequate for determining the relevance of the given neuropsychological defect to the person's life;

2. that neuropsychological assessment should not be a mere tabulation of test defined deficits, used in a more or less additive way to describe a patient's neuropsychological functioning;
3. that the fields of cognitive psychology, experimental neurophysiology and experimental neuropsychology can augment, in terms of methodology, the clinical armamentarium from which to evaluate patients in context of a theoretical framework;
4. that neuropsychological investigation in the rehabilitation setting requires a theoretical framework from which to evaluate patients by way of diverging methodological approaches so as to generate treatment strategies;
5. that neuropsychological functions are multi-dimensional, changing, and interactive, determined by dynamic forces within and external to the individual.

Neither the psychometric–statistical or the theoretical–clinical definitional processes need be exclusive. To determine the amount and pathway of the recovery of function, it is important to have some quantification beyond subjective impression, but quantification of relevant qualitative aspects of neuropsychological function. Nonetheless, these numerical values cannot be confused with outcome in rehabilitation. Metric changes in neuropsychological functioning are not in themselves of relevance to the patient who wishes functionally to re-adapt better. The extent to which metric values reflect the conditions and processes which enable the patient functionally to re-adapt or compensate, the more useful that particular neuropsychological measurement technique is for the rehabilitation setting. Finally, the rehabilitation neuropsychologist should not presume that the direction of rehabilitation will be solely determined by the results of his or her evaluation. Patients themselves should and can play some part in determining *what* should be rehabilitated.

## Diverging philosophies on neuropsychological rehabilitation: how are we rehabilitating?

As could be predicted, the way in which we go about rehabilitating neuropsychological difficulties follows from the way in which we define them. Neuropsychological rehabilitation in the United States appears to have two schools of thought, which can be described as reductionistic and dynamic, and which correspond respectively to psychometric–statistical definitions and theoretical–clinical definitions of neuropsychological function. In the abstract, these represent polarities on a continuum but in practice most rehabilitation techniques, or programs, have elements of both. The dichotomy is useful, however, for contrasting the diverging assumptions and intentions behind the two rehabilitative strategies.

Characteristics of the reductionistic approach to neuropsychological rehabilitation include a focus on the components of the neuropsychological defect in question. Typically these are derived from an analysis of test or material characteristics. Furthermore, it is typically assumed that restoration of function of a given component will add to the overall system(s) to which this component contributes. The componential additivity of these neuropsychological functions sometimes assumes a developmental sequence, a divisibility of cerebral mechanisms, or what is assumed to be a hierarchy of function. Typically, reductionistic approaches are concerned with specific neuropsychological functions such as perceptual organization. However, Craine and Gudeman (1982) have detailed a highly reductionistic approach to the restoration of 'frontal lobe' functions, which traditionally have not been regarded as particularly specific or divisible.

As derived from psychometric and statistical thinking, reductionistic rehabilitation typically involves considerable practice to some normative criteria. Consequently, the rehabilitation goal inherent in reductionistic approaches to neuropsychological rehabilitation is, by way of practice to restore 'deficits' to some specific predetermined criteria. Finally, in reductionistic approaches to neuropsychological rehabilitation, the parameters and methods of training are typically clearly related to the characteristics of the materials or stimuli used to evaluate the patient. Diller and Gordon (1981) have referred to this approach as remediation, in contrast to rehabilitation which goes beyond the treatment of specific deficits and involves intervention methodologies derived from many other rehabilitation disciplines. This would suggest that for the remediation effects to have an impact on the patient's general functioning, additional therapeutic intervention, not part of 'cognitive remediation', is required.

One example of a reductionistic approach to neuropsychological rehabilitation has been provided by Gianutsos and Gianutsos (1979). In this study the authors utilized an experimental methodology derived from information processing research in cognitive psychology and applied it to the treatment of verbal recall defects among four brain-injured patients. While patients were clinically assessed using fairly standard neuropsychological techniques, the results of this evaluation had no bearing on their treatment. Rather, this study utilized the patient's performance on the training task itself as baseline criteria and outcome criteria, with no indication of whether or not the gains, or lack thereof, on the training tasks related to any other indices of cerebral efficiency, or the patient's functional status. The methodology employed was based on a specific component inherent in information processing approaches to memory, irrespective of patient characteristics. Furthermore, all four patients were treated in the same way, except for variance in terms of the timing of experimental mnemonic training, as dictated by the requirements of a single case multiple baseline methodology.

Gasparrini and Satz (1979) have provided evidence that left-hemisphere-injured subjects with deficits in paired associate word list recall could improve recall relative to left hemisphere control subjects using visual imagery techniques, and that the improvement was attributable to the imaging process itself and not the effects of verbal mediation. In this study all 15 were given the same training procedure, irrespective of their performance on the baseline neuropsychological measures, irrespective of the individual neuropsychological measures, and irrespective of the individual neuropsychological sequelae. Nonetheless, the results of this investigation would suggest that the technique of visual imagery to improve word lists recall is sufficiently robust such that individual differences, in terms of neuropathological or neuropsychological characteristics, are irrelevant. This investigation, like that of Gianutsos and Gianutsos (1979), provides data which suggest that brain-injured patients can improve brain-based neuropsychological functions, as determined by designated metric definitions, which is encouraging given historically prevailing assumptions, but fail to provide evidence that such improvements represent a clinically significant change in the patient's functional adaptation.

More encouraging results were obtained by Weinberg et al (1977). In their study a group of patients with right hemisphere stroke received 20 hours of what could be described as standardized, and reductionistic, treatment. Treatment consisted of teaching the patient, using standardized treatment techniques, to:

1. turn his head to the left so as to orient to visual data which were initially in the left visual field to the right visual field;
2. provide anchors in the left side of visual space from which to orient;
3. decrease the density of stimuli which would pull the subject to the left side of visual space; and
4. modify the patient's visual tracking and scanning.

Aspects of training are decidedly componential, and the emphasis in terms of training methodology was clearly determined by the materials utilized. As compared with controlled subjects who received traditional rehabilitation, these investigators found that the experimental training methodology significantly influenced non-treated, academic performance of patients with right cerebral lesions. Furthermore, these authors argued that using a systematic approach to the treatment of such disorders, restoration of function can occur through neuropsychological rehabilitation of 'deficits', rather than resorting to compensatory strategies.

Similar thinking has been applied to the treatment of patients with traumatic brain damage. Ben-Yishay and Diller (1983b) have described a series of training components that are 'administered in a specific order'. The patient moves from these 'modules' as a function of their having reached specific 'criterion levels of performance' or plateaued at some level below criterion. The contents of these task hierarchies (the cognitive modules) were derived from various theoretical conceptualizations. Ben-Yishay et al (1979) described five methodological procedures for the treatment of attentional disturbances which are based upon 'phenomenological analysis augmented by clinical didactic considerations'. These authors suggest that these components of treatment increase, as the patient progresses in terms of *tasks*, in complexity along a theoretically derived hierarchy. These authors also included pre- and post-treatment criterion measures in the evaluation of a single case, and demonstrated significant improvement on the non-trained criterion measures, which included traditional psychometric as well as functional variables.

Dynamic approaches to neuropsychological rehabilitation start with a different set of assumptions. There is little emphasis upon the absolute level of performance on specific neuropsychological measures. Rather, the level of performance of practical tasks is analyzed as a function of the overall constellation of neuropsychological, social, and other functions, and by how, or under what conditions, the level of performance may be impaired. It follows that dynamic approaches to neuropsychological rehabilitation do not utilize a preconceived treatment sequence. While the dynamic approach to rehabilitation may include some repetitive practice on given exercises or training materials, the way in which those materials are used depends upon overall patient characteristics rather than specific characteristics of the patient or of the training materials themselves. As a function of the patient's change and evolution, either on a minute-by-minute or day-by-day basis, the treatment sequence may be altered and interventions may be made from various levels. Dynamic conceptualization of the neuropsychological rehabilitation process also places more emphasis upon the therapist–patient relationship. Meltzer (1983), a clinical psychologist who suffered brain damage, has recommended to therapists that ' . . . more important than the rehabilitation techniques used is the relationship with you . . . .' Such approaches to rehabilitation maximize attention to individual differences – not only differences among levels of functioning within the individual, but the relations between the patient and significant others. In summary, dynamic approaches to neuropsychological rehabilitation are characterized less by 'remediation' and more by the larger perspective of rehabilittion.

Dynamic thinking in neuropsychological rehabilitation has nonetheless resulted in the development of some specific techniques oriented at facilitating the recovery of neuropsychological function. Trexler and Zappala (1985) have suggested that these address what could be referred to as more *general* neuropsychological defects which are dependent upon the integrity of the central nervous system as a whole. Gross et al (1982) have developed a number of strategies which can be characterized as dynamic techniques. These latter authors refer to the treatment of 'simultaneous information processing' defects by way of 'Interference Resistance Training', 'Conditional Responses', and 'The Empathic Dialogue'. These techniques focus on the flexibility of thinking and the re-automatization of filtering and contextual processing. The Empathic Dialogue is a group technique focused on the difficulty most brain-injured individuals have integrating all relevant information inherent in social communication, resulting in a propensity to respond in concrete and automatic ways. In all of these techniques, a notable difference, as compared with reductionistic techniques, is that the outcome in terms of patient performance is never strictly sought or determined on the basis of normative criteria. Rather, the focus of training is to improve the patient's overall functional re-adaptation; that may begin to occur within the therapy session itself or gradually emerge in a variety of contextual situations. Gross et al (1982) have provided some tentative outcome data that show the positive effect of such training experiences on psychometric measurement of new learning, flexibility of thinking, and memory.

So as to exemplify dynamic approaches to the remediation of a specific neuropsychological defect, a computer program developed at The Center for Neuropsychological Rehabilitation will be described. It was noted that many of the patients with diagnoses of brain trauma or stroke had interrelated defects of spatial analysis and recall. It was thought that the processes of spatial analysis and recall should not be addressed separately through different remedial tasks as the pathology which gave rise to these disorders simultaneously affected neural systems subserving both analysis and recall. Furthermore, the extent to which analysis and recall were affected differed from patient to patient. The Visual Analysis and Spatial Recall Task (VASR) has three components, including a scanning and identification of visual targets phase, a recall phase, and a recognition phase. In phase one the patient is presented with target and distractor stimuli. These target and distractor stimuli are presented on the computer monitor and are any combination of linguistic or spatial figures, arranged randomly or in a structured configuration, and at any spatial density as indicated by the needs of the patient. Depending upon the pathology, patients may present with defects in visually identifying details, systematically scanning, differentiating similar linguistic or spatial stimuli or organizing a strategy, depending upon the degree and type of frontal lobe and other involvement. The task was designed in such a way that it can be modified for the neuropsychological profile of each patient. In phase one the subject's task is to identify each target, either from memory or by comparison with a displayed model. Following the completion of phase one, phase two begins with the presentation of a blank screen. On the screen the patient is to place the targets in the array in which they were originally placed, without the distractors. In the final phase the patient is presented with four arrays and asked to indicate which of the four was the original array of target stimuli. Following the completion of all phases, a printout includes a hard copy of the original visual display of target and distractor stimuli, the spatial sequence of target identification, the time required, the array the subject constructed in phase two, and his or her accuracy on recognition in phase three, as well as other qualitative aspects of his or her performance. The conditions under which patients perform the task can be determined by the nature of the pathology and hence the neuropsychological defects, their progress, as well as by the functional progress they make in other situations which depend upon spatial analysis and recall.

One of the inherent limitations of a dynamic approach to neuropsychological rehabilitation is the difficulty in performing empirical research, other than outcome studies focused on global adaptation in a variety of functional situations. Since no patient receives the same treatment, in the same way, by clinical necessity, it is difficult to employ rigorous methods of empirical research using strict metric definitions of outcome. Efficacy research with dynamic, as well as reductionistic approaches to neuropsychological rehabilitation, must of course concern themselves not only with neuropsychological levels of performance, but with patient-relevant functional criteria as well. Methods imported from ethnology may ultimately prove useful for rehabilitation outcome research.

Prigatano and his associates (Prigatano, 1984) have recently completed an outcome study which addressed not only neuropsychological test performance, but *in vivo* psychosocial adjustment. Their outcome study shows that severely impaired traumatic head-injury patients can improve neuropsychological status, as well as reduce emotional distress, following intensive neuropsychological rehabilitation. A focus on the functional outcome of patients who are beyond the spontaneous recovery period is a methodological perspective which holds considerable promise for the future.

A model has been proposed (Trexler, 1983) which incorporates both reductionistic and dynamic approaches to neuropsychological rehabilitation. In this approach, there are essentially four dimensions of the rehabilitation process, which to some extent may be sequential, but overall greatly interact and vary as a function of individual patient characteristics. These four dimensions include:

1. the promotion of patient awareness, labeling and identification of their neuropsychological defects in both in vitro and in vivo environments;
2. the treatment of general neuropsychological defects, such as overall information processing and attentional systems;
3. the treatment of specific neuropsychological defects, such as perceptual difficulties or language problems (in a reductionistic and remedial manner); and
4. the promotion of integration and generalization to the patient's environment, whether it be at home or in a vocational setting.

These four dimensions are not assumed to follow in any standardized sequence; they may occur simultaneously within any one therapeutic session, and they do not represent an assumed hierarchy of neuropsychological function. The initial rehabilitation efforts with a given patient may deal with the specific neuropsychological defects rather than the promotion of awareness or labeling of the presenting neuropsychological defects, or the psychosocial adjustment of the patient, depending upon what is most clinically relevant. This model is offered as a general conceptualization of the components of the neuropsychological rehabilitation process, and when incorporated with the schema provided in the previous section (Fig. 2.51 and Table 25.1) incorporates what Diller and Gordon (1981) describe as 'remediation' and 'rehabilitation'.

At the present time, reductionistic approaches to neuropsychological rehabilitation predominate in the United States. This can be seen as attributable to the psychometric–statistical prevailing philosophies in American neuropsychology. Furthermore, the current status of American neuropsychological thinking has in part been influenced by the importation of neuropsychologists into the rehabilitation setting, where neuropsychologists and rehabilitation professionals have had different conceptualizations about the goals of rehabilitation. As has been mentioned, neuropsychologists have typically emphasized specific brain–behavior performance whereas rehabilitation professionals have particularly been concerned with re-adaptation at a functional level.

There is obviously a striking need for further outcome investigation in neuropsychological rehabilitation. Which approach to neuropsychological rehabilitation one utilizes will influence the research methodology. Individuals approaching rehabilitation from a dynamic perspective will tend to utilize single case designs since all patients are treated differently, making statistical group comparisons of questionable utility. The definition of outcome will also differ. The strict psychometric–statistical approach to neuropsychological rehabilitation outcome involves expression in terms of numeric quantifications relative to normative performance. Theoretical–clinical approaches to neuropsychological rehabilitation will rely on *in vivo* and more global assessments. Spiers (1982) has pointed out, at least with regard to assessment, that neither approach 'is of necessity unscientific . . . '. These two approaches differ in terms of what can be considered "relevant, primary data . . . ' and that both approaches are capable of statistical analysis. This author goes on to suggest that the statistical assumption of the normal distribution may have limited application to neuropsychology: We do not expect a normal distribution of neuropsychological defects following specific lesions. Rather, neuropsychological theory and research suggest that particular kinds of behavioral disorders are predictable given the type of pathology and their location. This knowledge base can help define a given patient's neuropsychological functioning irrespective of normative statistical criteria. Ultimately, combined approaches with reductionistic and dynamic approaches to neuropsychological rehabilitation will hopefully generate new ideas, techniques, methodologies, research, and programs, beyond a recapitulation of historical assumptions, in neuropsychological rehabilitation.

## PROGRAMS IN NEUROPSYCHOLOGICAL REHABILITATION

This section will address itself to a review of two programs of neuropsychological rehabilitation in the United States. These two programs were selected for review because of differences in program philosophy, program organization, and treatment methods which highlight diverging approaches to neuropsychological rehabilitation in the United States.

## The Center for Neuropsychological Rehabilitation, Indianapolis, Indiana

### *History and philosophy*

The Center opened on December 5, 1983. Its recent history was preceded by an evolution at The Hook Rehabilitation Center, Community Hospital of Indianapolis, which began with the formal development of the Neuropsychology Service in 1979. The Neuropsychology Service provided not only diagnostic information but also treatment and rehabilitation recommendations. In 1981 the Cognitive Rehabilitation Program was developed as a collaborative effort between the Neuropsychology Service and the Department of Occupational Therapy. The intent of this program was to provide services to patients in The Hook Rehabilitation Center based upon neuropsychological formulations of their defects and with an emphasis on 'cognitive' functions, such as attentional processing, not explicitly addressed by other therapeutic modalities. It became clear, however, that as patients attained medical and physical stability, and therefore were of necesity discharged, persisting neuropsychological sequelae seriously impaired their long-term readaptation. So as to address these persisting neuropsychological difficulties, the Center was developed.

The clinical services provided at the Center have been developed based primarily upon three assumptions. The first assumption was that it was critical to understand, in each patient's case, the neurobehavioral determinants of recovery. It was thought that a patient-specific conceptualization of the effect of neuropathology on general, particular and interactive neuropsychological functions would serve as the framework from which to derive rehabilitation strategies. Neuropsychological tests were therefore of value only to the extent that they assisted the neuropsychologist in formulating this conceptualization. Secondly, it was assumed that the interaction between neuropathological, neuropsychological, psychological, and social factors determined how a given defect in cerebral processes was expressed at any one moment. Therefore, rehabilitation strategies should be responsive to and stimulate variations in any one of these factors, in view of the effects on overall performance or adaptation. The final assumption was that the relationship between the therapist and the patient was an important determinant of outcome. A therapeutic relationship which permits changes in the many aspects of the patient's life to emerge, and one where the therapist feels free to address these various aspects, was thought of as the context from which facilitation of recovery of function and re-adaptation could occur.

Center staff are selected not only on their professional competencies in the areas of functional neuroanatomy and determinants of recovery and experience, but also upon their flexibility and ability to form relationships with patients and staff.

*Clinical and research programs*

The rehabilitation services provided at the Center emphasize, as has been discussed, the therapist–patient relationship. As a consequence, each patient admitted to the program is assigned a primary therapist. The primary therapist will see the patient at least 1½–2 hours per day and will determine what other activities the patient is involved in each day. Furthermore, the primary therapist is the main liaison with the family, although the therapist may utilize other resources within the Center for family therapy or education.

There are three components to the Center, which include the Aphasia and Related Disorders Program, the Cognitive Disorders Program, and the Vocational Entry Program. Depending upon the primary difficulties of the patients, they will be assigned to either the Aphasia or Cognitive Disorders Program, although in cases of traumatic aphasia, both. Furthermore, depending upon his or her priorities and readiness, the patient may simultaneously spend part of his or her time in the Vocational Entry Program. There are a variety of on going groups at the Center, in which the patient participates. However, the order and duration in which a patient would attend a particular group depends entirely upon the patient, and there is the absence of a predetermined sequence of such experiences. Groups at the Center include the Self-Regulation Group, Memory Skills Group, Functional Skills Group, Psychotherapy Group, Language and Communications Group, Vocational Skills Group, and a weekly Community Meeting. Through the Vocational Re-Entry Program patients may be placed in positions in private industry throughout the metropolitan area, which range from upper level management to manual labor jobs, for purposes of evaluation and training. If the patient has a previous employer who is receptive to the person returning, the staff will collaborate directly with the previous employee. A more detailed description of each group, the three clinical programs, and their relatedness has been offered elsewhere (Trexler, 1985).

The patient population attending the Center is not defined by any specific strict criteria other than the patient must be medically stable, not have a progressive neurologic disease, and not have a history of major psychiatric illness. The patients with diagnosis of cerebrovascular accident, traumatic injury, infectious disorders, and hypoxic encephalopathy are the most typical. The age of Center patients ranges from 14 to 58, with the most common being 20 and 35. The average length of stay has been approximately 3½ months, although this has varied from 2 to 9 months. Patients are admitted to the Center following complete neuropsychological examination, neuroradiological examination, evaluation by physiatry, and thorough review of medical records. The patient and the family are then evaluated at the Center for a three-day period, where the patient is evaluated by many of the staff, in group and informal situations. The family is asked to attend so as to begin to integrate them into the treatment process. At the end of this evaluation day, an admission conference is held which includes the patient, family, and staff. During this meeting the patient's medical and neuropsychological status is reviewed and a recommendation made to the patient and the family as to whether the patient should be admitted. At that time, the expectations and goals of rehabilitation are discussed and initial plans are developed. Patients are discharged from the program when they have attained a level of functioning which is commensurate with their and their families' expectations. Typically, patients are seen periodically after discharge so as to evaluate the success of their readaptation as well as to make further recommendations.

The Center has developed and implemented a comprehensive database, which includes pre-morbid personological data, neuropathological, neuropsychological, functional daily living, vocational, family rating, and treatment variables. Patients are evaluated at admission, discharge and 12 month follow-up. Through these efforts the Center studies determinants of outcome, degree, and permanence of social, behavioral, and vocational outcomes and other more experimental issues. Research findings are now being analyzed.

## The New York University Stroke Rehabilitation Programs

### *History and philosophy*

The initial work concerning the remediation of perceptual disorders of right hemisphere stroke patients was begun in 1972, by a research team headed by Dr. Leonard Diller. This team of investigators began studying the approximately 125 acute left hemiplegics admitted to the Institute of Rehabilitation Medicine of the New York University Medical Center each year. This team of psychologists were assigned patients, along with the patient's daily assignments to other rehabilitation therapies, including physical and occupational therapy. Further, because of the research goals, all patients were seen by a neurologist to ensure that all patients included in the studies had lesions confined to the right cerebral hemisphere. Patients were randomly assigned to either an experimental group, those who received perceptual remediation from the research team, or to traditional occupational therapy services.

The focus of these investigations has been on 'remediation' of cognitive and perceptual disorders, as opposed to the more global activity of rehabilitation. Diller and Gordon (1981) describe remediation as 'procedures designed to provide patients with the behavioral repertoire needed to solve problems or to perform tasks that seem difficult or impossible'. In this context, remediation refers to the treatment of specific deficits observed through standardized observations, whereas rehabilitation refers to the total spectrum of services that a brain injured person may require, such as speech pathology, vocational counseling, and so forth. The experimental evolution of approaches to the remediation of perceptual disorders associated with right hemisphere stroke had four phases (Diller & Weinberg, 1977), which included:

1. the development of metric instruments which would serve to define or diagnose the deficit;

2. the development of a taxonomy of response styles;
3. delineation of the stimulus and response properties of the task which determined the extent of the observed deficit; and
4. development of specific training methods, which were based upon task stimulus and response properties, for experimental analysis.

This rational approach to remediation of perceptual disorders yielded some of the first statistical data verifying that functions of the brain could be improved, beyond what spontaneous recovery or other traditional rehabilitation efforts may promote, with systematic behavioral (neuropsychological) intervention. Weinberg et al (1977) unequivocably demonstrated that disorders of reading and writing due to visual scanning deficits can be successfully treated. They also (Weinberg et al, 1979) demonstrated that the sensory awareness and spatial organization defects, particularly in more severely impaired right brain damage patients, could also be successfully treated. Furthermore, these investigators also demonstrated that, when the visual scanning, sensory awareness, and spatial organization deficits associated with right hemisphere stroke were simultaneously treated, the outcome was superior to addressing them one at a time.

*Clinical and research programs*

Given the success attained with modifying disorders associated with right hemisphere stroke, the remediation techniques used with the experimental (treatment) groups could no longer be withheld for ethical reasons from any patient in the Institute of Rehabilitation Medicine with this diagnosis. Consequently, research activities by Dr Diller and his associates have evolved along two directions. The first concerns the development of metric tests and treatment methods for disorders of arousal, depression and affect recognition among patients with right hemisphere stroke. The second research activity is focusing on the assessment and remediation of arousal and perceptual deficits associated with bilateral damage to the brain. These research efforts are incorporating some of the remedial modules for deficits in arousal that were developed for traumatically brain injured patients (Ben-Yishay et al, 1979) with the protocols for the remediation of perceptual deficits derived from the stroke rehabilitation program.

Separate from the research teams, the Department of Behavioral Sciences also offers clinical services to inpatients and outpatients of the Institute of Rehabilitation Medicine. Staffed by three psychologists and one intern psychologist, this program offers remediation services to appropriate patients as well as consultative services to the rest of the treatment team. One of the psychologists serves as a psychotherapist, so a patient may receive treatment from two psychologists at the same time. The remediation services offered may be derived from techniques developed in previous research, but situation-relevant alterations of task conditions and methods are often synthesized for individual patients. The contributions of the psychologist may also include applying therapeutic strategies to social and vocational situations.

Treatment is provided in hourly sessions, and inpatients are seen three to five times weekly and outpatients one to two times weekly. The length of treatment ranges from a few months to a year or more. Each in-patient stroke victim typically receives 35–45 hours of remedial work. Attempts are also made to collaborate with the family of the patient to promote practice at home of specific remedial exercises.

## CONCLUSIONS

This is a fruitful epoch for neuropsychological rehabilitation in the United States. New models of care, clinical programs, conceptualizations and paradigms, and, gradually, empirical studies are emerging. The prognosis for improving functional readaptation for at least some patients with neurological diagnoses seems to be better as a consequence. In the meantime, it appears that in the process, we are learning more about brain–behavior relationships while restoring function, albeit in some cases in an unquantifiable way, to brain-injured persons. The past 10 years have advanced our understanding of neuropsychological rehabilitation by slow but steady progress. The next 10 years seem likely to further our knowledge exponentially. Central questions for future efforts are, 'what are the predictor variables of response to intervention, and for whom?' and 'what methods are feasible and cost-effective for what kind of patient?'

### REFERENCES

Anderson D W, McLaurin R L The national head and spinal cord injury survey. The Office of Scientific and Health Reports, NINCDS, NIH, Bethesda, Maryland 20205

Ben-Yishay Y, Diller L 1983a Cognitive deficits. In: Rosenthal M, Griffith E R, Bond M R, Miller J D (eds) Rehabilitation of the head injured adult. F A Davis, Philadelphia, p. 167–183

Ben-Yishay Y, Diller L 1983b Cognitive remediation. In: Rosenthall M, Griffith E R, Bond M R, Miller J D (eds) Rehabilitation of the head injured adult. F A Davis, Philadelphia, p. 367–380

Ben-Yishay Y, Rottok J, Diller L 1979 A clinical strategy for the systematic amelioration of attentional disturbances in severe head trauma patients. New York University IRM Behavioral Science, Rehabilitation Monograph No. 60

Caplan B 1982 Neuropsychology in rehabilitation: its role in evaluation and intervention. Archives of Physical Medicine and Rehabilitation 63: 362–366

Cope D N 1982 Conclusions. In: Head Injury Rehabilitation Project final report. A report to the National Institute for Handicapped Research from the Institute for Medical Research, Santa Clara Valley Medical Center, 751 South Bascom Avenue, San Jose, California 95128

Craine J F, Gudeman H E 1981 The rehabilitation of brain functions: principles, procedures, and techniques of neurotraining. Charles C Thomas, Springfield

Crockett D, Clark C, Klonoff H 1981 Introduction–An overview of neuropsychology. In: Filskov S B, Boll T J (eds) Handbook of clinical neuropsychology. John Wiley, New York, p. 1–37

Diller L 1984 The rehabilitation of perceptual disorders. A presentation at the Fourth Annual International Symposium on Models and Techniques of Cognitive Rehabilitation, Indianapolis, March 31

Diller L, Gordon W A 1981 Interventions for cognitive deficits in brain-injured adults. Journal of Consulting and Clinical Psychology 49: 822–834

Diller L, Weinberg J 1977 Hemi-inattention in rehabilitation: the evolution of a rational remediation program. In: Weinstein E A, Friedland R P (eds) Advances in neurology. Vol. 18. Raven Press, New York, p. 63–82

Eysenck H J 1967 Intelligence assessment: a theoretical and experimental approach. British Journal of Educational Psychology 37: 81–89

Filskov S B, Goldstein S G 1974 Diagnostic validity of the Halstead-Reitan neuropsychological battery. Journal of Consulting and Clinical Psychology 42: 382–388

Gasparrini B, Satz P 1979 A treatment for memory problems in left hemisphere CVA patients. Journal of Clinical Neuropsychology 1: 137–150

Gianutsos R, Gianutsos J 1979 Rehabilitating the verbal recall of brain-injured patients by mnemonic training: an experimental demonstration using single case methodology. Journal of Clinical Neuropsychology 1: 117–135

Golden C J 1978 Diagnosis and rehabilitation in clinical neuropsychology. Charles C Thomas, Springfield

Goodglass H, Kaplan E 1979 Assessment of cognitive deficit in the brain-injured patient. In: Gazzaniga M (ed) Handbook of behavioral neurobiology. Vol. 2: Neuropsychology. Plenum Press, New York, p. 3–24

Gross Y A 1982 Conceptual framework for interventive cognitive neuropsychology. In: Trexler L E (ed) Cognitive rehabilitation: conceptualization and intervention, Plenum Press, New York, p. 99–114

Gross Y, Ben-Nahum Z, Munk G 1982 Techniques and application of simultaneous information processing. In: Trexler L E (ed) Cognitive rehabilitation: conceptualization and intervention. Plenum Press, New York, p. 223–238

Heaton R K, Pendleton M G 1981 Use of neuropsychological tests to predict adult patients every day functioning. Journal of Consulting and Clinical Psychology 49: 807–821

Jennett B, Teasdale G 1981 Management of head injuries. F A Davis, Philadelphia

Lezak M D 1983 Neuropsychological assessment. 2nd ed. Oxford University Press, New York

Luria A R 1966 Higher cortical function in man. 2nd ed. Basic Books, New York

Luria A R, Majovski L V 1977 Basic approaches used in American and Soviet clinical neuropsychology. American Psychologist 32: 959–968

McNamara J R 1979 Behavioral psychology in medicine: an introduction. In: McNamara J R (ed) Behavioral approaches to medicine: application and analysis. Plenum Press, New York, p. 1–8

Meltzer M L 1983 Poor memory: a case report. Journal of Clinical Psychology 39: 3–10

Moscovitch M S 1979 Information processing and the cerebral hemispheres. In: Gazzaniga M S (ed) Handbook of behavioral neurobiology. Vol. 2 Neuropsychology. Plenum Press, New York, p. 379–446

Prigatano G P, Fordyce D J, Zeiner H K, Roueche J R, Pepping M, Wood B 1984 Neuropsychological rehabilitation after closed head injury in young adults. Journal of Neurology, Neurosurgery and Psychiatry 47: 505–513

Reitan R M 1974a Assessment of brain behavior relationships. In: McReynolds P (ed) Advances in psychological assessment Vol. 3 Jossey-Bass, San Francisco, p. 186–242

Reitan R M 1974b Methodological problems in clinical neuropsychology. In: Reitan R M, Davison L A (eds) Clinical neuropsychology: current status and applications. Winston and Sons, Washington D C, p. 19–46

Spiers P A 1982 The Luria-Nebraska Neuropsychological Batterey revisited: a theory in practice or just practising? Journal of Consulting and Clinical Psychology 50: 301–306

Stanton K M, Pepping M, Brockway J A, Bliss L, Frankel D, Waggener S 1983 Wheelchair transfer training for right cerebral dysfunctions: an interdisciplinary approach. Archives of Physical Medicine and Rehabilitation 64: 276–280

Thomas J D, Trexler L E 1982 Behavioral and cognitive deficits in cerebrovascular accident and closed head injury: implications for cognitive rehabilittion. In: Trexler L E (ed) Cognitive rehabilitation: conceptualization and intervention. Plenum Press, New York, p. 27–62

Trexler L E Introduction and program description. Presented in a symposium entitled case studies in neuropsychological rehabilitation. Proceedings of the International Neuropsychological Society, Copenhagen, June 13, 1985

Trexler L E 1983 Introduction to brain function and cognitive rehabilitation. A pre-symposium institute presented at the Third Annual International Symposium on Models and Techniques of Cognitive Rehabilitation, Indianapolis

Trexler L E, Zappala G 1985 Emerging trends in neuropsychological rehabilitation. In: Formica M M (ed) Trattato di Neurologia Riabilitativa. Marrapese; Rome

Wechsler D 1955 Wechsler Adult Intelligence Scale, manual. Psychological Corporation, New York

Wheeler L, Reitan R M 1963 Discriminant functions applied to the problems of predicting cerebral damage from behavioral testing: a cross validation study. Perceptual and Motor Skills 16: 681–701

Weinberg M A, Diller L, Gordon W A, et al 1977 Visual scanning effect on reading related tasks in acquired right brain damage. Archives of Physical Medicine and Rehabilitation 58: 479–486

Weinberg M A, Diller L, Gordon W A, et al 1979 Training sensory awareness and spatial organization in people with right brain damage. Archives of Physical Medicine and Rehabilitation 60: 491–496

# 26

Anton Leischner

# Neuropsychological rehabilitation in West Germany

## HISTORICAL SKETCH

Neuropsychological rehabilitation had its beginnings in Germany in the late 19th century when aphasic patients were retrained by phoniatrists, the most prominent of whom were Fröschels, Gutzmann and Seeman. After the First World War rehabilitation units for soldiers with traumatic brain wounds were established in Frankfurt (K. Goldstein), Bonn (W. Poppelreuter), and Munich (M. Isserlin). In the Second World War specialized units were given the responsibility for the care and rehabilitation of brain-injured military personnel. Disturbances directly after the war led to a curtailment of operations but a new center was established in Langenberg in 1948 and later Bonn in 1953. There has been a steady expansion of rehabilitation facilities so that at present there are about 30 major centers in West Germany. Some offer rehabilitation services to both aphasic and non-aphasic patients with brain disease, while others on the rehabilitation of aphasic patients, a circumstance fostered by the passage of a law in 1961 specifying that all individuals with speech defects have a legal right to treatment. This law made the foundation of the Bonn clinic for language disturbances possible.

## DIAGNOSTIC PROCEDURES

The first step in diagnosis is a physical and neurological examination which serves to: identify the underlying pathology; determine whether medical or surgical intervention is indicated before rehabilitation is instituted; and ascertain whether there are any contraindications to rehabilitation such as serious systemic disease or dementia. The severity of an aphasic disorder is not in itself considered to be a contraindication.

The second step in diagnosis is a neuropsychological assessment in which both verbal and non-verbal abilities are evaluated. The assessment is accomplished both by administration of test batteries and by clinical examination. One of the more widely used aphasia test batteries is the Aachener Aphasietest (AAT) which has been well standardized and which generates quantitative measures. Aphasia test batteries have also been developed in

Göttingen and Tübingen. German versions of the Schuell and Goodglass–Kaplan batteries, and the Token Test of De Renzi and Vignolo, are available for use.

Equally important in diagnosis is the clinical examination, an individualized procedure in which the questions posed to the patient in interview are adapted to his education, occupation, and interests. The distinctive advantage of this approach is that it evokes the patient's optimal level of function since he is motivated to express himself on topics of vital significance to him.

## GENERAL FEATURES

Almost all rehabilitation centers have an inpatient service. After discharge patients who reside near the clinic may be offered outpatient services. A few clinics offer only outpatient treatment. Inpatient treatment is preferred because of the opportunity afforded for close observation and for diverse types of rehabilitation.

Speech and language retraining for an aphasic patient in an inpatient clinic is likely to consist of one 45-minute session daily for 8 to 12 weeks. Some facilities, such as the Max-Planck-Institut in Munich may keep patients as long as 9 months. The number of patients treated depends upon the size and resources of the clinic. The Bonn Clinic has 20 beds reserved exclusively for aphasic patients; this seems to be about the norm for the larger clinics. The smaller clinics have a case-load of 5–15 patients.

Outpatient clinic patients are generally seen for a 45 minute session two or three times a week, with the length of treatment extending from 18 to 24 months. The training program in some centers is divided into blocks of about 20 sessions followed by a rest period during which the patient's progress is evaluated and the treatment plan is reviewed. In most inpatient clinics a speech therapist will treat about eight patients at any one time. In the better-equipped centers the number is reduced to five or six patients, to allow the therapist more time for preparation of sessions. Therapists in outpatient clinics have larger case-loads because they see patients less frequently and treat a variety of speech disorders.

The background of training of aphasia therapists varies widely. The majority have been trained in logopedics ('speech pathology' in the United States) but the basic training of a substantial minority is in linguistics, general or special education, or psychology. A few physicians also engage in speech therapy. Thus the situation in Germany is different from that in most other countries where aphasia therapy is almost exclusively the province of the logopedist.

Individual treatment is the preferred mode of aphasia therapy in all clinics. However, many centers provide group treatment for selected patients. These groups, consisting of three to five patients, are formed on the basis of the presenting symptomatology. Thus a small group of patients with prominent word-finding difficulties, with impairment in understanding oral speech, or with articulatory defects, will be formed, and exercises and procedures directed toward the specific difficulty will occupy the group session.

Physiotherapy, gymnastics, and occupational therapy are common procedures. The extent to which praxic disabilities, constructional impairment, perceptual and spatial deficits, and attentional disturbances are treated is quite variable and is essentially dependent upon the resources of a particular clinic. Practice in copying figures, drawing, painting, clay modelling, and block assembling have been found to be effective in alleviating constructional and visuospatial disabilities. Conversely, aphasic patients without perceptuomotor defects are encouraged to utilize diverse non-verbal actions to express their thoughts and intentions (cf. Leischner & Pendzialek-Langer, 1974). Special exercises to improve concentration, memory, perception, and the capacity for independent living are included in the programs of many clinics. In some clinics autogenic training and psychotherapy are offered when they are judged to be indicated.

Social therapy is a recent addition to the treatment program of the Bonn Clinic. A group of up to 15 aphasic patients is formed under the supervision of a social worker. They visit museums and attend concerts and the theatre. In so doing they once again learn to use public transportation, how to order a meal at a restaurant, and the use of money. They go on small excursions and attend evening social gatherings. Thus the aphasic patient is rescued from his social isolation and the way is prepared for his reintegration into social and cultural life.

Some institutes provide facilities for active participation in sports. A few have kitchens in which patients can reacquire their cooking skills. Very few offer a patient retraining in his own occupation.

## METHODS OF SPEECH THERAPY

As has been mentioned, the direction taken by speech therapy rests on an initial diagnostic evaluation, the components of which are:

1. the diagnosis of the underlying pathology(e.g., occlusion of the left middle cerebral artery;
2. the clinical neurological status (e.g., right hemiplegia);
3. the neuropsychological evaluation (e.g., sensory–amnesic aphasia with agraphia, alexia and acalculia).

The therapist can then decide where activity must be focused on the basis of the neuropsychological evaluation.

This survey of treatment programs for aphasics at the various clinics indicates they all are linguistically orientated and modality-specific with the choice of training procedures depending upon the specific symptom picture. Over the course of the years a number of clinics have developed distinctive treatment programs.

One example is the aphasia rehabilitation program of the Neurological Clinic in Aachen developed by Poeck and his associates, in which a distinction is made between a reactivation phase and a consolidation phase in treatment. In the reactivation phase the deblocking method of Weigl is employed to arouse suspended speech mechanisms. This is particularly appropriate for severe aphasics at the beginning of treatment. Procedures are later modified as priority is given to the attainment of specific objectives and inductive learning is facilitated. Specific aspects of linguistic performance become the focus of training, e.g., the minimal phonological contrasts between two words, lexical relationships, constraints in word selection, and combining parts of speech. The consolidation phase of treatment begins after various linguistic skills have been completely or partially reacquired. This phase consists of facilitating the transfer of these skills to situations other than that of the patient–therapist interaction. Thus the difficulties encountered when there are several speakers in a conversational setting, when the other speaker is not sensitive to the limitations of the patient, or when the patient must speak under time pressure have to be faced. Role-playing is used extensively in this stage of treatment. When it is evident that some abilities will not be regained fully, compensatory strategies are taught. Alleviation of disturbances of attention and concentration are also part of the program.

Another example of a distinctive treatment program is that of Kotten in the Bonn clinic. The restoration of speech is based first on deblocking and then on the reorganization of specific speech functions. Various methods are utilized to evoke speech functions and to ensure that these functions once again are part of the patient's verbal behavior, the particular method employed being dependent upon the type of aphasic disorder manifested. To accomplish the specific goals of a rehabilitation program for an individual patient, training materials and tasks are assembled with due regard for his normal speech environment and his particular interests. An instructive exposition of Kotten's methods will be found in the monograph of Engl et al (1982).

The rehabilitation program of the Freiburg clinic has a number of noteworthy features. The first aim in treatment is to eliminate perseverations and automatisms in speech. Then the most prominent symptoms of the motor aphasic or sensory aphasic are attacked. Communication with global aphasics is initiated by placing emphasis on improvement in understanding speech and augmentation of vocabulary. A special program of training in which the still intact motor capacities of the upper extremities are utilized to advantage is set up for 'articulatory' aphasics.

The neuropsychological division of the Max-Planck-Institut for Psychiatry in Munich has developed its own distinctive treatment program. Stimulation therapy is initiated in the acute phase of the disorder. When the symptom picture stabilizes, attention is focused on the remediation of specific deficits. Special attention is paid to disturbances in reading and writing. In the chronic phase of the disorder the patient is provided with exercises that are relevant to the particular circumstances of his everyday life.

Treatment methods that were originally developed in other countries are utilized in many clinics. The most frequently adopted techniques include the deblocking method of Weigl, the preventive method of Beyn, the activation method of Schuell, the programmed learning techniques of Sarno, and the melodic intonation therapy of Sparks, Helm and Albert. Some institutes employ the programmed therapy of Von Stockert and the methods described by Braun, Springer, and Weniger.

The outcome of treatment is typically evaluated by repeating the assessment given at the beginning of treatment and comparing pre-and post-treatment levels of performance. Counseling of the patient's relatives as the patient leaves active treatment is almost universal. Some clinics arrange for follow-up home visits, the registration of patients in social centres, and the formation of self-help groups.

The establishment by Braun of a national association of aphasic patients and their families represents a particularly noteworthy development in post-treatment care. This association, which has over 30 regional chapters in different cities, publishes an information bulletin dealing with the social and legal problems of individuals with speech handicaps.

## CONCLUDING COMMENT

Despite the increasing number of rehabilitation units in West Germany the possibilities for treatment of aphasic patients has not yet been fully realized. Neither the number of therapists nor the available clinical facilities meet present needs. Both additional rehabilitation units for the rehabilitation of patients with aphasia and related neuropsychological deficits and additional training facilities for therapeutic personnel are required to meet these needs.

## MAJOR PUBLICATIONS ON REHABILITATION IN WEST GERMANY (1960–1983)

Braun R 1966 Sprachliche Rehabilitation Aphasischer in der Praxis. In: Sprachheilpädagogische und hirnpathologische Probleme bei der Rehabilitation von Hirn- und Sprachgeschädigten. Tagungsbericht Köln, Arbeitsgemeinschaft fur Sprachheilpädagogik. Wartenberg, Hamburg, 46–51

Braun R 1973 V Vorschläge zur Therapie von Aphasien. Die Sprachheilarbeit, Beiheft 3. Wartenberg, Hamburg

Braun R 1973 Allgemeine Richtlinien zur Behandlung der Aphasien. Beschäftigungstherapie und Rehabilitation 3: 32–41

Braun R 1976 Die Behandlung der Wernicke-Aphasie. In: Peuser G (ed) Interdisziplinäre Aspekte der Aphasieforschung. Rheinland-Verlag, Köln, pp. 17–24

Braun R 1983 Umgang mit Aphasikern im häuslichen Bereich. In: Kommunikation zwischen Partnern, Beiheft 'Aphasie', hrsg. von der Bundesarbeitsgemeinschaft 'Hilfe fur Behinderte'. Düsseldorf, 91–108

Cramon D v 1982 Der Weideraufbau der Sprechfunktionen nach traumatisch bedingtem Mutismus. In: Müller E. (ed) Das traumatische Mittelhirnsyndrom und die Rehabilitation schwerer Schädelhirntraumen. Springer, Berlin, 262–265

Cramon D v 1983 Prognostische Faktoren der Aphasie. In: Busch G, Eissenhauer W (eds) Leistungsdiagnostik und Rehabilitation von organischen Hirnschädigungsfolgen. Braun, Karlsruhe: 79–89

Dahmen W, Mattes K 1981 Selektive Schreibstörungen nach spontaner Subarachnoidalblutung. Nervenarzt 52: 598–601

DeBleser R, Weismann H 1981 Übergang von Strukturübungen zum Spontanen Dialog in der Therapie von Aphasikern mit nichtflüssiger Sprachproduktion. Sprache-Stimme-Gehör 5: 74–79

Engl E M, Kotten A, Ohlendorf I, Poser E 1982 Sprachübungen zur Aphasiebehandlung. Ein linguistisches Übungsprogramm mit Bildern. Marhold, Berlin

Heinrichs P v, Hinckeldey S, Poeck K 1982 Beratung von Aphasikern und deren Angehörigen. Rehabilitation 21: 18–20

Huber W 1978 Sprachliche Spezialisierung des menschlichen Gehirns. Schlussfolgerungen für die Therapie von zentralen Sprachstörungen. Sprache-Stimme-Gehör 2: 69–75

Huber W, Kerschensteiner M, Mayer J 1977 Untersuchungen zur Prognose und Methode der Therapie von Entwicklungsaphasie. Nervenarzt 48: 40–44

Huber W, Mayer J, Kerschensteiner M 1978 Phonematischer Jargon bei Wernicke-Aphasie. Untersuchung zur Methode und zum Verlauf der Therapie. Folia Phoniatrica 30: 119–135

Ingenbleek B 1983 Probleme der ambulanten Versorgung von Aphasikern nach der Entlassung aus einer Fachklinik. Diplomarbeit, Universität Dortmund

Kotten A 1976 Die kommunikative Funktion non-verbaler Umwegleistungen. In: Peuser G (ed) Interdisziplinäre Aspekte der Aphasieforschung. Rheinland-Verlag, Koln: 57–70

Kotten A 1976 Therapy of the so called 'telegraphic style'. In: Nickel G (ed) Proceedings of the Fourth International Congress of Applied Linguistics, vol. 3. Hochschul-Verlag, Stuttgart; 599–607

Kotten A 1977 Unterschiede im Beachten räumlicher und zeitlicher Präpositionen. Folia Phoniatrica 29: 270–278

Kotten A 1979 Sprachtherapie als Kommunikationssituation. In: Peuser G (ed) Studien zur Sprachtherapie. Fink, München; 27–43

Kotten A 1979 Verbale Umwegleistungen be Aphasikern. In: Peuser G (ed) Studien zur Sprachtherapie. Fink, München; 147–164

Kotten A 1980 Therapeutische Beeinflussung von Paraphasien. In: Gloning K, Dressler W U (eds) Paraphasie. Untersuchungen zum Problem lexikalischer Fehlleistungen. Fink, München; 35–51

Kotten A 1981 Aufbau eines linguistisch strukturierten Übungsprogramms zur Aphasietherapie. In: Kuhlwein W, Raasch A (eds) Sprache: Lehren–Lernen, Bd 1. Tübingen, 89–97

Kotten A 1981 Aphasietherapie: Linguistisch gesteuerter Wiedererwerb der Muttersprache. In: Peuser G, Winter S (eds) Angewandte Sprachwissenschaft: Grundfragen–Bereiche–Methoden. Bouvier, Bonn, 361–390

Kotten A 1982 Aphasietherapie schwer Hirngeschädigter. In: Müller E (ed) Das traumatische Mittelhirnsyndrome und die Rehabilitation schwerer Schädelhirntraumen. Springer, Berlin, 249–252

Kotten A 1983 Aphasietherapie: Kommunikation oder Drill? In: Althoff D-W (ed) Mündliche Kommunikation: Störungen und Therapie. Scriptor, Frankfurt, 105–121

Kotten A 1983 Aphasie therapie: Kommunikation oder Drill? In: Althoff D-W (ed) Mundliche Kommunikation: Störungen und Therapie. Scriptor, Frankfurt, 105–121

Kotten A 1983 Aphasietherapie unter linguistischen Gesichtspunkten. In: Kommunikation zwischen Partnern, Beiheft 'Aphasie', herausgegeben von der Bundesarbeitsgemeinschaft 'Hilfe für Behinderte', Düsseldorf, 34–56

Leischner A 1960 Zur Symptomatologie und Therapie der Aphasien. Nervenarzt 31: 262–271

Leischner A 1963 Grundsätzliches zur Behandlung der Aphasien. Die Sprachheilarbeit 8: 2–13

Leischner A (ed) 1970 Die Rehabilitation der Aphasie in den romanischen Landern nebst Beiträgen zur Aphasieforschung. Thieme, Stuttgart

Leischner A 1972 Sprachstörungen und ihre Behandlung. Deutsche Krankenpflegezeitschrift 4: 180–186

Leischner A 1979 Aphasien und Sprachentwicklungsstörungen. Klinik und Behandlung. Thieme, Stuttgart

Leischner A, Linck H-A 1967 Neuere Erfahrungen mit der Behandlung von Aphasien. Nervenarzt 38: 199–205

Leischner A, Pendzialek-Langer J 1974 Die Bedeutung konstruktiver Leistungen, insbesondere des Zeichnens und Malens, für die Rehabilitation der Aphasie. In: Wieck H H (ed) Psychopathologie musischer Gestaltungen. Schattauer, Stuttgart, 149–165

Linck H-A 1970 Ein Beitrag zur Behandlung der Aphasien. In: Leischner A (ed) Die Rehabilitation der Aphasie in den romanischen Ländern. Thieme, Stuttgart, 83–88

Merx W 1973 Behandlungsmöglichkeiten von Aphasien vaskularer Genese unter besonderer Berücksichtigung der Sprachheilkundlichen Behandlung. Medical Dissertation, Bonn University

Ohlendorf I 1976 Agrammatismus und Kommunikation: zur Sprechsprache von motorischen Aphatikern. In: Peuser G (ed) Interdisziplinäre Aspekte der Aphasieforschung. Rheinland-Verlag, Köln, 127–142

Peuser G (ed) 1979 Studien zur Sprachtherapie. Fink, Munchen

Poeck K, Huber W, Stachowiak, F J, Weniger, D (1977) Therapie der Aphasien. Nervenarzt 48: 119–126

Poeck K 1982 Modern methods of aphasia therapy. Paper presented at the 7th Annual Meeting of the Japanese CVD-Society, Hirosaki

Poeck K (ed) 1982 Klinische Neuropsychologie. Thieme, Stuttgart

Poeck K, Spiecker-Henke M 1982 Sprech- und Sprach- störungen bei neurologischen und psychiatrischen Krankheiten. In: Biesalski P, Frank, F (eds) Phoniatrie-Pädaudiologie. Physiologie, Pathologie, Klinik, Rehabilitation. Thieme, Stuttgart; 193–226

Rohricht J, Springer L, Weniger D 1978 Therapie der globalen Aphasie. Sprache-Stimme-Gehor 2: 96–98

Roth V M 1982 Dialogtraining in der Therapie schwerer Aphasien. Sprache-Stimme-Gehör 6: 125–127

Roth V M 1982 Sprachphilosophie und Sprachtherapie im System der Familie. In: Kuhlwein W, Raasch A (eds) Stil: Komponenten-Wirkungen. Kongressberichte von der 12. Jahrestagung der Gesellschaft für Angewandte Linguistik. Tübingen, 116–122

Roth V M 1983 Aphasie als Dialogstörung für beide Gesprächspartner. Fachblatt der Logopäden des Kantons Bern, Themaheft 'Aphasie'. Redaktion: B. Campiche

Roth V M 1983 (ed) Sprachtherapie. Publikationsreihe der Gesellschaft für Angewandte Linguistik e.V, Tübingen

Schuchardt, G 1975 Erfahrungsbericht aus einer Nachsorgeklinik für Hirnbeschädigte unter Berücksichtigung der neuartigen Substanz Piracetam. Therapiewoche 25: 43

Springer L 1979 Zur Anwendung der Deblockierungsmethode in der Sprachtherapie. In: Peuser G (ed) Studien zur Sprachtherapie. Fink, München, 462–474

Springer L, Weniger D 1980 Aphasietherapie aus logopädisch-linguistischer Sicht. In: Bohme G (ed) Therapie der Sprach-, Sprech und Stimmstorungen. Fischer, Stuttgart, 190–207

Sturm W, Dahmen W, Hartje W, Willmes K 1983 Ergebnisse eines Trainingsprogramms zur Verbesserung der visuellen Auffassungsschnelligkeit und Konzentrationsfähigkeit bei Hirnschädigung. Archiv für Psychiatrie und Nervenkrankheiten 233, 9–22

Temp K 1983 Spontane und therapeutisch beeinflusste Aphasieremission. Diss med, Universität Bonn

Wächter, H. (1980) Der anthropologische Aspekt in der Aphasietherapie. Staatsarbeit, Universität Dortmund

Weniger D (1979) Die Behandlung aphasischer Sprachstörungen. In: Scholz J F (ed) Rehabilitation als Schlüssel zum Dauerarbeitsplatz. Rehabilitationskongress Heidelberg 1978. Springer, Berlin

Weniger D, Huber W, Stachowiak F J, Poeck K 1980 Treatment of aphasia on a linguistic basis. In: Sarno M T, Hood O (eds) Aphasia. Assessment and treatment. Almqvist & Wiksell, Stockholm

Witzke C 1979 Sprachfördernde Materialien bei aphasisch Gestörten. Staatsarbeit, Universität Dortmund

Zihl J, Cramon D v, 1979 Restitution of visual function in patients with cerebral blindness. Journal of Neurology, Neurosurgery and Psychiatry 42: 312–322

Zihl J, Cramon D v, 1979 The contribution of the 'second' visual system to directed visual attention in man. Brain 102: 835–856

Zihl J, Cramon D v, Pöppel E 1978 Sensorische Rehabilitation bei Patienten mit postchiasmatischen Sehstörungen. Nervenarzt 49: 101–111

Zihl J, Cramon D v, Pöppel E 1979 Rehabilitation von Sehfunktionen bei Patienten mit cerebralen Läsionen. Bericht über den 31. Kongress der Deutschen Gesellschaft für Psychologie. Hogrefe, Göttingen, 430–434

Zihl J, Poppel E, Cramon D v 1978 Rehabilitation visueller Funktionen bei Patienten mit Ausfällen im Bereich des zentralen Sehsytems. Zeitschrift für Medizinische Psychologie 3: 223–224

# Index